BOURGEOIS EQUALITY

DEIRDRE NANSEN MCCLOSKEY

Bourgeois Equality

HOW IDEAS, NOT CAPITAL OR INSTITUTIONS, ENRICHED THE WORLD

THE UNIVERSITY OF CHICAGO PRESS ❧ CHICAGO AND LONDON

DEIRDRE MCCLOSKEY is distinguished professor of economics, history, English, and communications at the University of Illinois at Chicago and the author of sixteen books, including *The Bourgeois Virtues, Bourgeois Dignity*, and *Crossing: A Memoir*.

The University of Chicago Press, Chicago 60637
The University of Chicago Press, Ltd., London
© 2016 by The University of Chicago
All rights reserved. Published 2016.
Printed in the United States of America

25 24 23 22 21 20 19 18 17 16   1 2 3 4 5

ISBN-13: 978-0-226-33399-1 (cloth)
ISBN-13: 978-0-226-33404-2 (e-book)
DOI: 10.7208/chicago/9780226334042.001.0001

LIBRARY OF CONGRESS CATALOGING-IN-PUBLICATION DATA

McCloskey, Deirdre N., author.
    Bourgeois equality : how ideas, not capital or institutions, enriched
  the world / Deirdre Nansen McCloskey.
      pages   cm
    Includes bibliograpical references and index.
    ISBN 978-0-226-33399-1 (cloth : alkaline paper)
    ISBN 978-0-226-33404-2 (e-book)
    1. Technological innovations—Economic aspects. 2. Income
  distribution—History. 3. Cost and standard of living—History.   I. Title.
  HC79.T4M4 2016
  338'.064—dc23
                                                    2015035276

♾ This paper meets the requirements of ANSI/NISO z39.48-1992 (Permanence of Paper).

CONTENTS

The Three Volumes Show That We Are Rich Because of an Ethical and Rhetorical Change

Why are we so rich? Who are "we"? Have our riches corrupted us?

"The Bourgeois Era," the series of three long books here completed—thank God—answers

- first, in *The Bourgeois Virtues: Ethics for an Age of Commerce* (2006), that the commercial bourgeoisie—the middle class of traders, inventors, and managers—is on the whole, contrary to the conviction of the "clerisy" of artists and intellectuals after 1848, pretty good, and pretty much always has been so in human history;

- second, in *Bourgeois Dignity: Why Economics Can't Explain the Modern World* (2010), that the modern world was made not by the usual material causes, such as coal or thrift or capital or exports or imperialism or good property rights or even good science, all of which have been widespread in other cultures and other times, but by very many technical and some few institutional ideas among a uniquely revalued bourgeoisie, on a large scale at first peculiar to northwestern Europe;

- and third, in this volume, *Bourgeois Equality: How Ideas, Not Capital or Institutions, Enriched the World*, that a novel way of looking at the virtues and at bettering ideas arose in northwestern Europe from a novel liberty and dignity enjoyed by all commoners, among them the bourgeoisie, and from a startling revaluation by the society as a whole of the trading and betterment in which the bourgeoisie specialized. The revaluation, called "liberalism," in turn derived not from some ancient superiority of the Europeans but from egalitarian accidents in their politics 1517–1789. That is, what mattered were two levels of ideas—the ideas in the heads of entrepreneurs for the betterments themselves (the electric motor, the airplane, the stock market); and the ideas in the society at large *about* the businesspeople and their betterments (in a word, that liberalism). What were *not* causal were the conventional factors of accumulated capital and institutional change—which happened, to be sure, but were largely dependent on betterment and liberalism.

The upshot since 1800 has been a gigantic improvement for the poor, such as many of your ancestors and mine, and a promise now being fulfilled of the same result worldwide—a Great Enrichment for even the poorest among us.

These are controversial claims. They are, you see, optimistic. For reasons I do not entirely understand, the clerisy after 1848 turned toward nationalism and socialism, and against liberalism, and came also to delight in an ever-expanding list of pessimisms about the way we live now in our approximately liberal societies, from the lack of temperance among the poor to an excess of carbon dioxide in the atmosphere. Antiliberal utopias believed to offset the pessimisms have been popular among the clerisy. Its pessimistic and utopian books have sold millions. But the twentieth-century experiments of nationalism and socialism, of syndicalism in factories and central planning for investment, of proliferating regulation for imagined but not factually documented imperfections in the market, did not work. And most of the pessimisms about how we live now have proven to be mistaken. It is a puzzle. Perhaps you yourself still believe in nationalism or socialism or proliferating regulation. And perhaps you are in the grip of pessimism about growth or consumerism or the environment or inequality.

Please, for the good of the wretched of the earth, reconsider.

Let me tell you what the trilogy argues and how each of the three books answers the others. The project is one long, complicated argument. It is complicated not because I am hiding the ball but because the argument covers a lot of history and economics and politics, and depends on many sorts of evidence, historical and literary and quantitative. I'm an economist, and the question of why we grew rich and what we should think about the enrichment turns in part on economic facts and concepts. Therefore I offer from time to time little explanations directed at non-economists of why so many economists admire markets and profit and productivity. But I'm also a historian, and the scientific question here is historical. Therefore throughout I offer, too, some recent and internationally comparative perspectives on historical research, offerings directed at nonhistorians, and even at some of my beloved colleagues in history. Yet I have also been a professor of English and of communication, and I've been paid to teach philosophy a bit too. Therefore I do not neglect to report the evidence from the humanities— what the Germans call *die Geisteswissenschaften* and the French *les sciences humaines*—about economies and their histories, reports directed at whomever will listen. No wonder the books are so long.

Within each book you can see the argument in fair detail by consulting the table of contents. In the first book a brief summary—no more than four lines—appeared under each entry in the table of contents. In the second book I hit on the idea of outlining the argument in declarative sentences that serve as chapter titles and are repeated in the running heads. If you get confused—I have myself, often—take a look. Keep your eye on the ball.

The trilogy chronicles, explains, and defends what made us rich—the system we have had since 1848, usually but misleadingly called modern "capitalism." The system should rather be called "technological and institutional betterment at a frenetic pace, tested by unforced exchange among all the parties involved." Or "fantastically successful liberalism, in the old European sense, applied to trade and politics, as it was applied also to science and music and painting and literature." The simplest version is "trade-tested progress."[1] Many humans, in short, are now stunningly better off than their ancestors were in 1800. And the rest of humanity shows every sign of joining the enrichment, the "innovism."

A crucial point is that the greatly enriched world cannot be explained in any deep way by the accumulation of capital, as economists from Adam Smith through Karl Marx to Thomas Piketty have on the contrary believed, and as the very word "capitalism" seems to imply. The word embodies a scientific mistake. Our riches did *not* come from piling brick on brick, or bachelor's degree on bachelor's degree, or bank balance on bank balance, but from piling idea on idea. The bricks, BAs, and bank balances—the capital accumulations—were of course necessary. But so were a labor force and liquid water and the arrow of time. Oxygen is necessary for a fire. But it would be at least unhelpful to explain the Chicago Fire of October 8–10, 1871, by the presence of oxygen in the earth's atmosphere. Better: a long dry spell, the city's wooden buildings, a strong wind from the southwest, and, if you disdain Irish immigrants, Mrs. O'Leary's cow. The modern world cannot be explained, I show in the second volume, *Bourgeois Dignity: Why Economics Can't Explain the Modern World*, by routine brick-piling, such as the Indian Ocean trade, English banking, canals, the British savings rate, the Atlantic slave trade, natural resources, the enclosure movement, the exploitation of workers in satanic mills, or the accumulation in European cities of capital, whether physical or human. Such routines are too common in world history and too feeble in quantitative oomph to explain the thirty- or hundredfold enrichment per person unique to the past two centuries.

Hear again that last, astonishing fact, discovered by economic historians over the past few decades. It is: in the two centuries after 1800 the trade-tested goods and services available to the average person in Sweden or Taiwan rose by a *factor* of 30 or 100. Not 100 percent, understand—a mere doubling—but in its highest estimate a factor of 100, nearly *10,000 percent*, and at least a factor of 30, or 2,900 percent. The Great Enrichment of the past two centuries has dwarfed any of the previous and temporary enrichments. Explaining it is the central scientific task of economics and economic history, and it matters for any other sort of social science or recent history.

In this third volume I try to show that the massively better ideas in much of technology, such as textiles and food preparation, and in some institutions, such as universities and forward markets, not capital accumulation or government policies or union organizing, provide the explanation. As a wise man put it, humans recently have "invented the method of invention." How so? The ideas for the inventions, I claim here, were released for the first time by a new liberty and dignity for commoners, expressed as the "equality" of the book's title—that is, by the ideology of European liberalism. Ideas of equality accomplished a most surprising thing.

The great oomph of liberty and dignity can be shown by contraries. The linguist Kyoko Inoue explains how a Western notion of "individual dignity" gained a certain following in Japanese society during the early twentieth century, especially among the few Japanese Christians.[2] Yet when the Japanese word for character or dignity (*jinkaku*) was used in the MacArthur-imposed constitution after World War II, most Japanese still viewed it as expressing rank, as in the older English plural, "dignities"—something like the opposite of the recent Western idea of dignity to be accorded to everyone, equally. Thus the constitution's assertion of "dignity" for women was misunderstood (usually innocently) as merely reaffirming the *low* rank of women in the

Japanese hierarchy. The persistent denial of full dignity to half the population has not been good for the Japanese economy—at a time when the old heartland of liberalism in northwestern Europe has inched closer to realizing its radical nineteenth-century ideal that all men *and women* are created equal.

The modern world was not caused by "capitalism," which is ancient and ubiquitous, as for example in Japan itself during the seventeenth century. The modern world was caused by egalitarian liberalism, which was in 1776 revolutionary, being at the time most prevalent in in places like the Netherlands and Switzerland and Britain and British North America— though even in such islands of liberalism a minority view. Then it spread. The Great Enrichment, 1800 to the present, the most surprising secular event in history, is explained by a proliferation of bettering ideas springing from a new liberalism, against the *jinkaku* of rank.

The enrichment, I repeat, is recent. Some centuries before 1800 a few technological ideas had started to be borrowed by Europe from China and other economies to the east and south—paper, for example, and gunpowder, and the silk worm, and the blast furnace. But from the seventeenth century onward, and especially after 1800, the political and social ideas of liberalism shockingly extended the technology, through equality of liberty and dignity in Holland and Britain and Belgium and above all in the United States, and then beyond. The economic historian Joel Mokyr in a new book chronicles the improvements in communication and the welcoming of novelties that made for a freewheeling and largely egalitarian Republic of Letters after 1500, and especially after 1600.[3] The outcome of such rhetorical developments was a technological explosion, especially after 1800, that radically improved on Europe's old overseas borrowings. The Great Enrichment is not to be explained, that is, by material matters of race, class, gender, power, climate, culture, religion, genetics, geography, institutions, or nationality. On the contrary, what led to our automobiles and our voting rights, our plumbing and our primary schools, were the fresh ideas that flowed from liberalism, that is, a new system of encouraging betterment and a partial erosion of hierarchy.

Since capital readily accumulates in response to a genuinely bettering idea, and is not therefore the initiating cause, the fraught C-word, "capitalism," does not make many appearances here. The dishonored B-word, "bourgeois," though, appears all over the place, most prominently in the titles of all three volumes. "Bourgeois" was taken self-consciously into English from French. As an adjective applying to the precisely urban middling sort I am talking about it has been employed in English from the early eighteenth century, along with the vaguer phrase that eventually came to dominate, "middle class."

One task of the trilogy here, starting with the first volume, *The Bourgeois Virtues*, is to revalue the people of this middle class, or bourgeoisie—the entrepreneur and the merchant, the inventor of carbon-fiber materials and the contractor remodeling your bathroom, the improver of automobiles in Toyota City and the supplier of spices in New Delhi. The second volume then turns to economic history, and the third now to social and intellectual history, to show in detail that the ideas imagined by the bourgeoisie had arisen in the eighteenth century out of a new liberty and a new dignity accorded to ordinary people. Democracy of rights in voluntary trade and in polling booths, a democracy giving commoners a voice in the church and in the economy and in politics, made people bold, liberating them to have a go in business.[4] In the historical lottery the idea of an equalizing liberty and dignity was the winning ticket, and the bourgeoisie held it.

Yet after the failed revolutions in Europe during the hectic year of 1848—compare 1968—a new and virulent detestation of the bourgeoisie infected the artists, intellectuals, journalists, professionals, and bureaucrats—the "clerisy" I've mentioned, as it was called by Coleridge, on a German pattern. The Germans word was *Clerisei*, or later *Bildungsbürgertum*, meaning the cultivated and reading enthusiasts for *Kultur* as against the commercial and bettering bourgeoisie.[5] The clerisy of Germany, Britain, and especially France came to hate merchants and manufacturers and indeed anyone who did not admire the clerisy's books and paintings. Flaubert declared, "I call bourgeois whoever thinks basely." He wrote to George Sand in 1867, "*Axiome: la haine du bourgeois est le commencement de la vertu,*" which is to say, it is an axiom that hatred of the bourgeois is the beginning of virtue.[6]

In 1935 the liberal Dutch historian Johan Huizinga noted that the hatred had become general among the clerisy:

> In the nineteenth century, "bourgeois" became the most pejorative term of all, particularly in the mouths of socialists and artists, and later even of fascists. . . . How useful it would be from time to time to set up all the most common political and cultural terms in a row for reappraisal and disinfection. . . . For instance, *liberal* would be restored to its original significance and freed of all the emotional

overtones that a century of party conflict has attached to it, to stand once again for "worthy of a free man." And if *bourgeois* could be rid of all the negative associations with which envy and pride, for that is what they were, have endowed it, could it not once more refer to all the attributes of urban life?[7]

Such automatic sneering at the bourgeoisie needs to stop. It is an unattractive brand of self-hatred, since most of us, as owners and sellers of at least human capital, and, in our pension funds or house equity, of financial and physical capital, are bourgeois. True, if one insists on using the word "bourgeois" as, say, Jean-Paul Sartre and Simone de Beauvoir used it, to mean the worst and most inauthentic types of town life in France circa 1950, then it is not going to be much of an intellectual feat to conclude that bourgeois life leads straight to . . . well . . . the worst and most inauthentic types of town life in France circa 1950. But I urge you to stop using the word as a term of contempt, and to start using it scientifically and colorlessly to mean "owners and managers in town, risk takers or word workers, big or small in their capital, disproportionately literate and numerate, earning a living by conversation and calculation." Then we can find out by actual inquiry whether or not it is virtuous to hate them.

Like the mandarins of old China or *les honnêtes hommes* of early modern France, the members of the modern clerisy view themselves as uniquely ethical on account of their book learning, including book learning about ethics—or at least their daily reading of *Le Monde* or the *New York Times*. The notion that a person who truly grasps the meaning of "ethics" will in fact *be* ethical was Socrates's claim by way of Plato. In view of the numerous highly learned and book-reading but unethical people one meets, one rather doubts it. Yet the clerisy embraces the Platonic notion. It flourishes, for example, in the attitude of Dutch bureaucrats in the city halls, who view themselves as well qualified by arts degrees and ethical superiority and subscriptions to *NRC Handelsblad* for the job of protecting the sadly ignorant inferior classes from the ravenous capitalists down in *de markt*.

In the eighteenth century certain members of the clerisy, such as Voltaire and Tom Paine, courageously advocated our liberties in trade. And in truth our main protection against the ravenous has been just such competition in trade—not City Hall or Whitehall, which have had their own ravenous habits, backed by violence. During the 1830s and 1840s, however, a much enlarged clerisy, mostly the sons of bourgeois fathers, commenced sneering at the economic liberties their fathers were exercising so vigorously, and commenced advocating the vigorous use instead of the state's monopoly of violence to achieve one or another utopia, soon.

On the political right the clerisy, influenced by the Romantic movement, looked back with nostalgia to an imagined Middle Ages free from the vulgarity of trade, a nonmarket golden age in which rents and stasis and hierarchy ruled. Such a conservative and Romantic vision of olden times fit well with the right's perch in the ruling class, governing the mere in-dwellers. Later, under the influence of a version of science, the right seized upon social Darwinism and eugenics to devalue the liberty and dignity of ordinary people, and to elevate the nation's mission above the mere individual person, recommending, for example, colonialism and compulsory sterilization and the cleansing power of war.

On the left, meanwhile, the cadres of another version of the clerisy—also influenced by Romance and then by their own scientist enthusiasm for historical materialism—developed the illiberal idea that ideas do not matter. What matters to progress, the left declared, is the unstoppable tide of history, aided (it declared further, contradicting the unstoppability) by protest or strike or revolution directed at the ravenous bourgeoisie—such thrilling actions to be led by the clerisy. Later, in European socialism and American Progressivism, the left proposed to defeat bourgeois monopolies in meat and sugar and steel by gathering under regulation or syndicalism or central planning or collectivization all the monopolies into one supreme monopoly called the state. In 1965 the Italian liberal Bruno Leoni (1913–1967) observed that "The creation of gigantic and generalized monopolies is [said by the left to be] precisely a type of 'remedy' against so-called private 'monopolies.'"[8]

While all this deep thinking was roiling the clerisy of Europe, the commercial bourgeoisie—despised by the right and the left, and by many in the middle, too, all of them thrilled by the Romantic radicalism of books like *Mein Kampf* or *What Is to Be Done*—created the Great Enrichment and the modern world. The Enrichment gigantically improved our lives. In doing so it proved scientifically that both social Darwinism and economic Marxism were mistaken. The genetically inferior races and classes and ethnicities proved not to be so. They proved to be creative. The exploited proletariat was not immiserized. It was enriched. In the enthusiasm for the materialist but deeply erroneous pseudo-discoveries of the nineteenth century—nationalism, socialism, Benthamite utilitarianism, hopeless Malthusianism,

Comtean positivism, neopositivism, legal positivism, elitist Romanticism, inverted Hegelianism, Freudianism, phrenology, homophobia, historical materialism, hopeful communism, left anarchism, communitarianism, social Darwinism, scientific racism, racial history, theorized imperialism, apartheid, eugenics, tests of statistical significance, geographic determinism, institutionalism, intelligence quotients, social engineering, slum clearance, Progressive regulation, cameralist civil service, the rule of experts, and a cynicism about the force of ethical ideas—much of the clerisy mislaid its earlier commitment to a free and dignified common people. It forgot the main, and the one scientifically proven, social discovery of the nineteenth century—which was itself also in accord with a Romanticism so mischievous in other ways—that ordinary men and women do not need to be directed from above, and when honored and left alone become immensely creative. "I contain multitudes," sang the democratic, American poet. And he did.

New ideas from the bourgeoisie, and behind them new and encouraging ideas *about* the bourgeoisie and then about all of the commoners together, made the Great Enrichment. The trilogy here defends such an ideational hypothesis against a materialism long dominant.

The first volume, whose subtitle, *Ethics for an Age of Commerce*, gives away its theme, asks, Can a life in business be ethical? Can it be governed by virtues that include a businesslike prudence but are not limited to it? The answer, in executive summary, is Yes. Prudence is the virtue of profit, planning, know-how, *savoir faire*, common sense, efficiency. It's good to have. We teach it to our dogs and children. "Look both ways when you cross the street." "Study the balance sheet." "Provide, provide." But ethics in business goes beyond the virtue of prudence, and should. Actual businesspeople, being people, exhibit on their best days also love and justice and courage and hope and faith and temperance, and not only for instrumental reasons. The bourgeoisie is not composed entirely of the idiotically prudence-driven characters in a *Dilbert* comic strip.

The Bourgeois Virtues, in other words, repudiates the economist's obsession with prudence only, isolated from the other virtues. Philosophers and theologians observe that if a virtue is narrowed down and isolated it becomes a vice. Since the 1930s an army of "Samuelsonian" economists, the ones you hear most about, and most of my teachers, has undertaken to narrow down and isolate our economic lives to what it is pleased to call rationality. Samuelsonian thought describes modern economists of the so-called mainstream—modeling exclusively with "constrained maximization," in which the only virtue acknowledged is prudence.[9]

Not every worthy economist is Samuelsonian. An embattled countersquad of economic thinkers, with quite varied politics, has in the twentieth century included Joseph Schumpeter, Ludwig von Mises, Friedrich Hayek, Thorstein Veblen, John R. Commons, John Maynard Keynes, John H. Clapham, Frank Knight, Eli Heckscher, Gunnar Myrdal, Antonio Gramsci, Luigi Einaudi, Joan Robinson, Kenneth Boulding, Ronald Coase, Paul Sweezy, Alexander Gerschenkron, John Kenneth Galbraith, George Shackle, Robert Heilbroner, Theodore Schultz, Albert Hirschman, Bert Hoselitz, Bruno Leoni, Noel Butlin, James Buchanan, Thomas Schelling, Robert Fogel, Amartya Sen, Elinor Ostrom, Israel Kirzner, and Vernon Smith. They practice what could be called (Adam) Smithian economics, or what has lately been called "humanomics." It posits merely a mild tendency to enter on a new project when there might be a net benefit to be earned, leaving plenty of space for the practice also of love, justice, courage, hope, faith, and temperance. Genuine rationality among humans, as noted recently by social psychologists such as Jonathan Haidt and Nicholas Epley, and by the rest of us since the Epic of Gilgamesh, is *not* prudence only.[10]

A few economists are beginning to explore systematically such an economics, inviting back into the story a complete human being, with her ethics and language and upbringing.[11] For example, I am. The trilogy here exhibits a killer app of such an integration of quantity and quality, the sciences and the humanities, economic experiments and literary analyses, yielding—I hope you will come to believe—a plausible explanation of how we became rich in body and spirit.[12]

Yet I have to admit right off that "my" explanation is embarrassingly, pathetically unoriginal. It is merely the economic and historical realization, in actual economies and economic histories, of eighteenth-century liberal thought. But that, after all, is just what the clerisy after 1848 so sadly mislaid, and what the subsequent history proved to be profoundly correct. Liberty and dignity for ordinary people made us rich, in every meaning of the word.

The first, ethical volume repudiates also the *anti*-economist's obsession with the *vice* of prudence, narrowed down and isolated from the other virtues, the vice we call "greed." Greed is not good. But neither does it especially characterize the bettering world of the modern bourgeoisie, whether in a small business or in a corporate giant. Greed is ancient and human—

greed for gold, glory, power, position, sex. When Karsten Bernick in Ibsen's first bourgeois drama, *Pillars of Society* (1877), comes to his ethical senses in act 4, he declares, "Even if I haven't always gone after profit [contradicting the simplest version of greed in the Samuelsonian theory], nonetheless I'm aware now that a hunger and craving after power, status, and influence has been the driving force behind most of my actions."[13] Yes, all that, and sex too, since the caves, the hunger and craving that is exactly, in the absence of balancing justice and love and temperance, the vice of greed.

Trade-tested betterment since 1800 came in part, of course, from prudence and profit, which would indeed, without other virtues in attendance, constitute the Marxian or Samuelsonian economist's "rationality" and the anti-economist's "greed." The success of the experiment in honoring prudence raised the prestige of the executive virtue. But the betterment came also from the other virtues—hope, justice, courage, love, faith, and temperance—and raised the prestige of commercial versions of these, too. Corporations such as Merck, UPS, Walt Disney, and Lockheed-Martin had by early 2014, out of a sense of commercial justice and not merely out of instrumental calculation, stopped giving money to the then-homophobic Boy Scouts of America. Likewise, Shell Oil and Campbell Soup allowed in their health-care plans for gender-reassignment surgery. Some few others of the Fortune 500 have not been slow to provide opportunities for women and minorities (hmm, well: in 2014 fewer than 5 percent of the CEOs of S & P 500 companies were women, with more men with the first name "John" than all the women combined). And in the way that business has sometimes been ahead of government in ethical seriousness, so have small businesses sometimes been ahead of the large ones. In other words, a businessperson in the modern world, contrary to the materialist views of the Marxian or Samuelsonian economists and of their antigreed enemies, is not ordinarily a Mr. Max U—*Max*imizing his *U*tility—a sociopathic manipulator of the vending machines called "other people."[14] On the contrary, the businessperson walks with others, talks with them, entangled for good or ill in their stories and their metaphors. What news on the Rialto?

The trilogy's second volume, *Bourgeois Dignity*, which again gives away its punch-line in the subtitle, *Why Economics Can't Explain the Modern World*, examines in detail the capital-accumulation and worker-exploitation and other proffered causes in the materialist tales of the British Industrial Revolution, and shows their lack of quantitative oomph. Materialism can't explain the Industrial Revolution of the eighteenth century. Especially it can't explain the Great Enrichment that followed in the nineteenth. The book shows by the method of residues that bettering ideas, and especially ideas *about* betterment—the "bourgeois dignity" of the title—not mainly material interests, drove the modern world. Material interests and most of the institutions expressing them were ancient, and unchanging, and weak in force. What changed was ideology.

The British Industrial Revolution was a glorious start. All credit is due. Yet such novelty-rich revolutions had happened occasionally before, in fifth-century Athens or twelfth-century Song China or fifteenth-century Italy.[15] What differed this last time was the follow-on, the explosive Great Enrichment of ordinary people, arising from the loosening a Great Chain of Being that had trammeled most humans since the invention of agriculture, keeping men in hand-and-back work and women in arranged marriages. After the loosening and the consequent Enrichment, the son of a freight conductor could became a professor of government at Harvard, the son of a tailor a professor of law at Yale, the daughter of a conservative Southern lawyer a liberal professor of law, philosophy, and classics at the University of Chicago.

Why? The causes were not (to pick from the apparently inexhaustible list of materialist factors promoted by this or that economist or economic historian) coal, thrift, transport, high male wages, low female and child wages, surplus value, human capital, geography, railways, institutions, infrastructure, nationalism, the quickening of commerce, the late medieval run-up, Renaissance individualism, the First Divergence, the Black Death, American silver, the original accumulation of capital, piracy, empire, eugenic improvement, the mathematization of celestial mechanics, technical education, or a perfection of property rights. Such conditions had been routine in a dozen of the leading organized societies of Eurasia, from ancient Egypt and China down to Tokugawa Japan and the Ottoman Empire, and not unknown in Mesoamerica and the Andes. No: routines cannot account for the strangest secular event in human history, which began with bourgeois dignity in Holland after 1600, gathered up its tools for betterment in England after 1700, and burst on northwestern Europe and then the world after 1800.

Take the routine of property rights, emphasized, for example, by the economist Daron Acemoglu and the political scientist James Robinson in

Why Nations Fail (2012). The trouble with their emphasis is that most societies have always enforced property rights. It is what we mean by a "society." In Mesopotamia two millennia before the common era the cities enforced property rights, as did the societies of ancient Israel, the Viking lands, T'ang China. For that matter the hunter-gatherers and animal herders—First-Nation beaver hunters and Aboriginal plant gatherers and Sami reindeer followers—also enforced this or that institution of property, when it mattered, and when the enforcement did not grossly violate their other ethical convictions. When societies failed to enforce the property rights suited to their ethics, they dissolved into wars of all against all.[16]

What then, one naturally asks, was the special ingredient that made routine enforcement of property rights or routine building of canals or routine access to the sea or routine mining of coal so nonroutinely fruitful in the Great Enrichment? The second volume answered, as *The Bourgeois Virtues* had shown in applied ethics, and as *Bourgeois Equality* shows now in social and intellectual history, that the special ingredient was a change in ethics concerned with other people's behavior. Note the definition of ethics involved—not individual-on-herself ethics alone, but "social" or "conjective" or "I-and-Thou" ethics, that is, articulated judgments about others. Humans as individuals didn't get better, or worse; not much. But they did radically change, in the conversation of humankind, the attitudes toward other humans. What began to characterize northwestern Europe in the seventeenth and eighteenth centuries was not so much new ethics at the level of individual responsibility, though perhaps that improved a little, encouraging and benefiting from arm's-length trading. Much more important was a change at the social and rhetorical level: "You made a fortune trading with the East. Good." Or: "That fellow invented a new plastic cooling fan for automobiles. Good." In other words, the new liberty and dignity for commoners was a sociological event, not a psychological one, and originated in a changing conversation in the society, not at first in psychological self-monitoring by the individual. People in Holland and then England didn't suddenly start alertly attending to profit. They suddenly started admiring such alertness, and stopped calling it sinful greed.[17]

In any case, an institution such as Acemoglu and Robinson think crucial—or a canal or school or coal mine that others think crucial—works well not merely because of good official rules of the game, what Samuelsonian economists call the "incentives" or the "budget lines." An institution works, if it does, mainly because of the good ethics of its participants, intrinsic motivations powerfully reinforced by the ethical opinion people have about each other.[18] The typical human, it has been shown by careful experiments on our own species and on other great apes, is much inclined to indignation and punishment (though other animals punish too) in order to shame and scorn defectors. A woman is willing to punish defectors in ways that entail even the sacrifice (from the Latin, "make holy") of her own profits.[19] Humans have a sense of justice (as the primatologist Frans de Waal argues, so also do some other animals, if less elaborately), a sense of appropriate behavior toward other people and especially *in* other people. They will go to lengths to praise and reward manifestations of the virtues—prudence, temperance, courage, justice, faith, hope, and love—and to blame and punish the corresponding vices. The Blessed Adam Smith called such matters of internalized ethics the "impartial spectator"—though a spectator who then gets up on stage to act, for the moral sentiments and the wealth of nations.

A society can craft an official rule against cheating in business. Such a rule would be a "good institution." It's even necessary, to discourage the simplest game-theoretic defections and to generate "Schelling points" around which business can gather. True, Hasidic diamond dealers on 47th Street between 5th and 6th Avenues in New York get along without official rules. But the rest of us find the rules helpful institutions. Yet if the rules are enforced with a nudge and a wink among people who ignore simple honesty or who sneer at the very language of ethics, and who are not effectively condemned by the rest of society for doing so, as in a corrupt Chicago during the 1890s or a corrupt Shanghai during the 1990s, the economy won't work as well as it could. The society won't be, say, Iowa or Sweden, which do about as well as humans can in gently shaming and disciplining corruption. Friends help friends unfairly in Iowa and Sweden, admittedly. But in Italy and Ecuador people take such corruption a good deal further.[20] The extreme absence of a good impartial spectator in the breast, as in the Soviet Union and now in Russia again, makes the written constitution a dead letter.

The crux, that is, is not black-letter constitutions, the written-down constraints, the budget lines, but how the constitutions came about ethically and how they are sustained in social ethics—a continually renegotiated dance. It is located out in the language games in which people play as much as in their solipsistic "utility functions."[21] When a society or its elite earnestly wants the rules of the game to work, and talks *about* them a lot, and scolds violators from an early age, the constitutions usually do work—pretty much regardless of imperfections in the written-down rules and incentives, especially if the imperfections fall within the usual range of human folly. The political scientists Elinor and Vincent Ostrom at Indiana University showed repeatedly that a situation that would in Samuelsonian economics always be assumed to be a hopeless case of free riding and the tragedy of the commons, such as the overexploitation of the Los Angeles aquifer, can often be solved by sustained talk among serious-minded, ethically disciplined people.[22] It was true as well in medieval English villages, which in 1968 the ecologist Garrett Hardin supposed were instances of the hopeless case. Ethics undergirds water rights, grazing rights, civil and criminal laws, marriages, friendships, children's games, adults' games, clubs, traffic, science, business deals, constitutions—a point that political theorists from Machiavelli and Hobbes through James Buchanan and Martha Nussbaum, in their eagerness to devise a theory mainly out of prudence only, have tended to overlook.[23]

The working of the U.S. constitution, for example, has always rested on such ethical grounding. Its crises have arisen from deep disputes about ethics, such as that between the ethics of the dignity of all people regardless of condition of servitude and the ethics of honoring private property in slaves, or that between the ethics of the right of a woman to control her body and the ethics of the right of a fetus to be born. In January 2001, following the long-contested vote for the presidency, the Democratic candidate, Al Gore, who had won the popular vote in November but not the electoral college, hung by chad in Florida, conceded defeat, when the conservative majority on the Supreme Court spoke. So far the institutions reached. A rule of the game is that a majority of the Court gets the last word. But suppose Gore had not conceded. It was not automatic that he would do so, or written down somewhere in a self-interpreting text. Nor was his decision to concede the election wholly explicable in terms of the incentives facing him, at any rate not the sort of incentives that a Samuelsonian or Marxian economist would admire. Gore's wanting the good of his country came out of his personal and social ethics, learned at his mother's knee. So did the acceptance by other Democrats of his defeat, with more or less good grace. The rest of us heartily commend them, and congratulate the mothers who taught them so well. That too was a social part of the ethical dance. We do not view good people like Gore as mere suckers, missing a chance. We honor them, sociologically.

The Roman Republic fell because ethics no longer supported its constitution, and a Cicero who did not make the first move in a game of prudence-
only was accounted a fool and was put to the sword. Athenian democracy
was doomed when early in its long war with Sparta, as Thucydides put it,
"words [such as 'justice'] lost their meaning."[24]

The working of any institution depends on such socially supported ethics
beyond incentives. To be sure, rules and incentives and opportunity costs are
helpfully explicit. Yet they can be corrupted at any level, from board room to
shop floor. For serious results the people of any institution, whether a hotel
or a university, need to be to some degree seriously ethical from top to bottom, which is why economic development at a high level, or for that matter
running a hotel or a university at a high level, is difficult. The participants in
an institution or a society needn't be saints. Quite corrupt economies, such
as Britain's in 1716 or Greece's in 2016, can nonetheless perform reasonably
well by the standard of their times. But to achieve their full promise they
need to be sufficiently attentive to the impartial spectator, a sufficiency that
can be quantified. All participants, from the CEO to the hotel maid, need
to be a little proud of their work and willing to try to do it pretty well, and
to be ashamed when a customer or a boss points out an evident failure. You
can measure it. And when you find it egregiously bad you can fire the male-
factor, or jail him, unless he is protected by force or fraud and a misused
monopoly of violence.

Even so, if a substantial minority of the people available for hiring do
not have the right kind of impartial spectator in their breasts, and are put
beyond instruction by bad child-raising or bad labor laws or bad courts or
bad privileges protected by the state, you are stuck with a badly functioning
economy, such as Russia's early and late. In an almost vacant coffee shop in
Moscow in 2013 a customer asked politely that the loud rock music, pleasant
to the young staff but irritating to old folk, be turned down. The waitress was
shocked that a customer would have an opinion. She indignantly refused.
Thus was made evident the seventy years of changing the nature of man
under socialism. Ethical persuasions, especially about other people, arous-
ing a hardwired indignation about ethics, are foundational, and can work in
good or bad ways.

The trilogy, in other words, argues against the prudence-only obsessions
of the economists and of their enemies. Within economics it argues against

the factually dubious assertion from the political right that technological betterment comes automatically from private property.[25] And it argues against the logically dubious assertion from the political left that the betterment comes automatically from artificially high wages.[26] Both are what the economists Friedrich Hayek and Vernon Smith, among others practicing a humanomics, call "constructivist," as against "ecological."[27] There was little that was constructivist, automatic, material, Samuelsonian, Marxian, institutional, or predictable about the releasing of human creativity from ancient trammels in the eighteenth and, especially, the nineteenth centuries. All praise, then, to a betterment tested in voluntary trade of electricity supply for bread, or labor for doctoring services, permitted by new social and political ideas.

We're back, you see, to the first volume and the bourgeois virtues, and especially to the new praise in the eighteenth century for the commercial virtues as perceived in other people. The modern world was made by a slow-motion revolution in ethical convictions about virtues and vices, in particular by a much higher level than in earlier times of toleration for trade-tested progress—letting people make mutually advantageous deals, and even admiring them for doing so, and especially admiring them when, Steve Jobs–like, they imagine betterments. Note again: the crux was sociology, not psychology. Trade-and-betterment toleration was advocated first by the bourgeoisie itself, then more consequentially by the clerisy, which for a century before 1848, I have noted, admired economic liberty and bourgeois dignity, and in aid of the project was willing to pledge its lives, fortunes, and sacred honor. After 1848 in places like the United States and France and Japan, the bulk of ordinary people came slowly to agree. By then, however, as I also noted, much of the avant-garde of the clerisy worldwide had turned decisively against the bourgeoisie, on the road to twentieth-century fascism and communism. Yet in the luckier countries, such as Norway or Australia, the bourgeoisie was for the first time judged by many people to be acceptably honest, and was in fact acceptably honest, under new social and familial pressures. By 1900, and more so by 2000, the Bourgeois Revaluation had made most people in quite a few places, from Syracuse to Singapore, very rich and pretty good.

One could argue, as Joel Mokyr does, that what mattered for betterment was the change in outlook among a technical elite. An essay he wrote recently with the economic historians Cormac Ó Gráda and Morgan Kelly puts it this way: "What counted above all was [Britain's] highly skilled mechanics and engineers, who may not have been a large proportion of the labor force."[28] If one is speaking of the proximate cause, surely he's right. Mokyr's heroes are "the top 3–5 percent of the labor force in terms of skills: engineers, mechanics, millwrights, chemists, clock- and instrument makers, skilled carpenters and metal workers, wheelwrights, and similar workmen."[29] One could hardly have such revolutionary machines for the manufacturing in bulk of the wood screw and the nut-and-bolt without men like Henry Maudslay (1771–1831), already educated in making machines. A twenty-two-year old male student of economic history, one "Donald" McCloskey, found hilarious the remark by a historian of the lathe, a Dr. Holtzappel: "Mr. Maudslay effected nearly the entire change from the old imperfect and accidental practice of screw making . . . to the modern exact and scientific mode now generally followed by engineers; and he pursued the subject of the screw with more or less ardor and at an enormous expense until his death in 1831."[30] But Holtzappel was right, and supports Mokyr's argument that a tiny elite mattered and that profit making was not its entire motive.

Yet where did such a technical elite come from, with its education and ardor and expense? In Holland and Britain and the United States it came from ordinary people freed from ancient suppressions of their hopes. Such freeing is the sole way of achieving a sufficient mass of technically literate folk, oriented not toward rare luxuries or military victories but toward the ordinary goods of peacetime for the bulk of ordinary people—iron bridges, chemical bleaching, weaving of wool cloth by machines powered by falling water. The problem in, say, France in the eighteenth century was that the engineers came from the younger sons of its large nobility, such as Napoleon, educated for military careers.[31] In Britain, by contrast, a promising lad from the working class could become a bourgeois master of new machines and of new institutions, as an engineer or an entrepreneur. Or at least he could do pretty well as a clockmaker or spinning-machine mechanic. In Britain and its offshoots the career of the enterprising bourgeois or the skilled worker, in the fashion of Napoleon's army or Nelson's navy, was open to talent. John Harrison (1693–1776), the inventor of the marine chronometer, which solved by machine the problem of finding longitude in the wideness of the sea, against the arrogantly enforced demand by the elite that it be solved in the heavens by elite astronomy, was a rural Lincolnshire carpenter. His first clock was made of wood.[32] Similarly, Maudslay of the screw-making machine, two year younger than Napoleon and thirteen years younger than Nelson, began work at twelve filling cartridges at the Royal Arsenal, becoming then a blacksmith, and by age eighteen a locksmith, and more. The British working man carried the baton of a field marshal of industry in his rucksack.

Mokyr is taking as given a structure that in fact had a vibrant modern history, a history driven by the new and bizarre ethic of human equality of liberty in law and of dignity in esteem. The economic historian Karine van der Beek believes she is supporting Mokyr when she concludes with persuasive evidence that "the innovations and technological changes that were taking place in eighteenth century England increased the demand for these high quality mechanical workmen."[33] But her case is the opposite of Mokyr's, which is that what caused the betterment was the supply. The entirely new ethical context, I am claiming, made the demand for the engineers and entrepreneurs grow its own supply, when ardor and opportunity made the supply seem worth having. The opportunities themselves arose from a new equality in law and in society, encouraging new ideas for Dutch wholesale trade or new ideas for English coal mining. The new and liberal, if partial, equality in Holland and Britain and especially in the United States—for all the lingering sins of pride and snobbery and slavery—allowed many of the ordinary, and extraordinary, to have a go. The economic historian Peter Mathias's "having a go" then produced in the Great Enrichment a veritable idea-explosion: for example, about nitroglycerine, dynamite, gelignite, TNT, and C-4.

One could argue, again, as the French economist Thomas Piketty and most economists do, that growth depends on capital accumulation—not on a new ideology and the bettering ideas that such an ideology encouraged, and certainly not on ethics supporting the ideology. Piketty, like many American High Liberals, European Marxians, and traditional conservatives, is irritated precisely by the *ethical* pretensions of modern CEOs. The bosses, he writes, justify their economic gains by placing "primary emphasis on their personal merit and moral qualities, which they described [in surveys] using terms such as rigor, patience, work, effort, and so on (but also tolerance, kindness, etc.)."[34] As the economist Donald Boudreaux puts it, "Piketty prefers what he takes to be the more honest justifications for super-wealth offered by the elites of the novels of [the conservatives] Austen and Balzac, namely, that such wealth is required to live a comfortable lifestyle, period. No self-praise and psychologically comforting rationalizations by those early

nineteenth-century squires and their ladies!"[35] Piketty therefore is gratified
to note, from a conservative-progressive height, that "the heroes and heroines
in the novels of Austen and Balzac would never have seen the need to compare their personal qualities to those of their servants." To which Boudreaux
replies, "Yes, well, bourgeois virtues were not in the early nineteenth century
as widely celebrated and admired as they later came to be celebrated and
admired. We should be pleased that today's [very] high-salaried workers
brag about their bourgeois habits and virtues, and that workers—finally!—
understand that having such virtues and acting on them is dignified."

The theory of great wealth espoused by the peasantry and proletariat and
their *soi-disant* champions among the leftish clerisy is non-desert by luck or
theft. Likewise, the theory of great wealth espoused by the aristocracy and
their own *soi-disant* champions among the rightish clerisy is desert by inheritance, itself justified by ancient luck or theft, an inheritance we bloodline
aristoi should receive without psychologically comforting rationalizations.
By contrast, the theory of great wealth espoused by the bourgeoisie and its
friends, the liberal economists such as Smith and Mill and Friedman and
Boudreaux, is desert by a skill in supplying ethically, without force or fraud,
what people are willing to buy.

The bourgeois virtues are doubtless exaggerated, especially by the bourgeoisie and sometimes even by its friends. But for the rest of us the results of
virtue-bragging have not been so bad. Think again of the later plays of Ibsen,
the pioneering dramatist of the bourgeois life. The bank manager, Helmer,
in *A Doll House* (1879) describes his clerk caught in forgery as "morally lost,"
having a "moral breakdown."[36] Helmer's locutions throughout the play are
saturated with the ethical rhetoric we have come to call "Victorian." It is also
"bourgeois." Helmer's wife Nora, whose rhetoric is saturated with the same
ethics but is not so businesslike, commits the very same crime. Yet she commits it in order to save her husband's life, not as the clerk does for what she
views as amoral profit. By the end of the play Nora leaves Helmer, a shocking
move among the Norwegian bourgeoisie of 1879, because she realizes that
he instinctively would not have exercised the loving ethics of protecting her
from the consequences of a forgery committed for love, not profit. No satisfaction in the dollhouse, in the end. An ethical bourgeoisie—which is what
almost all of Ibsen's plays after 1876 examine, as later did the plays of Arthur
Miller and the novels of Philip Roth—has complicated duties. But anyway

the bourgeoisie talks about virtue all day long, admires it, and sometimes achieves it.

The original and sustaining causes of the modern world, in other words, were ethical, not material. They were the widening adoption of two mere ideas, the new and liberal economic idea of liberty for ordinary people and the new and democratic social idea of dignity for them. The two linked and preposterous ethical ideas—the single word for them is "equality," of respect and before the law, their theory being liberalism—led to a paroxysm of betterment.

Such equality, understand, is not to be taken in the style in which some in the French Enlightenment took it, as equality of material outcome. The French definition is what the left and the right unreflectively use nowadays in their disputes: "You didn't build that without social help, so there's no justification for unequal incomes." "You poor folk aren't virtuous enough, so there's no justification for your claim of equalizing subsidies." But the more fundamental definition of equality—praised especially in eighteenth-century Scotland after the place awoke from its dogmatic slumbers—is the egalitarian opinion people have of each other, whether street porter or moral philosopher.[37] Adam Smith, a pioneering egalitarian in this sense, described the Scottish idea as "allowing every man to pursue his own interest his own way, upon the liberal plan of equality, liberty and justice."[38]

It would be a good thing, *bien sûr*, if a society following the Scottish and liberal plan produced a French and Pikettyan equality of material outcome. And in fact—old news, this, though surprising to some—it largely has. By the only relevant ethical standard, most people in liberal countries have basic human rights and basic comforts in antibiotics and housing and running water, compliments of the astonishing betterment coming from liberty and dignity for ordinary people. Forcing now, by state violence, an equality of outcome, in an illiberal, "French" style—cutting down the tall poppies, envying the silly baubles of the rich, imagining that sharing income is as efficacious for helping the poor as sharing a pizza is for a nice party among friends, treating poor people as sad children to be nudged or compelled by the mandarins of the clerisy—often has had, we have found, a high cost in damaging liberty and dignity and slowing betterment. Not always, but often.

Anthony Waterman, the historian of economic thought, notes that as soon as the advocates for French-style equality stray from their sailing plan that inequality is simply evil, they founder on a consequentialist rock (on which John Rawls had in 1971 placed a lighthouse): "From the standpoint of economic efficiency, *is inequality* [by a French definition] *always a bad thing?* May it not sometimes confer social benefits against which the evils they report must be set as an offset? [Thus Rawls.] If so we should have what rejoices the heart of every [Samuelsonian] economist: an optimization problem."[39] Waterman points out that competition for "positional goods," such as a top standing at Harvard, a competition necessarily inegalitarian in its result, can, as Smith and other eighteenth-century liberals claimed, benefit the whole society. To quote Smith, it "rouses and keeps in continual motion the industry of mankind."[40] In historical fact the introduction of the Scottish plan of equality of liberty and dignity, beginning with the economic liberty of the bourgeoisie, has regularly led, as in the histories of Hong Kong and Sweden and France itself, to an astounding betterment and to an equality of genuine comfort. The poor have acquired automobiles and hot and cold water at the tap and color TVs denied in earlier times even to the rich, and have acquired political rights and social dignities denied in earlier times to all but a small portion of the rich.

The ideas of equality led to other social and political movements not uniformly adorable. Hannah Arendt remarked in 1951 that "equality of condition . . . [is] among the greatest and most uncertain ventures of modern mankind."[41] Alexis de Tocqueville had said much the same a century earlier. And Scottish equality has a harsh, even tragic, side. It entails equal reward for equal merit *in a marketplace in which others, by freedom of contract, can also compete.* As John Stuart Mill put it in *On Liberty,* "Society admits no right, either legal or moral, in the disappointed competitors to immunity from this kind of suffering; and feels called on to interfere only when means of success have been employed which it is contrary to the general interest to permit—namely, fraud or treachery, and force."[42] Yet in the real world, unhappily, if the poor are to be raised up, there is no magic alternative to such competition. An ill-advised and undercapitalized pet store, into which the owner pours his soul, goes under. In the same neighborhood a little independent office for immediate health care opens half a block from a branch of the largest hospital chain in Chicago, and seems doomed to fail the test of voluntary trade. Although the testing of business ideas in voluntary trade is obviously necessary for betterment in the economy (as it is too by nonmonetary tests for betterment in art and sport and science and scholarship), such failures are deeply sad if you have the slightest sympathy for human projects, or for humans. But at least the pet store, the clinic, the Edsel, Woolworth's, Polaroid, and Pan American Airlines face the same democratic test by trade: Do customers keep coming forward voluntarily? Does real income rise?

We could all by state compulsion backed by the monopoly of violence remain in the same jobs as our ancestors, perpetually "protected," though at $3 a day. Or, with taxes taken by additional state compulsion, we could subsidize new activities without regard to a test by voluntary trade, "creating jobs" as the anti-economic rhetoric has it. Aside even from their immediate effect of making national income lower than it could have been, perpetually, such ever-popular plans—never mind the objectionable character of the violent compulsion they require—seldom work in the long run for the welfare of the poor, or the rest of us. In view of the way a government of imperfect people actually behaves in practice, job "protection" and job "creation" often fail to achieve their gentle, generous purposes. The protections and the creations get diverted to favorites. Laws requiring minority or female businesses to be hired, for example, tend to yield phony businesses run in fact by male whites. In a society run by male whites or inherited lords or clan members or Communist Party officials, or even by voters not restricted by inconvenient voting times and picture IDs, the unequal and involuntary rewards generated by sidestepping the test of trade are seized by the privileged. The privileged are good at that.

The double ideas of liberty and dignity, summarized as Scottish equality—being political liberalism in a mid-nineteenth-century definition—mattered as causes of the Great Enrichment more than any fresh material incentives, real or fancied. The new ideas mattered more than wars or trade or empire or financial markets or accumulation or high wages or high science. The Bourgeois Revaluation ushered in a Bourgeois Deal: "Let me creatively destroy the old and bad ways of doing things, the scythes, ox carts, oil lamps, propeller planes, film cameras, and factories lacking high-tech robots, and I will make *you-all* rich."

The Bourgeois Deal became, unevenly, the ruling ideology. The Deal crowded out earlier ideologies, such as ancient royalty or medieval aristocracy or early modern mercantilism or modern populism. The bettering society of liberalism, when true to itself, was not led by the great king or the barons or the bureaucrats or the mob, all of whom took their profits from zero-sum and the monopoly of violence. It was led by the consumers, and served by betterers tested by peaceful trade, who came in bulk from low-status parts of the society—barbers, laborers, carpenters, linen weavers. They took their profits from a big positive sum, produced by water-powered sawmills and hand-puddled wrought iron. A bettering bourgeoisie, if not protected by the clerisy's theories of regulation or planning, could not seize for itself the old monopoly of violence. There were too many entrants, too many fresh bourgeois ready to drive down the price. Producers and consumers invented and improved the steamship and the widespread secondary school, the telephone and the Internet. It enriched us all.

This final volume, then, *Bourgeois Equality*, asks why such ideas about bourgeois betterment shifted so dramatically in northwestern Europe, and for a while only there. After all, "betterment" and "improvement" and especially "innovation" were long seen in Europe as violations of God's will or as unsettling heresies (the medieval sin was *curiositas*, which nowadays we honor extravagantly), such as Galileo peering at the moons of Jupiter and arguing therefore by analogy, in readable Italian rather than learned Latin, that the earth circles the sun. Surprisingly, in northwestern Europe and later elsewhere, betterment tested by success in domestic and foreign trade—and, as I've said, in scientific, artistic, sporting, journalistic, and political "markets" as well—came to be seen as splendid heroism, such as Henry Ford's assembly line or Steve Jobs's iPad. Why did Leonardo da Vinci in 1519 conceal many of his (not entirely original) engineering dreams in secret writing, whereas James Watt, of steam-engine fame (famous too for his fiercely defended antibetterment patents), would in 1825, six years after his death, be honored with a planned statue in Westminster Abbey?[43] Why did bourgeois Shakespeare in 1610 sneer loftily at the bourgeoisie, yet gentrified Jane Austen in 1810 smiled amiably at it?

The answer to why England or why Europe, I argue here, does not lie in some thousand-year-old superiority, such as English common law, or in the deep genetic ancestry of Europeans. It lies rather in the surprising, black-swan luck of northwestern Europe's reaction to the turmoil of the early modern—the coincidence in northwestern Europe of successful Reading,

Reformation, Revolt, and Revolution: "the Four Rs," if you please.[44] The dice were rolled by Gutenberg, Luther, Willem van Oranje, and Oliver Cromwell. By a lucky chance for England their payoffs were deposited in that formerly strife-suffering nation in a pile late in the seventeenth century. None of the Four Rs had deep English or European causes. All could have rolled the other way. They were bizarre and unpredictable. In 1400 or even in 1600 a canny observer would have bet on an industrial revolution and a great enrichment—if she could have imagined such freakish events—in technologically advanced China, or in the vigorous Ottoman Empire. Not in backward, quarrelsome Europe.

The Renaissance, by the way, much to be admired for other reasons, was not one of the democratically and economically relevant Rs. It yielded innovations, all right. But the test it applied for valuing them was aristocratic, not bourgeois. Grand though its innovations were—human dissection, perspective drawing, Palladian architecture, and the printing of edited Greek classics, among my favorites—they were not democratic betterments and did not improve the lives of ordinary people, at any rate not for a long time.[45] They had little to do with the remarkable Industrial Revolution or its astonishing follow-on, the Great Enrichment.

A result of the Four Rs of Reading, Reformation, Revolt, and Revolution was a fifth R, a crucial Revaluation of the bourgeoisie, first in Holland and then in Britain. The Revaluation was part of an R-caused, egalitarian reappraisal of ordinary people. (Such egalitarianism was not, you see, the central teaching of an Italian Renaissance which elevated the ideal, such as da Vinci's Vitruvian Man, and which disdained the average, such as Garrison Keillor's Norwegian Bachelor Farmer.) I retail here the evidence that hierarchy—as, for instance, in St. Paul's and Martin Luther's conviction that the political authorities that exist have been instituted by God—began slowly and partially to break down.

The cause of the bourgeois betterments, that is, was an economic liberation and a sociological dignifying of, say, a barber and wig-maker of Bolton, son of a tailor, messing about with spinning machines, who died in 1792 as Sir Richard Arkwright, possessed of one of the largest bourgeois fortunes in England. The Industrial Revolution and especially the Great Enrichment came from liberating commoners from compelled service to a hereditary elite, such as the noble lord, or compelled obedience to a state functionary, such as the economic planner. And it came from according honor

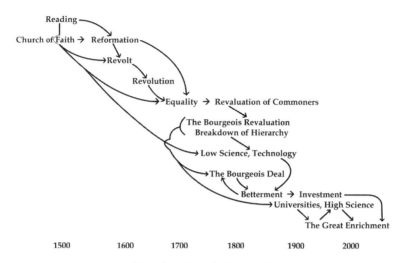

FIGURE 1. The Four Rs caused liberal equality, which caused the Bourgeois Revaluation, which caused the Great Enrichment.

to the formerly despised of Bolton—or of Ōsaka, or of Lake Wobegon—commoners exercising their liberty to relocate a factory or invent airbrakes.

Over the past few centuries the legal liberation and social honoring, together, did the trick, as figure 1 illustrates, in Holland and England, then in Austria and Japan. Now they are doing the trick with astonishing force in Taiwan and South Korea, China and India.

ACKNOWLEDGMENTS

Over twenty years of imagining and ten years of writing, the projected scale of the series has varied from one to six volumes. In a bad moment I thought of calling a six-volume version a "sexology," achieving thereby large sales through fraud and a tasteless mix of Latin and Greek. The thought did not meet the test of bourgeois virtue. I settle here for a trilogy, and modest sales, and say at its end, *laus Deo*.

I offer *laus* also to the embarrassingly large number of people who have straightened me out on the change in the attitude in northwest Europe circa 1700 about our bourgeois life and on the astounding consequences of the change. I will try here to offer praise especially to those who have not been acknowledged in the two earlier volumes (in the present volume, note, many are acknowledged in footnotes to the text). Please write to me at deirdre2 @uic.edu if you find that I have overlooked a conversation or correspondence I should not have. Doubtless I have, and I am mortified by the thought.

The Earhart Foundation of Ann Arbor, Michigan, a noteworthy exception to the coastie modishness of its sister foundations, has long helped my work. I thank in particular there David Kennedy, Ingrid A. Gregg, and Montgomery Brown.

The faithful and insightful encouragement of Donald Boudreaux of George Mason University has been especially inspiriting. Tom Palmer of the Atlas Economic Research Foundation arranged for a Chinese translation in 2016 of *Bourgeois Dignity* and has in other ways promoted worldwide what are laughingly called my "ideas." The Mercatus Center at George Mason, under its director of academic affairs Claire Morgan, has vetted all three volumes in extremely valuable mini-conferences. The attendees know that my thoughts have, to put it charitably, evolved. The philosopher Stanley Cavell admitted, "I never get things right, or let's rather say, see them through, the first time, causing my efforts perpetually to leave things so that they can be, and ask to be, returned to."[1] That describes my own presentations in the three conferences, at an early and inchoate stage of each volume. Those who gave me advice on how to get things right, often in more than one of the conferences, were Paul Dragos Aligica, Erik Angner, Peter Boettke, Donald Boudreaux, Richard Boyd, Jason Brennan, Art Carden, Gregory Clark, Henry Clark, Jan de Vries, Pamela Edwards, Ross Emmett, Jack Goldstone, Regina Grafe, Thomas Haskell, Robert Herritt, Margaret Jacob, Noel Johnson, Alan Levine, Leonard Liggio, Allan Megill, David Mitch, Claire Morgan, John D. Mueller, Jerry Muller, John Nye, Sandra Peart, Gary Richardson, Carlin Romano, Alan Ryan, Paul Solman, Virgil Storr, Scott Taylor, Jennifer K. Thompson, and Werner Troesken, with Joel Mokyr (my ally in the ideational turn in economic history), who was very helpful at the conferences on the other volumes and provided detailed commentary *in absentia* on this last.

The economics professor and journalist Art Carden has written with me a popular version of the trilogy, *Leave Me Alone and I'll Make You Rich: How the Bourgeois Deal Made the Modern World*. His enthusiasm and insight have been most encouraging. Graham Peterson, a graduate student in the Department of Sociology at the University of Chicago, was at UIC an extraordinary undergraduate student of mine, carrying on the tiny tradition of libertarians willing to listen sympathetically to Marxians, conservatives, Samuelsonians, and other misled friends. He offered many points of criticism and extension.

Some of the matter in chapter 51 comes from a paper with my friend and longtime collaborator Arjo Klamer and in chapters 57 and 58 from a paper with my friend and former student Santhi Hejeebu. Most of the writing here, though, has not been published elsewhere, with the exception of chapters 13–15 on neo-institutionalism, which appeared in another form as "Max U versus Humanomics: A Critique of Neo-Institutionalism," *Journal of Institutional Economics*, Spring 2015, 1–27; chapters 19–22 on Smith, which appeared in another form as "Adam Smith, the Last of the Former Virtue Ethicists," *History of Political Economy* 40, no. 1 (2008): 43–71; parts of chapter 41, from "Happyism: The Creepy New Economics of Pleasure," in the *New Republic*, June 28, 2012; and parts of chapter 51 on words in the economy, which appeared in another form as "How to Buy, Sell, Make, Manage, Produce, Transact, Consume with Words," the introductory essay in *How Language Is Used to Do Business: Essays on the Rhetoric of Economics*, edited by Edward M. Clift (Lewiston, NY: Mellen Press, 2008).

The summer seminars of the European Doctoral Programmes Association in Management and Business Administration (EDAMBA) have for two decades let me try out ideas on unsuspecting PhD students of business in Europe. I thank Hans Siggaard Jensen, Eduard Bonet, Pierre Batteau, and Jens E. Jorgensen for their invitations and encouragements. Christer Lundt and my students and colleagues at the University of Gothenburg in Sweden for five sessions during the late 2000s, and the visitors' program arranged by Ingela Palmgren and administered by Robin Biddulph, mightily stimulated my thinking about comparative economic history. A week organized by Helene Ahl teaching a graduate course at Jönköping University in Sweden and a week organized by Alessandro Nuvolari teaching a graduate course at the Scuola Superiore Sant'Anna of Pisa had similar effects.

At my home 2000–2015 at the University of Illinois at Chicago, my singular Department of History, especially in its Wednesday Brownbag, was patient with my ruminations over the years. My Department of Economics at UIC was amiable toward my mixing of the humanities with the mathematical social sciences. And the two other departments from which I also recently retired at UIC, of English and of Communication, let me gladly learn and gladly teach the human sciences.

Joel Mokyr, as I said, and Robert Wuetherick gave me astoundingly detailed and useful comments on this volume. Tyler Cowen and Jack Goldstone made helpful suggestions at a late stage. Jonathan Feinstein and Gregory Clark participated in an illuminating electronic discussion of *Bourgeois Dignity* at Cato Unbound, a blog of the Cato Institute, as did Matt Ridley, who has been cordially encouraging in other ways as well.

By the miracle of e-mail I have had advice from Ajit Sinha of IGIDR in Mumbai, Allan Tulchin, and Gary North. Recently Sanjeev Sabhlok, Adam Gurri, and James Pethokoukis have blogged favorably on my work, and have corresponded with me helpfully. My *vriendinnetje* Marijke Prins helped me think through the use of a locution unpopular in some circles, "the market."

I have given talks based on my evolving notions recorded in the present volume at January meetings of the American Economic Association in 2011, 2012, and 2013; at the Escuela Superior de Administración y Dirección de Empresas, my intellectual home in Barcelona, in 2011 and on other occasions; and at numerous other venues. In 2010: Segundo Congreso Latinoamericano de Historia Económica, Mexico City; Loyola University of Chicago; Economic History Seminar, All Souls College, Oxford; London School of Economics, Department of Economic History; Ratio Institute, Stockholm; Stockholm School of Economics, Heckscher Lecture; Free-Market Road Show (Barbara Kolm, director); Engelsberg Seminar, Sweden; Oxford Libertarian Society, Oxford; Society for Advances in Behavioral Economics, San Diego State University; Beloit College; Social Science History Association, Chicago; Jepsen School of Leadership Studies, University of Richmond.

In 2011: American Sociological Association, Chicago; keynote address to World Economic History Congress, Stellenbosch, South Africa;; Association of Private Enterprise Education, Bahamas; Christopher Newport University; James Madison University; Pennsylvania State University; Dennison University; Middlebury College; Latin American and Caribbean Economic Association, Santiago, Chile; Centro de Estudios Publicos, Santiago; Harvard University, Program on Constitutional Government; European Economic History Association, Dublin; Scandinavian Economic History Association, Gothenburg; keynote to European Group for Organizational Studies, 27th Colloquium, Gothenburg; Odyssey Lecture, Political Theory Project, Brown University; Social Science Festival (S3F), Salamanca, Spain; Thematicus Veerstichting, St. Peter's Kerk, Leiden; Technical University of Munich; Audimax of the University of Halle; University of Leipzig; Technical University of Hamburg.

In 2012: James Madison College of Michigan State University; Vrij Universiteit, Amsterdam; Pennsylvania State University; Legatum Institute, London; University of Denver; College of Charleston; Copenhagen School of Business; Collegium Helviticum, Zurich; History of Economic Thought Conference, Melbourne; keynote to Australian Economics Association, Victoria University, Melbourne; keynote to International Schumpeter Society conference, Brisbane; Francisco Marroquin University, Guatemala; IMCA seminar, Lugano, Switzerland; Lauchlin Currie Lecture, Universidad Nacional de Colombia, Bogota; Universidad de los Andes, Bogota; Oslo Business

School; American Council of Learned Societies, Philadelphia; Fondazione Cini, Venice; Bocconi University, Milan; Scuola Superiore di Sant'Anna, Pisa; Heilbroner Memorial Lecture, New School, New York City; New York University; Pacific Lutheran University, Tacoma; Fourth Adam Smith Forum, Moscow.

In 2013: Ratio Institute, Stockholm; Centre for Business and Policy Studies, Stockholm; University of Victoria, Canada; Louisiana State University; Radboud University, Nijmegen, Netherlands; Poroi (Project on Rhetoric of Inquiry), University of Iowa; Ramon Llull University, Barcelona; Universitat Autonoma de Barcelona; IE Business School, Madrid; University of North Carolina, Chapel Hill; Department of Economics, University of Missouri at Kansas City; St. Petersburg State University, Russia; conference on Rhetoric and the Possible, Northwestern University; Southern Illinois University, Department of Economics; Tocqueville Program, Indiana University; Ohio University, Athens, Ohio; John Boynton Lecture, Centre for Independent Studies, Sydney; Society for Heterodox Economics, University of New South Wales; Economic Society of South Australia; Crawford Lecture, Australian National University, Economic Society of Australia; University of Western Australia; Reserve Bank of New Zealand; Business School, Wellington University, New Zealand.

In 2014: Centre for Civil Society, New Delhi; University of Nebraska at Lincoln; Ohio State University; Kings College, London; Transatlantic Law Forum, Bucerius Law School, Hamburg; University Kiel, Germany; Centre for Policy Studies, Thatcher Conference, Guildhall, London; Department of Communication, University of Leeds; Mt. Pelerin Society meetings, Hong Kong; Rethinking Economics conference, New School, New York City; Istituto Bruno Levi meeting of the Mises Conference, Sestri Levante, Italy; Institute for Advanced Sustainability Studies, Potsdam, Germany; Wissenschaftskolleg of Berlin; Work and Human Life Cycle seminar, Humboldt University, Berlin.

Bart Wilson and Jan Osborn of Chapman University involved me in their brilliant teaching of humanomics (a word that Bart coined and that he and I are exploring). Douglas Mitchell, who among other achievements in his career can be credited with preserving qualitative sociology in the United States, has been my friend and editor at the University of Chicago Press now for a quarter century, encouraging my mad projects of the qualitative combined with the quantitative human sciences. Joel Score copyedited the manuscript with the energy and taste I have come to expect from the Press. And my mother, Helen McCloskey, has kept the faith, as she always does.

Speaking of faith, Anthony Waterman, friend, economist, and fellow Anglican, gave me valuable comments on the Jane Austen chapters and on other aspects of the volume. My spiritual director, the Rev. Brian J. Hastings, helped me discern the rough unity of my faith and my science. And some other Anglicans (or "Episcopalians," as we Americans had to start calling ourselves after Independence), Ross Emmett and Robert Sessions, have taught me what I was trying to say. For the Anglican Middle Way I thank God—you'll want to know, incidentally, that She is a middle-aged, black, lesbian woman with a working-class accent of Doncaster.

What Is to Be Explained?

PART I

A Great Enrichment Happened, and Will Happen

1

THE WORLD IS PRETTY RICH,
BUT ONCE WAS POOR

It had never happened before—a world in which many people, from Belgium to Botswana, have pretty good food and housing and education. We've not yet achieved, God knows, an earthly paradise. A little over seven billion people inhabit the planet. One billion of them live still in nations of economic hell: a loaf of moldy bread, some curdled milk, bad schools, bad shelter, bad clothing, bad sanitation. Most people in Haiti or Afghanistan live so, as do, in richer countries, many of the very poor. God knows that too.

Until 1800, though, such a hell was what everybody except a handful of nobles and priests and merchants expected, year after terrible year. We have achieved over the past two centuries for ordinary people worldwide, materially speaking, unevenly, for the first time, a pretty good purgatory.[1] The whole world's average income, for example, now approaches that of present-day Brazil, or of the United States in 1941. Since 1800, in other words, and especially since 1900, the goods and services available to the average human being, and the scope for a full human life, have startlingly expanded.[2] The event justifies its label, "the *Great* Enrichment."

Never in material terms had anything so Great as the Enrichment occurred—never to the mass of a population, not in the glory of Greece or the grandeur of Rome, not in ancient Egypt or medieval China. Startlingly, Brazil is now better off, on average, than the metropolises of the mightiest world empires before 1939. In the many and burgeoning very rich countries, such as Sweden or the United States, the value of goods and services made, earned, and consumed per person, without allowing for the radically improved quality of most goods and many services (cleaner food, better medicine), is three or four times higher even than the historically unprecedented world average.

Some Swedes and some Americans are still poor. But most aren't. The extremely high average has overwhelmed inequality so far as the standard of genuine comfort is concerned. It gives to the rich, the middling, and the poor alike a roof over their heads, plentiful food and clothing, long life expectancy, reasonable hours of work, literacy, dignity—all of which were prospects and satisfactions denied to most humans until well after 1800. The signs are good that if we keep our wits about us we can, within a few generations, achieve for everyone on earth the riches of Sweden and America. All the formerly poor can enjoy bourgeois incomes and can pursue, if they wish, the spiritual enrichment that such an income permits. We're on the way to a pretty good material paradise.

Look at the numbers.[3] Average daily expenditures by Haitians and Afghans, expressed in present-day U.S. prices at "purchasing power parity"—and so allowing for inflation and the relevant exchange rates among currencies—are well below $3 a day, which before 1800 was what the average human more or less everywhere expected to make, earn, and consume.[4] So it had been, always, back to the caves. Imagine living each day on the cost, spread over all your activities, of a half gallon of milk. If you've been to Liberia or Afghanistan it's not hard to imagine. Today, after two centuries of increase, recently accelerating, the world figure, an average that includes even the extraordinarily poor Liberians and Afghans, has arrived at an unprecedented $33 a day—roughly, I say, the Brazilian level.[5]

Like all the figures, the $3 and the $33 are corrected, I emphasize, for exchange rates and inflation. They are expressed, as the economists put it, in "real" terms, and therefore are comparable—or comparable enough for the scientific point being made here. The figures are supposed to include (however imperfectly when applied to earlier economies) not only what you buy in the marketplace but whatever goods and services you make or grow for yourself.[6] No one should put faith in the second or third digits of such an estimate, which may variously under- and overestimate the value of homework, care work, the environment, better health, and better quality of goods. But for the economic and historical science attempted here the great alteration of the first digit suffices. It is stunning.

Since 1800 the ability of humans to feed and clothe and educate themselves, even as the number of humans increased by an astonishing factor of seven, has risen, per human, by an even more astonishing factor of ten. Do the math, then, of total production. We humans now produce and consume *seventy*—7 × 10—times more goods and services worldwide than in 1800. Some people view this figure with alarm and speak of environmental degradation. But the news is mainly good. With seventy times more production, no wonder we can cultivate new economies of scale and reap their benefits through free trade. And no wonder we can harness the ingenuity of the larger population to get better antibiotics and better automobiles. No wonder we can clean up the air and the water, and turn forests into nature preserves.

In the best-run countries, such as France or Japan or Finland, all of which not so long ago were $3-a-day poor, real income per person, conventionally measured, has by now increased to roughly $100 a day. Income has risen, that is, not by 30 percent but by a *factor* of thirty (I will repeat the point until you feel it on your pulse), which is to say many hundreds of percent. It is not a doubling or a tripling of the material scope of a human life. Such routine increases, desirable as they are, have occurred many times before in world history, only to fall back again to $3 a day when the good times passed. Income now is *thirty to one hundred* times more than our ancestors could manage, and no falling back about it. The OECD, the Organisation for Economic Co-operation and Development, a club of reasonably well-off free-trade democracies with average earnings of about $100 a day per person, has now thirty-four members, containing nearly one-sixth of the world's population.[7] To be overprecise about the fifth-grade arithmetic involved, a factor of thirty for income growth in the OECD countries from 1800 to the present means a rise of 2,900 percent. Think conservatively of the Enrichment, if you wish, and call the increase merely 2,000 or 1,500 percent. Any such order of magnitude of enrichment justifies the word "great."

The Enrichment since 1800 shows in all the evidence. (It better, if it's so Great.) Real per-person income in Brazil is now, I repeat, about the same as it was in the world-beating United States in 1941, or in the still-recovering postwar Britain in 1959.[8] Two centuries ago fully four out of five U.S. adults worked to grow food for their families and for the remaining nonagricultural fifth. Now a single American farmer feeds three hundred people. Since 1800 worldwide the life expectancy at birth has doubled. World literacy is tending toward 100 percent. On Indian TV in 2014 an optimistic advertisement noted that for every adult illiterate in that bettering if still very poor country there are seven little children who can read a story. The scope of human life has widened, and bids fair to go on widening. All the instruments agree that most humans are massively better off now than their ancestors were two centuries ago.[9]

You will perhaps doubt that the Great Enrichment happened, or that it was so great, or that it will continue—or doubt that it is justified, in view of environmental decay and consumerist excess. But the evidence, regarded without prejudice, is overwhelming. From about 1800 to the present the world's economy did something good, which looks to be permanent and looks to be justified. If contrary to the evidence we cling to our prejudices about economic history—our view that the Industrial Revolution was impoverishing, or that the Great Enrichment was an irremediable environmental disaster, or that Europe is rich only because of poverty in the Third World, or that the new rich are always getting relatively richer, or that after all any enrichment is vulgar—we will mistake how we got here and will give mistaken advice on how to move forward. We will betray the remaining poor of the world.

The prejudices, which is to say our justifying discourses, would not matter if the issue were divergent judgments about, say, the latest ice cream flavors from Ben and Jerry's. We could then, in the easygoing English phrase, "agree to disagree." Chocolate Therapy versus AmeriCone Dream. Whatever. But the judgment about whether the System has worked for ordinary people, and why or why not, is too important to leave to personal fancy or to prideful skepticism or to a political identity adopted in late adolescence, never to be reconsidered in the light of new evidence or mature understanding, reaffirmed daily by the particular group of shouters and sneerers we tune into on cable TV. If we are to help the remaining poor of the world, as ethically speaking we should, the political judgment needs to be made soberly and scientifically.

The Great Enrichment is the most important secular event since the invention of agriculture. It has restarted history. It will end poverty, as for a good part of humankind it already has. Surprisingly, though, economists and historians from left or right or center can't explain it. Perhaps their sciences and their politics need revision.

∞

Our great-great-great-great-great-great-grandparents were very poor, which had in turn been the lot of their ancestors since time out of mind. In the sweat of thy face shalt thou eat bread, till thou return unto the ground; for out of it wast thou taken. The good old days, in other words, were for ordinary people horrible to a degree that is hard now for residents of $80-a-day countries such as Italy or New Zealand to appreciate. The historian David Gilmour notes that from 1375 to 1795 the great city of Florence experienced famine prices every five years or so.[10] In 1879 the French literary historian Hippolyte Taine expressed the horror in a vivid metaphor: "The people are like a man walking through a pond with water up to his chin. . . . Old-fashioned charity and newfangled humanity try to help him out, but the water is too high. Until the level falls and the pond finds an outlet, the wretched man can only snatch an occasional gulp of air and at every instant he runs the risk of drowning."[11] The British writer and literary historian Graham Robb, who quotes Taine, details the poverty of parts of rural France even in the improving nineteenth century. Over the winter in Burgundy the vineyard men hibernated, and not merely figuratively. An official reported in 1844 that "these vigorous men will now spend their days in bed, packing their bodies tightly together in order to stay warm and to eat less food."[12] Robb remarks that in French agriculture in the nineteenth century "slowness was not an attempt to savor the moment." Economists have long recognized that the world's poorest agriculturalists often run out of energy before they run out of money, the more so when they are afflicted by malaria and tuberculosis and other debilitating diseases.[13] The ploughman homeward plods his weary way. "A ploughman who took hours to reach a field," writes Robb, "was not necessarily admiring the effect of morning mist. . . . He was trying to make a small amount of strength last for the working day, like a cartload of manure spread over a large field." Even in fast-enriching Sweden, whose economy grew after the liberalization of the 1860s faster than any economy except Japan's, the novelist Vilhelm Moberg remarked of his childhood around 1900 in the countryside that he could bring to mind only the long summers. In winter "the children in a smallholder's cabin . . . were too badly clothed to stand the cold. . . . Life in winter was quite literally shut in: we dozed by the open fire and slept through many hours of the [very long Scandinavian] night: it was, for children, a quiet vegetating in the darkness under the low cabin."[14]

The Australian poet and cultural-literary critic Clive James struck the right note. During the nineteenth century tuberculosis afflicted the poor especially, but also the middle and upper classes. The aristocrat Alexis de Tocqueville, for example, died of it in 1859, as in 1850 had his bourgeois-liberal ally Frédéric Bastiat.[15] The working-class poet John Keats died of it too, in 1821, age twenty-five, before his pen had gleaned his teeming brain. James wrote, "Today's young tourists of a literary bent, when they pass, on the Spanish Steps in Rome, the window of [Keats's] last resting place, are being granted insight into the fearful realities of a world without antibiotics." (In 1943 the recently invented penicillin was two years away from being widely available for civilian use. My own kidneys bear the damage from the only alternative, sulfa drugs, of which the correct dose for an injured infant was poorly understood.) To grasp "the suddenness and randomness of God's wrath" in former times, James writes, we need to get inside the lives of our ancestors, "a trick of the mind . . . by which we can imagine how it must have felt when the only possible way to view reality without the benefit of religious faith was to despair."[16] In 1917 in a backwater of a definitely enriching Sweden, the potato crop failed and some of the poorer people starved to death.[17]

So it was from the beginning to 1800, and in most places for many a painful year thereafter. In the opening lines of *Christ Stopped at Eboli* (1945), the painter, doctor, and writer Carlo Levi described the poverty he saw when he was banished by the fascist state in 1935–1936 to a pair of villages in far southern Italy—"that other world, hedged in by custom and sorrow, cut off from History and the State, eternally patient, . . . that land without comfort or solace, where the peasant lives out his motionless civilization on barren ground in remote poverty, and in the presence of death."[18]

It was an ancient and terrible business, as it is still in Chad and Bangladesh, and on the homeless streets of Chicago and Amsterdam, too. For nearly all of humanity's time on earth the average amount of food and education and antibiotics and the rest per person stayed at subsistence, at $1 or $3 or $5 a day expressed in today's prices, or in exceptional times, briefly, $6 or $8 a day. Thus it had been, in 1800, during the two thousand or so centuries since the mitochondrial Eve (and about the same span, as has recently been discovered, since her good friend the Y-chromosome Adam[19]). Or during the thousand or so centuries since the invention of full language. Or during the hundred or so centuries since the invention of agriculture. Or during the eight or so centuries since commerce had revived in the West. Or during the three or so centuries since Europeans had ventured by sea to Africa and India and the New World. Pick whatever period down to 1800 you want. For a long, long time nothing much happened to the economic misery of the average Jill.

She and her friend Jack could perhaps trap or purchase a little meat to go with their bread, or pick nuts to go with their grubs, but they lived in a wretched little hovel, or a tent, or a cave. Poor people (and some not-so-poor people) lived in literal caves even in France and Italy until well after World War II, for example at Matera in the arch of Italy's foot. Jill before 1800 had two sets of clothing at most, or a string skirt. In the Jericho of Pre-Pottery Neolithic times, around 10,000 BCE, 40 percent of the burials were of infants or children.[20] In ancient Rome, on the 50-50 bet that a Jill survived to age fifteen, she could expect then to live on to age fifty-two—as against eighty-five for the same bet now.[21] Nowadays in rich countries, and in many very poor countries, almost all of a woman's children survive to the fifteen-year-old starting line. In ancient Rome, by contrast, a third of Jill's numerous children died before their first birthdays.

It had ever been so, as it is now in rural Ethiopia (one of the African cradles of *Homo sapiens*). Real income might go up for a while. In the richest parts of China and Europe in their most prosperous times it might rise for a while to $6 or $8 a day.[22] But as my mother's generation puts it, "even $7 a day is no bag of bluebirds." And then it would revert to $3 a day.

The old imperialist vision of China and India as always and anciently and particularly overrun with starvelings is a recent back-projection. The back-projecting had unhappy consequences during the 1960s and 1970s in the eugenic excesses of the family-limitation movement and of the Chinese single-child policy.[23] The historian Niall Ferguson, for example, favors the back-projection, despite recent work by historians such as Takeshi Hamashita and Christopher A. Bayly showing that trade in the Chinese seas and the Indian Ocean was large, and that in the eighteenth century the lands around them were prospering.[24] For most of history a dense population such as that in the lower Yangtze Valley or the lower Rhine or the lower Ganges signaled that a place was doing comparatively well in aggregate—albeit less wonderfully well for the Jack or Jill at the bottom of the ruck. The Ganges Plain, for example, was rich around 1600, at the height of the Mughal Empire, when the economic historians Stephen Broadberry and Bishnupriya Gupta reckon it reached 61.5 percent of the British GDP per capita—admitting that British real income was then at one of its lowest points.[25] But in most eras the people of north India were $3- or $1-a-day poor on average, as were all the other commoners on the planet since the beginning. The economic historian Bozhong Li makes a case that the Netherlands and the lower Yangtze were qualitatively comparable in 1800, though he does not in the paper venture on direct comparisons of incomes.[26] In a paper with Jan Luiten van Zanden, though, he concludes that by 1800 Dutch real income per person was double that of this richest of Chinese regions.[27]

Doubling or even tripling was possible, then, an instance of (Adam) Smithian growth, as the economic historians put it, coming up to the world-beating standard of Holland in 1800. But the vastly greater enrichment since 1800, a growth by factors of ten or thirty or one hundred, was out of the question. One hundred percent, yes, maybe 200 percent, if you were in the Scottish Highlands and reformed your society to match the habits of Holland. But 9,900 percent? Never.

You can tell the same story on a smaller geographical scale about what is now Belgium and the Netherlands. In 1568 the Low Countries were rich by the miserable standards of Europe, which is why Philip II of Spain wanted to go on taxing the place. Tax revenues from his Dutch- and French-speaking subjects thereabouts sometimes exceeded his silver revenues from the New World (though neither was enough to prevent the European hegemon from engaging in controlled defaults on numerous occasions, so uncertain were the fortunes of Spanish wars[28]). Two and a half centuries later, by 1820, the Netherlands was still the richest place in the world, with Britain only recently equaling it, while the southern part of the Low Countries (what was shortly to become Belgium) was smartly industrializing—but still at merely $6 or $8 a day. It meant ample bread but not much meat. Secondhand clothing if you were poor. Untreatable disease. Some education, but for most people not beyond a little reading of the Bible or the latest scandal sheet. Few books, few panes of glass, few shoes, horses, chairs—all expensive in hours of labor to get. No bag of bluebirds.

You would not want $3 a day, or $7, even if everyone around you had the same. When people can vote with their feet to escape it, they do. Most North Koreans who can, do. The Nigerian men selling handbags on the streets of Venice (*Vu cumprà?* "Wanna buy?") have done so most courageously. More descendants of the people in Carlo Levi's pair of *mezzogiorno* towns, Aliano and Grassano, now live in Argentina than in their home district of Lucania.[29] Levi's people, residing in the middle of the Italian foot, had heard the improbable boast of the city of Eboli (over to the west, on the shin of the Italian leg) that Christ had stopped there (*Cristo si è fermato a Eboli*). The hopeless Lucanese in the 1930s remodeled the boast into a bitter antijoke. Yes, Christ had stopped in *Eboli*—but he had gone no further, not bothering to take the branch line east to visit Lucania. Levi, who as an Italian and Jew and anti-fascist had little patience with the widespread modern notion of the State as benevolent savior, writes:

> None of the pioneers of Western civilization brought here his sense of the passage of time, his deification of the State or that ceaseless activity which feeds upon itself [thus the Great Enrichment]. No one has come to this land except as an enemy, a conqueror, or a visitor devoid of understanding.[30]

FOR MALTHUSIAN AND OTHER
REASONS, VERY POOR

In 1798 Thomas Robert Malthus (1766–1834), an Anglican priest with an interest in economics, was irritated by the extravagant and anticlerical claims of the French revolutionaries and their British allies that a new day had dawned, without religion, a day overflowing with utopian promise. "Bliss it was in that [French] dawn to be alive," sang William Wordsworth, "But to be young was very heaven." To which the Reverend Malthus retorted: rubbish.

Malthus undertook to explain for the first time why the enrichment of the poor had not happened by then, and why, according to the logic of the newly invented and previously optimistic political economy, even a modest enrichment would not happen ever, especially with the Poor Law subsidizing poverty, unless people adopted what he called "preventive checks" on population growth, what came to be called "birth control."[1] Even these, he said, would not do all that much for the average person. In the first, 1798 edition of *An Essay on the Principle of Population* (later editions were less pessimistic, but it is the first edition that has for two centuries ruled people's minds) Malthus claimed that what had kept people poor since the caves was not divine malevolence or royal extraction but human sexual intemperance and irremediable economic scarcity—which is to say, original sin and loss of Eden and all our woe.[2]

Up to 1798 the Malthus of the first edition was correct. Zero-sum ruled. As Malthus's inspiration, Joseph Townsend, had put it twelve years earlier, "In the progress of society it will be found that some must want; and then the only question will be this: Who is most worthy to suffer cold and hunger, the prodigal or the provident?"[3] Townsend argued on the basis of animal models (which later inspired Darwin by way of Malthus) that "the quantity of food . . . regulates the numbers of the human species." And the quantity of food, as some modern Malthusians still believe, was strictly limited. The "principle of population," as it was known among the classical economists of the early nineteenth century, had kept most of our ancestors since the caves living on that $3 a day, and many on less. In the slums of Edo or Calcutta they slept on mats in the street. People wandered the *veldt* or the outback or the jungle. They were hungry, crowded into tenements in Naples or Glasgow or Guangdong. They lay sick for weeks on a straw cot. They died young, ignorant though clever, violent if strong.

The average income seldom pushed much above $3 a day, and always temporarily, because betterment had come slowly, not at the frenetic pace after 1800. Here some betterer would devise a new use of iron or of Roman roads, there another could devise a new use of coal or of accounting. But the betterments were too small to wrench incomes up and—startlingly—to wrench birth rates down. Again and again, then, population growth and the consequent diminishing of returns were given time to overwhelm the too-slow accumulation of new ideas. As the economic historians Nico Voigtländer and Hans-Joachim Voth put it recently:

> In a Malthusian economy the race between technology and population size is the turtle against the hare—technological change can almost never rise fast enough to overcome the deleterious effects of population growth. The same logic applies for institutional improvements. They, too, can improve the mapping from resources to output, just like technological advances—but it is highly unlikely that institutional improvements outpaced the ability of human populations to grow.[4]

They observe that before 1800 the average rate of betterment was never higher than half a percent per year, and according to the economist Oded Galor more like one-tenth of one percent, yielding at best a rise of 64 percent per century.[5] But populations could grow at 3 percent per year, which is 1,800 percent per century. The turtle didn't stand a chance.

In engineering lingo, the $3 a day—plus or minus $2, say—was a "homeostatic equilibrium" and worked the way your thermostat does. Average income in olden days might occasionally rise a little above $3, as it did in Holland and Britain during their commercial thrusts of the early modern era, or in many places worldwide when potatoes from the New World were suddenly introduced. But soon the rise would lead women to have more children, and more of the children would survive to have children themselves. In Ireland at the time Malthus was writing, for example, such a rise in population was happening, fueled by Ireland's (in fact) nourishing diet of milk and potatoes. At length the Famine of 1845–1850 descended.[6]

What the Malthus of 1798 could not have known, considering the frailty of social statistics in his time, is that the falling birth rate in France betokened a demographic transition to smaller family sizes; or, indeed, that in Britain itself the recent rapid population growth, *without* sharply falling wages, had already betokened quick enough betterment through new ideas for sawmills and seed drills and colonizing overseas to offset diminishing returns.

The usual story had been that the supply of labor grew too fast, that when wages rose so did birth rates, and then in a generation or two, according to the Malthusian logic of entry to an ecological niche in a world of diminishing returns, the real wage would be pushed down again to subsistence, to $5 or $3 or even $1 a day. Predator-prey relationships work that way. If foxes can freely enter a place temporarily abundant in rabbits, the foxes will eventually kill and eat so many rabbits that the return on hunting falls and the new, overlarge, fattened population of foxes gets pushed back to its former level by starvation and, especially, by infertility.[7]

So it was with people preying on the land, or on one unreliable crop, such as potatoes in Ireland: "The praties they grow small over here. / We dig them in the fall / And eat them skin and all / Over here." Perhaps British incompetence, and long-standing British malice in protecting British interests against Irish competition, worsened *an Gorta Mór*, the Great Hunger. But there is no doubt that with Irish fertility unrestrained—the original Malthusian sin—population had exceeded the carrying capacity of Ireland. The crop had done poorly many times before, as early as 1739. Mokyr and Ó Gráda have shown that up to 1845, a 50 percent failure of the potato crop had usually meant merely that the pigs starved (which is why highlanders, who were mainly herders, survived dearth better than lowlanders wholly dependent on field crops: if the crops the highlanders ate or sold failed, their pigs or cattle were a store of value, and of food). In the Great Hunger, though, the crop failure was 90 percent, and the people starved too.[8] In the late 1840s one million out of Ireland's eight million souls died of starvation and disease.

Another million—especially those with the money to do so, or relatives established abroad—escaped to Boston or Liverpool, to Canada or Chile. Irish population has never recovered its level in 1845, unless you include the tens of millions of Irish descendants in land-rich places abroad, such as my father's family. Malthus was confirmed.

Diminishing returns on labor applied to fixed land would always be immiserizing, said the Malthus of 1798. The notion was taken up with grim enthusiasm by other classical economists, such as David Ricardo and Karl Marx. True, Malthus in later editions, beginning in 1803, as the historian of economic thought Ross Emmett has argued, believed that a rational restraint on procreation could permit some modest growth of income. "Biology could never be conquered," Emmett writes, "but within the right institutional context, reason could interrupt its career." For a time, that is. But the classical economists came to believe that there would soon be an end to conquering, a "stationary state." As Anthony Waterman puts it, "Malthus' first [1798] *Essay* made land scarcity central, and so began a century-long mutation of 'political economy,' the optimistic science of wealth, to 'economics,' the pessimistic science of scarcity."[9]

And in historical fact, diminishing returns in a nonglobalized world had been in the past powerfully immiserizing, in just such a simple Malthusian way. When the population of Europe rose by a factor of two between 1000 and 1350 CE, real wages fell by a third. (Remember that in the shorter period since Malthus the population has not merely doubled but grown by a factor of *seven*.) After the Black Death of 1348–1350 and its recurrences, which drove the population in many places down by a third or a half, real wages of farm laborers doubled. But when, by 1600, population recovered, European real wages again collapsed, to half their previous peak.[10] Dante's time and, after two centuries of rise and one of heavy fall, Shakespeare's time were two low points in how much bread the wage of an ordinary European could buy. Think of India and China in their worst eras, with coolies pulling rickshaws, the way porters in Italy and England once carried the rich in sedan chairs.[11]

The only hope, said Malthus, and that a faint one, was to keep population down by restraining reproduction, the preventive checks, an exercise of reason in the right institutional context, about which Emmett notes Malthus was a tiny bit hopeful. A grim form of state-enforced preventive checks, far from Malthus's preferences in the matter, became in the 1960s the policy of

India and China, I have noted, inspired by eugenic ideas hatched in Germany, Britain, and the United States in the late nineteenth century and implemented wholesale in Scandinavia and Germany and some U.S. states by fascists and progressives in the 1930s. Yet with fixed land and turtle-slow technological change such preventive checks could not in the long run help all that much. No wonder the classical economists were pessimistic about the prospects for a significant betterment in the human condition. "No possible form of society," Malthus had written gloomily in 1798, "could prevent the almost constant action of misery upon a great part of mankind, if in a state of inequality, and upon all, if all were equal."[12]

No wonder, too, that Malthus-out-of-Townsend was the inspiration for Darwin's brutally accurate theory of natural selection. Plants and animals have no way of applying "reason" to interrupt the career of nature. Their rate of betterment, being slow and biological rather than quick and social, is never frenetic enough to overcome the immiserizing force of diminishing returns after entry into a niche. Therefore adult coots (*Fulica atra*) have evolved to grow impatient after a few days with their large broods, and to drown the weaker chicks, leaving two or three out of the eight or so hatched.[13] Preventive checks. Humans do the same, as one can see from the imbalances in many poor countries in surviving girls as against boys. Drown the infant girls.

An alternative mechanism of homeostasis (Greek: "identical position"), tending to the same, sad, $3-a-day conclusion, posited that larger populations made for denser settlements, which by overcoming fixed costs of movement made for cheaper transport, which had the unhappy side effect of spreading disease.[14] Smallpox was spread by such densities of humans and of their domestic animals, as later was the White Plague of tuberculosis. Look at Ebola in 2014, leaping from country to country by airplane. The Black Death may be another case in point. It arose in densely populated China, or perhaps among the Mongols further north and west, spreading during the 1330s throughout the Chinese Empire and undermining the prestige of the Mongols ruling there. By 1348 it spread widely in Europe, killing, as in China and intermediate points, more than a third of the population and shaking the social order.[15] The Black Death, by Malthusian logic, sharply raised the real wage all over Eurasia. And in dense places the recurrences of the plague, which ended in northern Europe only around 1700, kept people fearfully off balance. The economic historian Guido Alfani argues that Italy continued to be hit by plague even after 1700, in the countryside as much as in the towns, at the moment that northwestern Europe was beginning to prosper a little.[16]

The other mechanism keeping the poor in poverty was class violence, such as Rousseau adumbrated in his seminal attack in 1754 on private property. Half a century later, Malthus, though a friend of private property, viewed property as characteristic of the uneven distribution of income in a "civilized," that is, an arable-crop, society.[17] Although bands of hunters-gatherers and independent-minded herder/highlanders might escape lordship, arable farmers in their dense and fixed populations in the lowlands could not. If you followed the plow you followed the local lord, perforce. Marshall Sahlins and other anthropologists have long observed that compared to an arable farmer a hunter-gatherer typically had an easier life, at least in the Holocene, after the ice, and in warm places. He worked fewer hours a week for his food than someone tied down to the abundance of crops. The abundance, according to the logic of lordship, went to priests and knights and other people able to make good with sword and horse their claim to ownership of the land. It did not go to most of our ancestors, the poor.[18] The philosopher Gerald Gaus notes the consequence, namely, "the extraordinarily rapid displacement over most of the world of small-scale egalitarian culture with agricultural-based states and empires that were hierarchically organized. This political development almost reversed, in the blink of an eye, the egalitarian culture in which humans evolved."[19]

Farmers were ideal victims for any specialist in violence who happened along, expropriating any surplus over $3-a-day bare subsistence.[20] That a temporary surplus in the ripening fields was easy to detect added to the hazards of immobility.[21] Land-based nomads on horses, such as the Mongols, led by a Mongolian Genghis or a Turco-Mongolian Tamerlane, preyed on farmers such as the Iranians or the Chinese or the Russians, becoming their long-term khans.[22] Sea-based nomads or pirates likewise went where the money was, as did the mysterious Sea Peoples of the late second millennium BCE in the eastern Mediterranean, or the Vikings two millennia later in the North Sea and the Baltic and beyond, or the well-organized descendants of the Vikings, the Normans, who ranged even further afield. In short, if diminishing returns or disease-breeding density didn't do the sad trick of keeping most of us at $3 a day, violent hierarchy did.

∾

Why during the long, long run before 1800 did ordinary people do no better? Because, considering the stately pace of betterment before the Great Enrichment, the Malthusian, homeostatic equilibrium was about $3 a day. Until 1750 or 1850, and even later in the poorest places, the Reverend Malthus of the first *Essay* looks sadly wise.

3

THEN MANY OF US SHOT UP THE BLADE OF A HOCKEY STICK

Then after 1798—as economic historians have discovered over the past few decades—life in quite a few places got better. Slowly, and then quickly, and by now with unstoppable, ramifying, worldwide force, it got much better. Material life got better not merely for Europeans or imperial powers or Mr. Moneybags, but for ordinary people from Brooklyn to Beijing.

The betterment stands in human history as that Great Enrichment, the most important secular event since we first domesticated squash and chickens and wheat and horses. The Enrichment has been and will continue to be more important historically than the rise and fall of empires or the class struggle in all hitherto existing societies. Such perennial fascinations of historians, entranced by the *realpolitik* that accompanies empires rising and classes struggling, had little to do with our enrichment. Empire did not enrich Britain. America's success did not depend on slavery. Power did not lead to plenty, and exploitation was not plenty's engine.

The real engine was the expanding ideology of liberty and dignity that inspired the proliferating schemes of betterment by and for the common people. Liberty and dignity for ordinary projectors yielded the Bourgeois Deal: "You accord to me, a bourgeois projector, the liberty and dignity to try out my schemes in voluntary trade, and let me keep the profits, if I get any, in the first act—though I accept, reluctantly, that others will compete with me in the second act. In exchange, in the third act of a new, positive-sum drama, the bourgeois betterment provided by me (and by those pesky, low-quality, price-spoiling competitors) will make *you* all rich." And it did.

The ideology supporting the Bourgeois Deal displaced that of the Aristocratic Deal: "You honor me, an aristocrat by natural inequality, and give me the liberty to extract rents from you in the first act, and in the second and in all subsequent acts. I forbid you under penalty of death to seek competitive 'protection.' By the third act of the zero-sum drama, if you have behaved yourself, and have pulled your forelock or made your curtsey as I ride by, I will not at least have slaughtered you." It was extortion, not protection. As an economic historian put it, reacting in 1971 to the claim by an economic theorist that feudal lords had offered "protection" to peasants, "The possibility that the main, if not the only, danger against which the peasant very frequently was in need of protection was the very lord is not mentioned."[1]

The bourgeois, voluntary, egalitarian, bettering ideology writ across a society is recent, and therefore cannot be put down to ancient risings of empires and strugglings of classes, or to biological evolution on a scale of centuries. We did not become rich at the time of the rise of trade, which is paleolithically ancient, or upon the establishment of towns and the agricultural state and the legal protection of real property, which are less ancient but nonetheless many millennia old, or in long times of peace, which has characterized life in economically stagnant places as much as in Europe 1815–1914. An ideological change did it, and recently. In northwestern Europe the strange idea grew up that aristocracy (the rule of the best by descent) and theocracy (the rule of priests) and even plutocracy (the rule of the present rich) were all nasty. What replaced them in people's ideology, slowly, was the rule of the better technique, allowing free entry to compete with the monopolies that the aristocrats or the plutocrats had arranged under the aegis of a captured government. The new ideology in places like Britain and Belgium around 1800 favored a "betterocracy," or, if you want the pure Greek, a "kaluterocracy."

The profit going to the betterers was promptly undermined, unless governmental monopolies and governmental protectionism intervened. The economist William Nordhaus has calculated that betterers nowadays earn in profit only 2 or 3 percent of the social value of their inventions.[2] If you are Sam Walton bettering the retail trade in the matters of inventory control and purchasing contracts, the 2 percent yields a great deal of money. But 98 percent at the cost of 2 percent is nonetheless a pretty good deal for the rest of us. The gain from macadamized roads or vulcanized rubber, then modern universities, structural concrete, and detergent, and then the airplane and the transistor, enriched even the poorest among us.

The new ideology of kaluterocracy spread quickly. In modern conditions of communication (invented by the bourgeoisie, with helpful inputs from secret police eager to read their gentlemen's mail), quickness rules. As Gaus put it, summarizing the work since 1985 by Peter J. Richerson and Robert Boyd and other proponents of group-level evolution (which was until the 1980s considered rank scientific heresy), "Group-beneficial norms can spread much more quickly within a group via copying or imitation; major cultural changes can occur within 200 years (or indeed considerably less)."[3] And they did, starting in Holland in the sixteenth century and spreading to England in the eighteenth, and now, two hundred years on, spreading to China and India.

For example, the lower end of the world's present income distribution, the bottom billion out of seven, as Ó Gráda has documented, has seen a dramatic decline of famine.[4] In the European Middle Ages a killing famine in the favored south of England came every ten years or so.[5] The last widespread, killing famine in southern England was 1597, in northern England 1623, in Scotland the 1690s, in France 1710, in Germany, Scandinavia, and Switzerland 1770–1772, in Ireland the late 1840s, in Finland 1866–1868.[6]

The upper middle of the present-day seven billion—perhaps two billion, double the population of the world in 1800—live in countries in the mold of Greece or Taiwan or Israel. The average income of such places exceeds $80 a day, which is to say two and a half times the present world average, and twenty-six times the world average in 1800. Hans Rosling, a Swedish professor of public health, calls $80 "the Washing Line," because at that level a household can have an electric washing machine, freeing women from exhausting wash days.[7] Deborah Fallows reports on a study of material aspirations among the upper bourgeoisie in China: "In the 1950s and 1960s . . . a watch, a bicycle, and a sewing machine. In the 1970s and 1980s . . . a color television, a fridge, and a washing machine. . . . By the late 1990s . . . foreign holidays, . . . computers and cars, and [the wherewithal] to buy their own houses."[8] In 1943 in Lansing, Michigan, my mother, a young middle-class woman, would wash the family's clothing by hand down in the basement, using tubs with washboards. My grandfather, an electrical contractor, was dismayed and bought her a small electric washing machine. One of Donna Leon's mystery novels set in Venice portrays chief inspector Guido Brunetti in 2012 noting to the department secretary, Signorina Elettra, that people in olden days were miserable: "They'd probably give you anything you asked for," he declares, "in exchange for a washing machine." Signorina Elettra laughs in agreement: "*I'd* give you anything. . . . I suspect that most people—at least the women—would willingly renounce their right to vote in exchange for a washing machine."[9]

And the higher, electric-*drying* end of present-day incomes, over $120 a day, enjoyed now by about half a billion people worldwide, a group growing rapidly each year in number and in share of the world population, and set to become in a few generations the typical human, supports a flourishing life of loft apartments, art museums, higher education, adventure holidays, spiritual exercises, Donna Leon mystery novels, and all the ennobling and not-so-ennobling goods and services of a modern bourgeois town.

In other words, when we economic historians lecture to undergraduates we emphasize an anti-Malthusian message of hope—that average human welfare has shot up startlingly since 1800. A graph of average income over time resembles an ice-hockey stick, with tens of thousands of years spent tracing the long, horizontal handle. Then finally, after 1800, history reached the business end of the hockey stick and shot up the blade. A video by Rosling, "200 Countries, 200 Years, 4 Minutes," makes the optimistic point, illustrating the transition from misery to hope.

The successful countries are "bourgeois," whether or not they also have capacious social safety nets, such as universal health care. Contrary to the usual myths of capitalism versus socialism, the United States has, if correctly measured, a social safety net almost as generous as, say, France's. And "socialist" Sweden even nowadays is bourgeois and "capitalist," and not much less so than the United States. Sweden allows property and profits. It allocates most goods by unregulated prices. The Swedish government, though busybody by historical standards—as are most governments nowadays—does not own much of the means of production. Unlike socialistic Americans, both Democrats and Republicans, who intervened to save General Motors and Chrysler during their post-2007 troubles, the Swedish government refused to bail out Saab Motors (sold in 2010 by that same GM) when it went bankrupt. Nor did the Swedes object when the Chinese bought both bankrupt Saab and solvent Volvo. All "Swedish" cars are now Chinese. Occupational choice in Sweden is free, though encumbered as it is in the United

States by cartels of doctors and electricians. Trade-tested betterment is honored, though heavily regulated, as it is also in the United States. Corruption is low, much lower than in most states of the United States, though with a correspondingly high level of intrusive "transparency" from government looking into private matters.[10] Inheritance in Sweden is not the admired path to social status, as it also is not in the United States. Like most Americans, most Swedish people live in big towns, though decamping to red-painted shacks in the woods for their long summer vacations. Swedes are honest and bourgeois. And they are, conservatively measured, thirty times richer than their ancestors were in what was in 1800 one of the poorest countries in Europe.[11]

Material growth in goods and services is not the only relevant sign of allocates the Great Enrichment. The word "enrichment" has a highly relevant secondary meaning of spiritual growth.[12] As the economists Ronald Coase and Ning Wang put it in their peroration to *How China Became Capitalist* (2013), "When the markets for goods and the market for ideas are together in full swing, each supporting, augmenting, and strengthening the other, human creativity and happiness stand the best chance to prevail, and the material and spiritual civilizations march on firm ground, side by side."[13]

Many of the clerisy on the left and on the right lament the mass character of modern society, agreeing for example with the leftish Australian economist Geoffrey Harcourt, who wrote in 1994 that trade-tested betterment has stunted "the Christian (and humanist) virtues of altruism, cooperation, tolerance, compassion." The conservative German economist Wilhelm Röpke in 1958 claimed similarly that mass democracy and enrichment has made for "a situation in which man can have no spiritual or moral life."[14] Tocqueville, Matthew Arnold, and José Ortega y Gasset lead the list of hundreds of members of the clerisy during the past century and a half who have deplored from above the Enrichment's failure to enrich. But contrary to such talk from left and right, and from above, the ability to seek the virtues of altruism and cooperation and to have a spiritual or moral life have in fact come from the enrichment of the masses. We have more pilgrim souls now. Mass-produced food and mass-produced education have on the whole elevated modern life, not corrupted it.

The economists and especially the economic historians know it, in their quantitative way. For example, illiteracy fell from over 90 percent of the world's adult population in 1850 to 20 percent in 2000, and by 2010 was down to 13 percent for adult women and 8 percent for adult men.[15] The fall in illiteracy means that the absolute number of literate people has risen since 1850 by a factor of about forty, some 3,900 percent. The rise exceeds the 900 percent rise in worldwide real income per head when the presently poor countries are included. No wonder there are vastly more visits to art museums (on the order of a hundred million attendees per year) and new book titles published (2.3 million per year, about 30 percent in English[16]).

Abraham Lincoln's mother and father were illiterate, yet he became the poet president and his son Robert graduated from Harvard. Such leaping up the social scale by educational enrichment did happen before 1800, occasionally. It is often said that Cardinal Woolsey was the son of a butcher—though it appears in fact that the butcher was also a rich merchant. Thomas Cromwell's father was a blacksmith—though in fact also a cloth merchant. The Chinese examination system allowed the son of a peasant to rise, occasionally, though the sons of the rich, now as then, were usually better prepared to take the exams.

After 1800, though, such leaping up became more common. Father Andrew Greeley (1929–2013), a mystery novelist and academic sociologist at the University of Illinois at Chicago as well as a priest, noted in *The American Catholic: A Social Portrait* (1977) that the second- and third-generation descendants of poor Irish and Italians immigrants to the United States by then trailed only Jews in educational attainment. You can confirm it by looking at the last names beginning with Mc- and O'- or ending with -a, -i, -e, or -o in any list of distinguished Americans today. The descendants of ditch-diggers and lumberjacks are now CEOs and senators. Of one hundred U.S. senators in 2014, on a rough survey four had Italian last names, six Jewish, and fifteen Irish.

Adult literacy and years of schooling are combined nowadays to measure the knowledge leg of the three-legged stool of the "human development index." Technically speaking the index is a geometric average of measures of knowledge, of real income, and of how long people live. All of these elements are rising and some are accelerating. Years of life, for example, have shot up, as I have noted, from an expectation at birth worldwide of less than thirty years in 1800 to fifty-two years in 1960 and to seventy years in 2010, including even very poor places. As a result of declining child mortality and of female control of reproduction, as Rosling shows in another of his amazing videos, birth rates in Bangladesh have fallen almost to replacement levels.[17]

During the recent period of intense globalization, access to clean water has dramatically improved. The distance to drinkable water is one of the heaviest burdens on the world's poorest women, together with the hand-washing of clothes, which itself requires reasonably clean water. The women of Levi's Italian villages in 1936–1937 "stood erect with the stately posture of those accustomed to balancing heavy weights on their heads"—the daily water or the wet clothes.[18] The carrying of burdens on the head had the cost by age forty or so of agonizing arthritis of the neck. The United Nations' Millennium Development Goals, set forth in 2000, aimed to "halve, by 2015, the proportion of people without sustainable access to safe drinking-water and basic sanitation." The goal was achieved five years early. The Modi government of India, elected in 2014, vows to supply toilets and corresponding sewers to the tens of millions of Indians now accustomed to defecating in the open.

Murder rates are down, even in the gun-toting US of A, in the short run since the 1990s and, even more dramatically, in the long run since the 1800s. Murder rates in medieval English villages were higher than in the most violent police districts in today's United States.[19] Addiction to alcohol is down too. American men in the early Republic toted their muzzle-loaders in a whiskey-soaked haze. In early modern cities in Europe, beer drinking absorbed from a quarter to a half of the entire crop of grain. The historian Richard Unger reckons that present-day beer consumption per person among Belgians ("among the most avid beer drinkers in the world") is half that of European city dwellers in the Middle Ages and early modern times.[20] Think of Monty-Pythonesque peasants and bourgeois, and worse, sword-bearing gentry and aristocrats, stumbling around inebriated all day long. European drinking and drunken brawling before the Great Enrichment makes Joe Six-Pack with his concealed-carry Glock .22 seem a model of temperance. Admittedly, medieval beer guzzling and early American whiskey imbibing had additional reasons in hygiene: alcohol kills germs and parasites in water, and had done so in the West since the earliest times. In the East the making of tea with boiled and thereby sterilized water had a similar latent function. And the worldwide use of silver goblets among the rich likewise killed some germs in the water.

Colonial Americans, already pretty rich, extended this last technique, tossing silver coins into their barrels of drinking water; silver coins, too, were the preferred replacement for bone removed by trepanning to relieve pressure on the brain.

Broadening travel is now more common, the jet plane and especially the jumbo jet having reduced the hours of work required to buy a trip. In 1959 we bourgeois Americans went to Europe by sea. The percentage of people with advanced degrees has shot up since the 1960s and is hugely higher now than it ever has been. We live in an age of the artist and scholar and scientist, and can expect much more when China and India and then the rest become rich and educated. The world has now more college graduates, more serious spiritual inquirers, more creative improvers of goods and services, more artists, musicians, professors, journalists, critics, and poets, and above all more appreciators of such arts and sciences and designs and spiritual exercises than all such folk combined in world history up to, say, 1950, and probably up to 1970. And we have more of them in percentage terms, too, since enrichment makes the risk of a life in art easier to venture on, even beyond providing a market for the product. Go to the Third Fridays open house at the Zhou B Art Center on West 35th Street in Chicago and stand amazed (holding a plastic cup filled with not very good white wine) at the number and quality of paintings and sculptures exhibited there. Every big city in North America and Europe has dozens of such centers. Little Fredericton, New Brunswick, has at least one, at which you can listen to folk music and admire painters at work.

Or consider the emergence of a Nature-worshipping environmentalism that would have been viewed as a crazy luxury in the hardscrabble times of 1800 or even of 1933. The economist and student of theology Robert Nelson calls environmentalism the new religion of the West (a West that nonetheless, outside of places like Poland or the United States, imagines itself to be irreligious). He wrote recently that in the twentieth century

> secular religions, such as Marxism, the American progressive "gospel of efficiency," and other forms of "economic religion" were the leading influences on government policies around the world. In economic religion, "efficiency" and "inefficiency" take the place of "good" and "evil." Towards the end of the century, still another secular religion, environmentalism, challenged the economic gospels—questioning the whole idea of "progress."[21]

The economist and think-tank maven Fred L. Smith Jr. speaks of "eco-paganism": "Most environmentalists do not, of course, see themselves as pagans," he writes. "Yet many do espouse a watered down form of pantheism which elevates nature to near the status of a deity."[22] By now the good people of rich and secular places such as Sweden, though contemptuous of the chidish absurdity (as most Swedes believe it to be) of their ancestors' worship of a Lutheran God, have found their transcendent in the worship of Nature, and spend their Sunday mornings devoutly gathering mushrooms and lingonberries in Nature's forest.

The Great Income Enrichment, that is, has allowed higher virtues of faith and hope and love, manifested in art and religion and lingonberries, to flourish, yielding a Great Spiritual Enrichment. In Chicago, Columbia College's arts programs are booming, as is the School of the Art Institute and UIC's School of Design, and the Music Conservatory of Roosevelt University. Our children, rich by historical standards, have become artists of paint and film, of music and video games. A poster promoting Columbia College pairs the slogan "Live your passion" with a photo of a young man fingering his electric guitar. The harvest is what the anarchist and communist and socialist visionaries in the nineteenth century predicted would happen following the abolition of private property and trade—except that the spiritual enrichment followed from the Great Income Enrichment that arose from property-encouraged and trade-tested betterment, not from their abolition. We are experiencing in the twenty-first century a worldwide explosion of high culture, out of "capitalism."

AS YOUR OWN LIFE SHOWS

You doubt it's as rosy as I say. I sympathize with your skepticism. You are bombarded daily with confidently asserted pessimisms, back-projected to the beginnings of the modern world, in the newspapers and on TV and in the latest Chicken-Little book from a respected (noneconomic) scientist. As the science writer Matt Ridley, like me a (rational) optimist, puts it:

> I find the world is full of people who think that their dependence on others is decreasing, or that they would be better off if they were more self-sufficient, or that technological progress has brought no improvement in the standard of living, or that the world is steadily deteriorating, or that the exchange of things and ideas is a superfluous irrelevance.[1]

Such pessimism is favored perhaps by our genetic inheritance of sharp attention to dangers.[2] It certainly sells books and TV shows and newspapers. News is by definition mostly bad, and modern media tell of disasters from all the wide world. Romanticizing the good old days, compared with which our latter days look so shabby, has been standard since the Romantic movement, and anyway was a conventional trope among the Greeks and Hebrews and Hindus celebrating an age of gold. Science fiction and horror fiction, offshoots of Romanticism, have tended since their invention in the nineteenth century to predict dystopias, reflecting the pessimism about the disturbing betterment current at the time. Consider Mary Shelley's *Frankenstein; or, The Modern Prometheus* (1816), H. G. Wells's *The Time Machine* (1895), John Wyndham's *The Day of the Triffids* (1951), or Matt Damon and Jodie Foster in *Elysium* (2013). It is a rare science-fiction writer, a Robert Heinlein or an Ursula K. Le Guin, who does *not* see the future as a version of scientific mischance or class struggle or imperial fascism or, most recently, environmental catastrophe.

But look around at the material betterments since 1800 in such places as your own room, located in a high-rise unbuildable before the 1880s with a condominium agreement first invented in Puerto Rico in 1958:

the twenty ballpoint pens stuffed into a mass-produced coffee cup, pens and cups greatly cheapened after World War II,

the electric lights much brighter and more convenient than candles or kerosene lamps,

the running water and sewer system, making possible the indoor toilet that your great-aunt's farm in Illinois in 1930 did not have,

the central heating rare even in rich Britain before 1970,

the thin TV screen hanging on the wall with access to many hundreds of idiotic programs,

the magnesium ladder standing over in the corner, safer and in terms of work-hours-to-buy cheaper than anything comparable available before 1960,

the family photos, better than the cutout profiles available in 1800,

the scissors for making cutouts, hanging on a nail on a hardwood bookcase imported from the other side of the world in container ships invented in 1957—things all cheaper in hours of work per item than they were in 1800 or 1960,

the cheap but serviceable paper on which to scribble grocery lists for the Trader Joe's store, driven to in a car that is cheaper in labor-hours than a horse and wagon in 1850 or a bicycle early in its improvement in 1880,

the safety pins and staplers, invented in the nineteenth century,

the machine-made quilt on your advanced mattress, better aesthetically and functionally than most handmade quilts and down mattresses available in 1900,

the faux-hardwood flooring, produced by better band saws and better veneers made with better scalpers of logs and better glue,

the dropped ceiling, which so pleasantly covers the pipes for fire sprinklers and the wiring for smoke detectors,

the lovely mass-produced carpeting,

the lucid plate-glass window,

the organized distribution to and from Whole Foods of that bowl of apples over there, the scattered books written by a multitude of highly educated people,

the copies of scholarly articles on modern economic growth, copies made by xe-
    roxing, invented in 1959 and costing now a small fraction in labor-time-to-
    buy of what it cost then,

the fine quality of the inexpensive book you now hold,

the ease of access to the Kindle edition if you were too cheap to buy the book,

the contact lenses that allow you to read it,

the computer on which you take admiring notes about it,

the college sheepskin on the wall, the acquiring of which allows you to grasp the
    book's profundity,

and even the better aluminum studs behind the wall, preventing the better wall-
    board painted with better paint and affixed with better cordless screwdrivers
    from caving in when you punch it out of sadly misled vexation at some of the
    more irritating factual claims in the book.

All this. And note how all of it arose over the past two centuries only, in a
trade-testing economy.

It did not arise from the government or from unions, as fine as such institutions are in other ways. I do earnestly believe that government "has a
role," as my friends on the left relentlessly put it to me. For example, I admire
the Civil Rights Act of 1964, especially its overturning of legal segregation,
and the Voting Rights Act of 1965, overturning voter suppression. And as for
unions, I belonged when I was seventeen to the National Maritime Union,
and now in old age I belong enthusiastically—reacting to the union-busting
folly of our local version of bureaucracy run mad in the "administrative university"—to a union for professors at the University of Illinois at Chicago,
affiliated with the American Federation of Teachers, AFL-CIO. You gotta go
down and join the union. I'm a union maid.

But I do not imagine that expanding the government or joining the union
will *radically* improve the material condition of my people, rich or poor.
That would be mistaken economics and mistaken history. The enrichment
came mainly from bourgeois liberty and creativity unbridled, not from piling up constraints on voluntary deals or from redistributing what income
we get from the deals. Wages and working conditions, after such shocking
enrichment, are in fact determined largely by supply and demand, not by
regulations passed by Congress or by struggles on the picket line. All boats
do rise. Professors and artists and child-care workers, whose productivity

has not increased for millennia, benefit from being substitutes in the long run for farmers and truck drivers and medical doctors, whose productivity during the Great Enrichment has risen enormously. A professor with an antique technology of chalk-and-talk could have instead entered farming or medicine, which means that she must earn, roughly at least, what such utterly transformed jobs earn. The professor cannot earn in equilibrium one-tenth, say, of what farmers earn, not because it would be unfair but because she could move, as the poet Robert Frost did in the early twentieth century, between farming and teaching. A ten-to-one differential is not sustainable if a sufficient number of people can move. Such reasoning was Adam Smith's chief analytic contribution to the emerging political economy of the eighteenth century.

If such an economic analysis were not roughly true in the world, one could not explain why Walmart employees, not unionized, make conservatively measured twenty times what the average South Asian employee makes. The explanation is obviously not solidarity forever or bargaining skill, or the more stringent regulatory constraints that Walmart faces in the United States. Walmart would not be in business if the legally required minimum wage were thirty times what it earned from hiring a laborer, no more than it would if the minimum wage were raised to $300 an hour. The gap between the United States and South Asia arises not from acts of Congress but from the economist's "marginal productivity theory," the commercial demand for labor determined by how much money for the employers the average employee produces in an extra hour of work. Marginal, or for that matter total, productivity depends on how fully an economy has been able to take advantage of bourgeois betterment. Trade-testing of new ideas, not government-regulating or union-joining, did it.

The English colonists in North America at first lived on $2 a day. The historical reconstruction of the Plimouth Plantation in southeastern Massachusetts shows how the settlers lived in the 1620s—drafty, unplastered walls, without glass windows, enclosing the sole room on the ground floor, and up a ladder to a sleeping loft. Six people lived there (in northern Europe typically there were also cows in the back for additional heat, and smell). The mother had one skirt for Sunday and one or two for the rest of the week. The newcomers faced disease, often fatal, in the first, "seasoning" generation, and smallpox and dysentery were ongoing threats, especially to children. The television series *Colonial House* in 2004 showed people trying to live in the way of pioneers in Maine in 1628, to similar effect. It was no bag of bluebirds. (True, in America, as was not the case among most Europeans at the time, there was from the beginning usually sufficient food, though still reliant on the harvest. Smith was right to note in 1776 of the English colonies that "a dearth has never been known there."[3])

Yet by 2011 the average resident of the United States consumed, correcting for inflation, $132 a day, sixty-six times more housing, food, education, furniture than in 1620—a betterment of 6,500 percent. Such a figure is conservatively measured, not allowing for the better quality of today's goods and services. The rise is a great deal larger per person if you adjust for the better quality of modern medicine (antibiotics, painless dentistry) and travel (cars, airplanes) and lighting (incandescent bulbs and now LEDs) and knowledge (philosophy and literature, physical science and, yes, economics). Such bettering would yield, according again to the always useful economist William Nordhaus, a factor as high as the rough yet justifiable figure at the upper end of the possibilities I keep mentioning, a factor of 100.[4] Thomas Babington Macaulay (1800–1859), with a longer perspective than his depressed contemporaries the classical economists, remarked in his *History of England from the Accession of James the Second* (1848):

> It is now the [Romantic] fashion to place the Golden Age of England in times when noblemen were destitute of comforts the want of which would be intolerable to a modern footman, . . . when to have a clean shirt once a week was a privilege reserved for the higher class of gentry, . . . when men died faster in the lanes of our towns than they now die on the coast of Guiana [thus seasoning illness]. We too shall, in our turn, be outstripped. . . . It may well be, in the twentieth century . . . that laboring men may be as little used to dine without meat as they now are to eat rye bread; that sanitary police and medical discoveries may have added several more years [try thirty more, Tom] to the average length of human life; that numerous comforts and luxuries which are now unknown, or confined to a few, may be within the reach of every diligent and thrifty working man.[5]

In the reign of Marx and materialism, 1890–1980, it was the fashion to deprecate Macaulay as hopelessly optimistic about progress. In the same extraordinary year of 1848 in which Macaulay published the first volume of his *History*, John Stuart Mill published the first edition of his *Political Economy*, in which he predicted merely modest betterment, modest in view of diminishing returns and the principle of population. Even in its last edition, 1871, when the betterment was becoming obvious, Mill did not modify his restrained and un-Macaulayite enthusiasm for the twentieth century to come. But Macaulay, not Mill, was more correct in his predictions, and his post-dictions. The anti-Whig-history pessimists, from Mill to Herbert Butterfield, were mistaken (as Butterfield himself eventually conceded, becoming himself a Whig historian). Fernand Braudel, the soft-left French historian of "capitalism," observed that even the rich in olden times suffered a world in which "heating was still poor, ventilation derisory."[6] In a rich modern economy even quite poor people have access to vaccination, air conditioning, automobiles, painless dentistry, reliable birth control, the Internet, and flush toilets. The aristocrats attending on the very Sun King himself at Versailles in 1715 had access instead to smallpox, hand-held fans and open windows, bumpy carriages, dentists with big pliers, leaky condoms, a small list of censored books, and relieving themselves in the chamber pots of *Le Palais*.

You are doubtful still. Open, then, your own closet. Compare it with the volume and quality of clothing possessed by even the richest woman in Plimouth in 1620, or for that matter the above-average woman in Amsterdam in 1800, or all but the extremely well-off in London in 1900 (if you doubt that last, watch the 1999 BBC's series *1900 House*; or while in London visit for a view of eighteenth-century life the Dennis Severs House for its family of Huguenot-descended silk weavers).

Further, a good deal of our present flow of income in the rising number of rich countries goes into consumer durables (as the economists call them), things that yield services over time rather than being, like pizza or movie tickets or copies of the *Printer's Row Journal*, used up in a day or a week or a year. The very fact of our massive expenditure on consumer durables betokens an enriched population, which can invest in long-lived items such as cars and granite kitchen counters instead of hustling to get today's food and drink. Look around at your bedroom. The $2,000 Tempur-Pedic mattress and the $500 Bose clock radio beside it contain together as much productive power as the entire average yearly income of a person in Ghana or Pakistan or Kyrgyzstan.

The point is stronger still, since the average age of U.S. consumer durables of your house, except for the house itself, is merely a little over four years.

Every four and a half years the automobile or the coat or the Bose is, on average, bought again, even though many of the "old" items have no secondhand market to offset the cost of novelty. Such churning of consumer durables is not peculiar to the United States. In Japan the tiny living spaces are refurnished frequently, and the unfashionable furnishings, such as working color TVs and entire bedrooms sets, are left at the curb to be picked up by junk men specialized in the trade.[7] Your mattress and the Bose together could pay for every fourth year of a Pakistani income. Select a few other items—a fridge, say, or that bedroom set, and you're set for many, many years of Pakistani life. At a higher income, at say the world's and Brazil's average of $33 dollars a day, if you sold your $220,000 average American house (supposing you owned it clear of a mortgage) and took a small apartment or a shack in a *favela* in Rio you could live on that sale alone for fully eighteen years of leisure at the U.S. average income in 1941, playing soccer barefoot on the beach at Copacabana.

In other words, modern economic growth emerged only in the last couple of centuries out of 1,500 centuries, or out of 500, or 100, or 10, or 5. A Malthusian could only predict—from the sevenfold increase of world population 1800 to the present—a homeostatic reversion to $3-a-day misery, or worse. Some still do, while trumpeting their status as Scientists devoted to facts. Our beloved friends the environmentalists and our less-beloved friends the population-control mavens cling to the Malthus of 1798 as their guide.

They have been gravely mistaken. Just about the time that Malthus so persuasively explained it, the old Malthusian constraint, luckily for us, began to dissolve.[8] Nowadays, and contrary to a Malthusian belief still widely credited, having more humans on the planet is good for the rest of us.[9] The whole of humankind, and no European imperium or class exploitation about it, broke decisively with the homeostatic equilibrium of being poor and sick. Trade-tested betterment exploded.

5

THE POOR WERE MADE
MUCH BETTER OFF

The two centuries of uplift happened most significantly not to the aristocrats or the landlords or the priests of the old ruling class, who were rather up-lifted already, but to the commoners, your ancestors and mine. The economist Joseph Alois Schumpeter (1883–1950) noted in the 1940s that "Queen Elizabeth owned silk stockings."

> The capitalist achievement does not typically consist in providing more silk stockings for queens but in bringing them within the reach of factory girls in return for steadily decreasing amounts of effort. . . . The capitalist process, not by coincidence but by virtue of its mechanism, progressively raises the standard of life of the masses.[1]

By now Schumpeter's point is still more obviously correct. The "mechanism" he had in mind is the entry of fresh entrepreneurs, driving the labor-hour price of things down, down, down, to the annoyance of the first betterers, who would rather have patent monopolies, such as Thomas Edison persistently sought.

W. Michael Cox and Richard Alm in 1999 documented the driving down, and recently Donald Boudreaux has reprised their argument using various catalogues from Sears, Roebuck (a company itself overtaken by the entry of entrepreneurs from Target, Walmart, Best Buy, Home Depot, Nordstrom's Rack, and other betterers, but in 1956 still dominant): "Sears' lowest-priced no-frost refrigerator-freezer in 1956," notes Boudreaux, "had 9.6 cubic feet of space, and sold for $219.95 (in 1956 dollars)."

Because the typical production-line worker back then earned $1.89 per hour (in 1956 dollars), an average American in the mid-1950s had to toil 116 hours to buy this refrigerator-freezer. Today, Home Depot sells a similar refrigerator-freezer for $298 (in 2013 dollars). Earning $20.14 per hour, an average American worker today works 15 hours to buy that appliance.[2]

That's 116 hours versus merely 15, an 87 percent decline in the real cost of living by work. The widespread notion that times were better for ordinary Americans in the 1950s than they are now could use some fact checking.

Yes, the rich got richer, 1800 to the present—they too spend less to buy a much better color television now than they did in 1975, and get a much better commute in their chauffeur-driven vehicle now than in 1800. But so did the poor get richer, much richer, at first in the late nineteenth century in such pioneering countries as Britain and France, and then in a wider world. Even in 1776 Adam Smith could claim that because of the elaborate division of labor and the trade that accompanied it "the very meanest person in a civilized country" had the advantage of "the easy and simple manner in which he is commonly accommodated":

> Compared, indeed, with the more extravagant luxury of the great, his accommodation must no doubt appear extremely simple and easy; and yet it may be true, perhaps, that the accommodation of an European prince does not always so much exceed that of an industrious and frugal peasant, as the accommodation of the latter exceeds that of many an African king, the absolute master of the lives and liberties of ten thousand naked savages.[3]

Smith knew next to nothing about African kings, and one may doubt the literal truth of the comparison in 1776 (it had become a common figure of argument after the Age of Exploration, used for example by John Locke). But the Great Enrichment made it true.

The subsequent enrichment of the very meanest person in Scotland was, I have frequently noted, 9,900 percent. It can only be explained by vastly greater productivity per worker, which is to say by a startling speeding up since 1800 of trade-tested betterment.[4] The exactitude of the 9,900 percent is silly: we do not know such a figure even to two significant digits. Its non-silly import, though, and the reason I'll keep using it, is that we have in fact benefited mightily from a *very* large percentage increase of productivity over the base in 1800.

One thousand percent, 5,000 percent, 10,000 percent—take your pick. It is anyway orders of magnitude of uplift that cannot be explained by little uplifts from improved static efficiency or little uplifts by reductions of worker exploitation. The Great Enrichment did not happen because of union demands or government regulation or routine exploitations or routine investments. Such routines, about which so much politics of left and right turns ("Raise the minimum wage!" "Protect the investing class!"), can't deliver 9,900 percent, whether one-by-one or in combination. If they could, the Great Enrichment would have happened earlier and elsewhere, since thrift and exploitation and investment, and for that matter occasional outbreaks of democratic demands for higher wages, are routine in human history.

The uplifting since 1800, in other words, was distinctly positive-sum, a free lunch, the sort of event the management theorist Mary Parker Follett dubbed in 1925 a win-win. She elsewhere said that the best democracy is not the rule of the majority but a search for agreement.[5] The easiest way of finding agreement is to find a win-win deal, which economists call "Pareto improving." The deals were possible because of radically new ideas, such as the betterments of steam and steel or of fertilizer and antibiotics or of voting and education—betterments, and voting and education, *not* encouraged in an old world long in the grip of an anxious and arrogant elite able to enforce its self-protectionisms. The economic and political betterments, and the intellectual children and grandchildren and great-grandchildren of the betterments, were imagined, produced, financed, tested, and sold by the middle class.

It didn't happen, I repeat, because of elite science.[6] As Ó Gráda put it recently, "The foremost inventor-entrepreneurs of the Industrial Revolution were of rather modest, artisanal origins."[7] Elite science made us richer only quite late in economic history, long after 1850. And anyway the eventual successes of useful science itself came from a Scottish equality and a resulting Great Enrichment that gave British design engineers and German organic chemists from modest backgrounds a shot at fame and riches. Without liberty and dignity for ordinary people the anxious elite would have suppressed commercial improvements, such as Wedgwood's pottery (Wedgwood despised patents, and only had one) or Edison's movie camera (his patent on movies, among the fully 1,093 he acquired, was partly overturned only in 1902, and for good in 1917), which in the event were brought within the reach of factory girls in return for steadily decreasing amounts of effort.

The Great Enrichment after 1800 came from human creativity unleashed by liberty and dignity for ordinary people, through trade-tested betterment resting on a new equality in the eyes of others, and spread by the overturning of monopoly in competition. On the supply side, the creativity of ordinary people now able to become extraordinary was released. On the demand side, the tastes of ordinary people were indulged, in cheap watches and Model T Fords and no-press shirts. The philosopher Karl Popper called the trade-oriented novelty of the modern world the "open society," and the politico-economic theorists Douglass North, John Wallis, and Barry Weingast call it the "open-access" society.[8] The *ORDO* liberals of pre- and postwar Germany called it "a competitive order" or a "social market economy" (which, however, they believed required a strong government to keep it from descending into monopolies, as indeed it had in Germany).[9] Whatever it is called, such a society, thronging with free conversations easily joined, made for a creativity that disturbed the rules of the game—rules designed, unsurprisingly, by the elite in favor of the old rich. The open economy created numerous *nouveaux riches*, such as James Watt and Robert Fulton. Both eventually failed to protect their monopolies. Fernand Braudel argued to the contrary that capitalism was inherently and permanently monopolistic. But *les nouveaux hommes* were themselves competed against by still newer rich, to the benefit, in the third act, of us all, à la Schumpeter and Nordhaus. A patent or copyright monopoly, to be sure, must be broken for the poor to benefit. But aside from overlawyered definitions of so-called intellectual property, for the most part it has been.[10]

The mechanism that raised up the poor is not a trickle down of expenditures from rich people. One hears such an argument from the right—even, alas, from Adam Smith on a rare bad day, in one of merely two uses in his published writings of the phrase "invisible hand."[11] One hears too a Keynesian form of trickle *up* from the left, as from the well-meaning Robert Reich in the *Nation* magazine: "If consumers don't have adequate purchasing power, businesses have no incentive to expand or hire additional workers [note Reich's desideratum: jobs]. Because the rich spend a smaller proportion of their incomes than the middle class and the poor, it stands to reason that as a larger and larger share of the nation's total income goes to the top, consumer demand is dampened."[12]

Reich's reasoning supposes that the point of an economy is jobs, jobs, jobs, and that spending assures jobs. The writer Pascal-Emmanuel Gobry calls such a view "productionist," as against "creativist," and admits (as I do) that in the very short run it is true.[13] The economy in the short run is indeed a treadmill of production and consumption that can stop running if whacked with a sledgehammer, as for example the Greek economy was in 2015 when the banks were closed. In a year of mass unemployment caused by great whackings—1933 in the United States and Germany, for example—the Keynesian trickle up from expenditure is correct. By all means, dig holes and fill them up and then dig them again, and pay the diggers/fillers with newly printed currency. (On the other hand, estimates of the "multiplier" on government expenditure even in 1933 have come in at below 1.0.) But in a more typical year of mismatched jobs and skills, the Keynesian argument is incorrect. Nor is it correct from peak to peak of the business cycle, for which only a creativist view makes economic sense. In the long run we get better off only by betterment, not by spending.[14] If spending worked, we could enrich ourselves endlessly by printing money and handing it out in steadily increasing sums to those high-spending poor—an unlimited miracle achieved merely by printing little portraits of George Washington. In nonmiraculous economies, during the long run and even in most of the short run, spending on an auto or TV has an opportunity cost of spending on food or education. There is no free lunch springing from a trickle down (as the Republicans say), or a trickle up (as the Democrats say), from mere spending. We get better by getting smarter, only, not by miraculous trickles up or down.

The Schumpeterian mechanism is the long-run one of open competition of betterments among the temporarily rich in Riverside orange groves and Manchester cotton mills and Chicago apartment developments and Swedish furniture stores that radically cheapens food and clothing and housing and furniture. It has nothing to do with trickling. Such openness to competition after 1800, and the cooperation that betterments require, made the economies that adopted it startlingly more productive, creating ten times, thirty times, a hundred times more goods and services, and to the poorest among us.

∞

Even in the already-advanced countries in recent decades there has been no complete stagnation of real incomes for ordinary people. You will have heard that "wages are flat" or that "the middle class is shrinking." But you also know that you should not believe everything you read in the papers.[15] This is not to say that no one in rich countries such as the United States is unskilled, addicted, badly parented, discriminated against, or simply horribly unlucky. George Packer's recent *The Unwinding: An Inner History of the New America* (2013) and Barbara Ehrenreich's earlier *Nickel and Dimed: On (Not) Getting By in America* (2001) carry on a long and distinguished tradition of telling the bourgeoisie about the poor, going back to James Agee and Walker Evans's *Let Us Now Praise Famous Men* (1944), George Orwell's *The Road to Wigan Pier* (1937), Jack London's *The People of the Abyss* (1903), Jacob Riis's *How the Other Half Lives: Studies among the Tenements of New York* (1890), and, the fount of such writings, Friedrich Engels's *The Condition of the Working Class in England* (1845).

They are not making it up. Anyone who reads such books is wrenched out of a comfortable ignorance about the other half. The wrenching comes also in fictional form, from John Steinbeck's *The Grapes of Wrath* (1939) or James T. Farrell's *Studs Lonigan* (1932–1935) or Richard Wright's *Native Son* (1940) or, in Europe, among the many observers of the Two Nations since the beginning of such a sensibility in the 1840s, Émile Zola's *Germinal* (1885), which made many of us into socialists. The wrenching is salutary. It is said that Winston Churchill, scion of the aristocracy, believed that most English poor people lived in rose-covered cottages. He couldn't imagine back-to-backs in Salford, with the communal outhouse at the end of the row. Wake up, Winston.

But waking up does not imply despairing, or proposing the overthrow of the System, if the System is in fact over the long run enriching the poor, or at any rate enriching the poor better than those other systems that have been tried from time to time. Righteous, if inexpensive, indignation inspired by survivor's guilt about alleged "victims" of something called "capitalism," and envious anger at the silly consumption by the rich, does not invariably yield betterment for the poor. Remarks such as "there are still poor people" or "some people have more power than others," though claiming the ethical high-ground for the speaker, are neither deep nor clever. Repeating them, or nodding wisely at their repetition, or buying Piketty's *Capital in the Twenty-First Century* to display on your coffee table, does not make you a good person. You are a good person if you actually help the poor. Open a business. Invest in a grocery store in an urban food desert. Invent a new battery. Vote for better schools. Adopt a Pakistani orphan. Volunteer to feed people at Grace Church on Saturday mornings. The offering of counterproductive policies, or the making of indignant declarations to your husband after finishing an article in the *Sunday New York Times Magazine*, does not help the poor.

The economy and society of the United States are not in fact unwinding, and people are in fact getting by better than they did before. The children of the sharecropping families in Hale County, Alabama, whom Agee and Evans objectified, to the lasting resentment of the older members of the families, are doing pretty well, earning money, many of their children going to college.[16] That even over the long run there remain some poor people does not mean that the system is not working for the poor, so long as the condition of the poor is continuing to improve, as it is, contrary to the newspaper stories and the pessimistic books, and so long as the percentage of the desperately poor is heading toward zero, as it is nationally in the United States, and worldwide. That people still sometimes die in hospitals does not mean that medicine is to be replaced by witch doctors, so long as death rates are falling and so long as the death rate would not fall under the care of the witch doctors.

And poverty is indeed falling, even recently, even in already rich countries. If income is correctly measured to include better working conditions, more years of education, better health care, longer retirement years, larger transfers such as Social Security and Medicaid, and above all the rising quality of the larger number of goods, the real income of the poor has risen, if at a slower pace than in the 1950s—which followed the wretched time-outs of the Great Depression and World War II.[17] The economist Angus Deaton notes that "once the rebuilding is done [as it was fully in, say, 1970], new growth relies on inventing new ways of doing things and putting them into practice, and this turning over of virgin soil is harder than replowing an old furrow."[18] In 2013 the economists Donald Boudreaux and Mark Perry noted that "according to the Bureau of Economic Analysis, spending by households on many of modern life's 'basics'—food at home, automobiles, clothing and footwear, household furnishings and equipment, and housing and utilities—fell from 53 percent of disposable income in 1950 to 44 percent in 1970 to 32 percent today." It is a point that the economic historian Robert Fogel had made in 1999 for a longer span.[19] The economist Steven Horwitz summarizes the facts on labor-hours required to buy a color TV or an automobile, and notes that "these data do not capture . . . the change in quality. . . . The 1973 TV was at most 25 inches, with poor resolution, probably no remote control, weak sound, and generally nothing like its 2013 descendant. . . . Getting 100,000 miles out of a car in the 1970s was cause for celebration. Not getting 100,000 miles out of a car today is cause to think you bought a lemon."[20]

Nor in the United States are the poor getting poorer. Horwitz observes that "looking at various data on consumption, from Census Bureau surveys of what the poor have in their homes to the labor time required to purchase a variety of consumer goods, makes clear that poor Americans are living better now than ever before. In fact, poor Americans today live better, by these measures, than did their middle class counterparts in the 1970s."[21] In the summer of 1976 an associate professor of economics at the University of Chicago had no air conditioning in his apartment.[22] Nowadays many quite poor Chicagoans have it. The terrible heat wave in Chicago of July 1995 killed over seven hundred people, mainly low-income.[23] Yet earlier heat waves in 1936 and 1948, before air conditioning was at all common, had probably killed many more.[24] The 2003 heat wave in non–air conditioned France killed 14,800 people, and 70,000 Europe-wide. Imagine what the London heat wave in June 1858 did.

6

INEQUALITY IS NOT
THE PROBLEM

Robert Reich argues that the problem must be measured by inequality, Gini-coefficient style, not by the absolute condition of the poor. "Widening inequality," he declares, "challenges the nation's core ideal of equal opportunity":

> Widening inequality still hampers upward mobility. That's simply because the ladder is far longer now. The distance between its bottom and top rungs, and between every rung along the way, is far greater. Anyone ascending it at the same speed as before will necessarily make less progress upward.[1]

Reich is mistaken. Horwitz summarizes the results of a study by Julia Isaacs on individual mobility 1969–2005: "82% of children of the bottom 20% in 1969 had [real] incomes in 2000 that were higher than what their parents had in 1969. The median [real] income of those children of the poor of 1969 was double that of their parents."[2] There is no doubt that the children and grandchildren of the English coal miners of 1937, whom Orwell describes "traveling" underground, bent over double walking a mile or more to get to the coal face, at which point they started to get paid, are much better off than their fathers or grandfathers. There is no doubt that the children and grandchildren of the Dust Bowl refugees in California are. Steinbeck chronicled in *The Grapes of Wrath* their worst and terrible times. A few years later many of the Okies got jobs in the war industries, and many of their children went to university. Some became university professors who think that the poor are getting poorer.

The usual way of talking about poverty relies on the percentage distribution of income, staring fixedly for example at an official-sounding but *relative* "poverty line." As the progressive Australian economist Peter Saunders observes, however, such a definition of poverty "automatically shift upwards whenever the real incomes [and hence the poverty line] are rising."[3] The poor are always with us, but merely by definition, the opposite of the Lake Wobegon effect—it's not that all the children are above average, but that there is a bottom fifth or tenth or whatever, always, in any distribution whatsoever. Of course.

It's not higher math. The philosopher Harry Frankfurt noted long ago that "calculating the size of an equal share [of income in the style of poverty lines or Gini coefficients] is plainly much easier than determining how much a person needs in order to have enough"—"much easier," as in dividing GDP by population and reporting with irritation that some people earn, or get, more.[4] It is the simplified ethics of the schoolyard, or dividing a cake among friends: "That's unfair."

But as Frankfurt also noted, inequality is in itself ethically irrelevant: "Economic equality is not, as such, of particular moral importance." In ethical truth we wish to raise up the poor to "enough" for them to function in a democratic society and to have full human lives. It doesn't matter ethically whether the poor have the same number of diamond bracelets and Porsche automobiles as do owners of hedge funds. It does, however, matter ethically whether they have the same opportunities to vote or to learn to read or to have a roof over their heads. The Illinois state consitution of 1970 embodied the confusion between the condition of the working class and the gap between rich and poor, claiming in its preamble that it seeks to "eliminate poverty *and inequality*."[5] We had better focus directly on what we actually want to achieve, which is equal sustenance and dignity, eliminating poverty, acquiring for all people what the economist Amartya Sen and the philosopher Martha Nussbaum call capabilities.[6] The size of the Gini coefficient or the share of the bottom 10 percent is irrelevant to the noble and ethically relevant and actually attainable purpose of raising the poor to a condition of dignity, Frankfurt's "enough."

The Liberal Lady Glencora Palliser (née M'Cluskie) in Anthony Trollope's political novel *Phineas Finn* (1867–1868) declares, "Making men and women all equal. That I take to be the gist of our political theory," as against the Conservative delight in rank and privilege. But one of the novel's radicals in the

Cobden-Bright-Mill mold ("Joshua Monk") sees the ethical point more clearly, and replies to her: "Equality is an ugly word, and frightens," as indeed it had long frightened the political class in Britain, traumatized by wild French declarations for *égalité*, and by the example of American egalitarianism (well . . . egalitarianism for male, straight, white, Anglo, middle-aged, high-income, nonimmigrant, New England mainline Protestants). The motive of the true Liberal, Monk continues, should not be equality but "the wish of every honest [that is, honorable] man . . . to assist in lifting up those below him."[7] Such an ethical goal was to be achieved, Monk the libertarian liberal would argue, not by direct programs of redistribution, nor by regulation, nor by trade unions, but by free trade and rights for women and tax-financed education—and in the event above all by the Great Enrichment, which finally in the late nineteenth century started sending real wages sharply up, Europe-wide. The absolute condition of the poor has been raised overwhelmingly more by the Great Enrichment than by regulation or redistribution. As the economic historians Ian Gazeley and Andrew Newell concluded in their 2010 study of "the reduction, almost to elimination, of absolute poverty among working households in Britain between 1904 and 1937": "The elimination of grinding poverty among working families was almost complete by the late thirties, well before the Welfare State." Their chart 2 exhibits weekly income distributions in 1886 prices at 1886, 1906, 1938, and 1960, showing the disappearance of the inflation-adjusted classic line of misery for British workers, "'round about a pound a week.'"[8]

Yet the left works overtime, out of the best of motives, to rescue its ethically irrelevant focus on Gini coefficients and the relative poverty line. A recent example of the leftish labor is the book by a French economist I have mentioned, Thomas Piketty's *Capital in the Twenty-First Century* (translated 2014), which was greeted with squeals of delight by the American and British left, and rapidly rose to number one on the *New York Times* best-seller list. Piketty claims that relative poverty is what matters, whether or not the poorest improve. "Just as we've been saying!" the left cried. "Eliminate poverty *and inequality*."

Much of the research on the economics of inequality stumbles on this simple ethical point, focusing on measures of relative inequality such as the Gini coefficient rather than on measures of the absolute welfare of the poor, on inequality rather than poverty, having elided the two. Speaking of the legal philosopher Ronald Dworkin's egalitarianism, Frankfurt observed that

Dworkin in fact, and ethically, "cares principally about the [absolute] value of people's lives, but he mistakenly represents himself as caring principally about the *relative* magnitudes of their economic assets."[9] Dworkin and the left commonly miss the ethical point, which is the liberal, Joshua Monk one of lifting up the poor. By redistribution? By equality in diamond bracelets? By codes for buildings or unions for trades? No: by the dramatic increase in the size of the pie, which has historically brought the poor to 90 or 95 percent of "enough," as against the small percent of enough attainable by redistribution without enlarging the pie. The economic historian Robert Margo noted in 1993 that before the Civil Rights Act "blacks could not aspire to high-paying white collar jobs" because of discrimination. Yet African Americans had prepared themselves, by their own efforts, up from slavery, to perform in such jobs if given a chance. "Middle-class blacks owe their success in large part to themselves," and to the increasingly educated and productive society they lived in. "What if the black labor force, poised on the eve of the Civil Rights Movement, was just as illiterate, impoverished, rural, and Southern as when Lincoln freed the slaves? . . . Would we have as large a black middle class as we do today? Plainly not."[10]

Piketty is alarmed by what he claims is the force of interest on inherited wealth causing inequality to increase. In 2014 he declared to the BBC's Evan Davis in an interview that "money tends to reproduce itself." Yet his own data suggest that only in the United States and the United Kingdom (with Canada) has inequality of wealth increased recently—a puzzle if money tends to reproduce itself, always, as a general law governed by his Ricardo-plus-Marx inequality-producing accumulation of financial capital, Piketty's master algebra of $r > g$. Inequality in fact goes up and down in great waves, 1800 to the present, which also doesn't figure in such a tale. Once a Piketty-wave starts it would, according to his logic, never stop, which means we should have been overwhelmed by an inequality-tsunami in 1800 CE or 1000 CE or for that matter 2000 BCE.

Nor does Piketty acknowledge entrepreneurial profit, the trade-tested betterment that through the Bourgeois Deal has made the poor rich. He focuses on the evil of rich people having seven Rolex watches by mere inheritance. Liliane Bettencourt, heiress to the L'Oréal fortune, in 2014 the wealthiest woman in the world, who "has never worked a day in her life, saw her fortune grow exactly as fast as that of [the admittedly bettering] Bill Gates." Ugh. Which is the sum of Piketty's ethical analysis.

The Australian economists Geoffrey Brennan, Gordon Menzies, and Michael Munger make a similar argument in a recent paper, written in advance of Piketty's book, that inheritance *inter vivos* of human capital is bound to exacerbate Gini-coefficient inequality because "for the first time in human history richer parents are having fewer children. . . . Even if the increased opulence continues, it will be concentrated in fewer and fewer hands."[11] The rich will send their one boy, intensively tutored in French and mathematics, to Sydney Grammar School and on to Harvard. The poor will dissipate what little they have among their supposedly numerous children.

Yet if on account of Adam Smith's hoped-for "universal opulence which extends itself to the lowest ranks of the people" all have access to excellent education—which is a proper subject for social policy—and if the poor are so rich (because the Great Enrichment) that they too have fewer children, which is the case, then the tendency to rising variance will be attenuated.[12] The economist Tyler Cowen reminds me, further, that "low" birth rates also include zero children, which would make lines die out—as indeed they often did, even in royal families, well nourished. Nonexistent children, such as those of Grand Duke of Florence Gian Gastone de' Medici in 1737, can't inherit either financial or human capital.

And the effect of inherited wealth on children is commonly to remove their ambition, as one can witness daily on Rodeo Drive, or in Bettencourt's daughter. Laziness from being rich too early is a powerful equalizer. Imagine if you had inherited ten million dollars at age eighteen, before your character was fully formed. It would have been an ethical disaster, as it regularly is for the children of the rich. However many diamond bracelets they have, most rich children don't bother to suffer through, say, a PhD in economics. Why bother? David Rockefeller did, to be sure (University of Chicago, 1940), but his grandfather was unusually lucky in transmitting a poor boy's values and a lifelong philanthropist's tastes to his son and then to his six John-Junior-begotten grandchildren. We prosperous parents of the Great Enrichment can properly worry about our children's and especially our grandchildren's incentives to undertake such efforts as a PhD, or serious entrepreneurship, or for that matter serious charity (Bettencourt's charitable foundation, by contrast with the Rockefellers', is comically niggardly, endowed with only one-half of 1 percent of her wealth).

And it is commonly the case, contrary to the focus of Piketty and of Brennan, Menzies, and Munger on inheritance, that the people with more

money got their more by being more productive, for the benefit of us all—
getting that PhD, for example, or being excellent makers of automobiles or
excellent writers of novels or excellent throwers of touchdown passes or
excellent providers of cell phones, such as Carlos Slim of Mexico (with a
little boost, it may be, from corrupting the Mexican parliament). That Frank
Sinatra became richer than most of his fans was not an ethical scandal. The
"Wilt Chamberlain" example devised by the philosopher Robert Nozick says
that if we pay voluntarily to get the benefit of clever CEOs or gifted athletes
there is no further ethical issue.[13] The unusually high rewards to the Frank
Sinatras and Jamie Dimons and Wilt Chamberlains come from the much
wider trading during the age of globalization and of mechanical reproduction, not from theft.[14]

For the poor in the countries that have allowed the ethical change to
happen, Frankfurt's "enough" has largely come to pass. "Largely," I say, and
much more than alternative systems have allowed. I do not say "completely"
or "as much as every honest person would wish." But I have noted that the
contrast between the condition of the working class in the United States and
in such avowedly social-democratic countries as the Netherlands or Sweden
is not in fact large, despite what you have heard from journalists and politicians who have not seriously looked into the actual statistics or have not
seriously experienced more than one country. The social safety net is, in
practice, rather similar among rich countries. But in any event the safety net,
with or without holes, is not the main lifter of the poor in the United States,
the Netherlands, Switzerland, Japan, Sweden, or the others. The way to the
lift is the Great Enrichment.

Boudreaux noted that a literal billionaire who participated in a seminar
of his didn't look much different from an "impoverished" graduate student
giving a paper about Gini coefficients. "In many of the basic elements of
life, nearly every American is as well off as Mr. Bucks [his pseudonym for
the billionaire]. If wealth differences between billionaires and ordinary
Americans are barely visible in the most routine aspects of daily life, then
to suffer distress over a Gini coefficient is to unwisely elevate ethereal abstraction over palpable reality."[15] Mr. Bucks undoubtedly had more houses
and more Rolls Royces than the graduate student. One may ask, though, the
cheeky but always relevant question: So what?

People are actually and ethically looking for a standard of what is enough
for a dignified life in a given society. How much dough is enough? To the

Dust Bowl refugees the minstrel Woody Guthrie sang, "California's a garden of Eden, / A paradise to live in or see. / But believe it or not / You won't find it so hot / If you ain't got the do re mi." You need the dough in the do re mi to buy the roof and the toilet and the food at California prices. Therefore Peter Saunders and others such as Horwitz and the theorists of capabilities propose to look at the goods poor people can buy and the rights they have. They ask: What's enough? Saunders determined "the items that are widely regarded as essential in today's [Australian] society," such as a telephone, a washing machine [thus the Washing Line], a separate bed for each child.[16] The "widely regarded" in his study comes from an opinion poll of Australians. If things go well by such a measure the level of Australian poverty can possibly fall. With an ever-rising relative poverty line it can never fall, which is nice for pessimists but silly as science or policy. If one uses a Gini coefficient, the measure of inequality becomes the level of diamond-encrusted-watch owning, excesses that are annoying and blameworthy but ethically irrelevant so far as state compulsion is concerned. After all, many private actions are blameworthy without triggering justifiable interference by the state—listening to NPR without pledging, or failing once again to go to the gym, or not eating your vegetables. Measuring rather the goods poor people can buy and the rights they have, public policy (that is, state compulsion) can focus on what actually matters to dignity, such as making schools work well, improving medical care, ending the War on Drugs, preventing voter suppression, changing the trade union–determined building code so that apartments can be built that the poor can occupy in a dignified way at a low rent.

Using Saunders's survey, for example, between 2006 and 2010 (which includes the world's Great Recession years, though at the time Australia was having a mining boom selling to China), the average number of items, out of the twenty-four the Australian public viewed as "essential," that were absent in single-parent households fell from 3.6 to 2.9. If things had got worse, with the number of absent essentials rising to 6.9 instead of falling to 2.9, Australians would have a justifiable basis for alarm, and some indication of what to do about it.

The postmodern French philosopher worshipped on the left, Michel Foucault (1926–1984), provides unlikely support for such thinking. Daniel Zamora, a Belgian sociologist, in an interview about his 2014 book *Critiquer Foucault* (Criticizing Foucault) reports that

Foucault himself met with [the conservative French economist Lionel] Stoléru several times when Stoléru was a technical advisor on the staff of [the right-wing French president] Valéry Giscard D'Estaing. An important argument runs through [Stoléru's] work and directly attracted Foucault's attention: in the spirit of [Milton] Friedman, it draws a distinction between a policy that seeks equality (socialism) and a policy that simply aims to eliminate poverty without challenging disparities (liberalism). . . . [Stoléru wrote:] "I believe the distinction between absolute poverty and relative poverty is in fact the distinction between capitalism and socialism."

Indeed. Solving absolute poverty came in fact from the Great Enrichment, and attempting to solve a logically insoluble relative poverty resulted in slow growth and the encouragement of an insatiable envy.

The result is general. Despite the clamor about poverty lines and Gini coefficients, nowhere in the past few decades except in war-of-all-against-all countries such as Somalia have conditions measured by a correct standard of "enough" worsened, even in notably unequal places such as Brazil, South Africa, Chile, China, or the United States. They have got better.

7

The nastiness of the Great Recession of 2008 and its slow-growth aftermath in the rich countries was hailed on the far left as being (at long last) the actual last crisis of capitalism. (I gently reply to them: So you have said, my dear friends, about every downturn since the Panic of 1857.) The Great Recession, nasty though it was, had a half dozen equally nasty cousins among the forty or so recessions since 1785. It caused less in human pain than, say, the depressions of the 1840s or the 1870s or the 1890s. And the Great Depression of the 1930s was much worse than any of these. The margin for surviving a depression in former days, even in comparatively rich countries, was much narrower. Before the full fruits of the Great Enrichment, real incomes were much lower than they were by 2007, and provision for unemployment insurance was weak—admitting that "friendly societies" in, say, Britain did part of the job, and that families often could take in Uncle Fred, bankrupted after one of Colorado's mining booms.

Yet in each of the forty-odd recessions since 1785, big or small, the real income of the poor and of the average wage earner was higher after the recession than it had been at the peak of the previous boom. In the three dozen or so ordinary recessions the previous peak was exceeded after the trough in about two years. Unhappily, it was not the case everywhere after the Great Recession of 2008. In the 1930s it had been even less so, disastrously, in the mismanaged recoveries from the Great Depression, especially in gold-obsessed France, Switzerland, and the United States. But in the Great Recession, despite the *Schadenfreude* expressed on the left, still echoing in such circles, the growth of real incomes did not stop permanently, even in the already developed and therefore necessarily slower-growing countries. Merely two years after the 2008 peak, real per-person income in the United States, for example, had grown beyond the peak (though not for the young, considering the job protections arranged by and for the middle-aged).[1] In the world as a whole, real income per person was fully 10 percent higher by 2011 than before the world crisis.[2] It had begun to exceed the 2008 peak by 2009. Here are some of the larger or more interesting countries arrayed by the years they took to match or exceed their previous peak in real per-person income (the peak being for most countries 2008, but 2006 for many of the worst performers):

TABLE 1. The Great Recession was not economic Armageddon: Years to recover from the Great Recession, for large and some small countries, measured by matching or exceeding the previous peak of GDP per head at U.S. purchasing power parity

Zero to 1 year	2 years	3 years	4 years or more
Australia	Brazil	**European Union**	Argentina*
Egypt	Canada	France	Bangladesh*
Israel	Chile	Mexico	China*
South Korea	Columbia*	Russia	Greece
Nigeria	Germany	UK	India*
Peru	Japan		Ireland
Poland	Mongolia		Italy
Taiwan	Indonesia*		Pakistan*
WORLD	USA		Philippines
Saudi Arabia			South Africa #
			Spain
			Turkey (2007 peak)
			Venezuela

* = peak occurred before 2008.
Source: World Bank figures corrected for inflation and purchasing power parity.

The eminent Marxist historian Eric Hobsbawm (1917–2012) gave in 2011 the conventional left-wing analysis of the Great Recession. In the peroration of a book republishing some of his essays, Hobsbawm decried how "the un-limited and increasingly high-tech economic growth in the pursuit of un-sustainable profit produces global wealth, but at the cost of an increasingly dispensable factor of production, human labor, and, one might add, of the globe's natural resources."[3]

The details of his rhetoric—tacking on a concern for "the globe's natural resources" with a "one might add"—show him, as Hobsbawm would have affirmed, to be an *old* leftist. He stopped being a dues-paying if unorthodox member of the Communist Party of Great Britain only a few months before it dissolved itself, in 1991. The "one might add" suggests a wariness toward the recent environmentalist modulation of the left, a modulation, as he suspiciously observed elsewhere in the same essay, "on a much more middle-class basis." The environmentalist, anticorporatist, antiglobalist, usually middle-class radicals exemplified by the Occupy movement and its Spanish model, *Los Indignatos*, were, he wrote, "anti-capitalist, though without any clear idea of capitalism." "It was almost impossible to identify what they proposed to substitute for it. This may explain a revival of what looks like Bakuninite anarchism."[4] From an Old Communist, "Bakuninite" is not a compliment.

But the main point of Hobsbawm's sentence is to cast doubt on the Great Enrichment. The left after Marx and Engels has always been, as Hobsbawm himself was in all his writings, strangely alarmed by economic growth. They have been alarmed even though economic growth was what in historical fact enriched the poor, not the nationalizing policies of the old Labourites and of the Communist Party, or for that matter the war-making policies of the Conservative Party and of the fascists, or the redistributive policies of the Liberal Democrats and of the populists. The radical left and the traditionalist right see economic growth as a vine smothering the world, a monopolistic kudzu, bringing on the cultural triumph of the West. (The traditionalist right glories in the cultural triumph of the West, at any rate if the rightist is a Thatcherite Westerner.) The hard-left Indian writer Pankaj Mishra lists in parallel with Hobsbawm the usual antigrowth claims: "the cultural homogeneity, or the other Trojan viruses—uneven development, environmental degradation—built into the West's operating software. . . . [And] the harshest aspects of American-style capitalism: the truncation of public services, deunionization, the fragmenting and lumpenization of urban working classes, plus the ruthless suppression of the rural poor."[5] Thus Mahatma Gandhi admired the foot-treadle sewing machine but viewed it as one of the few good innovations. No electricity or flush toilets. Stop growth now.

The antigrowth left, with the antigrowth right, is mistaken. (It does not mistake, though, that the fruits of the Great Enrichment have made the proletariat into a petty bourgeoisie, lamentably uninterested in revolution, and in its vulgar way now able to enjoy the goods and services formerly available only to the better sort of people. And it has made the poor into department-store and now Walmart customers, lamentably uninterested in making their women spin their yarn and weave it into cloth by hand.) Growth's "high-tech" feature, in Hobsbawm's way of putting it, makes certain laborers "dispensable," true—which is to say that people move from wretched assembly-line jobs at Ford near Detroit or at Volvo near Gothenburg to better jobs standing in a white coat monitoring robots, at the higher wages made possible by the higher tech. Or, mainly, they move to jobs outside the auto industry, the real rewards of which are now higher because people can buy the radically cheaper stuff made by the robots.

And if their new jobs are *not* higher paying it may be because the United Automobile Workers of America or the IF Metall union of Sweden had been able to extract monopoly profits from the company and therefore from consumers. Robert Reich, a reliable source of sweetly leftish errors of facts and ethics, declares that "the decline in unionization [of private companies] directly correlates with the decline of the portion of income going to the middle class."[6] But paying selected workers on the auto assembly line more than they can earn elsewhere, at the expense of other, sometimes poorer, workers buying autos, is hardly a formula for raising up the working class, or for that matter the middle class.

Walter Reuther, president of the United Auto Workers long ago, replied to a young manager enthusiastic about robots on the assembly line, "Tell me, those wonderful new robots—will they go out and buy cars from your company?" Reuther's, and Reich's, argument, though well intentioned, is fallacious, the "productionist" fallacy: trickle up. Employees of the auto companies are a trivial share of the auto-buying public. You can't create prosperity merely by buying from your own employer, hoisting yourself up by your bootstraps. The left's trickle-up economics is as illogical as is the right's trickle-down version. Neither focuses on what actually increases real income, which is bettered production.

The robots themselves are made by people who buy cars. Compared with horses, cars themselves are "robots." Yet the advent of cars did not produce mass unemployment because of insufficient demand for the output of blacksmiths and horse traders. Fundamentally, all tools—a blast furnace and a spinning jenny, or for that matter an Acheulean hand ax or a Mycenaean chariot wheel—are "robots," that is, contrivances that make labor more productive. Reich listed in 2014 the usual lineup of villains allegedly driving down American wages: "Automation, followed by computers, software, robotics, computer-controlled machine tools and widespread digitization, further eroded jobs and wages."[7] No they didn't. They raised real wages, correctly measured, according to the common sense that a human supplied with a better tool can produce more. If Rosie the Riveter gets better tongs to insert the rivets she gets higher wages, because employers have to compete for the now more productive worker, and she can give her children more to eat. If everyone gets better tools they move out of old jobs and produce more for everybody in their new jobs with the new tools.

After all, the point of an economy is production for consumption, not protection of existing jobs using old tools—horses, candles, hand-controlled drill presses. Any contrivance substitutes for raw labor, as does the cactus spine that the Galapagos finches use to dig grubs out of tree bark. The finches use "robots." In Afrikaans the word "robot" means what it means elsewhere, following its coinage from Czech (the original meaning is "required work"). But it is also the normal Afrikaans word for "traffic light." The traffic light substitutes for the labor of a policeman with white gloves on a pedestal. And in the third act such substitutions are good for workers as a whole, not bad.

In the literal second act of Ibsen's *Pillars of Society* (1877), one of the pillars, Karsten Bernick, the owner of a shipyard in Norway, scolds his foreman, Aune:

BERNICK. You don't know how to work with the new machines I had installed—or, better, you *won't* work with them. . . . Progress has to come from me, or it won't come at all.

AUNE. I also want progress, Mr. Bernick.

BERNICK. Yes, for your own narrow faction, for the working class. . . .

AUNE. What right do technology and capitalism have to introduce all these new inventions before society's trained a generation in how to use them? . . . I can't stand seeing one good workingman after another turned out to go hungry, all on account of these machines.

BERNICK. Hm. When printing was invented, a lot of scribes went hungry.

AUNE. How'd you like it, Mr. Bernick, if you'd been a scribe at the time?[8]

Aune articulates the program on the left to educate an entire generation of people to work with all conceivable robots before any are installed and tried. He believes the future can be laid down because we already know how it will turn out. Aune's program would stop the enrichment of the working class (the "narrow faction" constituting 90 percent of Norwegian society, then as now). By contrast, Bernick articulates the program on the right to let the bourgeoisie install whatever labor-abridging device it wishes and afterward train the workers, a bet on progress without quite knowing how it will turn out. In society's third act Bernick's has turned out to be the better program, because we pay the Bernicks to have such ideas, punishing them with bankruptcy when they are wrong. The Bernicks push for an unknowable future, which in the event has been massively good for the workers.

And indeed in the literal fourth act of the play an ethically renovated Bernick meets with gratifying cooperation from Aune:

BERNICK. I gave you too little time. [The ship under repair] needs a more careful job.
AUNE. Will do, Mr. Bernick. And with the new machines!
BERNICK. That's the way. But take special care and pains with it now. There's a lot with us that could stand some careful, painstaking renovation.[9]

It's a happy ending, a trifle twee. But after all, the new machines are in fact necessary for the happy result of enriching the workingmen.

The business profit that the left abhors—"in the pursuit of unsustainable profit," said Hobsbawm—is indeed temporary, "unsustainable." That's good, not bad, and is the reason why profits on American industrial capital fell from their "unsustainable" levels of about 15 percent per year after World War II, when the United States was the only big industrial economy left standing, down to a normal level of about 10 percent per year on the capital sum invested from the 1960s on, a level typical since industrialization began two and a half centuries ago. The reward for venturing, for example, on robotization—that is, toolmaking—has been eroded time and again, I say again, by competition driving down the rewards to the inventors of weaving machines and rolling mills and assembly lines, and leaving the fruits for the rest of us in much cheaper clothes and girders and automobiles measured by the labor time to buy them.

The left speaks as though such competition among capitalists for the dollar of the worker-consumer, keeping down profits on capital, is a bad idea. From both the socialist left and the nationalist right the feeling seems to be that competition by businesspeople vying to give you what you want is the same thing as competition by violence. The feeling misleads. Marshall Field of Chicago formulated the motto of his department store as "Give the lady what she wants." Giving the lady what she wants in a manner better than Goldblatt's or Carson, Pirie, Scott is not an act of violence. It is an act of seduction, a form of love, admittedly a self-interested form. Harry Gordon Selfridge, trained in Chicago by Field, continued after 1909 the seduction in his London store, becoming rich by competing for the love of the ladies with his new business plan, driving down the price of glamour.[10]

In *The Ladies' Paradise* (1882–1883), set in fictional 1864–1869, Zola makes a central character out of the perfected department store, a betterment dating from the 1850s, such as Le Bon Marché ("the good deal," still on offer). The owner of the bettering store, M. Octave Mouret, is describing to a Baron Hartmann (= Haussmann) how he is driving the old-fashioned sellers of fabrics out of business. The implied author uses a cup of anticapitalism (from the author of *Germinal*), a dose of misogyny, a pinch of regional prejudice, and a *soupçon* of anti-Semitism. (The passage, however, is from the pen also of the defender of Captain Dreyfus; it is in free indirect style, and cannot be taken as a straightforward report on the opinions of Zola himself.) Mouret boasts, "Why, we can sell what we like when we know how to sell! There lies our triumph." The implied author continues:

> And with his southern spirit, he showed the new business at work. . . . From counter to counter the customer found herself . . . yielding to her longing for the useless and the pretty. . . . Right at the summit appeared the exploitation of woman. . . . It was woman that they were continually catching . . . yielding at first to reasonable purchases for the household, then tempted by their coquetry, then devoured. . . . Through the very gracefulness of his gallantry, Mouret thus allowed to appear the brutality of a Jew. . . .
>
> "Once have the woman on your side," whispered he to the baron, and laughing loudly, "you could sell the very world."[11]

Unlike Balzac or Dickens or many other of the clerisy, Zola was not anti-capitalist out of mere ignorance about how trade-tested betterment worked. In his laboriously gathered notes for *The Ladies' Paradise* (he spent a month wandering in Le Bon Marché and its competitors overhearing conversations and interviewing its staff) he wrote, "A department store [smashes] all the small commerce of a neighborhood . . . but I would not weep for them, *on the contrary*: for I want to show the triumph of modern activity," of which Zola in his rational optimism by 1882 approved. The local drapers, like the local hardware stores facing Menards and Home Depot, "are no longer of their age, too bad for them!"[12] And good for the consumer.

The sociologist Georg Simmel—about the economy often more penetrating than his contemporary Max Weber—noted in 1908 that "usually, the poisonous, divisive, destructive effects of competition are stressed" (though it is *creative* destruction):

> But, in addition . . . competition compels the wooer who has a co-wooer, . . . to go out to the wooed, come close to him, establish ties with him. . . . To be sure, this often happens at the price of the competitor's own dignity and of the objective value of his product [that is, by driving down the price]. . . . [Yet] it achieves what usually only love can do: the divination of the innermost wishes of the other, even before he himself becomes aware of them. . . . Modern competition is described as the fight of all against all, but at the same time it is the fight of all *for* all.[13]

OR FROM THE RIGHT AND MIDDLE

And there are doubts from the right, too. Some students of the economy, such as Robert Gordon, Lawrence Summers, Erik Brynjolfsson, Andrew McFee, Edmund Phelps, Edward E. Gordon, Jeffrey Sachs, Laurence Kotlikoff, and Tyler Cowen, have argued recently that countries in the position of the United States, on the frontier of betterment, are facing a slowdown, with a skill shortage, and that technological unemployment will be the result.[1] Maybe. The economists would acknowledge that in the past couple of centuries numerous other learned commentators have predicted similar slowdowns—such as the Keynesian economists in the late 1930s and the 1940s, confident in their theory of "stagnationism"—only to find their predictions once again falsified by the continuing Great Enrichment.[2] The classical economists of the first three-quarters of the nineteenth century, Marx included, expected landlords, or in Marx's case capitalists, to engorge the national product. In a cartoon cover of the *National Review* by Thomas Reis, a supercool little Karl Marx with a Starbucks coffee in his hand and an MP3 player in his ear sports a T-shirt inscribed, "Still Wrong."[3] Right.

Marx supposed that wages would fall and yet profits would also fall and yet technological betterments would also happen. Such an accounting, the left-Keynesian and eventually Maoist economist Joan Robinson used to point out, is impossible. At least one, the wages or the profits, has to rise if technological betterment is happening, as it so plainly did. In the event, what rose were wages on raw labor and the return to *human* capital, owned by the wage-earners, not the bosses. The return to physical capital was higher than a riskless return on British or American government bonds, in order to compensate for the risk in holding the capital (such as being made obsolete by betterment—think of your computer, obsolete in four years). But the return on physical capital was anyway held down, I just noted, by competition among the proliferating capitalists, to its level of 10 percent. Imagine if real wages had experienced a similar history of stagnation since 1800. Instead they increased by a factor of twenty or thirty or one hundred.

Startlingly, the learned economists from the right of politics join their colleagues from the left in predicting that *machines* will cause low wages. They haven't yet. But soon. Tyler Cowen, for example, an economist I admire, spends many pages of his recent book *Average Is Over* (2013) describing breathlessly "the increasing productivity of intelligent machines," such as those used for dating services. Your fate is determined, he says, by how you answer the technological-unemployment question: "Are you good at working with intelligent machines or not? . . . This is the wave that will lift or that will dump you."[4] He concedes that "it was true in the great Industrial Revolution of the nineteenth century and it is true now: machines do not put us *all* out of work, as eventually machines will *create jobs*."[5] I italicize the words amazing in an economist of Cowen's ability. Not "all" jobs, he concedes. Well, actually, machines have put no one out of work who can move to another job, and on balance not anyway the bulk of workers, as you can see in the absence, 1848 to the present, of a rising reserve army of unemployed. The other italicized locution, "create jobs," is regularly a sign of a slot theory of labor supply and demand, which no economist since J. R. Hicks published *The Theory of Wages* in 1932 has believed. A job is a voluntary deal between a worker and a boss. It is the opportunity, not the job, that is "created" by a newly invented machine. Government can "create jobs" only by taxing some deal to subsidize another, with no net gain unless the government is wiser about trading opportunities than people in trade.

On the preceding page Cowen had characterized some things as "scarce" (high-quality labor with unique skills, for example) and others as "not scarce" (unskilled labor). It is a meaningless locution in economics. It's like saying that gold is scarce but water is not. No: they have a relative price, that is all. *Both* are scarce, in the sense that neither is free of opportunity cost, and it is meaningless to compare them, or apples and oranges, by the ounce, something Cowen teaches his students in Economics 1 during the third week of the course. And in any case the economics and the history say that in the long run unskilled and skilled people are substitutes. The unskilled benefit as much—more when the standard of genuine comfort is applied to rich and poor. Remember Robert Frost choosing at the margin between teaching and farming, which keeps the wage in each occupation within hailing distance of the other. And if goods and services are provided by machines we will still have "jobs," that is, ways of spending our time that other people will pay for—deciding what to buy, for example, or who to vote for or what is to be done or what machines to invent next, which cannot in its nature be eliminated by mechanization.

Later Cowen gives a chart of labor's income as a share of the total, showing an alarming fall since the 1970s. "If there is one picture that sums up the dilemma of our contemporary economy, it is that one."[6] But the chart is what we used to call a *Time*-magazine chart—it cuts off the top and bottom in order to exaggerate a relatively slight change. How alarming is the decline? It is a decline in Bureau of Labor Statistics numbers from 63 percent to 61 percent—a decline of labor's share by two percentage points of national income. On this Cowen erects his terrifying case that "average is over."

Something is driving intelligent economists out of their economic minds. Perhaps it is the short run, the first act. Before they have well lost their minds, some of them acknowledge what has been true of every economy since the beginning, that "jobs"—that is, opportunities for mutually advantageous exchange—adjust to the skills available. Better tools or better skills make for higher income in total. But if not, the economy finds something to do with the badly skilled. The principle is called comparative advantage, one of the few nonobvious propositions in economics.

Of course, if one raises wages artificially, by union or by statute, unemployment will result. The argument one hears from, say, Paul Krugman—that raising wages is good for the company because workers will work harder as a result—seems implausible, considering that the company in such a case would already have raised wages, for its own good. And working harder worsens the conditions of work. Both the company and the workers suffer. Cowen notes that one can observe "labor market troubles of the young" "in many countries."[7] Yes, one observes such troubles in Egypt and South Africa even more than in France and the United States, which suggests that laws protecting the employment of favored classes (old people, for instance, or government-approved union members, often grotesquely favored in poor countries), not the advanced machine tools of advanced economies, imitated in poor countries, are what is causing the troubles.

Joel Mokyr, a deep student of the history of technology, has recently offered some persuasive Whiggish assurances on the matter of slowdown,
observing that by now the sciences behind biology and computers and the
study of materials promise gigantic enrichment.[8] And Patrizio Pagano and
Massimo Sbracia argue that failures of previous stagnationisms—proposed
after every major recession, they observe—failed not so much in not anticipating wholly new technology as in not grasping the further rewards of
existing technology, such as, now, computers.[9] As Macaulay asked in 1830,
"On what principle is it that, when we see nothing but betterment behind
us, we are to expect nothing but deterioration before us?"[10] He continued:

> If we were to prophesy that in the year 1930 a population of fifty million, better
> fed, clad, and lodged than the English of our time, will cover these islands, that
> Sussex and Huntingdonshire will be wealthier than the wealthiest parts of the
> West Riding of Yorkshire now are, that machines constructed on principles yet
> undiscovered will be in every house, many people would think us insane.[11]

Whiggish and bourgeois and progress-minded and vulgarly pro-betterment
though Macaulay was, he was in his prediction exactly right, even as to the
UK population in 1930. If one includes the recently separated Republic of
Ireland, he was off by less than 2 percent.

And even the pessimistic, anti-Whiggish economists—"gloomsters," the
headline writers call them—would not deny that we have before us fifty or
a hundred years in which now middling and poor countries such as South
Africa and Brazil and Haiti and Bangladesh will catch up to what is already,
in the rich countries, a stunningly successful level of average real income.
Edward Phelps, among the pessimists, believes that many rich countries
lack dynamism.[12] But nowadays China and India, making up 37 percent of
world population, have become more free-market than they once were, and
therefore are quickly catching up, growing with notable dynamism at upward of 7 to 12 percent per person per year. All the economists who have
looked into the evidence agree that the average real income per person in
the world is rising faster than ever before.[13] The result will be a gigantic increase in the number of scientists, designers, writers, musicians, engineers,
entrepreneurs, and ordinary businesspeople devising betterments that spill
over to the now rich countries allegedly lacking in dynamism. Unless one
believes in mercantilist/business-school fashion that a country must "com-

pete" to prosper from world betterment, even the leaky boats of the Phelpsian undynamic countries will rise.

To appreciate what will happen in the world's economy over the next fifty or a hundred years it's a good idea to pause to learn the "Rule of 72." The rule is that something (such as income) growing at 1 percent per year will double in seventy-two years. The fact is not obvious without calculation. It just happens to be true. You can confirm it by taking out your calculator and multiplying 1.01 by itself seventy-two times. It follows that if the something grows twice as fast, at 2 percent instead of 1 percent, that something will double, of course, in *half* the time, thirty-six years—as a runner going twice as fast will arrive at the mile marker in half the time. Similarly, something growing at 3 percent a year will double in a third of the time, or twenty-four years. And so forth. The general formula, then, says something growing at N percent per year doubles in 72/N years. The approximation gets less exact for higher growth rates—clearly something growing at 72 percent per year won't double in a year—but for the growth rates we're considering, it's accurate enough.[14]

Consider some Rule-of-72 calculations. At 7 percent per year a real income will double in 72 divided by 7 years, or a little over 10 years; at 12 percent it will double in about 6 years. Even at the modest 4 percent per year per person that the World Bank implausibly reckons China will experience out to 2030 the result will be a populace almost twice as rich.[15] The specialists on China's economy Dwight Perkins and Thomas Rawski (2008) reckon a 6 to 8 percent annual growth out to 2025, by which time the average Chinese person will have a 1960s-U.S. standard of living.

China and India during their socialist experiments of the 1950s through the 1970s were so badly managed that there was a great deal of ground to be made up merely by letting people open shops and factories where and when they wanted to, without approval from the authorities. As Perkins pointed out in 1995, "When China stopped suppressing such activity, . . . shops, restaurants and many other service units popped up everywhere . . . [because] Chinese . . . had not forgotten how to trade or run a small business."[16] No genetic argument can be put forward that implies that Chinese or Indians or Africans or Latin Americans should do worse than Europeans permanently. The environmental limit can reasonably be expected to be overcome by serious environmentalists implementing serious technologies, such as carbon capture and nuclear power (India in 2014 bought ten nuclear reactors from Russia). No limit to fast world growth of per-person income is close at hand—not in your lifetime, or even that of your great-grandchildren. Then, in the year 2100, with everyone pretty rich, and hundreds of times more scientists and entrepreneurs working on improvements in solar power and methane burning, we can reconsider the limits to growth.

The environmental limit, which worries even the middle of the political spectrum, is often inferred from a use of merely mathematical arguments, which are identically true but scientifically irrelevant. "After all," it is said, "nothing can grow forever" when the practical limit is scores of times larger than the present level. The actual carrying capacity of the earth, as one can judge from such densely populated place as Holland or Java, is on the order of a hundred billion people, not the ten or eleven billion at which it will soon peak and then start falling in response to rising per-person incomes. "After all, resources are finite," the doubters continue, when what is a "resource," as Julian Simon showed, is ever changing in response to human ingenuity.[17] Bauxite ore was once useless dirt, but became valuable for making aluminum. Rare earths were not economically rare until they came to be used for computer batteries. Valuable whale oil became almost useless (and saved the whales) compared with the newly exploited oil from the ground. Black rock from the ground called "coal" was rediscovered many centuries ago in Europe and known two thousand years earlier in China to be useful for heating houses and making glass. Underground water inaccessible with old drilling techniques suddenly became minable, and its large if limited amount is soon to be supplemented, as it already is in some arid places, by ingenuity in finding ways to desalinate sea water cheaply, powered as in Western Australia by wind and sun. The man in the street thinks that countries are rich because of "resources," in which case Japan and Hong Kong would be poor and the Russian Federation and the Democratic Republic of the Congo rich. In a modern economy in which people on farms are 2 percent of population, presently used resources earn 5 percent or less of national income and do not determine much of its level.

The environmental limit looks to be solved by the ingenuity that caused the Great Enrichment in the first place. It will not be solved by some of the stranger anti-economic suggestions, such as Eating Local. As Robert Wuetherick asks, "What will be next? 100-mile-sourced medicines? 100-mile-sourced ideas? 100-mile-sourced economic history?"[18] Some of the more unreasonable environmentalists in this line have campaigned against genetically modified bananas delivering vitamin A, an innovation that could save seven hundred thousand children's lives each year and prevent three hundred thousand cases of blindness.[19]

Yet reasonable environmentalists have for decades been solving problems such as smog caused by soft coal for heating, or intelligence-reducing emissions from cars using lead-enhanced fuels, and will continue their virtuous labors with the hearty approval of us economists and calculators. After all, the goal is not growth-regardless, in the style of the North Carolina legislature in 2014 requiring science to be revised to make rising ocean levels appear less threatening or the governor of Florida issuing instructions that the phrase "global warming" be banished from official documents. The goal is *ethical* trade-tested betterment, such as making poor people rich, which has happened, or reducing inequality in essentials, which has also happened. Making people dangerously ill with bad air (or for that matter denying children life-saving genetically modified crops) is not ethical, or bettering. Nor is it something "the corporations" want. Nike and Toyota, unlike some governments, with their local monopoly of violence, do not want to sicken or kill us.

The rich countries decided to take seriously the threat to the ozone layer from air-conditioning fluid and hair spray (hair spray!), led by Margaret Thatcher the Conservative British prime minister (and a big user of hair spray), and now the ozone gaps at the poles are getting smaller. Waterways, which were open sewers until the development of effective waste treatment at the end of the nineteenth century, are in rich countries largely cleaned up.[20] Levels of particulate matter from burning coal for house heating in American cities in the 1930s and 1940s—American income per head then was, as I have noted, about the same as Brazilian income now—were comparable to those in present-day poor countries, and fell by the late twentieth century to an eighth of their previous level. In 1912–1913 a poor and therefore smoky Chicago was smothered in suspended particulates 50 percent higher than those in 58 poor Chinese cities in 1980–1993.[21] Since the use of soft coal in British cities was banned in 1954 and then more rigorously in 1968, the Royal Courts of Justice in now-rich London have been scrubbed to return to their original white stone facing. Little but rich Denmark spends a good deal of its riches on avoiding carbon-based fuel and is prominent, for example, in the world market in windmills.[22] As the libertarian columnist at the *Chicago Tribune*, Steve Chapman, reported: "Since 1980, carbon monoxide pollution in America has been cut by 83 percent, lead by 91 percent, and sulfur dioxide by 78 percent. But total economic output per person, adjusted for inflation, has risen by 77 percent. We've gotten greener and healthier as we've gotten richer."[23] If we care about the environment, then, let us become prudently and temperately rich. Then we can do some good.

What, then, about the polluting poor countries? Rising real income per person at such heady rates as 6 or 12 percent per year, with the level quadrupling in a generation, is understandably popular with ordinary Chinese and Indian people. Yet when their incomes went up, the formerly poor, such as the Danes and the Australians and the British, came to value the environment more. Sometimes, true, they have valued it irrationally, as for example by stopping nuclear power, which has made dirty old coal the fastest growing source of energy worldwide.[24] Yet China, bettering but still very poor, has now a vigorous environmental movement—a movement against coal, not against nuclear power—with numerous riots substituting for democracy. In a nervous response to the movement, and maybe even because it is good for people, the Chinese government in January 2014 started requiring fifteen thousand factories to report their air and water pollution in real time, and to release the results to the public.[25] If they actually do so (don't hold your breath; and when visiting Beijing, do), the Chinese standard of transparency in pollution control will be higher than in the United States. Also in 2014 China signed an agreement with the United States to work seriously on restraining the release of atmospheric carbon. China is now at a stage of industrialization similar to England's in the 1870s or the United States's in the 1890s, during which sulfur-laden coal smoke rising from Birmingham, Warwickshire, or from Birmingham, Alabama, was viewed not an occasion for rioting but as a *good* sign. In the 1940s, when my grandparents would drive to Chicago around the southern edge of Lake Michigan, they would note with pleasure the smoke rising from US Steel in Gary, Indiana—an improvement, they implied, over the shuttered mills of the 1930s.

Oil supply, too, is no long-term limit, as the failures of limits-to-growth predictions from the 1960s to the present have shown, and as fracked gas in Pennsylvania and oil sands in Alberta and deep discoveries in the Falklands/

Malvinas seas and in the Australian outback are showing again, whenever the price of oil rises. The rhetorical triumph of fossil fuel over nuclear power has, to be sure, worsened global warming. But this too can be overcome (some reasonable people have argued) by realizing that even Chernobyl, incompetently managed by the USSR, resulted in few fatalities (a onetime event of fifty-six direct fatalities and a few thousand shortened lives, it is claimed, which is two or three orders of magnitude smaller than the coal-caused deaths in the same region yearly). Fukushima resulted in still fewer fatalities, and Three Mile Island, unless you believe conspiracy theories on the left, none. We can return to an improved nuclear power—or, if you are optimistic, and understandably resistant to the evidence about nuclear power, and determined to stay spooked about the One Big Disaster, which French nuclear engineering has obviated—you can wait for clean coal, on which Southern Illinois University is feverishly working.[26] The present engineering is clear. France, with 80 percent nuclear power for its electricity, the cheapest in Europe, has one-fifth the carbon pollution of neighboring, coal-fed-if-green-obsessed Germany. In any case, however you come down on nuclear power, on what principle is it that, when we see nothing but betterment behind us, we are to expect nothing but deterioration before us?

Consider more Rule-of-72 calculations: If we take 9 percent as the combined annual per-person growth rate in the 37 percent of world population living in China and India, the rest of the world could have literally *zero* growth per person and yet the world's average growth per year of real income per person would be 0.37 × 9, or 3.3 percent, which is a little faster even than during the great postwar boom of 1950–1972. If the rest of the world were to grow merely at the subdued rates of 1973–2003 (namely, 1.56 percent per person per year conventionally measured, without allowance for improved quality), the world result, factoring in the Chinese and Indian marvels, would be (if the population share held up) (0.37 × 9.0) + (0.63 × 1.56), or 4.3 percent per year, the highest in history.[27] A rather lower sustained growth rate worldwide of, say, 4 percent per year per person would result in a doubling of the material welfare of the world's average person within a short generation (72/4 = 18 years), with economies of scale in world invention kicking up the rate in addition. In two such generations, just thirty-six years, that would mean a quadrupling, which would raise the average real income in the world to the levels attained in 2012 in the United States, a country that for well over a century has sustained the world's highest per-person income of any place larger than Norway. Pretty good. And it will be good for solving many if not all of the problems in the environment and in the society.

The resulting spiritual change, as I have noted, has been and will be as impressive as the material change. At the level of the purpose of a human life it is the more important outcome. For what is a man profited, if he shall gain the whole world, and lose his own soul? The sacred and meaning-giving virtues of hope, faith, and transcendent love for science or baseball or medicine or God are enabled by our riches in our present lives to bulk larger than the profane and practical virtues of prudence and temperance necessary among people living in extreme poverty. True, in our modern times even unworthy uses of our higher income—eating more Fritos, watching more reality TV— are better physically than in ancient times starving in beggary by the West Gate. Look again at falling death rates worldwide. But one would hope that the Great Enrichment would be used for higher purposes.

And, on the most hard-minded criteria, it has been, and will be. Enrichment leads to enrichment, not loss of one's own soul. The American journalist and essayist H. L. Mencken, no softie, noted in 1917 à propos of Sister Carrie's good fortune, that "with the rise from want to security, from fear to ease, comes an awakening of the finer perceptions, a widening of the sympathies, a gradual unfolding of the delicate flower called personality, an increased capacity for loving and living."[28] Nor was the University of Iowa economist Frank Knight a softie, yet he too spoke in 1923 about such an increased capacity: "As the standard of living rises, the economic interests of people are transferred more and more out of the sphere of fundamental needs into that of aesthetic and social gratification and pure experimentation."[29] And no blame attaches.

Know also a remarkable likelihood in our future. Begin with the sober scientific fact that sub-Saharan Africa has great genetic diversity, at any rate by the standard of the narrow genetic endowment of the ancestors of the rest of us, the small part of the race of *Homo sapiens* that left Mother Africa in dribs and drabs after about 70,000 BCE.[30] The lower diversity outside Africa comes from what geneticists call the founder effect, that is, the dying out of genetic lines in an isolated small group, such as those that ventured into west Asia and then beyond. The founder effect is merely a consequence of the small samples dribbling out, as against the big sample of the *Homo sa-piens* folk that stayed put in Africa. Any gene-influenced ability is therefore going to have more African extremes. The naturally tallest people and the naturally shortest people, for example, are in sub-Saharan Africa. The natu-rally quickest long-distance runners are in East Africa. The best basketball players descend from West Africans. In other words, below the Sahara the top end of the distribution of human abilities—physical and intellectual and artistic—is unusually thick. (Yet even in Africa the genetic variability in the *Homo sapiens* race appears to have been thinned repeatedly before the time of the modest emigrations, by population crashes, such as when the super volcano Toba in Sumatra went off, suggestively also around 70,000 BCE.[31] It reduced our *Homo sapiens* ancestors to a few thousand—a close call.)

The thickness of sub-Saharan abilities at the high end of the distribu-tion is a mere consequence of the mathematics. Greater diversity, which is to say in technical terms, higher variance, means that unusual abilities at both ends of the distribution, high and low, are more common. Exactly how much more depends on technical measures of genetic difference and their expression. The effect could be small or large depending on such measures and on the social relevance of the particular gene expression.

The high end is what matters for high culture. Sub-Saharan Africa, now at last leaning toward liberal democracy, has entered on the blade of the hockey stick, growing since 2001 in per-person real income by over 4 per-cent per year—doubling that is, every eighteen years. A prominent Nigerian investment manager working in London, Ayo Salami, expects an ideological shift among African leaders in favor of private trading as the generation of the deeply socialist anticolonialists born in the 1940s dies out.[32] The 6-to 10-percent growth rate available to poor economies that wholeheartedly adopt liberalism will then do its work and yield educational opportunities for Africans now denied them.

The upshot? Genetic diversity in a rich Africa will yield a crop of geniuses unprecedented in world history. In a century or so the leading scientists and artists in the world will be black—at any rate if the diversity is as large in gene expression and social relevance as it is in, say, height or running ability. Today a Mozart in Nigeria follows the plow; a Bashō in Mozambique was recruited as a boy soldier; a Tagore in East Africa tends his father's cattle; a Jane Austen in Congo spends her illiterate days carrying water and washing clothes. "Full many a gem of purest ray serene / The dark unfathom'd caves of ocean bear."

∞

We should expect during the next hundred years, then, a world spiritual change enabled by much higher real incomes. In fifty-four years at that conservative 4 percent per year, world income per person will rise by a factor of about eight—that is, 700 percent. The figure is not much below the factor of ten and the percentage of 900 by which conventionally measured income averaged over the rich and poor parts of the world has risen in the span of the fully *four* half-centuries since 1800. The growth rate will probably be higher than such a calculation assumes, when the increasing returns from discoveries shared worldwide is allowed for, and when more and more countries see the Chinese and especially the Indian light of liberty and dignity for the bourgeoisie, first lit in Holland and then in Britain. In fifty years, in other words, if tyrants, robbers, militarists, populists, Maoists, and the less thoughtful among socialists, regulators, end-state egalitarians, Bakuninite anarchists, and environmentalists do not break it, the businesslike blade of the hockey stick will have eliminated the worst of human ignorance and poverty, the malaria-crippled, soldier-raped, zero-schooling lives of the poorest among us. By the middle of our twenty-first century it will have resulted in a big bang of world culture, with sub-Saharan Africa by the early twenty-second century in the lead.

9

THE GREAT INTERNATIONAL
DIVERGENCE CAN BE OVERCOME

"But what about the poor right now in the rest of the world? Have you no pity?" Suppose you are an indignant member of the clerisy speaking in this way. You are an alert reader of the popular books and journals that focus on, and view with alarm, the distribution of income instead of the condition of the working class. You will have heard that "capitalist" globalization and neoliberalism have been bad for the world's poor, especially in the past few decades, on account of the evil ideas of economists such as Milton Friedman.[1]

Consider, though, the evidence to the contrary—that globalization and neoliberalism and Milton Friedman have in fact been good for the poor, in unprecedented fashion. There is still, admittedly, that bottom billion in Haiti and Burundi, out of the world population of seven billion, to which must be added many poor people even in rich and middling countries. We must find effective ways to help them lift themselves up. In our desire to help the poor, we bleeding-heart libertarians stand in solidarity with our social-democratic friends—if not usually agreeing with them on exactly which policies have actually helped the poor.

The contrast implied by the adverbs "exactly" and "actually," though, is with well-intentioned but erroneous policies that make us feel helpful even when they in fact damage the people we intend to help. Such faux policies include stoutly supporting "rational" central planning of the economy, or stoutly demanding more bureaucratic regulation when any disaster whatsoever occurs, or stoutly supporting trade unions that discriminate against blacks and women and immigrants and effective school teachers, or stoutly opposing Walmart selling groceries at low prices in poor neighborhoods that now lack grocery stores entirely. A bottom billion out of seven is a scandal. Let's fix it. But let's *actually* help the billion, not merely indulge our indignation and our conviction of ethical superiority by supporting policies that in fact make them worse off.

And know this. Forty years ago, before the recent liberalization of foreign trade and the dying out of central-planning socialism and the lessening of corrupt regulation, the situation was much worse than a bottom billion out of seven. In those unhappy days before the word "globalization" became common and before the word "neoliberalism" was known and before the wretched Washington Consensus and before the horrible Friedman got his Nobel Prize in economics, the world faced a bottom *four* billion out of a total human population of merely five, with no prospects.[2] The well-intentioned policies of job protection and import substitution and state ownership of the means of production had kept the poor very poor indeed.

Almost nowhere in the world, 1800 to the present, and contrary to pessimistic theories such as Malthusianism or Marxism or radical environmentalism, did real income per person decline for long, the rare exceptions being places with one-party socialism on the model of Kwame Nkrumah in Ghana and Nicolae Ceaușescu in Romania, or thuggish tyrants on the model of Robert Mugabe in Zimbabwe and Alexander Lukashenko of Belarus, or entirely uncontrolled robbers on the model of Somalia. In most places it is not true that "the rich get richer and the poor get poorer," amusingly cynical though it is to repeat the old proverb of a zero-sum society.

Since 1976, that is, most of the poorest people in the world have been getting better off almost every year. From 1981 to 2008 the share of the world's population living at the level of Afganistan, a horrible $2 a day (expressed as always, if roughly, in present-day U.S. prices allowing for the cost of living), fell from 70 percent to 42 percent.[3] The share of the world's population living on an appalling $1.25 a day, as in Liberia (the experiment in sending African-Americans with longer American lineages than most European-origin Americans "back to Africa"), fell from 53 percent to 22 percent. It fell, in other words, by more than half. From 2005 to 2008 even sub-Saharan Africa, for the first time since its independence from the colonial powers half a century earlier, shared on average in the betterment.

Not all of the recent uplifting, that is, can be accounted for by neoliberalization's top two success stories, China and India. Yet China's success since 1978 (from $1 a day, not alleviated by the ideal of a communist society advocated by Mao) and India's since 1991 (from a similar level, not alleviated by the ideal of *swadeshi*, or self-suffiency, advocated by Mahatma Gandhi and Nehru and the later Gandhis) do constitute a powerful anti–antiglobalization and anti-anti-Friedman argument. In 2013, for example, the new premier of China, Li Keqiang, no political liberal, hinted that if a new eleven-square-mile free-trade zone in Shanghai, one of twelve in prospect, worked as well as we Friedmanites think it will, the idea would be extended to the other places.[4]

If the four countries other than India and China among the BRIICS—Brazil, Russia, Indonesia, and South Africa, the BRIS—would adopt the Friedmanite ideas applied with such enthusiasm in India and China, they too would experience India's and China's transformative rates of growth in real per-person income, ranging annually from 5 to 12 percent. Such rates easily quadruple real income per person in a generation or so. (The doubling Rule of 72 implies a *quadrupling* Rule of 144, which is 2 times 72: something growing at, say, 6 percent per year will quadruple—which is to say, double twice—in 144/6 = 24 years, or one generation.) The quadrupling of any original per-person income in a generation or so would seem to justify the word "transformative." Yet Brazil, Russia, Indonesia, and South Africa have stuck with pre-Friedman ideas such as Argentinian self-sufficiency and 1960s British unionism and 1980s German labor laws and a misunderstanding of Korea's "export-led" growth.

The literature of the "middle-income trap," which speaks in particular of Brazil and South Africa, presupposes a mercantilist notion that growth depends on exports, which are alleged to have a harder time growing when wages rise.[5] The theory is defective, since the *absolute* "advantage" of low wages is irrelevant to the pattern of trade. The mercantist policies adopted by Brazil and South Africa to encourage this or that export depend, in other words, on denying comparative advantage. And anyway the literature on the middle-income trap focuses on externals when what matters mainly to the income of the poor is domestic productivity. Therefore countries such as South Africa with trade-denying laws, such as those that obstruct entry to new business and overregulate old business, drag along at growth rates of less than 3 percent per year per person—at which rate a mere doubling takes a quarter of a century and a transformative quadrupling fifty years. Slow growth yields envy, as the economist Benjamin Friedman has argued, and envy yields populism, which in turn yields slow growth.[6] In 2014 Venezuela ranked 182nd out of 189 countries in the world in the ease of doing business, Brazil 120th.[7] That's the real "middle-income trap."

Here are the data on the transformative, quadrupling rates of growth of China and India, and the nontransformative rates of the rest. Note the italicized years to quadruple:

TABLE 2. Annual rates of growth and *years to quadruple* in gross domestic product per person at purchasing power parity in constant 2005 international dollars of the BRIICS and the USA at the rates of growth experienced 1992–2002, 2002–2012, and over the entire twenty years, 1992–2012

Periods	China	India	Brazil	Indonesia	Russia	South Africa	USA
1992–2002	8.42%	3.38%	1.31%	1.87%	−0.682%	0.593%	2.18%
×4 in	*16 yrs*	*36*	*100*	*74*	*n.a.*	*230*	*63*
2002–2012	9.40%	5.98%	2.49%	4.15%	4.64%	2.26%	0.934%
×4 in	*15 yrs*	*23*	*55*	*33*	*30*	*61*	*150*
1992–2012	8.92%	4.92%	1.90%	3.01%	1.98%	1.43%	1.56%
×4 in	*15 yrs*	*28*	*73*	*46*	*70*	*98*	*88*

Methods and sources: I used continuous compounding instead of simple interest, so at 1.0 percent per year the rule to double is 69 years instead of 72, and so the rule to quadruple is 138 years instead of 144. Years to quadruple are rounded to two digits. Source for the underlying real GDP per person figures is the World Bank, http://data.worldbank.org/indicator/NY.GDP.PCAP.PP.KD?page=4.

Observe that among the BRIICS India is second only to China in per-person real growth. And observe that its best years were 2002–2012 (though 2012 itself was not so good). The best Indian years were not, as is sometimes claimed, the 1990s, before Congress Party liberalization had made all the progress it was going to make. In the early 2010s, unhappily, the Congress Party started once again to talk of populism and first-act equality and reregulation—for which it was punished in the elections of 2014 that brought the pro-growth Narendra Modi to power. But the decade just before the Party's apostasy from Milton Friedman was good for the poor and, yes, the rich of India. Anyway, at such rates, if sustained, as they show every sign of doing (the IMF predicted early in 2015 that annual growth there would be over 7 percent), Indian real income per person would quadruple in one long generation or two short ones. By 2020 or so, a majority of voters in India will be middle class, at any rate by the modest definition of "middle class" in a still very poor country.

The recent economic history of India and China suggests that liberalization—and not natural resources or foreign trade or government planning—causes the beneficent quadrupling. Only nine countries out of the world's 180 or so, a mere 2 percent of world population, match the Chinese and Indian record of real growth per capita of over 4 percent per year sustained over the three quinquennia up to 2010—Vietnam, for example, which adopted in 1986 a policy of "Doi Moi" (Renovation) to achieve a "socialist-oriented market economy," and Georgia, which between 2006 and 2014 jumped from 98th to 8th in the World Bank's "Ease of Doing Business" index, liberalization in spades redoubled and vulnerable.[8] (Vietnam in 2014 was in this respect mired at Georgia's old ranking of 99th.) Contrast the records of Brazil and South Africa, which have clung to subsidies and regulation and protectionism. The United States and the rest of the OECD world are already at the frontier of betterment and could be expected, as I have said, to grow only at moderate rates. Yet the U.S. rate during the 1990s exceeded some of the subdued rates of the BRIS. The BRIS account for 9 percent of the world's population, yet none of them, recently (2004–2013), has equalled the *world's* rate of growth of real GDP per capita, which was 4.8 percent—a very healthy level (a quadrupling in thirty years) that continued, notably, right through the Great Recession.[9]

The Great Enrichment is spreading to the world. True, in the nineteenth century places such as India and China experienced relative to the West a "Great Divergence," stagnating while the West shot ahead.[10] Until 1500, and in many ways until 1700, as the historian of technology Joseph Needham showed, China was the most technologically advanced country in the world, contrary to the old Eurocentric notion that the West has always been unusually ingenious.[11] Until 1700, and in some respects until 1850, most of the best technology, such as the blast furnace, was Chinese (and, in this particular case of large-scale production of iron, West African). Anesthesia is among the few dozen most important European betterments of the nineteenth century (Mokyr notes that it would not register as a rise in GDP, an instance of understatement of the Great Enrichment). Yet the Chinese were doing operations with anesthesia by drug and acupuncture two thousand years earlier.[12] Hundreds of years before the West the Chinese invented and used locks on canals to float up and down hills, and the canals themselves were until the nineteenth century four times longer than any in Europe.

Then after 1700 and especially after 1800 the West caught up to Chinese best practice, streaking ahead in betterment, and the Great Divergence commenced. The Divergence during the nineteenth century is probably explained partly by the comparative slowness with which betterments in northwestern Europe piled up at first, and then in many places by traditionalist or imperialist or populist objections to trade tests. The economists Diego Comin and Martí Mestieri show that the speed of first adoption of technologies has risen over the past two centuries, the lag from invention to poor-country adoption falling from about 120 years for spinning machinery and steamships to 13 years for cellphones and 7 years for the Internet.[13] Yet they also find that the time to spread in a country *after* first adoption has increased—perhaps from the increased autonomy of poor countries, with attendant pressures of populism to protect older techniques.

At a 7 percent rate of growth in per-person income—a rate available if people in now wretchedly poor countries will adopt liberty and dignity, such as the economic liberty to open a new convenience store or the social dignity accorded engineers who invent a new digital camera—the Divergence could be over in a couple of generations. Such a prospect is not hypothetical. It has happened again and again. Hong Kong's real income per head, which in 1948 was equal to that on the miserable mainland of China, now exceeds that of the United States. Routine supply, too, such as running a dry-cleaning shop with diligence or drilling for oil with intelligence, is best supported by allowing and encouraging ordinary people under law to make economic decisions for themselves, and by honoring the self-and-other-enriching outcomes of their decisions. As the Czech novelist and playwright Ivan Klíma put it, "America's wealth . . . is chiefly the result of the creative activity of free citizens. Americans are not to blame for Third World poverty, which is mostly due to . . . the demoralizing lack of freedom that most of the people there endure."[14] Give them economic liberty and social dignity and they will succeed—and often have in fact succeeded—as well as the Americans have.

A Great Convergence, in other words, is upon us.[15] The world's real income has accelerated, rising faster and faster, albeit with a sickening slowdown during the antibourgeois disorders of Europe and the world (1914–1950, with an extended engagement in some place down to 1989)—the disorders of nationalism, socialism, and, God help us, national socialism. The economic historian Leandro Prados de la Escosura has chronicled the late nineteenth-century and late twentieth-century rises in economic liberty. The fall in his figures during the grim three and a half decades after 1914 is stunning.[16] By contrast, the three decades after World War II, wrote Angus Maddison, "were a golden age of unparalleled prosperity," and not only in the West.[17] World real domestic product per person measured conventionally (without, that is, allowing properly for somewhat hard-to-measure betterments in the quality of goods) rose at nearly 3 percent a year, which implies a doubling of the material welfare of ordinary people every twenty-four years—that is, in a single generation. The later, less vigorous growth of 1973–1998, Maddison pointed out, was nonetheless higher than any earlier period except the unparalleled prosperity of the postwar boom. Now the world's growth rate of per-capita real income at purchasing-power parity, despite the Great Recession, I have noted, is 4.8 percent per year. However it is calculated it is notably faster than the golden age after 1945.

Nor are the world's poor paying for the growth. The economists Xavier Sala-i-Martin and Maxim Pinkovsky report on the basis of detailed study of the *individual* distribution of income that "world poverty is falling." They measure it person-by-person as against nation-by-nation. (The two methods, though, come to much the same conclusion.) "Between 1970 and 2006, the global poverty rate [defined in absolute, not relative, terms] has been cut by nearly three quarters. The percentage of the world population living on less than $1 a day (in purchasing-power-parity-adjusted 2000 U.S. dollars) went from 26.8% in 1970 to 5.4% in 2006."[18] The Great Recession slowed growth among the rich countries, but not much among the vigorously growing the poor countries.

We are converging on an enrichment of the poor.

Why Not the Conventional Explanations?

PART II

Explanations from Left and Right Have Proven False

10

THE DIVERGENCE WAS NOT
CAUSED BY IMPERIALISM

What does *not* explain the Divergence and the success of the West are the conventional "killer apps" that the historian Niall Ferguson, among others, claims were differentially strong in the West after 1500, namely, better science, better (domestic) competition, better property rights, a consumer society, and a European work ethic. These resulted, says Ferguson, in European "domination" of the rest of the world.

To the contrary, until the nineteenth century the apps were notably superior outside Europe—medicine was superior in China, for example, as were other applicable sciences, at any rate before the discoveries in Europe in and after the late nineteenth century of the germ theory, genetics, metallurgy, and organic chemistry, themselves the result of liberty and dignity permitting ordinary people to have an education, and a go. China's businesses in, say, 1700 faced healthy domestic competition more than those in a Europe broken up by tariffs and mercantilist monopolies. Taxes in China were uniform and transportation was good by international standards, which facts show up early in high correlations of Chinese prices of commodities north and south, east and west.

Political competition, Ferguson notes—and here he is correct, if conventional—was usually absent in China from the First Emperor on. Europe's fragmentation led to a beneficent intergovernmental competition for business, in the way American cities and states are forced to compete for business. It continued after 1800. Yet from an economic point of view the quarrel-provoking fragmentation of Europe was as much bad news as good. It led Europe to incessant wars. Murdering people and burning down their houses turns out to be bad for an economy. Some observers want such an obvious point to be wrong, and want to see an ill wind blowing good. The economic historian Patrick O'Brien, for example, argues that the (final stage of the 120-year) British anti-French world war, 1793–1815, was on balance good for the United Kingdom, making it more united and encouraging iron production. But it is hard to see how a peaceful two decades would not have been even better, without the diversion of a startlingly high proportion of GDP to warships and cannon and cannon fodder (which O'Brien has himself measured).[1] Voigtländer and Voth make a strange but not entirely implausible case that the Europeans unusual success at killing each other kept wages high, explaining thereby the First Divergence, which is to say (northwestern) Europe's high wages 1348–1800 compared with less sanguinary polities, such as China's.[2] Yet the best killing fields, such as Germany in the Thirty Years War, were not where growth flourished. One can doubt anyway that the First Divergence mattered very much to the Great Divergence of the nineteenth century. And the "good" was not so delightful for the numerous prematurely dead Europeans. On such accounting one could enrich the one surviving German by exterminating the rest.

Chinese property rights were anciently good. To repeat, however, the killer app of property rights characterizes any organized society, because that is what "organized" means. Ferguson may be relying for his account on the chronology of Douglass North and Barry Weingast, which attributes greatly improved property rights to the English Glorious Revolution of 1688.[3] Even if we insist on being Anglocentric, as North and Weingast are, the claim is false, and it would anyway be more appropriate to point to the English Civil War, four decades earlier, during which, for example, all existing domestic monopolies were abolished, or to the Statute of Monopolies (1624), in which Parliament declared, against the king, that the granting of new monopolies was "altogether contrary to the [common] law of this realm and [is and shall be] void," or indeed to *Darcy v. Allen* (1599, nearly nine decades before the revolution alleged by North and Weingast to have initiated good property in England). And it would make even more historical sense to point six centuries earlier, to 1239 and the ascension of Edward I, by which time English law for free subjects was largely in place.[4] In any case, there is no evidence that 1688 was the turning point in property rights—though it certainly was a turning point in parliamentary dominance, which brought on the Old Corruption. Compare Italy nowadays.

Further, the killer app of a "consumer society" is, on reflection, an empty category. For one thing, consumption does not expand production. To think so is to apply to the long run what is only true in the short, to believe that insufficient demand causing unemployment in 1933 is the same as bad labor law causing unemployment in 2016. It is the productionist fallacy. For another, as Dr. Johnson said in 1778, "Depend on it, sir, every state of society is as luxurious as it can be. Men always take the best they can get," in lace or food or education.[5] All societies, hunter-gathers no less than urbanites, consume beyond what is "needed." "Consumerism" is not special to the modern world, as cultural anthropologists such as Mary Douglas and Marshall Sahlins tell us.[6] True, the startlingly enriched people of the modern world can safely make more mistakes in purchases of dresses they never put on, and indulge in more hope that they will, this time, for sure, learn to play blues on that newly purchased guitar, after which it sits in the corner unused. But such consumption is a matter of quantity, not quality, a result of enrichment, not a cause.

As for the alleged killer app of a European work ethic (which could anyway hardly explain a rise of a factor of 100), everyone works hard, when not debilitated by malaria and the like. Here Ferguson may be relying on Max Weber's old notion, to be expected from a north-German Protestant in 1905, that Protestant Europeans worked harder than Catholic Europeans (such as Bavarians), not to speak of people in Hindu India or Confucian China. It is not factually correct, allowing again for debilitation. And without bothering with facts it would anyway seem unlikely, considering the starvation that attends the slothful in hardscrabble economies.

Ferguson declares above all, in line with a power-makes-for-plenty theory, that the apps permitted after 1500 a few European countries "to dominate the Rest [of the world]."[7] Note the year, claiming four and a half centuries of "domination."[8] He admits at one point that aside from the stagnant empires of Portugal and Spain the "domination" didn't really get going until rather late—in 1854, say, with the American treaty opening Japan, or 1858, with the crushing of the Sepoy Rebellion in India, or 1860, with the victory in the Second Opium War against China, a domination that came to an end in the defeats for colonialism after 1945. So the main "domination" lasted about a century. Yet a few pages later Ferguson is back to claiming that the West was able to "dominate the world for the better part of 500 years."[9]

In any case, on whatever time scale you wish to use, a "domination" of

India is not the same thing as an enrichment of Britain. Ferguson occasionally admits the point: "Empire is not a historically sufficient explanation
of Western predominance."[10] Actually, it had nothing to do with the West's
"predominance" if, in the way Ferguson sometimes speaks, he means "high
incomes." To suppose that the hurt from domination must somehow correspond to the economic gain from empire is a persistent error in thinking
about European imperialism, whether against it or in favor of it. The Indian
writer Mishra, in the course of a savage review in the *London Review of
Books* of what he claims are Ferguson's neo-imperialist notions (for which
claim Ferguson spoke of a suit for libel), presupposes a big "role of imperialism's structural violence in the making of the modern world."[11] But modern
prosperity, as India's vigorous recent experience of it shows, has nothing to
do with late nineteenth-century imperialism by Europeans. Mishra's anti-
imperialist error matches the pro-imperialist one. Mishra and Ferguson
slide together toward the same historical mistake—that Europe became rich
by "dominating."

It didn't. The appeal to "dominance" is a flaw in Jared Diamond's otherwise splendid book *Guns, Germs, and Steel* (1997). He plausibly argues on
geographic grounds that Eurasia was bound to be the scene for the Great
Enrichment. Because domesticable plants and animals could easily be shared
across the east-west orientation of Eurasia from Spain to Japan, and not
across the north-south orientation of the rest of the world, some place in
Eurasia and not New Guinea or Africa or the New World was going to be
the place originally with towns and writing and a chance at industrialization (although consider Mayan and Incas; consider African empires). But
then Diamond confuses enrichment of ordinary people based on trade-
tested betterment after 1800 with the merely financial "betterment" from
conquest after 1492, based on (primitive) guns, (non-intentionally spread)
germs, and (a little bit of expensive) steel, including horses and a loony
Christian conviction of superiority, inflicted by an aristocratic Spain on a
New World ill-prepared on all counts.

The persistent macho and deadly notion that power will cause plenty is
popular among historians. But the truth is the other way around: plenty can
budget for repeating rifles and ironclad ships, which lead to dominion over
palm and pine. Yet such dominion, like war itself, makes for scarcity, not
plenty. As the British Foreign Office kept warning during the scramble for
Africa, guns are expensive in housing and education forgone.

The "domination" on which Ferguson, Diamond, David Landes, Charles Kindleberger, Samuel Huntington, Ian Morris, and Paul Kennedy focus confounds empire with enrichment, violence with mutual benefit—the privilege of insulting the southern subalterns confused with high incomes for the Europeans back home. Mixing up political domination with economic enrichment has been an analytic mistake from the Hobson-Luxemburg left around 1900 to the Landes-Ferguson right around 2000. Europe became rich, and made the modern world, which reasonably promptly became the rest of the world's world, by its own betterments at home, not by stealing treasure from India or China or Africa, or even from Mexico and Peru so far as efficacy for European enrichment is concerned. Rich trades in products taking up a tiny share of national consumption, such as tea, china, tobacco, and spices, grew gratifyingly. A few wealthy merchants in Amsterdam and London lorded it over the rest. Average income in the commercial nations of Europe inched up, though at nothing remotely close to the frenetic rates established by massive technological and organizational betterment at home in the nineteenth century and beyond. As the French version of Adam Smith, Jean-Baptiste Say, put it in 1803, before imperialism became the fashion among the clerisy, "Dominion by land or sea will appear equally destitute of attraction, when it comes to be generally understood that all its advantages rest with the rulers, and that the [home] subjects at large derive no benefit whatever."[12]

The usual accounting of imperialism, in other words, is gravely mistaken. To say so is not to defend imperialism. The appalling history of European imperialism in Africa after 1885 sufficiently establishes its indefensibility. The point is merely that the undoubted exploitation of black mine workers in South Africa, the undoubted damage to the families of Maori or Zulu warriors mowed down by British settlers with guns, the undoubted condescension toward Indian cricket teams by the governing board of the English game, were none of them gains to Britons at home.[13] The economic effect of imperialism on ordinary Europeans has been shown repeatedly to be nil or negative.[14] Disraeli himself complained that "these wretched colonies . . . are a millstone around our neck."[15] A few British mining fortunes were made, a few viceroys educated at Christ Church College got their portraits up on the walls of the Senior Common Room, and quite a few twits from minor public schools got jobs in the Empire, with billiards and gin-and-tonics nightly at the Club. But the ordinary Scot or Cockney or Yorkshireman got nothing except the delight of seeing, by jingo, a quarter of the globe painted red. He paid taxes on beer and tobacco to support the Royal Navy, and then died on the Northwest Frontier in 1880 or on the Western Front in 1916 or in the Burmese jungles in 1943.

Economic growth in Europe had essentially nothing to do with what was in fact a small trade of the center with its Portuguese, Spanish, Dutch, British, French, and at last Belgian and German empires on the periphery. After all, during the Great Enrichment the European countries poor in overseas empire, such as Sweden and Austria, eventually grew smartly, too, getting their bananas for breakfast from trade rather than "domination." Europeans traded mainly with each other, and most of all with their countrymen, imperialism-free. The great bulk of their betterments were wholly domestic, such as improvements in sanitation and in state schools quite unrelated to glorious aggressions south and east of Suez.

And as to the late example of the "informal empire" of the United States, such quasi-imperialism has not benefited the average American—witness, for recent examples, Vietnam and the Second Iraq War. Interventions by guns or by diplomacy to protect American "interests" were focused on the interests that could buy presidents or congresspeople, or at any rate could buy enough newspapers or TV networks to spook the politicians: United Fruit, the oil companies, and the like.[16] The bulk of Americans then paid the butcher's bill (let us pass over in silence the masses of dead Guatemalans and Vietnamese and Iraqis). A tiny group of imperialists benefited. Empire can be a way to a few private fortunes, such as Cecil Rhodes's, but not to national wealth. As the free-trader John Bright declared in 1858, "This excessive love for the 'balance of power' [and 'America's role as the indispensable nation'] is neither more nor less than a gigantic system of out-door relief for the aristocracy of Great Britain" (and for the Southern military class and the military-industrial complex).[17]

In other words, ideas for new machines and institutions, inspired by an ethic of liberty and dignity for commoners, not the exploiting of empire or the building of military power, made Europeans rich. Power did not breed plenty.[18] The incessant wars of Europe, eventuating in the grand festival of power 1939–1945 with sixty-eight million dead, had modest civilian spinoffs yet occasioned massive diversion of resources from fruitful use. In justifying in the month of Pearl Harbor the supposition that power led to plenty, the Japanese prime minster Hideki Tojo was articulating a social Darwinist theory then widespread, and still to be heard in some quarters in the form of "competitiveness." "Our nation . . . stands at a crossroads," he declared, "one road leading to glory and the other to decline."[19] You can read similar power-or-decline rhetoric in most issues of *Foreign Affairs*, or in the works of historians drinking too deeply at the spring of Power and too little at that of Plenty, such as Landes, Kennedy, and recently Ferguson. The classical archaeologist Ian Morris, for example, following on his book of 2010, wrote an op-ed piece in 2014 entitled "In the Long Run, Wars Make Us Safer and Richer."[20] No, they don't. In 1923 Luigi Einaudi, the Italian liberal economist and the theorist of democratic Italy after fascism, noted that "before the [First World] war it was a favorite doctrine with nationalists that new, rising nations [for example, Italy itself, and Japan, Germany, and the United States] . . . were called to high destinies, to conquer territories, to become world Powers. . . . The war of new and rising nations against old and stationary . . . was erroneous both historically and economically."[21] The Declaration of the Intellectuals, signed by 352 German professors in 1915, said that it was reasonable to suppose that the German Empire required Belgium, Flanders, Ukraine, and overseas colonies to prosper.[22] The doctrine, unlike its victims, was hard to kill, reviving with Mussolini's imperial projects, Hitler's *Lebensraum*, and the theoretical agreement in the 1930s between the Japanese and the Americans that the only way for Japan to get oil was to conquer Indonesia. One hears it still, in exciting talk of power making for plenty. It is nonsense. Germany and Japan have prospered with trade, not aircraft carriers.

Quite another matter, though, is the strange curiosity of Europeans about the rest of the world, not matched by the rest of the world's curiosity about Europe. It yielded from the time of the Crusades through the Age of Exploration some notable augmentations in crops and machines and sciences. No one would deny that Europe's curiosity arrived often in a violent and imperial package. Yet it arrived often, too, by way of peaceful trade, such as the Silk Road. To have their Great Enrichment the Europeans did not have to follow a doctrine that one gets ideas and tea and oil only by conquest.

The point is that the empires near or far seldom yielded much loot, and what loot they did yield was temporary. Even when the empires paid off in coin the payoff was after all merely money, merely onetime claims to ownership dwarfed by annual domestic production, not permanent augmentations of the European ability to produce. The economic historian and dependency theorist André Gunder Frank, for example, spoke of Spanish silver "buying a ticket on the Asian train."[23] The phrase has a nice ring to it but is mistaken as economics. Giving silver and gold to the East in order to get imports of Asian cloth and porcelain did nothing to encourage betterment in the West. Money is a claim to capital, not capital itself. And in any case betterment, not capital, was the ticket that mattered.

The silver flowing to early modern Spain was a case of a political-economy-and-sloth version of the (ill-named) Dutch Disease, that is, oil riches that make the elite hostile to betterment: No thanks, we have all we want. And in any case, the silver extracted from the mountain of Potosí by a *corvée* imposed on natives was wasted by Spain in European wars. Imperial adventures did not yield plenty, merely more fighting. A clear gain from the Spanish ventures to ordinary Europeans, I noted, was the cheap and nourishing potatoes and tomatoes (and expensive and noxious tobacco, too). But they were brought also to China and India, by trade and the spread of ideas in seeds, not by conquest. If stout Cortez had failed, and if the Spaniards had been satisfied to trade with the Aztecs and Mayans and Incas instead of putting them to the sword, and to the *corvée*, the main, agricultural effects of the Columbian Exchange would nonetheless have taken place.

The European conquest of other parts of the world came in the sixteenth and seventeenth centuries from unusual daring (think again of Cortez, or Pizarro, or Clive of India) and from guns, germs, and steel. The greater triumph of imperialism awaited the nineteenth century, giving even little European countries like Belgium extensive empires thanks to gunboats, high-muzzle-velocity carbines, and well-ordered armies, backed by the intercontinental shipping by steam to deploy them quickly. Britain won the (Second) Boer War because it could after a while concentrate great masses of soldiers gathered from Home and Empire to defeat the Afrikaners, who at first had the upper hand in mobility and intelligence. Yet the late nineteenth-century empires were no more profitable than the Spanish and Portuguese empires of the sixteenth century.[24] The British got nothing from "winning" the Boer War—not even a slowing down of Afrikaner abuse of blacks and coloreds. In the long run, that is, it was plenty that bred power, not the other way around.

POVERTY CANNOT BE
OVERCOME FROM THE LEFT
BY OVERTHROWING "CAPITALISM"

I have occasionally used, because everybody chatters about it, the word "capitalism." Even more than "bourgeois" it acquired its prominence from Marx and his followers. (It is often remarked, correctly, that Marx himself does not in *Das Kapital* or in many other places use the word *Kapitalismus*. But let's not quibble: he does freely use *Kapital, Kapitalist, kapitalistisch*.)

We should drop the word, because it has led people astray. "Capitalism" insists on the erroneous conviction of early economists such as Adam Smith and Karl Marx that piling brick on brick is what made us rich. And it insists on the likewise erroneous conviction of Marx, building on stage theories by Montesquieu, Smith, and others, that the "capitalism" of accumulation is new, five centuries old, say, a new "stage" of history, instead of, as it is, an ancient human practice. We should replace "capitalism" with the non-snappy but accurate "trade-tested betterment"—or if you want a single word, "improvement" or "betterment" or even "innovism"—understood as the frenetic bettering of machines and procedures and institutions after 1800, supported by a startling change in the ethical evaluation of the betterings.

God won't tell us how to employ words. If we must use "capitalism," I propose, if God doesn't mind, that we employ it to mean simply "the background use of trade, very widespread in Africa and Latin America in 1800 CE, but not by any means unknown in China and Mesopotamia in 1800 BCE, and dating, truth be known, to 80,000 BCE or earlier in Mother Africa." It is the way Max Weber and Fernand Braudel used the word in all their works. "*Modern* capitalism" could then be used to highlight the strangely innovative and historically unique form that a trading society at last took—frenetically adopting technical and organizational betterments, a "modern capitalism" or, better, the "innovism" peculiar to the past couple of centuries.

But the new system to be analyzed does not consist of the anciently routine trading or the old class relations in medieval cities or ancient Greece. Nor is there anything novel about the big size of business or the detailed division of labor, which happened in ancient China in silk making and in ancient Rome in fish-sauce making. Nor is the novelty an accumulation of capital, which happened in the Old Stone Age. And even modified by "modern," the phrase "modern capitalism" can give heart to what the economist William Easterly calls "capital fundamentalists," those who mistakenly believe that the piling of brick on brick is what poor countries need.[1] They need betterment tested by voluntary deals, not the roads and port facilities that would follow easily if the alleged betterment were in fact profitable. My proposed substitute for "modern capitalism"—"trade-tested betterment at the frenetic post-1800 pace, and routine supply also governed by profit"—fits the history. A thirty- to hundredfold increase, between 1800 and the present, in the per-person ability to make goods and services is impossible through routine accumulation or routine exploitation. The increase can be called a "frenetic betterment" without violating the norms of language. "Betterment" or "innovism" at least gets us looking in the right direction. "Capitalism" turns us firmly away.

The Australian historian of economic thought Elena Douglas has persuaded me to question, further, in describing the release of creativity, the fashionable word "innovation." Her point is that "improvement" or "betterment," or indeed the more argumentative "innovism" or "progress," words I eventually settled on, focus more sharply on the actual help to ordinary humans of new ideas, as against the sheer novelty of the ideas. Novelty is easy. Let us start walking without stepping on the cracks in the sidewalk. Let us start blaming our troubles on witchcraft. Let us start having novel but socially unprofitable, governmentally compelled, and feed-corn-absorbing ethanol for our gasoline pumps. Actual help is not easy. Let us start having improved but thus far bureaucracy-blocked up-to-date computers for air-traffic control. Joel Mokyr, again, who is among the handful of my academic colleagues in economic history favoring the ideational approach (along with the historian Margaret Jacob, the sociologist Jack Goldstone, and such groundbreaking nonacademics as Jane Jacobs, Michael Novak, George Gilder, and Matt Ridley), makes the same point in speaking of the turn to *usefulness* in what he calls the Industrial Enlightenment. Yet Mokyr would agree that usefulness, too, needs a trading test, and that sheer innovation without the test is worse than useless, novelty without betterment—backyard blast furnaces, say.

The crux is the test in trade. Are people willing to pay for it? The phrase "*trade-tested* innovation" occurs in a few other contexts, such as Barbara Jones and Bob Miller, *Innovation Diffusion in the New Economy: The Tacit Component* (at p. 83). The procedures of a company called Jump Start promise "a trade-tested innovation to your team for ongoing management," while another, ISOKO, "promotes action-driven, market tested innovation" in Africa.[2] The closest to my use is in Clayton, Dal Borgo, and Hasekl (2009), which uses the exact phrase on page 11 and, more to the point, criticizes other definitions of innovation precisely for not thinking in terms of a trade test. They quote the definition in the OECD's authoritative Oslo Manual: "a technological product innovation is the implementation/commercialization of a product with improved performance characteristics such as to deliver objectively new or improved services to the consumer." The manual, they observe, makes a faint gesture toward the test of trade in the word "commercialization" but gives "objectively" no content. Mainly it supposes, as social democrats do, that we already know what is "improved to the consumer" without such a test. Ask the regulator or the planner. "Betterment," by contrast, gives the relevant context for us humans—a trading test of profit, allowing for externalities. Clayton and colleagues see that a trading test requires that the bettering increase national income, properly measured. They reckon that 61 percent of the growth in labor productivity 2000–2005 in the British sector of voluntary trade (excluding government, that is) was attributable to betterment.[3]

The communitarian political philosopher Michael Walzer declared in 1983 that "in a capitalist society, capital is dominant," that is, it is translatable into other sorts of things people want, such as political power.[4] But capital is not "dominant." Ideas are. Walzer is being misled, as so many are, by the very word "capitalism" into supposing that its mainspring is the accumulation of capital. The mainspring is rather new ideas for progress, which make some new, targeted accumulation profitable. In nearly every society the routine profit of "men about me that are fat, / Sleek-headed men and such as sleep a-nights" has been translatable into political power. It has nothing about it of the modern, which is the sense of "capitalist society" that Walzer wants.

Unusual profit awaits anyone at any time in history, such as "Yond Cassius [with] a lean and hungry look. / He thinks too much," who finds the ideas first and is courageous enough to invest in them—Mark Zuckerberg (and roommates) find Facebook, Henry Ford finds cheap cars, Andrew Carnegie finds cheap steel. As Luigi Einaudi wrote in 1943, summarizing the analysis in 1730–1734 of the Irish/French Richard Cantillon of the word "entrepreneur," what distinguishes the *imprenditore*, the entrepreneur, is not possessing and accumulating capital at a fixed interest rate, but "assuming the risk of acquiring the factors of production [such as land and labor and capital itself] at the price on the market . . . and of selling their product at an uncertain price."[5] Buy ideas low and hope that you can sell them high. It is different from clipping coupons or purchasing Congress, and has been understood to be so since 1730.

Likewise the Marxian sociologist Immanuel Wallerstein was being a trifle careless when he wrote in 1983 that "the word capitalism is derived from capital. It would be legitimate therefore to presume that capital is a key element in capitalism."[6] No, it would not. What we now, in retrospect, say about the early modern world does not by virtue of that saying become true. That we insist on ruminating on something called "capital" does not imply that its accumulation was in fact unique to modernity. It does not make true the Master's words: "Accumulate, accumulate! That [in the opinion of the classical economists whom Marx was attacking, though agreeing with them on the centrality of capital and its 'endless' accumulation] is Moses and the prophets."[7]

The word "capitalism" emerged in the late nineteenth century on the left of European politics, and eventually, in a turn the Dutch call a *geuzennaam* (literally, a "beggar name," assigned by ones enemies, such as "Quaker" or "Tory" or "Whig"), was adopted proudly by the right itself. Once the lineup of the politics had been settled, people left and right reckoned that they already knew the merely corroborative detail of the actual economic history backing up the politics. "Capitalism," educated people have believed since 1848, emerged in the sixteenth century. Accumulation proceeded until it yielded the Industrial Revolution of the eighteenth century. It corrupted all who touched it, said the left. It automatically enriched people through physical and human capital accumulation, said the right. Left-wing sociologists to this day believe that Marx and Engels in 1848 discerned the story correctly. Right-wing economists have joined them in the same persistently erroneous "stylized facts"—so much less troublesome than actual facts. Both left and right are enchanted by the just-so story that the Industrial Revolution was a "take off" and that physical accumulation, not ideology, was its fuel.

The American humorist Josh Billings long ago said, "It's better to know less than to know so much that ain't so." Acemoglu's and Robinson's *Why Nations Fail* (2012), to take a recent example of the persistence of the just-so story, has much in it with which to agree: Europe's advance was highly contingent; political and economic liberty are linked; economic growth can't get going in the midst of a civil war. But Acemoglu and Robinson expressly and even a little proudly rely on a startlingly out-of-date account of the Industrial Revolution. "Our argument about the causes," they assert, "is highly influenced by" a list of "scholars in turn . . . inspired by earlier Marxist interpretations" of the 1920s through the 1960s, such as R. H. Tawney, Maurice Dobb, and Christopher Hill.[8] The *locus classicus* of such interpretations, and the introduction of the very phrase "the industrial revolution" into English, had been *Lectures on the Industrial Revolution of the Eighteenth Century in England* (1884), delivered by a young university lecturer and ardent social reformer, Arnold Toynbee (1852–1883), in the year before his death at age thirty-one. Toynbee in turn depended on the story of triumph and tragedy put forward in *The Communist Manifesto*. For example, Toynbee declared that "as a matter of fact, in the early days of competition,"

> the capitalists used all their power to oppress the laborers, and drove down wages to starvation point. This kind of competition has to be checked. . . . In England both remedies are in operation, the former through Trades Unions, the latter through factory legislation.[9]

None of this is factually correct, though all of it fills the popular view of industrialization. There were no "early days of competition"—competition was common in any society of trade, as its enemies such as the medieval guildsmen sharply realized. Competition comes from entry, which is ancient, if annoying to the established rich. Supply and demand, not "power," is what determines wages, as one can see in the ups and downs of real wages in response to population downs and ups in the age of Malthus before 1798. The workers in the Industrial Revolution did not find their wages reduced, and did not starve. It is why the workers moved eagerly to cities, even though Manchester and Lille and Boston were still death traps of waterborne disease.

Competition, which sets entrepreneurs against one another for our benefit, needs to be encouraged, not checked. Wages were in fact rising and children were being taken out of English factories before the legalization of trade unions and well before the factory legislation began seriously to bite.

In other words, Acemoglu and Robinson are accepting an erroneous left-ish story of economic history proposed in 1848 or 1882 by brilliant amateurs, before the professionalization of scientific history, then repeated by Fabians at the hopeful height of the socialist idea, and then elaborated by a generation of (admittedly first-rate) Marxian historians, before thoroughgoing socialism had been tried and had failed, and before much of the scientific work had been done about the actual history—before it was realized, for instance, that other industrial revolutions occurred in, say, Islamic Spain or Song China, as Jack Goldstone argued in 2002: "Examined closely, many premodern and non-Western economies show spurts or efflorescences of economic growth, including sustained increases in both population and living standards, in urbanization, and in underlying technological change."[10]

The older historians of the left, indeed, wrote before the British Industrial Revolution itself had been closely examined. In 1926 the economic historian John Clapham showed, for example, that Britain in the mid-nineteenth century was no steam-driven factory. "At what point" during the Great Enrichment, he noted, "the typical worker may be pictured as engaged on tasks which would have made earlier generations gape is a matter for discussion. It may be suggested here that this point will be found some rather long way down the [nineteenth] century."[11] Gape-worthy steam power in Britain, for example, increased by a factor of fully ten from 1870 to 1907, a hundred years after the mills, most at first propelled by water, first enter British consciousness.[12] And in 1850 the bulk of goods and services, Clapham showed, were still provided in traditional ways outside the mills. Think of making chairs or making beds.

A foundational text in Acemoglu and Robinson's tale, they say, is a book by Paul Mantoux (1877–1956), frequently reprinted (which was a publishing decision, not a testament to scientific currency). "Our overview of the economic history of the Industrial Revolution," they declare forthrightly, "rests on Mantoux (1961)."[13] Note the date given. But Mantoux's book, written in 1906 and translated from the French once, in 1929, contains no historical science done after 1906. Mantoux was not himself an economist or an economic historian, but a professor of French history. He was a friend of Lloyd George and was the English translator for Clemenceau at the Versailles Conference. The comforting phrase "revised edition" in Acemoglu and Robinson's bibliography does not refer to the reported date of 1961. *La révolution industrielle au XVIIIe siècle* was last revised in its French edition, well before we knew much beyond Marx, Engels, and Toynbee's youthful anti-economic essay about the Industrial Revolution. We did not know, for example, Clapham's finding of the 1920s; or the finding of the 1950s that early factories had little to do with massive accumulations of capital (anticipated briefly in Weber 1905, p. 31); or the finding of the 1990s that such Smithian growth was common worldwide; or the finding of the 1960s through the 2010s that the Great Enrichment, not the Industrial Revolution, was the most amazing fact.

And yet even we Professional Economic Historians sometimes yield to the just-so story, which shows up in the same way, with citations to the same book of 1906 as up-to-date science. Ronald Findlay and Kevin O'Rourke in their book connecting power with plenty through foreign trade cite the book as "Mantoux (1962)" (they used another of the numerous reprintings).[14] The impression unintentionally conveyed is that Mantoux's book was up-to-date historical science six years after his death, and fifty-six years after its last revisions.

We need to get beyond just-so stories, beyond what the historian C. Veronica Wedgwood described in 1960 as "the various agreed fables which had served men well enough for several generations."[15] A good first step would be to abandon the word "capitalism" and the chronically erroneous fables that go with it.

We need, in other words, to contradict the usual anticapitalist fables. About Milton Friedman, for example. According to leftist lore, Friedman was a big advisor to General Pinochet in Chile. He was not: he had one conversation with Pinochet, telling him to pay attention to the money supply.

Or, to take a more academic example about this defender of market-tested betterment, in a famous article in the *New York Times Magazine* in 1970 Friedman argued, as the headline put it, that "The Social Responsibility of Business Is to Increase Its Profits."[16] Following the conventions of big-time journalism the headline, which is what most people know about the article, was not chosen by Friedman himself but was plucked out of the article by a clever writer of headlines. Friedman was in fact arguing that a society with more wealth can better pursue its transcendent goals, and that more wealth for such noble purposes is produced by maximizing profits. That is correct, and is part of the case for focusing on betterment rather than on distribution. (Margaret Thatcher once said, "No one would remember the Good Samaritan if he'd only had good intentions; he had money as well" to pay for the care of the man beaten and robbed.) Friedman further argued that a hired manager for Boeing who raises his social standing in Chicago by getting the corporation to give to the Lyric Opera is stealing money from the stockholders. That is correct too, and is clearly also an ethical issue. (Yet a contrary economic argument, which Friedman uncharacteristically overlooked, is that the ability to play the noble lord is part of executive compensation. The stockholders would have to pay the manager still more in cash than they do if they insisted that he not be allowed to give away some of the their money to worthy causes.)

But most people who have expressed shock or delight at Friedman's article have not realized that in the actual sentence from which the headline writer took the title Friedman adds a side constraint to the manager's fiduciary duty to the stockholders: "make as much money as possible *while conforming to the basic rules of the society, both those embodied in law and those embodied in ethical custom.*"[17] We need, as Friedman was in effect arguing, to balance all the virtues of courage and love and faith and prudence in an ethical business life. As a matter of fact, as *The Bourgeois Virtues* documents, most businesspeople are already ethical, contrary to the populist line that they are price-gougers, contrary to the Marxian line that they are carriers of an evil system, and contrary to the conservative line that they are anyway indecorous.

In any case, surely, we do not want lofty disdain for the bourgeoisie and their betterments, or ignorant hatred of their liberal defenders, to be preordained by the rhetoric since Marx of the very word "capitalism," or by the various agreed fables about it and about its defenders.

"ACCUMULATE, ACCUMULATE" IS
NOT WHAT HAPPENED IN HISTORY

The new economy of betterment that started to take hold in seventeenth-century Holland and eighteenth-century England and early nineteenth-century Belgium, northern France, and the United States was not mere accumulation, which as I've noted is as ancient as the fashioning of the Acheulean hand axes in bulk by *Homo erectus* and earlier by *Homo habilis* (that is, "tool-making human") from a little after 2 million years BCE. Our ancestors accumulated arrow points and animal-skin clothing, or they starved or froze to death. But their accumulation did not make for a Great Enrichment.

Accumulated capital becomes unusually, nonroutinely profitable only if it embodies betterment, innovism. As John Maynard Keynes pointed out, the return on capital could be driven down by investment to zero in a generation if there were no betterment.[1] Because he thought that by the 1930s betterments had been exhausted—as some during the 2010s have come to believe again—he thought that savings (which depend on income, he claimed, not on profit) would henceforth exceed profitable investments (which depend on the allegedly exhausted betterments), leading to perpetual unemployment unless the government substituted social investment for private.

Keynes was correct about the logic of the if-then statement: if no betterment, then profitable investments are speedily exhausted. The stationary state is achieved. All buildings and machines and educations that make economic sense have been accumulated. Further investment yields less than zero, net. Don't do it. And worry about the savings piling up. But a profitable use of savings or of retained earnings is easily found once a betterment is exogenously devised, itself in response to a mad optimism about progress or a newly permitted search for honor. Mere accumulation of capital is, as the economists say, "*endo*genous," Greek for "*internally* generated" from, say, how much savings are routinely made. The bettering ideas in technology and institutions were by contrast *exo*genous. As the economic historian and development economist Jeffrey Williamson put it in 1993, "It was the rise in the rate of return to private investment during the Industrial Revolution that encouraged savers to save more [and businesses to reinvest their profits more], and it was technological advance that drove the rate of return to private investment."[2] Any theory of a system depends on determining what is endogenous and what is exogenous. Newton's law of inertia declares that something moving under initial, given forces continues moving in the same fashion until the forces change. Likewise here. "The rise in the rate of return," coming from ideas springing from a new liberty and dignity for the masses, changed the economic forces. Accumulated capital was merely an intermediate factor expressing the forces, not an intrinsic, Aristotelian principle of motion.

Furthermore, the accumulated capital depreciates. Therefore a long-term accumulation, the piling up of capital over centuries, can't happen. With rare outliers of durability such as Roman roads or the Great Wall or the treeless environment arising from the fire-stick of the Aborigines, most physical investments, in houses and machines and drained fields, require frequent renewal or else they succumb to entropy. They fall apart. The fact of depreciation contradicts the sociologist Charles Tilly's influential book, *Coercion, Capital, and European States, AD 990–1990* (1990). Tilly supposed that capital accumulated in 990 CE, or 1700 CE, mattered for what happened in 1990 CE. It didn't. The sites of medieval accumulation in Italy became the laggard economies of the nineteenth century. During the same century the English economy, a backwater in the Middle Ages, flourished.

A house built in 900 or 1700 is dust by now, unless it has been repaired and restored again and again. The New Franklin Building was erected in 1914 as a printing plant but by 1983 had fallen into entire disuse. In 1979 the installation *The Dinner Party* by the artist Judy Chicago was first exhibited on its vacant top floor. Then in 1989 the shell was gutted and remodeled into sixty-five loft apartments, profitable because people were just beginning to move downtown and the betterment of reusing industrial buildings had become apparent. Otherwise, entropy. Anyone who has replaced the roof of her house knows that a house is a continuing and recent accumulation, like a garden, not to be acquired unmodified from past centuries. In the *Mahabharata*, the Achilles character Karna declares, "I see it now: this world is swiftly passing."[3] "Lay up not for yourself treasures upon earth," said Jesus of Nazareth, "where moth and rust do corrupt." St. Augustine was eloquent on the point: "All things pass away, fly away, and vanish like smoke; and woe to those who love such things!"[4]

What does not vanish like entropic smoke, aside from God, is knowledge, or the tacit knowledge in design or sport or art transmitted in practice, or the bookable knowledge of the formula for aspirin or the procedure for habeas corpus, and most particularly, with the greatest consequence, the information-plus-judgment embodied in the Bourgeois Deal. To be sure, knowledge does not always persist. Jared Diamond notes the forgetting of the bow and arrow among the aboriginal settlers of Australia.[5] Such forgetting comes from the low population densities of the pioneers, which lets lines of ideas die out, by a social analogy to the founder effect in genetics. Too few experts on using a bow and arrow teach too few students, and the art has a good chance of disappearing. After the legions withdrew and the Anglo-Saxons came to rule, the formerly Roman Britons lost in the fifth century coinage, mortared buildings, and knowledge of the potter's wheel.[6] During Roman times the baths at Bath had been reheated with coal, the use of which the English promptly forgot. Marco Polo, from sophisticated Venice, was astounded in the thirteenth century by the Chinese use of a black stone that burned like a log—though by that time the English themselves had started to burn coal they found on beaches from sea-worn outcrops, "sea coal."

But knowledge—unlike most treasures upon earth—has a chance of accumulating over centuries, as a few economists such as Paul Romer have realized at last, after economists had tried and tried to make the routine accumulation of physical or human capital, instead of the mysterious ways of human creativity, into the hero of modernity.[7] But then Romer turned the story back into a routine capital accumulation of ideas that would arise in any large city, from Ur to Istanbul, but did not. As the economic historian Maarten Prak remarked, "We should . . . never forget that during the premodern era perhaps as much as half of the world's urban population lived in Chinese towns and cities."[8] Wherefore not a Chinese Great Enrichment?

Nor was the new form of "capitalism" gradually emerging from the mist after 1600, and triumphant by 1848, a new greediness. Many people still believe so, and it is repeated in denunciations of modern bankers. But Max Weber and I dispute the belief: "The notion that our rationalistic and capitalistic age," he wrote, "is characterized by a stronger economic interest than other periods is childish."[9] The infamous hunger for gold,

> the impulse to acquisition, pursuit of gain, of money, of the greatest possible amount of money, has in itself nothing to do with capitalism. This [greedy] impulse exists and has existed among waiters, physicians, coachmen, artists, prostitutes, dishonest officials, soldiers, nobles, crusaders, gamblers, and beggars. One may say that is has been common to all sorts and conditions of men at all times and in all countries of the earth, wherever the objective possibility of it is or has been given."[10]

The novelty after 1600 in Holland and after 1800 in Europe generally was a cluster of ideas for betterment tested by voluntary trades with customers and with a resulting profitability, arising at a uniquely frenetic pace, sustained by an entirely new ideology of human equality. As Matt Ridley puts it, the outcome was that technological ideas had sex: "At some point in human history, ideas began to meet and mate."[11] The point was around 1800. The novelty was not the accumulation of capital but the accumulation of knowledge, protected by the newly accumulated ideology of the Bourgeois Deal. The Acheulean hand ax (in fact, more a knife and even a projectile than an ax) was unchanged for over a million years of accumulations, and was used even by an early *Homo sapiens*, before he put a haft on it. His descendants at length started polishing it into the beautiful objects of the Late Stone Age. But until then the axe was accumulation without any betterment at all.

What is unique about the past two centuries, I say yet again, is the gigantic betterment, not the routine capital accumulation that the betterment made profitable. Ridley in his books and TED Talks puts a picture of the axe and the computer mouse side by side. They are strikingly similar, because both are designed to fit snuggly into a human hand. But one was a technology frozen for 1.3 million years. The other is pure betterment, invented in 1963 and then creatively destroyed for our benefit after a mere fifty years, when motions of the hand over a watchful screen began to take its place. Who has a mechanical typewriter now? Who a black-and-white TV? Where are the skills of the telephone operators (350,000 in the United States in the late 1940s) or the elevator operators found in every tall building until the 1950s or the Latin-speaking diplomats and scholars (numbered in the thousands in 1600)? Such physical and human accumulations of capital have passed away, flown away, and vanished like smoke. But betterments in the knowledge of how to make computers or how to understand supply and demand for labor have abided. And unless we now kill it off, the Bourgeois Deal, too, abides.

Aside from a few isolated voices such as Schumpeter's and Mokyr's and Nick von Tunzelmann's and William Baumol's, economists have not much to say about the causes of the betterment.[12] Most keep trying to force betterment back into accumulation, spurning innovism. Matt Ridley has worried about "a deep incuriosity among trained economists . . . about defining what prosperity is and why it happened to our species."[13] He may not be giving sufficient credit to the discoveries by economic historians during the past seventy years and the revival of interest in historical economics during the past twenty years among otherwise historically incurious economists.[14] Yet forcing the story onto the Procrustean bed of capital accumulation does amount to a lack of curiosity about how prosperity depends on creativity. In 1959 the libertarian journalist John Chamberlain noted the lack: "People can only live creatively," he wrote,

> when cooperation is a matter of free election, of the voluntary approach. . . . Economists in general overlook the importance of the "x" of invention and the "y" of technological innovation. . . . The pace, the incidence, of disruption must remain a largely unknown quantity unless the economist can isolate the causes of invention, of creativity, itself.[15]

Therefore I suggest "the age of betterment" or a similar phrase to describe the modern world, not "the age of capital(ism)." There's nothing automatic about growth of capital in "capitalism," though since 1776 and especially since 1848 many people have believed there is. In particular, a large scale of *financial* accumulation has little to do with it. Only with the coming of railways was that part of betterment much dependent on financial markets. Little or nonexistent piles, such as those of a young John D. Rockefeller or a young Bill Gates, can grow at rates far above normal, if in a time and place of betterment that permits and honors the bourgeoisie, a business-admiring civilization. Before its coming, the big piles of financial capital, such as Spain's, were regularly dissipated in aristocratic posturing financed by taxes on the periphery and preserved by local elitism walled off by high transport costs.[16] The English king Henry II's partial conquests in Ireland, which later English kings seldom visited, were milked to staff armies and finance wars in France and Scotland and the Holy Lands.[17] The accumulated financial and human capital was seized or charmed out of the country: " 'Missus McGrath,' the sergeant said, / 'Would you like to make a soldier out of your son Ted?' "

There does not appear to be anything special—except that it occurred now in a business-respecting civilization—about the use of accumulated capital in the "modern capitalist" era. People used financial and real capital before 1800 if it seemed like a good idea, as for example in twentieth-century BCE Mesopotamia, in transactions recorded on clay. Profits were earned, as they were in the fifth-century BCE empire of commercial Athens. "The voluntary approach" in economic relations is very ancient, back to the buying of shell beads and obsidian knives. The trade was not small or confined to consumption by the rich. Obsidian, for example, a volcanic glass, was highly localized in supply but demand was widespread, for harvesting grain by sickle, among other uses of its exceptionally hard and sharp edges. The archaeologist Steven Mithen tells of the trading of shell beads for obsidian in the Middle East as early as 6,500 BCE and 9,600 BCE.[18]

The antiquity and ubiquity of trade is a commonplace among archaeologists and anthropologists. The Berndts in their classic of 1964, *The World of the First Australians*, noted under the rubric "Trade" that "there is [in traditional Aboriginal society] a more or less constant movement of goods. . . . The Lugga say they cannot make boomerangs properly: they prefer to import them. . . . Central Australian shields find their way to . . . the head of the [mid-Western Australia] Canning Stock Route [some hundreds of miles from the origin of the shields]. . . . Kimberly pearl shells [from the northwest coast] traveled right across Australia," as far as Eyre's Peninsula, fourteen hundred miles away as the crow flies.[19] And tens of thousands of years earlier, back in Mother Africa, at the beginnings of *Homo sapiens* culture, ornaments were brought by trade from seashores hundreds of miles away.[20]

Braudel, in 1979, concluded his three-volume study of the facts of "capitalism" by noting that, even in his idiosyncratic sense of the linking of local markets by international and high-profit and allegedly monopolized trade (his distinction of it from other forms of trade came more from leftish prejudice than from historical evidence), "capitalism" was ancient:

Throughout this book, I have argued that capitalism has been potentially visible since the dawn of history. . . . It would however be a mistake to imagine capitalism as something that developed in a series of stages . . . with "true" capitalism appearing only at the late stage when it took over production, and the only permissible term for the early period being mercantile capitalism or even "pre-capitalism." . . . The whole panoply of forms of capitalism—commercial, industrial, banking— was already employed in thirteenth-century Florence, in seventeenth-century Amsterdam, in London before the eighteenth century.[21]

Or, one might add, the whole panoply of forms of capitalism was already employed in Athens before the fourth century BCE, Rome before the third century BCE, China before the second century BCE.[22] The historical sociologist Eric Mielants is indignant that the French historian Jean Baechler writing his history of the *longue durée* (2002) "does not mention capitalism at all."[23] Baechler had it right.

No automatic machinery of accumulation got turned on in 1760. No "take-off into self-sustained growth" occurred as a result of higher saving rates making more capital, and more, and more. The absence of such machinery contradicts the mysterious claim of its centrality by Walt Rostow in 1960, at the height of capital fundamentalism, and it contradicts what is now again mysteriously claimed by recent capital-obsessed economists filling their blackboards with "growth theory." High savings rates in Italy in the nineteenth century did not result in economic growth, until late. Savings rates in Britain in the eighteenth century were in fact comparatively low.[24]

Growth that is "sustained" or "continuing" or "taking-off" is an economist's fancy leading us away from scientific insight. Economists favor it because it allows them to summarize economic history in a single equation. The metaphor promises that once the airplane lifts off the tarmac its flight is determined. Yet even in 1800 there was little determined about the coming Great Enrichment, as Joel Mokyr has argued more widely about technological change. It is a highly nonroutine event, not a machine of accumulation, that needs scientific explanation.

One can imagine counterfactuals that would have caused the Industrial Revolution to stall permanently around 1800, and crash, as so many had before—Song-dynasty prosperity, for example, flying into the turbulence of the Mongol invasion, and the Mongol high-flying itself, thrown off course by the Black Death. Suppose the French had succeeded in invading Britain in 1798 (when the Irish sang hopefully, "Oh, the French are in the bay, / They'll be here without delay"). French centralization, without the irritation of competition from Britain or the Low Countries, might have killed the trade test, substituting a test by experts in Paris. Or suppose that the left radicals or their enemies the reactionaries, both of whom were opposed to industrialization, had succeeded in throttling the infant.

Or suppose that the United States had not stood as a constant quasi-democratic and fully trade-testing challenge to Old Europe. The counterfactual is not remote if one attends to the Engerman-Sokoloff hypothesis that Latin America, by contrast, was saddled from its origins with a hierarchical society unable to reward and respect ordinary people.[25] In such a case the left in Europe would have had no model except the utopian side of the French Revolution, expressed later in the lunacies of Charles Fourier. The European reactionaries after 1815 might have kept forever the upper hand that they exercised so vigorously in Russia or the Austrian Empire, slowing down disturbing betterments such as railways. In the actual event, however, the liberal left could point across the Atlantic to the success of a government of the (male, nonslave) people, the ideology of which did not perish from the earth.

Nor does the capitalist machinery automatically exploit and alienate the proletariat. It didn't in the United States, which was and is in its working class notoriously antisocialist, and whose comparative wealth even in its poor argues against a theory of economic exploitation. The political writer David Ramsay Steele speaks of the crisis of socialist thought in the 1890s, by which time it was realized that the workers in Europe and the United States and Australia and Argentina were getting better off, and were not about to bring on the revolution.[26] In 1914 the lining up of socialist parties in Europe with their national declarations of war was as disturbing to thoughtful socialists as the parallel lining up of Catholic and Orthodox priests and Protestant ministers along the same nationalist lines was disturbing to thoughtful Christians.

We don't want to prejudge everything about the mechanisms and morals of "capitalism" merely because we have defined it the way Marx did in chapter 4 of *Capital* (at any rate according to the standard, and inaccurate, English translation) as "the restless *never-ending* process of profit-making alone . . . , this *boundless greed* after riches, this passionate chase after exchange-value."[27] The original German, it should be noted, says "solely the restless stirring for gain, this absolute desire for enrichment, this passionate hunt for value" (*nur die rastlose Bewegung des Gewinnes. Dieser absolute Bereicherungstrieb, diese leidenschaftliche Jagd auf den Wert*).[28] Key words in the English translation of such passages, such as "never-ending" (*endlos, ewig, unaufhörlich*) and "boundless" (*grenzenlos, schrankenlos*), appear nowhere in Marx's German. The normal German word for "greed" (*Gier*), which most people would attribute to Marx's theory, does not appear anywhere in the chapter. Indeed, *Gier* and its compounds (*Raubgier*, rapacity; *Habgier*, avarice; *Geldgier*, greed for money) are rare in Marx, in accord with his attempt to shift away from conventional ethical terms in analyzing "capitalism" and the bourgeoisie and the new world they were making— terms of disapproval that his favorite novelist, Balzac, for example, was free in using. Marx's rationalist and materialist scientism, the intellectual historian Allan Megill notes, prevented him from saying, "Here I am making a moral-ethical point," even in the numerous places in which he was.[29] The first 25 chapters in volume 1 of *Das Kapital*, through page 802 of the German edition (page 670 in the Modern Library edition of the 1887 translation into English), contain *Gier* and its compounds in Marx's own words a mere seven times (mainly in chapter 8, "Constant Capital and Variable Capital"), with a few more in quotations.

Yet the sneer at the bourgeoisie's endless/boundless greed is common enough, and Engels after all approved the English translation. Townspeople such as the bourgeoisie had long been despised, seen by the priest and the aristocrat as vulgar, associating with the urban mob. *Odi profanum vulgus*, "I hate the unholy mob," sang Horace in priestly style two thousand years ago, and claimed implausibly to spurn fashionable riches more burdensome than his farm in a lovely Sabine valley. The son of a freed slave, Horace adopted the social attitudes of his acquired knightly rank. Still today, as always, trade and betterment are threatened by the scorn of priest, knight, gentleman, poet, or thug, from Green to neo-Nazi.

And now too they are threatened from within the bourgeoisie itself by a foolish pride—pride, the master sin against the Holy Spirit—that elevates trading prudence to the exclusion of other virtues. The threat appears as the crudely "neoliberal," "greed-is-good" theory of behavior, encouraged by some economists and by all inside traders. The theory is the modern descendant of the Machiavellian moment of *Il Principe* and then the

Hobbesian-Mandevillean-Benthamite notion that it's enough to have prudence only—the restless stirring for gain, utility, self-interest.[30] But profit maximization is not in itself an ethic. It is prudence only, elevating one of the seven principal virtues into the only one. Money is good to have. Thomas Hardy quotes the medieval saying "Take, have, and keep are pleasant words."[31] But taking, having, and keeping do not give purpose to a full human life. Faith, hope, and love do.

13

BUT NEITHER CAN POVERTY BE OVERCOME FROM THE RIGHT BY IMPLANTING "INSTITUTIONS"

The facts do not support the old Eurocentric claim that places east of Vienna or Venice were simply conservative or ignorant or "traditional" or "hydraulic." They were economically vital societies, with a full panoply in 1500 of the legal institutions that recent economists and political scientists such as North and Greif and Acemoglu and Robinson have put forward as explaining the modern world. Genghis Khan achieved supremacy precisely by enforcing the rule of law among the Mongols themselves, introducing, for example, fierce penalties for stealing animals (which were the productive capital of the steppe nomads) or women.[1] The resulting *Pax Mongolica* of the thirteenth century imposed peaceful property rights on the largest contiguous land empire until then assembled, from Korea to Hungary. An Italian merchant in 1340 declared that the Central Asian routes under Mongol control were "perfectly safe, whether by day or by night."[2]

But conquest and a royal state were nothing like necessary. Of an Iceland without kings *Njàl's Saga* declares, *Með lögum skal land byggja*, "With law will the land be built," and so it was.[3] (The quotation is also the first sentence of the Danish Jutland law code of 1241, appearing to this day on Danish law courts, and it is the motto of the Shetland Islands and of the Icelandic police force.[4]) The motto continues with *en með ólögum eyða* ("and with bad laws [the land is] destroyed"). The law in the Icelandic case was enforced not by a state but by kin.[5] When Gunnar Hámundarson in *Njáls Saga* killed two members of the family of Gissur the White, Gissur's family was authorized by Icelandic law to kill him in turn, and eventually did. No one went to the police—in Iceland there being none. In other words, property rights and laws against murder are necessary, true, but by no means regularly dependent on centralization in kings.

Kings arose, claimed James VI of Scotland, soon to be James I of England, in *The True Law of Free Monarchies* (1598), "before any estates or ranks of men, before any parliaments were holden, or laws made, and by them was the land distributed, which at first was wholly theirs. . . . And so it follows of necessity that kings were the authors and makers of the laws, and not the laws of the kings."[6] James was mistaken in fact and logic. Recent experiments by Kimbrough, Smith, and Wilson and by Wilson, Jaworski, Schurter, and Smyth show property emerging without the "legal centralist" support that, say, James I of England or Douglass North of Washington University claim is necessary.[7] Nor is there archaeological or historical evidence for the Jacobean/Northian view. "It takes an overly narrow view of human history," Kimbrough, Smith, and Wilson write in another paper, "to argue that no property existed prior to the creation of law and the state, for both agriculture and animal husbandry far pre-date the state."[8] And Mokyr devastates the claim that rule of law in the eighteenth century depended in Britain largely on the state.[9] Mainly ethics—not mainly law—held societies together.

In any case, mere sets of laws—the "rules of the game" that North and his followers assert are the cause of our riches—are strikingly insufficient to explain the Industrial Revolution or the Great Enrichment. Neither the Mongols nor the freemen of Iceland experienced an explosion of betterment sufficient for a modern world. Many societies worldwide had in such matters thoroughly matched England in 1689. The ancient Near East, for example, had "norms and rules of behavior," writes the Assyriologist Norman Yoffee, and local powers to back them up. "Law codes [such as that of Hammurabi of Babylon, who had by the early eighteenth century BCE established a wide hegemony, which 'his' laws were meant to justify] were not the foundations of order in Mesopotamian society [because the order already existed, Yoffee argues, arising from the bottom up, à la Iceland] but were . . . instruments used to proclaim a [centralized] simplicity that did not exist."[10]

To say that the Great Enrichment was caused by good property rights, and not (as it was) by the unprecedented explosion of betterment out of the unprecedented ideas of liberty and dignity for ordinary people, is like saying that a fire in the barn was "caused" by the presence of the barn, not by little Joe smoking carelessly behind it. The Great Enrichment did not arise from good property rights, which existed all over, and anciently, and were anyway merely productive of efficiency, not revolution. It arose from revolutionary, trade-tested betterment, which was recent, frenetic, and uniquely northwestern European.

∞

Like the old Marxists, and the older Christians, the neo-institutionalists among Samuelsonian economists such as North want a theory that would have allowed them looking forward from, say, 1700 to lay down the future. They want the story of the Great Enrichment—the utterly strange magnitude of which they acknowledge, being competent economists and economic historians—to be one of "institutions," predictable in their "incentives."

Yet by "institutions" the economists do not mean what other social scientists mean by institutions, such as marriage or trade—which is to say, the good or bad dance of human lives, full of human meaning. (Mae West, the American comedienne of the 1930s and 1940s said, "I admire the institution of marriage. But I'm not ready for an institution.") Norms are ethical persuasions, bendable, arguable, interpretable. Rules are, well, rules, such as that bribes are illegal in Delhi, or that jaywalking is illegal in Evanston. The rules of bribery in Stockholm are probably the same as in Delhi, and the jaywalking rules in Berlin the same as in Evanston. The difference is ethics.

The English novelist and essayist Tim Parks, who has taught at university in Italy since 1981, notes that "it is extraordinary how regularly Italy creates . . . areas of uncertainty: how is the law to be applied?" The "culture of ambiguous rules" seems "to serve the purpose of drawing you into a mindset of vendetta and resentment. . . . You become a member of [Italian] society insofar as you feel hard done by, . . . [playing in] a gaudy theatre of mimed tribal conflict." He gives the example of *il furbo*, the crafty one, who jumps the queue in Rome to buy a ticket at the train station, in a way that would get him assaulted by grandmothers with umbrellas in Hamburg and by licensees with handguns in Phoenix. The law-abiding Italians groan at the tricks of *il furbo*, but do not act to protect the public good of queues. The protective reaction has been shown in experiments to be deeply human, contrary to the predictions of noncooperative game theory. The Italians, however, would rather be merely resentful, and therefore be allowed sometimes to take advantage of their own little acts of *furbismo*.[11]

Economists call ethics often by other names, such as "enforcement" or "probity" or "*informal* institutions." The new words, though, do not make

social life any less about the ethical convictions with which a group oper-
ates. "Norms" are one thing, "rules" another. The neo-institutionalists turn
their arguments into tautologies by melding the two. They end up saying,
"Social change depends on society." One supposes so, unless the weather
intervenes. "Informal constraints" are not informal if they are constraints,
and if they are "informally enforced" the theory has been reduced to a tautology, since any human action is now brought under institutions. The neo-
institutionalists have nothing nontautological to say about ethics, because
they have not read any of the immense literature on ethics since 2000 BCE,
including the literature of the humanities turning back to look at language.
They are unwilling to bring ethics seriously into their history and their economics. As one of them said genially to me, "Ethics, schmethics."

On the contrary, the historian of the medieval English economy James
Davis concludes that "without a proper understanding of the morality and
social conventions of the marketplace, the historian cannot understand the
influence of formal institutions," such as the assize of bread or the rules
of guilds. "In medieval England," Davis writes, a "pragmatic moral economy . . . was not a simple, efficient alignment of institutions and cultural
beliefs, but rather a heady and complex mixture of vested interests, pragmatism and idealism that varied according to the prevailing circumstances,"
ranging from the pressures of trade to the preachments from the pulpit.[12]
The political economists Guido Rossi and Salvatore Spagano have argued
plausibly that evolved custom works well in contexts without the printing
press, but that printed, black-letter law provides all parties with public information cheaply, and therefore leads to efficiencies.[13] Imagine how the tax law
of the United States would work if it were not written down. The argument
is surely correct. And yet, as Rossi and Spagano would probably concede,
printing still leaves a gigantic area in an economy for custom or ethics or
play, which is why the courts are filled with tax cases. And indeed black
letters never come with their own interpretation, a point that, for example, the literary critic and public intellectual Stanley Fish makes about legal
documents and about John Milton's poetry. He observes that interpretive
communities impart (at least a large share of) the meaning of a law or of a
poem.[14] And such communities can be called ethical (which includes bad as
well as good ethics). Yes, sometimes writing down the customs/ethics is a
clarifying improvement, in just the way Rossi and Spagano propose. A par-

allel point is the old and conservative one that argues for the educational function of written law. Yet Fish's point remains. Law is a conversation.

Or, I say, a dance. The economists want to narrow the word "institution" to fit their conception that a dance can be reduced to formulaic steps, maximization under constraints, rigid rules of the game known to all, the constraints being the institutions. That is, economists want formulaic, public incentives to be the main story.[15] One, two, three: ball change, brush, brush, side essence, riffle. True, part of a routine by Bill Robinson or Fred Astaire can be described after the fact by such a formula. But it's nothing without Robinson or Astaire. It don't mean a thing if it ain't got that swing.

It's hard to get through to economists on the point, so enamored are they of the Max U story of budget lines and incentives, which they have been taught since boyhood is a complete theory of choice. They have not read the opening pages of Aristotle's *Nicomachean Ethics*, for example, or the Exodus of the Jews, or the *Mahabharata* of the Hindus, all of which exhibit choice as a painful exercise in identity, by contrast with the snappy determinism of a so-called consumer facing a so-called budget line. At a conference in 2010 praising Douglass North's contributions, Mokyr wrote: "Institutions are essentially incentives and constraints [there it is: institutions as budget lines] that society puts up on individual behavior. Institutions are in a way much like prices [as I said] in a competitive market: individuals can respond to them differently, but they must take them parametrically and cannot change them."[16] Neat. Mokyr then in a footnote instructs me on price theory. I get the price theory. Price and property, the variables of prudence, price, profit, the Profane as I have called them, move people.[17] But the point is that people are moved not just by these *P* variables but by the *S* variables of speech, stories, shame, the Sacred, and by the use of the monopoly of violence by the state, the legal rules, the *L* variables. To speak metaphorically, most behavior, *B*, is explained by *P* and *S* and *L*, together:

$$B = \alpha + \beta P + \gamma S + \delta L + \varepsilon.$$

Such an equation (a serious model might have another functional form, but the point would be the same) is not wishy-washy or unprincipled or unscientific. The message is that the *S* and *L* variables are the conditions under which the *P* variables work, and the *P* variables modify the effects of the *S* and *L* variables. For example, the conservative argument that laws serve as education would connect *L* causally to *S*, by a separate equation.

When the price the Hudson Bay Company offered Indians in Canada for beaver pelts was high enough, the beaver population was depleted, in line with *P*-logic. But *S*-logic was crucial, too, making the *P*-logic relevant. As the economic historians Ann Carlos and Frank Lewis explain, "Indian custom regarding the right to hunt for food and other aspects of their 'Good Samaritan' principle mitigated against the emergence of strong trespass laws and property rights in fur-bearing animals; conflict in the areas around the Hudson Bay hinterland contributed to an environment that was not conducive to secure tenure, and attitudes towards generosity and even a belief in reincarnation may have played a role" in running against European property rules.[18] The institutionalist economist John Adams speaks of trading as an "instituted process," which puts it well.[19] The institution is the *S*, the process the *P*, the legal limits *L*. Or sometimes the other ways around: anyway, in general, all.[20]

You can get as technical as you want about it. For example, econometrically speaking in the linear specification here, if the *P* and *S* and *L* variables are not orthogonal, which is to say if they are not entirely independent statistically speaking, or alternatively if there is reason to believe that a combined variable such as *PS* has its own influence, then an estimate of the coefficients α and β that ignore *S* (or *PS*) will give biased results. Larger samples will not solve the problem. The bias is important if the *S* variables are important. If laws adjust to trading, to give another example, then *L* is affected by *P*, and an attribution of an exogenous effect of *L* would be biased.

The very phrase "the rules of the game" is an oxymoron. Even a literal human game played by *Homo ludens* (in Johan Huizinga's coinage) follows rules, but its successes come from creative testings of the rules, Donald Bradman's footwork, Bob Cousy's behind-the-back dribble, Pelé's bicycle kick. And outside of literal games the creative point is often stronger. People do *play* with what they are given, in language and religion and technology. Institutions alone, often conservative, always lacking in play, don't run the show.

BECAUSE ETHICS MATTERS,
AND CHANGES, MORE

In an interesting paper on the swift recovery of San Francisco from the earthquake of 1906 the economist Douglas Coate shows that the existing (and corrupt) political institutions of the city were shoved aside. The U.S. Army, stationed at the Presidio, patrolled the ruins for seventy-three days, and joined a committee of business and civic leaders to take charge of the city—actions that were, as Coate puts it delicately, "extralegal." Yet Coate quotes with approval in his conclusion a remark by the fine if conventionally Samuelsonian economist, Jack Hirshleifer: "Historical experience suggests that recovery [from a disaster] will hinge upon the ability of government to maintain or restore property rights together with a market system that will support the economic division of labor."[1] No. It was the ethics, and the ethos, of the Army and the committee, and nothing like "the ability of [legitimate] government" that saved the city, just as in 2005 it was private companies such as Walmart and Home Depot springing into action, not any level of government, that partially saved New Orleans during and after Katrina.[2] If in New Orleans the existing formal institutions, the "rules of the game," had been relied upon the result would have been further malfeasance by the institutions, such as the police department and the office of Mayor Ray Nagin, or the heck of a job done by the Federal Emergency Management Agency.

The ur-neo-institutionalist Oliver Williamson in his reflections on governmental bureaucracies, "public agency," calls ethics "probity," that is, "the loyalty and rectitude with which the . . . transaction is discharged."[3] Like all proper Samuelsonian economists, Williamson wants to reduce ethics to incentives: "Probity concerns will be relieved by governance structures to which reliable responsiveness can be ascribed," by which he means incentives that work to make it unnecessary for anyone actually to have probity. "Probity concerns," he claims, only arise in "extreme instances." "Breach against probity is better described as inexcusable incompetence or even betrayal. In the limit, such breach is punishable as treason."[4] Notice his suddenly hot language. His error is a common one in recent thinking about ethics, supposing that ethics is only about grand issues ("extreme") such as murder or abortion or outright fraudulence in accounting, *House of Cards* instances, one might say. Yet it is also about daily good will and professionalism—an accountant doing as well as she can, or a professor earnestly trying to tell the truth, or a New Orleans police officer not abandoning the city during Katrina.

Williamson claims repeatedly, as economists do when adhering to the dogma of *de gustibus non disputandum est*, that ethics always changes slowly. But there is no historical or experimental evidence for such a claim. Sometimes ethics, a matter of S and the ethical parts of L, changes quickly. Sometimes it doesn't. You have to find out. The ethics of labor-force participation by married women, for example, changed quickly in the United Kingdom during the 1960s and 1970s, partly because of the pill and partly because of an ideological upheaval, feminism.[5] The ethics of the Roman state in the late first century BCE did not change slowly from republican to imperial. The ethics of German Christianity in the early sixteenth century did not change slowly from a relaxed régime of indulgences to a rigorous Protestantism of congregational shaming. The ethics changed more quickly than the institutions, which is why we find Imperial Rome still pretending to have a powerful Senate and Anglican Protestantism still claiming (in this case with entire justice, I must say) to be a "holy, catholic, and apostolic church" back to St. Peter.

And, most to the point here, the British ethics evaluating trade and betterment in the late eighteenth century did not change from contempt to admiration slowly. In fact ethics (understood not as individual ethics à la Max Weber but as what is honored or dishonored by the society) is what changed quickly, not the institutional environment. A time traveler from England in 1630 or from Britain in 1730 would not have been astonished by the institutional arrangements of the United Kingdom in 1830—except for the shift before 1730 to the transcendent power of a (thoroughly corrupt) Parliament and the weakening by 1830 of the (thoroughly corrupt) king. The law courts worked as they had ("This is the Court of Chancery," Dickens intoned). Property rights had not changed. Criminal law was still fiercely slanted against the poor. The institutions, such as criminal, contract, property, and corporate law, changed *after* the ethical change, not before.

Institutions are frosting on the cake if they lack ethical backing—the bus driver taking professional responsibility for the plans and the lives of the sixty people under his care, or the politician resisting the well-placed bribe offered by a highway construction firm. Nor are these to be reduced always to the incentives of enforcement or reward. The dismissal or jail time help, as do the special medals worn by New Orleans police officers who did *not* abandon the city, but they depend in turn on upright prosecutors and managers. Consider the upright prosecutors and judges in Italy who went after the Mafia in the early 1990s, at the cost of their lives. *Quis custodiet ipsos custodes*, the Romans asked: who will enforce the very enforcers? Ideological change brings a new impartial spectator into the widespread habits of the heart, "socialized subjectivity," as Pierre Bourdieu and Loic Wacquant put it.[6] New egalitarian ideas in Europe—according to which bus drivers and politicians, professors and housewives, felt themselves empowered to be equally responsible—broke the cake of custom. Surprisingly, treating ordinary people as free and honorable made them by historical standards startlingly wealthy.

The neo-institutionalist economists have not really taken on the idea that ethical ideas can matter independently (sometimes) of incentives. The neo-institutionalists say they have taken it on, and become cross when some idiot claims they have not. But then they keep falling back into arguments that say that formal Institutions (let's symbolize them by N, since the other term, Ideas, also start with an I) suffice for growth (G)

$$N \rightarrow G$$

That is, (good) Institutions imply (positive) Growth. The neo-institutionalists in their actual scientific practice, as against their ornamental claims to be interested in ideas, are denying what I claim in the present trilogy, on the basis of masses of positivist, behaviorist, and Samuelsonian evidence, but also on the basis of the humanistic testimony of plays, novels, philosophy, biography, and ordinary human experience, namely,[7]

$$N \text{ and } D \rightarrow G.$$

N is Institutions, D is Ideas, in this case including ideas of ethics in the S-variables and perhaps law in the L-variables (though one could also put L into the institutions, if one viewed them as incentives rather than expressions of ideals). The Ideas, D, are to be thought of as "sound, pretty favorable ethical ideas about other people acting in voluntary trades and proposing betterments." Likewise, the Institutions, N, are to be thought of as "not perfect but, John Mueller–style, pretty good incentives, lining up with P variables."[8] What actually changed in the eighteenth century in Britain was D, pretty much—ideas, not institutions. N in fact didn't change much, and L hardly at all.

If one believes on the contrary with North and Acemoglu and others that, near enough, $N \rightarrow G$, then it follows in strict logic that not-$G \rightarrow$ not-N, and the hunt is on for institutions that failed, and kept nations failing. But if one believes that N and $D \rightarrow G$, then it follows in equally strict logic that not-$G \rightarrow$ either not-N (bad institutions) or not-D (bad ideas), or both. (This logical point in the philosophy of science is known as Duhem's Dilemma, and in a single line of symbolic logic disposes of the Samuelsonian falsificationism underlying modern econometrics and economic theory.) If so, the hunt is then on for either bad institutions or bad ideas, with no presumption that hunting for the bad-idea possibility is somehow less of a scientific priority.

I recognize the impulse to stick with a Max U version of institutions as first on the agenda, since in the 1960s I used to say the same thing to conventional, nonquantitative, noneconomic economic historians such as David Landes: "First, let's use measures of total factor productivity; then, if there's anything left over, we can look at the letter archives of British ironmasters." To my shame, I never intended to look at the letter archives, and did not. Samuelsonian economics, I thought, sufficed. So there.

To the claim that Northian institutionalism steps *beyond* Samuelsonian economics, I say again, as I have in fact been saying to dear Doug North now for thirty years, I think not: neo-institutionalism is Samuelsonian economics in drag. And its claim that earlier economists did not consider institutions is false. Earlier economists did consider institutions, and often in a much broader way than the neo-Samuelsonian–Institutionalists do—look at Fogel and Engerman on the institution of slavery, or Buchanan on the institution of government, or for that matter Marshall on the institution of the business firm or Smith on the institution of civil society.

Consider, for example, an institution that undoubtedly did encourage growth, namely, a large free-trade area in which a local interest could not block betterment. It was expressed in black-letter law in the American Constitution, and in practical terms was prevalent in Britain from Land's End to John o' Groats (though not until the 1780s also in John Bull's other island). Customs unions like the Zollverein or the Austro-Hungarian Empire were examples, too. So was the Chinese Empire. In other places local monopolies unchallenged by wide competition surely did *discourage* growth, which is to say not-N → not-G, from which one might want to deduce that G → N, that is, that if there was growth there must have been large free-trade areas. But the trouble is that even with a large free-trade area in black-letter law, irritating competition from across the mountains might inspire people to petition the state for protection. In fact, it does. In the United States, widespread state licensure laws for professions and the prohibition of branch banking have such a source. Without a strong ethical conviction such as spread in Britain and Ireland in the nineteenth century that such petitioning is bad or shameful, the black letters will be dead. N and D → G. Ideas matter, ideology matters, ethics matters.

It is not reasonable to keep asserting that North and Avner Greif and the rest *do* admit the force of ideas in their neo-institutionalist stories. In his *Understanding the Process of Economic Change* (2005), for example, North says repeatedly that he is interested in the source of ideas. Good. But instead of entering the humanistic conversation since cuneiform on clay, which has been for four millennia the main conversation about the source of ideas, he defers to "brain science" (about which, it must be said, he knows little). That is, North reduces ideas to matter, and then to the biological stimuli surrounding matter in the brain, every time. He takes the mind to be the same thing as the brain, which is the central error in the new phrenology of certain schools of brain science.

My own argument for the importance of ideas, D, might have had merely static effects.[9] That's right. But the historical point is that *the ideas and ideology and ethics changed. The institutions did not.* It is quite wrong, I repeat, to think that the institutions faced by British entrepreneurs in 1800 were radically different from the ones they faced in 1685. But ideas of what was honorable, appropriate, allowed among right-thinking folk, did change, radically. And the economic point is that ideas are intrinsically subject to economies of scale and therefore can yield dynamic effects able to explain factors of thirty or one hundred ("ideas having sex"), but institutions are often as not deeply conservative, and able to have *only* static effects having little oomph.

∞

Let me exhibit what can be learned from the humanities since 2000 BCE and the actual brain sciences since 1980 CE. The less dogmatic of the neo-institutionalists, such as Joel Mokyr and John Nye, seem on odd days of the month to believe in the North-Acemoglu prejudgment that $N \rightarrow G$. No ideas present. The less-dogmatic group calls ideas "culture," which is the vague way people talk when they have not actually taken on board the exact and gigantic literature about ideas, rhetoric, ideology, ceremonies, metaphors, stories, and the like since the Greeks or the Talmudists or the Sanskrit grammarians. They do not, as the artificial intelligence guru Nick Bostrom put a similar point sharply, "resist the temptation to instantaneously misunderstand each new idea by assimilating it with the most similar-sounding cliché available in their cultural larders."[10] The vague "culture" talk makes the mistake that Germany made for centuries, elevating *Kultur* to a ignorable, higher realm of ornamental distraction from real rhetoric—that is, from actual politics and human relations.[11]

One thing that is deeply superficial, so to speak, about the neo-institutional notion of "rules of the game," or constraints, is that it overlooks that the rules are under discussion. People in the hood, for example, hold that you should not talk to the cops. The cops devote great effort to changing the ethic of not being a snitch, not cooperating with The Man, not getting involved in someone else's business. The "broken windows" tactic recommended by George L. Kelling and James Q. Wilson is often held up as an example of incentives and constraints. No, it isn't. It's an example of trying to change the conversation, changing what people say to themselves or to each other when contemplating mugging the woman walking down the street: "Hmm. This place is pretty fancy. Must be heavily patrolled" or "Gosh. Things are nice around here. I better do what Mom said, and be nice." As Kelling and Wilson put it, "Vandalism can occur anywhere once communal barriers—the sense of mutual regard and the obligations of civility—are lowered by actions that seem to signal that 'no one cares.'"[12] We have recently seen how the policy leads the other way, too, alienating black and Hispanic men repeatedly rousted for selling cigarettes one at a time. The dance is unpredictable.

We humans have an unusual capacity, performed by what the philosopher John Searle has called a "status function," that is, a purpose performed by a person (such as a president) or a thing (such as a $20 bill) or an entity (such as a limited liability corporation) by virtue of a social agreement. He formulates the status function as "X is treated as Y in the context C." A corporation is to be treated as a person under the Fourteenth Amendment in the context of the United States after 1886. The crossing of the goal line by the ball is treated as a goal (one point) in the context of playing soccer.

Searle notes that any status function requires language. "Without a language," he writes, "you have only prelinguistic intentional states such as desires and beliefs together with dispositions."[13] The prelinguistic desires and beliefs are what economists call utility functions and constraints. Economics after Adam Smith, but not because of Adam Smith, has been determinedly prelinguistic. No talk, please: we're political economists. In Marx or in Samuelson the ethical valences expressed in language don't matter. What matters are desires and dispositions combined with powers. Yet Searle observes that the very powers come from speech. "To get to the point that you can *recognize* an obligation as an obligation," he observes, a social constraint as a social constraint, "you have to have the *concept* of an obligation, because you have to be able to *represent* something as an obligation, that is, something that gives you a reason for action independent of your inclinations and desires."[14] Notice the words I have italicized: "recognize," "concept," "represent." They play no part in a non-Smithian economics understood as not needing language. Game theory in economics is the claim that we can do without language and language-created meanings. Shut up and play the game, consulting your budget constraints and your preferences. Searle and I and even many of the brain scientists disagree with such a reduction. "Games and other nonlinguistic institutional phenomena," Searle writes, "can be explained only in terms of language. You can't use the analogy with games to explain language because you understand games only if you already understand language."[15]

Treating X as Y in the context C looks trivial, merely a figure of speech, mere talk. So it is, Searle argues, if it is merely a "linguistic institutional fact," such as "all unmarried men are bachelors." Speak of a man as something called a bachelor under the circumstances that he is unmarried and you are speaking English. But treating X as Y under circumstances C becomes a "nonlinguistic institutional fact," with consequences ("powers") beyond mere language when the circumstances and the person doing the treating have extralinguistic powers, themselves arising from agreed conventions (that is, arising from language).[16] Language establishes the meaning of the word "bachelor," but the extralinguistic context, C, creates the powerful consequences—that only a bachelor, who is treated so under the linguistic convention of the definition of "bachelor," can marry a woman (and under the former U.S. Protection of Marriage Act, only a woman). If he is already married, for instance, he thereby commits bigamy.

If I promise to review a book, the speech act of promising means . . . well . . . I hereby promise to review the book. Don't count on it. But if the extralinguistic context obtains that the editor is a dear friend of mine, the promise plus the context creates a power beyond merely linguistic meaning. It gives me a reason for action independent of and contrary to my inclinations and desires (my utility function) to work on my own book, or watch a cricket match. Under such a context C, my promise in the little society of editors and book reviewers now means I'll really do it. "Once you have a common language, you already have a society," declares Searle.[17] True. And therefore as the language changes, the sort of society one can have also changes. The language game, as Ludwig Wittgenstein put it, determines a form of life. As the word "honest" shifts, between 1600 and 1800, from aristocratic to bourgeois honor, the sort of deals we can make, the sort of action we can countenance, change. To call a man "dishonest" in an aristocratic society requires a duel with swords next morning. To call a man "dishonest" in a bourgeois society requires a suit for libel.

Economic betterment "counts as" (to use Searle's vocabulary) honorable only in the Bourgeois Era. Or to be exact, what was honorable in the Aristocratic Era was innovation without a trading test. No one asked, I have noted, whether a new machine of war was *profitable*. The post-1848 clerisy, those pseudo-neo-aristocrats of "merit," judge their merit in nontrade terms. The well-named "honorary" degrees count for more than high pay. I witnessed a discussion of a candidate for an academic job in which his success with a popular book *in addition* to his large and fine scholarly output was offered as a reason not to hire him. Profit makes a neo-pseudo-aristocrat of the clerisy feel dirty, if she cannot well conceal the dirt.

But Searle's analysis needs another word, which one might coin as "conjective," what we know together as against what we know inside an individual head or what we imagine to be God's objectivity. The conjective comes from human agreement or acceptance.[18] The Latin of the coinage is *cum* + *iactus*, that is, "thrown together," as we humans are in our mammalian cuddling, and especially in our conversation. "Institutional facts are typically objective facts," Searle writes, by which he means not that they are facts in God's eyes, but that in our human eyes they bite.[19] A $20 bill, to take his favorite example, buys $20 worth of stuff. It bites as deeply in our lives as does the physical fact that the bill falls to the ground if you let go of it. (And *after* it falls, what does mere physics—"brute facts," in Searle's way of talking—imply about its future location? It implies a mistaken prediction. Economics, by contrast, predicts that someone will pick it up, which is not something one could learn from its brute-fact, physical equilibrium on the floor. Thus the superiority of economics over physics.[20])

Searle continues: "Oddly enough, [the institutional facts] are only facts by human agreement or acceptance." I would reply: There's nothing odd about it, John, not in a world of the conjective. Raymond Tallis, himself a distinguished neuroscientist, reviewed favorably *Who's in Charge? Free Will and the Science of the Brain* by Michael S. Gazzaniga, whom he describes as "a towering figure in contemporary neurobiology." Tallis writes, sprinkling in phrases from Gazzaniga:

> Crucially, the true locus of this activity is not in the isolated brain but "in the group interactions of many brains," which is why "analyzing single brains in isolation cannot illuminate the capacity of responsibility." This, the community of minds, is where our human consciousness is to be found, woven out of the innumerable interactions that our brains make possible. "Responsibility" (or lack of it), Mr. Gazzaniga says, "is not located in the brain." It is "an interaction between people, a social contract"—an emergent phenomenon, irreducible to brain activity.[21]

And he concludes in his own eloquent words (Tallis is a published poet, too):

> We belong to a boundless, infinitely elaborated community of minds that has been forged out of a trillion cognitive handshakes over hundreds of thousands of years. This community is the theater of our daily existence. It separates life in the

jungle from life in the office, and because it is a community of minds, it cannot be inspected by looking at the activity of the solitary brain.

So much for phrenology as the only model for actual brain science.

Human agreement or acceptance, what the philosopher Michael Oakeshott called the conversation of mankind, is precisely what I call the conjective, as against the merely subjective. Searle argues persuasively that a society is glued together by conjective facts of the sort "*X* counts as *Y* in context *C*." Thus, a clergyman saying "I thee wed" counts as marrying two people in the context of a properly constituted marriage ceremony. As Stanley Fish often notes, such conjective facts are always contestable. Objective facts ("water is two molecules of hydrogen and one of oxygen") or subjective facts ("Ian Botham intends to hit a six") are not contestable. The physical facts of the world and the psychological states of human minds are "brute," to extend Searle's word, in the sense of being incontestable in their very nature, their "ontology," as the philosophers put it.[22] Physical constraints such as gravity, or intentional states such as a great love for vanilla ice cream, are not the sort of facts we can quarrel about once we have grasped in a humanistic inquiry their nature, their "qualia," as the philosophers also put it. All we can do then is measure, if we can, "quanta."

The conjective, by contrast, is always contestable and always in that sense *ethical*, that is, about "deontic status," Searle notes, "deontic" being about what we *ought* to do (the Greek means "being needful"). The clergyman might be argued to be not properly authorized to perform the marriage (look at the controversy about gay marriage), the definition of "U.S. territory" might be ambiguous (embassies abroad?), the goal might be disputed. If *any part* of the ball breaks the plane of the goal line is it a goal? Was the referee or the linesman in a position to judge?

"There is no 'I' taken in itself," wrote Martin Buber early in *I and Thou*, "No '*Ich an Sich*,'" beloved of the dogmatic methodological individualist. As the economist Bart Wilson points out, and as has been shown by Wilson and others in linguistic analysis and laboratory experiments, such a thing as "social preference" resides in our language games among ourselves, not within our isolated utility functions.[23] "The fundamental fact of human existence," Buber wrote in *Between Man and Man*, "is neither the individual as such nor the aggregate as such, but 'man with man.'"[24] It is neither subjective nor objective. ("Objective truth is not granted to mortals," said Buber at the espionage trial of Aharon Cohen in 1958, not perhaps the best thing to have said under the circumstances.) The conjective, the "between" in Buberian talk, is what we know in speech and meeting and dialogue, one human with another.

What Searle does not appear to understand, though, is that his formulation of a status function—"*X* is treated as *Y* in the context *C*"—is itself analyzable into a metaphor ("Treat the female child Jannike as Mommy") and a story ("We are playing house": once upon a time there was a house with a Mommy and a Daddy . . .). In a word, Searle's status function is an allegory. *Pilgrim's Progress* is an allegory of the metaphor of a spiritual life as a journey ("Treat a literal journey as a metaphor of spiritual challenge and development") with a story giving the metaphor a dimension of metonymy through time (successive events in a story are contiguous to each other, not *like* each other).

Searle correctly notes that human children "very early on acquire a capacity to do this double level of thinking that is characteristic of the creation and maintenance of institutional reality. Small children can say to each other, he notes, "Okay, I'll be Adam, you be Eve, and we'll let this block be the apple."[25] The psychologist Michael Tomasello and colleagues have shown in ape-human experiments that "human thinking [that is, the function of the mind, the "preference ordering" in the economist's jargon] is fundamentally cooperative." Human infants, for example, unlike their close cousins among the great apes, point. That is, they "form a 'we' that acts as a kind of plural agent" (Tomasello cites Searle in this connection). And children evaluate, engaging in "objective-reflective normative thinking." We have ethics in a real world of brute facts and human intentions.[26] Yet Searle is satisfied with calling allegory-making "an element of imagination" and "fantasy." He does not bring into play the research on the playful and deadly serious abilities of humans to form metaphors and metonymies.

So what? Well, let's get serious about "brain science" and let's acknowledge that the humanities, and higher culture generally, can shed light on "institutions." Searle says that "creating institutional facts" such as that professors, not the students, lead classes, or that walkers stay to the right on a crowded sidewalk, or that Elizabeth II is the queen of England, depends on "one formal linguistic mechanism."[27] The institutional facts "carry deontic powers," such as the (recognized) responsibility of the professor to lead the class or the (acknowledged) right not to be bumped into on a crowded sidewalk or the (accepted) power of Elizabeth to be informed weekly by the prime minister.[28] Ethics in daily life or in high science is a conjective matter of recognizing, acknowledging, accepting arguments by other humans. The institutionalist economists call the human arguments carrying deontic powers "constraints" or "rules of the game." Searle notes, citing his understanding of Durkheim, that "some social theorists have seen institutional facts as essentially constraining. That is a very big mistake." Whether Durkheim committed the mistake is not so clear. But North and associates certainly do commit it. Institutions, Searle is arguing, are not about regulating relations between preexisting people and objects. They are allegories about *creating* and *negotiating* entirely new power relationships between people.[29] It is what is magical about status functions. We Americans in 1776 declared our independence and thus fashioned a new relationship of power between King George and his former subjects.

In other words, it's more complicated than mere budget constraints between buying ice cream and paying the rent. The complexities have been observed for the past four millennia in folktales and recorded literature and debated in philosophy and theology and literary criticism, none of which the neo-institutionalists attend to. Searle points out that there are two kinds of rules: regulative rules ("Don't steal"; "Drive on the right"), which apply to already existing activities, and "constitutive" rules, which create the very activity ("Follow these rules and you are playing chess"; "Act in this way and you are being a proper bourgeois"). It is language, the combined metaphors and stories, that we use to create the allegories called institutions. If the science of economics, as the economist Virgil Storr argues (2008), needs meaning, it needs, deontically, not merely rules of the game or a phrenological version of brain science but the humanities, all the way up to the Department of English.

AND THE OOMPH OF INSTITUTIONAL
CHANGE IS FAR TOO SMALL

A story goes with the neo-institutionalist tale. Once upon a time, the neo-institutionalists say, Europe did not face the "right" incentives. Property rights were imperfect by comparison with modern times. On its face, it must be said, the story is strange. In the European Middle Ages all the land and husbands and eternal salvation were eagerly traded, and other, non-European societies often had better, not worse, property rights than Europe did. But set aside the factual problem for the sake of charitable scientific discussion.

Then in the neo-institutionalist story the incentives righted themselves, and the result was an increase of real income per person. By a factor of 100, or 9,900 percent. More strangeness. If mere incentives were all that stood in the way of correct allocation, then a reallocation, paying off routinely, predictably, in Samuelsonian fashion, 100-to-1 would presumably have happened, if only by accident, and even would have consciously occurred to someone, in the previous millennia, sometime, somewhere. It would have been a $100 bill lying on the floor of a $1- or $3- or $6-a-day society. The unique magnitude of the Great Enrichment, that is, tells against the economist's reliance on routine incentives. The cause had to be, on the contrary, something highly peculiar (for a while) to northwestern Europe, not a rearrangement of the old things prevalent in most civilizations, such as private property, rule of law, literacy, cheap exchange, or predictable investment.

No institution in 1800—not the state or the church or the university or the republics of science and of letters—rationally intended the frenetic betterment that since then has characterized the West and now the rest. It is another reason why the economist's Max U neo-institutionalism does not explain what it claims to explain. The economists want to reduce motivation to predictable Max U. If a graduate student in economics can in retrospect come up with a simple, "institutional" explanation of a phenomenon, it seems plausible that the people on the scene at the time could have spotted the $100 bill too. Yet the modern world, like the business cycle (and for the same reason), was not predictable. It depended on the new liberal notion of liberty and dignity, and their unpredictable results in betterment for all.

Postulate in charity, though, the partial failure of routinely predictable incentives. It is high charity, because virtues other than knowable, routine prudence obviously matter too. As the Christian economist Stefano Zamagni puts it, "Modern economic development did not occur due to the adoption of stronger incentives or better institutional arrangements, but mainly because of the creation of a new culture."[1] Or as the Indian businessman and public intellectual Gurcharan Das puts it, "Social scientists [under the influence of Max U thinking among economists] think of governance failures as a problem of institutions, and the solution they say, lies in changing the structure of incentives to enhance accountability. True, but these failings also have a moral dimension."[2] It is no surprise that an Italian and an Indian, from countries as corrupt as the United States was in the nineteenth century, make such an anti-neo-institutional point.[3]

Consider the supply of and demand for labor in a country.[4] Suppose that the opportunity cost of labor is upward-sloping, measuring the value of the next hour of labor in activities alternative to working inside the country, such as working abroad or taking one's ease. Now add into the diagram the demand curve for labor, which slopes downward because any extra labor gets employed in less urgent employments. Such a marginal product of labor curve, as labeled in figure 2, is the value in trade of the product of the last hour demanded. If there is no misallocation of labor the nation will be led to employ labor up to the point at which the two curves cross. At that point, the country's income will be as large as it can be, considering the known marginal product and the known opportunity cost of labor. (To speak more technically, total income is, up to a constant of integration, the integral under the marginal product curve out to the amount of labor employed—that is to say, it is the area under the partial derivative curve, known to economists as the marginal product of labor.)

And it will be good for the country as a whole to be at such a point of efficiency. What economists mean by "efficiency" is that the last hour of work

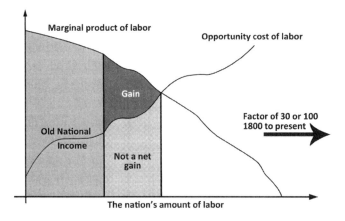

Gains of efficiency are dwarfed by the Great Enrichment 1800-present

FIGURE 2. Institutional change of a static sort cannot explain modern economic growth.

gets in the utility of goods just what it sacrifices in, say, an hour's worth of utility in taking one's ease. All previous hours therefore earn *more* than their opportunity cost, which is the reason to go just so far: to go further would not profit the society. The sum of consumers' and producer's surpluses—in this case the area between the marginal-product and the marginal-opportunity-cost curves—is maximized by letting exchange go all the way to the intersection of the curves. After all, that is what you individually do in allocating your own hours between labor and leisure. So too the country as a whole.

If misallocation causes too little labor to be employed, putting the economy at the vertical line to the left of the utility-maximizing equilibrium, there would be a potential gain of income forgone, the triangle labeled Gain, now measured in dollars. (Another technical remark: Why does it not include the trapezoid below Gain? Because the trapezoid is the value of the opportunity costs of labor—of taking one's ease or working abroad—of the work not employed at home, and is a gain to the workers enjoying it when out of the optimal allocation. The deadweight loss measured by forgone Gain, by contrast, is a gain to no one. It is, as economists say in honor of its prominent user, a Harberger Triangle.)

A government can impose policies that make the sadly forgone Gain compared to the income at the efficient point quite large. Nowadays, for example, North Korea is good at this. The clotted institutions of the *ancien régime* before the French revolutionary conquest could reduce trade on, say, the Rhine by a quite large percentage. The historian Robert Spaulding has estimated that French occupation of the banks of the river, which swept away or greatly simplified the old privileges and tolls and regulations, caused the volume and value of traffic from the base line of 1789 down to 1806 to triple.[5] The tripling, of course, was not a net gain to welfare measured in money. Part of it was trade diversion, not trade creation, and a good deal of it was merely formerly smuggled traffic coming into the full light of legality. Still, governments can be stupid for a long time, and can obstruct the achievement of quite large potential gains.

Yet on any reasonable view of how economies work a government can't, by laws *hampering* free exchange—which is the regulatory business of government—make the marginal product of labor *rise* by the factor of 100 of modern economic growth correctly measured, or even by the factor of 10 or 30 conventionally measured. The liberal French policies on the Rhine that reduced the misallocation that had led to a loss in the first place would yield gains small by comparison with the pre–good-régime income. The point is that the static assumptions of neo-institutional economics cannot have the quantitative oomph they claim in explaining the elephant in the room of modern social science, massive modern economic growth.

It would be amateurish for an economist to reply that compounded over two centuries a small change, 2 percent per year, say, adds up to a factor of 100 (or so). The static gain contemplated in neo-institutionalism is precisely *not* compounded. If railways increased national income by 2 percent, they did it once, not every year anew. Railways, as Robert Fogel noted long ago, were invented one time, not reinvented every year. And the amateur reply does not tell why the compounding only started in 1688 or 1800. It remains to discover why the society changed in fact to give a dynamic improvement of 2 percent *every, single* year.

Look at the diagram again, and note the big arrow labeled "Factor of 30 or 100, 1800–present." The big arrow, not the little gain from efficiency, is the order of magnitude to explain the modern world. That is, the great bulk of the enrichment of the modern world has not come (as some on the political right argue) from repairing technically inefficient institutions, and in any case could hardly come (as some on the political left argue) from laws further *hampering* free exchange. Misallocation has limits, and therefore repairing it—and, certainly, worsening it by excessive regulation—has a limit of gain far below the orders of magnitude of the Great Enrichment. Suppose a quite terrible government causing market failures and wretched property rights had reduced income originally by as much as 80 percent of its potential. In that case a perfectly wise government correcting all market failures and establishing ideal property rights would increase income by a factor calculated by dividing the Gain of 80 by the original, miserably inefficient 20, a factor of 4. Splendid. But the Great Enrichment was a factor not of 4, but of 10 or 30 or 100.

The repairing of incentives can have, to be sure, secondary effects of encouraging a betterment that does in turn produce enrichment. But the neo-institutionalists have no theory for this crucial step, the step of the creative production of novelties—except an ancillary theory claiming that patents transform novelties into routine property subject to routine accumulation. The theory has been shown to be false, in recent work by Dutton, MacLeod, Nuvolari, Mokyr, Boldrin, and Levine.[6] And if tiny efficiencies, 2 percent here or there, can have enormous dynamic effects, the model is instable. It would have yielded explosions in 400 BCE in Greece or in 1200 CE in China, and would not have waited, mysteriously, until 1800 CE in northwestern Europe.

In short, without something unique to northwestern Europe at the time—such as a novel liberty and dignity allowing ordinary people to have a go—the repairing of incentives can't produce much. Most of the enrichment came from the curves in question zooming out by gigantic magnitudes, as a result of spillovers from the whole world's trade-tested progress, originating from Smith's proposal for "allowing every man to pursue his own interest his own way, upon the liberal plan of equality, liberty and justice."[7] Liberalism led to the modern world by allowing the idea of electricity or the idea of skyscrapers or the idea of the stock exchange—not by the mere facilitating of property (as conservative economists recommend) or the mere hampering of property (as progressive economists recommend).

New Zealand, for example, is well governed. Italy is not. New Zealand has honest and efficient governmental institutions. Italy, strikingly, does not. In ease of doing business—which is low when the government vigorously obstructs private dealings or when its officials demand bribes—New Zealand ranked in 2010 and 2012 (among 183 or 185 countries) third from the top. Italy in 2010 ranked eightieth, slightly below Vietnam, and in 2012 seventy-third, slightly below the Kyrgyz Republic. In 2012, according to the Corruption

Perceptions Index of Transparency International, New Zealand was tied for first, the most honestly governed among 173 ranked countries. Italy was seventy-second.[8] In 2009 in the Economic Freedom Rankings, New Zealand ranked first in its legal system and fifth in its freedom from regulation. Italy in its legal system ranked sixty-third, just above Iran, and in its freedom from regulation ninety-fourth, just above the Dominican Republic.[9] Italian legal institutions, the exercise of the monopoly of legitimate violence—its L variables and the S variables supporting the L—are wretched.

Yet in real GDP per person New Zealand and Italy, in 2010, were nearly identical, at $88.20 and $86.80 a day, a little above Hans Rosling's Washing Line. One could argue that there is anyway an international correlation between income and governance. But the causation is in part the other way around—rich people demand better governance, which is certainly the story of more honest governance in American cities, 1900 to the present. And the oomph of the fitted curve is too small to explain much: that correlation "exists" does not answer the scientific question of its importance. The reason Italy and New Zealand differ so much in governance and so little in income is that Great Enrichment consists not of little efficiencies but of utterly novel betterments causing the marginal product of labor curve to zoom out, such as asphalt-paved roads, cheap screws and bolts, sewer traps in plumbing, screens on open windows, dental implants, widespread secondary schools, computers. Such betterments are so profitable that they get adopted at least in the private sector of even a badly governed economy, such as Italy's, with pretty satisfactory results. That is, the zooming out of the curves in the diagram, not the attainment of an efficient equilibrium, matters most.

There are limits. North Korea, again, shows what can be achieved by truly idiotic governance. Mao's Great Leap Forward beginning in 1958, with its communal kitchens and backyard blast furnaces, caused thirty to forty million deaths from starvation. It was gross misallocation, idiocracy. It may be possible, that is, to reduce even a very high income to $1 a day if the government goes completely insane, as governments have with some regularity been doing since they first came into existence. Witness Assad's Syria, or Nero's Rome, or the conquering Mongol's original plan (they soon came to their senses) of turning the rich agricultural fields of China into depopulated grazing grounds for their horses.

But in the other direction of change, by the quantitative standard of the Great Enrichment, a government can do little but get out of the way. If the economy starts with the usual somewhat imperfect rights to property and the usual modest corruptions, it cannot achieve anything resembling the 900 or 2,900 or 9,900 percent growth of modern economies 1800 to the present merely by improving routine efficiency, which is old, or by introducing routine mercantilism, which is also old, or, least of all, by merely wishing it and issuing propaganda that it has in fact been achieved, which was the old Red-Chinese formula. If a place is even moderately well governed, there has been historically, usually, nothing like a 99 percent idiocracy to recover from merely by allowing people to exercise routine prudence. A country achieves the Great Enrichment by allowing improvers to creatively destroy earlier ways of doing things. If the sultan throws a crazy inventor off a cliff, the Ottoman Empire will remain poor, however snappily it equalizes known marginal cost and known marginal valuation.

Yet liberty and dignity are not easy to achieve, because they require accepting the Bourgeois Deal of commercial profit and dignity, rejecting tribal protectionism, resisting the temptations of reasonable-sounding "planning" or "regulation," disbelieving the populist/Keynesian claim that free lunches abound, and embracing an ideological revolution toward equality for women and the poor and low-status castes that traditional societies and parts even of some modern societies resist. Norwegians only reluctantly adopted liberal economic values in the late nineteenth century, contrasting themselves with the frenetic liberalism of their numerous cousins in America.[10] You can see the tension again in Ibsen's plays, such as *Pillars of Society* (1877), in which crazy but enriching America is contrasted with sensible, sober Norway. The economic historian Stanley Lebergott wrote in 1984 about the American economy before the Civil War that "we must turn to the contribution made by the values of the people themselves":

> These values drove the "productivity" gains, for they prompted the American willingness to accept persistent novelty in production. Without such willingness Americans would never have put up with the costs of growth—job turnover, migration, high depreciation of machinery, destruction of business investments, and the harsh obsolescence of human skills and training. Visitors to the United States have long remarked how unusually willing Americans were to accept novelty in the economic process.[11]

It's the Bourgeois Deal.

Modern politics is a four-way tug of war between liberalism in the sensible part of the elite, socialism in the rest of the elite, traditionalism in the peasantry, and populism in the proletariat. Only liberalism works, but the others tug vigorously. As some French economists reported about slow growth in Madagascar, "Although the Malagasy people lay claim to democratic principles, they remain torn between the demands of a democratic and meritocratic nature and the traditional values that impose respect for the real and symbolic hierarchies they have inherited from the past."[12] The miracle is that France itself or, for that matter, honors-drenched Britain, both heavily regulated, are not instances. The miracle is explained by the easily appropriated idea of the Great Enrichment, the zooming out of marginal products. A government has to do *extremely* badly with its public institutions, worse even than Italy, to offset what can be gained from adopting chemistry, electric lighting, elementary education, automobiles, and computers.

Accepting the Bourgeois Deal and its supporting ethics is what caused the zooming out. Institutional change in the absence of such an ethic has not worked. It won't suffice, as the World Bank nowadays recommends, to add institutions and stir. You can set up British-style courts of law, and even provide the barristers with wigs, but if the judges are venal and the barrister have no professional pride and if the public disdains them both, then the introduction of such a nice-sounding institution will fail to improve the rule of law. The neo-institutionalists Acemoglu and Robinson report on an attempt to curb absenteeism among hospital nurses in India by introducing the institution of time clocks. The economists in charge of the experiment were sure that the bare incentives of the "right institution" would work. It didn't. The nurses conspired with their bosses in the hospitals to continue not showing up for work. Acemoglu and Robinson draw the moral that "the institutional structure that creates market failures" is what went wrong.[13] But the continuing absenteeism was not about institutions or incentives. A new institution with the right incentives had been confidently applied by the economists out of the tool kit of World Bank orthodoxy, and had failed. The failure was rather about the lack of an ethics of self-respecting professionalism among the nurses, of a sort that, say, Filipino nurses do have, which is why they are in demand worldwide. The time-clock experiment imagined P-only constrained through L, when humans are also motived by S.

Acemoglu and Robinson do not see that what failed was the new P-only theory of the economics profession: add institutions and stir. "The root cause of the problem," they conclude, was "extractive institutions." On the contrary, the root cause was ethical failure, in the presence of which no set of instituted incentives will work well, and under which extraction will persist. The institutions—time clocks and management practices, and the incentives they are supposed to impose, like incentives imposed on rats in a maze—were not the problem. The problem was defects in ethics and in the impartial spectator and in the professionalism of the nurses and their bosses.

As the Italian legal scholar Serena Sileoni pointed out to me, hermetically sealed legal reasoning since the Austrian legal theorist Hans Kelsen (1881–1973)—like hermetically sealed Samuelsonian economics since Léon Walras (1834–1910)—does not recognize the interaction of law and society, as for example in ethical indignation. "Pure" legal reasoning is assumed to work by itself, on its own internal logic, like the pure incentives that the neo-institutionalists claim. In legal history it is called "legal positivism." The legal scholar Richard Epstein, agreeing with the Italian lawyer and political philosopher Bruno Leoni, harbors a "suspicion of any positivist theory that treats the legal rules governing these various relationships as the arbitrary plaything of the state."[14] Make a law arbitrarily, set up incentives. Introduce time clocks. Problem solved. Thus economic neo-institutionalism.

Sileoni observes that in her native Italy, and in the many other countries lacking effective indignation against unethical behavior, not to mention such subcountries as Illinois and Louisiana with a similar lack, a problem with law cannot usually be solved by adding another law. In the civil-law tradition of Italy, for example, the ethical high ground is claimed for strict process, regardless of the absurdity of the outcome. Thus in Italian academic appointments the professors in the committee judge themselves blameless when the obviously worst candidate is chosen, so long as the choice was the result of punctilious conformity to process. The best candidate's file is incomplete—it does not contain her photograph, for example, as specified in the law. Cast her aside, even though everyone in the room agrees she is the best. An Italian building contractor is exempt from suit when his apartment block collapses if he has followed every procedure to the letter, checked every legal box, despite the spirit of the law having been ignored, as everyone knows with a shrug or a wink, by corrupt inspectors.

The regulatory state, outside of paradises of public ethics, I have noted, such as Sweden and Iowa, has similarly perverse effects. Sileoni's point is that the Italians or the Illinoisans have no ethics that effectively condemn absurd results and bad behavior. They laugh sardonically, shrug their shoulders, and say, *Sai com'è,* "You know how it is, in our 'Chicago Way,'" instead of expressing indignation in action by throwing the bums out. Another law added to the ineffective laws/incentives/institutions already in place will have no effect.

Italy has a centuries-long tradition of high professionalism evoked by money trades. Benvenuto Cellini bragged about the size of his cash commissions from the pope as much as he bragged about the quality of his statues and of his murderous swordplay (his *Autobiography* of 1563 contains a lot of bragging). Italy's state bureaucracy, by contrast, does not evoke a professionalism directed at serving the victim-citizen-customer. An uneven punctiliousness, enforced by *il pignolo,* the keeper of mechanical rules in the tax office or on the trains, has always been treated by the public as the enemy, someone to be outflanked. Tim Parks speaks of "the abyss in Italy between the private and public sectors, a psychological as much as an economic abyss." He contrasts the dismal service at the state-owned coffee shop in the central train station of Milan with the excellent service at a private bar near his university. The barman there says to Parks, "Every cappuccino I make must be the best the customer has ever drunk."[15] Such pride in craft and service in the private sector, eagerly adopting trade-tested betterment in accord with the Bourgeois Deal, innovism, is why Italy, or for that matter Chicago, is not so poor as its governance would imply. Not all economic activity is in the institutions of *Le Ferrovie dello Stato Italiane* or the Chicago Department of Streets and Sanitation. Institutions are not where the action is.

MOST GOVERNMENTAL
INSTITUTIONS MAKE US POORER

Well, then: is the action in the middle, in the "regulation" so attractive to the reasonable social democrat?

Not under most governments. One should, in prudence, if one really wants to help the poor, look along the chain of causation. In 1848 the French economist and journalist Frédéric Bastiat, whose writings deserve reading and understanding by the left if it is serious about understanding "capitalism," declared, "There is only one difference between a bad economist and a good one":

> The bad economist confines himself to the visible effect; the good economist takes into account both the effect that can be seen and those effects that must be foreseen. . . . Whence it follows that the bad economist pursues a small present good that will be followed by a great evil to come, while the good economist pursues a great good to come, at the risk of a small present evil.

Consider, for example, the visible and invisible effects, the seen and unseen, as Bastiat would put it, of channeling economic power through the keeper of the monopoly of violence, the government. The government is often, to take one effect, a poor chooser of nation-enriching projects on which to spend the tax money extracted from its subjects or the government-to-government foreign aid extracted from subects of richer nations. Or so it would seem from the great evils that so often come out of projects to invade Iraq in 2003 or irrigate farmland from the Caspian Sea. As one among a myriad of instances, the economist William Easterly details the disastrous effects of government-to-government foreign aid that paid for a dam-created lake in Ghana.[1] A government that gets its budget from foreign aid or from state-owned or state-taxed oil does not need to attend to the desires of its citizens. Look at Russia under Putin, or Nigeria under anyone. In Nigeria the byword for politicians, from a 1980s hit song, is "international thief-thief," or "ITT." In 2013 Nigeria still ranked 144th out of 177 countries in perceived honesty.[2] Channeling more money toward such a government is probably not going to improve public health and private welfare, any more than channeling money to a government dominated by people rich by inheritance from their violent ancestors or rich by the exercise of state-enforced monopolies, or for that matter channeling money to Mafia thieves. Before liberalism, almost all governments were thieves. The news to my gentle social-democratic friends is that most of them still are.

Honest governments are rare. The Norwegian government gets a good deal of its income from North Sea oil but is honest and therefore not subject to the resource curse in the style of Nigeria. But the state of Alaska benefits from oil, too, and is among the most corrupt of American states. Ireland has benefited greatly from subsidies delivered by the Common Market, but its governance is a little honest, and therefore the government has not become arrogantly corrupt from its subsidies. The same cannot be said of some of the other beneficiaries of the policy, such as Hungary under its "illiberal democracy" à la Putin, or the French farmers obstructing highways when they don't like the level of subsidies transferred to them from other citizens.

The "Corruption Perceptions Index" compiled by the respected organization Transparency International "ranks countries and territories based on how corrupt their public sector is perceived to be."[3] In 2013 the top 40 (out of 177 governments) scored above about 60 on a 1-to-100 scale, from Spain (scoring 59) and Poland (60) up to the most honest governments, Denmark and New Zealand (91). Those in between included the UK at 14th (scoring 76), Japan at 18th (74), the United States at 19th (73), Ireland at 21st (72), and France at 22nd (71). Among the governments ranked lower for perceived honesty were Hungary (47th), Saudi Arabia (63rd), and Italy (69th), and Nigeria, as I said, at 144th out of 177. The lowest were Somalia, North Korea, and Afganistan, each coming in at a score of 8.

Suppose, then, you reckoned that governments in the top 40 could be trusted with more money extracted from their citizens (I would agree with you that such a standard is not high). Yet—and here is the point—such governments rule a mere 14 percent of the world's population. That is, 86 percent of the world's seven billion subjects live under plainly corrupt governments, *governo ladro*, the Italians say, "thief government." Governments satisfying a more stringent standard, say the top 20—which includes the Unites States as whole, though some parts of it (Alaska, Mississipi, Louisiana, Tennessee, and Illinois, for example) would probably rank lower—rule a mere 10 percent of the people in the world.[4] Most governments in the world are corrupt. I am not saying "all," or "in every single respect," merely "most," enough to break the heart of an earnest social democrat who thinks that the way forward is to give more money and guns and regulatory power to the existing holders of the monopoly of violence.

The fact suggests that the projects of betterment enacted by governments, compared with voluntary deals made among consenting adults free of force or fraud, will fail, as they regularly have, because they are directed not at general betterment but at enriching special interests at the expense of the generality, or merely spending mindlessly what money the government can appropriate under the threat of violence.[5] The modern social-democratic habit of regarding the government as a wise and honest distributor of public goods ignores the unseen, the contents of Swiss bank accounts and the misdirected expenditures in aid of the prime minister's second cousin, which practices govern most of the world. It supposes that every government is like Denmark's, New Zealand's, or Finland's (which together govern 2 percent of the world's population), when most are instead like Russia's, China's, or India's (39 percent). In James Madison's words in 1787, "If angels were to govern men, neither external nor internal controls on government would be necessary."[6] Angels are rare, if unseen.

To take another ignoring of the unseen, consider the persistent claim by good Christians and other charitable folk, such as Pope Francis I, or indeed Saint Francis of Assisi, that poverty can be solved by a charity transferring by benevolence or by threat of violence large amounts of money from rich people and rich countries to the poor. It is generous of heart. But in a non-zero-sum world it is defective of head. The seen is good in the first act, and is certainly good for the souls and the self-regard of the givers of the charity. But by comparison with the mighty engine of the Great Enrichment, its unseen is at best feeble. And, at worst, a forced charity can reduce the income of the poor—as it has largely done, to repeat, in the case of foreign aid to irresponsible governments or state control of extraction of oil or copper, which frees tyrants from needing in the third act to consider their victims.

A related instance of failure to look down the chain of consequences to the third act, a failure of imagination in the same group of good people, is the proposal for a debt-forgiveness jubilee (Leviticus 25:8–34), enthusiastically endorsed in 2000 by many loving Christians. It would have, of course, made *future* loans to poor countries radically less likely. Their roads and ports to be financed by new loans would not get built even if the projects passed the test of trade-tested betterment.

A better way to give foreign aid, taking into account both the effect that can be seen and the effects that must be foreseen, Cormac Ó Gráda has suggested, is to allow some immigration to rich countries like Ireland or the United States, in which case the immigrants will send back gigantic remittances, targeted to families rather than to governmental officials.[7] Another is to cease protecting rich farmers in the United States and Europe, including Ireland and France and Hungary, by letting Latin America and Africa supply the global North with fruits, fibers, and vegetables. The gain in profit to poor southern farmers, it has been calculated, would be many times larger per year than all the private and public donations from north to south. To the bargain, Europeans would get cheaper fruits, fibers, and vegetables.

And the best way to give aid is to encourage poor countries to adopt liberal domestic policies, as China and India have, with their astonishing results. The actual enrichment of the poor, that is, has not come from foreign aid or regulation or taxing the rich or protectionism or trade unions or debt forgiveness, all of which, despite their undoubted first-act popularity among many on the left and some on the right, merely redistribute a constant pie, or yield a shrunken one. By contrast, economic growth—which is something people and their countries do mostly on their own, by way of the liberating and dignifying of trade-tested progress in a market stall or a little machine shop or a rise to great riches through betterments in making steel or supplying computer services or constructing skyscrapers in Hong Kong—has every time in the third act given the poorest a dignified life at a level unheard of in history.

"Regulation" has a sweet and reasonable sound. In a few angelic countries it does not damage income too much. Who would not want, the voters cry, the disturbing uncertainties of trading to be "regulated"? Voters have a deep and sometimes justified suspicion that markets are crazy, not orderly. And everyone would want belching smokestacks to be regulated, though not always by bureaucrats sent out from Paris or Washington or Brussels.

But "regulation" could also be described as high-handed and ignorant interference in the mutually advantageous deals contracted voluntarily among the miserable serfs of the state, interference at best inspired by antique theories of natural monopoly and using antique policies appropriate to obsolete technologies, and at worst by conspiracies to benefit existing rich people, backed by state violence. Much of regulation, looked at coldly, would fall under such a definition, if not immediately on its passage, then after a few years of technological change or regulatory capture. Regulation of electricity in the United States is a case in point, having ignored changes in technology since 1900.[8] The now-defunct Interstate Commerce Commission (1887–2005) regulated the new trucking industry after 1910 as though it was a branch of the old railway industry the Commission was "designed" to regulate. The policing of recreational drug laws would certainly be a case in point of state violence in aid of out-of-date medical opinion, not to speak of the objectionable character of interference in private activity, but so would the less obvious case of the regulation of medical drugs by the U.S. Food and Drug Administration, leaving American patients, and Ebola victims, without treatments—and not approving the addition of essential polyunsurated fatty acids to infant formula for premature babies. Look at the behavior of the Securities and Exchange Commission under Bush II, or indeed its longer history since its inception under the New Deal.[9] In the cotton portion of the U.S. farm bill of 2014, in an item known as the Stacked Income Protection Plan, cotton farmers, most of them quite well off, were guaranteed about 80 percent of "expected" revenue, with taxpayers covering most of the premiums for the so-called insurance, and with no limits on how much millionaire farmers could collect by thus farming the government, as they have since 1933.[10] To correct "market imperfections" (few of which have been shown to be very large) by calling in the regulatory state is to assume that the state's intervention is cheaper than the "imperfection." Often it is not, and in any case one would not want simply to *assume* that the state performs its regulations well, at any rate if one were not Swedish or Iowan. It is an empirical question.

It is an old story, robbery by regulation, and it has ever been so. Too commonly the state, as the economist Murray Rothbard used to put it, is a band of robbers into whose clutches we have fallen, at any rate if the robbers are not benevolent Robin Hoods of the Swedish or Iowan sort. The economic historian Robert Higgs puts it coolly: "Government as we have known it for the past few thousand years [is] a monopoly operating ultimately by threat or actual use of violence, making rules for and extracting tribute from the residents of the territory it controls."[11] Enthusiasts for more and more government need to explain to Higgs and me in what respect his definition is inaccurate. The Interstate Commerce Commission, supposed to keep down rail rates charged to farmers, was swiftly captured by the railways and commenced keeping rates up.[12] Because the rich and powerful run the government, the poor and other powerless have been regularly hurt by governmental regulation—even by such sweet-sounding regulations as evening closing of shops (making it hard for the working poor to have time to shop) or protections limiting the hours women could work (making it hard for them to hold supervisory jobs requiring one to come early and stay late) or building codes claiming to promote safety but instigated by building trade unions (making it hard to build inexpensive housing) or minimum wages (making it hard for blacks, immigrants, women, and nonmembers of craft unions to get paying jobs).

When, as in Argentina during the 1940s or Venezuela during the 2000s, a naïvely populist or socialist policy has taken hold—introducing often well-intentioned but always perverse policies such as subsidizing unprofitable industries or attacking markets and property and therefore attacking trade-tested betterment—income has grown more slowly than it could have; or, as it did in Cuba, income has declined. Declines of income are rare exceptions, and we pray that soon even such countries will reform in a bourgeois ideological direction, and join the blade of the hockey stick, in the way again of China and India—once also grotesquely mismanaged against "capitalism" in the name of the poor, a mismanagement that locked the poor into poverty.

We bleeding-heart libertarians wholly approve, incidentally, of the one-time-and- never-again attack on property called "land reform," such as Hernando de Soto's proposal to give property rights to squatters in slums.[13] We lament that land reform has not happened in every country in Latin America. But we lament, too, that our colleagues on the left have assailed de Soto's poor-friendly proposals with the same arguments that the left long applied, equally mistakenly, to the enclosure movement in eighteenth-century England—namely, that private property hurts poor people.[14] No, it doesn't.

When accompanied by liberalism, it helps them, massively. It makes their economies work well, and in the third act it enriches them all. Innovism.

Lightly regulated trades, in other words, contrary to a hardy populism suspicious of any trading, have on the whole been good, not bad, for the poor, for the women, for the powerless of the world. Such a claim, which is evident from the history of the world since Hammurabi, does not mean that every trading deal is ethical or that every bourgeois is virtuous, no more than anyone could reasonably suppose, unless she lives in Norway or Idaho, that every government regulation is ethical or every civil servant virtuous. The relevant comparison is not of some unattainable utopia of perfect trade-tested betterment with actual, imperfect government regulation. It is the comparison of the actual record of liberated trade, and the betterment it has brought to the powerless of the world, with the actual record of populism, fascism, socialism, and thick regulation bettering a few favored groups of the poor, every Party official, and most of the owners of the bigger enterprises able to corrupt the government, all at the expense of the rest. In the Russian Federation the antitrust agency is used to attack hundreds of the small firms that compete with influential giants. The literary critic Tzvetan Todorov reports that Margarete Buber-Neumann (Martin Buber's daughter-in-law), "a sharp-eyed observer of Soviet realities in the 1930s, was astonished to discover that the holiday resorts for ministry employees were divided into no less than five different levels of 'luxury' for the different ranks of the communist hierarchy. A few years later she found the same stratification in her prison camp."[15]

The comparison shows again that the one reliable good for the poor and powerless over the long run since 1800, or since 1980, has been the startlingly larger pie arising directly from the liberating and honoring of trade-tested betterment—as the economist-poet Robert Frost put it, "the trial by market everything must come to."[16] Well, not everything—not love, for example—though certainly such a trial by trade must come for New Hampshire apples and Christmas trees grown for profit. Private charity and public works, intergovernmental aid and union organization, all sound good in the first act of the political drama, in the run-up to the next election. Often the advocates for such policies have pure motives (though regularly the policies enrich corruptly selected groups, such as road contractors and members of the dominant political party). But good intentions alone do not serve to uplift the poor. Selling Christmas trees "beyond the time of profitable growth" (said Frost) doesn't uplift anyone. A pure heart and a subscription to the *Nation* or the *Guardian* do not suffice. We need the test of profit, reserving large nonprofit areas of life as appropriate. The goal is not to monetize everything, the charge the philosopher Michael Sandel levels against the post-Friedman world.[17] The goal is to enable the powerless, such as your ancestors and mine, to embark on a Great Enrichment, the better to achieve spiritual enrichment outside and inside the economy.

Daniel Zamora noted that in his later years, the left's hero, Michel Foucault, "was highly attracted to economic liberalism":

> he saw in it the possibility of a form of governmentality that was much less normative and authoritarian than the socialist and communist left, which he saw as totally obsolete. He especially saw in neoliberalism a "much less bureaucratic" and "much less disciplinarian" form of politics than that offered by the postwar welfare state.[18]

Another French leftist, Geoffroy de Lagasnerie, according to Zamora, "underlines [in a 2012 book] a point that to my mind is essential and goes to the heart of numerous problems on the critical left":

> [Lagasnerie] argues that Foucault was one of the first to really take the neoliberal texts seriously and to read them rigorously.... Sequestered in the usual sectarianism of the academic world, no stimulating reading had existed that took into consideration the arguments of Friedrich Hayek, Gary Becker, or Milton Friedman. On this point, one can only agree with Lagasnerie: Foucault allowed us to read and understand these authors, to discover in them a complex and stimulating body of thought.

Wise words of counsel to the left, from the left.

Let us, then, not reject the blessings of economic growth on account of planning or pessimism, the busybody if well-intentioned rationalism of some voices of the French Enlightenment or the adolescent if charming doubts of some voices of the German Romantic movement, fashionable though both attitudes have long been among the clerisy. As rational optimists, let us celebrate the Great Enrichment, and the rhetorical changes in freer societies that caused it.[19]

What, Then, Explains the Enrichment?

PART III

Bourgeois Life Had Been Rhetorically Revalued in Britain at the Onset of the Industrial Revolution

IT IS A TRUTH UNIVERSALLY
ACKNOWLEDGED THAT EVEN
DR. JOHNSON AND JANE AUSTEN
EXHIBIT THE REVALUATION

Why, then? Why did the world become dramatically richer in the two centuries after 1800? The second book of this trilogy, *Bourgeois Dignity*, showed that the answer is not material causes, since material causes are routine and run out of steam, literally. The Great Enrichment was nothing like routine and did not run out of steam. The book suggested instead a rhetorical cause. The first book, *The Bourgeois Virtues*, had already showed that the rhetoric and implementation of ethics does matter to the operation of trade-tested betterment. Consider, then, the scientific evidence for a Bourgeois Revaluation, a rhetorical and ethical change causing the proliferation of ingenious ideas for betterment.

Look at the table of contents here and you will see that I am going to tell the history backward, to answer the questions about causes and conditions implied by each lurch toward the modern world. Backward history is better for analysis, because it focuses sharply on Why. Straightforward narrative from time 0 to the present, good for many other purposes, faces the analytic hazard of false smoothness, 0 leading "inevitably" to 1, 1 to 2, and so forth. Narrative, in other words, has the problem that mere sequence (metonymy is the technical word) gives an impression that the questions of analysis (metaphor, models) have in fact, by that very sequence, been somehow solved.

The arrangement of the present book can be summarized thus (in a table of contents, to so speak, for the table of contents):

We were poor but now are rich. Why?
Answer: The change in attitude toward the bourgeoisie and creative destruction.
But why did they change?

Answer: The egalitarian accidents of 1517–1789. But why were they important?

Answer: Because earlier times were fiercely antibourgeois, being holy and
  hierarchical,

And they were so even though markets and "capitalism" have always existed,
  contrary to Karl Polanyi. And so, to return from ancient times to our own
  times:

Alarmingly, the clerisy after 1848 came to oppose all this good change.

Which is the danger.

Let me begin the backward history, then, with a couple of hard cases, lower
bounds, so to speak—two writers on the eve of the Great Enrichment who
would be expected to have contempt for money, enterprise, betterment, business, the bourgeoisie.

The first mildly surprising case of the pervasive change in rhetoric toward
1800 is the poet, critic, and playwright Samuel Johnson (1709–1784). Though
a Tory in much of his politics, Johnson was suspicious of the prideful aristocrats of his society and favorably disposed toward the bourgeoisie. True,
he said, of aristocratic occupations, at age sixty-nine in 1778, "Every man
thinks meanly of himself for not having been a soldier, or not having been at
sea. . . . The impression is universal: yet it is strange."[1] About the remark, his
eager young friend and biographer James Boswell comments, "Such was his
cool reflection in his study; but whenever he was warmed . . . he, like other
philosophers, whose minds are impregnated with poetical fancy, caught the
common enthusiasm for splendid renown." Johnson, when caught in aristocratic and Christian enthusiasm, wrote of the holy island off Scotland, "That
man is little to be envied whose patriotism would not gain force upon the
plains of Marathon, or whose piety would not grow warmer amid the ruins
of Iona."[2]

And yet in his own book about the tour that Boswell and he took, Johnson
the bourgeois noted of the violent and aristocratic traditions of the West of
Scotland that "a man who places honor only in successful violence is a very
troublesome and pernicious animal in time of peace."[3] As a writer he was not
dependent on churchly or aristocratic patronage, but was self-supporting
in the literary marketplace, a master of Grub Street (which he described in
his *Dictionary* as "much inhabited by writers of small histories, dictionaries,
and temporary poems"). A very lofty Lord Chesterfield had subscribed to

the *Dictionary* seven years earlier the absurdly unaristocratic sum of £10. Though half the annual income of a poor man at the time, it was pocket change by the standard of the noble lord's expenditure, and an embarrassment by comparison with the princely £1,575 that the Scottish and bourgeois printer William Strahan had arranged for Johnson to get at the beginning of the project. Yet at its conclusion, My Lord Chesterfield was discovered giving himself airs in the press as a patron of the now-successful *Dictionary*. Johnson was moved to write to him a declaration of bourgeois authorial independence from anything but trading, which indeed Johnson employed to support himself by subscription:

> I hope it is no very cynical asperity not to confess obligations where no benefit has been received, or to be unwilling that the public should consider me as owing that to a patron which providence has enabled me to do for myself.[4]

In the *Dictionary* itself he had described a "patron" as "commonly a wretch who supports with insolence, and is repaid in flattery." Let us be repaid in coin: "No man but a blockhead," he declared, "ever wrote except for money."[5] "There are few ways," he said again, "in which a man can be more innocently employed than in getting money." His interlocutor at the time, that same printer, Strahan, who also lived by trade and was a friend of bourgeois Benjamin Franklin (as Johnson, who detested the slave-driving Americans, was not), remarked, "The more one thinks of this, the juster it will appear."[6]

Johnson never indulged in the anti-economic, anticonsumerist cant so common among the clerisy after 1848, and common among the aristocracy and the literal clerics earlier. Remember what he said about men always taking the best they can get. To the easy supposition that money isn't everything, he replied, "When I was running about this town a very poor fellow, I was a great arguer for the advantages of poverty; but I was, at the same time, very sorry to be poor."[7] And he approved of innovation, in 1753, well before the word had gained prestige—"The age is running mad after innovation; all the business of the world is to be done in a new way; men are to be hanged in a new way"—and took an informed interest in new ways of brewing.[8] Decades earlier he had delivered the following encomium on hopeful projectors:

> That the attempts of such men will often miscarry, we may reasonably expect; yet from such men, and such only, are we to hope for the cultivation of those parts

of nature which lie yet waste, and the invention of those arts which are yet wanting to the felicity of life. . . . Whatever is attempted without previous certainty
of success, . . . amongst narrow minds may . . . expose its author to censure and
contempt; . . . every man will laugh at what he does not understand, . . . and every
great or new design will be censured as a project.[9]

It was a declaration against its enemies in favor of the bourgeois dignity and
liberty to improve. Such a declaration would have been nearly impossible
in 1620—although Francis Bacon, for all his aristocratic nastiness, was an
early robin in that spring. At about the same time as Johnson did, Benjamin
Franklin wrote to similar effect, with uncharacteristic bitterness: the attempts
of an improver such as himself "to benefit mankind, . . . however well imagined, if they do not succeed expose him, though very unjustly, to general
ridicule and contempt; and if they do succeed, to envy, robbery, and abuse."[10]
As Weber pointed out, the arrival of the creative destroyer "was not generally peaceful. A flood of mistrust, sometimes of hatred, above all of moral
indignation, regularly opposed itself to the first innovator."[11]

Consider at greater length a harder case.[12] It tests the hypothesis of a change
in attitude toward the dignity of money and moneymaking with another example that one would suppose leans *against* the hypothesis. It yields another
argument *a fortiori*.

The characters in Jane Austen's six mature and finished novels, published
between 1811 and the year after her death in 1817, are smallish landowners
and their pastors, the lesser rural gentry, with the army and the navy in the
wings. She never portrays, and hardly mentions, the heights of England's
tiny aristocracy. Her dedication of *Emma* in 1815 to the Prince Regent, for
example, was famously compelled. She writes to her niece Anna in 1814, "3
or 4 families in a country village are the very thing to work on."[13] We hear
nothing of dukes and duchesses, though a little more of the major county
gentry above the rank of the three or four families. The horrid Lady Catherine de Bourg of *Pride and Prejudice* "likes to have the distinction of rank
preserved," as evoked by her Norman-style name (though it is suspiciously
bourgeois: "of the city").[14]

Austen's people bring along with their place in the gentry an attitude of disapproval for the gaming tables and dueling grounds of the real aristocracy, or

the obsession with hunting and drinking among the county bloods. "Drunk as a lord" is still proverbial in England. In the early nineteenth century, as the historians Leonore Davidoff and Catherine Hall put it, the "claim [by the English bourgeois] to moral superiority was at the heart of their challenge to an earlier aristocracy."[15] Lord Brougham spoke in favor of the Reform Bill of 1832 extending the franchise to some small part of the urban bourgeoisie by describing the "middle class" (as he called it, in what was still felt to be a new phrase) as "the genuine depositories of sober, rational, intelligent, and honest [note the meaning, 'genuine'] English feeling."[16] Not aristocrats chiefly but middle-class people led the Radical and Evangelical agitations in Britain, especially educated bourgeois such as William Wilberforce, descended from a line of merchants at Hull. (True, actual cabinet posts were for long reserved mainly for dukes and their cousins, with a sprinkling of Celtic commoners to keep up the standard of eloquence.) Part of the embourgeoisement of England 1600 to 1848, as the historian Michael Thompson has argued, consisted of tempering the upper classes with bourgeois values.[17] The Third Duke of Bridgewater bridged water with canals carrying his coal. Even the less commercially active dukes took to serving as honorary board chairmen for gasworks and walking about in sober business suits (deriving in Austen's Regency period, 1811–1820, from Beau Brummell's fashion of men's clothing without aristocratic lace or glitter—to this day unaltered in its sober, bourgeois lack of ornament).[18]

In the other class direction, Austen barely mentions, at any rate by the standard of earlier or later novels such as *Tom Jones* (1749) or *Little Women* (1868–1869), servants and small children, who were in fact present in her home in large numbers. Her country villages seem empty of agricultural workers too, at any rate by a Thomas Hardy standard. The Two Nations are not Jane's concern. We hear of Mrs. Charles's nursery maid in *Persuasion*, but we do not hear her speak or hear of the small children under her care.[19] Jane's mother had eight children, six sons and two daughters. There are glimpses, and implied presence.[20] Yet the mobs of children or servants or farm workers do not have speaking parts.

Also rare are the capitalist farmers paying rents to the gentry—"yeomen" would be how the gentry referred to them. To speak of the "middle class" below the gentry, none of Austen's major characters are conventionally bourgeois, though some quite important secondary ones are—in *Pride and Prejudice*, for example, the Gardiners, aunt and uncle to Elizabeth Bennet, the protagonist. Uncle Edward Gardiner is in trade in London, where Elizabeth visits. Yet in Austen's finished novels no merchant or manufacturer is featured largely. True, the fact is less surprising when one realizes that Austen Country, like the Dickens City later on, was in the south, the deindustrializing part of England at the time—though London had only recently given up its place among the chief manufacturing areas in Europe, and was still the trading hub of empire.

The critic Markman Ellis asserts that "characters in Austen express a profound distaste for trade." Many do, but Austen's own opinion behind her ironies is plain and is by no means antibourgeois. Ellis is correct that "a consistent stream of conservative opinion throughout the eighteenth century continued to argue [against Addison, Steele, Defoe, Lillo, Fielding, Johnson, and, I am saying, Austen] that active engagement in commerce vitiated any claims to gentility."[21] The most ordinarily bourgeois figure in the novels is Robert Martin, the well-to-do yeoman suitor of Harriet Smith in *Emma*. At first Harriet "believed he was very clever, and understood everything. He had a very fine flock, and, while she was with them [that is, present with Martin and the wool buyer], he had been bid more for his wool than anybody in the country."[22] The protagonist Emma, who in her busybody way worries that if Harriet marries him "she might be required to sink herself [socially] forever," persuades Harriet not to accept his offer—until the end of the novel, when it is discovered that Harriet herself is in fact by parentage bourgeois (a father in trade, Austen reports with a touch of instable irony, "rich enough to afford her . . . comfortable maintenance . . . and decent enough to have always wished for concealment" of her parentage). Earlier, in chapter 4, Emma had slipped the stiletto in:

EMMA. Mr. Martin, I suppose, is not a man of information beyond the line of his own business? He does not read?

HARRIET. Oh yes!—that is, no—I do not know—but I believe he has read a good deal. . . . And I know he has read *The Vicar of Wakefield*. . . .

EMMA. A young farmer, whether on horseback or on foot, is the very last sort of person to raise my curiosity. The yeomanry are precisely the order of people with whom I feel I can have nothing to do. . . . A farmer can need none of my help, and is, therefore, in one sense, as much above my notice as in every other he is below it. . . . There can be no doubt of your being a gentleman's daughter, and you must support your claim to that station by every thing

within your own power, or there will be plenty of people who would take
pleasure in degrading you. . . .

HARRIET [mortified, and resolved suddenly not to accept Martin's offer]. To be
sure, he is not so genteel as a real gentleman.

Men of business, who are not, like real gentlemen—that is, as Emma says,
"born to an independence"—can with "diligence and good luck" become
rich, but will always appear in society "so very clownish." Independence in
the sense of literally or symbolically nonearned income was then the key
to gentility—land rents, clerical benefices, interest on government bonds,
returns on naval prizes gathered by bold preying on the French and their
trading partners, even the fees to private doctors and barristers billing in
patrician guineas (twenty-one shillings to the guinea) rather than plebeian
pounds sterling.

As the historian Gordon Wood notes, speaking of Ben Franklin's ambi-
tions to gentility, a gentleman was "independent in a world of dependencies,
learned in a world only partially literate, and leisured in a world of laborers."[23]
In America the admiration for the entirely and proudly leisured did not survive far into the nineteenth century. Later in the nineteenth century even
in lordly England it had largely broken down. In Trollope's *Phineas Redux*
(1874) the contempt for a man without an occupation, such as the aged Duke
of Omnium, is palpable. The heroine Madame Goesler, herself the widow of
a rich bourgeois (and Jew), by then "knew that no man should dare to live
idly as the Duke had lived." A minor character in the novel, Gerard Maule,
though not an aristocrat as was the duke, was according to Mrs. Atterbury
(of Florence, who "had been an intimate friend of Garibaldi") "the most in-
sufferably idle man who ever wandered about the world without any visible
occupation for his hours." "'But he hunts,' said Adelaide. 'Do you call that an
occupation?' asked Mrs. Atterbury with scorn."[24]

Austen's unfinished last novel, *Sanditon* (1817), though, does deal directly
and significantly with the working bourgeoisie. Jane's favorite brother, Henry
Thomas Austen (1771–1850), who was a successful banker for a dozen years
in London, had just gone bankrupt in the economic slump that followed the
defeat of the French. One wishes on that trivial ground, too, that Jane had
not died age at forty-one, in order to see what she would have done with
the revival of trade after 1817 and the gradual prominence of industry and
the coming of the bourgeoisie to self-conscious political power. The heights

of the bourgeoisie in London and in the ancient boroughs, to be sure, had *actual* power much earlier, as for example in the English Civil War. It was merely in their self-consciousness as a national class differentiated from commoners as a whole that after the Napoleonic Wars they awakened.[25]

Austen, that is, wrote in a bourgeois genre but did not on the whole bother with tradesmen. Within the tiny class that she examines, an antitrade snobbery is commonplace, even among the major characters when ethically misled. But the snobbery is regularly spoofed. Listen to the free indirect style in

> Mr. Gardiner was a sensible, gentlemanlike man [note: merely gentleman-*like*], greatly superior to his sister as well by nature as by education. The Netherfield ladies would have had much difficulty in believing that a man who lived by trade, and within view of his own warehouses, could have been so well bred and agreeable."[26]

The literary critic Marilyn Butler argued that Austen was, as Johnson was, a conservative figure, an anti-Jacobin: "The crucial action of her novels is in itself expressive of the conservative side in an active war of ideas."[27] But it was not exactly our early twenty-first-century ideological war. What we, with the French at the time, would call the "left" hardly existed in Britain until well into the nineteenth century—such was the horror in Britain of the revolutionary mob, and then Bonaparte, that a real leftism was hard to sustain. Decades before, in the Gordon Riots of 1780, the upper and middling orders, Whig or Tory, had been thoroughly terrified.

Other, older conservatives, such as the poet William Cowper, whom Austen joined many of her contemporaries in admiring, were not anticapitalist in a modern, leftish way. Yet the conservatives worried—as did Adam Smith—about the dangers of bourgeois excess. And even the Radicals worried about lower-class excess in the town, the Mob. In the eighteenth century most parties, leaving out Dr. Johnson, were classically antiurban, which is to say bucolically hostile to any massed humanity, much in the spirit of ancient pastoral poetry and present-day radical environmentalism. Thus Cowper in 1785:

> And burghers, men immaculate perhaps
> In all their private functions, once combined,
> Become a loathsome body, only fit

For dissolution, hurtful to the main.
Hence merchants, unimpeachable of sin
Against the charities of domestic life,
Incorporated, seem at once to lose
Their nature; and, disclaiming all regard
For mercy and the common rights of man,
Build factories with blood, conducting trade
At the sword's point, and dyeing the white robe
Of innocent commercial Justice red.[28]

In citing the passage, the literary critic Markman Ellis takes it as saying that "in its modern form, commerce had grown cruel and corrupting
in its search for profit at all cost."[29] Quite apart from the economic illogic
("profit at all cost"), his reading seems a back-projection of the hostility to
trade among the left clerisy after 1848, and especially among Departments
of English after 1968. It is not in the passage by Cowper, which is about the
evils of "man, associated and leagued with man," whether for aristocratic or
bourgeois or proletarian purpose. The bourgeoisie after all is composed of
"men immaculate perhaps / In all their private functions" and merchants
"unimpeachable of sin / Against the charities of domestic life" and commercial justice begins as "innocent," all of which would be highly unlikely
in descriptions written by a clerisy instructed by Marx. Jane Austen would
not have drawn a moral from Cowper, as Ellis does, that "in the calculating
spirit of trade . . . the enduring virtues of the English gentleman were narrowed, hardened and corrupted."[30] That's late nineteenth-century rhetoric, a
conservative nostalgia for the rule of gentlemen warmed by leftish prejudice
against trade, neither of which is Austen's politics.

In other words, Austen was not a pro-bourgeois writer, but neither was
she anticapitalist, no more than the man she called "my dear Dr. Johnson."[31]
In her more foolish characters what turns the virtue of prudence into greed
is the absence of balancing virtues of justice or love or faith or temperance.[32]
True, no celebration can be found in Austen of entrepreneurship or the
thrusting enterprise of new men—not at all, at least if we do not paste such
an attitude onto the fragments we have of *Sanditon*. But neither was she opposed to calculation or trade—merely favoring as its site the southern country village, with its urban branches of Bath, London, and Portsmouth. In
London she frequently visited the grand house of brother Henry when he

was banking. Henry acted as her literary agent before and after her death. Jane did not regard his business as shameful.

W. H. Auden mistakes Austen's economism the way Ellis does, writing in his "Letter to Lord Byron" of 1936:

> You [Byron] could not shock her more than she shocks me;
>> Beside her Joyce seems innocent as grass.
> It makes me most uncomfortable to see
>> An English spinster of the middle class
>> Describe the amorous effects of 'brass' [that is, money],
> Reveal so frankly and with such sobriety
> The economic basis of society.[33]

It is a misreading.

NO WOMAN BUT A BLOCKHEAD
WROTE FOR ANYTHING BUT MONEY

Economics is the science of prudence. And a cool prudence is the characteristic virtue of the bourgeoisie. Jane Austen was in such a sense an economist
in her life and in her fiction, a follower of sense. But prudence is nothing
like the only human virtue, even among the bourgeoisie—or so say Adam
Smith, Samuel Johnson, Jane Austen, and I. Jane is of the Bourgeois Era and
is not attacking "the essentially selfish nature of the commercial imperative,"
as Ellis puts it in his too-modern and too-leftish-leaning way (or, what is
the same thing, his too-early-medieval and too-monkish-leaning way).[1] Her
foolish characters are selfish, to be sure, the very word she uses in *Sense and
Sensibility* to describe Lucy Steele. Yet Austen understood that ethical self-
love—prudence—is indeed a virtue when balanced by other virtues. It slips
into selfishness, the sin of greed, only when not so balanced by sensibility.

And Austen in her literary trade certainly betrayed no worry that her
profits were greedy. Though they were trivial by the standard of Byron or
Scott or Maria Edgeworth, they were large enough to make her a little literary capitalist, as Johnson on a bigger scale had been decades earlier. It has
often been remarked that Austen is bourgeois in the sensible interest she
has in earning money and spending it prudently. The literary critic Edward
Copeland entitled all three of his contributions since 1986 to handbooks
for the study of Austen simply "Money."[2] The historian Oliver MacDonagh
observed that Jane "was accustomed from childhood to hear money matters discussed in informed and detailed fashion; and the lessons she learned
were driven home by her own comparative poverty."[3] Those of my undergraduate students who come from farms and other small businesses start

their study of economics with the same Austenian grasp of the value of money, which eludes students from more privileged homes (such as that of my parents when I myself started studying economics) in which Daddy mysteriously provides from a distant office. Austen tells her beloved niece, the heiress Fanny Knight, that *Mansfield Park* has sold out its first edition. "I am very greedy and want to make the most of it; but you are much above caring about money. I shall not plague you with any particulars."[4] Note Aunt Jane's amused self-deprecation in the use of "greedy," and the sharp turn in alluding to Fanny's wealth. In November 1812 she writes to a friend, "*Pride and Prejudice* is sold—[the printer/publisher] Egerton gives £110 for it [which was at the time a respectable lower-middle-class annual income]. I would rather have had £150, but we could not both be pleased."[5] But she *was* pleased.

Johnson said that no sensible man wrote except for money, and Austen embraced the principle. She expresses to her sister Cassandra her delight in making as much as £400 in total from her writings, twenty times the average annual income of a working family and only a little below what the big Austen household had lived on annually. As Marilyn Butler explained, she felt in her last six years, 1811–1817, that she was an Author, because she was making money at it.[6] It was her independence, in an age in which independence in a woman of the gentry or the upper bourgeoisie was controversial. Her profits bespoke a prudence, temperance, hope, and courage similar to that of her two naval-officer brothers. And it was a bourgeois standard, the *trade* test for literary progress in, say, the technique of free indirect style. When the buying public pays, you are a professional.

Austen's sailor brothers participated in money making without shame when they captained freelancing frigates rather than ships of the line. In chapter 8 of *Persuasion* (1818, Austen's last and posthumously published novel), Captain Wentworth (modeled on her brother, the Captain and at length Admiral Francis William) reminisces about his commercial triumph in capturing enemy vessels with his frigate: "Ah! those were pleasant days when I had the Laconia! How fast I made money in her." No man but a blockhead goes to sea except for money. And banker brother Henry became later an Anglican priest. In Austen's world it was no contradiction. (Nor need it be now, though we find it stranger than Austen did. I have a woman friend who retired from a career as a big-time commercial banker, University of

Chicago MBA in finance, dealing in $100-million loans, to become a Protestant minister of religion. We were amazed.) As Waterman has persuasively argued, in the early nineteenth century, before the rise of an anticommercial ideology among the European clerisy, there was nothing bizarre about such a mixed career.[7]

Observe, too—again there's little original about the observation, and the political scientist Michael Chwe has written a brilliant book discussing it in detail—that our Jane portrays highly strategic thinking.[8] She is in this way, too, bourgeois, in the honor or at least toleration accorded to such behavior. For one thing she examines, if on a tiny social stage, and always with her ironies, the idealism of ordinary life that characterizes modernity, and accompanies economics with its doppelganger, a strategic view of the world (as against a nonstrategic impulsiveness, or cluelessness). Though Langland or Chaucer centuries before had spoken of ordinary life and its imperative of prudence, in the meantime the literary romance (whose late representatives Austen makes fun of in *Northanger Abbey*, published also posthumously in 1818, though started two decades earlier) had spoken more and more of princes and magicians and ghosts on vasty castle walls. A new feature of the English novel from *Robinson Crusoe* (1719) forward, by contrast, is that before they venture the characters plan, strategize, consider, and agonize about their material situation.[9] And a new feature from *Moll Flanders* (1722) forward, again by Defoe, is that they do so in a social context.[10]

Of course actual people strategized in actual fact, always, from the caves onward, if they wanted to eat. We are talking here about what brought honor, not what actually happened. In a holy or heroic or peasant-habitual life you were supposed to act out of identity, not calculation. Wordsworth declared in his sonnet "Within King's College Chapel," composed in 1820, that "high Heaven rejects the lore / Of nicely-calculated less or more." Well: High Heaven might in 1820 reject it, as not honorably sacred—though Waterman, I've noted, thinks not. But ordinary people of the bourgeoisie, who were more and more the subject of European novels and plays, did not reject profane calculation, if it was exercised in an ethical framework.

The contrast is sharp with the medieval romance down to its parodic transformation in *Don Quixote*, with the Don dashing about to save an imagined princess or slay an imagined giant with nothing like the quasi-bourgeois prudence that Sancho Panza (sometimes) counsels. The noble Don just *does* things, straight out of his identity as a medieval knight errant. Sancho, as representative of the modern world, complains about the lack of calculation, but to no effect. The comic point of the book is that the Don is invulnerable to reason, calculation, cool rhetoric, conversation, not to speak of nicely-calculated less or more. (Yet in modern economic life the role of identity and impulse needs to be acknowledged, as the social psychologist Jonathan Haidt, the management theorist James March, the economic historian John Nye, and the economists George Akerlof and Robert Shiller have all affirmed. Not many business decisions could be made without identity and impulse.[11])

Austen laughs at thoughtless aristocratic gestures and Christian pseudo-martyrdoms. In Austen's novels, strategic thinking is the means, and if the end is wisely chosen (as it is at the last by the major and developing characters), all is well. Strategic thinking *balanced by other virtues* is the ticket to emotional maturity and to a good marriage. As early as age thirteen Jane was capable of Austenian irony and free indirect style about the whole business, and indeed about enterprise and tickets, writing of "Mr. Wilmot of Wilmot Lodge . . . the representative of a very ancient Family & possessed besides his paternal Estate, a considerable share in a Lead mine & a ticket in the Lottery."[12] Marriage was the literal business of a young woman of the gentry, the truth universally acknowledged. Though strategic thinking in the novels is absurdly undignified in the self-absorbed pursuit of prudence-only by many of the minor characters, it is dignified in the self-conscious ethical development by the major characters.

The science of economics had in Adam Smith and his French influences grown far beyond its definition in Aristotle and Xenophon as advice on how to run an estate, such as the king's, or Mr. Wilmot's. Bourgeois literature and bourgeois economics share the subject of calculation about ordinary, unwritten life. Alessandro Manzoni, the Italian Tolstoy, devoted an entire chapter of his masterpiece *I Promessi Sposi* (The Betrothed; 1827, 1842; chapter 12) to explaining the dire consequences in a famine of interfering with the grain market. An economist could reprint it for a lecture in Economics 101. Luigi Einaudi, who advocated commercial liberty, not regulation (*libertà vs. controllo di commercio*), wrote in 1919 that *I Promessi Sposi* was "one of the best treatises on political economy that has ever been written."[13] The master builder in Ibsen's play of 1892, Halvard Solness, achieves his profit and his transcendence by sitting on other people's lives, such as that of his gifted young draftsman. His worry about the young ("From the young . . . the change is coming. . . . Then it's the end of Solness the master builder") is worry about the creative destruction of entry, characteristic of a liberated economy, which the bourgeoisie advocates but then routinely seeks state protection from.[14]

In Austen the admiration for prudence is undercut, I say, when it shows as prudence *only*. The minor characters are often idiotically strategic, mothers pushing their daughters up the marital tree with a single-mindedness that would delight a Marxian or a Samuelsonian economist. Of Lucy Steele's success in the business of marriage in *Sense and Sensibility*, Austen writes, "The whole of Lucy's behavior in the affair, and the prosperity which crowned it, therefore, may be held forth as a most encouraging instance of what an earnest, an unceasing attention to self-interest, however its progress may be apparently obstructed, will do in securing every advantage of fortune, with no other sacrifice than of time and conscience."[15] Or, an anticipation of Mr. Gradgrind's marital argument to Louisa in Dickens's *Hard Times*, consider Reverend Collin's proposal to Elizabeth in *Pride and Prejudice*:

> My reasons for marrying are, first, that I think it a right thing for every clergyman in easy circumstances (like myself) to set the example of matrimony in his parish. Secondly, that I am very convinced it will add very greatly to my happiness; and thirdly—which perhaps I ought to have mentioned earlier, that it is the particular advice of the very noble lady whom I have the honor of calling patroness.[16]

But the major characters never talk in this prudence-only way. They talk not of a Marxian or a Samuelsonian but of a Smithian economics. I once responded to a male Samuelsonian economist who had suggested that the other six principal virtues could be absorbed into Prudence as a function $U = P$ [*Love, Justice, Courage, Temperance, Faith, Hope*] by asking him if he was married. He admitted he was. "And would you honor your wife," I then asked in effect, "by saying, 'I am very convinced our marriage will add very greatly to my happiness'?" He got the point. He must simply love, a separate matter, in which the beloved's happiness conquers all. Theologically speaking, such a love is a matter of grace, *agape*. As Adam Smith's best characters do as well, the major characters in Austen's novels, and their talk about their behavior, always mix prudence with simple love and justice and temperance and moral courage. At any rate by the last pages the major characters do finally achieve such an admirable ethical balance. They struggle ethically, which is the only drama.

∞

Austen commends, then, both sense *and* sensibility, as did Samuel Richardson, in *Pamela; or, Virtue Rewarded* (1740), and Manzoni and Ibsen later. They commend, that is, both prudence and love among the traditional principal virtues. Such are the virtues honored by most men and by all women of the bourgeoisie. Jane Austen is here strikingly bourgeois, understanding the word as praiseworthy, not merely another word for "vulgar and greedy."

In a business-respecting civilization—which I am suggesting Jane Austen stood smiling at the doorway of—the bourgeois is highly honored for his sense. Without making it his whole purpose in life (if he has sensibility, too), he strategizes, though not always correctly. Generals strategize (Greek *strategos*, "military general"). The Western bourgeoisie is fascinated by Sun Tzu's *The Art of War* (ca. fifth century BCE), busily reading it on airplanes, because it does *not* elevate to the chief virtue of a general/CEO an aristocratic Courage but rather a bourgeois Prudence:

11. What the ancients called a clever fighter is one who not only wins, but excels in winning with ease.
12. Hence his victories bring him neither reputation for wisdom nor credit for courage.
13. He wins his battles by making no mistakes.[17]

François Jullien wrote in 1996 in praise of such an ancient Chinese military and Western bourgeois notion of achieving success in war or business by upstream manipulation of the incipient—not waiting until heroic virtue is necessary, with events downstream tumbling by then with unstoppable force. Jullien notes that such a bourgeois way of life is prudent and effective. But in the Western sense it is unheroic. *The Art of War* is not about heroic gestures but, as Jullien puts it, "efficacy."

For the lack of heroism, however, Julien continues, "there is a price to pay. . . . To confront the world [in the Greek and Western style] is a way to free oneself from it. . . . [It provides] the substance of heroic stories and jubilation [and, he notes elsewhere, tragedy, too, which in the technical Greek sense is absent from Chinese tradition]. . . . Through resistance, we can make our way to liberty."[18] He argues that the Chinese sages were explaining—in more detail even than the Machiavelli of *The Prince*—how to be a successful tyrant. From this point of view it is no accident that the culture that gave us the stories of Prometheus, Achilles, and Antigone also gave us an idea, if an imperfect practice, of liberty. Tragedy, hopeless courage—Roland at the pass of Rencesvals, the 54th Massachusetts's assault on Fort Wagner, the Dutch battalion, if only it had acted with courage at Srebrenica in 1995—is the choice of the free human.

In the older Western tradition, honor accrues to the aristocratic gesture of an Achilles, not to the suspect-because-bourgeois upstream craftiness of an Odysseus. The good bourgeois in Austen has sensibility too, and will love, if not always wisely. But in Austen's novels *heroic* virtue is unnecessary. Events downstream are *not* tumbling with unstoppable force. Notice how impossible a carelessly aristocratic, Achilles-like sentiment is in an Austen novel. Responsibility, honor/honesty (in the bourgeois sense of keeping your word), and above all "amiability," a highly admired quality, dominate the scene. Edgy heroism of a *Boy's Own Paper* sort does not. Doubtless Austen's naval-officer brothers were heroic when it was called for, and urged their men once more unto the breach. Without physical courage you were un-likely to rise in His Majesty's Navy to the rank of admiral of the fleet, as Francis did (poor Charles had to settle for rear admiral).

The large army and especially the large navy of Austen's time provided quasi-aristocratic careers for the sons of the lower gentry and the upper bourgeoisie. The historian Peter Earle suggests that the incessant British wars of the long eighteenth century down to 1815, financed by a Dutch-style sinking of funds and an efficient tax system, "provided a useful niche for the younger sons of gentlemen, a trend which was eventually . . . to encour-age a snobbish disdain for business as the eighteenth century went on."[19] Earle is arguing that during the eighteenth century the antibourgeois feeling among the gentry and the upper bourgeoisie grew stronger, not weaker. A similar pseudo-aristocratization of the middle classes, with a similar conse-quence in reversing the admiration for a business civilization, happened in Europe during the nineteenth century on a much larger scale, as a side ef-fect of training officers for the gigantic, railway-enabled armies of the times, quickly mobilizable, as they were in August 1914. The German army in the Second World War (or for that matter, the First), wrote the military historian

R. A. Parker, was "distinguished by the high quality of leadership . . . among officers at every level, and among NCOs. The prestige of the army had meant that the cadres of the wartime army had been drawn from men of high potential."[20] The same could be said of the Japanese army and navy by the 1930s. Developed over a shorter period of time but with a useful background in the myth of the samurai, it was mobilized around the same highly nonbourgeois notion that what was needful was heroically conquered *Lebensraum*, in its case in Korea, Taiwan, Manchuria, Indonesia, "to increase economic resources and make them secure," as Parker puts it (without realizing its economic illogic), by the exercise of violence, not by the bourgeois virtues of exchange.[21]

But in Austen's social world the most necessary virtue, as in the Royal Navy, and in any navy that was going to succeed in an age in which the naval ship was a highly complex organization, the most elaborate machine in existence, was the bourgeois virtue of prudence—which is to say tactics and strategy, or game theory, as Chwe puts it. Naval officers were expected to do their utmost, and were shot if they did not, to encourage the others. But beyond a necessary courage unto the breach, or onto the quarterdeck, they were expected to be prudent. Unlike the accepted aristocratic practice of running a regiment in the army at the time, the running of a big sailing warship required strict attention to procedures usual in commerce. The ship captain had to provision with care, never miss a tide, navigate with skill, avoid the lea shore. From the time of Pepys in the late seventeenth century all officers in the Royal Navy were required to have had experience on the lower decks, starting as midshipmen at a tender age (Jane's sailor brothers both went to sea at age twelve). Nothing like this was required in the army. Though during the age of sail one's birth and social position mattered for promotion (Francis Austen got his promotions partly through the influence of Warren Hastings), there was no straightforward purchasing of commissions and promotions, as was practiced in the British army until 1871. At sea no wild charging for the guns was permitted, no throwing away of an expensively trained life upon useless but heroic gestures, no endangering a *Victory* of His Majesty's Navy costing £105,000 ($420 million in present-day terms) by being an innumerate, too-peasantly navigator or a foolhardy, too-aristocratic fighter.

Jane Austen and Adam Smith are both chiefly concerned, as the literary critic Elsie Michie argues, with both the good and the bad that can come

out of the possession of wealth and the pursuit of interest. Strategy is sometimes good, both Austen and Smith say, but not always, if at the sacrifice of
conscience. "The changes in the depiction of the rich woman as we move
from *Pride and Prejudice* to *Mansfield Park* to *Emma*," Michie writes, "show
Austen wrestling with the ambivalences we find in Smith's writings: the sense
that in a commercial culture the desire for wealth will be both beneficial
and harmful and the need to find a way to acknowledge and accept the uni-
versality of such self-interested impulses while at the same time imagining
psychological and social mechanisms that will keep them in check."[22] Surely.
Smith from the liberal side and Austen from the conservative side both worried about sense *and* sensibility.

In an ethical connection, what is most surprising is that Jane is not much
of a *Christian* novelist. Her characters, whether major or minor, make little of their Anglican Christianity. Hope and faith and love of God are the
"Christian" virtues, or so Christians have claimed from the earliest times,
without the bother of actually exhibiting such virtues much in practice. But
the Neoclassicism of the eighteenth century had put religion in its place—
without usually going all the way to the atheism that became so common a
century later among advanced thinkers such as Hardy or Zola or late Darwin. Yet even in an eighteenth-century context, Austen deals surprisingly
lightly with the transcendent. She was a daughter of a clergyman, courted by
clergymen, sister of two clergymen, and aunt or great-aunt-in-law to clergymen. As a friend put it to me, "In an Austen novel you can't spit without
hitting an Anglican clergyman." But she rarely mentions God, and in all her
books uses the official word for an Anglican clergyman, "priest," once only.[23]
True, the *OED* remarks on "priest" that "in the nineteenth century [it was]
more prominent in English regional [that is, Northern] use," the North being where the tiny group of English Catholics had persisted, supplemented
by Irish immigrants, which could explain its absence in Austen's Southern
novels. It became later "associated with High Church and Anglo-Catholic
circles." But that's the point: Austen is Broad Church, nothing like Anglo-
Catholic, not to speak of Evangelical, and makes little of her faith.

We know Austen's lack of religious fervor from other sources than her
mainly a-religious novels. (The heroine of *Northanger Abbey*, true, is a bit of
a Christian, but merely to set off the pagan absurdities of the gothic novel.)

Austen clearly was no Enthusiast, a word that was just then shifting under a new Romantic rhetoric away from its standard eighteenth-century meaning of "insane intemperance" to its present religious and secular meaning of "admirable if somewhat exaggerated faithfulness." Mainline Anglicans were temperate, not Evangelical. Austen writes to her niece, advising her on a suitor, "And as to there being any objection from his *Goodness*, from the danger of his becoming even Evangelical, I cannot admit *that*. I am by no means convinced that we ought not all to be Evangelicals, and am at least persuaded that they who are so from Reason and Feeling, must be happiest and safest."[24] Note the mix of Reason and Feeling, sense and sensibility—which shows Austen to have an entire lack of understanding of the unmixed Evangelical temper, Faith Before All. Austen, notes the literary historian Michael Wheeler, "eschews the kind of fervent religiosity that characterizes much of the religious fiction of her day."[25] Waterman argues for the salience "of Wilberforce's [the Wilberforce of the antislavery movement] profoundly influential *Practical View* (1797), which (combined with the terrible shock of the French Revolution) almost single-handedly brought the 'higher and middling classes' back to Christianity. There is a world of difference between the view of religion and the church evinced in *Northanger Abbey* [begun in 1798] and *Mansfield Park* [written 1811–1812]."[26] Yes: as I said, Austen was a conservative. Fervent religiosity is absent.

The three virtues of the classical and Christian seven that are missing from Austen—transcendent hope and faith and love of God—are the same one's missing from Adam Smith. (Austen appears to have got the gist of Smith only indirectly, if at all. Her father's considerable library of five hundred books might possibly have contained one of the two books Smith published. Waterman, who has gone into the matter of the circulation of *The Wealth of Nations* in detail, doubts it.) That is, she is not a Romantic novelist, even though she concerned herself exclusively with romance in its recent sense of "affairs of the heart." She does not take Art as a model for life, and does not elevate the Artist to a lonely pinnacle of heroism, or worship the Middle Ages, or adopt any of the other, antibourgeois themes of Novalis, Brentano, Sir Walter Scott, and later Romantics. Her *Northanger Abbey*, I repeat, first written, it appears, in the same year as Coleridge and Wordsworth's *Lyrical Ballads*, was a broad parody of the earlier and proto-Romantic gothic novel. The Rousseau-inspired Sentimental Revolution of the 1770s in England, dating from Henry Mackenzie's novel of 1771, *The Man of Feeling*, had anticipated German Romance. Romanticism around 1800 re-vived talk of hope and faith and a love for Art or Nature or the Revolution as a necessary transcendent in people's lives. But Jane would have none of it, neither Evangelical Christianity nor Romantic paganism. In cricketing terms appropriate to her southern villages at the time, she was middle and leg, playing conservative strokes off the back foot quietly down the pitch, with an occasional brilliant glide down to long leg.

Austen is gentry, not bourgeois. She provides nonetheless a model for good bourgeoisness—not sense alone, but combined with sensibility; not amiability alone, but also a prudent marriage. "I consider everyone," she de-clared in a letter in 1808, "as having a right to marry once in their lives for love, if they can."[27] But watch the balance sheet, dears. True, as I've said, in her completed novels she doesn't so much as mention stockbrokers or mill owners. Yet long after her death she has assumed a special place in the ethi-cal education of the English-speaking, bourgeois world, as in her apotheosis in the 1930s at the hands of the English critics F. R. and Queenie Leavis.

It would alarm many of her most devoted readers to say so, but her kind of people are the kind we want in our trade-testing society—her major peo-ple, that is, who do not follow the Marxian and Samuelsonian economists, as her minor people so often do, in relying on prudence only.

19

ADAM SMITH EXHIBITS BOURGEOIS
THEORY AT ITS ETHICAL BEST

Another and more conventional exemplar of the Bourgeois Revaluation is the Scottish professor of moral philosophy Adam Smith (1723–1790). He is grossly misunderstood by most economists, and by the Wall Street men sporting Adam Smith ties.

Smith's peculiarly eighteenth-century project was the making of an ethic for a commercial society, "wrestling with," to repeat Michie, "the sense that in a commercial culture the desire for wealth will be both beneficial and harmful." Commerce, the economist Albert Hirschman noted in *The Passions and the Interests* (1977), is for the first time seen to be amiable—as the French put it in the eighteenth century, *doux*, sweet. The "seen to be" served to protect bourgeois behaviors, such as opening a new trade in pepper or devising a new waterwheel, from the usual attacks by other bourgeois intent on government-sponsored monopoly or by aristocrats intent on keeping things as they so pleasantly are or by peasants or proletarians intent on getting some of the stuff by tip or gift or theft from the riches of the merchant or aristocrat.

In an early essay, which he did not carry into editions of his *Essays* beyond 1741–1742, David Hume proposed a project for the age: "I shall take occasion . . . to compare the different stations in life, and to persuade such of my readers as are placed in the middle station to be satisfied with it, as the most eligible of all others. These form the most numerous rank of men that can be supposed susceptible of philosophy; and therefore all discourses of morality ought principally to be addressed to them."[1]

Hume does not in fact in the essay go on to make such an address. After observing that the virtue of friendship is natural in the bourgeoisie, which is true enough, he turns to praising artists and scholars, losing sight of his numerous audience of the middle station. His aporia (as the professors of rhetoric would say) anticipates the chasm that opened up in Europe a century later between the bourgeoisie and its children of *la vie bohème*, and especially its sons. What is mainly striking in Hume's essay is the unfulfilled proposal to fashion a discourse of morality for the bourgeoisie.

Adam Smith fulfilled what his friend Hume proposed. No aporia there. It was Smith's intention in almost all of his writings published and unpublished to develop an ethic for a commercial society, a society of the middle station. Authorial intention, true, is not the same thing as authorial accomplishment. You can intend with all energy and earnestness to write the Great American Novel, but the intention is irrelevant to reading it as it actually, sadly is. Yet Smith did accomplish his intention, though the accomplishment has long been misunderstood by his children and grandchildren among economists, sociologists, and ethical philosophers. His temperate rhetoric is too cool and sensible and bourgeois, in the manner of Sun Tzu or Jane Austen, to work when seeking the favor of young people against the hot and aristocratic rhetoric of Rousseau or Marx. Although he made his intention unmistakably clear, his accomplishment has been occluded by the subsequent rise of utilitarianism and the reaction to it during the treason of the clerisy after 1848.

Saying that Smith intended an ethic for a commercial age is not the same thing as saying that he admired every ethical or political excess of the bourgeoisie. Economists have often Thatcherized Smith in this way, and read into the single throwaway line about "the invisible hand" an entire economistic, prudence-only, Benthamite philosophy: "Markets are always efficient," the economists declare with boyish confidence, "so they provide a model for all of social life." Always. Sell the children.

Against such simplemindedness Smith had written in 1759 *The Theory of Moral Sentiments*. Few economists or their enemies have looked into it. And although it can be viewed as the founding text of Western social psychology, few social psychologists have read it either. Its first sentence reads, "However selfish man may be supposed, there are evidently some principles in his nature, which interest him in the fortune of others, and render their happiness necessary to him, though they derive nothing from it except the pleasure of seeing it."[2] Smith goes on in the book to rebuke Hobbes and Bernard Mandeville explicitly and at length for their dependence on prudence only, and their reduction of all motivation to mere selfishness, Lucy Steele–style.

Still, in northwestern Europe by the middle of the eighteenth century the prudential arguments, often in simpleminded form, had come notably more into favor than they had been in the centuries of courage and faith. Therefore seventeen years after *The Theory of Moral Sentiments*, in *The Wealth of Nations*, Smith made the argument against the excess of bourgeois self-interest such as the mercantile system of protection, in cool, self-interested instruction, as matters of "police," that is, policy, that is, prudence. He warned, for example, that the interest of merchants and manufacturers is "always in some respects different from, and even opposite to, that of the public."[3] Smith therefore did not recommend rule by the bourgeoisie, and in fact supported the traditional politics of the landed classes. *The Wealth of Nations* was read at the time as an attack more on bourgeois schemes in pursuit of monopoly through government (which is perpetual) than on intrusive social engineering by government (which awaited the twentieth century), as in Hugh Blair's letter to Smith dated April 3, 1776: "You have done great service to the world by overturning all the interested sophistry of merchants, with which they have confounded the whole subject of commerce"[4] The "clamor and sophistry of merchants and manufacturers," declared Smith, "easily persuaded [the rest of society] that the private interest of a part, and a subordinate part of the society, is the greatest interest of the whole."[5]

So it has been with protectionism, whether aristocratic or bourgeois or proletarian, down to the present. Denis (or Dionysius) Papin (1647–ca. 1712) improved in 1688 on the Dutchman Christiaan Huygens's notion of a steam engine—"The steam cylinders," he pointed out, "could be used for a great variety of purposes"—and is supposed to have built in 1707, a century before Robert Fulton, a side-paddle steamboat (there is some doubt that he in fact did, but he had acquired the theory decades earlier and had certainly acquired at the time some sort of boat that was threatening to vested interests). Leibniz was impressed, and supported Papin's application to the Elector for permission to steam down the River Weser to Bremen. Permission was denied. The Elector himself may have encouraged the riverboat men to attack and destroy the boat, which they did. Papin escaped with his life to England. An American professor who read the correspondence between Papin and Leibniz wrote indignantly in an 1877 number of *Scientific American* that

Papin "was persecuted on account of the injury that ignorant and jealous people believed his inventions would inflict in the industries of the country."[6] In America in 1877, with some startling exceptions such as in the Jim Crow laws about to be implemented, the ignorant and jealous people did not, in the economy, have the upper hand.

Such protecting of existing interests from creative destruction was anciently usual. William Lee's stocking frame had been denied a patent by Queen Elizabeth and then again by James I on the grounds that it would injure the industry of hand knitting. (In the event perhaps the lack of a patent was for the better, compared, say, with Watt's fierce monopoly on the steam engine a century and a half later, or Edison's monopolizing three centuries on. Knitting by machine in fact spread in the guild-weak lands of England, and eventually even in guild-clotted France.) People in pre-Benthamite Europe saw the state as merely an instrument of the interests, nothing like a disinterested body, and certainly not an instrument of progress. When it attempted to be an instrument of progress, as in the case of the chronically meddling French state, it often chose wrongly, driven by mistaken theories and monopoly interests.

And so the more modern notion of the state versus monopoly (a notion devised in the late nineteenth century by what the legal historian Herbert Hovencamp has called the first law-and-economics movement) was in 1776 viewed as a category error.[7] The notion that the Hanoverian state could be a "countervailing power" to monopoly would have struck an eighteenth-century Scot as hilarious. After all, as Smith repeatedly emphasized in his book about interests, the state had created the monopolies in the first place. The state since then has not become less skilled at favoring one group of its citizens over another. The bourgeois mercantilism of which Smith complained thrives still in appeals to buy American or to protect gigantic farms in North Dakota raising beet sugar or in the hundreds of occupations protected by state-issued licenses.

Adam Smith, then, knew the interests well, spending the last third of his book of 1776 railing against them. But he knew the other truth too, the force of raillery, and knew that the clerisy can have a historical role for good or evil independent of the interests of a sector or a social group. Repeatedly private interests since then have attempted to reimpose mercantilism, using their influence on the state to extend under the Mickey Mouse Protection Act in 1998 the term of copyright from the life of the creator plus fifty years to life plus seventy years, a transfer from present consumers to distant and now rich and idle heirs of a long-dead Walt Disney, at the cost of the efficient use of images and songs in the present. Myriad Genetics patented in the mid-1990s the naturally occurring *BRCA1* and *BRCA2* genes, which signal a high probability of breast cancer, and in the United States has been able to prosecute researchers and companies trying to find betterments. William Murdock's anticipation of the railway locomotive in the early 1780s was killed off by Boulton and Watt's taking out a competitive patent on the same idea, digging into their deep pockets and then not using or licensing the idea.[8]

Yet in the Bourgeois Era even a person with bags of gold could not as often as he could in olden times delay a betterment. Robert Fulton (1765–1815) in the early 1810s got the New York state legislature to grant him a monopoly on all steam navigation in the state, and then extended his success to the entire trans-Appalachian west by corrupting the legislature of the New Orleans Territory—then as now no difficult feat. By 1817, however, the federal courts had broken the monopolies, owned by Fulton's heirs, as violations of the Constitution: only Congress, they said, could grant interstate monopolies.[9] So we must, as Smith said, and did, marshal our rhetoric against "the clamorous importunity of partial interest."[10] Indeed. Down with corporate welfare! Overcome the Congress-corrupting of the Walt Disney Corporation and Myriad Genetics! Prevent monopolies from using "regulation" and "consumer safety" and "rewards for research" as tools to block entry! Don't be fooled! *Aux presses d'imprimerie, citoyens!*

Yet in modern times the bigger danger than corruption by the bourgeoisie itself, real though the danger is, has been the reimposition of neo-aristocratic or neo-Christian notions of the proper place of business, expressed as nationalism or socialism, imperialism or racism. Such notions have in the twentieth century caused massive slaughters of people, massive violations of liberty, and massive impoverishments of the survivors: Mussolini, Lenin, Stalin, Hitler, Franco, Tojo, Mao, Castro, Ho Chi Minh, Pol Pot, Nkrumah, King Saud, Saddam Hussein, Kim-Jong-un—a dreary record. Corporate welfare and the patent and copyright system, by contrast, has so far merely given a few well-placed people seven houses. Irritating. Worthy of indignation. Well worth watching for its capacity in an era of international enforcement of the illiberal idea of "intellectual property" to close down betterment. Yet modern mercantilism has not been mass-murderous the way thoroughly nationalist and socialist or merely thuggish régimes have been. By comparison with compelled loyalty to the state, backed by police and soldiers, the nasty international corporation in the social imaginary of the left looks amateurish in its pursuit of more voluntary customers for its steam engines and steamboats, hamburgers and athletic shoes.

Wise up, said Smith in *The Wealth of Nations*. Get prudent nationally to offset the private interests of a subordinate part of the society. In 1600 no one in England, and still less in the decidedly unbourgeois Scotland of Mary or of her son James VI, or even in 1660 under her great-grandson Charles II, would have thought to write a two-volume *Inquiry into the Nature and Causes of the Wealth of Nations*, treating a nation as a prudent project for the self-betterment of a bourgeois society and especially of the poorest members of it. (Yet in 1662 Pieter de la Court wrote *Interest van Holland*, a best seller defending the free-trade policies and the republican government of the United Provinces. The Dutch were first.) By the eighteenth century the rhetorical ground in Europe had shifted, and Smith encamped on the new ground. The new bourgeois society that Smith theorized was pragmatic, prudent, non-utopian, and wary of both state power and monopolies—that is, it was Dutch and Scottish rather than French and German in its Enlightenment. It knew, as Louis Dupré put it, "what Voltaire knew," and what his French descendants often forgot, "how little reason directs human conduct."[11] (Yet Voltaire, despite his admiration for England, regarded China as the ideal, with reason-directed mandarins running the country—a characteristically French notion, one which already by Voltaire's time under the Bourbons had a long history.)

Even the more prudence-oriented of Smith's two books is not about prudence only. *The Wealth of Nations* waxes sympathetic for the natural right to dispose of one's labor, for example, beyond considerations of the prudent, income-raising effect of such a policy, and waxes wroth against the corruptions Smith attributes to "the commercial system" of protectionism. Prudence and justice, policy and indignation, together, fuel Smith's attack on laws prohibiting manufacturers from selling at retail and prohibiting farmers from selling to remote middlemen in the grain trade. "Both laws were evident violations of natural liberty, and therefore unjust; and they were both, too, as impolitic [that is, as imprudent] as they were unjust."[12]

Smith was particularly indignant about restrictions on a worker's right to use his labor as he saw fit. The English (not Scottish) Settlement and Removal Acts, which he understood as attempting to prevent poor people from overwhelming local systems of relief, would force the poor back to the parishes of their birth—literally removing and resettling them, cleansing by social class. There is doubt whether it actually happened on a large scale. But never mind: Smith's indignation at the trespass on a poor man's liberty was aroused. "To remove a man who has committed no misdemeanor from the parish where he chooses to reside is an evident violation of natural liberty and justice. . . . There is scarce a poor man in England of forty years of age, I will venture to say, who has not in some part of his life felt himself most cruelly oppressed by this ill-contrived law."[13] China nowadays has the same illiberal system. Compare the illiberal laws against illegal aliens working in the fields of Georgia or in the nursery schools of New York.

"The property which every man has in his own labor," Smith wrote, "as it is the original foundation of all other property [as Locke had said in 1689], so it is the most sacred and inviolable. The patrimony of a poor man lies in the strength and dexterity of his hands; and to hinder him from employing this . . . in what manner he thinks proper without injury to his neighbor, is a plain violation of this most sacred property."[14] Compare regulation of freely arrived-at deals in employment in order to protect trade unionists against non-unionists—by the minimum wage, for example (as against the better plan of the earned income tax credit). The word "sacred," note, is used by this unenthusiastic Christian twice in successive sentences. In view of such fervent egalitarianism, it is little wonder that Smith has recently been claimed by the political left.

Even in his book about prudence, in other words, as has been argued for some time by the philosopher Samuel Fleischacker (who is prominent among those claiming Smith for the left), Smith recommends for a commercial society an ethical engagement well beyond prudence only.[15] Smith is not Mandeville, nor Jeremy Bentham, nor Judge Richard Posner. Justice and temperance, with a bit of love and courage, must figure too. But as in Austen, or as in Johnson when not caught in the common enthusiasm for splendid renown, the virtues are not heroic or saintly. The political scientist Christopher Berry argues:

Whereas the premodern view sees a threat to virtue and liberty in the boundless uncontrollability of human bodily desires, modern, Smithian liberalism accommodates those desires. Virtue is largely domesticated or privatized. . . . Understood in this manner neither virtue nor liberty calls for superhuman qualities but are tasks in which every human partakes and for which every human is qualified [thus Smith's egalitarianism]. . . . They are less exclusive than the classical versions, which are, in comparison, elitist and sexist.[16]

It is how social teleology is brought into the virtues. The virtues are those of Hume's middling sort, not of titanic heroes—this against the view that "virtue" can only be attained by *hoi aristoi*, and that the rest of us should shut up and settle for getting along with our miserable, slavish lives. An economy and polity of middling people, with middling virtues, said Smith and Hume, will suffice.

Smith and his friends exhibited a bourgeois character, for example, in the plain style of calling each other "mister" rather than "doctor," as in Dr. Smith.[17] (Smith's LL.D. was honorary, conferred conventionally by the University of Glasgow during his professorship there.) Smith was inclined to "offices of secret charity," a most bourgeois inclination.[18] The Duke of Buccleuch, in whose entourage Smith traveled the Continent 1764–1766, admired him for "every *private* virtue," the sort of virtues an aristocrat would think well suited to a bourgeois.[19] On eighteenth-century suppositions, the public virtues—that is, the political virtues—were to be exercised mainly by aristocrats.

Of the seven principal virtues of classical and Christian theory, Adam Smith paid particular attention to three. His three books—two published and one intended—match the three. Prudence is the chief, if nothing like the only, virtue considered in *The Wealth of Nations*. Temperance is the chief, if again not the only, virtue considered in *The Theory of Moral Sentiments*. And justice was to be considered in a projected *Treatise on Jurisprudence*, the shape of which we can imagine from elaborate notes by Smith's students in courses given from his chair of Moral Philosophy in 1762–1763 and 1766.

Smith was using a model of social behavior something like that shown in figure 3.[20] As also in Aristotle and Kant, the Smithian model is distinguished from the model of the early Hume/Bentham/modern economist by the presence of, beyond animal passions, a second and a third motivating principle. They are socially enforced ethics (justice, command of others) and

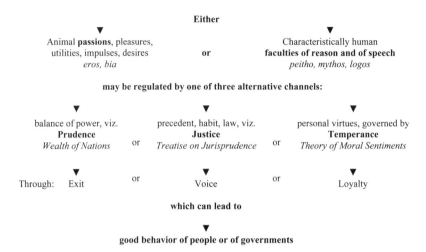

Either

▼

Animal **passions**, pleasures,
utilities, impulses, desires
eros, bia

or

Characteristically human
faculties of reason and of speech
peitho, mythos, logos

may be regulated by one of three alternative channels:

▼   ▼   ▼

balance of power, viz.   precedent, habit, law, viz.   personal virtues, governed by
Prudence   **Justice**   **Temperance**
Wealth of Nations   or   *Treatise on Jurisprudence*   or   *Theory of Moral Sentiments*

▼   ▼   ▼

Through: Exit   or   Voice   or   Loyalty

which can lead to

▼

good behavior of people or of governments

FIGURE 3. The Platonic/Smithian/Hirschmanian social model.

individual conscience (temperance, or what Smith more often called "self-command"). As within a single person, so within a *polis*, as Plato had argued at length in *The Republic*. There are no other ways than the three virtues of prudence, justice, and temperance, the model claims, by which passions in a *polis* may be satisfactorily translated into behavior.

Albert Hirschman famously characterized a similar choice as "exit, voice, and loyalty," distributed as in the figure. If you dislike, for example, the latest proposal for an optional American war you can take one of three routes. You can exit the political community, washing your hands of the matter and moving to Vancouver. Or you can exercise your voice before the courthouse and in the newspaper and at the polls, to change the policy. Or you can retreat to the quietism of personal virtue, tempering your dislike, seeing merit in the policy, staying loyal to the *polis* or the party. The Platonic-Smithian model here is of the same genre as Hirschman's, and makes the same point. It is this: that exit, or prudence, is not the only option that social science should consider in understanding how the passions are controlled.

Both models are contrary to the Marxians and Samuelsonians among economists, who spurn voice and loyalty, justice and temperance, in favor of prudence only. That is to say, the passions are not the only motivators of humans. Unlike cats and grass, which are also prudent, humans are open to reason and rhetoric.[21] If not, it would have been pointless for Smith to write at length about the foolishness of mercantilism or empire, as for Hirschman in his youth to write against the World Bank's policy for Latin America. The balance of power, that is, is not the only constraint on human passions.

"Realism" in foreign policy, for instance, asks that we think only of passions and then only in prudential terms. Be tough, it recommends, and "realistic." But it ignores the habits and laws of nations, a civic republicanism that can justify good behavior. And it treats with contempt the ethical channel and, worse, the rhetorical channel, calling it "preaching." The German-language writer Elias Canetti noted in his journal in 1943:

> There is nothing more unsophisticated [indeed, in the old, literal sense of the word] than the realism of cabinets and ministers, except for that of dictators, who regard themselves as even more realistic. In the struggle against frozen forms of faith, the Enlighteners have left one religion intact, the most preposterous of all, the religion of power. . . . In place of the dying religion of love, which it mocked with strength and wit [thus Nietzsche], . . . it announced: God is power; and whoever has it is his prophet.[22]

Thus, for example, the Chicago economist George Stigler (1911–1991), a fervent advocate of so-called rational models of politics, was opposed always to the premise of his friend and colleague Milton Friedman that people are open to reason, and that reasons therefore are worth giving. In the early 1970s at the University of Chicago I overheard Stigler and Friedman arguing amiably in the coffee room of the Social Science Building in just such terms. In effect they said:

FRIEDMAN. I am trying to persuade Americans to adopt free international trade.
STIGLER. Milton, you're such a preacher! Forget about persuasion. People follow
   their passions and their interests.
FRIEDMAN. I'm a teacher, George, and I believe in persuasion.
STIGLER. Less economist thou!

About 1990 I attended a little conference of rational-choice students of international relations held at the Center for Advanced Study in the Behavioral Sciences, that bastion of prudence-only social science. I was invited, I think, for my tough-guy [sic] reputation as an economic historian, though by then I had also been working on rhetoric for a decade. The organizers must have assumed that a Chicago School economist (such as I was and am, with amendments) would fall in with their talk-is-cheap, game-theoretic "realism." After listening for a day or so to one boyish claim after another that prudence-only sufficed I said, "But consider, guys, that nations speak to each other. Their talk has human meaning." Embarrassed silence.

The historian of economic thought Vivienne Brown notes in *Adam Smith's Discourse* (1994) that the talk of ethics in *The Wealth of Nations* is directed at the butcher and the baker and the politician in the ordinary business of their lives. Smith's talk there is of a "lower-order" ethics, she says, a matter of prudence only rather than of the great-souled practice of balanced virtues recommended in *The Theory of Moral Sentiments*.

But is Smith's discourse of morality ever really about lower-order prudence only? His ethical standard for the middle station is better shown than told, as in his first appearance in print, an unsigned memorial to a bourgeois friend, written in 1758, while at age thirty-five he was completing *The Theory of Moral Sentiments*:

> To the Memory of Mr. William Crauford,
>
> Merchant of Glasgow
>
> Who to that exact frugality, that downright probity and plainness of manners so suitable to his profession, joined a love of learning, . . . an openness of hand and a generosity of heart, . . . and a magnanimity that could support . . . the most torturing pains of body with an unalterable cheerfulness of temper, and without once interrupting, even to his last hour, the most manly and the most vigorous activity in a vast variety of business . . . candid and penetrating, circumspect and sincere.[23]

This is not an encomium to "profit regardless" or "I've got mine, Jack" or "prudence only." It praises bourgeois virtue. And bourgeois virtue, it suggests, is no oxymoron.

Glasgow in the 1750s and 1760s was a suitable place to launch a free-trade theory, says Dugald Stewart, Smith's younger contemporary and first biographer.[24] Smith was much acquainted with businessmen there. He recognized the desirability of developing an ethic of prudence and justice and temperance for a commercial age beyond the me-first ethic of mercantilism. And he stepped beyond traditional Christianity—though Smith, being what is now called a virtue ethicist, has in him a lot of St. Thomas Aquinas. And he stepped, too, beyond classical stoicism, which was another, if narrower, version of ancient virtue ethics.

Though there were eerie parallels in some Japanese thought at the time, it is hard to imagine Smith's writings outside of the eighteenth century in a commercial quarter of northwestern Europe. Smith shared with Kant and many others in the eighteenth century a willingness to philosophize without the hypothesis of God, raising the question of how to live a good life without God actively present. Both Smith and Kant answered, "by reason." But Kant's reason was a Platonic, absolute one, a closed aristocracy of proof. Vivienne Brown noted that Smith's reasoning about ethics was on the contrary dialogic and open. And I would add that his ethics was empirical, depending on a philosophical anthropology that Kant in his ethics would scorn. Smith's ethics, you could say, was Aristotelian and Aquinian, or social psychological, interested in how sacred and profane interact among actual denizens of this world, as against the ideal rational beings so charming to the Platonic and Ockhamite and Kantian thinkers.

Smith, for example, was obsessed, as Kant was not, with how language and its limits fit into a society of merchants, as against the older absolutes of saint or hero. Smith was a rhetorical theorist, explicitly and self-consciously. Smith's first job was teaching rhetoric to Scottish boys. He thought language was important even in an economy, and that it was not, as the game theorists nowadays suppose, merely cheap talk. The notion that ethical behavior should come out of an internal dialogue with a better self, named by Smith the impartial spectator, was natural to someone who believed language was foundational. The image is theatrical, of audience and player. The audience in a theater or the judge in a courtroom listen to the persuading talk. By contrast, Kant believed that a priestly and individual reason was foundational. Manfred Kuehn's biography argues that Kant modeled himself on an English merchant like the Scottish one Smith memorialized.[25] But Immanuel was no theorist of the chattering bourgeoisie. Adam was. "I will buy with you, sell with you, talk with you, walk with you, and so following."

20

SMITH WAS NOT A MR. MAX U, BUT RATHER THE LAST OF THE FORMER VIRTUE ETHICISTS

Smith, in other words, was mainly an ethical philosopher, directing his discourses of morality to readers placed in the middle station of life. The modern literature, from Knud Haakonssen (1981) through Charles Griswold (1999) and Samuel Fleischacker (2004, pp. xv, 48–54), says so, against the claim by the economists, believed for a long time (a belief embodied during the go-go 1980s in Adam Smith ties), that he was mainly an economist in the modern, prudence-only, anti-ethical sense. The taking of ethics out of Smith began immediately after his death, in a Britain reacting nervously to the French Revolution. To assure British authorities and British public opinion that the new political economy was not subversive, ethics was omitted. The historian of economic thought Emma Rothschild points out that the first generation of posthumous interpreters of Smith, such as Dugald Stewart and William Playfair, were at pains to prove that Smith was no friend of such Jacobin ideas as that workers should participate in politics.[1] A century and a half on, the Cold War inspired similar omissions, and it may be that during the American conquest of economics a fear of radicalism sustained the anti-ethical reading of Smith.

But another reason the economists' claim was accepted for so long, against decisive textual and biographical evidence, is that Smith practiced what for a long time after him was considered an *obsolete* sort of ethical philosophy, "virtue ethics." Mysteriously, virtue ethics evaporated from academic circles after the sixth and final, substantially revised edition of *The Theory of Moral Sentiments* (1759, 1790), which appeared to be Smith's own favorite of his two books. Since 1790, as though keyed to Smith's year of death, most ethical theory as practiced in departments of philosophy has derived instead from two other books published about the same time, one by Immanuel Kant (1785, down to, for example, Harry Frankfurt 2004) and the other by Jeremy Bentham (1789, down to, for example, Peter Singer 1993). A third and older tradition of natural rights, which influenced Smith too, by way of Locke and Pufendorf, finds favor nowadays among conservative and Catholic intellectuals.[2] And the contractarian theories of Rousseau, Locke, and Hobbes, to which Smith paid no favorable attention, have provided in our time a fourth, related, stream of narrow ethics paired with grand political theory, left or right.[3] But the fifth and by far the oldest and broadest stream is the virtue-ethical one. It flowed from Plato and especially from Aristotle in his *Nicomachean Ethics* (ca. 330 BC), with parallel streams in other cultures such as Chinese and Indian, meandered through the Stoics, mapped by Cicero (44 BC), and channeled into Christianity by Aquinas (ca. 1269–1272). After its submersion in 1790, it reemerged only in 1958.[4]

After Bentham, however, and especially after the anti-ethical turn in twentieth-century economics associated with Pigou, Robbins, Samuelson, and Friedman, most economists have interpreted Smith's praise of the virtue of prudence to mean what the economists meant by virtue, that is: you do uncontroversial good only by doing well. As the economist Frank Knight wrote in 1923, "The nineteenth-century utilitarianism was in essence merely the ethics of power, 'glorified economics.' . . . Its outcome was to reduce virtue to prudence."[5] Remember Canetti's strictures on the preposterous religion of power. Canetti remarked in 1963 that "all thinkers who begin with human wickedness [one version of prudence only] are characterized by enormous persuasiveness. . . . They look at reality point-blank and never fear calling it by its name. One does not notice until later that it is never total reality."[6] The realistic pessimism of Machiavelli, Hobbes, Mandeville, de Maistre, Giacomo Leopardi, Pablo Picasso, or T. S. Eliot before he found Christianity strikes people at first as discerning, and all you need to know. As Leopardi put it in the opening axiom of his posthumous *Pensieri*, "I say that the world is a league of scoundrels against men of good will," and then went on to make a pretty good case for its truth.[7]

The turn in economics toward prudence only was renamed in the 1930s the "new welfare economics," which attempted to build judgments about the economy on the supposition that virtue consists in prudence, with a special form of justice defined as a utility function for choosing among distributions of happiness among people. If all people are benefited, or could be benefited, the proposed policy is good. That is all ye know of ethics. Smith did praise prudence as a virtue, especially in his book about prudence. For example: "What is prudence in the conduct of every private family can scarce be folly in that of a great kingdom."[8] But in his other published book one can find hundreds of pages in praise also of other virtues, especially temperance or, in the unpublished *Lectures on Jurisprudence*, justice. And even in the *Wealth of Nations*, I have noted, unless one is precommitted to seeing its implied hero as merely a confused precursor to Karl Marx's Mister Money Bags or Paul Samuelson's Max U, one can find a good deal of ethical judgment more grown-up than "prudence suffices" or "greed is good."[9]

"Max U," remember, is a little joke, referring to the *Max*imization of *U*tility under Constraints that Samuelson laid down as the monopolistic principle of modeling in economics in his modestly entitled PhD dissertation and then book, *Foundations of Economic Analysis* (1947). Max (such a man, I venture to say, would be more sensible if he became Maxine) is literally a sociopath, reducing every experience to his own pleasure. He views everyone else as a vending machine. You put your money in and you get your pleasure out. In many parts of the economy, Max U has merits as a premise of behavior. If you are dealing with covered-interest arbitrage on the foreign exchange market you would be unwise to attribute much more than Max U to its participants. They will not be motivated by, say, love. They are motivated by the virtue of prudence, only.

But the economist's great love for the hypothesis that no one is motivated by, say, love reduces all virtues to vice, in particular the vice of pride, which is, to speak in theological terms, idolatry, the worship of self, Max U. In chapter 10 of his *Introduction to the Principles of Morals and Legislation*, Jeremy Bentham attempts just that, as Mandeville and Hobbes and Machiavelli had earlier. The "individualism" that so many observers think admirable about the modern world can be corrupted into Max U. It is possible to doubt that there was a "rise of individualism" in Europe independent of the Revaluation of the bourgeoisie—which is one other reason I doubt that the Renaissance, with its supposed birth of the individual, was crucial to the Great Enrichment.[10] Individualist Max U is ancient. Thus Gurcharan Das shows that the eldest of the Kauruvas in the *Mahabharata*, Duryodhana, is a slave to the vice of envy about his cousin Yudhishthira. The envy could be represented easily in individualistic, Max U form as "Duryodhana's utility is a function of the worldly consumption of Duryodhana minus that of Yudhishthira."[11]

Some economists, from Thorstein Veblen through Fred Hirsch (1977) down to Robert Frank (2005), have argued that "positional goods" are prevalent, making for an arms race in consumption that we must suppress by government action. But it seems dubious that social position bulks so large as a motive for consumption as to justify such use of violence-backed regulation. The professor claiming its large bulk would probably not apply it to much of his own consumption, such as to the lovely *pied-à-terre* he has in Manhattan. And the theorists of positional goods have not on the whole done the empirical science to show that envy matters for the economy as a whole. Frank asserts that "models that incorporate concerns about relative position predict an equilibrium with too much expenditure on positional goods, too little on non-positional goods."[12] Note the word "predict" and the promise, not fulfilled, of measurement in the phrase "too much." Frank offers some on/off "predictions" that, for example, imply too-large houses built. But he does not show that the too-large houses are not, say, a result of deductions in the tax system, and especially he does not show that the effect itself is large enough to justify massive intervention in personal choice.

And anyway to indulge envy by restricting your neighbor's consumption is to encourage a vice. Frank admits that "society does indeed have a legitimate interest in discouraging envy."[13] All vices are errors of seeking things of this world, which in Christian or Buddhist thought are precisely illusory. To pursue such things for their prudent utility is a fool's errand. "The human tendency to evaluate one's well-being by comparing it with that of another," Das writes, "is the cause of Duryodhana's distress."[14] Putting the other's well-being into one's utility function with a negative sign is not the solution. It's the problem. And so also is the indulging of envy, another form of me-first-ism, in socialist opposition to the Bourgeois Deal.

By contrast, a courageous man does not charge for the enemy's guns only for utility but for the very sake of being courageous. A loving woman does not love her husband only because he is amusing or is able to open tight lids on jars. She loves him for himself alone, and not his yellow hair. The virtues other than prudence—courage, love, justice, temperance, faith, and hope—are virtues, and not merely another way of getting prudent pleasure. They cannot be stuck into a utility function in the sociopathic or Benthamite way of Max U. They are in themselves separate, nonfungible virtues in a flourishing human life—a *human* life, not the life of a maximizing rat.

One way, therefore, to avoid vice is to turn away from the world, in the style of ascetics in all ages, from the Hindu sages in the forest to the Roman stoics, the desert fathers, and Julian of Norwich. It lays a cross on utility. But Gurcharan Das, the Dalai Lama, and Deirdre McCloskey would recommend instead, or also, that one stay engaged in the world, seeking an ethical version of the *vita activa*.[15] Such a course of life means thinking of prudence as a virtue but balancing it with the other, nonfungible virtues in a flourishing and truly human life. The hero of the *Mahabharata*, the virtuous if flawed Yudhishthira, is asked by the mother of the Pandavas, "Why be good?" He replies, "Were *dharma* ['virtue,' among other meanings] to be fruitless . . . [people] would live like cattle."[16] Precisely. His reply is exactly paralleled by Cicero lambasting the Epicureans—the ancient Mediterranean's version of Max U economists—as "those men who in the manner of cattle [*pecudum ritu*, literally, 'by the cattle's rite'] refer everything to pleasure" and who "with even less humanity . . . say that friendships are to be sought for protection and aid, not for caring."[17] Cicero is here referring to Aristotle's three sorts of friendship (*philia*)—friendship for profit, for pleasure, and, the highest and best, *agape*, for the friend's own sake.[18] Mammals and birds, who take care of their young, exhibit love (even crocodiles appear to). Mammals, and especially apes like us, have an array of emotional responses to distress in others, even in other species (a gorilla saving a little bird, for example), in a manner that Darwin understood but many others have long denied.[19] Yet the more elaborate forms of spiritual love and abstract justice and national courage seem nonetheless exclusively human. People could live lives of prudence only, the lives of prudentially evolved snakes or cattle. They would be without love, temperance, justice, courage, faith, and hope. And they would not be human.

Smith's system of the virtues of prudence, temperance, justice, courage, and human love, did not simply drop into his head one day while strolling along Canonsgate. He was using the ethical tradition of the West. From about 500 BCE to about 1790 CE, the ethical universe was described in Europe as composed of the seven principal virtues, resulting by recombination in hundreds of minor and particular virtues. The seven are a jury-rigged combination of the four "pagan" or "cardinal" virtues (courage, temperance, justice,

FIGURE 4. The seven principal virtues.

and prudence) and the three "Christian" or "theological" virtues (faith, hope, and love).

Jury-rigged or not, they are a pretty good philosophical psychology. The tensions among the seven, and their complementarities, too, can be expressed in a diagram (figure 4).

Minor if admirable virtues such as geniality or piety or patriotism can be described as combinations of the principal seven. A vice results from a notable lack of one or more of them. The seven are primary colors. They cannot be derived from each other, just as blue cannot be derived from red.

Contrary to various attempts since Hobbes to do so, justice cannot be derived from prudence only.[20] The other, minor colors can be derived from
the primaries. You can't derive red from maroon and purple, but blue plus
red does make purple. Blue plus yellow does make green. The Romantic and
bourgeois virtue of honesty, for example, is justice plus temperance in matters of speech, with a dash of courage and a teaspoon of faithfulness.

Aquinas was the master of such analyses of virtues and vices. He provides
scores of examples in showing that the seven are principal. "The cardinal
virtues," he declares, "are called more principal, not because they are more
perfect than all the other virtues, but because human life more principally
turns on them and the other virtues are based on them."[21] Courage plus prudence yields enterprise (a virtue not much admired by Smith, who recommended instead safe investments in agriculture).[22] Temperance plus justice
yields humility, prominent in Smith's theorizing, and underlying, in his own
character, as Fleischacker, Levy, and Peart argue, his principled modesty in
social engineering.[23] Temperance plus prudence yields thrift, which Smith
came to believe, erroneously, was the spring of economic growth.[24]

Notice the dimensions of the diagram, going from an ethical object of
the self at the profane bottom through an ethical object of other people in
the social middle up to an ethical object of a sacred transcendent, such as Art
or the White Sox or the Virgin Mary. Ethical philosophy since the sudden
decline of virtue ethics late in the eighteenth century has focused on the
middle, as though ethics consists entirely in how we treat other people. But
it consists also in how we treat ourselves and our sacred purposes. The sociologist Georg Simmel, whom I've commended for his economic insight, had
ethical insight too: in 1907 he described compliance with religious commandments as arising from either "egotistical reasons" (the profane at the bottom), "an altruistic nature" (the social middle), or "the objective relation
between God and ourselves" (the sacred).[25] The very word "ethics" is from
the early Greek for "character," on all three levels. In theorizing since 1790
in the West two of the three levels get neglected, resulting in an unbalanced
focus on one of the virtues, such as prudence only or love abiding, alone.
The virtue-ethical thought is an old one, at least as old as the notion that we
are God's creatures, and therefore owe to ourselves integrity and owe to Him
(or Her) worship.

The diagram also has a left side and a right, ranging from the virtues of
autonomy (Greek for "self-rule"), such as courage, to those of connection

(Latin for "bind together"), such as love, and the dozens of nonprincipal virtues formed by combining the principal virtues on the left or middle or right, such as ingenuity or thrift or solidarity. In song and in story the one side is masculine, the other feminine, but only in song and in story. Women practice courage, after all, and men love.

From the seven principal virtues, I say, Adam Smith chose to admire especially for his moralizing of the bourgeois life four and a half. He chose the four pagan and Stoic virtues of courage, temperance, justice, and prudence. To these he added, as the half, a part of the Christian virtue of love, the part that his tradition—such as that of his teacher at Edinburgh, Francis Hutcheson—called, against Mandeville and in favor of Shaftesbury, "benevolence." In expositing Plato's system, for example, Smith enumerates the pagan four, "the essential virtue of prudence," the "noble" virtue of courage, "a word [*sophrosune*] which we commonly translate temperance," and "justice, the last and greatest of the four cardinal virtues."[26] In expositing Stoicism he repeats the four, also with approval, speaking of virtue as "wise [that is, practically prudent: Greek *phronesis*], just, firm [that is, courageous], and temperate conduct."[27]

And then he speaks of benevolence toward people, the secular half of a whole (the whole of love would have included a love for the transcendent, which Smith sidesteps). "Concern for our own happiness recommends us to the virtue of prudence; concern for that of other people, the virtues of justice and beneficence," "the first . . . originally recommended by our selfish, the other two by our benevolent affections."[28] *Bene-volent*, "well-wishing," is what we expect from the good person who attends to the middle level in the diagram. An impartial spectator develops within the breast, which "in the evening . . . often makes us blush inwardly both for our . . . inattention to our own happiness [prudence, temperance, and parts of courage], and for our still greater indifference and inattention, perhaps, to that of other people [justice, the other part of courage, and secular love]."[29] Think of regret for the pizza gobbled, or the insult half unintentionally given.

Notice in Smith the hint of explicitness in dividing virtues into feminine and masculine: "The man who, to all the soft, the amiable, and the gentle virtues, joins all the great, the awful, and the respectable, must surely be the natural and proper object of our highest love and admiration."[30] We admire such a man's virtues as both Christian and Stoic, peasantly and aristocratic, feminine and masculine, private and public. In *The Theory of Moral Sentiments* Smith asserts, "Our sensibility to the feelings of others, so far from being inconsistent with the manhood of self-command [that is, temperance], is the very principle upon which that manhood is founded."[31] Manhood. The combination is not altogether convincing. But you could take a feminist view of Smith.

Smith particularly admired what Hume had called the "artificial" virtues, the three on which any society must rest, namely, temperance, prudence, and justice. His admiration shows, I have noted, in his life plan to write a great, thick book about each. The other two virtues of the Smithian five were courage in, say, enterprise and secular love in, say, family arrangements. The two stood apart from Smith's central concerns for the artificial three essential to public life in a modestly progressing commercial society. Smith detested buccaneer commerce, with its overemphasis on manly but imprudent courage. And as feminist students of the matter have noted, he did not put a great deal of emphasis on family love. Although he expected to get the materials for his dinner from the regard to their self-interest of the butcher, the brewer, or the baker, he neglected to observe that he expected it, too, from the love of his mother Mrs. Smith in arranging to cook it.

THAT IS, HE WAS NO REDUCTIONIST,
ECONOMISTIC OR OTHERWISE

The alternative and novel systems of prudence-only, or love-only, or anything-else-only, as Smith argued at length, did not work well. Narrowing a theory of ethics down to merely one of the seven virtues—the modern economist specializing in selfish prudence, for example, the modern theologian in transcendent love—does not do the ethical job. I have noted that Smith in *The Theory of Moral Sentiments* declares himself on the issue early, indeed in the first clause of the book—"How selfish soever man may be supposed"—then proceeds to show in the next 330 pages that a specialized selfish account, identical to the one nowadays so popular among economists and evolutionary psychologists, does not suffice.

On the fifth page he again attacks prudence only: "Those who are fond of deducing all our sentiments from certain refinements of self-love think themselves at no loss to account" for sympathy. The supposed egoist rejoices in expressions of approval of his projects, and is downcast by expressions of disapproval. "But both the pleasure and the pain are always felt so instantaneously, and often upon such frivolous occasions [for example, in a theater, as he later notes, or in an account from a remote history, or when the child is about to fall down a well], that it seems evident that neither of them can be derived from any such self-interested consideration."[1] And so Smith argues throughout, against ethical reduction.

A man following propriety exhibits in a temperate way all the principal virtues. That is, he shows a balance of them, or selects the subset appropriate to the occasion. The Third Earl of Shaftesbury had in 1699 and later editions of his book inveighed against the one-virtue systems of, say, Hobbes and

Mandeville: "Whoever is in the least versed in this moral kind of architecture will find the inward fabric so adjusted . . . that the barely extending of a single passion too far or the continuance . . . of it too long, is able to bring irrecoverable ruin and misery."[2] (Had he lived to 116 years of age, Shaftesbury would also have inveighed against the one-virtue systems of Kant and Bentham, and he would have been driven to distraction by the one-virtue analyses of their modern followers, such as most analytic philosophers and almost all Samuelsonian economists.) Balancing of the virtues is not cloistered, but takes place in the practice of the *vita activa*. Sunday mornings in church, as the Dutch economist and social theorist Arjo Klamer puts it, the virtuous person exercises chiefly the virtue of spiritual love, Saturday nights on the dance floor the virtue of self-asserting courage, and Mondays through Fridays at her job in the bank the virtue of thoughtful prudence.[3]

Virtue ethics was revived after Elizabeth Anscombe's 1958 essay "Modern Moral Philosophy." The revival has been led notably by English-speaking, female analytic philosophers, such as, today, Julia Annas of the University of Arizona. Ethics is the largest part of analytic philosophy having a feminine voice, a voice heard more and more since the 1950s, though still in less volume than the masculine. (In such a history Alasdair MacIntyre counts as an honorary woman.) The revival has directed attention to the desirability of talking about a set of virtues directly, rather than talking in Enlightenment style only of an allegedly universal, and singular, maxim. "It would be a great betterment," wrote Anscombe, "if, instead of 'morally wrong,' one always named a genus such as 'untruthful,' 'unchaste,' 'unjust.'"[4]

But where do you stop in listing the virtues of truthfulness, chastity, justice, and the like? A list of 170 virtues would be so detailed as to be useless. Some virtue ethicists after 1958 appear to have had no definite list in mind, or an unhelpfully long one. An instance is the inchoate listing of capabilities proposed by my friendly acquaintances Amartya Sen and Martha Nussbaum. They deserve full marks for pushing the discussion in the right direction, away from snappy utilitarianism, Max U, prudence only. Yet one wishes they had a more coherent list.

Modern ethical philosophy has indeed two opposite faults of quantity. The one is to let virtues proliferate, leaving us to struggle with the 170 words for "virtues" in the main headings of "Class Eight: Affections" in *Roget's Thesaurus* (edition of 1962). The list recalls the 613 commandments of orthodox Judaism, as counted by Rabbi Hillel (d. 10 CE), but is less coherent. Kant and Bentham (and, indeed, the Talmud) imposed a healthy discipline on such aimless proliferation. But Kant and Bentham veered toward the other fault of quantity, which Shaftesbury had anticipated: acknowledging too *few* virtues to fit the stories of our lives—narrowing an ethical system down to, for example, one virtue only, the Good, or the categorical imperative, or the greatest utility. The reductive impulse is to choose one of the seven, such as prudence or love or justice, to stand for all.

The point is worth stressing here because Smith's definite four and a half virtues, and his emphasis on their joint cultivation by the impartial spectator, puts him solidly in the older tradition of virtue ethics, which worked hard to refine a limited, but not too limited, list. Smith's four and a half out of the seven classical virtues are counted from the bottom of the virtues diagram, noting again that Smith's secular love leaves off love's transcendent half. Smith's good plan is to stop, as Epictetus or Aquinas did, with a moderate yet comprehensive list of principal virtues. With Aquinas's seven, which align pretty well with the actual psychological characteristics of human beings, you know better what you are talking about than with Max U's one. Aquinas's seven, or Smith's four and a half, constitute a mean, perhaps even a golden one, between $N = 1$ and $N = 170$, or 613.

As a virtue ethicist Smith disliked reductions. "By running up all the different virtues . . . to this one species of propriety [namely, 'the most real prudence'], Epicurus indulged a propensity," he noted, "which philosophers . . . are apt to cultivate with a peculiar fondness, as the great means of displaying their ingenuity . . . to account for all appearances from as few principles as possible."[5] It is Ockham's Razor, with which so many male philosophers have cut themselves shaving. Parsimony, after all, is not the only intellectual virtue. In his very method, Smith recommended a balance of the virtues— historical relevance balanced with parsimony, justice in summarizing other philosophers balanced with hope to go beyond them. And therefore in substance he avoided the utilitarian pitfall—into which Hume gazed fondly and into which Bentham eagerly leapt, and in which Samuelsonian economists wallow happily—of reducing all other virtues to prudence only.

All right. Smith analyzes good and bad not as a specialized prudence or justice or temperance but as a proper balance among four and a half of the seven Aquinian virtues. We will not grasp his argument, or understand what bourgeois life actually is, if we insist on making it lie down on a Kantian or a utilitarian or even a Lockean-contractarian bed, as analytic philosophers amateur and professional have long tried to do.

But something is missing. In choosing his four and a half virtues Smith drops the two transcendent virtues of hope and faith, and also the transcendent, higher half of love, *agape*, which goes beyond a love for people or things here below. In the matter of love Smith stops (in the precise Greek) with *eros* or *philia*. There is no question that he realized what he was doing, for he knew perfectly well that hope and faith and *agape* were principal virtues in Christian thought. The classification would have been clear even in secondary descriptions of Scholastic thought—even if Smith did not have a direct understanding of St. Thomas Aquinas's role in the construct, not to speak of that of Thomas's teacher, St. Albert the Great. But if someone lacks "strengths that forge connections to the larger universe and provide meaning," in the words of the modern psychologists of happiness Christopher Peterson and Martin Seligman, she does not have a fully human life.[6] As the Anglican theologian Richard Hooker put it in 1593, "Man doth seek a triple perfection: first a sensual . . . then an intellectual. . . . Man doth not seem to rest satisfied . . . but doth further covet . . . somewhat divine and heavenly."[7]

The reasons Smith neglected the divine and heavenly hope, faith, and *agape* are not obscure. He shared with Enlightenment figures such as Hume and Voltaire an aversion to any alleged "virtue" that could be seen as conventionally religious. Hope and faith seemed to advanced thinkers in the eighteenth century to be horribly conventionally religious, and anyway dispensable. Let us build a new world free from religious superstition, they cried, free from the wars of sects, free from the meddling of priests and dominies. Let us dispense with the silliness of "faith" and "hope" and transcendent "love," and establish a new faith on the hope for transcendently lovable reason and propriety.

The Christianity that Smith opposed was the rigid Calvinism still influential in Scotland at the time, no longer ascendant but able (with some help from the benevolent Francis Hutcheson) to keep atheists such as Hume out of university chairs, and the Catholicism that could in France still warrant the conviction and torture to death of a Protestant, Jean Calas, alleged on slender evidence in 1762 to have murdered his suicidal son to prevent the son's conversion to the ruling Catholicism. The Protestant religious fanatics with whom Smith's Lowland Scotland had recently had experience, along with the Catholic traitors to the Hanoverian succession with whom High-land Scotland had flirted, impute "even to the great Judge of the universe . . . all their own prejudices. . . . Of all of the corrupters of moral sentiments . . . faction and fanaticism have always been by far the greatest."[8] Smith wanted, as did Hobbes, Locke, Vico, Hume, Kant, and Bentham, to bring ethics down to earth: "The most sublime speculation of the contemplative philosopher," Smith declared, "can scarce compensate the neglect of the smallest active duty." One can hear him including the theologian and any other advocate for the transcendent in that phrase "contemplative philosopher." Compare Hume's sneering at "divinity or school metaphysics" and the "monkish vir-tues." Thus Hobbes without God, Vico without God, Hume without God, Kant without God, Bentham without the slightest regard for God.

But sheer anticlericalism, fierce against the Knoxite dominies or the pa-pist priests, can't be the whole story. The philosopher Charles Taylor has argued persuasively for a shift around 1700 from an ethic of being to an ethic of acting.[9] The virtue of everyday "acting," which "gives our own produc-tive life order and dignity," is a matter of courage, temperance, justice, and above all prudence.[10] The virtue of sacred "being" is a matter instead of faith, hope, and transcendent love: *Quo vadis?* Where are you going? What's the point? Taylor argues that the Enlightenment, whether French or Scottish, adopted "a procedural conception of the right," reaching its highest expres-sion in Kant (and something like its lowest in Bentham). Smith was part of the procedural expression, leading to the liberal plan of live and let live. The sociologist Douglas Porpora, using Taylor, laments the world we have lost. We have sustained since 1700, he writes,

> a pervasive loss of emotionally moving contact with a good that is ultimate, a contact that was once provided by the sacred. . . . As a consequence, the whole of our lives is without any overarching moral purpose. . . . This hardly means that we are all immoral. It does mean that our sense of morality has become largely procedural.[11]

Later he summarizes Taylor as chronicling a modern "age in which everyday life is valorized, not on some higher plane of transcendental purpose"—not, that is, on the identity supplied by the theological virtues. Adam Smith's error was the error (but also the glory) of the Enlightenment, trying to lib-erate us from transcendence by sneering at it or, at best, silently setting it aside in favor of procedural maxims such as the impartial spectator or the categorical imperative or the greatest utility.

But hope and faith and transcendent love slip back into Smith, as into Kant and the rest of the liberals wary of a God term, though by a back door unobserved. The impartial spectator, or the Kantian or even the Benthamite equivalent, are not merely behavioral observations about how people develop ethically. They are recommendations. The very idea of a "recommendation" depends on faith and hope and transcendent love—articulated, for example, out of the faithful identity of an urbane resident of Edinburgh, politically hopeful for a rather better society, sweetly loving the imagined result. As Fleischacker notes, "When we ask after the 'nature' of human beings we are looking for what human beings 'really' want, beneath the surface trappings. . . . Human nature always includes what people aspire to, for Smith; it is never reduced [as in the economist's version of utilitarianism] to the desires they merely happen to have."[12]

And how, one may ask, was this faithful and loving hope, this aspiration to full humanity that no human can long deny, to be achieved in a commercial society? Answer: through admitting even in a commercial society the seven virtues—or Smith's four and a half, with hope and faith and transcendent love knocking at the back door.

AND HE FORMULATED THE
BOURGEOIS DEAL

Smith and the rest of the more optimistic of the economists 1700 to 1848 were busy providing a theory of innocent contributions to the well-being of the world arising from the genius of the natural merchant. They explained how the cooperation and the competition of people innocently getting money leads to the division of labor and the wealth of nations, at least to the modest degree that Scotland could imitate the contemporary paragon of bourgeois virtue, Holland. Smith was by no means appalled that in places like Holland or Scotland or England or Pennsylvania the people got money. A quarter century before Napoleon sneered at the "nation of shopkeepers," Smith declared that "to found a great empire for the sole purpose of raising up a people of customers may at first sight appear a project fit only for a nation of shopkeepers. It is, however, a project altogether unfit for a nation of shopkeepers; but extremely fit for a nation whose government is influenced by shopkeepers."[1] He was not sneering at commercial trades. He noted that "England, though in the present times it breeds men of great professional abilities in all different ways, great lawyers, great watch makers and clockmakers [and thus the instruments of the Industrial Revolution], etc., etc., seems to breed neither statesmen nor generals."[2] (Though true enough in 1776, the age of Lord North and Gentleman Johnny Burgoyne, the remark would a few decades later look strange, with Pitt, Nelson, and Wellington among the statesmen, admirals, and generals in charge.) On the contrary: "There are more natural parts and a stronger genius," he wrote, "requisite to make a good lawyer or physician"—and a merchant of Glasgow, surely—"than to make a great monarch."[3]

Yet Smith is concerned to avoid an ethics of what the market can bear, the worst of bourgeois behavior. He encompasses the paradox that a conscience—his impartial spectator—has a social origin yet can stand against the worst of society. "When we first come into the world," he writes, meaning into the social world, "we are accustomed to consider what behavior is likely to be agreeable to every person we converse with, to our parents, to our masters, to our companions."[4] It is an adolescent plan. Yet a mature person abandons "the impossible and absurd project of rendering ourselves universally agreeable."[5] "The weak, the vain and the frivolous, indeed, may be mortified by the most groundless censure or elated by the most absurd applause. Such persons are not accustomed to consult the judge within."[6] The man o' independent mind, / He looks and laughs at a' that.

In similar fashion St. Thomas spoke of a faculty of "synteresis" (Greek, "watching closely"; the Scholastics for some reason spelled it with a D, "synderesis"), the conscience, a third thing beyond nurture or nature, beyond upbringing or original sin. (We call original sin nowadays "genes," and congratulate ourselves for our lack of merely medieval theology.) Synteresis, or Confucian sprouts of character, or the germ of an impartial spectator, resolves with free will the nature/nurture paradox. An ignorant woman can by her good will be more virtuous than many a proud doctor. In some theologies emphasizing a free will, a virtuous pagan can enter Paradise. It is similar to the way the brain is supposed to work in modern theories. The brain is begun by biology but then becomes in part self-healing, self-directing, self-educating. Thus people born blind train their visual cortexes for substitute uses. Smith and St. Thomas take the sunny view that we can bend our will to virtue and can self-heal—this in contrast to the pessimistic line of St. Augustine, Martin Luther, John Calvin, Jonathan Edwards, and Stephen Pinker in articulating the betting odds that we are probably hopeless sinners lacking grace in the hands of an angry God. "Grace," says Aquinas to the contrary, "does not abolish nature; but perfects it."[7] You could use it as a motto in a paper on epigenetics.

Smith, then, is less a neo-Stoic, as he has often been called, than he is a secular follower of Aquinas, the urban monk making room for the active life. Stoicism is above all antibourgeois, even antisocial—proud and heroic and solipsistic. Its founder, Zeno, is an early example of a recurrent character in bourgeois culture, the antibourgeois son—Zeno's father appears to have been a Cypriot merchant. Zeno's follower, the slave Epictetus, advised, "Wish [events] to happen as they do happen; and you will go on well." It is the op-posite of the bourgeois's busyness, and the opposite of a prudence of cost versus benefit measured by what other people are willing to pay in a trade. "Whoever then would be free, let him wish nothing," Epictetus declares. "For this is yours, to act well the character assigned to you; to choose it, is another's."[8] His *Enchiridion* begins, "Of things, some are in our power, and some are not. In our power are opinion, pursuit, desire, aversion, and in one word, whatever are our own actions. Not in our power, are body, property, reputation, command, and, in one word, whatever are not our own actions."[9] Epictetus recommends that we deal only with those things "in our power," as he claims them to be.

Yet his list of things *not* in our power is precisely the list of things the bourgeois reckons *are* in his power—body, property, reputation, command. Epictetus articulates the ethic of an emperor or a slave, aristocrat or Christian, in a zero-sum and hierarchical society. You have a heroic character or an immortal soul, and especially you have a fixed place in society, given to you by the grace of the gods, or of God. Do well with your gift, but don't expect much. In aristocratic and peasant theory you do not make yourself and cannot advance in condition. Forget about trade-tested betterment. The so-called Law of Jante (*Janteloven*) in Scandinavia is just such a peasant sensibility (it comes from a Danish novel of 1933): do not think you are better than other people. No free will. What matters is your moral luck, your genes, your original sin, your fate. Above all never declare your honesty. The Law is a rule of temperance, against any excess, as in bragging, and contrasts with the rule of blowing your own horn in the United States. In Denmark there was an attempt to set up a web page on which honest businesses could sign up to declare their honesty. No one signed up, because to do so would violate *Janteloven*, showing paradoxically by pridefulness that they were *not* honest. Likewise, when an American politician prefaces a statement with "Frankly," watch out for nonfrankness to follow.

Smith's ethical theory, then, is not stoic in its theory of society. Furthermore, in a commendable sense it is deeply social. It does not recommend bowling alone. Metaphors of accounting were part of bourgeois education and had long been the metaphor of Protestant self-education, as in Robinson Crusoe's meditations. Smith wrote in his letter to Gilbert Elliot some months after the first publication of *The Theory of Moral Sentiments*, "Man is considered as a moral, because he is regarded as an accountable being.

But an accountable being, as the word expresses, is a being that must give an account of its actions to some other, and that, consequently, must regulate them according to the good liking of this other." Though the accountable being "is, no doubt, principally accountable to God [says Smith with his mild faith so far from the quarrelsome Calvinism of earlier Scotland], in the order of time, he must necessarily conceive of himself as accountable to his fellow creatures."[10] Said Rabbi Hillel, standing on one foot, "What is hateful to yourself, do not do to your fellow man. That is the whole Torah; the rest is commentary." The impartial spectator of the good person's imagination is a substitute for the Deity.

And then Smith makes a sweet and characteristically eighteenth-century argument for why "the author of nature has made man the immediate judge of mankind":

> If those infinite rewards and punishments . . . were perceived as distinctly as we foresee the frivolous and temporary retaliations which we may expect from one another, the weakness of human nature, astonished at the immensity of objects too little fitted to its comprehension, could no longer attend to the little affairs of this world; and it is absolutely impossible that the business of society could have been carried on.[11]

It is a thought derived from the natural theology and the bourgeois activity recently elevated—that business should take precedence over salvation, lest you improperly use one of God's creations, yourself, while praying on a pillar in the desert. Therefore God in his wisdom has arranged moral sentiments to make the little affairs of the world more convenient, and noncorrupting, *doux et sacré commerce.*

An ethical yet commercial society would inspirit its people in the uptake of betterments. It is plausibly said that Leonardo da Vinci's time was too early for, say, flying machines (though it is not quite true—medieval monks tried flying machines, though they walked with limps thereafter). Smith does not much emphasize technological betterment. In fact, as I have noted, he initiated the overemphasis on sheer capital accumulation, brick upon brick in Amsterdam, that has misled economists since. But sweet commerce, intellectual cooperation, and competition in trade, wrote the economist Friedrich Hayek in 1979, "is as much a method for breeding certain types of mind as anything else: the very cast of thinking of the great entrepreneurs would not exist but for the environment in which they develop their gifts."[12] Imagine Bill Gates stuck in Shakespearean England. Smith did at least respect merchants and manufacturers, recommending a society in which their (modest, Holland-imitating) betterments could flourish. Being an egalitarian, he believed, in Hayek's words, that "the same innate capacity to think will take a wholly different turn according to the task it is set," that of being the philosopher or the street porter, a courtier or an improver.[13]

What of it?

This: Smith had two invisible hands, two outcomes of (in his uncharacteristically clumsy phrase) "the obvious and simple system of natural liberty."[14] One was the invisible hand of the marketplace, whose effects are occasionally noted in *The Wealth of Nations*. For example, to mention Smith's most original economic contribution, the marketplace in labor equalizes the wage-plus-conditions in Scotland with those in England, within social and legal limits, because people move from one place to the other until it is so, as though directed by an invisible hand. Likewise the invisible hand gently pushes people out of their solipsistic cocoons to consider what is valued in trade by other people. "Every individual . . . neither intends to promote the public interest, nor knows how much he is promoting it."[15] Smith scorned interference in the affairs of workers and bourgeois, writing, for example, that "it is the highest impertinence and presumption . . . in kings and ministers to pretend to watch over the economy of private people."[16] The private person "intends only his own security; and by directing that industry in such a manner as its produce may be of the greatest value [in terms of what others are willing to pay], he intends only his own gain," though a gain from providing goods and services for others, and for the benefit in profits earned of the circle of family and friends close to him.[17] Smith is not recommending selfishness, merely the literal minding of one's own business. He concludes that the private person "is in this, as in many other cases, led by an invisible hand to promote an end which was no part of his intention," namely, the nation's modest prosperity—and, though it was no part of Smith's intention, accidentally promoting something entirely new, the Great Enrichment.

The passage is not (as imagined by recent economists, having read one or two excerpts from *The Wealth of Nations*, and back-projecting from later theorizing) merely a poor approximation to our modern understanding of

the pretentiously named First and Second Theorems of Welfare Economics.[18] And especially Smith's invisible hand does not mean, as Mandeville had
asserted in 1705, that "Thus every part was full of vice, / Yet the whole mass a
paradise." "Intending one's own security" for family and friends is not a vice,
especially when achieved, as it must be a achieved if profitable, "in such a
manner as its produce may be of the greatest value" to others.

Fleischacker, a philosopher, I have noted, of the left and a prominent
student of Smith, argues that when Smith writes about the regard to their
own interest of the butcher, the brewer, or the baker he is appealing not to
a theory of selfishness but to the faculty of imagination, using the theatrical
metaphor so prominent in Smith's other book.[19] Put yourself in the position
of the butcher, in imagination, says Smith; or allow yourself to feel spontaneously, as he called it according to Scottish social thought, "sympathy." Fleischacker's argument persuades, especially in view of the strongly egalitarian
strain that characterized the Sage of the Lowlands. Schumpeter noted in 1949
Smith's suspicion of both landlords and businessmen: "His sympathies [note
the word] went wholly to the laborer who 'clothes everybody and himself
goes in rags.'"[20] We are to view each other, even if poor, as equal members of
the social/theatrical cast of characters and members of the social audience,
alternating our roles in fact and especially in imagination.

The impartial spectator, then, develops Smith's other invisible hand, the
social one as against the economic. We become polite members of our society by interacting on the social stage—note the word, "inter-acting." Smith
in the *Theory* did not believe, as his teacher Hutcheson did, that in achieving social peace and prosperity we can depend on natural benevolence—we
would call it genetically hardwired cooperation (for which, by the way, in
case you don't believe the evidence of four millennia of poetry, drama, religion, novels, proverbs, folktales, philosophy, theology, and history, there is
by now a good deal of recently gathered positivistic experimental and obser-
vational evidence). Nor did he believe, as many economists still understand
him to do, in a fuzzy version of Mandeville's hardwired opposite of cooperation, a macho competiveness, greed is good.

Against inherited niceness or nastiness, as I have noted, Smith repeatedly
emphasized in *The Theory of Moral Sentiments*, as he did also in *The Wealth
of Nations*, that during their lives people change, shaped by society and, it
may be, by their own impartial spectator. In the phrase appropriate to a time
of apprenticeships, people were "brought up to a trade." They started the

same, said Smith the radical egalitarian. As boys the future porter and the future philosopher are little different, he observed—this against the pretensions of aristocrats that the Little Lord got his nobility from his blood.[21]

And whether porters or philosophers, people play on a social stage all their lives, and respond to the other actors *ex tempore*. It is the creativity of real conversation. People, Smith said, are on the bourse all the time, talking, talking: "Everyone is practicing oratory on others through the whole of his life."[22] Such commerce, whether social or financial, changes how we behave. It is like a mountain torrent over time rolling and smoothing its pebbles. It is the French *doux commerce*, such as in Montesquieu's commendation of trade: "Commerce polishes and sweetens [*adoucit*] barbarian ways."[23] That is, you have to live in the world to become civilized. You are neither a sweetly noble savage, in the style of Hutcheson or Rousseau, nor a selfish warrior of all against all, in the style of Hobbes or Mandeville. You are a social, even a theatrical, product in your complexity. Bring the isolate into society, wrote Smith in 1759, "and all his own passions will immediately become the cause of new passions. He will observe that mankind approve of some of them, and are disgusted by others. He will be elevated in one case, and cast down in the other."[24] Think of a child coming to ethical maturity, if he does.

All right. But what makes Smith and his virtue-ethical theory significant for the Bourgeois Revaluation? In 2011 the economist Peter Boettke, commenting on a pessimistic book by Tyler Cowen, argued that Cowen is merely showing that the economy involves a continuing struggle among the Three Ss: Stupidity, Schumpeter, and Smith.[25] Clearly, Stupidity runs much of our private and especially our public lives—and keeps economists and family counselors fully employed. Boettke would argue that (because by historical accident for quite a while after the New Deal there were powerful Schumpeterian and Smithian offsets to Stupidity) people have come to believe in magic—that spending causes growth or that obstructing by act of Congress deals among people makes the people better off. The second S, Schumpeter, with his "Austrian" emphasis on betterment, had got it right on creative destruction, such as Henry Ford's destroying the exclusively high-class car industry or Charlie Parker's destroying swing jazz or Pablo Picasso destroying Postimpressionism. Schumpeter's views, especially in his youthful book on entrepreneurship (1912), supplemented by Israel Kirzner's more profoundly

Austrian views on alertness (1973, 1979), inspire my own book, and its critical predecessor, *Bourgeois Dignity*.[26] Boettke means by the third S, "Smith," the exploitation of the usual efficiencies, "Smithian" growth as we have come to call it, distinct from the Schumpeterian progress I emphasize here. The two contributors to growth, Schumpeterian and Smithian, are at one end of the tug-of-war rope. Growth-killing Stupidity is at the other end.

Boettke agrees with Cowen that if Schumpeter and Smith do not offset the Stupidity of most government policies, as they rather easily did in the boom after World War II (so great had been the accumulation of unused betterments in the time-out of the 1930s and the 1940s, as the economic historian and social theorist Alexander Field argues), then Stupidity on the other end of the rope wins.[27] As the libertarian legal theorist Richard Epstein observed in a foreword to translated essays by Bruno Leoni, the Stupidity of, for example, job protection against the uncertainties of unregulated deals for hiring will fail in its purpose: "The vaunted certainty of their legislative protection does not hold up against the systematic shrinkage in the size of the pie that their own initiatives brought on. Others get a smaller share of a smaller pie and lose immediately."[28] We need to watch out for Stupidity. Urgently.

We watch out in our language. Smith's contribution was to embed society and economy in metaphors of drama, oratory, persuasion, conversation, commerce, trucking, and bartering. We talk as we trade, he said, and we do so in response to other people's talk. It is a conversation, or as I have said a dance. Smith is not about the attainment of efficient equilibria, efficient causes. He is not indeed about efficiency much at all, despite the appropriation of "Smithian" to describe routine exploitation of known efficiencies. At heart he is about the fruitfulness of conversation. Better conversations, even about economic policy, are matters of ethics. True, Smith had no idea what astounding creativity his doctrine would help unleash in the world. His Smithian, as against Schumpeterian, theory of betterment was far too pessimistic about what was possible when human liberty and dignity were grown up. China was in his day specialized too, but was having nothing like an industrial revolution, not to speak of a great enrichment, for lack of full liberty and dignity.

Above all Smith's ideas at length made popular an ideology of the Bourgeois Deal. Unlike the laissez-faire physiocrats of France, he did not make the analytic mistake of attributing all wealth to land (though he did make numerous other analytic mistakes, as Schumpeter insisted: overstressing capital accumulation, thinking of value as labor power, and demoting services as against commodity production).[29] He was properly suspicious of the bourgeoisie's attempts to protect and manipulate its commerce, with a little help from the Royal Navy. He became nonetheless the chief apologist for the world that commerce made:

> Every man, as long as he does not violate the laws of justice, is left perfectly free to pursue his own interest his own way, and to bring both his industry and capital into competition with those of any other man, or order of men. The sovereign is completely discharged from a duty . . . of superintending the industry of private people, and of directing it towards the employments most suitable to the interest of the society.[30]

No choosing of winners. No protecting of trades.

One can ask why it was so important to exhibit the merits in two stout volumes of what was "obvious and simple" if it was so obvious and simple. One thereby gets closer to Quentin Skinner's point about the history of ideas: "We can only study an idea by seeing the nature of all the occasions and activities—the language games—within which it might appear."[31] The reference to "language games" is an appropriation of Wittgenstein Mark II; later in the same essay Skinner appropriates with the same purpose the language of J. L. Austin's illocutionary force, the speaker's intent in a language game.

The (obvious and simple) description of the language game and therefore of Smith's illocutionary intent is that earlier observers were terrified by the prospect of an egalitarian society of people going about their businesses, but Smith was not and was intent on showing its innocence. In Smith's time, and now again in the regulatory state, few believed that a masterless society would be possible. The haunting fear by governing elites supported by worried citizens stirred up by an antitrade clerisy was then, as it still is, that ordinary people will do bad things if left alone. Unless overawed by the threat of state violence in police or planning or regulation, ordinary people, especially the lower classes, will spurn priests, stop paying their rents and taxes, not save enough for old age, kill each other, not buy enough insurance, speak against the government, appear with hair uncovered, refuse military service, drink to excess, commit unnatural acts, use naughty words, chew gum, smoke marihuana—committing in sum, as Bill Murray put it in *Ghost Busters*, "human sacrifice, dogs and cats living together, mass hysteria." A progressive or a conservative program of heavy regulation is a first-night-in-Ferguson-Missouri notion of keeping order. It is the justification of all tyranny, hard or soft. "Women will go wild if not confined," the chieftain says, and then insists on burqas and honor killings.

In matters of religious belief and in matters of economic betterment and in matters of clothing style, almost everyone before the tolerant Poles and Dutch in the sixteenth century or the reluctantly tolerant English in the early eighteenth century or the anyway ungovernable Americans of the late eighteenth century were persuaded that liberty meant license. The Congregationalists of Massachusetts were horrified by the religious liberties that Roger Williams permitted in Rhode Island. Western Christians, as against Orthodox or Coptic or Ethiopian, partook of St. Augustine's unhappy contribution to theology, the doctrine of original sin, man's first disobedience, and the fruit of that forbidden tree. As late as 1776 most Europeans, and most non-Europeans, believed that lifting lordship and regulation from fallen humans would result in opening the gates of hell, as in paintings by Lorenzetti or Bosch supporting a conservative program of mastering by powers and principalities. Many conservatives of the left and the right still believe so.

Sometimes, of course, the fear is justified. Humans certainly do sometimes behave as though they were fallen creatures—for example, in a traffic jam in Boston or in a free-fire zone in Syria. But defection from a social order is mainly prevented, well short of enforcement by state violence, by incentives to behave yourself out of simple prudence—for example, losing repeat business if you cheat your customers—and most powerfully by the Man Within, the impartial spectator, the deep human desire to be good. The child psychologist Jerome Kagan concluded that "humans spend most of their waking hours trying to find, or create, evidence that affirms that they rightfully belong to the category 'good person.'"[32] Smith argued in *The Wealth of Nations* for the *trading*-encouraged motive of prudence to be good, and he had argued in *The Theory of Moral Sentiments* to the same end, for the *self*-enforced motive of faithfulness to the impartial spectator. Had he got around to it, he would have argued in a *Treatise on Jurisprudence* for the role of a *state*-enforced motive of justice. In Smith's thinking the public virtues are prudence, justice, temperance. These three abide. But the greatest of these is temperance, the self-command leading to a self-conception that one is a good person.

It was a striking, egalitarian innovation for Grotius, Pufendorf, and Smith's teacher Hutcheson to declare, tentatively, for masterless men, governed not merely by law and hierarchy but by trade and ethics. It justified the bourgeois projector and a policy of laissez faire. Late in the childhood of the laissez-faire idea Smith sneered at mercantilism and its expert "man of system . . . [who] seems to imagine that he can arrange [by state compulsion] the different members of a great society with as much ease as the hand arranges the different pieces upon a chess-board. He does not consider that . . . every single piece has a principle of motion of its own."[33]

Smith was reacting here against a view of society and economy entirely dominant in 1776, and still vibrant down to the present—the proposition that a law on the books can say where taxes will actually fall, or that government can pick winners, or that consumers need to be corrected in their consumption (recently revived in proposals to "nudge" people), or that natural liberty in running airplanes or grocery stores or an education in medicine needs to be closely regulated lest we fall into human sacrifice, dogs and cats living together, mass hysteria.

Smith was (to pick up on one of Skinner's criteria of interpretation) intending "to subvert . . . one of the more fundamental moral commonplaces of political life in his time."[34] That is why Smith had to *argue* for the merits for his obvious and simple lack of state-imposed system. And his eventual rhetorical and ideological success, achieved slowly, and long after his death—though still under dispute nightly on MSNBC and Fox News (both of them neo-Puritans, influenced, if only they knew it, by Western Christianity and its gloomy assessment of human spontaneous orders)—was crucial for making the modern world.

BEN FRANKLIN WAS BOURGEOIS, AND HE EMBODIED BETTERMENT

Such an ethic was a natural project in the eighteenth century for a Lowland Scottish Enlightenment, or indeed for an even more marginal Coastal American Enlightenment. It can be seen vividly in a figure such as Benjamin Franklin in far Philadelphia.

Both locales, as earlier in the Netherlandish provinces of Zeeland and North and South Holland, were laird-light, and were commercial without being wholly ignorant of philosophy. The theory of the bourgeoisie came from the margins, away from courts and princes, far from Paris or London or Brussels and their proud men of system and hierarchy. It is emblematic of the mechanism involved that Voltaire, a friend of kings and of their mistresses, was induced in 1726 to examine British commercial virtue on-site precisely by his banishment from Paris and its courtly environs, a banishment (and a beating) occasioned by an insult to a well-connected aristocrat. He located his estate prudently in far Ferney, nearly in Switzerland—not in the central places of Versailles or Paris (though with time off in Frederick the Great's court), the better to flee to the Swiss republics if the agents of the French king showed up. He purchased Ferney with his profits as a playwright and a grasping speculator. From it he preached the bourgeois ethic of cultivating one's own garden.

Franklin shows the ethic flourishing on the furthest margins. His *Autobiography* (which is most of what outsiders know of Ben, if they get beyond what they have heard of "The Way to Wealth"), first drafted in 1771, was initiated as counsel for his son (though the father a few years later broke with him permanently, because the son was a Tory and a Crown Governor opposed to the Revolution). The book was not finished until much later. Part 1 first saw light, in French, in 1791, then in English, in England, in 1793. Parts 1, 2, and 3 were published in a defective form by Franklin's grandson in 1818, and in their full canonical version only in 1868, with all four parts. Yet since its beginning it has had fully four hundred editions, becoming symbolically the First Book of the Nation.[1]

In 1940 W. H. Auden sang:

> Out of the noise and horror, the
> Opinions of artillery . . .
> . . . the smell
> Of poor opponents roasting, out
> Of LUTHER's faith and MONTAIGNE's doubt,
>
> . . .
>
> Emerged a new *Anthropos*, an
> Empiric, Economic Man,
> The urban, prudent, and inventive,
> Profit his rational incentive
> And Work his whole *exercitus*,
> The individual let loose
> To guard himself, at liberty
> To starve or be forgotten, free
> To feel in splendid isolation
> Or drive himself about creation
> In the closed cab of Occupation.[2]

In Philadelphia Ben Franklin lived a bourgeois life, which Auden views with a disdain characteristic of the post-1848 clerisy. But it is a life Adam Smith (who knew Franklin) would have praised. A century ago Max Weber made the point by using the Franklin of the *Autobiography* as the very type of the secularized Calvinist—though he is commonly understood to have believed that such a Franklinite person was mainly a prudent accumulator of capital rather than, as he was, a courageous projector of trade-tested betterments, with the aid of excellent political skills. It is not quite what Weber said, but the impression persists that hard work and saving is all that the Protestant ethic consists in.[3]

About the same time as Weber, D. H. Lawrence believed he saw in Franklin what he hated most, the man of a bourgeois society, "the sharp little man. . . .

The pattern American, this dry, moral, utilitarian little democrat."⁴ "Dry." It might be said that Lawrence, having a worse sense of humor even than many other of his fellow modernists in literature, was not well equipped to read Franklin. Viewing the "pattern American" in such a way is a persistent European error. Fifty years earlier Charles Baudelaire had assailed Franklin as "the inventor of the ethics of the shop-counter, the hero of an age dedicated to materialism."⁵ The humorless assault continues down to the present. The literary historian Franco Moretti recently swiped at Franklin in the European-conventional fashion as "grim" (he cannot have read many of Ben's writings).⁶ Admittedly the characterization was also routine among the better sort in Franklin's homeland, and started early. The Federalists of the early Republic detested Franklin. Poe and Hawthorne assaulted him in print as vulgar.⁷ "A penny saved is a penny earned" summarizes him, they said. And so to the present. In the selling of retirement homes the "Benjamin Franklin close" is the argument made to the doubtful client that it is prudent to buy such a home, because it is an asset to pass on to one's children.

But the characterization as dry and grim and utilitarian is mistaken. Franklin was, to be sure, a successful businessman. Baudelaire had asserted that "civilized man finds himself confined within the narrow limits of his specialty ['the closed cab of Occupation,' the usual sneer by the clerisy directed at people employed in making goods and services for other people]. . . . [He] has invented the doctrine of Progress to console himself for his surrender and decay; while primitive man, a feared and respected husband, a warrior obliged to personal valor, . . . comes closer to the fringes of the Ideal."⁸ I think not, and neither did Franklin. Work was not his whole practice, and he did not in fact drive about in the closed cab—not that Occupation is such a terrible practice. And Baudelaire cannot have had much experience with "primitive man" if he regarded such a man as close to the fringes of the Ideal. Baudelaire and Lawrence are only two of the numerous European mis-underestimators of Franklin: Auden, as quoted; Moretti; and, surprisingly, the Scottish philosopher Alasdair MacIntyre, who has spent most of his career in the United States yet nonetheless chimes with Lawrence's antibourgeois and anti-American reading of the *Autobiography*.⁹

Franklin was, on the contrary, a great—indeed after age forty-two a full-time—negotiator and projector for public purposes unrelated to business ambition. He succeeded in them by learning early to "put myself as much as I could out of sight." He explains the tactic prudentially, as men did in those first days of doing without a restlessly active God: "The present little sacrifice of your vanity will afterwards be amply repaid."[10] But that he uses here such prudential rhetoric of cost and benefit does not mean he was in fact the monster of prudence-only that Baudelaire and Lawrence imagined. For the City of Brotherly Love, Franklin carried into practice public paving, street lighting, night watchmen, a newspaper, a lending library, a hospital (financed by a matching grant, which he invented), the University of Pennsylvania, the fire department, and a self-improving discussion group of working-class fellows; for the colonies as a whole and for the new nation he helped start eighteen paper mills, a private postal service, the American Philosophical Society, the American Foreign Service; and for the world at large he invented bourgeois virtues, bifocals, the glass harmonica, the flexible catheter, the Franklin stove, the library chair, lightning rods, a map of the Gulf Stream, the electric battery, the wave theory of light, and the theory of electricity.

He says for all this that he was amply "repaid." But in what coin? Honor, good repute, the good of his community—motives that a warrior obliged to personal valor would recognize, or a saint obliged to nature's God, but not a mere machine of profit and accumulation. Franklin did not think business demeaning. On the contrary, it was a useful platform from which to launch into civic republicanism unrelated to money profit. (Compare Milton Friedman.) His attitude contrasted with that of Southerners at the time, who believed that "it would derogate [that is, undermine even in law] greatly from [a young gentleman's] character to learn a trade."[11] Although Franklin spent his life becoming a gentleman in the eighteenth-century sense of the word, a man of leisure devoted to public service, as Gordon Wood documents, he was never ashamed of his trade.[12]

The metaphor of being "repaid" for a present sacrifice, as though a loan at interest, typifies Franklin's businesslike manner of theorizing. But it does not typify his life. His prudential rhetoric has misled antibusiness readers of his *Autobiography*. "Character" in his theory—but not, I am claiming, in his actual behavior—is a capital project, to be built at present sacrifice for future cash reward. The theory was a commonplace of the Bourgeois Era, emerging for example in *Tom Brown's School Days*, though in a peculiarly pseudo-aristocratic form. The reformed English "public" schools, such as Rugby, were bourgeois in their emphasis on accumulated (human) capital in character, as against natural merit by inheritance. Franklin recommends building good character on personal prudential grounds: "I had therefore a tolerable character to begin the world with," Franklin writes. "I valued it properly, and determined to preserve it," as he preserved the capital in his printing business.[13]

But the theory is misleading. Franklin—like Adam Smith in his book of 1776 counseling a nation—speaks of prudence more than he speaks of love, esteem, or solidarity. If you ignore Franklin's actions, and ignore his other writings (in the way economists have ignored Smith's actions, such as his frequent and large contributions of charitable funds, and have ignored *The Theory of Moral Sentiments* and his other writing), you might infer that Franklin believed only prudence mattered. And yet, it has been observed, this supposedly Max U Ben, at age seventy, joined a revolution, helping to write and then signing a document that could have had him hanged, drawn, and quartered.

The absence of prudence-only in Franklin's actual behavior, as against his theorizing, shows in the tension between a short- and long-run prudence. (An economist notes that the distinction is meaningless, since the long run is a sequence of short runs, but no matter.) Franklin speaks of his friend William Coleman, "then a merchant's clerk, about my age, who had the coolest clearest head, the best heart, and the exactest morals, of almost any man I ever met with. He became afterwards a merchant of great note, and one of our provincial judges."[14] Doing well by doing good. But note that the tests Franklin here applies would be agreeable to Smith's impartial spectator or his encomium to the merchant of Glasgow, extending beyond mere short-run worldly success—yet (quoth Ben) not inconsistent with it, either.

The prudence-only reading is not entirely unjustified by the text of the *Autobiography*. Franklin, for example, always gives a prudential excuse for good will, as though he expected his readers to be cynical about earnest claims of love: "These friends were afterwards of great use to me, as I occasionally was to some of them."[15] Wood notes that in the eighteenth century (and indeed earlier in English, according to the *OED*) "friend" was commonly a euphemism for "patron" or "client," and Franklin played both traditional roles with great skill.[16] It took Romance and Evangelicalism among the clerisy of Europe to bring Love back into repute.

But a manly self-regard in Franklin's circle is in fact hedged by love, if not Love. Franklin in his youth was much impressed by the fallacious cynicism of Mandeville's claim that vice was just as good as virtue for keeping an economy prosperous. Greed is good, and anyway the life of man. Franklin, however, eventually abandoned such theories—as have many people after a larger experience of life, at any rate if they have not pursued a PhD in economics or become members of the Communist Party. The friends whom he claims in the *Autobiography* to be merely useful "continued their regard for me as long as they lived."[17] Such constancy bespeaks not a friendship of interest or amusement, which in Franklin's prudential rhetoric is justificatory, but rather Aristotle's third and highest friendship, for the friend's own sake, which plays no official part in Franklin's rhetoric. Of a spendthrift friend he says, "He owed me about 27 pounds, . . . a great sum out of my small earnings." It was above the average annual income at the time. To give an idea of the size of the debt think of $50,000 nowadays. "I loved him notwithstanding, for he had many amiable qualities."[18] The L-word gets out. Though he loved him almost for his own sake, he meant here that the fellow was a good companion, a lower motive for love. Franklin cannot in 1771—standing with a genial smile a little to the side of an explicitly Christian framework for ethics—quite admit that he simply loved the rogue. He claims instead that, after all, his friend was amusing, the second kind of friendship in Aristotle's triad.

Again, in urging other printers to keep their presses clear of libel and personal abuse—printers then were publishers—he ends with an argument from narrow prudence. The printers "may see by my example, that such a course of conduct will not on the whole be injurious to their interests."[19] Yet even here, as elsewhere, Franklin's rhetoric keeps slipping away from its prudence-only theory. Like Smith thundering at violations of natural right when liberty of employment or of investment was blocked, Franklin thunders at printers filling their newspapers with private altercations, which "pollute their presses and disgrace their profession." The thundering is not the discourse of a cool and consistent utilitarian, free from moralizing, focused on prudence without churchy appeals to justice or love.

Smith and Franklin put their ethical talk in businesslike terms likely to appeal to eighteenth-century men before the Sentimental Revolution. Franklin claims, as does Smith, to care more about the consequences of ethical behavior than about its purity of intention. A pure intention is secular grace, much valued by Kant and ethicists following in his train. Good will, said

Kant, "would shine like a jewel for itself, as something that has its full worth in itself. Utility or fruitlessness can neither add to nor subtract anything from this worth."[20] A good will is not to be justified by works. It is a free gift of God, suited to religions of the Messiah from the Abrahamic trio to environmentalism and the animal rights movement. However bad the unintended consequences in this world, a pure soul and good intentions promise a reward in another, if only an imagined world of duty. (One stands amazed that some writers on Kant persist in claiming that his Pietist upbringing has no relevance for understanding his ethical philosophy.)

Franklin and Smith would agree with Kant only at the level of Sunday preaching—which they did not disdain, though none of the three was rigorous in attendance. On business days from Monday to Saturday, as again Arjo Klamer put it, what matters is the impartial spectator shaping a good character for future use. Or indeed—to think prudentially but in the short run—what matters for business during the business week is the spectator, impartial or not. Franklin scandalizes a Christian of his own time, or a secular but ethically serious humanist of our own, in making his famous little joke about his struggle with the sin of pride: "I added humility to my list [of virtues to be cultivated when a young man]. . . . I cannot boast of much success in acquiring the *reality* of this virtue; but I had a good deal with regard to the *appearance* of it." (The editor of Franklin's papers, Claude-Anne Lopez, remarked once that Franklin will lack a fully adequate biography until someone with a lively sense of humor attempts it.)[21]

Sincerity, the virtue most admired by Romantics, does not figure much in Franklin, or in Smith. True, the seventh of Franklin's thirteen virtues to guide daily life is exactly "Sincerity," but he gives it a narrow and pre-Romantic range: "Use no hurtful deceit. Think innocently and justly; and, if you speak, speak accordingly."[22] It is not the deep sincerity of Heine or Shelley, the hero unburdening his soul. It is not Lawrence's "Sincerity," written explicitly against Franklin's by a late-Romantic enemy of the bourgeoisie: "Remember that I am I, and that the other man is not me."[23] Franklin's sincerity is "honesty," again defined in a bourgeois way as keeping one's commercial promises, to be defended as prudential and social: "I grew convinced that truth, sincerity and integrity in dealings between man and man, were of the utmost importance to the felicity of life."[24] It's nothing like the Romance of one's unconquerable soul.

Franklin's list of virtues in his little account book as a young man does not reflect all the bourgeois virtues he reveals in the rest of the *Autobiography*, and for which he was known to the world. Perhaps the list was trimmed in piety toward conventional Christianity, and certainly it is defective in being a young man's inexperienced theorizing. But for whatever reason it misses a good many virtues practiced by Franklin the bourgeois. To be sure, it does not miss every one of the bourgeois versions of the virtues. The virtues numbered two through six out of the thirteen are those of an actor in trade, and mainly irrelevant to virtue in a pagan or Christian or Romantic mode: "Speak not but what may benefit others or yourself"; "Let each part of your business have its time"; "Resolve to perform what you ought"; "Waste nothing"; "Lose no time." The bourgeois part of the list drove Lawrence, as a founder of the new aristocracy of literary modernism, to angry distraction.

At virtue number seven, though (that "Sincerity"), Franklin's list loses its bourgeois cast, ending with "Humility: Imitate Jesus and Socrates"—which Franklin admits was a later addition. The list is deistic, not Christian. Nor is it Stoic, though Franklin modeled himself on Cicero in some ways (leaving out Cicero's disastrous habit of making jokes at another person's expense, to the person's face). Like Smith's uneasy relation to the theological virtues, nothing in the young Franklin's list corresponds to hope and faith and *agape*, and of the four pagan virtues only justice and temperance are present.

Among the missing in Franklin's explicit list of virtues are the bourgeois versions of prudence and courage—commercial profit and commercial enterprise. Yet Franklin exhibited these to an unusual degree. And it is after all the point of his book to recommend them to young men who wish to become, like him, "honest instruments for the management of . . . affairs."[25] As a boy, he said, "I was generally a leader" and had "an early projecting public spirit."[26] Defoe's *Essay on Projects* (1697), he writes, was an early influence.[27] He became the best printer in the colonies (he modestly implies) and a man of wealth not by following Christian or aristocratic virtues but by following bourgeois virtues, the ones sometimes recommended in the Hebrew Bible. He quotes Solomon on the reward to virtue in this world ("Length of days is in her right hand, and in her left hand riches and honors") and on "calling," the very passage that Max Weber most emphasized: "Seest thou a man diligent in his calling: he shall stand before kings."[28] Franklin the printer had in the long length of his days the satisfaction of remembering his riches and honors, an American businessman diligent in his calling, who stood before kings.

Another bourgeois virtue Franklin omits from his list, although he (and Adam Smith) practiced it famously, was amiability (a favorite of Austen's too, and again not meaning the literal Latin "lovability" in any lofty sense). By his own account, he made friends for use and amusement with astonishing ease: "The Governor, seeming to like my company [though Franklin was at the time a mere teenager], had me frequently to his house"; "I had shown [to a Quaker woman on the boat to Philadelphia as a boy] an obliging readiness to do some little services which impressed her I suppose with a degree of good will towards me."[29] Again he is spinning the events as prudent, as mere investments. But he was more than crafty. Franklin is not describing a Hobbesian world of defectors in a prisoner's dilemma—as the modern clerisy, in ignorance of business practices, has so commonly imagined the world of business to be—but a world that presumes, until supplied definite evidence to the contrary, that we are willing to cooperate. Alexander Field, again, has written on the theme, arguing that such a premise of cooperation is in fact hardwired into humans by group selection.[30]

Franklin in fact marshaled cooperation all his life, and was in this an ideal bourgeois. Cooperation, not competition, is the creative side of a life of betterment by testing trade. The members of the clerisy, especially of the European clerisy, take amiability, especially in its American version, to be simply a false rhetoric, the little con. On either side of the Atlantic they believe, and often practice in their own lives, a rule of harshness carried into their business as deans and scholars and teachers and book reviewers. And when they venture into the agora they carry an unbusinesslike harshness into their economic business. It's just business, says the proud member of the clerisy. That's why I, a professor, happily free from the corruptions of the marketplace, feel justified to cheat when practicing my own corrupt little market business on the side—as did the much-admired art critic Bernard Berenson (1865–1959), cheating about the provenance of paintings he received large amounts of money for evaluating.

In such a theory the highest virtue (from Latin *vir*, male human) is being tough. The turn back to quasi-aristocratic values (apparent for example in Machiavelli) has become especially an obsession of American men and their female imitators, and especially American academic men. A professor of economics at Harvard was caught in 2006 stealing manure and was arraigned on charges of trespassing, larceny, and malicious destruction of property. Another professor of economics at Harvard, on a rather grander scale, was sued by the Department of Justice in 2000 for advising the Russian government in a way immensely profitable to his wife. Mere property; mere business; Max U. Though both men lost their named chairs, the university did nothing else, even to the professor harvesting millions from his advice to the Russian government. Indeed it defended him with its own lawyers at great expense. Harvard professors of economics, especially those who are personal friends of the president of the university, have no need for ethics in mere, vulgar business.

An actual life in business, on the contrary, must be filled with honesty and humor, and especially with humility before the demands of the customers, and must be highly selective with tricky dealing. Business life is not solitary, poor, nasty, and brutish—or else, Franklin would say, bowing to the new religion of prudence, it will be short. Nor does a bad life give evidence, much valued by humans, affirming that the businessperson rightfully belongs to the category "good person."

Another and central bourgeois virtue of Franklin was address—rhetoric. Franklin was not an aristocratic orator. "I was [as a young man, and still in old age] but a bad speaker, never eloquent, subject to much hesitation in my choice of words." He and George Washington were well known for their taciturnity in public assemblies, though both were also well known for the weight of their words when they did speak. Yet Franklin was a great persuader in private business, or in the salons and coffeehouses of Philadelphia, Versailles, and London. Here too his life followed Smithian lines, the Smith who placed the faculty of speech along with that of reason at the origins of the propensity to truck and barter.

The theorizing of a bourgeois life was taking place in America and Scotland, even Naples, rather than in Paris or London where the best theorists more usually held court. It would otherwise seem strange that sociology, economics, jurisprudence (and while we're at it, geology among the physical sciences—though not the older and courtly physics or astronomy) were first expressed in English by Scots, and new theories of history and criminology in Italian by Neapolitans and Milanese. To speak of the Scots, the likes of Hutcheson, Hume, Smith, Ferguson, the law Lord Kames (Henry Home)

were not country bumpkins unaware of preference and privilege. Smith, the son of a revenue officer, was himself from 1778 a royal appointee collecting the import taxes he had recently deprecated. He had spent six years, though not happily, at Oxford. He was the tutor for years to the second Duke of Buccleugh's son and heir, on the young man's long grand tour. He was fluent in the rhetoric of Your Lordship's most obliging and most humble servant, Adam Smith. Franklin was too. Franklin played to the hilt the role of the coonskin-capped, backwoods philosopher, especially while in France. But when he did stand before kings he played the game of the royal court with skill, and to the advantage of his country.

Yet Smith and Franklin, and Jane Austen as well, and most of their friends, were not of the court party, and they were not surrounded at home by the literal nobility. Their daily acquaintances were businessmen and lawyers, or in Jane's case the lesser gentry. Few territorial lords. They were not fashionable people. One could hardly be fashionable in Edinburgh by the highest cosmopolitan standard, and certainly not in Glasgow or Philadelphia or the village of Steventon, when the main political action in the Anglosphere was in London (nor could one do so in Naples or Milan when the main intellectual action in the Romance languages was in Paris: therefore Neapolitans and Milanese during the eighteenth century and beyond were prominent in social theorizing). Smith writes, "Are you in earnest resolved never to barter your liberty for the lordly servitude of a court, but to live free, fearless, and independent? There seems to be one way . . . and perhaps but one. Never enter the place."[31] It was ancient advice. Juvenal spoofed the "aged, genial Crispius"(compare Shakespeare's Polonius)—as the perfect courtier, "not a citizen able / To speak freely the words of his heart, and his life to hang upon the truth. / And so saw many winters he saw, and his eightieth / Solstice, by such weapons safe even in that lofty hall."[32]

Bourgeois, Lowland Scotland or bourgeois, tiny Philadelphia, not the great cosmopolis, was the place for such anti-Crispiuses of the eighteenth century, despite flirtations abroad: "Though I am happy here," wrote Smith to Andrew Millar from France in 1766, "I long passionately to rejoin my old friends. . . . Recommend the same sober way of thinking to Hume. He is light-headed, tell him, when he talks of coming to spend the remainder of his days here."[33] From London a few years before Hume had claimed that "Scotland suits my fortune best, and is the seat of my principal friendships; but it is too narrow a place for me."[34] Perhaps it was too narrow for Hume, but not for a man who was actually carrying out a theory of the middle station, ethical and economic.

Smith was just as aware as Hume of the inconsequence of Scotland beside England and France: "For though learning is cultivated in some degree in almost every part of Europe," he wrote in the first and failed attempt at an *Edinburgh Review* (1755–1756), "it is in France and England only [and specifically in Paris and London] that it is cultivated with such success or reputation as to excite the attention of foreign nations."[35] But it was on just such a margin as Scotland or Philadelphia that one could take seriously the ordinary business of life, undistracted by the lordly servitude of a court, with its daily excitements of great decisions being made. Washington, DC, has just such an effect on American academics, distracting them from their job of theorizing. The economic historian Alexander Gerschenkron (1904–1978), who never bartered his scholarly liberty at Harvard in favor of the court, had a friendly but critical attitude toward his colleague John Kenneth Galbraith (1908–2006), who spent more time in the lofty halls than in the library. When Galbraith, expecting admiring praise, told Gerschenkron excitedly in 1961 that he had accepted an offer from President Kennedy to become ambassador to India, the Harvard scholar replied, "Oh, Ken, Ken, what a disaster! You might as well have taken down your pants in the middle of Harvard Square."

As the popular historian Arthur Herman puts it, "Scottish merchants and capitalists, like their American counterparts, recognized the advantages of a laissez-faire private sector far earlier than the English or the other Europeans."[36] North Holland, which again lacked glorious courts by the standard of Paris, or Brussels earlier, was in fact the pioneer. It was never at the court of the Great King that bourgeois theory could develop, which is perhaps why the successful empires of China and Turkey and North India were deficient in bourgeois theory. A theory of the middle station in life could develop in the first century CE at commercial and Christian Corinth, not academic Athens; in the Middle Ages at profit-focused Florence and Venice, not Rome or Constantinople or Istanbul; in the seventeenth century at Ōsaka, not Edo; in the seventeenth and eighteenth centuries at commercial Amsterdam and Edinburgh, not Versailles or Westminster or even the Hague.

The least aristocratic places, more admiring of the bourgeoisie, are the second cities. They're not always many miles from the *cosmopoleis*, but they feel the distance intensely. Think of the aristocratic airs of the clerisies of New

York or Washington compared to the big shoulders of Chicago; or think of the artists of modern Amsterdam or the bureaucrats of the Hague compared to the businesslike rolled-up sleeves of Rotterdam; or of the proud bureaucrats and politicians of Rome and Madrid compared with the entrepreneurs full of *saggezza/seny* in Milan and Barcelona. In the secondary places, away from every pretense of firstness by traditional standards, away from the lofty court, the bourgeoisie could theorize in confidence about itself.

The theory thus birthed was one of practical betterment short of utopia, by contrast to the mischievous religious-socialist/apocalyptic-revolutionary view of the Enlightenment in France that would prove so damaging to the twentieth century. Militant utopian Christianity had been the catastrophe of seventeenth-century Europe in the way that militant utopian post-Christianity, and lately militant utopian Islam, has been the catastrophe of our times. Utopia makes perfection the assassin of the merely good. The bourgeois, coming to honorable dignity in the eighteenth century, wanted neither enthusiastic religion nor massive social experimentation—merely betterment, cultivating one's own garden, in accord with Dr. Pangloss's chastening precept and Dr. Johnson's Tory pragmatism and Dr. and Mr. Smith's Scottish theory and Miss Austen's novels and Dr. Franklin's life.

BY 1848 A BOURGEOIS IDEOLOGY
HAD WHOLLY TRIUMPHED

If in the Bourgeois Revaluation the bourgeoisie in fact rose sharply in prestige, along with its central virtue, a prudence exercised in trade; and if the aristocracy's central virtue of battlefield or courtly courage declined in dominance; and if the change in values resulted in an obsession with betterment tested by willingness to buy the products, then the evidence ought to appear all over Dutch and British and American and then other bourgeois societies, in all manner of testimonies.

It does. Odd testimony to the bourgeois character of the British, for example, is that lethal dueling ended there fifty years before it did on the Continent. The last known proper duel on English soil occurred in 1852, and in Scotland a little earlier.[1] When in Trollope's *Phineas Finn*, set in 1866–1867, the choleric nobleman Lord Chiltern insists that his friend Phineas duel him with pistols, they have to go to Belgium to do it, and secretly. In far America, Andrew Jackson in 1806 engaged in a duel to defend his wife's honor, killing his opponent and taking a bullet he carried thereafter. The practice died out in the bourgeois United States after the Civil War, to survive as mere vendetta and brawling, especially in the mountain South and its lowland offshoots (Jackson himself was from what David Hackett Fischer called "borderers," their origin being the violent clans of the Scots-English Border, an origin still evident in high rates of murder for honor in the South[2]). The allegedly commonplace dueling of cowboys on the street of Laredo and Tombstone was a myth created for the amusement of working-class boys and then bourgeois men.[3] It hardly ever happened—not in the bourgeois cow- and mining-towns of Kansas and Arizona ruled by peace-loving merchants and landowners.

By contrast, in France and Germany and more so to the east and south, formal duels with their highly unbourgeois definition of honor survived late into the nineteenth century. An Italian member of parliament was finally killed in 1898 in his *thirty-fifth* duel. Marcel Proust fought an absurd duel in 1897 to defend his honor against the charge that he was gay (no one was hurt, which by then in France had become the norm). Still more absurdly, Schumpeter when teaching in 1909 at the University of Graz in Austria fought a duel with sabers, fencing fraternity-style in padded clothing and helmets to prevent serious injury, against a university librarian who had resisted letting Schumpeter's students get easy access to books (the librarian was nicked, Schumpeter "won," and they became fast friends).

Less sensational proofs that in Britain the Bourgeois Era had well begun by the early nineteenth century come from a modern classic of English social history, *Family Fortunes: Men and Women of the English Middle Class, 1780–1850* by Leonore Davidoff and Catherine Hall (1987), a multigenerational portrait of two provincial families. The families were the Cadburys of Birmingham, who were Quakers selling tea, coffee, and at last a chocolate drink and much later, after crucial betterments in packaging made them possible, chocolate bars; and the Taylors of Colchester in the east of the country, who were Evangelicals making and selling engravings and books. "Serious Christians" the families were, both. The "conflicting ideals of masculine leadership [that is, aristocratic display versus bourgeois domesticity] came to a head over the issue of dueling. The use of the sword in issues of private honor symbolized all that was repellent to their pacific, religious and commercial sense of the middle-class provincial."[4]

"It is surely no accident," wrote Donna Andrew in 1980, "that it was an Evangelical, Thomas Gisborne, in his *Duties* [*An Enquiry into the Duties of Men in the Higher and Middle Classes of Society in Great Britain: Resulting from Their Respective Stations, Professions, and Employments*, 1794] who was among the first writers to use the term 'middle class.' Much of the evangelical literature was specifically addressed to this group and helped it to identify itself and its responsibilities."[5] She is not literally correct, since the first quotation for "middle class" in the *OED* is in fact 1745—"bourgeois" being a little earlier. But the historian Dror Wahrman, as I have noted, argues that it was not until the Napoleonic Wars that the middle class was differentiated much from the lower and common people, especially in its self-image.[6] The early quotations in the *OED* entry therefore speak of "people of the middle or inferior classes" (1756). For the very word "class," the *OED* notes that "higher and lower *orders* were formerly used," until around 1800, when "orders" in this sense appears to die out except in ironic use.

The middle class was elevated to the degree that even royals such as George III behaved so. Davidoff and Hall note that King George "in his later life . . . had embraced all those virtues increasingly adopted by the middling sort: piety, dignity, honesty [in a modern definition], and the love of a proper domestic life."[7] His eldest son, the long-suffering Prince Regent (and then George IV), attacked middle-class values (and attacked, too, his wife Charlotte, who espoused them). But his younger brother, the Duke of Clarence (and then William IV), called a royal truce, and Farmer George's granddaughter Victoria embodied bourgeois values. As the historian of religion Diarmaid MacCulloch remarks, "If ever there was anything resembling the 'Protestant work ethic,' it came out of [eighteenth-century, Anglican-based] Methodism and the Evangelical Revival rather than the sixteenth-century Reformation."[8] The bourgeoisie's "rejection of landed wealth as the source of honor and insistence on the primacy of the inner spirit," write Davidoff and Hall, "brought with it a preoccupation with the domestic as a necessary basis for a good Christian life."[9] MacCulloch uses as an emblem of the same theme Hannah More (1745–1833), the fantastically successful writer of plays, poems, and religious tales recommending domestic virtue, who "set patterns for the moral seriousness which was the preferred public self-image of most nineteenth-century Britons," the effect of which "did not wear off until the 1960s."[10] The new, bourgeois "gentleman," dressed in a sober suit of black, with no lace, and was a Christian, not a gambler.

The word "gentleman," sense 2a in the *Oxford English Dictionary*, is "a man in whom gentle birth is accompanied by appropriate qualities and behavior; hence, in general, a man of chivalrous instincts and fine feelings," with an instance as early as 1386, in Chaucer. The lexicographers of Oxford note further that "in this sense the term is frequently defined by reference to later derived senses of 'gentle,'" that is, mild mannered, an early and unusual use being

1552. Yet much more usually until modern times the word "gentle" continued to mean "from the upper class." In their book *Shakespeare's Words: A Glossary and Language Companion* (2002) David and Ben Chrystal put "gentle" among their selection of the hundred most frequently encountered words that would mislead a modern reader of the Bard. They define "gentle" simply as "well-born."[11] The alternative spelling and pronunciation, "genteel," meant much the same as "gentle" in seventeenth-century English, "appropriate to persons of quality," as in the *OED* quotation from Pepys, writing in 1665: "we had the genteelist dinner." In its various shades of meaning recorded in the *OED*, "genteel" becomes in the eighteenth century a bit of a joke, and was and still is used "chiefly with sarcastic implication." Thus Jane Austen says of an unfortunate family that was, in Emma's opinion (spoofed in free indirect style), "of low origin, in trade, and only moderately genteel."[12] Note Austen's gentle, and genteel, touch of irony about the distinction.

The mid-Victorian businessman and moralist Samuel Smiles held up as his ideal, in the final chapter of *Self Help* (1859), "The True Gentleman." Yet the way Smiles mixes aristocratic, Christian/democratic, and bourgeois notions of gentlemanliness is not the main line of the word until late. Smiles's modern assertion on the last page of his book that "Gentleness is indeed the best test of gentlemanliness" may serve well enough now in our egalitarian times, but it originated in the crazy notions of Levellers in the 1640s or Wat Tyler's mad talk in 1381 that rank and birth should not matter: "When Adam delved, and Eve span / Who then was the gentleman?" Likewise in *Tom Brown's School Days* (1857, set in the 1830s) fictional Tom's father intends only that little Tom will "turn out a brave, helpful, truth-telling Englishman, and a gentleman, and a Christian."[13] Even Mokyr slips when he echoes Smiles on the gentle gentleman and then applies it anachronistically to the eighteenth century. Such a late bourgeois notion has nothing to do with the self-confident society of sneering rank and birth that Shakespeare's gentlemen praised, or that Eton College practiced well into the eighteenth century, or that still in the eighteenth century associated the gentleman with sword-carrying and sword-using, and still anyway into the nineteenth with a lack of an occupation.

Around 1700 the rhetoric began slowly to change in earnest—and "earnest" is the word. Until then English people thought it quite absurd to claim, as Smiles did, that gentlemanliness "may exhibit itself under the hodden grey of the peasant as well as under the lace coat of the noble."[14] Smiles's "hodden

grey" [that is, undyed homespun cloth from unsorted white and black wool]
is an unmarked quotation from Burns's leveling poem of 1795, "A Man's a
Man for a' That": "What though on hamely [homely] fare we dine, / Wear
hoddin grey, an' a that; /Gie [give] fools their silks, and knaves their wine; /A
man's a man for a' that." But Burns's talk is modern, democratic, revolutionary, the talk of the Scottish kirk meeting, where any devout man could speak
up, or of the Scottish marketplace, where a poor man's penny was as good as
the penny of "yon birkie ca'd [that assertive fool called] a lord." The very word
"noble" was transformed by egalitarian Calvinists in the seventeenth century
into a spiritual condition, "true nobility," as against merely high and inherited
social status.[15] The change in rhetoric was historically unique, the honoring
of people who claimed no privilege of robe or sword and merely worked at
the business of ordinary life, serving rather than being served ("helpful," said
Tom Brown's father, "truth-telling" in a bourgeois way), yet finding honor in
such tasks. It signaled the shift to a bourgeois civilization—which came (as
causes must) before the material and political changes it gave rise to. Said
Burns, "The pith o' sense an' pride o' worth / Are higher rank that a' that. /
Then let us pray that come it may, / (As come it will for a' that,) / That sense
and worth, o'er a' the earth, /Shall bear the gree [shall be superior], an' a' that."
It was a change in ethics, a change in earnest talk about the good life, spreading at length to poets and plowmen, and finally to politics and policy.

By the end, by 1848, famously, in Holland and England and America and
their imitators in northwestern Europe, a busy businessperson was routinely
said to be good, and good for us, except by the angry and as yet tiny antibetterment clerisy, gathering especially in France and Germany. The new form
of betterment, dating from its precursors in the northern Italian city-states
around 1300 to the first modern bourgeois society on a large scale in Holland around 1600 to a pro-bourgeois ethical and political rhetoric in Britain
and its North American offshoots around 1776 to a world-making rhetoric
around 1848, grew for the first time in history at the level of big states and
empires to be acceptable, even honorable, even virtuous.

A good thing or bad, this triumph around 1848 of the bourgeois virtues in
the realm of rhetoric, and then in the realms of exchange?

In a commercial world, for one thing, we bump regularly against strangers, but the strangers become friends. To my friends (as indeed some of them

are) the communitarians I say: your sweet ends are achieved precisely by commerce. The legal historian Henry Maine a century and a half ago made the still-sensible argument that distaste for fraud implies the existence of a general trust: "If colossal examples of dishonesty occur [and we feel them indeed to be 'colossally' bad], there is no surer conclusion than that scrupulous honesty is displayed in the average of the transactions."[16] Muckrakers are liable to draw the opposite, and erroneous, conclusion: that a fraud is typical of the whole barrel. Arthur Miller remarked of the proto-McCarthyite attack on his play *All My Sons* (1947, two years before *Death of a Salesman*), "If the . . . play was Marxist, it was Marxism of a strange hue. Joe Keller is arraigned by his son for a willfully unethical use of his economic position; and this, as the Russians said when they removed the play from their stages, bespeaks an assumption that the norm of capitalist behavior is ethical."[17]

The growth of trade, I would argue, promotes virtue, not vice. Most of the clerisy—themselves, as Bismarck described them with disdain, having "no property, no trade, no industry"—think the opposite, that it erodes virtue.[18] And yet we all take happily what trade gives, which is polite, accommodating, energetic, enterprising, risk-taking, trustworthy people having some property, trade, and industry—not bad people. Sir William Temple attributed the honesty of Dutch merchants in the seventeenth century "not so much [to] . . . a principle of conscience or morality [here he is mistaken], as from a custom or habit introduced by the necessity of trade among them [here he is correct], which depends as much upon common-honesty [note the use of 'common' here, 'honesty' unmodified still connoting the aristocratic], as war does upon discipline."[19] In the Bulgaria of socialism before 1989 the department stores had an armed policeman on every floor—not to prevent theft but to stop customers from attacking the arrogant and incompetent staff charged with selling shoddy goods that instantly fell apart. The way a salesperson in an American store greets a customer makes the point: "How can I help you?" The phrase startles some foreigners. It is an instance in miniature of the bourgeois virtues.

You can see the bourgeois virtues by contrast with the aristocratic or Christian ones. The virtues listed here in table 3 are those attributed to the class, not necessarily those it actually exhibits. Even taking the calumnies of the clerisy against the bourgeoisie at face value, an ethics of greed for the almighty dollar is not the worst. It's better, for example, than an ethics of slaughter with patrician swords or plebeian pikes. Of Johnson's remark that

TABLE 3. The classes and the virtues

Aristocrat/patrician	Peasant/plebeian	Bourgeois/mercantile
pagan	Christian	secular
Achilles	St. Francis	Benjamin Franklin
pride of being	pride of service	pride of dealing
honor	calling	integrity
forthrightness	candor	honesty
loyalty	solidarity	trustworthiness
courage	stoicism	enterprise
wit	jocularity	humor
courtesy	reverence	respect
propriety	benevolence	consideration
justice	fairness	responsibility
foresight	wisdom	prudence
self-restraint	frugality	thrift
love	charity	affection
grace, *sprezzatura*	dignity	self-possession
subjective	objective	conjective

there are few ways in which a man can be more innocently employed than in getting money, Hirschman noted, "The very contempt in which economic activities were held led to the conviction, in spite of much evidence to the contrary, that they could not possibly have much potential in any area of human endeavor and were incapable of causing either good or evil."[20] The "evidence to the contrary" was not so great in 1776. Adam Smith at the time, I have noted, saw only a modest growth arising from peaceful specialization. Later it became overwhelming.

The property developer, TV personality, and Republican politician Donald Trump, to take an extreme example, offends. But for all the criticism he has provoked, and for all his unusual opinions about Barack Obama's nationality and Mexican immigrants and numerous other matters, he is not a thief. He did not get his millions from aristocratic cattle raids, acclaimed in bardic glory. He artfully made, as he put it in his first book, deals, all of them voluntary.[21] (In a *New Yorker* cartoon a father explains, "Yes, I do make things, son. I make things called deals.") Trump did not use a .38 or a broadsword to get people to agree. In his account he bought the Commodore Hotel low and sold it high because Penn Central, Hyatt Hotels, and the New York City Board of Estimate—and behind them the voters and hotel guests and politicians—put the old place at a low value and later found the new place, trumped up, to have a high value. Trump earned a suitably fat profit for seeing that a hotel in a low-value use could be moved into a high-value use. An omniscient and benevolent central planner would have ordered the identical move. Even a Trump, in other words, does good by doing well. Look at his magnificent addition in 2008 to the Chicago skyline along the main branch of the Chicago River (spoiled in 2014 by the addition of enormous letters on the building reading TRUMP). That building, too, earned him a pretty penny, the pennies showing what to do next in the way of trade-tested betterment.

In Thomas Mann's first successful novel, *Buddenbrooks* (1901), Tom Buddenbrook (he is throughout called informally "Tom") becomes the head of his north German bourgeois family and "the thirst for action, for power and success, the longing to force fortune to her knees, sprang up quick and passionate in his eyes."[22] But success at bourgeois occupations, even that of a bourgeois novelist, is success in mutually advantageous deals, deals in which Tom the grain merchant delights—not the successful slaughter or successful double-dealing recounted in the literature of aristocrats or of peasants. Think of Odysseus's trickery in escaping the Cyclops or Jack's trickery in stealing from the giant.

And even from a strictly individual point of view the bourgeois virtues, though not those of Achilles or Jesus, are not ethical zeroes. Greece even in Homer's time was a commercial society, and one sees a trace of the merchant in the story of Odysseus's wanderings. As a later poet put it, the Greek trader venturing into the Atlantic beyond the Pillars of Hercules, "unbent sails / There, where down cloudy cliffs, through sheets of foam, / Shy traffickers, the dark Iberians come; / And on the beach undid his corded bales." The common honesty of a society of merchants in fact goes beyond what would be strictly self-interested in a society of rats, as one can see in that much-maligned model of the mercantile society, the small Midwestern city.[23] A reputation for fair dealing is necessary for a roofer whose trade is limited to a city of fifty thousand. One bad roof and he is ruined. A professor at the University of Iowa refused to tell at a cocktail party the name of a roofer in Iowa City who had at first done a bad job for her (he redid the job free, at his own instigation) because the roofer would be finished in town if his name got out in such a connection. The professor's behavior itself shows that ethical habits can harden into ethical convictions, the way a child grows from fear of punishment toward consulting an impartial spectator, the man within the breast. An unethical person would have told the name of the roofer, to improve the story. After all, the professor's own reputation in business was not at stake.

The motto of the Buddenbrook family was "My son, attend with zeal to thy business by day; but do none that hinders thee from thy sleep at night."[24] Remember Milton Friedman's motto, "conforming to the basic rules of the society, both those embodied in law and those embodied in ethical custom." It is the bourgeois's pride to be "a fair-dealing merchant," with "quiet, tenacious industry," to "make concessions and show consideration," to have "assured and elegant bearing, . . . tact and winning manners," a "liberal, tolerant strain," with "sociability and ease, and . . . remarkable power of decision at a division" in the town assembly, "a man of action," making "quick decision upon the advantageous course," "a strong and practical-minded man, with definite impulses after power and conquest," but by no evil means.[25] "Men walked the streets proud of their irreproachable reputation as business men."[26] Is it so evil to hope that "one can be a great man, even in a small place; a Caesar even in a little commercial town on the Baltic"? I think not. What is wrong with "the dream of preserving an ancient name, an old family, an old business"?[27] Not much, at any rate by comparison with the blood spilt by aristocrats defending a nine-hundred-year-old name, or the blood spilt by the clerisy-in-charge inspiring and then leading mass slaughters during the twentieth century. On the contrary, preserving by continuous betterment a business of making mutually advantageous trades is good for the rest of us, the Bourgeois Deal.

Increasingly in the eighteenth and then especially in the early nineteenth century, the elite and then a wider swathe of European public opinion did embrace the Bourgeois Deal. For the first time a public opinion—an audience made up of citizens (though not by any means all the adult male in-dwellers, and few women)—began to matter in European politics. It was one of the causes of the rhetorical change.

In 1953 the anthropologist Sol Tax lamented that "Europe and its offshoots embraced a business civilization," but Guatemala had not. The Europeans did, 1600–1848. Much later—though first in the United States and Australia—the former peasantry and proletariat also adopted bourgeois values, and started calling themselves when queried "middle class." Mostly what changed, however, was not actual behavior but the opinion the rest of the society had of it. As Mokyr puts it, "By the time of Queen Victoria's ascent to the throne, [Britain] had . . . learned to appreciate the free market." Such an ideological change, "the mother of all institutional change, needed to take place before economic growth was to become the norm rather than the exception."[28] The outcome was the Bourgeois Era and the Great Enrichment. Long and widely may it spread.

PART IV

A Pro-Bourgeois Rhetoric Was Forming in England around 1700

THE WORD "HONEST" SHOWS THE CHANGING ATTITUDE TOWARD THE ARISTOCRACY AND THE BOURGEOISIE

The best question one can ask of a scientific proposition—or for that matter of an ethical or aesthetic one—is How Do You Know? (Milton Friedman used to ask it regularly in the Money Workshop at the University of Chicago during the 1970s, striking terror into the hearts of students and colleagues.) Clive James, though a literary chap, admires it in the form of "the scientist's unsleeping attention to the question of what constitutes evidence."[1] Let us not sleep when numbers from the past march by, or at least can be force-marched by.

But neither should we sleep when words from the past do so. The trouble with word-evidence, of course, is that people—and chimpanzees and camouflaging plants—can be dishonest. (Quite unlike, for example, the latest fair and balanced numbers reported on Fox News.) That is, people can fashion a gap between what they say and what they mean, especially if the faking or the irony doesn't cost much to perform. "I just *love* that outfit!" can mean in the right circumstances, "Thank God you got rid of that hideous orange dress!" Words—and my claim is that the initiating change leading the Great Enrichment *was* in words—can be cheap talk (as it is put, I have noted, by the Samuelsonian economists), which is to say, *merely* words, bloviation. (Jesting aside, the numbers, too, can be fake or misleading or irrelevant, a lesson that the best numerical scientists also know.) But it is in their words, as Charles Taylor put it, that people "imagine their social existence, how they fit together with others, how things go on between them and their fellows, the expectations which are normally met, and the deeper normative notions and images which underlie these expectations."[2] Numbers tell how much is in a classification. Words tell what we mean when we count.

The evidence for the rhetorical change toward a bourgeois civilization, then, has to catch people talking unawares. If you simply ask them outright they are liable to affirm indignantly that they are decidedly against the vulgar bourgeoisie, and remain enthusiastic advocates for old-fashioned aristocratic or Christian virtues. We need verbal thermometers of the change in civilization that made the modern world.

Start with a word once surprisingly redolent of aristocratic civilization but nowadays thoroughly bourgeois. Lots of English words have such a history.

In English our bourgeois word "honest" once meant *not* mainly "committed to telling the truth" or "paying one's debts" or even "upright in dealing," but mainly "noble," even "aristocratic," or sometimes "dignified," in a society in which only the nobles were truly dignified. After all, what aristocrat would bother with merely propositional truth or procedural uprightness when style, gesture, heroism, dignity, loyalty to persons, and social position are the life of man?

Honestus in classical Latin never meant telling the truth or keeping one's word. For such concepts, uninteresting in a society obsessed with honor and nobility, the Romans used the word *sincerus* ("pure," from Indo-European "one growth"). In the Roman Empire the *honestiores* were the people who mattered—not because they made a habit of telling the truth but because they were rich and honorable. In England latterly they were not always rich. In 1430 an English lady—the word "lady" indicated then high social standing, not as it does now in polite modern talk any adult female—asked for a loan to pay for "honest [i.e., dignified and suitable to her rank] bedding, without which mine husband's honesty [honor, dignity] and mine may not be saved." Well short of its application to the literal nobility, an ecclesiastical court in 1574 required of a defendant of much lower social standing than the "lady" of 1430 that he find to testify to his character six "honest men . . . such as have six or eight oxen a piece and keepeth ploughs of their own" (these being substantial yeomen).[3]

The modern and secondary meaning of truth-telling and keeping one's word (a "truth-telling Englishman"), whether or not of high or at any rate upright and sincere social rank, does occur in English as early as 1400. But the meaning of honorable by virtue of high social standing is still dominant in Shakespeare's time and quite lively until the eighteenth century. Shakespeare uses the ambiguity of the two meanings—"worthy of social honor" and "truth-telling"—in many places, for example in *Cymbeline*. The loyal servant Pisanio says to himself that he must dissemble to remain true to a wider truth: "Wherein I am false, I am honest [that is, honorable and genuine]; not true, to be true" (that is, not truth-telling, yet faithful; 4.3.42).

Observe likewise the double meaning in Pisanio's verbal play of "true," which nowadays usually means "in accord with the facts, propositionally accurate." In a society running on personal loyalty it had meant originally "loyal to a person," as in present-day German *treue* and still in English "love me tender, love me true," or the older English "pledge my troth," cognate with "truth." The *OED* gives as the first and oldest meaning of "true," "steadfast in adherence to a commander or friend, . . . to one's promises," and labels it "somewhat archaic." It is cognate also with "truce," for example. All these faith-words—lief, belief, true, troth, truce—originate in Germanic languages as expressions of attachment to people or to God, not to propositions such as $F = ma$ or "It's raining." The very word "belief" is cognate with "love" and Latin *libido*, from Indo-European *leubh-*, "to like, to desire." The rare old English word "lief," as in "I had as lief do it," is a cousin to "belief" (with cognates in all Germanic languages, as in Dutch *liefs*, "loving regards," ending a letter to a close friend). Christian "belief" was therefore a loving commitment to God, not a set of modern and propositional "beliefs."

Waterman has argued that in the 1820s the economist and soon-to-be archbishop Richard Whately was working to bring orthodox Anglicanism and economics back together, after their separation by Benthamite radicals. Whately declared in 1828 (as St. Augustine had also declared) that "the Bible . . . was not designed to teach men astronomy, or geology, or, it must be added, political economy, but *religion*."[4] And the word "religion" itself, as a classically trained man such as Whately would have vividly known, is again not about propositional dogma such as the virgin birth or papal infallibility, but a word of commitment, from the Latin "re-bind," possibly from an Indo-European root meaning "collect."

The Augustinian and the Whatelyan teaching goes on. The religious writer Karen Armstrong argues in a recent book that the scientific revolution and

correlate movements in the seventeenth century led to a propositional redef-
inition of Christian "faith" in Western Europe, as against the ancient "affective spirituality," which was a commitment to God, or "religion as practice"
of a collectivity, rather than propositional dogma.[5] After 1600, she writes,
"there would soon be no place in the new Europe for the skepticism of Montaigne or the psychological agnosticism of Shakespeare. By the beginning of
the seventeenth century, the notion of truth had begun to change."[6] Earlier,
Luther had explicitly denied the propositional definition of faith: "Faith does
not require information, knowledge, and certainty," he wrote, "but a free
surrender and joyful bet on His unfelt, untried, and unknown goodness."[7]
Commitment. I pledge my troth. But in the seventeenth century propositional dogma and a "natural theology" attaching faith to science triumphed
among advanced thinkers, who started to speak of a watch found in a field
as implying a watchmaker—disastrously, says Armstrong, because it transformed the joyful bet into "believing," in the modern sense, as many as six
impossible things before breakfast. It led to the scornful, if ignorant, attitude of modern atheists, with their digs at naïve believers. Thus Peppermint
Patty in the Peanuts strip affirms that "I believe!" in Linus's faith in the Great
Pumpkin, "*because*," she declares in italics, "*I'm superstitious*."

Back to "honest," then. In Shakespeare's time a phrase such as "honest,
honest Iago" in *Othello* mainly meant, with a certain coy ambiguity, that
the lying, motivelessly malignant Iago, a high-ranking soldier by profession,
was "honorable, noble, warlike, even at least in behavior aristocratic."[8] The
famous definition of a "diplomat" by Sir Henry Wotton (1568–1639) plays on
the ambiguity: "an honest man sent to lie abroad for the good of his country." "Honest" here means "noble, distinguished," but dances prettily with
"lie" in its nonpostural sense. The old phrase in men's mouths, "an honest
woman"—thus Desdemona in *Othello*, repeatedly, an ironic commentary
on her husband's suspicions—preserves the original meaning of the word
"honest," with adjustments for a woman's place in a male system of honor.
Anne Boleyn refused Henry VIII's advances unless he married her: "I would
rather lose my life than my honesty."[9] Charles I on the scaffold, 1648, said
he was "an *honest* man and a good King, and a good Christian." He did not
mean that he kept to his business bargains or told the truth, which chronically he did not. He meant that he was noble, aristocratic, worthy of honor.
Thus too his enemy John Milton: the sole occurrence of "honest" in the second edition of *Paradise Lost* (1674) comments on Eve's nakedness before her

disobedience. "Then was not guilty shame, *dishonest* shame / Of nature's works, honor dishonorable."[10]

In the Crystals' *Shakespeare's Words* four definitions of "honest" are given, of which the closest to the modern sense, straightforward "truth-telling," is number 3, "genuine," as in the 'umble servant Davy's appeal for an occasional indulgence toward knaves in the second part of *Henry IV*: "if I cannot once or twice in a quarter bear out a knave against an honest man, I have but a very little credit with your worship. The knave is mine honest [that is, genuine] friend, sir; therefore, I beseech your worship, let him be countenanced."[11] Even here an "honest man" is honorably dignified compared with a knave (cognate with German *Knabe*, a mere boy). The other three definitions in *Shakespeare's Words* relate straightforwardly to elevated and even knightly honor.

In 1571 John Northbrooke, preaching against dueling, noted with irritation that "if a man be a roister, and knowing how to fight his fight, then he is called [mistakenly, he was arguing] by the name of honesty."[12] And so to Shaftesbury in 1713, a late occurrence in the aristocratic sense—unsurprisingly from an aristocrat resisting the bourgeois claim by his teacher Locke that individual experience, not sociality, writes on the blank slate—looks into what "honesty or virtue is, considered by itself."[13] The two words, "honesty" and "virtue," have merged. Alexander Pope in his Preface to Samuel Addison's play *Cato* (1712), also uses the word "honest" in its aristocratic sense: "With honest scorn the first famed Cato viewed / Rome learning arts from Greece, whom she subdued." And likewise, in the play itself, the noble Juba asks indignantly, "Can such dishonest thoughts / Rise up in man! wouldst thou seduce my youth / To do an act that would destroy my honor?" (2.5.35–37).

Yet "honesty" had already in some usages lost its air of gentility. As early as at the Putney Debates in 1647 within the New Model Army the word was used repeatedly in its nonaristocratic sense. "Honest" and its compounds appear frequently in the recorded text, thirty-eight occurrences, especially in Cromwell's lengthy, property-admiring interventions, and the word has already started to be specialized down to its bourgeois sense of just, sincere, upstanding.[14] Three-quarters of a century later, in *Cato* (3.5.45–46, two of the four instances), Cato scolds his mutinous troops—no gentlemen, they—with "Learn to be honest men, give up your leaders, / And pardon shall descend on all the rest." But the meaning keeps slipping back to nobility. Addison himself, in *The Spectator*, no. 293 (Tuesday, February 5, 1712), wrote: "The famous

Gratian, in his little book wherein he lays down maxims for a man's advancing himself at Court, advises his reader to associate himself with the fortunate . . . which, notwithstanding the baseness of the precept to an honest [that is, noble, high] mind, may have something useful in it for those who push their interest." John Dennis's *Remarks upon Cato* (1713) complained that "the honest simplicity and the credulity of [the hero] Juba" is not rewarded.[15]

Contrast, thirty-seven years later, *Tom Jones* (1749). Fielding uses "honest" only four times in one of the first English novels to be accounted such by professors of English, all in the first of its eighteen books: "the honest and well-meaning host"; "these honest victuallers" (both in chap. 1); "he lived like an honest man, owed no one a shilling" (chap. 3); and "a good, honest, plain girl, and not vain of her face (chap. 8).[16] All mean "upright, sincere," with by then an old-fashioned and even parodic air. By 1749 they have nothing to do, as forty years before they often still did, with honorableness in a nobleman's or a gentleman's sense. In Johnson's *Dictionary* (1755) the senses of "honest" given are (1) "upright; true; sincere" (that is to say, the bourgeois definition), (2) "chaste," and (3) "just; righteous; giving to every man his due." Not "noble" or "of deservedly high social status." Yet also under "honesty" Johnson quotes Temple late in the previous century giving a definition and the recent etymology. "Goodness, as that which makes men prefer their duty and their promise before their passions or their interest, and is properly the object of trust, in our language goes rather by the name of honesty, though what we call an honest man, the Romans called a good man [thus *vir bonus dicendi peritus*, the rhetor in Quintilian]; and honesty, in their language, as well as in French [and I am saying in earlier English], rather signifies a competition of those qualities which generally acquire honor and esteem."

The idea of "honest" dealing in trade comes from merchants and tradesmen (such as Quakers, the first merchants to post fixed prices instead of continuing the bargaining, which they viewed as violating the commandment that thou shalt not lie), never from the gentry or the aristocrats. Adam Smith admired honesty, sincerity, truth, candor in a fashion foreign to Shakespearean England. In Smith's books of 1759 and 1776 "honest" means "upright" or "sincere" or "truth-telling," never "aristocratic." Even a poor man, he argues in *The Theory of Moral Sentiments*, is constrained not to steal by "the man within": "there is no commonly honest man who does not more dread the inward disgrace."[17] In Shakespeare "commonly honest" would commonly be an honest contradiction in terms and "honest but poor" an absurdity, if the poor man was not a distressed gentleman. "Honest but poor" was not old-southern-English talk but eighteenth-century Scots-Lowland talk, as again in 1795 in Burns's "The honest man, though e'er so poor, / Is king of men for all that." (As early as 1732–1734, to be sure, Alexander Pope in the Fourth Epistle of *The Essay on Man*, line 247, declares Burns-style, that "An honest man's the noblest work of God." Yet be careful—the "noblest" work, and no mention of poverty.)

In *The Theory of Moral Sentiments* Smith writes, "The man who indulges us in this natural passion, who invites us into his heart, who, as it were, sets open the gates of his breast to us, seems to exercise a species of hospitality more delightful than any other."[18] Smith's usage anticipates a Romantic faithfulness to the Self, and an honest willingness to set it open, as in Wordsworth, when democratic sincerity comes fully into its own. By contrast, any Othello or Hamlet who opened the gates of his breast would invite a fatal wound. Even in Shakespeare's comedies it was prudent to dissimulate. Shakespeare again and again—sometimes favorably, sometimes unfavorably—exhibits instances of what we would call perfidy, treason, dissembling, mistaken identity, cross-dressing, dishonesty. There is no play of his in which bourgeois "honesty" is honored.

By the late eighteenth century at last, then, "honest" had changed. In Henry Mackenzie's *The Man of Feeling* (1771), which initiated the proto-Romantic novel in English (Mackenzie, by the way, was like Burns a Lowland Scot), the thirteen instances of "honest" (or "dishonest") never connote the old, high-status sense.[19] Nine times it means "upright" in a way that includes all social classes, twice it means "genuine," and twice "not cheating." In the eight works of Jane Austen, written from 1793 to 1816 (including *The Watsons*, 1804, unfinished, and her early and unpublished *Lady Susan* [something of a first draft for *Sense and Sensibility*] but not including her last, unfinished *Sanditon*), "honest" occurs thirty-one times.[20] It means "upright" on six occasions, dominantly in the old phrase "honest man," but never in Shakespeare's dominant sense, "of high social rank, noble, gentle." Another third of the time it means "genuine," as in "a real, honest, old-fashioned boarding-school" (*Emma*), far indeed from "honest" as "honor worthy of high status." In its dominant modern sense of "truth-telling," it occurs a third of the time, in the meaning "sincere."

In the Trollope novel of 1867–1868, the title character Phineas Finn is a twenty-something quasi-gentleman, the son of an Irish doctor, no aristocrat, though dealing daily with aristocrats as a high-flying member of the Parliament of 1867. He worries whether he could "bid [his friend] Lord Chiltern come home to woo Violet Effingham, and instantly go forth to woo her for himself. He found that he could not do so—unless he told the whole truth to Lord Chiltern. In no other way could he carry out his project [of wooing Violet] and [yet] satisfy his own idea of what was honest." The word here and elsewhere in the novel (it is a prominent word, with seventy-two occurrences in various forms in the Oxford World Classics 711-page duodecimo edition) means "honorable" as well as "truth-telling." In writing to his friend, Phineas declares, "I am endeavoring to treat you well" (by confessing his own love to Violet). He opens the gates of his heart. Without such Romantic candor, "I should feel myself to be false." And a couple of pages later in replying to Violet's implied question, whether Lord Chiltern would behave less gruffly if she allowed him to court her, "Phineas knew that in this emergency [an honest answer to such a question about his friend being against his own interest in courting her] it was his especial duty to be honest."[21] He could have bad-mouthed Lord Chiltern to Violet but would not then have been telling the truth, being honest. In the novel some of the non-gentlemen, too, such as the politically Radical owner of young Phineas's rooming house, Jacob Bunce, evince honesty (and are so described), as indeed do most of the characters in this far from cynical novel of politics and romance. Phineas shows an uncynical bourgeois sensibility, too, by worrying about his debts and paying them as promptly as he can, by contrast with his friend the Honorable (that is, the younger son of a Irish lord) Laurence Fitzgibbon, who contemptuously evades the bill collector, exploiting to the full, as Phineas will not, the immunity that both men possess as members of Parliament.

The 1934 *Webster's New International Dictionary* labels "honesty" in sense 1, "held in honor," as archaic, with the example of "honest" (chaste) as in an "honest woman." It labels "honesty" in sense 1a, "honor," also as obsolete. The adjectival form "honest" in the dominant sense 2 means, say the American lexicographers, fair, upright, truthful, "as, an honest judge or *merchant*, [or an honest] statement" (my italics).[22] No talk of aristocrats or gentlemanly warriors and their "honest" war-making. In the Aristocratic Era "honest" is a matter of inherent or achieved status. In the Bourgeois Era it becomes behavioral and contractual. Status yields to contract, earl to entrepreneur.

The shift from "honest" meaning "in being, honorable, high-status" to "in behavior, truth-telling, as in a contract," was, moreover, not merely English. Surprisingly, the shift occurs in all the commercial languages of Europe, with the suggestive exceptions, it may be, of Spanish and Polish. English is Germanic in a good deal of its structure (though not in how it the verb places), and thoroughly Germanic in its homely vocabulary of bread and hearth, kith and kin. But in its elevated vocabulary of politeness, prudence, and politics, as a French friend of mine likes to say, it is merely French or Latin spoken with a strange accent. Thus "honest" comes in Middle English from Old French *honeste*, and drives out the Old English word for the same idea, *árfæst* or *árful*, "respected, virtuous" or *árlic* (honorable"); *ár* is "honor, dignity, glory," cognate with general Germanic words for honor, all pronounced "air").

In Romance languages, including English in the mouths of the Norman upper classes, the honesty-word meant the same honorable thing—and nothing like mere bourgeois integrity or telling the truth or paying your debts. In English, French, Italian, Spanish, and so forth the word is derived, I noted, from the Latin *honestus*, itself from early Latin *honos*, "reward, honor, high rank." Thus in the first book of Castiglione's *The Book of the Courtier*, written after 1508 and published in 1528, words or compounds of *onesto* occur in the Italian eight times, and always mean "honorable" in a gentlemanly sense or, in the case of women, "chaste" (or, ironically, unchaste, as in *cortegiane oneste*, which is to say, "cultivated courtesans").[23] They never mean "truth-telling" or even commonly "honorable" in the modern meaning that might apply to mere peasants or merchants. In *The Prince* (written in 1513) *onesto* occurs three times (unsurprisingly rarely in a book devoted to prudence only). One time it means "just" ("the goal of the common people is more *onesto* than that of the nobles, the latter wishing to oppress and the former wishing to not be oppressed"). Another time it means "decent or appropriate" ("the soldiers . . . could not put up with that *onesto* way of life to which Pertinax wished to discipline them"). And one more time it means, with dis-, "dishonorable" ("men are never so *disonesti* to turn on you with such obvious ingratitude").[24] Not bourgeois truth telling.

Thus too French *honnête* still in the sixteenth and seventeenth centuries meant what Shakespeare and Castiglione and Machiavelli meant by "honest" and *onesto*. The imposer of the French legislative attitude toward *bon usage*, François de Malherbe (1555–1628), appealed to the linguistic standard of *honnête* men, that is, a nobility or at least a gentry worthy of honor. He was outraged when beggars would address someone as a "noble gentleman," since the word *gentilhomme* already entailed the notion of nobility, and the phrase was therefore an irritating and even insulting redundancy, in suggesting that a gentleman might *not* be noble.

The historian George Huppert notes that in the "Age of Tartuffe," as he puts it, the *honnête homme* loses his strictly aristocratic air but comes instead to exemplify the intellectual fruits of a century of "the style of Paris"—skeptical, anticlerical, pointing forward to Voltaire and the eighteenth-century Enlightenment.[25] "Religious zeal is an embarrassment" to the *honnête homme*, who was an enemy of the Counter-Reformation and therefore an enemy of the state when, as periodically in France, the state was captured by the *dévôt* party. The *honnête homme*'s "morality is that of the pagan authors," the *auctores* (Latin "authorities," leading through French to English "authors"). "Reasonable, courteous, tolerant and well-intentioned towards others," Huppert writes, "one pictures him holding Montaigne's *Essais*." The *Essais* became, Huppert observes, quoting late sixteenth-century and early seventeenth-century praise for it, "*une bréviaire des honnêtes gens*," the only religious instruction needed by a cultivated man. *Honnête* was shifting from praising dukes to praising humanists.

But not yet shopkeepers. In Molière's *Le Bourgeois Gentilhomme* (1670), sixty-five years after *Othello*, the romantic lead, Cléonte, uses *honnête* in the same way that Shakespeare did, with much talk of *honneur* associated with it. The idiotic bourgeois wannabe gentry, M. Jourdain, asks Cléonte if Cléonte is a *gentilhomme*, which meant not "gentleman" as we American democrats would use it now but "of gentle birth, an aristocrat" in the purchasable sense of French society at the time. The recent *Oxford-Hachette* labels *gentilhomme* "historical," with the sole meaning of a member of the gentry or aristocracy. (English "gentry" is of course cognate in its French origin with "gentle," and both originate ultimately in Latin *gens*, a race—a superior one). Cléonte replies at length to My (Foolish) Sire Jourdain:

> No one scruples to take [falsely] the name [of *gentilhomme*], and usage nowadays seems to authorize the theft. For my part, . . . I find that all imposture is unworthy of an honest man [*honnête homme*], and that there is a bit of cowardice in disguis-

ing what Heaven has born us into . . . and to give the impression of that which we are not. I was born, certainly, of parents who held honorable [*honorable*] position. I achieved honor [*l'honneur*] in the armed forces through six years of service. . . . [But] I say to you frankly [*franchement*, not *honnêtement*, as still often in French and English, though "honestly" is taking over] that I am not at all an aristocrat [*gentilhomme*].[26]

A few lines later Madame Jourdain advises her fool of a husband, who wishes "to have an aristocrat as son-in-law," that "your daughter would do better to have an *honest* [that is, honorable] man, rich and well-favored [*un honnête homme riche et bien fait*] than a beggarly and poorly built aristocrat" (*gentilhomme*). Stick with your caste, and watch your purse.

And the usual French word for what we call "mister" (from old "master"; Italian *messer*), or "gentleman," as in democratic phrases such as "ladies and gentlemen," is another piece of hierarchical talk brought down to earth: "my senior, my superior," "my sire," "sir," *monsieur*. In French even in the 1830s it had not been brought down entirely. The bourgeois protagonist in Balzac's *Le Père Goriot* (1835) should have been called *Monsieur* Goriot, but was demoted to *le Père* (the old father, merely) by his loss of wealth.[27] The hero of Stendhal's *The Red and the Black* (1830), Julien Sorel, a craftsman's clever son employed as tutor to the children in the household of a local worthy, triumphs in chapter 6 by earning the title *Monsieur*. At first the *Monsieur* is bestowed by his employer merely because he wishes that the newly hired tutor appear more dignified, to overawe his children: "And now, *Monsieur*— for by my orders everyone in this house is to address you as *Monsieur* . . . ." The other servants are at first reluctant to do so, since they know that Julien is merely the son of a sawyer in town. But shortly he overawes them all with a display of his command of the New Testament in Latin: "This scene earned for Julien the title '*Monsieur*': the servants themselves dared not withhold it from him."[28]

In the big *Hachette-Oxford* nowadays both *honnête homme* and *honnête femme* are labeled obsolete. *Honnête* itself is translated as "honest, decent, fair." The more normal modern French for the English "honest," as applied to a person, is *intègre*, *sincere* (compare the Roman usage), *franc* (flatteringly cognate with *La France*—the *franci*, the spear holders in Germanic, being the free men of Gaul). Yet the old word pops up remade for bourgeois contexts still. One who is honest in the sense of truth-telling about (something) is said *être honnête au sujet de (quelque chose)*. The adverb "honestly" in a bourgeois sense is *honnêtement*. And the English commercial proverb, "honesty is the best policy," is rendered in French as *honnêteté est toujour recompense*, honesty is always rewarded. Would that it were true, honest though it might be.

La Dizionario di Lingua Italiana of 1990 notes of *onesto* that it means in modern Italian *moralmente integro* but had once a now obsolete (*arcaico*) meaning of "deserving honor," *degno d'onore*.[29] It notes, too, the derivation from Latin *honos*, that is, "honor" in the sense of reward for noble military deeds. Looking at it from the other direction, in both the *Concise Cambridge Italian Dictionary* of 1975 and the bilingual *Il Nuovo Ragazzini*, the synonym of *onesto* does appear, though late in the list of Italian words rendering English "honorable," and then in the modern sense, namely, commercially "honest," not in the original sense, the *Ragazzini* says, of "having aristocratic honor, that is, high rank justified by noble blood or by military or other noble deeds."[30]

Thus English and the commerce-drenched Romance languages from 1600 to the present embody the shift from "honor" meaning "aristocratic" to merely bourgeois "reliable."

26

AND SO DOES THE WORD *"EERLIJK"*

What is most surprising, however, confirming a deeper significance for the coming of a bourgeois civilization of trade-tested betterment, is that an identical shift occurs in non-English Germanic languages. In those languages, too, during Shakespeare's or Molière's or Cervantes's time, the words for "honest" and "honesty" evoke noble honor, though coming out of an entirely different linguistic root than in the Romance languages and in an English overwhelmed by Norman French. In Dutch, for example, the root is spelled *eer*, "noble, aristocratic"; it has cognates (with the same pronunciation of English "air") in all the West and North Germanic languages spoken now and earlier, from Iceland and Sweden south to Switzerland and Austria, including Old English (but not, it seems, in the extinct East Germanic languages such as Gothic). Though derived from a quite different root, the word *eerlijk* follows the same modern trajectory as do the words derived from Latin *honestus* in English, French, and Italian. Both Romance and Germanic languages start at the same aristocratic place in their expressions of honor in, say, 1500, and arrive at the latest by 1800 in a different, and commoner and even bourgeois, place.

When the bourgeois southern Netherlanders printed in 1516 the medieval romance *Heinric en Margriete van Limborch*, they averred that Sir Heinric would achieve *eer*, honor, by paying his debts generously: *so sal men eer van u spreken*, literally "so shall people honor of you speak," if you act as a bourgeois who pays his bills and not only as a knight who chronically does not.[1] But the tale is still of knights and their ladies, of whom *eer* is routinely spoken. In the twenty-first century, German *Ehrsucht*, once honorable "honor-seeking," has become to mean "excessive ambition" (*Ehrgeiz* is nor-mal, restrained ambition). The Dutch *eer* and German *ehre* still nowadays mean "noble, honorable, high-status, aristocratic"—like English "honorable" when used among would-be aristocrats on the dueling grounds. And the word persists, as it does in English and French, in dead metaphors remem-bering hierarchy. "*Meine Ehre heißt Treue*" (My Honor is Loyalty; note *treue*) was taken as the motto of Hitler's SS. Using it as a noun, the Dutch say *de eer aandoen om*, "to do [me] the honor of." Or an old-fashioned German politely answering the telephone will say, *Mit wem habe ich die Ehre zu spreken?*— "With whom do I have the honor to speak?"

But in Dutch and in German the addition of *-lijk/-lich* (-like) yielded an *eerlijk/ehrlich* that eventually comes to mean simply "honest," in the same sense as the modern English commendation of the truth-telling necessary for a society of merchants to work. Thus too Danish and Norwegian *ære*, honor (but be careful: *ær* without the *-e* means "duck"!), parallels *aerlig*, hon-est (like Old English *árlic*, "honorable").

The surprising fact, in short, is that both the Germanic languages and the commercial daughters of Latin developed from their respective root words meaning "high-status, worthy of honor" a new word appropriate to an in-creasingly bourgeois society meaning instead "truth-telling, worthy of trust." Thus the alternative Swedish ennobling word *heder* (the Icelandic cognate is *heiðra*) means both "honor" and, with a commercial twist, "credit," and with *-lig* "honest" (equivalent to *ärlig* from the other root, less usual in Icelandic). That is to say, in the seventeenth and early eighteenth centuries in both of the western and northern European families of Germanic languages the pri-mary and older and Iago-ite meaning of "noble, warlike, courteous, worthy of being honored," fades, leaving mainly our modern notion of "that deals uprightly in speech and act . . . that will not lie cheat or steal."[2]

The title of the English poem of 1705 by Shaftesbury's opponent, Bernard Mandeville, is *The Grumbling Hive: or, Knaves Turn'd Honest*. Mandeville—who not incidentally, though writing in English, was a Dutchman—meant by "honest" nothing like "partaking of nobility," but instead "not cheating," in the modern sense, *eerlijkheid*. He cynically condemned such behavior as naïve and socially profitless: "Then leave complaints: fools only strive / To make a great an honest hive."[3] The honest/honor split appears to be not sharp in Spanish, as one might have expected in a society obsessed with honor in an old-fashioned sense. Spanish follows Mother Latin in using for English "honest" *sincero*. By 1800 at latest, by contrast, many Romance and all Germanic languages have come to use the honesty word to mean pretty much exclusively "sincere, upright, truth-telling, reliable for a business deal."[4]

Honesty now means honesty.

If you can stand any more of this sort of evidence, consider that translations of the New Testament register the change, too, though unevenly. In many recent translations of the Parable of the *Unjust* Manager into English, the word "honest" is used in the sense of "upright, plain dealing." Thus the New Revised Standard Version (1989) of Luke 16:8 is "And his master commended the *dishonest* manager." The *New English Bible* (1961) has "And the master applauded the *dishonest* steward." The New International Version (1973–1984): "The master commended the *dishonest* manager." Thus also the Weymouth NT and the World English Bible. But the original Greek is *adikias*, literally "un-*just*." The New American Standard (1960–1995), the Darby Version, and Young's [old] Literal Translation use "unrighteous," and Douay-Rheims and Webster's use the wholly Greek-justified "unjust." (The Basic English Bible makes do with plain "false.")

In the era in which English "honest" meant "high-status," however, the word "honest" was *never* used in its modern sense of "fair-dealing." Thus the King James (1611) version of Luke 16:8 speaks of the "*unjust*," not the "*dishonest*" steward. (On the other hand, the merely seven occurrences of "honest" in the King James, all in the New Testament, appear to mean "righteous" [as in Greek, *dikos*, just] in the sense of following the law, of Moses or of Jesus, not high-status or even aristocratic.)

Not so incidentally, as Diarmaid MacCulloch argues, the Latin of the Vulgate uses *justitia*, as in Romans 1:17, for what in Luther's Bible is translated (from the Greek, in which the word is *dikaios*) as *Gerechtigkeit*, righteousness (you see the English cognates of *recht* in "right," or "upright"). The Latin *Justitia*, however, actually meant something *made* upright, like the derived word in printing, "justify," in the sense of *making* the right margin of a printed book straight, not ragged. Luther took it to mean ("in a literally crucial difference," as MacCulloch puts it, making a learned joke about the cross) *declaring* someone to be upright. That is, *Gerechtigkeit* is *declared* by God ("imputed" is the theological word), and it is therefore a matter of God's grace alone. It is not a virtue *made* by men out of the (after all) hopelessly sinful, unworthy person (following Augustine's talk of original sin). Thus Protestant theology, entire.

To return to "honest." In other languages having the same problem with the older meaning of "honest" it is similar. The old States' Bible of the Dutch (1618–1619) calls the steward *onrechtvaardigen*, "unrighteous." Some versions of Luther's Bible (say, 1545) calls him *den ungetreuen Verwalter*, the *unfaithful* manager [note again the use of the word cognate with English "true" in the sense of "faithful," as in the SS motto], a mistranslation in context (since in the original Greek *pistos*, "faithful," occurs two verses down in contrast, not in parallel, to *dikos*). But anyway it is not *unehrlich*, modern "dishonest"—which in 1545 would have suggested the irrelevant "not of high status." The modern (1912) Luther and the Schlachter (1951) give, as the Dutch does, *ungerechten*, "unrighteous." A recent translation into Afrikaans calls the manager *oneerlike*, that is, "dishonest" in the modern sense, as in modern Dutch.[5] But a 1953 Afrikaans version was using the more true-to-the-Greek *onregverdige*, "unrighteous," as did earlier in the twentieth century Norwegian (1930) and Swedish translations (1917).[6]

In French the old Martin and Ostervald (1744, though in a 1996 revision) use "unfaithful" and the Darby uses the Greek-justified "unjust." The French Jerusalem Bible uses the modern *malhonnête*. In Italian the steward (or "factor" in older English, cognate with the Italian *fattore*) is in the Giovanni Diodati Bible (1649) *l'ingiusto fattore* and in the Riveduta (1927) *il fattore infedele*. No *disonesto* about him, with its whiff in olden times of low breeding. The modern Catholic Vulgate uses "unfair" following the Greek—not following the Latin for "dishonest" in the modern sense, which would be the opposite of *sincerus*, *probus*, *simplex*, *antiques*, *frugii*, depending on the shade of meaning. Spanish translations simply call him *malo* and leave it at that.

The sociologist Norbert Elias noted in his book of 1939 the same shift. "*Courtoisie*, *civilité* and *civilisation* mark [in French] three stages of a social development," that is, from distinction by membership in a court, to distinction by membership of a restricted urban society, down to a universalization of, say, table manners by an entire society, rich and poor, urban and rural.[7] Likewise, I am claiming, the changing fortunes of "honesty" signals that the old civilization, which was dominated by warriors and latterly by courtiers, required above all a word for rank. Our civilization, by contrast, dominated by merchants and latterly by manufacturers and recently by risk capitalists, requires instead a word for reliable truth-telling. Honesty is, as the philosophers and linguists put it, a conversational "implicature" of a society in which exchange is honored and would not function well without it. Nowadays the fancy and steadily growing word is "transparency."

And so from 1600 to 1691 to 1776 to 1848 this new civilization in northwestern Europe came into being, in its words.

The English, I say, had been notorious in the age of Sir Francis Drake and Queen Elizabeth I for a proud, decidedly unbourgeois way of talking and acting. In August 1588 Elizabeth astride her horse in full armor in Tilbury Field professed to have no doubt, as the Spanish Armada sailed up the English Channel, that "we shall shortly have a famous victory over those enemies of my God, of my kingdom, and of my people":

> I am . . . resolved, in the midst and heat of the battle, to live or die amongst you all, to lay down my life for my God and for my kingdom and for my people, my honor [note the word], and my blood, even in the dust. I know I have the body but of a weak and feeble woman, but I have the heart and stomach of a king and a king of England too.

You can imagine what the effect on the assembled men was of such royal "honesty," if entirely unrealistic, and even in a bourgeois sense dishonest, considering that the enemies of her kingdom were the best soldiers in Europe, led by Parma, the best general in Europe. Waiting impatiently in Flanders the Spaniards had double the number of seasoned troops already aboard the Armada heading to pick them up, which two armies joined would have crushed the English, who had not won a major land battle against Continentals since Verneuil in 1424. Elizabeth's declaration was aristocratic cheek. (And, as the literary critic Mary Beth Rose observes of this and other speeches by the Virgin Queen, she exhibited still more cheek in her "rhetorical technique [which] involves appeasing widespread fears about female rule by adhering to conventions that assume the inferiority of the female gender only in order to supersede them."[8]).

As late as 1657 the scholar Joshua Poole in his quotation book, *The English Parnassus*, admired his fellow Englishmen as "bold, audacious, adventurous, warlike." Although the limited taxing powers of English and Scottish kings kept them from much national involvement in Continental wars until the 1690s, individual Britons maintained a Europe-wide reputation as volunteers or mercenaries recruited from what Francis Bacon early in the seventeenth century called "a choleric and warlike nation."[9] A Flemish-origin businessman (and postmaster) in the London of the previous century had declared of the wannabe-aristocratic English that "the people are bold, courageous, ardent and cruel in war, but very inconstant, rash, vainglorious, light and deceiving, and very suspicious, especially of foreigners, whom they despise."[10] Of these qualities only courage and the despising of foreigners survived the embourgeoisement of England. Jeremy Paxman, who is among the numerous tellers of the tale to use the Fleming's words, remarks that by the nineteenth century the English had come to be viewed as having on the contrary "honesty [in our modern and bourgeois sense], prudence, patriotism, self-control, fair play and courage."[11] "It's not cricket" is far from "we shall shortly have a famous victory over those enemies of my God, of my kingdom, and of my people." Evidently something had changed. The language changed early.

So also in the matter of attitudes toward trade. "Credit" comes from *creditus*, "believed." Each of the hundred-odd quotations in the *Oxford English Dictionary* illustrating the noun and the verb date from after 1541, but during the sixteenth century most of the commercial uses of the word show hostility toward it. An act of 34–35 Henry VIII (that is, 1542) noted that "sundry persons consume the substance obtained by credit of other men." Shame on them (the scolding has lasted down to populist assaults on credit, such as the anthropologist David Graeber's book in 2011, and the Syriza Party in Greece in 2015). But by 1691 Locke is using neutral, businesslike language: credit is merely "the expectation of money within some limited time."

Roger Holmes has pointed me to Felicity Heal and Clive Holmes, *The Gentry in England and Wales, 1500–1700* (1994).[12] He well summarizes their evidence:

> They point to the change in funerary monuments ("marmorialized gentlemen") from those of the sixteenth to those of the later seventeenth century. Effigies of the deceased in armor give way to one's wearing Roman togas or contemporary clothes. . . . Gervase Holles insisted he "would not scrape a chimney sweeper out of my pedigree" and castigated those who refused to acknowledge "those honest [note the new usage] ancestors whose industry prepared the way to our better

condition." . . . "By the end of the [seventeenth] century," Heal and Holmes write, "Sir Robert Atkyns, writing his history of Gloucestershire, took it for granted that 'very few families continue to flourish above three generations, therefore there are few families above a hundred years standing.'"[13]

Sir Robert's remark is confirmed by Gregory Clark's recent research into the persistence of occupational (low status: Smith) and Norman (high status: de Bourg) names in England over centuries.[14]

We are just beginning in economic history to take seriously ideas and their trace in language. But economists and economic historians, recovering from the age of materialism, 1890–1980, have had a hard time of it. An interesting paper in 2012 by Plopeanu, Foldvari, van Leeuwen, and van Zanden on the stages of the connection between books and progress puts the word "ideas" in scare quotes throughout. It reminds me of how Gary Becker in his classic papers on the prudence-only theory of marriage put the word "love" in scare quotes, to indicate how doubtful he was that it mattered much to the mutually beneficial exchange of food preparation and auto repair between F and M. In a similar vein the economist Ajit Sinha has pointed out in personal correspondence that I "provide 'evidence' from literature and the like for the existence of the idea of bourgeois dignity during this period. But then, I suppose, one could also provide even more evidence of lack of bourgeois dignity in the literature of the same period. In that case, how does one decide which one represented the dominant culture of the period?" Yes, though note the positivist sneer in the scare quotes on "evidence" that is not framed as a scientifically irrelevant test of "significance." In any age one is going to find praise or blame for bourgeois virtues, and vices, somewhere. The charmingly passionate old men peddling copies of the *Socialist Worker* on street corners will be glad to tell you about the vices. The questions are: What the ratio of praise to blame found in documents that are salient or honored or revealing? Does it change? And does the change matter for betterment?

What I do claim, correctly I think, is that it is much easier to find talk about the bourgeoisie at betterment-favoring ratios after 1700 and especially after 1800 than before, and easier in Britain until the 1980s than in, say, China or India. When varied evidence—Sinha's "and the like"—piles up in a free society, we are justified in concluding that the society changed. The economist

Nimish Adhia has shown that the leading Bollywood films changed their heroes from the 1950s to the 1980s from bureaucrats to businesspeople, and their villains from factory owners to policemen, in parallel with a similar shift in the ratio of praise for trade-tested betterment in the editorial pages of the *Times of India*. Adhia quotes the leaders of an newly independent India. Mahatma Gandhi declared that "there is nothing more disgraceful to man than the principle 'buy in the cheapest market and sell in the dearest.'" Nehru agreed: "Don't talk to me about profit. Profit is a dirty word."[15] Did the change from hatred to admiration of trade-tested betterment make possible the Indian reforms after 1991? Clearly without some sort of change in opinion the Congress Party would not in a democracy have been able to liberalize the economy. The result of the liberalization was a growth rate of 7 percent per person per year, as against what the Indians had bitterly called the "Hindu rate of growth" of 1 percent per year during the first four decades after independence. I am making for the Great Enrichment the same case that Adhia made for late twentieth-century India.

DEFOE, ADDISON, AND STEELE
SHOW IT, TOO

The prestige of prudence, then, as against that of the characteristically aristocratic or Christian virtues, such as courage and faith, rose sharply in England. By the middle of the eighteenth century British people—especially the men—delighted in claiming prudence for their own behavior and fell in love with a cynical supposition that others were motivated similarly, lacking in a merely feminine love. I have noted that Mandeville in 1705 had upvalued the actions of the selfish, a kind of reduced prudence. And Benjamin Franklin and Samuel Johnson, among others, accounted for their own behavior in prudential terms, rather than in aristocratic or religious terms, and went about prudently measuring the Gulf Stream and Scottish castles.

The voice of the English novelist, beginning with Daniel Defoe (1661–1731), is bourgeois too, and focused on prudence—that is to say, the ordinary business of life, its know-how, its *savoir faire*. The eighteenth and especially the nineteenth-century *roman* eventually comes to be focused on the middle-class home, in sharp contrast to adventure yarns focused on court, castle, and battleground, long called "romances" (whence the standard French, Italian, Swedish, Dutch, and German word, *roman*, for what the English, Portuguese, and Spanish called the "novel," a purveyor of novelties). A "romance" was given new vigor by Romantic novelists and poets such as Sir Walter Scott and late Goethe. The Greeks and Romans had written novels about mundane matters, such as dinner parties, but the genre died out along with Rome's grandeur and corruption. The Japanese from the twelfth century had modern-seeming novels, written famously by women, though focusing on courtly life. And at about the same time, during the Islamic

Golden Age, the novel was a common genre, if similarly focused on the court. The Chinese—hundreds of years before the Europeans caught on, as usual—had been gathering folktales and official histories into proper novels, such as the *Romance of the Three Kingdoms* (early Ming dynasty), though these also focused mainly on the great and good and their exploits. As with many other technologies, such as pottery and gardening and mathematics, the Europeans in the seventeenth and eighteenth century laboriously reinvented, reverse-engineered, and then improved upon literary genres practiced for centuries in places more advanced than backward Europe.

Defoe's version arose out of broadsheets and pamphlets relating the novelties of prodigious storms and terrible murders, and out of a rich devotional literature by English Puritans, such as *Pilgrim's Progress* (1678 and later editions).[1] The leading case is Defoe's *Robinson Crusoe* (1719), which combined prodigies with devotion, though in a style so realistic that it could plausibly be presented to the naïve as a factual memoir. J. M. Coetzee's narrator in *Foe* (1986) urges Crusoe to write in Defoe's style: "When you made your needle [as Crusoe did in Defoe's novel] . . . by what means did you pierce the eye? When you sewed your hat, what did you use for thread? Touches like these will one day persuade your countrymen that it is all true, every word."[2] The touches evoke *savoir faire*, knowing how to do. Defoe also wrote in his realist style *Journal of the Plague Year* (1722) and, astonishingly in the same year, his masterpiece of the proto-novelistic genre, *Moll Flanders*—Defoe was a one-man publishing house of bourgeois propaganda, such as *The Complete English Tradesman* (1726).

Novels are associated in every way with the bourgeoisie, an old point in literary criticism, made most enthusiastically from the 1930s on by left-wing critics, but also from the center by Ian Watt, who noted in *Robinson Crusoe* "the dynamic tendency of capitalism."[3] The European novel later became news about the middling sort practicing creative destruction—the bettering merchants and craftsmen and yeoman farmers—a class that had earlier been thought unworthy of attention. As Coetzee put it recently in his introduction to an edition of *Robinson Crusoe*, "for page after page—for the first time in the history of fiction—we see a minute, ordered description of how things are done."[4] How things are done, that *savoir faire*, is precisely the virtue of prudence, which Defoe praised in all his writings. Defoe's imagination, as a nineteenth-century French critic wrote on the eve of the clerisy's reaction against all things bourgeois, was that of a man of business.[5]

Look at Crusoe selecting what to load on his first trip with his raft from the wreck of the ship, of which he was the sole survivor:

> It was in vain to sit and wish for what was not to be had, and this extremity roused my application. . . . My raft was now strong . . . my next care was what to load it with. . . . This put me on rummaging for clothes, . . . but I took no more than I wanted for present use, for I had other things which my eye was more upon, as first tools to work with on shore.[6]

The rational bourgeois is a calculator making rough-and-ready choices about what to put next on the raft. The details of the style contribute to the emphasis on choice under scarcity—a contrast to the stories of shipwrecks in the *Odyssey* or the *Aeneid* or the early books of the Hebrew Bible over which hover gods willing to perform miracles of abundance. Defoe's and Crusoe's world is naturalistic, in a manner we have come to call "realistic." The story is filled with realistic disappointments, signaled often by an ominous "but." "There had been some barley and wheat together" on the wreck, "*but*, to my great disappointment, I found afterwards that the rats had eaten or spoiled it all."[7] "I went a-fishing, *but* caught not one fish that I durst eat of."[8] The "but" is realistic, unsentimental, aware of life's scarcity, as the earlier romance was not. It is the economist's and the bourgeois's favorite conjunction.

The realist novel perfected by the English and then successively by the French and the Italians and the Russians and the Germans was hard to fit with nonbourgeois cultures. As Coetzee said in an essay about the twentieth-century Egyptian novelist Naguib Mahfouz, the realistic novel devalues tradition—"it values originality, self-founding," in the way one founds a business, not putting high value on the traditions of an ancient family. Jane Austen begins *Persuasion* (1818) in free indirect style making gentle fun of "Sir Walter Elliot of Kellynch Hall . . . who, for his own amusement, never took up any book but the Baronetage [which listed all the upper gentry, not the few peers of the realm but those below them who on coming of age would nonetheless by heredity be called Sir]; . . . there his faculties were aroused into admiration and respect, by contemplating the limited remnants of the earliest patents [of hereditary entitlement, sold by James I on a large scale from 1611 on]."[9] Sir Walter was looking back fondly to an aristocratic age in which the hereditary sirs were memorialized in recumbent statues in full armor atop their tombs, not by mere modest plaques on the church wall.

By contrast, the realistic novel, Coetzee continues, "imitates the mode of the scientific case study or the law brief rather than the hearthside fairy tale." Just when the realistic novel was being devised, the scientific revolution was gaining prestige. The novel, writes Coetzee, "prides itself on a language bereft of ornament," reaching its height in Hemingway's one true sentence. It focuses "on the steady, prosaic observation and recording of detail," as in Robinson Crusoe's struggles with the raft and a failed canoe he built. *Robinson Crusoe* "is just the kind of vehicle," Coetzee concludes, "one would expect Europe's merchant bourgeoisie to invent in order to record and celebrate its own ideals and achievements."[10] (There is some slippage here: it was above all the sons and especially the daughters of the literal gentry, or the literal clergy, who wrote the novels, not the children of merchants. And so, except for Defoe, the best of the English novel in the eighteenth and nineteenth centuries does not directly celebrate buying low and selling high.) The recent turn to magic realism and postmodernity in the novel, as for example in Gabriel García Márquez or Isabel Allende, registers the strongly *anti*bourgeois feelings of the twentieth-century clerisy, especially in Latin America.

It was the historian Paul Langford in 1992, titling his survey of English history 1727 to 1783, who revived Blackstone's epithet for the English as "a polite and commercial people." Langford attacks repeatedly the more usual notion that the age of the Whig grandees was ruled by the values of the aristocrat.[11] The "seeming passion for aristocratic values," for example, evinced in the vogue for the spas, such as Bath, and later the seaside resorts, such as Brighton, "depended on a middle class clientele, the upper middling sorts described in Jane Austen's novels. Britain in the eighteenth century was a plutocracy if anything, and even as a plutocracy one in which power was widely diffused, constantly contested, and ever adjusting to new incursions of wealth, often modest wealth." As early as 1733, Langford claims, "the shopkeepers and tradesmen of England were immensely powerful as a class." "Bath owed its name to the great but its fortune to the mass of middling."[12]

Such cultural embourgeoisement of England started in the late seventeenth and early eighteenth centuries. The first voices in English theorizing the event are Joseph Addison and Richard Steele, in their much-imitated magazine briefly issued, *The Spectator* (555 daily numbers, each about 2,500 words, from March 1711). "With *The Spectator* the voice of the bourgeois," Basil Willey declared in 1964, "is first heard in polite letters, and makes his first decisive contribution to the English moral tradition." Addison was "the first lay preacher to reach the ear of the middle-classes." (Defoe reached the ear of the less educated of the middling sort.) "The hour was ripe for a rehabilitation of the virtues [against Restoration cynicism], and [Addison and Steele] were the very men for the task."[13] Decades later the Dutch, who a century earlier had originated the praise for bourgeois virtue in northern Europe, returned the favor of the Addisonian project, under the heading of "*Spectatorial* Papers" (*Hollandsche Spectator*, 1731–1735; *Algemeene* [Universal] *Spectator*, 1742–1746; and *De Patriot*, 1742–1743), in explicit imitation and against a perceived corruption of the bourgeois virtues—the wannabe-aristocratic vices of nepotism, French manners, effeminate men, and sleeping late.[14]

Addison's play *Cato: A Tragedy* (1713) became astoundingly popular among the bourgeoisie of the eighteenth century. Since it is the story of one Roman aristocrat, Cato, opposing another, Julius Caesar, one wonders why. One could say the same of Shakespeare's unbourgeois plays, which were performed to large audiences of London shopkeepers and their wives; or for that matter, one could say it of cowboy and detective stories nowadays, delighting middle-class male audiences who wouldn't think of riding herd or staking out.[15]

The young hero Juba in *Cato* announces the ennobling Roman project:

> To make man mild, and sociable to man
> To cultivate the wild, licentious savage
> With wisdom, discipline, and liberal arts—
> The embellishments of life; virtues like these
> Make human nature shine, reform the soul,
> And break our fierce barbarians into men.[16]

The project of *Cato* in 1713 is just that, and identical to that of *The Spectator* two years before—to tame the "barbarous" interests of war and loot by preaching sociable virtues. At a loftier level, Shaftesbury's implied audience in his *Characteristics of Men, Manners, Opinions, Times* (1699, 1711) is his fellow aristocrats. But Addison and Steele were speaking instead to the middling sort. The values of an aristocratic society lingered, but down to the present have been reused to ennoble the commoners' lives of lawyer-ing or merchanting. The early eighteenth-century English theorists recast aristocratic civic republicanism into a new way of public life admired and practiced by the bourgeoisie.

The character of Cato himself appeals to bourgeois notions of libera-tion from subordination to the quality. The cry of liberty in the eighteenth century was necessarily a cry for the benefit of the bourgeoisie. It is a con-ventional point, but true, that the aristocracy and gentry did not require liberation, and for a long time no one but a handful of radicals such as the Levellers or Paine or Burns or the left wing of the French Assembly took seriously the liberty of the rest. Increasingly during the eighteenth century in Britain and more so in the nineteenth century the typical heir to an aris-tocratic title, or his lower-status imitator, was seen by the bourgeoisie as a gambling, arrogant fool. The country gentleman was often portrayed as il-literate, devoted to his dogs and hunting, in the mold of Squire Western in Fielding's *Tom Jones* (1749) (and in contrast there to the admirable Squire Allworthy) or Sir Pitt Crawley in Thackeray's *Vanity Fair* (1847–1848) or Lord Chiltern in Trollope's Palliser novels of the 1860s and 1870s. And there-fore a noble, abstemious, republican patriot like Cato the Younger could be applauded by bourgeois audiences. A battle between aristocrats at the close of the Roman Republic is reappropriated in the play for its uses in dignifying the bourgeoisie.

Addison's play, and his *Spectator* with Steele, anticipated by forty years Adam Smith's sociable and impartial spectator. The play's themes of theatri-cality, imagination, and idealized spectators are echoed in *The Spectator* 231's declaration that "in our solitudes, we should fancy that Cato stands before us, and sees everything that we do" and the earlier statement, in *Spectator* 10, that his work is addressed to "everyone who considers the world as theatre, and who desires to form a right judgment of those who act in it." *The Spec-tator*, at least—no such commercial theme could be admitted into *Cato*—anticipated the Turgotian and Humean and Smithian approval of economic activity: "Riches and plenty are the natural fruits of liberty," *Spectator* 287 declared, "and where these abound, learning and all the liberal arts will im-mediately lift up their heads and flourish."[17] Such a declaration is impossible in the mouth of a Shakespearean character. In the 1720s "Cato" was used as the pseudonym for the authors John Trenchard and Thomas Gordon advocating a Lockean freedom of speech and conscience. Cato became therefore a (somewhat strange) symbol of radical libertarian thought, such as opposition to Madison's ideas for the federal Constitution in 1787 and 1788, or the Cato Institute, founded in 1977.

Consider the contrast between Addison's *Cato* of 1713 and Shakespeare's *Julius Caesar* of 1599 or *Antony and Cleopatra* of 1606, also retellings of the fall of the Roman Republic. In *Julius Caesar* the tyrant is the hero, and the public sin of Brutus, an "honorable man" (again the word "honor"), is his rebellion against such a constituted authority as Caesar's. It is a theme one would expect in anxious Elizabethan and Jacobean times. In *Cato*, by contrast, what is damned is the courting of the mob by Caesar. It is precisely the middle ground of liberty for the middling sort that made *Cato* so useful to the bourgeoisie. In the hands of the American founding brothers "tyranny" was an appeal against imperial power exercised by Tories, but it was also an appeal against the ignoble mob. The Federalist politicians of the early American Republic, such as Madison and Washington, eager readers of *Cato*, expected a continuation of the rule of the educated best, their virtuous selves in particular. John Adams of Quincy and Boston, a lawyer who famously won a case against precisely the ignoble mob wishing to execute British soldiers doing their duty, gloried in *Cato*. The play was echoed in many an outburst by revolutionary Americans: "what pity is it / That we can die but once to serve our country!"[18]

Louis B. Wright's old *Middle-Class Culture in Elizabethan England* (1935) is surely correct in claiming that the education of the English bourgeoisie during the sixteenth and seventeenth centuries—the scholarly and even scientific habits that Deborah Harkness (2007) has recently emphasized—makes the "sudden" emergence of a literate and confident class in the late seventeenth and early eighteenth centuries less surprising. True, Wright was mistaken when he wrote, "The gospel of work, one of the most significant articles of the bourgeois dogma, was promulgated with great earnestness during the period of Puritan supremacy and paved the way for the later apotheosis of business which has colored the entire outlook of the modern world."[19] What made the modern world was ingenuity, not slogging. But what matters here is how society in general came to feel about the sort of work a businessman did, whether ingenuity or slogging—and about that he is surely correct. No doubt the merchant had always and everywhere urged himself and his fellows to work at accounts and correspondence late into the night. But as long as a "gentleman" is still defined to have no vocation beyond rattling swords and composing sonnets, the fullness of the Bourgeois Revaluation has not been reached.

THE BOURGEOIS REVALUATION
BECOMES A COMMONPLACE, AS
IN *THE LONDON MERCHANT*

The Bourgeois Revaluation begins slowly, against resistance. The literary historian John Loftis had argued that the eighteenth-century theater testifies to a new admiration for the bourgeoisie.[1] The economist Jacob Viner, while commending Loftis for his energy in research, offered in 1970 "the simpler hypothesis . . . that as soon as merchants came to the theatre in sufficient numbers the dramatists would provide fare which would retain them as customers."[2] Viner thus appeals to the rise of the bourgeoisie in its simplest economistic form—not as a rise in prestige originating in the superstructure but a rise in sheer numbers originating in the base. As I said, from 1890 to 1980 we were all a bit Marxian.

But the relation between actual and implied audience is seldom without ambiguity. In *Star Wars* and *The Godfather* and *The Sopranos* and *The Wire* none of the heroes or antiheroes are typical of their massed audiences. Shakespeare systematically flattered his aristocratic and especially his royal audiences, but his actual audience, I have noted, included the massed merchants of London. *Wall Street* (1987) assaulted financial "capitalism," but many a financial master of the universe along with his victims gloried in the movie. As Charles Taylor notes, such materialist history as Viner's is less persuasive than any number of ideational alternatives—for example, that "it more and more dawned on governing elites that increased production . . . was a key to . . . military power," as shown for example by Tsar Peter apprenticing himself in the shipyards of Holland.[3]

The cultural task was to bring the bourgeoisie out into the daylight of honor. Even now the task (which is mine as well) is not entirely finished, three or four centuries after its beginnings. It begins in Amsterdam and Rotterdam and other Dutch -dams around 1700, and a century later is imitated in royal London. (Remarkably, it happens in Japan too, about the same time, but only in the merchant academies of Ōsaka and not in the center of power in Edo.)[4] The comedies of the Restoration after 1660 in England still sneered at the bourgeoisie, as Shakespeare and his contemporaries had sneered. Lawrence Stone and Jeanne C. Fawtier Stone observed in their book *An Open Elite? England 1540–1880* (1984) that during the seventeenth century any attempt to claim the honored aristocratic values for the bourgeoisie failed, dying "of its own . . . implausibility, and . . . crushed under the avalanche of satirical plays and pamphlets . . . in which the figure of the merchant continued to be portrayed in stereotypical terms that went back to antiquity." But matters changed, I have said, in the age of *The Spectator*. Early in the eighteenth century, the Stones continue, "at the hands of men such as Addison and Steele . . . [the overseas merchant at least] was now portrayed as a responsible and sober citizen, . . . whose commercial activities were recognized as . . . the basis of the nation's prosperity and greatness."[5]

Not without exception. Addison wrote in *The Spectator* about what he regarded as the dangers of commercial success: "Having no fears to alarm them from abroad, [they] indulge themselves in the enjoyment of all the pleasures they can get into their possession; which naturally produces avarice, and an immoderate pursuit after wealth and riches."[6] We hear echoes of such antimarket clichés, I've noted, in present-day alarms about consumerism. Addison had quoted in the same number Dryden's translation of Persius's *Satires*:

> Of pepper, and Sabean incense, take
> With thy own hands, from the tired camel's back,
> And with posthaste thy running markets make.
> Be sure to turn the penny; lie and swear,
> 'Tis wholesome sin: But Jove, thou say'st, will hear.
> Swear, Fool, or starve; for the dilemma's even:
> A tradesman thou! and hope to go to heaven? (5.131)

Such talk echoes down the eighteenth century, a civic-republican counterpoise to the new admiration for commerce. People worried that riches were "softening," and took to admiring, bizarrely, not the commercial glory of Athens but the anticommercial hardness of Sparta. We see it still in conservative historians touting the plenty they claim arises from a ravishingly attractive Power, and warning about the decline the West and the Clash of Civilizations. Take up the white man's burden. Little of the rhetoric against the bourgeoisie and its activities is new.

In Johnson's *Dictionary* a "cit," from "citizen," is "a pert low townsman," and in the *OED*, it is said to have been used "more or less contemptuously, for example to denote a person from the town as opposed to the country, or a tradesman or shopkeeper as distinguished from a gentleman." The first three citations in the *OED* are 1633, 1673, and 1674. The word would have arisen in reaction to the seventeenth-century and early eighteenth-century empowerment of the bourgeoisie at first from Hampden's breast or Cromwell's sword—though the most influential parliamentarians arrayed against the king during the Civil War had not been cits but gentry accustomed to bearing arms. Cromwell himself was, for example.

The newly defined "squirearchy," distinguished now among the larger category of "the middling sort" below the aristocracy, would have such a word as "cit" frequently in its mouth, to sneer at the bourgeoisie sitting below them in the Great Chain of Being. In Steele's play of 1722, *The Conscious Lovers*, a merchant of Bristol, Mr. Sealand ("sea-land," which about covers it), replies to the rural gentry's sneer:

> Sir, as much a cit as you take me for, I know the town, and the world. And give me leave to say that we merchants are a species of gentry [note] that have grown into the world this last century, and are as honorable, and almost as useful, as you landed folks, that have always thought your selves so much above us. For your trading, forsooth, is extended no farther than a load of hay, or a fat ox. You are pleasant people, indeed, because you are generally bred up to be lazy. Therefore, I warrant you, industry is dishonorable [to you].[7]

Acknowledgement of the sneer and the corresponding bourgeois cringe was still there—in the word "cit" itself, and in the sarcastic "almost as useful" in evaluating the mercantile "species of gentry" against the country version. Mr. Sealand duels verbally with the other and even higher status gentry in the play, a Sir John Bevil, and Steele arranges for Sealand to win:

SIR JOHN BEVIL. Oh, Sir, . . . you are laughing at my laying any stress upon descent. But I must tell you, Sir, I never knew anyone but he that wanted [that is, lacked] that advantage turn it into ridicule.

MR. SEALAND. And I never knew anyone who had many better advantages put that into his account.

Even Sealand's witticism is expressed in the bourgeois language of accounts. The other gentry in the play are disturbed about a marriage with a bourgeois (act 5, scene 1):

MYRTLE. But is he directly a trader at this time?

CIMBERTON. There's no hiding the disgrace, sir; he trades to all parts of the world.

MYRTLE. We never had one of our family before who descended from persons that *did* anything.

That the audience in 1723 would *laugh* at "*did* anything," though, signals a social alteration.

Voltaire wrote with similar sarcasm ten years later, "I will not, however, take upon me to say which is the most useful to his country, . . . the powdered lord, who knows to a minute when the king rises or goes to bed . . . or the merchant, who . . . from his counting house sends his orders into Surat or Cairo, thereby contributing to the happiness and convenience of human nature."[8] And still later, Johnson, again, affirmed the innocence of the getting of money. And much later, in 1844, on the eve of the Great Conversion against betterment among the elite of American writers (such as his friend Thoreau), Emerson wrote:

There are geniuses in trade, as well as in war. . . . Nature seems to authorize trade, as soon as you see the natural merchant. . . . The habit of his mind is a reference to standards of natural equity and public advantage; and he inspires respect, and the wish to deal with him, both for the quiet spirit of honor [note the word] which attends him, and for the intellectual pastime which the spectacle of so much ability affords.[9]

∞

Early in that bright morn of bourgeois honor, in 1731, George Lillo (1693–1739), a jeweler of London, wrote *The London Merchant; or, The History of George Barnwell*, his second play and his first success. It inaugurated the bourgeois tragedy, which reaches its artistic height in Ibsen's and Miller's plays and Dreiser's and Updike's novels. The very name of the genre is an absurdity by earlier dramatic standards, since only the mighty could fall in the way required by a Greek tragedy (or so Romantic theoreticians such as Schiller were later to say). The absurdity was imitated in France and Germany a quarter century after Lillo in the *bürgerliches Trauerspiel* ("bourgeois mourning play") or Diderot's *drame bourgeois*. In Spain, catholicized (by way of five French adaptions in 1748, 1757, 1758, 1769, and 1781), *The London Merchant* was remade into four Spanish versions, in 1776, 1783, 1785, and 1787—one of the Spanish playwrights supposed that a French translation was the original.[10] It was an important work Europe-wide.

The plot was drawn from an old street ballad, set in the Armada time of 1588—Britain in 1731 had recently been at war with Spain again. Eighteen-year-old George Barnwell, apprenticed to a good merchant of the city, is tempted by a Mrs. Millwood, a whore, to steal from his master, of the bourgeoisie, for money; and then he murders his uncle, of the gentry, for money. In the Child ballad version:

"Nay, I an uncle have;
At Ludlow he doth dwell;
He is a grazier, which in wealth
Doth all the rest excel.

"Ere I will live in lack,
And have no coin for thee,
I'll rob his house and murder him."
"Why should you not," quoth she.[11]

Barnwell and Mrs. Millwood both end on the gallows, though Barnwell at least is blessed by true repentance.

The tale was well enough known that the "fine, powdered sparks" (in the phrase from the poet laureate Colley Cibber's "Epilogue" to the play) who attended the first performance brought along broadsheet copies of the poem, which Lillo had hawked around the town by way of advertising on the day before its opening. The antibourgeois sparks intended to laugh. But Colley's son Theophilus claimed that they stayed to weep.

The play is described by literary critics as "almost militant in its pride in the middle class."[12] "Honest merchants," declares the elder merchant in the play, who is absurdly named "Thorowgood," "at some times contribute to the safety of their country, as they do at all times to its happiness."[13] (Note "happiness" is here applied to merely material well-being.) Thorowgood then asserts boldly what was still contested in the 1730s, that "as the name of merchant never degrades the gentleman, so by no means does it exclude him."[14] The playwright lays it on thick. Thorowgood instructs his other, and virtuous, apprentice "Trueman" (there you go again, Lillo), "If . . . you should be tempted to any action that has [even] the appearance of vice or meanness in it, upon reflecting upon the dignity of our profession you may with honest scorn reject whatever is unworthy of it." (Note "honest," now applied to a bourgeois.) The big merchants dealing in foreign goods had come to stand at the height of bourgeois dignity. "The method of merchandising," declared Thorowgood, is not "merely as a means of getting wealth [but] a science. See how it is founded in reason, and the nature of things, how it has promoted humanity. . . . by mutual benefits diffusing mutual love from pole to pole."[15]

Forty years later, in Richard Cumberland's sentimental comedy of 1771, *The West Indian*, a character addresses the elderly merchant, Stockwell (epithets as names were at the time conventional stagecraft): "A merchant of your eminence, and a member of the British Parliament, might surely aspire, without offense, to [marry] the daughter of a [rich gentry, a West Indian] planter."[16] In 1731 such a hierarchy-offending proposal had been more controversial, and Lillo had therefore to claim virtue for his merchant more insistently. In the same opening scene of *The London Merchant*, Thorowgood, just before his exit, instructs his assistant to "look carefully over the files to see whether there are any tradesmen's bills unpaid." Like the death of Little Nell, it would require a heart of stone to read the set-up scenes of the play without laughing. But in seriousness, is it not a matter of virtue to pay, even at the tradesman's entrance? What kind of person accepts the wares of tradesmen and then refuses to give something in return? No merchant he. The law acknowledged it. A literal aristocrat, a "peer of the realm," could not be arrested or imprisoned for debt. A bourgeois assuredly could.

Thorowgood's eligible daughter in *The London Merchant* continues the aggressively pro-bourgeois propaganda, refusing to make an appearance among "men of quality." "The man of quality who chooses to converse with a gentleman and merchant [note the mixing] of your worth and character," she says, "may confer honor by doing so, but he loses none."[17] And later Thorowgood instructs the good apprentice, named, remember, Trueman, against Max U: "I would not have you only learn the method of merchandise . . . merely as a means of getting wealth." Trueman replies as though he were John Bright or Richard Cobden defending free trade in the nineteenth century: "I have observed those countries where trade is promoted and encouraged do not make discoveries to destroy, but to improve, mankind." It's the McDonald's Theory, that two countries with McDonald's fast food never fight with each other (falsified recently by Ukraine and the Russian Federation). Trueman and Thorowgood then launch on mutual assurances about the desirability of European trade: "It is the industrious merchant's business to collect the various blessings of each soil and climate, and, with the product of the whole, to enrich his native country." Wonderful.

The good apprentice Trueman is praised by his master in bourgeois style: "I have examined your accounts. They are not only just, as I have always found them, but regularly kept and fairly entered. I commend your diligence." In this matter the bad apprentice Barnwell is found to be disastrously deficient, though he had once been promising in bourgeois virtues. Trueman recalls of the younger Barnwell that "never was life more regular than his: an understanding uncommon at his years; and open, generous manliness of temper; his manners easy, unaffected, and engaging." He remarks sadly on his wayward colleague, "Few men recover reputation lost—a merchant, never."

The pro-bourgeois propaganda has a decidedly tacked-on air. The play uses frequently the word "interest," which is to say, mere prudence only, always opposed to the others virtues. Barnwell condemned in his cell declares that it is "not my interest only, but my duty, to believe and to rejoice in that hope" of heavenly forgiveness.[18] Lillo was attempting to shift tragedy from "princes distressed and scenes of royal woe" to "the circumstances of the generality of mankind," though he was not quite up to the standard of Ibsen in such stuff.[19] Yet the play was much admired, especially by people whose native language was not English (compare the French admiration for Edgar Allan Poe and Jerry Lewis). In Germany it served as a model, I have noted, for a middle-class drama, and G. E. Lessing declared in 1756, "I would infinitely prefer to be the creator of *The London Merchant* than the creator of [Gottsched's 1732 conventional tragedy based on French models and Addison's *Cato*] *Der sterbende Cato*."[20]

Polly Stevens Fields offers a feminist reading, noting that Mrs. Millwood, the whore, is the active agent in the play: "Millwood is hardly the 'girl who can't say no' from the male fund of fantasy; rather, she knows that her only commodity is her body. . . . We may meaningfully regard Millwood, not Barnwell, as 'The London Merchant' of the title."[21] Compare Moll Flanders, that woman of commerce. Mrs. Millwood could be speaking of merchants relative to "men of quality" as much as of women relative to men when she says, "We are no otherwise esteemed or regarded by them but as we contribute to their satisfaction."[22] In a ferocious scene in which Mrs. Millwood is seized by the authorities she declares the revenge of women on men: "To right their sex's wrong devote their mind, / And future Millwoods prove, to plague mankind!"[23]

The conventional hierarchies of gentry versus bourgeois, and even male versus female, are bending in 1731. At length they will break.

BOURGEOIS EUROPE, FOR EXAMPLE, LOVED MEASUREMENT

The economic historian Werner Sombart (1863–1941) observed in 1913 that "not only was Holland the model for all middle-class virtues, but for exact calculation also." [1] Holland has been known for both down to the present. For instance, the first person in Europe to suggest that accounting could be applied to the affairs of an entire nation, as though the nation were a business firm, appears to have been the popularizer of the decimal point and the discoverer of equal temperament in musical scales, the Dutch mathematician and statesman Simon Stevin(us) (1548–1620). Among other bourgeois schemes, Stevin persuaded the city of Amsterdam and the king of Sweden to adopt double-entry bookkeeping. [2]

Public calculation is characteristic of the bourgeois world, such as the political arithmeticians of the seventeenth century, first in Holland and then in England and then in France. The theory of probability came out of an aristocratic fascination with games of chance, but the fascination quickly became plebeian too, applied to thoroughly bourgeois projects such as fire insurance. In England, calculation had to be learned. As late as 1673 Sir William Temple, gob-smacked, was observing of the Dutch that "the order in casting up [that is, accounting for] their expenses, is so great and general, that no man offers at [that is, attempts] any undertaking which he is not prepared for, and [is not] master of his design before he begins; so as I have neither observed nor heard of any building public or private that has not been finished in the time designed for it." [3] How strange, and Dutch, and bourgeois.

The English were by then starting to adopt such rationality, or at least claiming to do so. Samuel Pepys became an influential rationalizer of the

Royal Navy under Charles II and James II, working steadily, as I've noted, against gentleman-appointees with no naval experience and no ability to calculate latitude.[4] When in 1688 the stadholder William invaded England to stop the Catholic and pro-French king of England from surrounding the Netherlands, the job was done with the Dutch bourgeois method of casting up, and stunned the world. In 1690 Sir William Petty announced his method of Dutch-English political arithmetic: "The method I take to do this is not yet very usual. For instead of using only comparative and superlative words and intellectual arguments I have taken the course (as a specimen of the political arithmetic I have long aimed at) to express myself in terms of number, weight, or measure; to use only arguments of sense."[5] It was a manifesto for a Dutch and quantitative and bourgeois age.

The coming of bourgeois statistics altered the rhetoric of politics. By 1713, as the economic historian John Nye explains in his history of British-French commercial relations, the British importers of Spanish and Portuguese wine had long benefited from the prohibition on imports of French wine into Britain, adopted as a war measure. By then Britain and France had concluded their bloody quarrel over the Spanish succession. A bill in Parliament proposed therefore to drop the wartime preferences for Spanish and Portuguese as against the formerly dominant French wines. Unsurprisingly the existing importers of Spanish and Portuguese wines—there were by then, of course, no legal importers of French wines to speak up for the profits of the French trade—objected strenuously. A river of pamphlets spilled out a rhetoric of accounting and quantities. It was the first time, Nye notes, following the historian G. N. Clark, "that the newly collected statistics on British trade [inaccurate to some considerable degree because of the smuggling of the illegal products under discussion] entered the political debate in a substantial way," serving "as a basis for the mercantilists' published statements of economic doctrine." Note the year: in now Dutch-imitating England, 1713, it was the first time that a debate over British policy claimed to depend on number, weight, measure, and arguments of sense.

The wine trades with Portugal, wrote one defender of the status quo, for example, "have as constantly increased every year as we have increased the demand for their wines, by which means the navigation and seamen of this kingdom have been greatly encouraged." If French wines are allowed back into Britain, went the usual productionist argument, the navigation and seamen will be ruined, because "small ships and an easy charge of men can fetch wines from France." It reminds one of the spoof by Bastiat in the 1840s of productionist arguments in favor of breaking bulk at Bordeaux in a proposed Paris-to-Madrid railway. On such "Keynesian," trickle-up grounds of providing employment for carters and hotels in Bordeaux, Bastiat noted, one could justify breaking bulk at every little town along the route, absorbing all the productive powers of France and Spain into one great "negative railway."

Or again, in the same pamphlet of 1713, it is argued that "the greatest part of those ships [idled if they have only a short route to France to work on] must lie and rot, or come home dead freighted," resulting in a rise in freight rates on British exports, to the detriment of the country's treasure by foreign trade. Another British pamphleteer reckoned that "the advantage to the French nation by having such a vent for their wines" was very great. He offered a number by way of argument of sense: "The French king . . . would give a million of money to procure" it.[6] Another reckoned that

> formerly the king of Portugal prohibited the importation of cloth into his king-
> dom. . . . [The] prohibition was taken off on consideration that Portugal wine
> should pay [in Britain] one third less duty than French. . . . Should the duty on
> French wines be lowered . . . we very much fear that the French king will take
> the opportunity of introducing his subjects' cloth into Portugal, which being of a
> thinner manufacture than the cloth of this nation, may be fitter for that country
> and their Brazils. . . . We may forever lose the cloth trade in that kingdom[7]

"Constantly increased." "The greatest part of those ships." "A million of money." "One third less duty." In June of 1713 the bill to relax the duties on French wine was rejected, purportedly on such rational grounds of numerical reasoning. The official statistics were dubious, the quantitative arguments on both sides nonsensical, the social accounting mistaken, the economics positively wacko. Yet a rhetoric of quantitative prudence ruled.[8]

A rhetoric of calculation since the seventeenth century, however, does not mean that Europeans actually were or are or will be rational. Many social scientists following Sombart or Weber have mistakenly supposed that Europeans became in fact freshly prudent in 1600 or 1713 or 1914 or whenever. They suppose that a new skill with numbers and with accounts meant that the Europeans even outside the countinghouses had discovered true rationality. Such an instrumental rationality is claimed to characterize the modern world. Franco Moretti notes that in claiming objectivity Weber himself liked to quote the Latin tag *sine ira et studio*, without anger or partisanship.[9] But wait: Weber was quoting not a rationalized and quantitative modern man but Tacitus (65–120 CE; *Annals* 1.1).

Samuel Johnson was in 1775 typical of his age and gender in reporting the size of everything he encountered in his tour of the West of Scotland. (He liked chemical experiments too.) He used as a measuring device, I've noted, his walking stick, though eventually he lost it and was disabled from reporting the dimensions of every castle he encountered. Three decades earlier he had used a typically bourgeois numerical joke in promising to finish his *Dictionary* in three years by himself unaided, instead of the forty years that forty French scholars spent to complete the comparable dictionary of French: "This is the proportion. Let me see; forty times forty is sixteen hundred. As three [man years] is to sixteen hundred, so is the proportion of an Englishman to a Frenchman." He actually took nine years. Let me see: as nine is to sixteen hundred. . . .

By the 1850s the conservative critics of bourgeois betterment, such as Charles Dickens, who favored south Britain's inherited money over the wretched factories of north Britain (most of Dickens's later plots are resolved by inheritance), were becoming very cross about the statistical figure of speech. Dickens made fun in *Hard Times* (1854) of counting lunatics like "Thomas Gradgrind, sir—peremptorily Thomas—Thomas Gradgrind. With a rule and a pair of scales, and the multiplication table always in his pocket, sir, ready to weigh and measure any parcel of human nature, and tell you exactly what it comes to. It is a mere question of figures, a case of simple arithmetic."

The bourgeois world claims nonetheless to be ruled by little else than quantity. Dickens was arguing about and against the spirit of the age. In chapter 15 of *Hard Times* Gradgrind is trying to persuade his daughter Louisa to marry Mr. Bounderby by the mere batty citation of facts, only facts:

> You are, we will say in round numbers, twenty years of age; Mr. Bounderby is, we
> will say in round numbers, fifty. There is some disparity in your respective years,
> but in your means and positions there is none; on the contrary, there is a great
> suitability. Then the question arises, Is this one disparity sufficient to operate as a

bar to such a marriage? In considering this question, it is not unimportant to take into account the statistics of marriage, so far as they have yet been obtained, in England and Wales. I find, on reference to the figures . . .

And so forth. Counting can surely be a nitwit's, or the devil's, tool. Among the more unnerving exhibits in the extermination camp at Auschwitz are the books laid out for inspection in which Hitler's executioners kept neat records on every person processed.

Instrumental rationality with calculation, that is, characterizes the rhetoric of the modern world. The blessed rage for quantitative order, however, did not make the Europeans more sensible than their ancestors, or more sensible than the non-Europeans—who after all invented and used "Arabic" numerals and the abacus long before the Europeans did. The Europeans discovered in the seventeenth and eighteenth centuries how to *talk* rationality, which they later applied with enthusiasm to counting the weight of bird seeds one could fit into a Negroid skull. The numbers and calculation and accounts do appeal to a rhetoric of rationality—"arguments of sense." But they do not guarantee its substance. During the heyday of scientific modernism 1910–1970, the Europeans, with the British in the lead, went mad with rational counting, on the analogy with their startling successes in quantitative engineering, such for example as bombarding German trenches at the Somme with a carefully calculated weight of the wrong kind of shells.

Counting is not in itself a sin of modern life. It is an expression rather of the high prestige in the modern world of the characteristically bourgeois virtue of prudence. Counting is only a sin (as are other pieces of prudence) when practiced without the other virtues in attendance, such as justice and temperance. Admittedly it often is so practiced, with claims that counting by itself suffices, that numbers contain their own interpretation, as in the startlingly widespread malpractice of tests of "null hypothesis significance testing" in the absence of a loss function—as, for example, the splendid-sounding but mass-lethal practice of "evidence-based medicine," which will cause your own untimely death.[10] In any case bourgeois Europe showed its love of bourgeois profit-and-loss in its love of numbers, and by inventing the statistical chart and the decadal census of population and all the imposing if often mistaken rhetoric of accounting and R-squares.

In few cases were the numbers actually relevant to instrumental rationality. Bureaucracies in railroading and steel making and universities and the National Security Agency collected masses of numbers. But most of the numbers were beside the point in deciding whether to expand, contract, hire, build, prosecute, assassinate, bomb, or arrest. Accounting, after all, is necessarily about the past. It is a story. Yet business and governmental and personal decisions are, of course, about the future, which usually is in im portant respects unknowable. As Yogi Berra, and Niels Bohr, said, "It's hard to predict. Especially about the future."

What the modern fascination with charts, graphs, figures, and calculations does show, in other words, is that moderns especially *admire* prudence. It does not show that they always practice it. To suppose mistakenly that calculation is the same thing as practicing rationality might be called the "Max Weber rationality attribution error." Body counts in Vietnam did not show that American policy there was in fact prudent. What changed from Shakespeare's time to Dickens's time was principally the rhetoric of quantification, and the social prestige of people like merchants and engineers and political economists and natural philosophers who specialized in it. The rise in quantification announced the modern world. The rise in the prestige of quantification ornamented it. Neither made it.

THE CHANGE WAS IN SOCIAL HABITS
OF THE LIP, NOT IN PSYCHOLOGY

Tocqueville claimed in *Democracy in America* that "habits of the heart" and "habits of the mind" are "the whole moral and intellectual state of a people."[1] I wish to argue rather that it is the habits of the *lip* that shape the habits of the mind and heart, and that rhetoric therefore is fundamental. We can know the rhetoric of an age, the habits of the lip, by reading its literary and other written products. We can from this infer the habits of the corresponding minds much more directly than can any brain scientist of the new phrenology. And for historical purposes the brain scientists' hypotheses are literally untestable, because the brains we wish to scan are dead. And in any case the phrenological procedure does not scan what we wish, which is minds, not brains. Humanistic techniques are mind-scanning.

What changed 1600–1848, and dramatically, as we can learn from the techniques of a humanistic science, was the high- and low-cultural attitude toward trade, numbers, betterment, and the bourgeoisie. Economic versions of the virtues, such as a rhetoric of prudent calculation of costs and benefits or a hopeful attitude toward industrial novelties or a just acceptance of ethically acquired profits, first in Holland and then in England, and a little earlier in England's remote American colonies, and then later in England's impoverished neighbor, Scotland, came to be fully respectable, honorable, admired, permitted, encouraged—not obstructed and disdained.

It was not the induced thriftiness in the individual businessperson that mattered (contrary again to Marx and Weber), but the admiration, or at any rate toleration, by the rest of the society for a bourgeois life of creating economic value. One "creates" economic value by buying low and selling high, that is, by moving coal and ideas from a place in which they are not highly valued to a place in which they are, if transport and transaction costs do not offset the gross profit.

Weber's error was to suppose that "accumulate, accumulate" enriched the modern world when what did so was a new and favorable rhetoric regarding business, which led to betterments, which led to profitable investment out of savings easily assembled. Weber's *secundum mobile* of "worldly asceticism" leading to high rates of capital accumulation was not what made the Great Enrichment. Ideas and the resulting betterment did, with capital accumulation (and labor, and oxygen in the air, and liquid water in the seas) in attendance. As the sociologists Victor Nee and Richard Swedberg put it, "The enduring legacy of Weber's scholarship is perhaps not so much the Protestant-ethic thesis, but the view that the mechanisms motivating and facilitating today's [and the seventeenth-century's] capitalism are rooted not in the materialist domain of incremental capital accumulation, but in the realm of ideas and institutional structures."[2] What makes Weber charming to many readers (a later figure, Karl Polanyi, charms them for the same reason) is the combining of spiritual/ideological causes with material/economic consequences. The linguist Benjamin Whorf's hypothesis, too, that a language such as Hopi yields people who think differently, attracts similar loyalty for similar reasons. All of them, Weber, Polanyi, and Whorf, proved mistaken in their details—however correct they were in claiming that spirit and ideology and language do matter.[3]

The economist Virgil Storr attributes five themes to *The Protestant Ethic and the Spirit of Capitalism* and admits that only one of them—that "capitalism" can take on a variety of forms—has stood the tests of historical and economic criticism.[4] The admission runs contrary to his enthusiastic defense of other of Weber's theses, though he does calls the variety-of-forms the "central" thesis.[5] Yet it is true that different societies engaging in business, from the Middle-Paleolithic trade in flint through so-called state capitalism of the Russian sort, have been supported by different "spirits" (Weber's *Geist*, what Marx called ideology and I call rhetoric). The real *Geist* or spirit or rhetoric of modern "capitalism" is the admiration for and acceptance of trade-tested betterment.

The new attitude ("spirit" again) had stupendous economic consequences. As Tocqueville put it in 1853, "The sentiments, the ideas, the mores [*moeurs*] . . .

alone can lead to public prosperity and liberty."[6] Max Weber's own words, even in *The Protestant Ethic*, can be appropriated: "Capitalism appeared in China, India, Babylon, the ancient world, and Middle Ages . . . [but] just that particular [modern] ethic was missing in all these cases."[7] Weber thought the new ethic was of endless accumulation as "an end in itself" (Weber 1905, pp. 17, 18, 34, 48; an antibourgeois calumny originating, I have noted, in Aristotle). He was mistaken, as I hope the present book and *Bourgeois Dignity* will persuade you.[8] The new ethic was of betterment, novelty, risk-taking, creativity, democracy, equality, liberty, dignity. Indeed, Weber himself grasped the point, though he sometimes wrote as though he did not, and his readers have taken the routine line. His own words may again be appropriated:

> The question of the motive forces in the expansion of modern capitalism is not in the first instance a question of the origin of the capital sums which were available for capitalistic uses, but, above all, of the development of the spirit of capitalism. Where it appears and is able to work itself out, it produces its own capital and monetary supplies as the means to its ends, but the reverse is not true.[9]

Such social virtues are what China nowadays often lacks and must find in bulk if it is to get much beyond $20 a day. India already has them—except in the sadly crucial matter of equality of castes.

In other words, it was not a change in the psychology of the bourgeoisie that explained regional differences, whether inside England or between England and, say, France. It was a change, I affirm, in the sociology. As Swedberg observes in a book on Tocqueville, who had it right, Tocqueville's "theory of entrepreneurship is social rather than individualistic in nature."[10] It was not what was instinctively inside people's heads that mattered, since it varies little in humans ("I want more of that"), but what was on their lips, about other people ("Those wretched Browns, you know: they are such vulgar people, in trade"). As the economic historian Eric Jones put it recently, "Culture, in the sense of bourgeois values [Jones here means psychological dispositions], has not been shown to differ systematically by region."[11] Nor have such values been shown to differ by much else, if "values" are taken to be the dispositions of the bourgeois working down in the marketplaces of Les Halles or Tlatelolco. "Buy low, sell high" is not a modern invention. It has been the basis of trade, always. And *Homo sapiens* has been a trader, always.

Weber's theory turned the discussion of entrepreneurship toward how psychology is supposed to have changed around 1600, when in fact what changed in Europe in early modern times, starting in Holland, was the sociology and its corresponding politics. It was not a matter of a new sort of human but a new sort of talk about long-existing sorts of humans. The first scientific studies of entrepreneurship, such as those emanating after World War II from the Harvard Business School, made the Weberian mistake, claiming that the prevalence of a particular psychology in a population is the key to economic growth.[12] The key is rather whether the law and the society praise or damn invention and enterprise and betterment. As Jones again says, "Industrialization . . . is seen to result from political and ideological change bearing on investment markets [though I would say not investment markets (since investment, though necessary, is routine) but mechanical and institutional betterment, which at the pace since 1700 or 1800 was anything but routine]. . . . The English elite were coming more decisively to embrace market ideology."[13] And "the English elite came to accept market competition among its members, embracing what is called [by North, Wallis, and Weingast] an open access order."[14]

Weber's argument that anxieties about salvation drove Calvinists to save more and work more is attractive, as I said, because it combines a spiritual spark with a materialist kindling. Most readers are thrilled by such dual-sourced intellectual fires. But Weber's choice of kindling was mistaken, since betterment, not investment, was the maker of the modern world (as I said, he sometimes speaks the same way; sometimes not). And the choice of the spark was mistaken too, as has been shown repeatedly since Weber wrote. Contrary to his understanding of the theology, the theologian Reinhold Niebuhr wrote in 1952, "Prosperity was not, according to the Puritan creed, a primary proof or fruit of virtue." "When men do not see and own God but attribute success to the sufficiency of instruments," declared Urian Oakes, a Congregational minister in Cambridge, Massachusetts, and president of Harvard College from 1675 to 1681, "it is time for God to maintain his own right and to show that He gives and denies success according to His own good pleasure."[15] Grace, not works, makes a man rich. Niebuhr saw "the descent from Puritanism to Yankee in America . . . [as] a fairly rapid one. Prosperity which had been sought in the service of God was now sought for its own sake [Aristotle again]. The Yankees were very appreciative of the promise in Deuteronomy: 'And thou shalt do that which is right and good in the sight of the Lord: that it may be well with thee, and that thou mayest go in and possess the good land which the lord swore unto thy fathers'" (6:18). "According to the Jeffersonians," Niebuhr continued, "prosperity and well-being should be sought as the basis of virtue":

> They believed that if each citizen found contentment in a justly and richly re-warded toil he would not be disposed to take advantage of his neighbor. The Puritans regarded virtue as the basis of prosperity, rather than prosperity as the basis of virtue. . . . [T]he fusion of these two forces created a preoccupation with the material circumstances of life ['happiness' was the word in favor] which ex-pressed a more consistent bourgeois ethos than that of even the most advanced nations of Europe."

Away from northwestern Europe and its offshoots as late as 1848 the eco-nomic virtues were still not respectable, not at any rate in the opinion of the respectable classes. Right up to the Meiji Restoration of 1868, after which the rhetoric in Japan changed with lightning speed, elite opinion scorned the merchant. In Japanese Confucianism, I have noted, the ranking from top to bottom was the emperor (who recovered his power in 1868), the sho-gun (1603–1868), the daimyo, the samurai, the peasant, the craftsman, the merchant, the night-soil man, and last of all Koreans. A merchant in Japan and China and Korea was not a "gentleman," to use the European word, and had no honor. The historian F. W. Mote observes that in China as early as the ninth century BCE "legal barriers" to bourgeois advancement "simply could not longer be maintained." "By Song times [960–1279]," he continues nonetheless, "the attitudes underlying the anti-merchant bias of an earlier social ideal still lingered (as indeed they did until the end of the imperial era [in 1911]), but the legal restrictions were largely abolished." Liberty but not dignity. Yet "the old ideal pattern still affected their lives, most directly by inducing them to imitate the patterns of scholar-official's lives . . . and to in-vest family wealth in land."[16] It was likewise the case around 1600 in England. And indeed in the eighteenth century in China, as in England, the gentry and the merchant class become so entangled by marriage and apprentice-ship and landholding that the Confucian contempt—or in England the con-tempt by the aristocracy and gentry—was laid aside.[17] The development is not simple, but the tendency is clear: a place must revalue the bourgeoisie or else it must become accustomed to economic stagnation. One is not surprised to find, after the recent Fukushima disaster, the modern Japanese clerisy, hostile anyway to the bourgeoisie, recommending that Japan abandon nuclear power and become accustomed to stagnation: Ikezawa Natsuki offered a poem entitled "Toward a Serene Poverty."[18]

A central (if rare) misstep in Simmel's *The Philosophy of Money* (1900, 1907) is the assertion of a "psychological feature of our times which stands in such a decisive contrast to the more impulsive, emotionally determined character of earlier epochs. . . . Gauging values in terms of money has taught us to determine and specify values down to the last farthing."[19] In a word, thriftiness reigns now, as against the warm noncalculativeness of earlier folk. The assertion is false as actual behavior, and is of a piece with Weber's claim around the same time that a rise of rationality characterizes the modern world. On the contrary, as soon as people learned to write they started keeping more or less rational accounts, or vice versa. Writing comes out of accounts, and out of magical spells, both rational in their own terms. Thus around 1280 CE one Walter of Henley, well before our modern times devoted to gauging value in money, wrote in French an estate manual for English lords filled with quantitative prudence of a wholly rational sort.[20] So was Mesopotamia four millennia earlier filled with quantitative prudence in accounts.

Nowadays the behavioral economics of, say, Dan Ariely does a job of demolishing claims of individual rationality in moderns. Yet it too commits the Weberian mistake of focusing on individual psychology instead of group sociology and market economics. The experimental economics of Vernon Smith, Bart Wilson, Erik Kimbrough, and others, by contrast, works always with groups, showing that a wisdom of crowds often prevails over psychological shortsightedness and calculative confusion. And, by the way, it makes a good case that property arises without the help of the state or the nudging of the clerisy.[21]

Irrationality is always with us. Ernest Renan, professor of Hebrew at the Collège de France from 1862, most famous for his claim that Jesus was a good chap if a trifle primitive and oriental, declared that "we must make a marked distinction between societies like our own, where everything takes place in the full light of reflection, and simple and credulous communities," such as those that Jesus preached in.[22] The Great War was at length to make such European claims to the full light of reflection look bizarre. One is dumbfounded that anyone can still believe in an unusual rationality or prudence or thriftiness of behavior in the modern European world, a belief still widespread even after the second of the world wars initiated by Europeans during the twentieth century. As Gandhi might have put it if asked what he thought about European rationality, "It sounds like a good idea."

In fact people always and everywhere have been more or less rational and more or less impulsive, both. They'd better be, or they starve or get eaten. The social psychologist I have mentioned, Jonathan Haidt, illustrates the point with the image of the elephant and the driver. The elephant is emotion, the driver something like the economist's rationality. Both are necessary to get the log carried from the river to the sawmill. A medieval English peasant was poor not because he was irrationally imprudent but because he lived in a society before the new ideas of liberalism, the Bourgeois Revaluation, the Bourgeois Deal, and the resulting Great Enrichment. Likewise the Mayan peasant or the Pakistani laborer are as rational as they can be. To put it in the old framework, humans exhibit the seven virtues, and the numerous corresponding vices—all, including prudence but also love and justice and courage (with which Haidt, who honors the humanities in a way some of his colleagues in social psychology do not, would agree). But until the humans came to admire *commercial* versions of each, their economies crept along at $3 a day.

Humans have always thought in terms of money. There was no such thing as "monetization," another of the myths of pioneering German scholars inspired by Romance, because societies always have money, whether or not they have coinage. Cigarettes served as money in POW camps, and still do in prisons. In hunter-gatherer societies there is always something—blankets or arrow points—that serves as a medium of exchange or a store of value or an item with which to establish status. In herding societies cattle buy wives. In Mesopotamia before coinage one paid by clipping off a bit of silver from a coil. In medieval England the pervasiveness of a money economy shows in handbooks I mentioned such as *Walter of Henley* and the *Seneschaucy*, directed at estate management for the aristocracy. A parallel literature in China predated such European books by hundreds of years, printed on cheap paper.

In 1900 the Simmel of *The Philosophy of Money* had little way of knowing how mistaken his notions of the "rise of the money economy" were to prove in actual as against philosophical history. At that time only a few pioneers such as the legal historian Frederic William Maitland, reading the actual cases in English courts in the high Middle Ages, had it right. During the century of professional history after 1900 it has been established beyond cavil that in olden times everything was for sale, for cash. (Such a claim runs against the agreed fables, true, but no one who reads medievalists from Maitland through Raftis and Herlihy down to any number of economic histories can seriously doubt it.) Poor and rich people in 1300 appear to have thought in money values down to the last farthing. So it was anciently elsewhere. So it is now, except that after the Great Enrichment the numerous well-off among us do not have to calculate so carefully. Commercialization is nothing new.

Where Simmel was correct, however, is again that attitudes and commonplace rhetoric *about* prudence and temperance did change, 1600–1800. As the historian of Russia Richard Pipes put it, "Sometime during the period in European history vaguely labeled 'early modern,' there occurred a major break in the attitude toward property."[23] The Low Countries were in their greatest time the point of contrast to an older rhetoric of disdain for property, trading, and finance ("unless I profit from them," said the aristocrat under his breath). Well into the eighteenth century Holland served as a model for the English and Scots of how to be bourgeois, and especially how to talk about being bourgeois.

31

AND THE CHANGE WAS
SPECIFICALLY BRITISH

I have noted that Mokyr has written that the Enlightenment was obsessed with *useful* information. He is right—a test of "usefulness" in ordinary life being characteristically bourgeois. But wait. The economist Peter Boettke observes in this connection that what registered the items that people thought "useful" was trade-determined prices, though of course only for the profane, not for sacred items such as art or family or science. The trade test, in which prices are negotiated, is the essential other half of the revolution of profane betterment. "Useful" is not given by the essence of a coat or a sark, or by the wark o' the weavers. The labor theory of value, or any other essentialism in attributing profane value, is mistaken. Usefulness in ordinary good and service is to be measured, as economists got clear in the 1870s (too late for Marx), only from the money value that people are willing to put on coats or sarks in exchange for other goods, at any rate for goods that do enter commerce (the exceptions are called by economists "corner solutions" and by normal people the sacred). There is no profane value beyond use value. As the Ashkenazi Jewish-American financial maven Leo Melamed was told by his father in Lithuania, "You cannot determine value except in the real marketplace, which is where the people are." As irritating as it is, trading value is not inside a loaf of bread or inside an hour of housework. It is determined out where the people are, because profane value comes from what humans value, not from the thing itself. Decades later the junior Melamed applied his father's wisdom to organizing in Chicago the first market for financial futures.[1]

Demand therefore does have a role in the Industrial Revolution, and later in the Great Enrichment, by a back door, the one marked Traded Values Registered Here. Earlier industrial revolutions in Europe and elsewhere probably had similar shifts in values among their impulses—think of luxury goods in the Italian Renaissance, or the impact of Muslim sophistication on crusading Europe, or the reception of Chinese culture in Korea and Japan. The economic historians Maxine Berg and Pat Hudson have emphasized the great extension in Britain during the eighteenth century of small luxuries coming from foreign trade, beginning emblematically in the seventeenth century with coffee and the coffeehouses.[2] The economic historian of the Dutch Republic, Jan de Vries, likewise argues that what he calls with characteristic wit the "industrious" revolution arose out of the lust in Holland and England and New England for new goods, such as Chinese porcelain and Windsor chairs.[3] But such distinguished historical students of the demand side in the seventeenth and eighteenth centuries would readily admit that the demand for coffee or chairs does not *itself* an industrial revolution make, much less a great enrichment. If it could, a historian can point out, it would have happened earlier and elsewhere, because waves of new goods for consumption are historical commonplaces. And an economist can point out—as I myself have pointed out in British economic history since 1970 repeatedly, without much influencing those of my colleagues eager to talk in a Keynesian way about trickle down or trickle up—that shuffling from one use of the society's inputs of labor and capital and land to another use does not *much* change the efficiency of the inputs.[4] It is a dramatically large change in real income per person we are trying to explain. Dramatically improved methods of production (steam, electricity, electronics, universities) of dramatically novel products (porcelain in bulk, educated people, cotton for underwear, upholstered furniture, modern corporations, recorded sound, air travel, antibiotics, word processors) made the modern world. Not a shuffling arising from shifts in the pattern of demand.

Being obsessed with useful information giving power over nature, as Mokyr puts it, was not new in the eighteenth century, not precisely.[5] What changed was what was deemed useful. In this deeper sense the pattern of demand, the values in the heads of consumers—that is to say, as economists strangely put it, a change in "tastes"—was indeed a shaper of industrial revolutions, if not a deep cause. When war horses and cathedrals were valued, they were what was useful, and knowledge about them was useful knowledge and much sought after with money offers. In 1200 CE knowledge of how to breed big destriers, coursers, and rounceys able to carry a fully armed knight was useful and therefore valued in the market for horses, where the people were. In 1300 a stonemason with skill in carving gargoyles possessed useful and therefore profitable knowledge, which he sold for money, about which we have detailed records. In 1400 a church in possession of a piece of the true cross or located by the grave of Saint Thomas Becket was a "useful" place to go, and people sought it obsessively at their own expense, "the holy blisful martir for to seke, / That hem hath holpen whan that they were seeke." When in the 1520s eternal salvation was highly valued, people bought it, and fought for it, and smote those with alternative theories about it.

English people continued in the eighteenth century to value eternal salvation. What changed is that preachers such as the American William Bentley and later the British (and then American) Joseph Priestley commenced telling them from the pulpit that God intended us also to flourish on earth and to enjoy its fruits, to seek happiness. The ascetic coloring of *Il Penseroso*, if it ever had amounted to much in the economy, was bleached out with chlorine.

The rising class in the English sixteenth and seventeenth century was not the (urban) bourgeoisie only, but the gentry, viewed as one of two classes of land-rich "gentlemen"—the leading characters in novels by the Fieldings and the Austens, themselves standing just below England's small aristocracy. Yet a mere hundred years after Shakespeare, I have said, the English, surprisingly, were busy transforming themselves away from admirers of the gentry and aristocracy and into admirers of the bourgeoisie. In the 1690s, with a Dutch king, the English William of William-and-Mary translated from Willem van Oranje, the British proceeded in a rush to adopt Dutch institutions such as excise taxes, a central bank, a national debt, an aggressively anti-French foreign policy, a stock market, and a free press. The wonder is that they didn't adopt the Dutch language. What they admired, and sought, had changed, quickly. They undertook to cease being inconstant, rash, vainglorious, light, and deceiving. The very word "businesslike," always used as a commendation, dates from 1771 and Henry Mackenzie's *The Man of Feeling*: Miss Atkins in the novel is introduced by her landlady to "a grave business-like man"—though ironically he proves to be a john, the landlady being a procuress.[6]

During the decades up to 1700 the effective rulers of Britain became in theory and practice more and more mercantilist, drifting away from a much earlier fiscalism under which the King cared only about his own revenues, mainly from his estates or from whatever traditional imposts he could revive. And then by the end of the eighteenth century the rulers became even a little bit free in trading. Anyway they became, after the sixteenth and early seventeenth century, more and more concerned with *national* profit and loss, instead of ensuring this man's monopoly profit and that woman's church attendance, and always the monarch's glory through revenues for war. Temple noted in 1672 of the great nations of Europe that during and before the Thirty Years War "their trade was war." But "since the Peace of Munster, which restored the quiet of Christendom in 1648, not only Sweden and Denmark but France and England have more particularly than ever before busied the thoughts and counsels of their several governments . . . about the matters of trade."[7] The English were first in line to adopt this Dutchlike subordination of politics to trade. As Montesquieu put it in 1748, "Other nations have made the interests of commerce yield to those of politics; the English, on the contrary, have ever made their political interests give way to those of commerce."[8] In truth not "ever," but by 1748, often.

The Chinese nowadays say that before 1978 the Communist cadres talked only of class war, but after 1978 they talked only of economic success. " 'Seeking truth from facts' became the Party's new guideline," Ronald Coase and Ning Wang observe. "Getting rich became glorious."[9] The post-1978 mottoes of the Chinese Communist Party echo in a discordant key the empiricism, liberty, and dignity that was newly popular in northwestern Europe after about 1700. Europe went from talking only about God and hierarchy to talking only about the economy and national strength. In both cases the change was made possible by political competition. The *xian* (townships) of China compete nowadays for the latest computer factory. In early modern times the towns of the Netherlands or of England competed for the latest textile factory. Coase and Wang argue that the Chinese reform came from the bottom up, being merely permitted by Beijing, not designed. It was true also in Europe, especially during the nineteenth century. In the medicine of the 1830s purging and bleeding and myths of bodily humors gave way to a more prudent "therapeutic nihilism," preparatory to a new science advancing on Galen. Similarly in the politics of the 1850s the old mercantilism gave way to a more prudent laissez faire. Both were justified on the principle that we know too little to intervene with abandon. We had better experiment cautiously, allowing diverse evolution, and assessing the results. "When China's

32 provinces, 282 municipalities, 2,862 counties, 19,522 towns and 14,677 villages," Coase and Wang report, "threw themselves into an open competition
for investment and for good ideas of developing the local economy, China
became a gigantic laboratory where many different economic experiments
were tried simultaneously."[10]

What was said in aid of national economic strength was often wrong, and
contained holdovers from an earlier, mercantilist rhetoric. Like the Europeans early and late, the Chinese theorists of "socialist market economy" were
irrationally obsessed with exports. And like the Europeans early and late,
the Chinese were often tempted to protect state enterprise by law. A bizarre
example is a local regulation recently enacted in a Chinese town famous
for making distilled liquor under which the townspeople were themselves
required to consume large quantities of the product. It was the up-by-your-
bootstraps theory of productionist mercantilism in all ages, heard on the left
in the United States, as I've noted, when speaking of Henry Ford paying high
wages, "so that his workers could buy the cars." Yet the Chinese Communist
Central Committee did permitted what Coase and Wang call a "Revolution
from the Margins." The main topic, once upon a time in Europe and recently
in China, became national income, not godly or aristocratic or revolutionary glory.

Such an ordering of ideas was by 1600 second nature to the Dutch. In the
century to follow it had to be learned slowly by the English. As late as 1694
Robert Viscount Molesworth lamented, "Shall we forever retain the ill character they give us of the most mutable and inconstant nation of the world?"[11]
The actual change in individual behavior was not great. The rest of the world
continued to be shocked by the aristocratic/peasant brutality of British soldiers, into the nineteenth century and beyond. Consider the bold Black and
Tans suppressing Irish rebellion in 1920, or the massacre at Amritsar in British India in 1919. A little if rich island did not paint a quarter of the world
red, nor did it win two world wars, with a little help from the French, the
Americans, and the Russians, by sweetly bourgeois persuasion alone. But
the change in rhetoric in Britain toward bourgeois collaboration, as against
aristocratic rivalry, was great and was permanent and was finally softening.

A long-evolving thesis in English history claims that on the contrary Britain long espoused a "gentlemanly capitalism," which is claimed to have been
hostile to bourgeois values.[12] Right through late Victorian times and beyond,
it is said, betterment was undermined by polo-loving and estate-yearning.

Such a thesis seems doubtful. True, always in England the aristocracy and gentry have had a prestige that is amusing or puzzling or dazzling to the Scots and especially the Americans and the Dutch and other more plebeian enthusiasts for the bourgeois virtues. As Hume noted in 1741, "While these notions prevail, all the considerable traders will be tempted to throw up their commerce, in order to purchase . . . privileges and honor."[13] But from 1741 to the present the quantitative judgment in Hume's "all" has proven to be mistaken. Not anything like "all" of the English bourgeoisie have lusted after noble privilege—this in contrast to France of the *ancien régime*, for example. In any case, the people translated to the honor of "Sir Roderick" or "Baron Desai" have been replaced from below by hordes of new bourgeois.

And it has always been strange to lament the economic "failure" of the first industrial nation, allegedly caused by a persistent desire to play cricket as a gentlemen as against a mere paid "player."[14] Britain has remained from 1707 to the present among the richest countries on earth.[15] In 2010, allowing for the actual purchasing power of local currencies, the United Kingdom had a gross domestic product per person of $38,700 a year (that is, $106 a day), ranking tenth in the world among substantial countries (excluding mere city-states such as Singapore, which would be better compared with the richer parts of southeast England, and excluding oil states with few official citizens). It was by such a standard a little behind Sweden and a little ahead of Germany, far behind the United States and a good deal ahead of Japan.[16] All such countries were roughly four or five times richer per person than Brazil. The UK was 3.7 times richer than the African success of Botswana, in southern Africa, and 94 times richer than the African catastrophe of Zimbabwe next door. From the time of atmospheric steam engines to the present, England and Scotland together have been world centers for invention: modern steel, radar, penicillin, magnetic resonance imaging, float glass, and the World Wide Web, to name a few.[17] A surprisingly high percentage of the world's inventions still come out of a "tiny" Britain of sixty-three million rich and highly educated souls.

Why Britain? For one thing, the change in British rhetoric about the economy came out of the irritating successes of the Dutch. The successes of the Dutch Republic were startling to Europe. The Navigation Acts and the three Anglo-Dutch Wars by which in the middle of the seventeenth century

England attempted in mercantilist, trade-is-war fashion to appropriate some Dutch success to itself were the beginning of a larger English project of emulating the burghers of Delft and Leiden. "The evidence for this widespread envy of Dutch enterprise," wrote the historian Paul Kennedy in 1976, "is overwhelming."[18] Likewise the historian Matthew Kadane recently accounted for the English shift toward bourgeois virtues by "various interactions with the Dutch."[19] The English at the time put it in doggerel: "Make war with Dutchmen, peace with Spain / Then we shall have money and trade again."[20] Yet it was not in fact warring against the Dutch that made England rich. Wars are expensive, and the Dutch *admiraals* Tromp and De Ruyter were no pushovers. It was imitating them that did the trick.

Thomas Sprat, in his *History of the Royal Society* of 1667, early in the project by some Englishmen of becoming Dutch, attacked such envy and interaction and imitation. He viewed it as commendable that "the merchants of England live honorably in foreign parts" but "those of Holland meanly, minding their gain alone." Shameful. "Ours . . . [have] in their behavior very much the gentility of the families from which so many of them are descended [note the sending of younger sons into trade]. The others when they are abroad show that they are only a race of plain citizens," disgraceful cits. Perhaps it was, Sprat notes with annoyance, "one of the reasons they can so easily undersell us."[21] Possibly. John Dryden in 1672 took up Sprat's complaint in similar words. In his play *Amboyna; or, The Cruelties of the Dutch to the English Merchants* the English merchant Beaumont addresses the Dutch: "For frugality in trading, we confess we cannot compare with you; for our merchants live like noblemen: your gentlemen, if you have any, live like boers."[22] Yet Josiah Child, arguing against guild regulation of cloth, admired the Dutch on nonaristocratic, prudential grounds: "if we intend to have the trade of the world we must imitate the Dutch."[23] Better boers we.[24]

PART V

Yet England Had Recently Lagged in Bourgeois Ideology, Compared with the Netherlands

32

BOURGEOIS SHAKESPEARE
DISDAINED TRADE AND
THE BOURGEOISIE

To the intense irritation of French and German and Japanese people, England, with parts of Wales and lowland Scotland and a few scattered parts of Ireland in attendance, has been since about 1700 the very fount of bourgeois virtues and most particularly their acceptance by the rest of society. Admiration for British merchants, British investors, British inventors, British bankers, and British economists led to the Great Enrichment. Only in the twentieth century have the British passed along some of their international duties to their American cousins, as now the Americans pass them to the East. Even now the United Kingdom, despite its long love affair with the Labour Party's Clause IV promising nationalization, is by historical and international standards a capitalist paradise. In the Heritage Foundation's Index of Economic Freedom the United Kingdom ranks 14th out of 178 countries worldwide, between Luxembourg and the Netherlands, 5th out of the 43 European countries, and would rank higher if the index did not punish it, in accord with libertarian orthodoxy, for allowing so much of its income to flow through the government.[1] Despite Britain's long relative "decline"—the word is a misapprehension based on biological metaphors and the happy fact that once-British inventions such as steam engines and bicycles and antibiotics have proven over the past two centuries rather easy to imitate—it remains even today, I say again, among the most rich and inventive and innovative societies on earth.[2]

One view is that Englishmen have always been good capitalists, eager to learn about crossbows from the Italians and gunpowder from the Chinese and how to make silk from both. On this view the historical anthropologist

Alan Macfarlane was substantially correct in his *Origins of English Individualism* (1978, of which in 1979 I gave an admiring review in the *Journal of Political Economy*) that English people were "individualistic" in their personal and trading lives. The implication of Macfarlane's view, and that of many other students of the medieval English evidence, is that the North-Weingast and now Acemoglu-Robinson attribution of the invention of property rights to the Glorious Revolution of 1688 is gravely mistaken.

But how can one make such a view of antique individualism comport with the evident fact that something did change radically at about the same time as the Glorious Revolution, the something being a new attribution of dignity and liberty to the betterers among the bourgeoisie? The answer is that the society Macfarlane praises as individualistic in the thirteenth century (and before: Macfarlane goes back to Anglo-Saxon times) was also deeply *hierarchical*. It is hierarchy, I have argued—the Great Chain of Being, in the Elizabethan theory, plain in every play of Shakespeare and his contemporaries—that was the main obstacle to betterment. It is another reason the Renaissance is irrelevant to the Industrial Revolution and the Great Enrichment, for the Renaissance gloried in hierarchy. Around 1700 any sort of social equality—"the liberal plan of equality, liberty and justice"—was a startling novelty.[3] The Leveller Richard Rumbold, facing his execution in 1685, declared, "I am sure there was no man born marked of God above another; for none comes into the world with a saddle on his back, neither any booted and spurred to ride him."[4] Few in the crowd gathered to mock him would have agreed. A century later, many would have. By 1985 virtually everyone did.

Medieval England—with medieval France and Italy and Germany—was already a society of laws, and in particular of property rights. Property laws are necessary but they are nothing like sufficient for the startling betterment that begins in the Industrial Revolution and eventuated in the still more startling Great Enrichment of the past 150 years—all of which, embarrassingly for the North-Acemoglu orthodoxy in economic history and development, happened a century or more after the allegedly sharp improvement of property rights out of 1688. A society can be individualistic in a thoroughgoing way but still honor only noblemen, not letting ordinary people have a go at spinning jennies and desktop computers. Roman sculpture (as a conventional if not obviously sound line in art history claims) was "individualistic" in a way that Greek sculpture, which is said to have dealt in ideal figures, was not. Yet at Rome, as in Shakespeare's England, rank told above all.

Aristocratic England before its embourgeoisement was, on the whole and in its theory of itself, hostile toward betterment tested in trade. Betterment of the society at large was inconceivable in a zero-sum world, and betterment of position by an individual disturbed the Great Chain of Being. The literary critic Katherine Eiseman Maus, writing in 2002 on Philip Massinger's play of the 1620s, *A New Way to Pay Old Debts*, notes that "such an ethos, which resists innovation and sees agents of change as presumptuous, influences Massinger's methods of characterization":

> Some critics complain that his characters do not develop. . . . Such critics assume that novelty is interesting and that a writer who depicts change is more skillful than one who does not. In Massinger's worldview, however, development is not a desideratum. . . . [A leading character in the play] could do better, Massinger implies, to know his place and stick to it.[5]

Thomas More, who in 1516 had recommended a nightmarish society of slaves, which was achieved at last in fascism and communism, was pleased that "the use as well as the desire of money being extinguished, much anxiety and great occasions of mischief is cut off with it, and who does not see that the frauds, thefts, robberies, quarrels, tumults, contentions, seditions, murders, treacheries, and witchcrafts, which are, indeed, rather punished than restrained by the severities of law, would all fall off, if money were not any more valued by the world?"[6] The USSR in May 1961 made economic crimes of mutually advantageous exchange subject to a death penalty (rather like the United States making the economic crime of buying and selling certain drugs subject to a life-destroying penalty), and it was not until 2003 that China removed the death penalty for being a millionaire—though by then it was a law unenforced, as was most of its constitution. China had officially recognized private property in 1998.

Once a writer's pens or brushes get filled he seem to have a hard time restraining eloquence against trade and money and betterments tested by profits in money that the bourgeoisie earns: the frauds, thefts, robberies,

quarrels, tumults, contentions, seditions, murders, treacheries, and witchcrafts. A traditional peasant-and-aristocrat resentment of the bourgeois
middleman comes out in volume, as nowadays in highly capitalist Sweden
in much of its popular fiction and television shows.

In Scotland in 1552–1554 the character Deceit in Sir David Lindsay's
court play *A Satire of the Three Estates* explains in fifty-four lines how he has
helped merchants to cheat, for instance:

> I taught you merchants many a wile,
> Upland wives for to beguile
> Upon a market day.
> And make them think your stuff was good,
> When it was rotten, by the Rood [that is, by the Cross],
> And swear it was not sway [so].

> I was always whispering in your ear,
> And teaching you for to curse and swear,
> What your gear cost in France;[7]
> Although not one word was true. And more:
> I taught you wiles many-fold:
> To mix the new wine with the old. . . .
> To sell right dear and buy goods cheap,
> And mix rye meal among the soap,
> And saffron with olive oil.

The play bulges with such vituperation of crafts and merchants, unsurprising
at the time from the pen of a man called "Sir." The speech of another character, Falsehood, before he is hanged, fills seventy-eight lines with light weights
and high prices on offer from the townsmen (with thirty lines thrown in for
a thieving shepherd and a "good common thief"): "then all the bakers will
I curse / That mixes bread with dust and bran / And fine flour with barley
meal," and "Adieu, ye crafty cordiners, / That sell the shoes over dear," and so
on and so forth, down to Barbara Ehrenreich and Naomi Klein.[8]

The Elizabethan world picture, and the Great Chain of Being, was a conservative ideology or political rhetoric, which is to say a system of ideas and
their expressions supporting those in power. Queen Elizabeth gave a short
speech in Latin to the heads of Oxford University on September 28, 1592,

ending with "Each and every person is to obey his superior in rank. . . . Be of one mind, for you know that unity is the stronger, disunity the weaker and quick to fall into ruin."[9] Everyone must have a master, and dignity for every person consists in obedience, not a disturbing enterprise. Ulysses in *Troilus and Cressida* gives the conventional analysis:

> Degrees in schools, and brotherhoods, in cities,
> Peaceful commerce from dividable shores,
> The primogenity and due of birth,
> Prerogative of age, crowns, scepters, laurels,
> But by degree stand in authentic place?
> Take but degree away, untune the string,
> And hark what discord follows. (1.3. 103–110)

The theme of Shakespeare's *Coriolanus* is the same, the Great Chain of Being expressed as the body politic, and the nobleman's pride at being the head and belly and arms of the body. The figure of the social body as a defense of hierarchy, as John Filling notes, was ancient.[10] Shakespeare has his classical characters use it with enthusiasm. The senator and patrician Menenius Agrippa in the first scene of *Coriolanus* defends the belly of the body, which has been blamed by the mob as taking without giving:

> MENENIUS. The senators of Rome are this good belly,
>   And you the mutinous members; for examine
>   Their counsels and their cares, digest things rightly
>   Touching the weal o' the common, you shall find
>   No public benefit which you receive
>   But it proceeds or comes from them to you
>   And no way from yourselves. What do you think,
>   You, the great toe of this assembly?
> FIRST CITIZEN. I the great toe! why the great toe?
> MENENIUS. For that, being one o' the lowest, basest, poorest,
>   Of this most wise rebellion, thou go'st foremost.[11]

Such noble pride does not disappear even in bourgeois England.[12] But after 1776 the obedience to superiors as the chief political principle, or the subordination of the great toe to the belly or brain, becomes less prominent than it was in 1600. In the United States nowadays it is affirmed chiefly by certain members of the country club.

In Shakespeare's England, then, the bourgeois virtues were not respectable. Sneered at, rather. (This despite Will's own economic success in the business of running theater companies.) The only one of Shakespeare's plays that speaks largely of merchants offers no commendation of what was supposed to be the bourgeois virtue of thrift. Shylock's "well-worn thrift" is nothing like an admired model for behavior. In the aristocratic Bassanio it is the lack of thrift, the "disabling of his estate," itself viewed as amusing and blameless—since had he but the means he could hold a rival place with the wealthy and aristocratic suitors for Portia's hand—that motivates the merchant Antonio to make his foolish blood bargain in the first place. No blame attaches, and all ends well, except for the Jew.

This does not mean that Shakespeare's contemporaries did not acknowledge the acquiring of money, or did not want income. Shakespeare charged money for theatergoers to get into the Globe. Shakespeareans and their imagined characters, like most people in any age, were desirous of more of it. Bassanio was, for example. But economic power could express itself honorably only in the aristocratic notion that Lord Bassanio simply deserved the money from his lands or borrowings or gifts from friends or marrying well or any other unearned income he could assemble and then gloriously spend. Shylock was to be expropriated to enrich others—never mind such bourgeois notions as incentives to thrift or work or betterment, with its attendant virtues of prudence and a commercial justice that even Shakespeare realized was foundational at Venice.

The gentry and especially the aristocracy in Shakespeare's England discounted bourgeois thrift and scorned the bourgeois work that earned the income with which to be thrifty. As late as 1695 the English economic writer Charles Davenant complained that "if these high [land] taxes long continue, in a country so little given to thrift as ours, the landed men must inevitably be driven into the hands of . . . usurers."[13] The unthrifty were landed English gentlemen puttin' on the style. Francis Bacon had been in Shakespeare's time the very type of such a man, given to "ostentatious entrances, arrayed in all his finery, and surrounded by a glittering retinue," greedy, chronically unthrifty, always in debt, and surrendering to the temptation therefore to misuse the Lord Chancellor's mace, when finally his ambition achieved it, by soliciting bribes from both sides in legal disputes.[14] As Pope wrote in

1732–1734 in *The Essay on Man* to those who admired Bacon, "If parts allure thee, think how Bacon shin'd, / The wisest, brightest, meanest of mankind." Not bourgeois virtue.

In 1621 in England the scholar and cleric Robert Burton wrote fiercely, in *The Anatomy of Melancholy*:

> What's the market? . . . A vast chaos, a confusion of manners, as fickle as the air, *domicilium insanorum* [abode of madmen], a turbulent troop full of impurities, a mart of walking spirits, goblins, the theatre of hypocrisy, a shop of knavery, flattery, a nursery of villainy, the scene of babbling, the school of giddiness, the academy of vice; . . . every man is for himself, his private ends, and stands upon his own guard. No charity, love, friendship, fear of God, alliance, affinity, consanguinity, Christianity, can contain them. . . . Our *summum bonum* is commodity, and the goddess we adore *Dea moneta*, Queen money, . . . money, greatness, office, honor, authority; honesty is accounted folly; knavery, policy; men admired out of opinion, not as they are, but as they seem to be.[15]

Well. If many people believed this, and acted on it, a modern economy would be impossible. If dignity was not accorded to transactions in trade and to the betterments that the bourgeoisie brings forward to the test of profit, and if the liberty to trade and to invent were scorned, and if liberty to compete were not the test of anyone's betterment, then the modern world would have languished at 1621.

My claim is that the old, antibourgeois view—the exceptions, I have said, came early among the Italians and Catalans, and then the Bavarians such as the Fuggers of Augsburg, and the northern Hanseatic League and above all the Netherlanders—dominated the public rhetoric of Scotland and England until the very late seventeenth century, that of France until the late eighteenth, that of most of Germany until the early nineteenth, that of Japan until the late nineteenth, that of China and India until the late twentieth. The belief I say is ancient, and it persists in some circles even into the Bourgeois Era.

If trading were in fact a scene mainly of adulterated flour and over-dear shoes, a matter of making upland wives think your stuff was good when it was rotten, a theater of hypocrisy ruled only by lying and plotting, then no one of faith or justice or indeed of common prudence would venture to take part in it. The self-selection would drive out all faithful people, by a mechanism the economists call, following George Akerlof, the "lemons" effect. If the only automobiles that come be traded, Akerlof observed, are those that work badly and therefore are lemons fit only to be sold off to suckers (an auto that has been in a serious crash, for example, though "repaired"), then everyone will come to suspect that *any* automobile put up for sale is likely to be a lemon.[16] The medieval historian James Davis makes the same point: "If unremitting suspicion [which he finds especially in literary and religious comments on petty traders] reflected the opinion of all medieval market users then exchange would have been very difficult, . . . requiring constant (and costly) surveillance."[17] If only deceitful Scottish tradesmen, or English knaves and men admired out of opinion rather than for who they really are, can succeed in the secondhand market for horses, then everyone will come to suspect that any horse put up for sale is likely to be rotten, impure, overdear, and dissembling. Make sure you look in the horse's mouth and count the teeth. Watch for blue eyes. In an auto chassis watch for signs of welded breaks. Or, better, don't buy a horse or car at all. Walk, and remain at $3 a day.

Something is strange here. Lindsay and Burton could not actually have maintained such a view without self-contradiction. After all, they bought their ink and quills to scribble away at *A Satire of the Three Estates* or *The Anatomy of Melancholy* in a market, and sustained themselves with wine purchased in a market supplied from France with *Dea moneta*, and rode on purchased horses when they could, and if really wealthy and citified were carried in hired sedan chairs or in self-owned carriages. A modern who holds such antimarket views faces the same self-contradiction, buying paper and ink and computers in the marketplace to produce the *Socialist Worker*, or driving her recently purchased Mercedes to meetings to overthrow capitalism.

Burton himself could not sustain it. The other eighteen instances in his book of the word "market" (all coming after the first passage attacking the very idea) refer to market*places*, not the abstract concept, analogous here to Vanity Fair, and do not carry connotations of nattering by walking spirits. Anyway, such blasts against greed are standard turns in literary performances from the *Iliad* (1.122, 149) and the prophet Amos (2:6–7, 5:10–12, 8:4–6) down to the novels of Sinclair Lewis and the TV show *American Greed: Scams, Schemes, and Broken Dreams*. They must be satisfying to write, because there is a great supply of them; and the demand, too, seems brisk.

In its very conventionality, however, Lindsay's speeches and Burton's paragraph typify the rhetorical obstacle to a modern economy. The sneer by the aristocrat, the damning by the priest, the envy by the peasant, all directed against trade and profit and the bourgeoisie, conventional in every literature since ancient times (though there is some doubt concerning Mesopotamia), have long sufficed to kill economic growth. Only in recent centuries has the clerisy's prejudice against trading been offset and partially disabled by economists and pragmatists and the writers of books on how to win friends and influence people.

Consider the analogy with other prejudices. Anti-Semitism was "merely" an idea, unless implemented in Russian pogroms during the 1880s or in Viennese politics during the 1890s. But lacking the mere idea, and its long history in Europe, and its intensification in the nineteenth century, the Russian pogroms and the Viennese newspaper articles and their spawn after 1933 would not have happened. Hitler, although not much of a reader, was an intellectual in the sense that hole-in-corner dealers in ideas on the blogs are nowadays. Ideas, especially about art and architecture, mattered to Hitler and motivated him, which made him a member of the clerisy, alas. (The committee that turned down his application in 1907 to become a student at the Vienna Academy of Fine Arts bears a heavy weight of historical guilt.) The coming of the idea of praise for bourgeois values, or at least toleration for them, resembles the ending, or the moderating, or at least the embarrassing, of anti-Semitism. And it is no hot news that antitrade prejudice and anti-Jewish prejudice are connected at the hip. Ideas mattered. That ideas mattered didn't mean that legal and financial implementation was a nullity, or that self-interest never motivated a Czech seizing the house of an exterminated Jew. But ideas are not, as the economists believe, merely cheap talk with no impact on social equilibria.

Or consider racism in America. The hypocrisy of Lindsay's or Burton's antimarket blasts while trading with their friend Nat the stationer for ink can be compared, as Virgil Storr has observed, with talking about African-Americans being quite terrible on the whole, as burglars of houses and rapists of white women—except my cleaning lady, who is a good one, or except my friend from church, whom after long acquaintance I hardly remember is one, or Sammy Davis Jr., who after all was Jewish. "All merchants are crooks," writes Storr in free indirect style, "but this chap I deal with isn't so bad."[18] Or consider prejudice against women. My daughter deserves respect, says the virulent sexist. But those others are fat pigs, dogs, slobs, and disgusting animals.

Or to return to the main point—the prejudice against business so crippling to economic growth—the unreflective hypocrite will declare, "My local grocer is a good fellow, but in general they're cheats." Yet for a Great Enrichment the middleman in the marketplace or in the corporation requires the same liberty and dignity as does the betterer in the laboratory or the saxophonist at the Jazz Showcase. All of them sell dear and buy cheap, the one routinely with, say, food, the other creatively with ideas, whether of furniture or saxophone riffs. The idea-betterment must be tested by what people will trade for it, or else it is a mere fancy that will on balance reduce welfare. The central error of comprehensive socialism or the regulatory impulse is to suppose that betterment does *not* need to be tested by trade, that no discoveries are to be made by performing cash tests on millions of individual and idiosyncratic people about what they value, that we already know everything we need to know to satisfy and protect the consumers. Therefore it seems right and proper to hand over the regulation of the economy to the state—that is, for the state to act, in John Kenneth Galbraith's brilliant rhetoric of 1952 (which installed the notion in the minds of American Democrats) as a "countervailing power," a perfectly unbiased referee, between unions and businesses.

The point is that the prejudice against the middleman, the boss, the banker—vile things—if it gets beyond cheap talk, and it often does, can stop cold all discovery, betterment, and creative destruction. Smith and Schumpeter are stymied. Stupidity comes to reign. It needs to be contradicted, and in Britain in the eighteenth century it was.

33

AS DID ELIZABETHAN
ENGLAND GENERALLY

It is not merely by Shakespeare that a modern bourgeois and his trading activities were disdained in soon-to-be-bourgeois-accepting England. The Elizabethan playwright Christopher Marlowe in 1592 has Barabas, the despicable Jew of Malta, asking ignobly, "Who is honored now but for his wealth?" We are to sneer at such an attitude. The equally despicable Governor of Malta in the play declares on the contrary, as an aristocrat conventionally would, that "honor is bought with blood and not with gold," though neither Barabas nor the Governor exhibit much in the honor line.[1]

Thomas Dekker's popular comedy in the same era, *The Shoemaker's Holiday*, is claimed by the literary critic David Bevington to be, in contrast, pro-bourgeois: "No play better celebrates bourgeois London."[2] I think not quite, and neither, really, does Bevington—not in the way "bourgeois" came shortly to be understood. The hero of Dekker's play, Simon Eyre (ca. 1395–1458), was in historical fact a draper who had risen to be Lord Mayor of London in 1445. Dekker's play of 1599, which shifts Eyre's trade to shoemaking, was presented before Queen Elizabeth, and its success may have provoked Shakespeare to write *The Merry Wives of Windsor*. Eyre in the play is a "professor of the *gentle* craft" of . . . mere shoemaking, a joke common at the time, and persisting into the nineteenth century, turning on the absurdity of a shoemaker being "gentle," that is, born to a family of high position in the Great Chain of Being. I have noted that the word was "originally used synonymously with noble," as the *OED* puts it, in the way *gentil* in French and *gentile* in Italian still are.[3] In the play the absurdity of calling such a humble job "gentle" is drawn on again and again (1.30, 1.134, 1.219, 3.4, 3.24, 4:47, 7:48). Eyre's curious catchphrase, "Prince am I none, yet am nobly born"—taken in form from *Orlando Furioso* and in application to Eyre and the "gentle craft" from a contemporary novel—underlines the extent of Eyre's rise in the social hierarchy.[4] The "shoemaker's" very name, Eyre, is a homonym of Dutch *eer* or German *Ehre*, "honor" in an aristocratic sense, which must have amused the Dutch-origin Dekker. (The playwright's name, Dekker, is Dutch even in spelling, and means [roof] "Thatcher," a nice historical irony. Dekker exhibits his Dutch origin by showing an accurate knowledge of the language of the merchant republic so irritating to aristocratic England.)

What is admired in the play is honorable hierarchy and its stability, not the bourgeois upheavals, creative destruction, and wave of gadgets to be commended in the eighteenth century and especially in the nineteenth. Bevington observes that Dekker's Eyre "is not 'middle class' in the nineteenth-century sense of the term, since his values remain stubbornly and proudly those of his artisan origins."[5] Eyre starts as a jolly and indulgent master, dealing sharply only once (7.74, 7.77–78)—and this in a minor matter involving how *much* beer he is going to buy in order to overreward his workers. He stays that way. No sharp-eyed entrepreneur he.

The "Lord" Mayor is so called because he becomes a knight by virtue of the office. In keeping perhaps with the historical facts about Simon Eyre the playwright never raises him to *Sir* Simon. Though Eyre rises quickly to alderman, to sheriff, and last and most gloriously to Lord Mayor, he speaks right to the end of the play in mere prose, not in blank verse, five beats to the unrhymed line. The convention of Elizabethan drama was that the comic figures below the gentry and nobility do not normally speak in verse.[6] Eyre's journeyman Ralph Damport, for example, is bound for military duty in France, which ennobles a man. As Henry V says before Agincourt, "For he today that sheds his blood with me / Shall be my brother; be he ne'er so vile, / This day shall gentle his condition."[7] The mere journeyman Ralph, then— who gets spoken lines in the play only after his noble service in the army is decided upon—speaks in blank verse. Yet when he returns from the wars, now a sad and comical cripple, it's prose for demobbed and denobled Ralph (18.15). Ralph's wife Jane, likewise, nobly resisting courting by an actual gentleman while her proletarian husband is at the wars, also thereby rises above the commonality of prose.

The romantic lead in the play, Rowland Lacy, is nephew to the very grand Earl of Lincoln, and is therefore gentle by blood. He disguises himself as un-gentle Dutch "Hans" in order to secretly court Rose Oatley, daughter of a Sir Roger Oatley, who is at the outset the reigning Lord Mayor. The faux-Hans speaks in comical Anglo-Dutch—and in plebeian prose. That Rowland to begin with is seen as a ne'er-do-well, or even Dutch, paradoxically emphasizes his deeply inherited English nobility, as it does in spendthrift Bassanio in *The Merchant of Venice* or slumming Prince Hal in *Henry IV* (soon to succeed his father to become Henry V, noble in more than blood). It would be unseemly for an aristocrat, especially a young one, to bother with a sober prudence and temperance suitable to the mere bourgeoisie. Blood will tell. When "Hans" is revealed at the end of the play as Rowland Lacy, the nephew of an earl, to be knighted by the king himself, it's back to the nobility of English blank verse.

And so throughout. Every character is slotted by form of language into a proper place in the Great Chain of Being. Eyre and his sharp-witted wife Margery, for example, use the familiar "thou" (like *tu* in French) to address the journeyman shoemakers, but the formal "you" with their superiors (and "you" for plurals in both registers: *vous*). The reinforcement of the Great Chain appears all over Elizabethan and early Jacobite drama, and shows even in its rare exceptions. The bizarre feature of the Jews Barabas in Marlowe's *The Jew of Malta* and Shylock in *The Merchant of Venice* is their eloquence before social superiors. As the literary critic Lynne Magnusson points out, a comic effect in Shakespeare is achieved more usually by the middling sort (and Jews in Europe were at best middling) trying to speak posh, and fail-ing disastrously.[8] Like Dogberry in *Much Ado About Nothing*, the common-ers stumble about when speaking to the quality, and always their stumbling takes place in prose. By contrast, the Jews Barabas and Shylock have no such problem with elevated fluency, and almost always speak in blank verse: "But stay! What star shines yonder in the east? / The lodestar of my life, if Abigail." The limited experience of Englishmen with the despised Jews—expelled from England in 1290, Jews were not officially readmitted until 1656—must have made doubly impressive the contrast with the low comic figures speak-ing idiotically in prose.

That is, the honoring of hierarchy by Dekker, and by Shakespeare and by Marlowe, is nothing like "bourgeois" in the disruptive sense that Marx and Schumpeter understood it.

∞

Payment pops up all over *The Shoemaker's Holiday*, the stage direction "Giving money" being second only to "Enter" in frequency. Bourgeois?

No. In keeping with the emphasis on social hierarchy in the play and in the time and place in which it was written, the money transfers are almost always payments by a superior to an inferior, not deals between equals in the bourgeois marketplace. They are tips, expressing hierarchy, as they do now in Britain and the United States, as against, say, egalitarian Australia. We are not witnessing a celebration of "bourgeois" dealings in a modern sense, in which one equal dealer buys from another—"equal" at least in that a shilling is a shilling.

The giving of money in *The Shoemaker's Holiday* celebrates the Great Chain of Being. For example, jolly old Eyre gives a tip to his social inferior Ralph on his way to war, and the foreman Hodge and another, higher journeyman immediately also do so (1.218, 225, 229). When Eyre is elected sheriff, the cheeky journeyman Firk brings the good news and gets tipped by Mrs. Eyre (10.132), who is bourgeois and therefore above Firk in the Great Chain. Early on, the reigning Lord Mayor Sir Roger Oatley promises to get an aldermen to shower £20 on Rowland, the young noble, if he will but take up his commission as an officer and leave to fight in France (1.66–67). Oatley wants the wastrel safely away from his daughter Rose (as the Earl of Lincoln explains at 1.71–73). It's the usual comic material—before the Great Enrichment made such a plot irrelevant—of thwarted lovers circumventing their rich fathers, the only source of high incomes in a stagnant economy of status. Twenty pounds in 1599 was a large sum, far in excess of an unskilled workman's yearly wages. The same £20 gets circulated forty lines later by Rowland himself, to undermine the very elders who gave it. Likewise the gentleman Hammon offers the same magnificent sum, £20, to proletarian Ralph, back from the wars, if he'll only sell his chaste wife Jane to Hammon. It's no go, because Ralph is a good fellow, and yet Hammon then proves his own nobility by reaching down the social order to give the incorruptible couple the £20 tip anyway (18.97). The Earl of Lincoln and Sir Oatley keep trying to make cash work against love (8.49, 9.97), giving bribes to the same "noble," that is, blank-verse chap. Again at 16.97 cash payment tries to work against love, and, by the conventions of comedy in all ages, it fails.

So the middle class is held in its subordinate realm of prose, accepting the position with good grace. The money transactions in the play have nothing to do with ordinary business, much less with the financing of creative destruction. They reinforce status differentials, as a tip or a bribe given to lesser folk. Income is taken to be bullion in the style of mercantilists, such as the economic writer Thomas Mun in the 1620s: "One man's loss becomes another man's gain."[9] The world's wealth was conceived then as zero-sum—not such a foolish supposition before the Great Enrichment. Holland in Mun's theory or Dekker's play was bound to rise while England declines. Money circulates in aid of hierarchy, in the manner of the league tables of "competing" nations about which modern mercantilists in business schools and on the financial pages like to talk. Thus in our own day the "rise" of China (average per-person income in U.S. terms, $20 a day) is imagined to imply that the United States ($130 a day) will "fall."

Circulation in the play does not lead to specialization and certainly not to betterment. Shakespeare's people bettered themselves not as their descendants some decades later did by reinventing, say, the ancient Chinese technique of thin-walled cast iron but by robbing their inferiors or by amusing their superiors—witness Sir John Falstaff in *1* and *2 Henry IV* and in *Henry V* and, impelled by Dekker's success, in *The Merry Wives*. The playwright here is celebrating not mutual betterment but social climbing premised on zero-sum.

The modestly positioned Simon Eyre does at last become Lord Mayor, an office of great expense. To be an alderman, sheriff, and especially Lord Mayor of London required considerable wealth already accumulated. Yet Eyre does not achieve the wherewithal through entrepreneurial vigor and bourgeois betterment, or even the hard work that Mun in the 1620s noted in the Dutch and claimed was lacking in the English. Nor does Eyre achieve it through the personal incentives praised in 1825 by an observer of the Lord Mayor's show: "It is not . . . by what the *Lord Mayor* feels in his coach but by what the *apprentice* feels as he gazes at him, that the public is served."[10] He achieves the office by sheer luck, as though a shoemaker had won the Illinois State Lottery.[11] In the traditional story on which the play was based Eyre gets rich by chancing on a wrecked Dutch ship, whose contents he buys cheaply and sells dearly. It's mercantilist zero-sum, one man's misfortune being another man's enrichment.

Thomas Deloney's contemporary novel, *The Gentle Craft, Part I*, appeared two years before the play by Dekker and was a source for him, providing, I've noted, the tagline "Prince am I none." In the novel it is Eyre's wife who sees the entrepreneurial opportunity and urges him to seize it. Deloney explains that she "was inflamed with the desire thereof, as women are (for the most part) very covetous. . . . She could scant find in her heart to spare him time to go to supper for very eagerness to animate him on to take that bargain."[12] The word "bargain" here means a *good* bargain, which the *OED* first records in 1516. As the historian Laura Stevenson (O'Connell) put it in 1976, "By attributing all the innovation to Mistress Eyre, Deloney can celebrate Eyre's later achievements as a wise, just, and charitable rich man without having to portray him at first as an entrepreneur who has sullied himself by conjuring up a questionably honest business deal."[13]

Honorable (that is, "honest") riches are achieved by collecting rents on land, not by mutual dealing, and certainly not by inventing plate glass or dropped ceilings or a stock market. In an aristocratic society, as in a sacred society of charitable Brahmins, or in a socialist society imagined by the modern clerisy, actual *business* deals are presumed to be *dis*honest, in both the old sense of "undignified" and the modern sense of "not fair dealing." Recall Gandhi's judgment on national-income-raising business: "There is nothing more disgraceful to man than the principle 'buy in the cheapest market and sell in the dearest.'"

In *The Shoemaker's Holiday*, Eyre is elevated in the Great Chain by Lady Luck. Numerous people above him in the chain just happen to die, and his wife and his foreman just happen to put the shipwreck in front of his nose. Mortenson notes that Dekker's play is a version of the pastoral, shifted to London. Off-stage throughout there occur highly nonpastoral wars (which cripple Ralph, and to which Rowland Lacy honorably adjourns at the end), deaths (aldermen especially), and the loss of the Dutch merchant ship that enriches Eyre. As Mortenson puts it, "Dekker creates a grim world and encourages us to pretend that it is a green one."[14]

In a world after Eden, then, God gave the shoemaker Simon Eyre abundance, and he "gives it back," in the unhappy phrase so often on the lips of charitable American billionaires. (They did not steal what they have, and usually got it by their own effort in supplying us with things we desire, and therefore in justice they should not speak of "giving back" as though they took it illegitimately in the first place.) Bevington notes that "his ship literally comes in."[15] As to the rhetoric of the economy, then, Dekker's play is conservative. The machinery differs entirely from that in the increasingly common pro-bourgeois productions in English after 1690.

The theatrical history of *The Shoemaker's Holiday* eerily parallels that of *The London Merchant* 132 years later, and the contrast between the two exhibits the change in attitude. Like Dekker, George Lillo was of Dutch origin (Lillo was apparently the son of a Dutch jeweler). Like Dekker's play, Lillo's was after its initial success performed yearly for the benefit of the young bourgeois of the city, invariably at Christmas down to 1818, and often also on the Lord Mayor's Day in November. Like *The Shoemaker's Holiday*, it was "judged a proper entertainment for the apprentices, etc., as being a more instructive, moral, and cautionary tale than many pieces," as the original producer and star of *The London Merchant*, Theophilus Cibber, put it. And in the manner of *The Shoemaker's Holiday* Lillo's play is clumsy, below the best standard of its age. *The Shoemaker's Holiday* looks amateurish beside Marlowe's *Doctor Faustus* of 1588–1589, for example, not to speak of most of Shakespeare. And *The London Merchant* likewise looks amateurish beside John Gay's *The Beggars' Opera* of 1728. Yet both amateurish plays were startlingly successful. From 1702 to 1776 *The London Merchant* was the third most often produced English play.[16]

The plays are similar, then. But they differ radically in their valuation of the bourgeoisie. The change between *The Shoemaker's Holiday* of 1599 and *The London Merchant* of 1731 reflects a change in popular opinion about the middle class, which one may with justice call the Bourgeois Revaluation. An already-wealthy Eyre had to put a little pep into the Lord Mayor's show, and to exhibit therefore his liberality, an aristocratic virtue praised in Dekker's time at all levels of English society. Eyre reflects on his good luck: "By the Lord of Ludgate, it's a mad life to be a lord mayor. It's a stirring life, a fine life, a velvet life. . . . This day my fellow 'prentices of London come to dine with me too; they shall have fine cheer, gentlemanlike cheer. I promised . . . that if ever I came to be mayor of London, I would feast them all; and I'll do't, I'll do't, by the life of Pharaoh. By this beard, Sim Eyre will be no flincher."[17] He promises "gentlemanlike" cheer to non-gentlemen—tipping again. A faithful man, he does not forget his "fellow" apprentices. Laura Stevenson explains, "The godly rich man was not a man who was engaged in the pursuit of wealth; he was a man already wealthy." "The calling of the rich man was the calling of the public servant, preacher, or teacher," as it had always been.[18] William Perkins, a Puritan preacher at the University of Cambridge whose numerous works were collected and published in 1616–1618, declared that "if God gives abundance, *when we neither desire it nor seek it*, we may take it, hold it, and use it. . . . But [the businessman] may not desire goods . . . more than necessary, for if he doth, he sinneth."[19] Article 12 of the 5th Main Point of Doctrine of the English translation of the orthodox Calvinist Canons of Dort emanating from the Netherlands in 1619 explains how the Chosen might come to be assured of their chosenness: "This assurance, . . . so far from making true believers proud and carnally self-assured, is rather the true root of humility, of childlike respect, of genuine godliness, of endurance in every conflict, of fervent prayers, of steadfastness in crossbearing and in confessing the truth, and . . . provides an incentive to a serious and continual practice of thanksgiving and good works." Spending on good works is good, if blamelessly acquired—preferably by God's accidents to shipping.

The ancient claim, dating from Aristotle's *Politics* and repeated in Marx and Weber and recent critics of commercial society, is that what is wrong with money is that it tends to be accumulated "without limit." To give charity and do other good works, by contrast, is to impose limits, by a gospel of wealth. Stevenson criticizes the historian Christopher Hill (1912–2003), writing at the height of the prestige of historical materialism, who according to her "did not realize that once a man reached a certain point of affluence, the Puritans [and the other English people of the time, and the Anti-Remonstrants of the Netherlands, and in historical order, the Israelites, the Romans, the medieval Christians, the nineteenth-century clerisy, and the Carnegies, Warren Buffetts, and Bill Gateses] insisted that he be diligent in a calling which involved not making money, but spending it."[20] It was a Protestant theme—as indeed it had been a Catholic theme among Florentine bankers worried about their taking of usury, building baptisteries out of their fortunes. And likewise the robber barons in America. Donald Frey writes in a review of Olivier Zunz's *Philanthropy in America*:

> The Methodist admonition to "earn all you can, save all you can, give all you can" surely influenced more Americans than Carnegie's "Gospel of Wealth" ever did. Yet, by the time Zunz picks up the story [in the late nineteenth century], religion is more a minor player than the lead actor. The naïve reader might conclude from

Zunz's book that [American] philanthropy sprang full-grown from rich entrepreneurs, who started foundations for no reason other than that they could.[21]

It was long a religious routine to deny dignity to the pursuit of wealth and grant it only to the pious spending.

And so it went in all the plays and novels of Shakespeare's time. The novelist Deloney, who died in 1600, speaks in his last bourgeois production about one Thomas of Reading, a good rich clothier, but tells nothing of the entrepreneurial activities leading to his wealth, only of his acts of charity and good citizenship after acquiring it. "Far from using the preacher's approval of abundant wealth and diligent work as a doctrine which encourages poor boys to make good," writes Stevenson, "Deloney uses Puritan morality as a retreat from the spirit of capitalism."[22] Similarly, the English clerisy in the nineteenth century, portrayed by George Eliot in 1871–1872 as seeking their noncommercial callings in a sadly commercial land, reverted to the earlier and Puritan model.

Such piety continued to be in tension with trade-tested betterment even in the bourgeois nineteenth century in the bourgeois United States in bourgeois occupations. In Horatio Alger's novels the poor boys made good, as in *Struggling Upward, or Luke Larkin's Luck* (1868). Note the "luck," resembling Lord Mayor Eyre's. Alger's Luke was "the son of a carpenter's widow, living on narrow means, and so compelled to exercise the strictest economy."[23] Luke achieves business success only with a tremendous struggling upward, fully 144 pages of it, in which he is polite, industrious, abstemious, and on and on in what was to be called Weberian style (inaccurately, as I have noted: Weber emphasizes the spirit, and sometimes notes that startling betterment is its outcome). Yet, again in the manner of Simon Eyre in a traditionally antibourgeois society, and in Weber's account, too, Luke is *not* entrepreneurial in the bolder sense that made the modern world. He invents nothing. He ventures nothing. Commercial hope and courage and prudence are not his. He does not engage in trade-tested betterment. He merely works hard—as people of all sorts have been doing since the beginning and especially since agriculture. The Filipino song declares (in English) that, "Planting rice is never fun, / Bent from morn 'til set of sun." The truth is that stoop labor or high savings rates or the strictest economy are not the essence of our betterment since 1800.

By contrast, Alger's contemporary in England, Samuel Smiles, who was himself a successful businessman and an admirer of entrepreneurial engineers such as George Stephenson and Isambard Kingdom Brunel, understood that riches came from substantive betterment tested by profit, not from the zero-sum luck of finding a Dutch wreck or being favored by a tip from the already-rich or by getting a hand up from an older man. Alger did not understand it. The usual identification of a "Horatio Alger story" with entrepreneurship is mistaken. Alger was the son of a minister, a graduate of Harvard, and briefly a minister himself. He knew nothing of the business world and had no affection for the mania for betterment characteristic (said Tocqueville and many others) of his America. After a scandal and disgrace involving boys in his charge, Alger embarked on his writing career with *Ragged Dick* (1867). All the Alger novels have the same plot. His boys get their start by impressing an older man—in *Struggling Upward*, for example, Luke impresses a Mr. Armstrong, named a "merchant."[24] Virtue is achieved through hard work on the one side, and on the other side through possessing Armstrongian wealth by God's grace and giving it out to suitable objects of largess, especially to attractive boys. It is not achieved by creative destruction.

With few exceptions (such as Smiles), the theorists of betterment, or the ministers criticizing it, or the writers of 110 novels for boys, didn't know betterment in business from practicing it themselves. Unlike love or even war, serious business seems to stop the telling. Multatuli's novel *Max Havelaar* (1860) was a Dutch *Uncle Tom's Cabin*, testifying against exploitation in the Dutch East Indies. The first narrator is a comically self-absorbed dealer in coffee—the most famous line in Dutch literature is the opening of the book: "I am a dealer in coffee, and live at 37 Lauiergracht." He explains with some warmth why he had previously not engaged in such an unbusinesslike business as writing novels:

> For years I asked myself what the use of such things was, and I stand amazed at the insolence with which a writer of novels will fool you with things that never happened and indeed *could* never happen. If in my own business . . . I put out anything of which the smallest part was an untruth—which is the chief business in poetry and romance—[my competitor] would instantly get wind of it. So I make sure that I write no novels or put out any other falsehoods.[25]

Back at the dawning of a Dutch-imitating enterprise in Britain, Daniel Defoe, whose business was journalism and propaganda, had characterized himself as a similarly secular Puritan, suspicious of fiction—though he re-sembled the dealer in coffee at 37 Lauiergracht in being self-contradictory in his suspicion. He wrote in *Serious Reflections of Robinson Crusoe*, one of his two follow-ons to *Robinson Crusoe* (Defoe never admitted that anything he wrote was fiction), "This supplying a story by invention is certainly a most scandalous crime."[26] Then Defoe, and the literal-minded merchant-narrator of *Max Havelaar*, proceed to transmit the truth to be discerned in just such a novel. The European novel developed a special, nonpastoral connection with literal truth. In truth no "falsehoods" come from Multatuli, but an effective exposé, written not by the dealer in coffee (the dealer is a framing device), of the horrors of Dutch colonialism. A business-respecting civilization that had not misplaced the virtues could in pioneering Holland become guilty about its excesses.

ARISTOCRATIC ENGLAND, FOR
EXAMPLE, SCORNED MEASUREMENT

One countable piece of evidence that bourgeois values were scorned in England until the early eighteenth century is the unfashionability in the time of Shakespeare or Dekker of reasoning by count. A century ago Sombart made the point that in the Middle Ages in Europe "the handling of figures was very primitive."[1] Europe had to learn to count with Arabic (really, Indian) as against Roman numerals. The Italians led. Yet Sombart observed that "as late as 1299 the use of Arabic numerals was forbidden by the brethren of the [Florentine] Calimala guild," although "Italy was the first in the field as the land where commercial arithmetic was in vogue."[2] In the North the leaders in counting were the Dutch, and not merely as a technique but as an attitude toward a commercial and calculating life, so unlike the mad, gentlemanlike life of an English Lord Mayor.

It has recently been realized, further, that medieval Europe was peculiarly backward in such matters: China was far ahead in numeracy. A'Hearn, Baten, and Crayen argue that literacy and numeracy before and after 1800 was high in China, confirming the earlier work by Ronald Dore (1965) on neighboring Japan and by Evelyn Rawski (1974) on China itself.[3] Numeracy can be judged by observing the peculiar fact of "age-heaping," that is, the frequency with which people report their ages in round numbers as 40, 25, or 55 instead of the more accurate 41, 24, or 53, instances collected from the tons of social documents reporting such replies, as in Qing records of the reported ages of people involved as victims or perpetrators of crimes, ages in soldier lists from the Qing army, the reported ages of Chinese immigrants to the United States, and so forth. A'Hearn, Baten, and Crayen fall in with the recent orthodoxy about "institutions," but they observe, too, that a deeper "ideological change" was important in bringing economic fruit to the relatively literate and numerate.

Shakespeare's works record an aristocratic refusal to calculate. Think of Hamlet's indecision, Lear's proud impulsiveness, King Leontes's irrationalities in *A Winter's Tale*. Even Antonio the merchant of *The Merchant of Venice* makes the bargain impulsively, on account of his deep friendship. Such behavior is quite unlike the prudent examining of ethical account books even in late and worldly Puritans such as Daniel Defoe, or in their still later and still more worldly descendants such as Benjamin Franklin.

The premodern attitude—which survives nowadays in many a nonquantitative modern—shows in a little business between Prince Hal and Sir John Falstaff. The scene is fictional early fifteenth century; *1 Henry IV* was written in London at the end of the sixteenth century. Either time will do. Prince Hal, disguised in a stiffened linen cloth called buckram, had been the night before one of the merely two assailants of Falstaff and his little gang of three other thieves. The princely two had relieved the four thieves of their loot just taken. Falstaff, after a token resistance, had fled in terror, as had his confederates. One of them, Gadshill, and poor old Jack Falstaff, recount the episode to Prince Hal, without realizing that it was the prince himself who attacked them. Here among the low life even the prince—though soon to become noble and blank-verse Henry V—speaks in prose:

FALSTAFF. A hundred upon poor four of us.

PRINCE. What, a hundred, man?

FALSTAFF. I am a rogue if I were not at half-sword with a dozen of them, two hours together:

GADSHILL. We four set upon some dozen—

FALSTAFF [to the PRINCE]. Sixteen at least, my lord.

GADSHILL. As we were sharing [the loot], some six or seven fresh men set upon us.

FALSTAFF. If I fought not with fifty of them, I am a bunch of radish. If there were not two- and three-and-fifty upon poor old Jack, then I am no two-legged creature. I have peppered two of them. Two I am sure I have paid [that is, mortally injured]—two rogues in buckram suits. Four rogues in buckram let drive at me—

PRINCE. What, four? Thou saidst but two even now.

FALSTAFF. Four, Hal, I told thee four. I took all their seven points in my target
    [shield], thus.

PRINCE. Seven? Why, there were but four even now.

FALSTAFF. In buckram. These nine in buckram that I told thee of—

PRINCE. So, two more already.

FALSTAFF. [As swift as] a thought, seven of the eleven I paid.

PRINCE. O monstrous! Eleven buckram men grown out of two![4]

Yet in 1783 Boswell says to Johnson: "Sir Alexander Dick tells me, that he
remembers having a thousand people in a year to dine at his house; that is,
reckoning each person as one, each time he dined there."

JOHNSON. That, Sir, is about three a day.

BOSWELL. How your statement lessens the idea.

JOHNSON. That, Sir, is the good of counting. It brings every thing to a certainty,
    which before floated in the mind indefinitely.

BOSWELL. But . . . one is sorry to have this diminished.

JOHNSON. Sir, you should not allow yourself to be delighted with error.[5]

Something had changed. As Johnson wrote elsewhere, "To count is a
modern practice, the ancient method was to guess; and when numbers are
guessed they are always magnified," in the style of true Jack Falstaff, plump
Jack Falstaff.[6] Johnson the classicist knew what he was talking about. The
economic historian Gregory Clark has reviewed the startling evidence from
tombstones that wealthy if illiterate and innumerate ancient Romans, for
example, didn't know their own ages. In the style of fabled Methuselahs the
innumerate among the Romans would grossly exaggerate the age at death
of old folk, with every sign of believing their own miscalculations.[7] The lack
of precision in counting persisted among the ignorant. When Casanova escaped from prison in Venice in 1757 he went to Paris, where he lighted on a
promisingly gullible female victim, the Marquise d'Urfe. But she was already
captivated by another gentlemanly scoundrel, the Comte de Saint-Germain,
who had persuaded her to believe he was three hundred years old.[8]

The bourgeois boy in Northern Italy from earliest times and later elsewhere in Europe did learn to multiply and divide, somehow, or else he went
bankrupt. He had to use an abacus, and skillfully, as I've noted, and could
multiply and divide on it. Presumably the same was true earlier at Constan-

tinople and Baghdad and Delhi, not to speak of Ōsaka and Guangzhou. The height of mathematical ability in an ordinary European man or a commercial woman by the eighteenth century was the Rule of Three, which is to say the solving of proportions: "Six is to two as N is to three." It is the first step in algebra. Without getting the Rule of Three down pat one could hardly deal profitably as a merchant with the scores of currencies and systems of measurement even in the big and unified countries of Europe, and the scores of systems in the German lands. Interest, eventually compounded, was calculated by table. Mistakes were common.

Numeracy, then, was always advanced among the bourgeois, who had to calculate to live. The Dutch, I repeat, led the way, and ordinary Dutch folk around 1600 thought quantitatively. In Britain by 1757 even among people not in business a common numeracy was perhaps more advanced than in, say, France. Johnson laid it down that "no man should travel unprovided with instruments for taking heights and distances," as he himself used his walking stick.[9] Boswell reports a conversation in 1783 in which Johnson argues against constructing a wall around a garden on calculative grounds, the garden not being productive enough to bear the expense of the wall—the same calculation at the same time, by the way, was surprisingly important for the enclosure movement in English agriculture. "I record the minute detail," writes Boswell, "in order to show clearly how this great man . . . was yet well-informed in the common affairs of life, and loved to illustrate them."[10] The point is that he loved to illustrate them *quantitatively*, quite contrary to the routine in earlier centuries.

Because of his friendship with Mr. and Mrs. Thrale, who ran a large London brewery, Johnson turned his quantitative mind to their hopes. In 1778 he writes, "We are not far from the great year of 100,000 barrels [of porter brewed at the Anchor's brewery], which, if three shillings be gained from each barrel will bring us fifteen thousand pounds a year [an immense sum, much larger than Mr. Darcy's income in Jane Austen's *Pride and Prejudice*]. Whitbread [a competing brewery] never pretended to more than thirty pounds a day, which is not eleven thousand a year."[11] Calculate, calculate. That is the good of counting. And this was from a literary man.

No wonder that "by the early nineteenth century," as Leonore Davidoff and Catherine Hall note, "foreign visitors [to England] were struck by this spirit: the prevalence of measuring instruments, the clocks on every church steeple, the 'watch in everyone's pocket,' the fetish of using scales for weighing everything including one's own body and of ascertaining a person's exact chronological age."[12] Praise for calculation was becoming slowly a Europe-wide trope, along with its Romantic flip side of sneering at any calculation. The self-satisfied merchant Young Werner in Goethe's *Wilhelm Meister's Apprenticeship* (1796) declares, "What [immense] advantages does [the genuine merchant] derive from the system of book-keeping by double entry! It is among the finest inventions of the human mind; every prudent master of a house should introduce it into his economy."[13] A good account brings every thing to a certainty, which before floated in the mind indefinitely, though the literary clerisy will sneer.

Such an idea of counting and accounting is obvious to us, in our bourgeois lives. It is part of our private and public rhetoric, and we laugh at quantitative exaggerations, though perhaps not as easily as Shakespeare did, so much do we honor counting. The point is that counting had to be invented, both as a technique and as an attitude. What we now consider quite ordinary arithmetic entered late into the educations of the aristocracy and the clergy and the nonmercantile professions. Johnson advised a rich woman, "Let your boy learn arithmetic"—note the supposition that the heir to a great fortune would usually fail to do so—"He will not then be a prey to every rascal which this town swarms with: teach him the value of money and how to reckon with it."[14] In 1803 Harvard College required, naturally, fluency in both Latin and Greek of all the boys proposing to attend. Yet only in that year did it also make arithmetic a requirement.

Consider such a modern commonplace as the graph for showing, say, how the Dow Jones average has recently moved. (*New Yorker* cartoon: a man sitting in front of a wall chart, on which an utterly flat line is graphed, declares, "Sometimes I think it will drive me mad.") Aside from the "mysterious and isolated wonder" of a tenth-century plotting of planetary inclinations, the political scientist and graphing guru Edward Tufte observes, the graph appeared surprisingly late in the history of counting. Cartesian coordinates were "invented" by Descartes himself in 1637, unifying geometry and algebra, perhaps from the analogy with maps and their latitudes and longitudes. (Much of this was invented centuries before in China, though the Europeans were innocent of the fact.) But graphical devices for factual observations, as against the plotting of algebraic equations on Cartesian coordinates, were first invented by the Swiss scientist J. H. Lambert in 1765 and more influentially by the early economist William Playfair in two books at the end of the eighteenth century, *The Commercial and Political Atlas*, 1786 (the time series plot and the bar chart) and *The Statistical Breviary Shewing on a Principle Entirely New the Resources of Every State and Kingdom of Europe*, 1801 (the pie chart; areas showing quantities; exhibiting many variables at one location), "applying," as Playfair put it, "lines to matters of commerce and finance."[15] Contour lines for heights on maps were only invented for Europeans in 1774 by the pioneering Scottish geologist Charles Hutton, in aid of a survey of a Scottish mountain.[16]

Obsession with accurate counting in Europe dates from the seventeenth century. Pencil and paper calculation by "algorithm" (named after the home district of a ninth-century Arabic mathematician) and its generalization in algebra (*al-jabr*, the reuniting of broken parts) depended on Arabic numerals (from India), with place value and a zero (from Arabic *sifr*, emptiness). True, the abacus, dating it may be from the third millennium BCE and certainly from the first millennium CE from Japan to Spain, with versions in Mesoamerica, makes rapid calculation possible even without place-value notation on paper. But with Roman-style numerals without place value you cannot multiply or divide by written-down algorithm. Even addition and subtraction is difficult—though the abacus made all this easy.

Only in the sixteenth and seventeenth centuries did Arabic numerals spread widely to Northern Europe. Admittedly, the first European document to use Arabic numerals was as early as 976. The soon-to-be Pope Sylvester II—or rather "the 2nd" (ca. 940–1003)—tried to teach them, having learned them in Moorish Spain. His lessons didn't take. The merchant and mathematician Leonardo Fibonacci reexplained them in a book of 1202. The commercial Italians were using them freely by the fifteenth century, though often mixed with Roman.[17] But before Shakespeare's time 0, 1, 2, 3, . . . 10, . . . 100, as against *i, ii, iii,* . . . *x,* . . . *c,* had not spread much beyond the Italian bourgeoisie. The Byzantines used the Greek equivalent of Roman numerals right up to the fall of Byzantium in 1453. And still in the early eighteenth century Peter the Great was passing laws to compel Russians to give up their Greek numerals (α, β, γ) and adopt the Arabic.

In England before its bourgeois time Roman numerals prevailed. Shakespeare's opening chorus in *Henry V*, two years after *1 Henry IV*, apologizes for showing battles without Cecil B. DeMillean numbers of extras: Yet "a crooked figure may /Attest in little place a million; / And let us, ciphers to this great accompt [account], / On your imaginary forces work." The "crooked figure" he has in mind is not Arabic "1,000,000," but merely a scrawled Roman M with a bar over it to signify "multiplied by 1,000": 1,000 times 1,000 is a million.

The historian Peter Wardley has pioneered the study of numeracy in England by the use of probate inventories, statements of property at death available in practically limitless quantities from the fifteenth century onward. He has discovered that as late as 1610 even in commercial Bristol the share of probates using Arabic as against Roman numerals was essentially zero. By 1670, however, it was nearly 100 percent, a startlingly fast change.[18] Robert Loder's farm accounts from about the same time, in Berkshire 1610–1620, used Roman numerals almost exclusively before 1616, even for yields of grain. In 1616 Loder started to mix in Arabic, as though he had just learned to reckon in them. He continued to use Roman numerals for the years, because calendar years, like regnal years, or Elizabeth II or Superbowl XX, are not subject to calculation.[19] English official accounts did not use Arabic numerals until the 1640s. "On the church at Chedworth in the Cotswolds," Eric Jones notes, "there are dates of the 1490s carved in Arabic form, probably having been introduced by Italian merchants who came there to buy wool."[20]

Fra Luca Pacioli of Venice popularized double-entry bookkeeping at the end of the fifteenth century, and such sophistications in accounting rapidly spread in bourgeois circles. The metaphor of a set of accounts was nothing new, as in God's accounting of our sins, or the three servants in Jesus's parable (Matt. 25:14–30) rendering their account of their uses of the talents— the Greek original uses *logon*, the word "word" being also the usual term for "commercial accounts": "My soul more bent / To serve therewith my Maker, and present / My true account, lest he returning chide." Bourgeois boys actually carried out the Puritan program of accounting numerically for one's sins, as in the young Franklin's scorekeeping.

We must not, though, be misled by the absence in Olden Tymes of widespread arithmetical skills or formal accounts into thinking that our ancestors were merely stupid. Recent neuropsychology shows that a spatial sense of a large number of trees being fewer than a very large number is hardwired into pigeons and people, regardless of whether they can do their multiplication tables with precision in their heads. Shepherds had every incentive to develop tricks in reckoning, as in the old Welsh system of counting sheep, perhaps from how many sheep the eye can grasp at a glance. The myth is that all primitive folk count "one, two, many," and a tribe in Brazil has been cited as evidence, somewhat dubiously. People are not innumerate when they think it matters, though some do count in strange ways, because it doesn't.

Large organizations counted perforce. Sheer counts had often a purpose of taxation—St. Luke's (false) story about a decree from Caesar Augustus that all the world should be taxed, for example; and in 1086, William the Conqueror's Domesday Book. We owe our knowledge of medieval agriculture in Europe to the necessity in large estates to count, in order to discourage cheating by subordinates. The Bishop of Winchester's two-score manors 1211–1349 CE required accounting if the servants were not to make off with the silver.[21] We know less about agriculture a little later in Europe because the size of giant estates went down after the Black Death of 1346–1353 and the consequent fall in the ratio of rents to wages, and such accounting was therefore less worthwhile.

Calculation, in other words, is the skeleton of common prudence. But the aristocrat scorns calculation precisely because it embodies ignoble prudence and is so very bourgeois. The claim that businessmen are peculiarly tempted to evil, odd on its face, but common to Christianity and Confucianism and some other theories of the good life, perhaps arises from the very computability of profit. Computability in money makes—or seems to make—*maximizing* possible, whereas the scholar, the farmer, the craftsman, the bureaucrat, even the emperor do not have a maximand easily measured. They study, they cultivate, they fashion, they govern, they judge, but the merchant, as Aristotle observed with disdain, can pursue a calculated profit.[22]

Courage, the aristocrat's defining virtue, is noncalculating, or else it is not courage but a version of mere prudence. Henry V prays to the god of battles: "steel my soldiers' hearts; / Possess them not with fear; *take from them now / The sense of reckoning*, if the opposèd numbers / Pluck their hearts from them" (4.1.270–73). And indeed his "ruined band" before Agincourt, as he had noted to the French messenger, was "with sickness much enfeebled, / My numbers lessened, and those few I have / Almost no better than so many French" (3.6.132–34). Appalling thought. Yet on the Feast Day of St. Crispian his numbers of five or six thousand did not prudently flee from an enemy of some twenty-five thousand.

One reason, Shakespeare avers, was religious faith, as Henry says to Gloucester, "We are in God's hand, brother, not in theirs"—though in the play, as in many others of Shakespeare, the Christianity sounds a trifle formulaic, unless exhibited by (suspiciously Catholic) monks. The other virtue called upon—a much more serious matter to the aristocrats there assembled—was courage: "'tis true that we are in great danger; / The greater therefore should our courage be." Shakespeare emphasizes in 1599 these two Christian/aristo-cratic virtues of faith and courage, those of the Christian knight—and not, for example, the mere prudence of the warhorse-impaling stakes which on Henry's orders the plebeian archers had been lugging through the French countryside for a week.[23] Prudence is a calculative virtue, as are, note, justice and temperance. They are cool. The warm virtues—love and courage, faith and hope—the virtues praised most often by Shakespeare, and not praised much by bourgeois Adam Smith a century and a half later, are specifically and essentially noncalculative.

The play does not tell what the real King Henry V was doing in the weeks leading up to Agincourt on Sunday, October 25, 1415. It tells what was ex-pected to be mouthed by stage noblemen in the last years of Elizabeth's En-gland, a place in which only rank ennobled, and honor to the lowborn came only through loyalty to the nobles. Before the storming of Harfleur in the play Henry declared, "there is none of you so mean and base, / That hath not noble luster in your eyes" (3.1.29–20). And before Agincourt, as I noted, he repeats the ennobling promise, "be he ne'er so vile, / This day shall gentle his condition" (4.3.64–65) "Vile," too, has in it an idea of rank, from Latin *vilis*, base, cheap. ("Village" and "villein," and modern "villain," though, come from a different root, *villa*, farmhouse—though in a society of ranked castles and urban towers, a village-dwelling villein [a peasant] is vile, too.)

Out of earshot of Henry, the king's uncle grimly notes the disadvantage in numbers: "There's five to one; besides they all are fresh." At which the Earl of Salisbury exclaims faithfully, "God's arm strike with us! 'tis a fearful odds." The king comes onto the scene just as the Earl of Westmoreland is continu-ing the calculative talk: "O that we now had here / But one ten thousand of those men in England / That do no work today!" (4.3.17–19). To which Henry replies, scorning such bourgeois considerations, "If we are marked to die, we are enow [enough] / To do our country loss; and if to live, / The fewer men, the greater share of honor." And he ends his noble stem-winder with

And gentlemen in England now a-bed
Shall think themselves accursed they were not here,

And hold their manhoods cheap whiles any speaks

That fought with us upon St. Crispin's Day. (4.3.66–69)

Picture how that bit, late in World War II, intoned by Laurence Olivier on the stage of the Old Vic, played to the London audience. It is not a bourgeois, prudential rhetoric, and counts not the cost. We shall never surrender.

35

THE DUTCH PREACHED BOURGEOIS VIRTUE

What made bourgeois quantification conceivable was the "rise" of the bourgeoisie in northwestern Europe. But the rise was itself more than a matter of numbers. True, the share of the population plausibly counted as bourgeois rose. Yet the "rise" was above all a rise in dignity, expressed in public opinion, and of liberty, obtained by reformation and revolution. Otherwise you are back in China or the Ottoman Empire or the rest of Europe before 1700, in which, after all, there were many conurbations with large absolute numbers of bourgeois.

The first large bourgeois nation of the North proved its dignity by being ethical, and being far from blasé or cynical about the good and bad of trade. In the eighth century "Frisian" was a synonym for "trader"—and for "Dutchman," too, since the languages nowadays called Frisian and Dutch had not yet diverged (and had only recently diverged from English), and Frisia strictly speaking was not confined as it is now to the northern Netherlands.[1] The Jews, the "Italians," and the Frisians were the international traders of the Carolingian Empire around 800. The Dutch in turn became, in the High Middle Ages, the tutors of the other northerners in trade and navigation. The seagoing Dutch in later centuries gradually taught the English to say skipper, cruise, schooner, lighter, yacht, wiveling, yaw, yawl, sloop, tackle, hoy, boom, jib, bow, bowsprit, luff, reef, belay, avast, hoist, gangway, pump, buoy, dock, freight, smuggle, and keelhaul. In the last decade of the sixteenth century the busy Dutch invented a broad-bottomed ship ideal for commerce, the *fluyt*, or fly-boat, and the German Ocean became a new Mediterranean, a watery forum between the lands of the Germanic speakers—the English, Scots, Norse, Norn, Faeroese, Danish, Low German, Frisian, Flemish, and above all the Dutch—who showed the world how to be bourgeois.

The shores of the German Ocean seemed in, say, 98 CE an unlikely place for town life and the bourgeois virtues to flourish. Tacitus at least thought so. Tacitus claimed that the *Germani*, and the wild *Batavii* among them, used cattle rather than gold and silver as money, "whether as a sign of divine favor or of divine wrath, I cannot say"(in admiring the *Germani* he was criticizing civilized greed).[2] "The peoples of Germany never live in cities and will not even have their houses adjoin one another," in sharp contrast to apartment-dwelling Romans at the time.[3] And he claimed it was precisely those whom Dutch people later looked on as their ancestors, the Batavians, who were the first among the *Germani* in martial virtue (*virtute praecipui*).[4]

The modern Dutch therefore dote on Tacitus, and named the capital of their conquests in the East Indies Batavia. Yet the Dutch and the Belgians, though sufficiently warlike in the cockpit of Europe, have been since the fifteenth century at the latest, I say, the first large, northern European *bourgeois* people. The Dutch Republic, the northern half of the Low Countries, the part that successfully defied the Spaniards, was and even still is a "nation" in a loose sense. Despite shows of drunken enthusiasm, *Oranje boven*, "Up with the Orange," on the monarch's official birthday, Holland is to this day not as nationalistic as are England and France. The modern master of Dutch history, Johan Huizinga (his name is Frisian) believed that Holland's prosperity came not from the warlike spirit of the Batavians of old, or in early modern times from the Protestant ethic or the spirit of capitalism, or from more modern nationalism, but from medieval liberties—an accidental free trade consequent on the worthless character of Dutch mudflats before the techniques of water management were perfected, and the resulting competition among Dutch free cities after the breakup of Carolingian centralization.[5] It was always about trade, not battle. "We [Dutch] are essentially unheroic," Huizinga wrote:

> Our character lacks the wildness and fierceness that we usually associate with Spain from Cervantes to Calderòn, with the France of *The Three Musketeers* and the England of Cavaliers and Roundheads. . . . A state formed by prosperous burghers living in fairly large cities and by fairly satisfied farmers and peasants is

not the soil in which flourishes what goes by the name of heroism. . . . Whether we fly high or low, we Dutchmen are all bourgeois—lawyer and poet, baron and laborer alike.[6]

In the sixteenth century the lethality of the revolt against Spain stripped away the aristocracy, which in the seaward parts of the northern Netherlands had been thin on the ground to begin with. Many aristocratic families died out, by the logic of what evolutionary biologists call the Galton-Watson process. Start with a small, English-style aristocracy and go to war a lot, and eventually the number of surviving males in the noble Family Berg can easily hit an absorbing barrier at zero. After the northern Dutch speakers had made good their defiance of the Spanish, as early as 1585—though it was not made official until 1648—they lacked a king, and so the aristocracy could not be refreshed.

What was left to do the ruling was the *haute bourgeoisie*, the class of big merchants and bankers—very *haute* in such a compacted, urbanized place at the mouth of three of northwestern Europe's larger rivers. Yet such *regenten*, regents, for all their pride in humanistic learning and their hard-eyed rule over the mere "residents" without political rights (*inwoners*), were not aristocrats, either in their own or in the public's opinion. Like the earlier elites of the south in Venice or Genoa, they never disdained trade. They were not in their self-image soldiers or courtiers. All that the *regenten* shared with a literal European aristocracy was riches and political power. That's not an "aristocracy" or even a gentry in the sense that Europeans understood it from the time of the first Greek cities down to Eton College and the German *Junkers*. The offices of the regents were not literally inherited. The regents were businesslike and numerate. They were not embarrassed by their bourgeois or even lower roots—burgermeister Franz Hendrickszoon Oetgens, for example, the corrupt builder of an expanding Amsterdam in the early seventeenth century, as Chicago was corrupt in its own golden age of expansion in the late nineteenth century, began life as a mason.

The mudflats became rich cities without, so to speak, anybody noticing, and by the time Philip II, with the Duke of Alva and others in Spanish pay, sprang to attention it was too late. The place of big European cities, true, was still the Mediterranean. In 1500 three out of the (merely) four cities in Europe larger than present-day Cedar Rapids, Iowa (population 100,000), were Mediterranean ports, two of them Italian: Venice and Naples, with Constantinople, the fourth being Paris. Of the twelve in 1600 half were still Italian (Palermo and Messina, for instance, had become biggish cities).[7] Yet it is indicative of stirrings in the German Ocean that Antwerp temporarily in the mid-sixteenth century, and London permanently by 1600 and Amsterdam by 1650, broke into the over-100,000 ranks.

By the early seventeenth century the tiny United Provinces contained one and a half million people, as against about six million in Britain and over eighteen million in France. The population ratio was 1:4:12, but the 1 supplied much of the shipping of Europe. And in absolute numbers more Dutch people (360,000 or so) lived in towns of over 10,000 in 1700 than did English people four times as numerous. The United Provinces were bourgeois, all right.

"Holland is a country where . . . profit [is] more in request than honor" was how in 1673 Temple concluded chapter 5 of his *Observations upon the United Provinces of the Netherlands.* The "honor" that Temple had in mind was that of a proud gentry or aristocracy. Yet the profit more in request—shamefully in the view of the English better sort—was not achieved at the cost of the Dutch bourgeoisie's soul. It was not a sin to be bourgeois.

The question is whether Holland was in fact made worse in spirit for being so very bourgeois. In the town-hating, trade-disdaining rhetoric of some Christianity and aristocracy, and nowadays of more or less all of the clerisy, Holland would be corrupted utterly by riches earned from gin, spices, herring, and government bonds. It would be "bourgeois" in the worst modern sense. Was such a town-ridden place less ethical than its medieval self, or less ethical than its contemporary and still aristocracy-dominated societies like England or France?

For the sixteenth and especially the seventeenth century, and for the independent north rather than the Spanish-retained south of the Low Countries, I could rest the case by pointing to the art historian Simon Schama's *Embarrassment of Riches*, which argues that "the [northern, polder-draining] Dutch feared literal drowning," "in destitution and terror," a worry that was "exactly counterbalanced by their fear of drowning in luxury and sin . . . distinguishing between proper and improper ways of making fortunes, and the concept of wealth as stewardship."[8] The fuller story begins earlier, in the southern Low Countries, up on dry land. The student of Dutch literature

Herman Pleij has argued that "the virtues associated [in the sixteenth cen-
tury] with capitalism and the Reformation were not new . . . [but] had already
been setting the tone for more than two centuries in Brabant and Flanders,"
south of the provinces of Holland and Zeeland proper.[9] He has studied the
rise of urban literature in the southern Low Countries, 1350–1550. The literature "played an active role in forming, defending and propagating what
came to be called middle-class virtues, which revolved around . . . practical-
ity and utilitarianism." The virtue was what I and the virtue-ethical tradition
call prudence—the Dutch-speaking Lowlanders also called it French-origin
prudence, using the Romance word because (strangely) Germanic languages
have always lacked an exact parallel.[10]

   The tradesmen and burghers were of Arras, Brussels, Louvain, Antwerp,
Ghent, Bruges. All except for Arras, in France, are now in Belgium. The
southern Lowlanders used existing models to point a bourgeois tale: as Pleij
observes, "a knight could, in fact, be perceived as an aspiring entrepreneur."[11]
Thus *Heinric en Margriete van Limborch*, the thirteenth-century romance
of knights and their ladies I mentioned, was printed in 1516 for the south
Netherlandish bourgeoisie with such commercial amendments as having
Heinric instructed, on achieving his knighthood, to "pay generously whenever you travel," as dusty merchants were in the habit of doing. Honor lay
not merely in the knightly fighting and hunting and wooing of the original
text, but the traveling and especially now in 1516 the honest paying of the
merchant readers.[12]

The art historian R. H. Fuchs notes that by the Golden Age of the seventeenth century in the northern Netherlands the painting of pictures was infused with ethics. After the sixteenth century, as printing cheapened, the
Calvinist and bourgeois Netherlanders eagerly bought "emblems"—secular
etchings illustrating proverbs with an ethical, or sometimes an anti-ethical,
point. Fuchs shows an example from 1624 of a mother wiping her baby's bottom: *Dit lijf, wat ist, als stanck en mest?* "This life, what is it, if [not] stench
and shit?" Such stuff is especially prevalent early in the seventeenth century,
it would seem, when Dutch painting had not yet separated itself from written texts (as another art historian, Svetlana Alpers, has argued vigorously—
against the "iconological" readings I am going to retail here[13]).

A painting such as Bosschaert's *Vase of Flowers* (1620) looks to a modern eye to be merely a bouquet that an Impressionist, say, might paint from life, though painted in Holland in the seventeenth century with much more attention to surface detail than the Impressionists thought worthwhile. But under instruction one notices—as the bourgeois buyer would have noticed without instruction, since behind his canal house he cultivated his own garden—that the various flowers would bloom at different times of year. Therefore the bouquet is botanically impossible.[14] Something else is going on. The iconologists among art historians favor a theological interpretation: "To every thing there is a season, . . . A time to be born, and a time to die; a time to plant, and a time to pluck up that which is planted" (Ecclesiastes 3:1–2). "That in principle," writes Fuchs, "is the meaning of every [Dutch] still-life painted in the seventeenth or the first part of the eighteenth century."[15]

I said that there are opponents to Fuchs's view (and the view of many other students of the matter, such as E. de Jongh, whose work is seminal). For example, Eric Sluijter joins Svetlana Alpers in skepticism. He notes a 1637 poem by the Dutch politician and popular poet Jacob "Father" Cats (1577–1660), which portrays painters as profit-making and practical, and therefore presumably uninterested in preaching (though one could reply that one could make profit among a religious bourgeoisie by selling it moralizing paintings, the way Hollywood sells moralizing movies). He analyzes in detail one of the few contemporary writings on the matter, from 1642, by one Philips Angel, who was lecturing to the painters of Leiden. The conclusion Sluijter draws is that "it is difficult to find anything in texts on the art of painting from this period that would indicate that didacticism was an important aim."[16] The argument of the skeptics, in other words, is that secret meanings, if no contemporary saw them, might not in fact be there. Sometimes a cigar is just a cigar.

Fair point. The purpose of paintings would not be, as the iconological critics think, *tot lering en vermaak*, "to teach and delight," a goal reflected in museum guidebooks nowadays—this from the Renaissance humanism tracing to classical rhetoric and Cicero, two of the offices of rhetoric being the same *docere et delectare* (the third is *movere*, to move to political or ethical action).[17] At least the purpose would not be *ethical* teaching, delighting, and moving. Perhaps, as Alpers argues, it was essentially scientific, showing people how to see.

But even Alpers and Sluijter would not deny that a still-life of a loaded table with a conch, book, half-peeled lemon, half-used candle, vase lying on its side, and (in the more explicit versions) a skull, signifying all the works that are done under the sun—such as Steenwijck's painting of circa 1640, entitled simply *Vanitas*—was a known genre, to be read like a proverb. Pieter Claesz's still life of 1625/1630 in the Art Institute of Chicago is filled with symbols of Holland's overseas trade—olives, linens, sugar, lemons—to the same end. All is vanity and vexation of spirit, saith the preacher. And in truth it does not matter much whether or not the Dutch painters knew they were making ethical tales, so long as their audience experienced them that way. Such a point is similar to that of the "new" literary criticism of the 1940s and 1950s. A poem or painting can have an ethical effect, or any other artistic effect, without it being self-consciously inserted by the poet or painter.

Fuchs and his tradition persuade outsiders like me better than do the skeptics. Think of the conventions of painted "realism." We ignoramuses in art history are liable to view realism as a simple matter of whether the people in the picture appear to have "real" bodies (though rendered on a flat canvas, with paint: hmm) or instead have half-bodies of fishes or horses, or wings attached for flying ("fantasy"); or whether you can make out actual objects apparently from this world (again admittedly painted on that flatness) or not ("abstraction"). If it is merely realism, under a naïve theory, then there is no ethical burden in the paintings. They are merely pretty, and pretty accurate, pictures of the world around us. How nice, and how real. And how irrelevant, it would seem, for the ethical history of the first large bourgeois society in Europe.

Fuchs observes on the contrary that what he calls "metaphorical realism" was the usual mode of early Golden Age painting, showing (barely) possible figures or scenery that nonetheless insist on referring to another realm, especially a proverbial realm, with at least a declared ethical purpose. The same is true of much of French and British realism in painting of the early to mid-nineteenth century, such as Ford Maddox Brown's *Work* (1852–1863, in two versions) or, in France, what the slightly mad painter Gustave Courbet called "real allegories." The art historian Richard Brettell notes that Courbet, and then the more accomplished Manet, put aside the academic conventions of mythology in favor of apparently contemporary scenes, but made pictures nonetheless "ripe with pictorial, moral, religious, and political significance."[18]

Two centuries earlier the Dutch pioneers of metaphorical realism, or "real" allegories, would depict for ethical purposes a merry scene of disordered home life, such as Jan Steen's painting of circa 1663 *In Luxury Beware* (itself a proverbial expression: *In weelde siet toe*).[19] Such a scene became proverbial. A "Jan Steen household" still means in Dutch a household out of control. The painting is littered with realistic metaphors. Even an untrained and non-Dutch eye can spot them: while the mother-in-charge sleeps, a monkey stops the clock, a child smokes a pipe, a dog feasts on a pie, a half-peeled lemon and a pot on its side signal the *vanitas* of human life, a woman in the middle of the picture with the deep *décolletage* of a whore stares brazenly out at us, holding her full wine glass at the crotch of a man being scolded by a nun and by a man dressed as a religious conservative, and a pig has "stolen the spigot of the wine barrel" (another literal proverb, Fuchs explains, for letting a household get out of control).

The Golden Age of Holland, in other words, though thoroughly bourgeois was ethically haunted. Oil paintings in the Netherlands in the seventeenth century were like plays in Shakespeare's London, or books of sermons in the eighteenth and nineteenth centuries, or the European novel before modernism, or pulp novels in the early twentieth century, or movies in the movie palaces of the 1930s, or TV in the twentieth century, or rock music and county music, or romance fiction for women and science-fiction or legal or spy novels for men down to the present. All were immensely popular art forms in which people thought about their ethical values.[20] Despite the pull of Mammon—or perhaps because of its pull, the way we late in the Bourgeois Era feel it and resist it—the Hollanders talked of ethics day and night.

The age was still one of faith, much more so, in fact, than the Middle Ages. Ordinary Europeans in the Middle Ages were barely Christian. People in 1300 who might take communion once a year, if then, were less religious than their spiritually aroused descendants in the sixteenth century, in the Reformation, as in *gereformeerd* Holland, with newly devout Catholics and Jews mixed in. The transcendent therefore keeps bursting into Dutch art. Rembrandt's intense sympathy with his subjects, so unlike the cold if entrancing observation of, say, Vermeer, imparts a more than conventional piety to Rembrandt's numerous religious paintings. One thinks of holy parallels in seventeenth-century English poetry, especially from Anglican priests such as John Donne and George Herbert or Puritans such as John Milton.

"Sweet day, so cool, so calm, so bright" in Herbert (1633) ends with "Only a sweet and virtuous soul, / Like season'd timber, never gives; / But though the whole world turn to coal, / Then chiefly lives." The literary English and the painterly Dutch reaching for God both seem to come to a climax of earnestness around the middle of the seventeenth century. Poetry and painting in the century and a half of renewed faith after 1517 was not mere entertainment (*delectare*). It had literally deadly serious work to do, of teaching and moving (*docere et movere*), justifying God's ways to man, to be sure, but also, as a historian of an earlier generation, Hugh Trevor-Roper, observed, of doing politics (*regere*). A. T. van Deursen again instances Cats, who began as a poet of emblem engravings and who "wanted to instruct his readers through moral lessons. . . . Those who desired something more erotically tinted would have to learn Italian"—or buy an Italian or South Netherlands painting.[21] Nothing means merely what it seems. Everything in the poem or painting points a moral.

By the late seventeenth century all this earnestness collapses into cynical exhaustion in both England and Holland, similar to the collapse circa December 1910 in the high valuation of earnestness characteristic of the Victorians.[22] An urbane reaction follows in, say, the English poet John Dryden, and in late Golden Age Dutch painters, as after 1910 in Pound, Picasso, and then Charlie "Bird" Parker.[23] Schama notes that after about 1660 Dutch painters shift from religious or moralizing allegory to "the business of everyday life."[24] A century later the keys to the early seventeenth-century moralizing in both poetry and painting had been mislaid. Similarly, the late eighteenth-century Romantic literary critics in England had no idea what John Milton was on about, because they had set aside the rigorously Calvinist theology that structured his poetry. Milton was misread by even so spiritual a reader as William Blake, who imagined, for example, that Satan was the hero of *Paradise Lost*. Romantic Samsons had by then pushed apart the two pillars van Deursen spoke of, Christianity and pagan literature. The ethical building had collapsed.

In looking at their national paintings even the Dutch critics of the eighteenth century had lost the emblematic keys (admitting again that skeptics such as Alpers and Sluijter think there were no keys to be lost in the first place). Foreigners had no chance at all. Gerard Terborch, for example, had painted at the height of the Golden Age, around 1654–1655, a scene in a brothel in which a young man bids with a coin for a whore, her dress lovingly rendered satin and her back turned to the viewer. The procuress facing the viewer goes about her business. And on the table sits a *vanitas* still life. The scene was conventional—Vermeer did one, for example, two if you include *Officer and Laughing Girl*, painted around 1657 in a different arrangement, similar to a painting of 1625 by van Honthorst named by him *The Procuress* (in which a lute is offered: *luit* in Dutch, Fuchs explains, can mean either the musical instrument or a vagina). Yet by 1809 in *Elective Affinity* Goethe is interpreting the Terborch painting as a scene of a father (that is, the john) admonishing his daughter (the whore) while the mother (the procuress) averts her eyes modestly.[25] Goethe is not to be blamed. An eighteenth-century engraver had retitled the work *Paternal Admonition*, and blotted out the coin in the client's hand. Likewise Goethe, in the style of Blake, misunderstood Milton's Satan as a Romantic hero, and Hamlet as such a hero, too. We have here a change in sensibility, away from a "realistic" and sexually candid yet soberly bourgeois engagement with a world still vividly illuminated by Christianity.

The painters themselves as much as the critics misplaced the ethical keys. Fuchs shows the metaphoric realism of the Golden Age giving way in the mid-nineteenth century to a pictorial realism, that is, a realism not of the soul—remember the flowers with differing times to pluck up that which is planted—but of the eye. Or of the mechanized eye. The *camera obscura*, it has only recently been discovered, played a large role in painting from the Renaissance on. When photography was invented the artists followed suit en masse. Like a snapshot (though it would be some time before photographic chemicals were fast enough to really allow a *snap* shot) the subjects just happen to be in the frame of the picture, as in Gustave Caillebotte's masterpiece in the Art Institute, *Paris Street, Rainy Day*(1877). The bourgeois walkers in his painting of an intersection in the newly built quarters are glimpsed just at that moment, which will in an instant dissolve meaninglessly into another moment. A different level of reality is not breaking in from above (though one might well argue that impressions such as Caillebotte's carried their own *vanitas* message). In the early Industrial Age the ethical transcendent was rejected. In the early Golden Age it was passionately embraced.

The Dutch were not bourgeois if the word is taken to mean (as it is nowadays on the lips of the clerisy) vulgarly unconcerned with ethics and the transcendent, Matthew Arnold's "Philistines." It is emphatically not how *de burgerij* of the Golden Age thought of themselves.

36

AND THE DUTCH BOURGEOISIE
WAS VIRTUOUS

Nor was Holland especially corrupt in its politics. To the contrary. The word "corruption" commonly means "activities involving payment that we do not like." Corruption violates our notions of the nonprudential virtues. It is unjust, unloving, unfaithful behavior in aid of prudence, that is, profit. It is a spilling of our profane into our sacred. Unless we are socialists, we do not regard paying for milk as corruption. But by Western European standards the paying of a customs officer in cash under the table to get out of a Romanian airport with your camera intact is. "Corruption," then, is by now a fancy word for distasteful self-interested behavior.

In its political rhetoric, at least, Holland declared for virtue and against corruption. It is hardly a stringent test. But the northern, literate Protestant nations on the North Sea were instances of democracy, at least of a highly limited "democracy" among the full citizens of the towns. The Dutch Republic was an insult to the monarchies surrounding it, more so even than the older and less imitable places without monarchs, such as Novgorod (until 1477), the cantons of Switzerland, the Republic of Genoa, and the Most Serene Republic of Venice. The kingless rule of towns was in the sixteenth and seventeenth centuries an irritating contrast to the divine right of kings being articulated with new theoretical fervor by Spanish Philip II and then Scottish/English James VI/I and then French Louis XIV. As a nation of traders—but also earnest Christians and big buyers of ethically instructive art—the Dutch emphasized what is supposed in the rhetoric of the royalists then and the high clerisy now to be impossible: the virtuous and republican bourgeoisie.

In 1764 the English satirist Charles Churchill, a friend of the inventor of modern English radicalism, John Wilkes, wrote a poem against everything he didn't like, producing for example, a long, homophobic blast against "catamites," and against French luxury and Spanish dogmatism and Italian "souls without vigor, bodies without force" (all of these were commonplaces). T. S. Eliot once called Churchill's lines "blundering assaults." But Churchill paused in his assaults to accord rare praise, difficult to read as sarcasm:

> To Holland, where Politeness ever reigns,
> Where primitive Sincerity remains,
> And makes a stand, where Freedom in her course
> Hath left her name, though she hath lost her force

The Holland of the Golden Age, that is, had decayed by 1764 into a less aggressive, though still wealthy, place. Yet:

> In that, as other lands, where simple trade
> Was never in the garb of fraud arrayed
> Where Avarice never dared to show his head,
> Where, like a smiling cherub, Mercy, led
> By Reason, blesses the sweet-blooded race,
> And Cruelty could never find a place,
> To Holland for that Charity we roam,
> Which happily begins, and ends at home.[1]

The first large bourgeois society in Northern Europe was well known for its Charity.

Yes, but was the ethical emphasis merely a show? Surely the Dutch of the Golden Age didn't actually carry out their painted and poemed project of the virtues? Surely the bourgeois then as now were mere hypocrites, the comically middle-class fools or villains in a Molière play; or, worse, in a Balzac novel; or, worse still, in a late-Dickens novel; or, worst of all, in a Pier Paolo Pasolini or Paolo Virzi film, n'est-ce pas?

No, it appears not. Ce n'est pas vrai. Not in Holland, nor in some other places. As a referee of the present volume put it, "being wickedly good at commerce needn't render people wicked." Trading did not corrupt, for example, the charity of trade-saturated Holland. "Charity seems to be very national among them," as Temple wrote at the time.[2] Only the Quakers in England cared for their poor the way an ordinary Dutch city did. The historian Charles Wilson noted in 1968 that "it is doubtful if England or any other country [at least until the eighteenth century] could rival the scores of almshouses for old men and women, the orphanages, hospitals and schools maintained by private endowments from the pockets of the Dutch regents class."[3] The fact is indisputable.

But its interpretation has made historians uneasy. Their problem is that like everyone else in the age of prudence-admiring since 1700 or so, and especially in the age of historical materialism 1890–1980, historians have not been comfortable with a rhetoric of the virtues. Any act of love or justice or temperance is to be reinterpreted, every time, as somehow an act of prudence. "I'm not helping you because I love you, understand. I'm helping you so that you will later help me." A dear and highly ethical friend of mine commented on a news story about a man rushing into a burning building to save a stranger: "Yes: if I do it for him, he will do it for me." The parable of the Good Samaritan is reduced to self-interest.

One manifestation of the reduction is Tocqueville's notion of "enlightened self-interest," in chapter 8 of volume 1 of *Democracy in America*, entitled "How the Americans Combat Individualism by the Principle of Self-Interest Rightly Understood." "The principle," he wrote, "perhaps prevents men from rising far above the level of mankind, but a great number of other men, who were falling far below it, are caught and restrained by it." It is how an aristocrat might view the surprising fact that bourgeois people, too, appear to have honor. But Tocqueville's argument, though widely admired, is a false analogy of ethical behavior with economic exchange. The Americans, he is claiming, do good out of self-interest. The historian of political theory Lucien Jaume in his study of Tocqueville notes that an earlier tradition from Helvetius and Rousseau believed that "virtue can be achieved only by uniting the individual interest with the general interest."[4] Helvetius and Rousseau believed that such a general will would arise by a mystery of solidarity, which has inspired the left ever since. Tocqueville was trying to clear up the mystery with a more bourgeois argument from self-interest. Yet his clarity is self-interest wrongly understood. Economists such as Mancur Olson (1932–1998) have pointed out that no merely selfish individual, if that is what we are being asked to posit, would be motivated to ethical behavior. Later, illiberal theorists and practitioners, who would have appalled Tocqueville, came to realize that if one *does* posit a prudence-only Max U at the level of individuals the general will can only be achieved by state violence—which they therefore embraced with enthusiasm.

Any historian who listens a little to modern economists takes on some of the prudential rhetoric of the dismal science, without quite grasping the illogic of collective action. Anne McCants, for example, begins her book on *Civic Charity in a Golden Age: Orphan Care in Early Modern Amsterdam* (1997) with a discussion of how hard it is to believe in altruistic motives among such tough bourgeois and bourgeoises as the Dutch. A compassionate motivation for transfers from the wealthy to the poor is said to be "unlikely" and "can be neither modeled nor rationally explained." By "rational" she seems to mean single-mindedly following monetary prudence only. By "modeled" she seems to mean put into a Max U framework that a conventional Samuelsonian economist would be comfortable with. Compassionate explanations—contrary to Mr. Max U—McCants writes, are "not to be lightly dismissed as implausible." But then she lightly dismisses the compassionate explanations, with a scientific method misapprehended, albeit in a way that some economists do misapprehend it—altruism, she says, holds "little predictive power." She has adopted the ugly little orphan Max U, fathered by the economist Paul Samuelson over in another building at her Massachusetts Institute of Technology.

"After a long tradition of seeing European charity largely as a manifestation of Christian values," McCants is relieved to report, "scholars have begun to assert the importance of self-interest."[5] Her own interpretation of the Amsterdam Municipal Orphanage is that it was "charity for the middling," a species of insurance against the risks of capitalism.[6] The bourgeois said to themselves, as it were, "There but for the grace of God go our own orphaned bourgeois children. Let us therefore create an institution against that eventuality. We do so *not* because it is just, but merely out of prudence, self-interest rightly understood." As Hobbes put it in reducing all motives to self-interest, "Pity is imagination of fiction of future calamity to ourselves, proceeding from the sense of another man's calamity."[7] McCants makes as good a case as can be made for such a strictly Hobbesian view of the human virtues. But as a matter of method the virtue of prudence does not have to crowd out temperance, justice, love, courage, faith, and hope, not every time, not 100 percent.

The unease of modern historians in the presence of nonprudential virtues shows in the leading historian of the Dutch Republic writing in English, Jonathan Israel. He devotes six pages in one of his massive books, *The Dutch Republic: Its Rise and Fall* (1995), to the Golden Age poor law. It was, he admits at the outset, an "elaborate system of civic poor relief and charitable institutions . . . exceptional in European terms."[8] The assignment of the poor to each confession, including the Jews (and even eventually in the eighteenth century the Catholics and much later the socialists and now the Muslims), foreshadows the so-called pillarization (*verzuiling*) of Dutch politics, reinforced by the theologian and prime minister Abraham Kuyper in the late nineteenth century. Each pillar is accorded sovereignty in its own domain, and therefore assigned responsibility for compassion toward its own poor. (Kuyper's notions, unhappily, were taken up by Afrikaner sociologists and theologians studying in Holland in the early twentieth century as justification for their own theory of apartheid.)

"But," Israel claims, "charity and compassion . . . were not the sole motives."[9] And then he lists all the prudential, self-interested reasons for taking care of the poor, ignoring as McCants does the problem of any such collective action in a society of Max U people. His first item seems the least plausible— that "the work potential of orphans" was worth marshaling. Oakum picking could scarcely pay for even the first bowl of porridge. Israel turns then to civic pride among towns and social prestige inside a town to be got from running a "caring, responsible, and well-ordered" set of institutions. The innumerable commissioned paintings of this or that charitable board of governors, scores of them hanging now in the refurbished Rijksmuseum in Amsterdam, do suggest that the pride and prestige was deemed worth getting in the Golden Age of the northern Netherlands. But it is hard to see how such rewards to vanity can be distinguished from the virtue of charity itself, at any rate if we are to limit our historical science in positivistic style to "predictive power." If caring is *not* highly valued by the society, then doing it in well-ordered institutions will not earn social prestige. Caring then would be a matter of mores, not institutions. We have a word nowadays for a high value of caring: "charity."

"At bottom," though, Israel continues—and now we approach the prudential axiom—the alleged acts of charity were "rather effective instruments of social control," by supporting the deserving poor (that is, our own Dutch Reformed poor in Rotterdam, say). Or as Simmel put it in 1908, we give charity "so that the poor will not become active and dangerous enemies of society."[10] The policy amounted, say Israel and Simmel, to bribing the poor to behave themselves, in the style of Bismarck inventing the modern welfare state.[11] The historian Paul Langford makes a similar assertion about the flowering of charity in England. The hospitals and foundling homes of the eighteenth century were "built on a foundation of bourgeois sentiment mixed with solid self-interest."[12] Merely prudent, you see, mysteriously overcoming the incentives to free riding that such a class interest faces. The "charitable" members of the Dutch and English bourgeoisie, rightly understood, were not really charitable at all. They were simply canny, the rascals.

Such arguments would not persuade, I think, unless one were determined to find a profane rather than a sacred cause for every act of charity—100 percent, right from the start. When the materialist/functionalist argument is made in historical works it is it usually unsupported by reasoning and evidence, in a field of the intellect that prides itself on providing reasoning and evidence. Bismarck, by contrast, actually said, on many occasions, and in circumstances in which the Prussian and the German imperial politics of the time made it plausibly efficacious, and in which he could with his own powers achieve the result he intended, that he made old-age insurance thoroughly national in order to attach a dangerous class to the idea of monarchy.[13] McCants does offer a little reasoning and evidence for her hermeneutics of suspicion, but that is what makes her book unusual. When putting forward such a point the majority of historians, such as Israel and Langford, don't. The lack of factual argument signals that the suspicion is being brought into the history from the outside.

No one, even such fine historians as Israel and Langford and McCants, explains exactly how "social control" or "self-interest" was supposed to result from giving large sums of money to the poor. Sometimes it has worked. We Americans have repeatedly tried to prevent Haitians from fleeing to Florida, for example, by invading Haiti and forcing money on its elites, which we imagine trickles down to the poor. We have done so all over our southern borders, though it often hasn't had the prudent result promised by realists in foreign policy. But no historian of Holland or Britain tells how civic charity might have had such a result—after all, it is a cliché of studies of revolution that the poor revolt when their condition is improved, not when it gets worse—or offers evidence that cynical charity was in fact efficacious. A vague if strictly materialist and prudential suspicion unsupported by fact or logic is made to suffice. The burden of proof is supposed to fall on people who take the Dutch at their word that they gave money to the poor out of charitable impulse. But why that burden of proof?

It doesn't compute. The question arises, for example, why other nations did not have the same generous system of charity (as some scattered cities in fact did) if it was such an obviously effective instrument of social control, requiring no proof of its efficacy from the historian, if it was in fact so utterly self-interested that any fool could see its utility. If its utility is so evident to historians four centuries after the event, presumably contemporaries before the eighteenth century in France and England could have seen it too. London in 1600 was almost as rich as Amsterdam, and had as many poor people. But at the time it gave little charity. Scotland likewise had no way aside from beatings to deal with tinkers and the unemployed, and did not think to develop elaborate provision for them to survive the winters.

In the Netherlands from the sixteenth century on, by contrast, acts of love, justice, and, yes, prudence were astonishingly widespread. True, here and there similar levels of love and justice and also political will to curb masterless men are recorded in England, and were regularized by the Elizabethan Poor Law. Yet Israel ends his discussion by implying that in 1616 fully 20 percent of the population of Amsterdam was "in receipt of charity," either from the town itself or from religion- or guild-based foundations.[14] The figure does not mean that the poor got all their income from charity, merely that one fifth of the people in the city received something, perhaps a supplement in the cold and workless times of year. Jan de Vries and Ad van der Woude, who are more skilled with statistics than Israel, put the figure lower: "In Amsterdam as many as 10 to 12 percent of all households received at least temporary support during the winter months." The figure is comparatively high—though duplicated in some few other parts of Europe (and more generally in Muslim lands following the *zakat*), I repeat, if nowhere on such a wide scale as in the United Netherlands—and is only low by the standard of a modern and northern European welfare state. De Vries and van der Woude note that "it is the steadiness of charitable expenditure . . . that distinguishes Dutch practice from other countries, where most financing . . . was triggered by emergency conditions."[15]

In the little cities of the Low Countries, public charity was by the Golden Age an old habit. Geoffrey Parker notes that by the 1540s in Flanders one-seventh of the population of Ghent was in receipt of poor relief, one-fifth at Ypres, one-quarter at Bruges.[16] Cynically prudential explanations of such loving justice seem tough-minded only if one thinks of prudence as tough, always, and love as soft, always, and for some reason you as a historian want to be seen as tough, always. The charity was no small matter. It was unusual in the European context and it is hard to see as prudence only. It might not be spiritual love, true *agape*. But neither is it prudence dissembling in sweet words, mere greed in disguise.

The Netherlands was above all the European frontier of liberalism. John Locke, finally publishing in the 1680s, was in many respects a culmination of *Dutch* theorizing and, more, of Dutch practice. He spent five years of fearful exile in Holland before returning to England with the Dutch *stadhouder* Willem, now also the English king. Locke had absorbed in Amsterdam, Utrecht, and Rotterdam the results of the country's liberal thought and practice from Erasmus through Episcopius and De La Court to Bayle. He stayed two years in Rotterdam with the English Quaker merchant Benjamin Furly and was friendly with the Arminian theologian Philip van Limborch, both of whom typified the liberal side of opinion gathered in the comparatively tolerant Holland of the 1680s.[17] Locke's publications started there and began then to flow in earnest (though many of them were in draft much earlier). The famous first essay on toleration (1689) was published initially for van Limborch at Gouda. And a little later the Third Earl of Shaftesbury, too, another Whig theorist and ethicist, and a student, I have noted, of Locke—found the Netherlands similarly congenial.

In the United Provinces a wide and old Erasmian humanism was real, and persistent, and virtuous, down to the present day. The broad-church attitudes of Erasmus had become a permanent if not always dominant feature of Dutch intellectual life before the coming of Reformed Protestantism, and they survived its excesses. In uncouth Scotland, by contrast, Huizinga notes, Calvinism descended in the mid-sixteenth century in the form of a century-and-a-half night of orthodoxy, before an intellectual dawn in the early eighteenth century.[18] In the Dutch controversies of the seventeenth century "Scottish" was a byword for unethical and self-destructive intolerance.[19] In its Dutch version, Calvinism "was held in check," wrote Charles Wilson, "by the cautious Erasmian obstinacy of the ruling merchant class.

Liberty of thought, in a remarkable degree, was preserved. Europe . . . was to owe an incalculable debt to the Erasmian tradition and to the dominant class in the Dutch Republic by whose efforts it was protected."[20]

All this was surely not crudely self-interested in the way that the historical materialists would wish. Wilson begins his praise of "the Erasmian strain, the belief in reason and rational argument as a means of moral betterment and a way of life" by quoting Huizinga on such qualities as "truly Dutch."[21] That such opinions are old and liberal does not imply in strict logic that they are mistaken. An amused cynicism about such noble themes in history is not always in order, not every single time. The cynicism usually comes out of a feeling in academic circles that mentioning transcendents such as God or Honor is disreputable and unscientific, regardless of the gigantic amount of evidence that beliefs about transcendents move people—such as the transcendent of Scientific History or of Politically Engaged History moving the most cynical of historians. The Dutch *stadhouders*, regents, poets, and intellectuals acted and wrote for self-interested reasons, sometimes, as Our Father in heaven knows. But they also acted and wrote for faith, hope, love, temperance, justice, and courage. *Onze Vader in de hemel* knows that, too.

37

FOR INSTANCE, HOLLAND *WAS* TOLERANT, AND NOT FOR PRUDENCE ONLY

Nor was the exceptional Dutch virtue of tolerance—dating from the sixteenth century and full-blown in the theories of Grotius, Uytenbogaert, Fijne, and especially Simon Episcopius in the 1610s and 1620s—a matter entirely of prudence. The Dutch stopped burning heretics and witches in the 1590s, early by European standards. The last burning of a Dutch witch was 1595, in Utrecht, an amusement which much of the rest of Europe—and Massachusetts, too—would not abandon for another century. Some forty thousand witches died in Europe, 1400 to 1800.[1] In the fevered 1620s hundreds of German witches were burned every year. In 1697 in Scotland one Thomas Aikenhead, aged nineteen, a student at the University of Edinburgh, was tried and hanged for blasphemy, for denying the divinity of Christ—alleged by one witness, and part of a youthful pattern of bold talk. The event was the last hurrah of what Arthur Herman calls the ayatollahs of the Scottish Kirk.[2] Afterward the ayatollahs were gradually pushed onto the defensive.

By contrast, the thirteenth article of the Union of Utrecht in the new United Netherlands had stipulated 120 years before Aikenhead's execution that "each person shall remain free in his religion," and that (though observing suitable privacy, since religion was still a matter of state) "no one shall be investigated or persecuted because of his religion."[3] They were not even to be "investigated"—much less hanged or burned. In 1579 it was a shocking assertion. It could not be expected to be literally followed, and was not. But by the admittedly low Christian standards of the times, the Dutch were then and later astonishingly tolerant. Only contemporary Poles and Transylvanians equaled them, and Muslims regularly.

The Dutch case could not until the late seventeenth century properly be described as complete "toleration." The obvious test case was Judaism—though Catholicism, as the religion of the Spanish enemy or of the French sometimes-enemy, was usually treated in Holland with more hostility. That same Grotius (who was no twenty-first-century liberal) advised against liberal treatment of the Jews. But the States General in 1619 decided, against his advice, that each Dutch town individually should decide for itself how to treat them, yet forbad any town to insist that Jews wear special clothing. No yellow stars of David. True, it was not until 1657 that the Dutch Jews became actual, full-rights subjects of the Republic. But by comparison with their liabilities down to the nineteenth century in Germany or England, not to speak of Spain and Portugal, the Dutch Jews were exceptionally free. In 1616 Rabbi Uziel (lately of Fez in Morocco) remarked with gratitude that the Jews "live peaceably in Amsterdam," where "each may follow his own belief," though he "may not openly show that he is of a different faith from the inhabitants of the city."[4] It is the melting-pot formula of not being permitted to wear special clothing, of the sort that in 2003 a fiercely secular France affirmed in respect of head scarves for Muslim schoolgirls. Jews in Holland in the seventeenth century suffered no locking up in ghettos at night, as, for example, in Venice or Frankfurt at the time; no expropriations and expulsions, as in 1290 in England—an England supposed, especially by Englishmen with scant knowledge of other places, to be the nursery of every free institution. In England the practicing Jews ("practicing" lets out David Ricardo and Benjamin Disraeli) were not entirely emancipated to serve in Parliament until 1861.

The earliest significant case of religious toleration was in Hungarian Transylvania, whose Diet in the town of Torda declared in 1568 that "no one is permitted to threaten to imprison or banish anyone because of their teaching, because faith is a gift from God."[5] The act would have applied even to a Unitarian, such as Thomas Aikenhead of Edinburgh or, secretly, Isaac Newton of Cambridge, had they had the good fortune to live in Transylvania. In Britain until the Doctrine of the Trinity Act in 1813 Unitarians were discriminated against or, early on, hanged. Diarmaid MacCulloch explains the Transylvanian toleration as arising from the princes wanting to mollify the varied faiths of their nobility. It was a political compromise similar to Henri IV's efforts at the time in France. Indeed, France itself until 1685 and the Revocation of the Edict of Nantes, MacCulloch notes, "represented *western*

Europe's most large-scale example of religious pluralism," though by the end of the seventeenth century the French had "created one of Europe's most impressive Counter-Reformations."[6]

So too Poland, on about the same schedule. The Poles had as early as 1573, five years after Torda and six year before the Treaty of Utrecht, declared religious liberty in the Warsaw Confederation, and forced on subsequent kings the so-called Henrician Articles maintaining it. The Polish declaration was characteristic of the Erasmian strain there, in the manner of the tolerant Dutch. The Sejm, the gathering elected by the startlingly large numbers of "nobles" in Poland (the *szlachta*, 10 percent of the population, samurai-style), declared that "Whereas in our Commonwealth there is no small disagreement in the matter of Christian faith [compare Transylvania], and in order to prevent that any harmful contention should arise from this, as we see clearly taking place in other kingdoms [in France the St. Bartholomew's Day Massacre of Protestants had happened the year before, and the candidate for the elected king of Poland was the brother of the same French king who had encouraged the massacre], we swear to each other . . . we will keep the peace between us."[7] And they did. Erasmus long before had written to the Archbishop of Canterbury that "Poland is mine." In Poland the Jews, for example, had been protected by law since the thirteenth century.

And so it was in Poland—until the seventeenth century, the Deluge, as the Poles call it. King Sigismund II Augustus (reigned in Poland 1548–1572) had declared that he wished to be "king of the people, not their consciences."[8] "When the tower of Cracow's Town Hall had been rebuilt in 1556," the historian Adam Zamoyski writes, "a copy of Erasmus's New Testament was immured in the brickwork," as testimony to liberal values in Poland in the sixteenth century.[9] And Grotius remarked that "to wish to legislate on religion is not Polish."[10] But, Zamoyski continues, "when the same tower was repaired in 1611 the book was replaced by a Catholic New Testament. . . . One vision of life was replaced by another. . . . The spirit of inquiry"—seen, for example, in Mikołaj Kopernik (1473–1543), the German-speaking Pole known to Europe as Copernicus—was replaced "by one of piety. . . . If Erasmus was the beacon for all thinking Poles in the 1550s, the Jesuits were the mentors of their grandchildren."

It is not, to be sure, quite so simple. The Jesuits in the first instance were agents of intellectual progress, attracting the Unitarian aristocrats in Poland because of the superior education for their sons offered by the unusually sophisticated order. But in 1632 the tolerant oath of 1573 was amended. Other faiths such as Unitarianism and Orthodox Christianity and Judaism were now merely "graciously permitted" to be exercised, and Catholicism was "mistress in her own house." Henceforth, as in contemporary France, the Protestants in particular were to be viewed as foreigners, and enemies of the nation.[11]

"Then, only Holland survived as a haven of tolerance," wrote the philosopher and intellectual historian Stephen Toulmin, "to which Unitarians and other unpopular sects could retreat for protection."[12] Consider, for example, the Dutch events immediately following August 23 in the same year, 1632, in which the Poles turned away from Erasmian toleration. Frederik Hendrik, Prince of Orange—but no king, mind you, merely the elected "holder" of the Dutch cities: he was "prince" of Orange, in southern France, not of the Netherlands—took the southern Lowlands and Catholic city of Maastricht from the Spaniards. Yet he permitted there for a time the continued free exercise of the Catholic religion. The poet and dramatist Vondel of Amsterdam, the Dutch Shakespeare, his family expelled when he was a child from Antwerp for being Anabaptists, was by 1632 not yet a Catholic convert. But he was active in support of Grotius and other even more forward thinkers in favor of toleration. So he wrote a poem for the occasion of Maastricht's conquest praising the Prince's triumph and tolerance, in contrast to the dagger of the Italian Duke of Parma in Philip II's service, who in the same city a half century before had drunk the "tasty burghers' blood."[13]

And so the Dutch are again, nowadays, tolerant. Since the 1960s, after a long period of conformity to the Dutch Reformed Church, tolerance in the Netherlands is having a second golden age. Outside the train station in Hilversum, the center for Dutch radio and TV, stands a block of stone set up after the Second World War representing praying hands, with the word carved on its four sides in Dutch, Russian, Spanish, and English: "tolerance," in the Dutch *verdraagzaamheid* (from *dragen*, "to bear," in the way that "toleration" is from the Latin "to bear," *tolerare*). *Verdraagzaamheid* is the central word in the civic religion of modern Holland, in the way that "equality" (*jämlikhet*) is in the civic religion of Sweden or "liberty" in the civic religion of the United States. That is, it does not always happen, but it is much admired in the abstract, and much discussed.

The clerisy in Holland down to the present reacts uncomfortably to praise for its country's tolerance, especially for the new sort of tolerance that has grown there among Catholics after Vatican II 1962–1965 and among Protestants after the startling decline of church attendance in the Dutch Reformed Church. A society heavily influenced by Dutch Reformed *dominees*, as until the 1960s the Netherlands was, is not, for example, going to be tolerant of gays or marihuana. There was an antihomosexual hysteria in the Netherlands in 1740–1742—after which, however, the Dutch were ashamed, quite unlike most others who indulged in violent homophobia.

The Dutch journalist Michael Zeeman notes that the post-1960s anticlerical movement was more successful in the Netherlands than anywhere else.[14] The transformation from a churchgoing, respectable society circa 1960, divided into "pillars" by religious group and stratified by class, to the present-day freewheeling Holland has been astounding, not least to the Dutch themselves. The Dutch reply to praise for their new tolerance of gays and atheists with an uncomfortable "Yes, but [*Ja, maar*, they say] you don't know how intolerant we *really* are." Progressive Dutch people nowadays move directly to embarrassments—for riches, for slavery, for imperialism, for the handing over of the Dutch Jews during the war, for a successful capitalism, for their army's cowardice at Srebrenica, for their less educated countrymen's reaction to Muslim immigrants in the 1990s and especially in the 2000s. "We're not *really* so tolerant," they repeat.

To which foreigners, now as in the seventeenth century, reply that the Dutch perhaps don't grasp how *really* lacking in toleration the competition is. In the seventeenth century most visitors were appalled, not delighted, by religious toleration in the United Provinces. The notion of one king/one religion was still lively, and still seemed worth a few dead heretics—one-third of the population of Germany, 1618–1648, say. Israel observes that foreigners then as now tended to judge the Dutch character by the metropolises of Amsterdam and Rotterdam rather than by the lesser and less liberal parts.[15] But even with such a reporting bias the Dutch were exceptionally tolerant by seventeenth-century European standards, as they were exceptionally charitable. Henri IV of France had attempted before his assassination in 1610 to bring a gentle skepticism worthy of his friend Montaigne to undecidable religious questions. Huguenots, in his view (he had been raised as one), could be loyal Frenchmen, no "nation within a nation."[16] But later rulers, especially the cardinal-rulers Richelieu and Mazarin, chipped away at the tolerations of the Edict of Nantes (1598) until it was officially revoked, with the disastrous consequences for economic betterment in France.

One can argue in the easy and cynical way of our times that some of the tolerance of, say, Frederik Hendrik came from mere prudence in a political game, especially the game so skillfully played over many generations by the House of Orange. That's true. Dutch *stadhouders* like Frederick Hendrick were in effect the elected presidents of particular provinces, drawn usually and then exclusively from the *Huis van Oranje-Nassau*. Frederick Hendrick was *stadhouder* of the provinces of Holland, Zeeland, Utrecht, Gelderland, and Overijssel, 1625–1647. It is a cliché of sixteenth- and seventeenth-century European history that religion was used by state-builders, sometimes startlingly cynically, as when *Cardinal* Richelieu arranged on behalf of a *Catholic* French monarchy for secret and then public subsidies to the Swedish *Lutheran* armies fighting a war to the death, claimed to be religious, against the *Catholic* Habsburgs. It makes the head spin. Dutch politics was dominated for a century by the question of whether the Netherlands should become a Christian city on a hill, as the radical Calvinists wished, and as they believed they had achieved in the Republic of Geneva, as also in early Massachusetts and in Scotland under the Stuart kings. The conservatives in the Netherlands railed against tolerating the "libertines [as the orthodox called the liberals], Arminians [followers of the liberal Dutch theologian Arminius], atheists, and concealed Jesuits."[17] Against this devout plan of imposing orthodox Calvinism, the princes of Orange sometimes joined with the Erasmian and tolerant upper bourgeoisie, the regents. Yet at other times the *stadhouders* supported the Calvinist orthodoxy. It depended on political convenience, often. Religion, to repeat, was politics. Soon after the triumph at Maastricht, for example, Frederik Hendrik found it convenient to abandon his liberal friends and take up again with the rigorist anti-Catholics. Maastricht was for a while worth a mass. And Amsterdam was then worth suppressing one. So much for principled toleration.

But principle in the seventeenth century was not usually tolerant, as the Dutch and Frederick Hendrick sometimes pragmatically were. If you want to insist on material, pragmatic, interested causes for everything you could say what is true—that businesspeople need in prudence to be tolerant, at least superficially, if they are to earn their livings from dealing with the irritatingly foreign foreigners. Venice had been for centuries one example; New York—once, remember, *Nieuw-Amsterdam*—has been for a couple of centuries another. The first of the *stadhouders* in revolt against Spain, William of Orange, had noted in 1578 that it was desirable to go easy on, of all things, the Calvinists, "because we [Dutch] are necessarily hosts to merchants . . . of neighboring realms who adhere to this religion."[18] A century later Temple, representing England during an uneasy truce in its own religious wars, praised the Netherlands, "every man following his own way, minding his own business, and little enquiring into other men's; which, I suppose, happened by so great a concourse of people of several nations, different religions and customs, as left nothing strange or new."[19]

The scale—"so great a concourse"—mattered. By the seventeenth century the citizens of Amsterdam alone owned many more ships than did citizens of the comparably tolerant Venice. By 1670 about 40 percentage of the tonnage of European ships was Dutch, "the common carriers of the world," as Temple wrote. (The fact persisted: even nowadays a large share of the long-distance trucking in Europe is in Dutch hands; the Dutch of Chicago in the nineteenth century were teamsters, and one still sees in Chicago on local trucks disproportionately many Dutch names).[20] The liberal pamphleteer Pieter de la Court (of the illiberal town of Leiden), Israel recounts, urged in 1669 "the need to tolerate Catholicism and attract more immigrants of diverse religions . . . to nourish trade and industry."[21] Similar appeals to prudence had been made by the pioneering liberal pamphleteers of the 1620s. The Leideners weren't interested.

Competition among cities of the Netherlands, to be sure, led to toleration. Comprehensive laws over wide areas nowadays have sometimes *reduced* international competition, as do EU rules from Brussels standardizing chocolate and cheese, running against what economists call the Tiebout Effect of qualitatively varied jurisdictions competing by mobility.[22] If a skilled Catholic was discriminated against in Leiden he could move to Amsterdam, as many did. As a result, even *Catholics* with skills to exercise fled to the mainly Reformed north, and the southern city of Antwerp under continued Spanish rule declined economically—with a little help from a blockade of the River Scheldt by the fleets of the Dutch Republic, and then in 1648 by a clause in the Treaty of Maastricht.

All right. If the prudence of competing jurisdictions makes people good in other ways too, we'll take it. But rationalize in a cynical, Samuelsonian-Marxian way as you will, the Dutch liberal regents and the Dutch owners of ships had ethical reasons, too, for persisting in their tolerance. Likewise their more strictly Calvinist enemies, the so-called Counter-Remonstrants, had ethical reasons for persisting in their lack of tolerance. Both sides were in part spiritually motivated. That people sometimes lie about their motives, or also have prudent reasons for their acts, or are misled, does not mean that all protestations of transcendent motives are so much error, blather, cheap talk, hypocrisy, or false consciousness. People are partly motivated by prudence, to be sure. But that does not imply—though many young, male economists think it does—that all human motivation must therefore be reduced to freakonomics prudence, and that a claim of motivation from temperance, justice, courage, faith, hope, and love, and their sinful opposites, is mere womanly chatter. In 1725 Bishop Samuel Butler was already complaining about "the strange [and then recent] affectation of many people of explaining away all particular affections and representing the whole of life as nothing but one continued exercise of self-love."[23] "It is the great fallacy of Dr. Mandeville's book," wrote Adam Smith in 1759, "to represent every passion as wholly vicious [that is, a mere matter of profit-making prudence and self-interest] which is so in any degree and any direction."[24] And so down to Marxian and Samuelsonian and Beckerian economics.

Contrary to the prudence-only model, we have always known, and have recorded since the invention of writing, that intrinsic virtues beyond prudence—love, justice, temperance, and the rest—are parts of what motivate adults. Internalization of ethics beyond having a profitable career is the way children become ethical adults. As the psychologists put it, the "internal locus of control," as against an external one, is what characterizes maturity and professionalism.[25] "Incentivizing" sounds tough and businesslike and is taught relentlessly in modern business schools, to the point of recommending that their faculty members be assessed for their scholarship by the "impact factor" of journals they publish in rather than by actually reading and assessing what they have written.[26] But it is at best a partial account of humanity, and tends to corrupt its internal locus. If you give children a quarter for doing their homework you make them into Max U–only adults. If you give money to professors for turning up to class or writing the next article, which are their internalized duties as professionals, you are treating them like trained parrots. They are liable to start acting like parrots.

"Religion is a complex thing," wrote Trevor-Roper, "in which many human instincts are sublimated and harmonized [he was channeling the secularism of the age of Freud and anthropology], and political ambition is only one among these." When the advanced liberal ("libertine") Dutch theorist Simon Episcopius wrote in 1627 that only "free minds and hearts . . . are willing to support the common interest," perhaps—startling thought—it is what he actually believed, and for which, against his prudential interests, he was willing to risk his life.[27] Perhaps, in the way Amartya Sen puts it, Episcopius showed "commitment"—what others since the beginning of writing have discussed as the virtues other than prudence. In other words, perhaps it is not only his pocketbook but his spirit that was motivating Episcopius. At least more than zero percent.

This is obvious. It would be strange indeed to explain by material interest alone the more than century-long madness of religious politics in the Low Countries after the Beggars' Compromise of the Nobility in 1566. As the sociologist of religion Rodney Stark puts it, "most instances of religious dissent make no sense at all in terms of purely material causes; they become coherent only if we assume that people did care."[28] In the early and mid-twentieth century the rhetoric of progressive and a good deal of conservative writing of history, I have noted, wished always to remake the sacred into the profane, every time, and to see motives of class and economics behind every professed sentiment. Thus Charles Beard's *An Economic Interpretation of the Constitution* (1913) or Georges Lefebvre's *Quatre-vingt neuf* (The Coming of the French Revolution, 1939) or Christopher Hill's *The English Revolution 1640* (1940). It was a reaction against the nationalist tradition of Romantic writing of history, such as, for example, the American historian John Motley's *Rise of the Dutch Republic* (1855–1867). During 1890–1980 even non-Marxians such as Trevor-Roper wished to slip in at the outset a quantitative estimate of 100 percent for profane prudence. Trevor-Roper added to the concession to the sacred just quoted ("political ambition is only one among" the instincts sublimated in religion) an estimate that "in politics it is naturally by far the most potent."[29] Well, sometimes. You don't know on page 3. You need to check it out factually, allowing at least for the possibility of some theory of human motivation other than prudence-only being to some degree potent. I imagine Trevor-Roper had this item in mind when he mentioned in a preface to the substantially unrevised edition of the book in 1962 "certain . . . crude social equations whose periodic emergence will doubtless irritate the perceptive reader" of his maiden book.

Stark takes on the notion that the doctrine of an active God could not really be why people became Muslims or Protestants or why they burned people at the stake—or went to the stake October 16, 1555, at Oxford declaring, "Be of good cheer, Mr. Ridley, and play the man. We shall this day light such a candle by God's grace in England as I trust never shall be put out." Surely, as a materialist history and sociology from 1890 to 1980 would say without evidence, "At bottom the economic argument must have constituted, more than any dogmatic or religious discussions, the principal motive of the preaching of heresy."[30] Surely, wrote even the theologian H. Richard Niebuhr in 1929, the quarrels among sects in, say, Holland were phony, a result of "the universal human tendency to find respectable reasons for a practice desired from motives quite independent of the reasons urged."[31] As Bakunin had declared in 1869, ahead of the curve, "No one at all interested in the study of history could have failed to see that there was always some great material interest at the bottom of even the most abstract, the most sublime and idealistic theological and religious struggles. No war of races, nations, states or classes has ever been waged with any purpose other than domination."[32] Replies Stark, No, and gives much evidence for his view: "These translations of faith into materialism are counterfactual," by which he means, in a bad sense, "mistaken."[33]

When the wish to see every behavior as prudence-motivated makes little scientific sense, as often in the Dutch case, it should not be indulged. The battle over toleration in the Netherlands went on for a long time. Israel observes that it was not finally thoroughly resolved in favor of tolerance until around 1700, as it was then too in England (with the exception of heavy civil disabilities for people not conforming to the established Church of England, and worse in conquered Ireland), in Scotland (with the exception of anti-Catholic prejudice justifying even now the beating up in Glasgow of a Celtic supporter), in France (with the exception in the eighteenth century of an occasional show trial of a Protestant), and in the German-speaking states (with the exception of a lush growth of anti-Semitism).

The hypothesis that European religious toleration was merely a reaction to the excesses of the seventeenth century was expressed explicitly by the historian Herbert Butterfield, for example in his posthumous essay *Tolera-*

tion in Religion and Politics (1980): toleration "came in the end through exhaustion, spiritual as well as material."[34] But as the historian Perez Zagorin
points out, if toleration were in fact "unaccompanied by a genuine belief,"
then the labor of two centuries by Zagorin's heroes Erasmus, More, Sebas-
tian Castellio, Dirck Coornhert, Arminius, Grotius, Episcopius, Spinoza,
Roger Williams, John Goodwin, Milton, William Walwyn, Locke, and Bayle,
exhaustion would not have mattered.[35] Exhaustion, observe, didn't stop
Catholic France so late as 1685 from revoking Nantes. The doctrinal enemies
of the Huguenots were not governed by prudence only, or else they would
not have banished a quarter million of the cream of French craftsmanship
and entrepreneurship to Holland, England, Prussia, America, Ireland, and
the Cape Colony. Exhaustion didn't stay the hand of anti-Catholic rioters
in London as late as 1780, or anti-Catholic Know-Nothings in the United
States as late as the 1850s, or the Ku Klux Klan, first after an exhausting Civil
War and again as a Klan revived in the 1920s. Some people in Europe and its
offshoots, Protestant and Catholic both, were willing to carry on and on and
on with their *fatwas*. People are. In South Asia mobs of Muslims and Hindus
kill each other routinely out of conviction, not always profit. The bully boys
shouting at blacks sitting nonviolently at lunch counters in Greensboro,
North Carolina, in 1960 were motivated by faithful ideology, not pecuniary
prudence. The point here is that an increasing number of people, especially
in bourgeois and tolerant Holland, as early as the late sixteenth century, or
as early as Erasmus at the beginning of the century, were willing to argue
and even die for the opposite of exclusivity in religion—*verdraagzaamheid*.

Zagorin's fourteen-man list of honor shows that ideas mattered as much
as did prudent reaction to disorder. The fourteen names are the seventeenth-
and eighteenth-century men to whom he accords chapter sections in his
book, *How the Idea of Religious Toleration Came to the West* (2003). Six of the
fourteen were Dutch, and the Frenchman Bayle spent most of his adult life
as a professor in Rotterdam. That makes half merely in the tiny Netherlands.
True, Episcopius was banished to Antwerp and settled in France for a few
years, though he returned to the Republic in 1626. Grotius escaped from a
Dutch prison in a barrel. I didn't say that the Netherlands in 1620 was as
tolerant as it is now. I said it was more tolerant than other places in Europe
at the time. The first large bourgeois society was virtuous by the standard of
an intolerant Europe.

Being bourgeois is not an ethical disaster.

PART VI

Reformation, Revolt, Revolution and Reading Increased the Liberty and Dignity of Ordinary Europeans

38

THE CAUSES WERE LOCAL,
TEMPORARY, AND UNPREDICTABLE

Eric Hobsbawm summarized Antonio Gramsci: "The basic problem of the revolution is how to make a hitherto subaltern class capable of hegemony, believe in itself as a potential ruling class and be credible as such to other classes."[1] Just such a revolution in beliefs happened slowly in northwestern Europe between 1517 and 1789. The notion that commoners, and in particular a bourgeoisie devoted to trade-tested betterment, could be capable of hegemony was thought an absurdity in the early sixteenth century, outside of the scattered merchant republics. By the year of the adoption of the American Constitution and the beginning of the French Revolution the belief was still radical but ready to be tried. And by 1869 the anarchist Bakunin looking back observed that "the bourgeois of the [eighteenth] century had sincerely believed that in emancipating themselves from the monarchical, clerical, and feudal yoke they would emancipate all the people along with them. And this naïve and sincere belief was the source of their heroic audacity and all their marvelous power."[2]

The entirely fresh credibility of commoners as rulers, even in royal France and England, and in particular among them the bourgeois commoners, is what needs to be explained. But note: it was a rhetorical change. And human rhetoric, being language, is deeply unpredictable. It is not, as the more simpleminded of Hobsbawm's and Gramsci's comrades in the Communist Party believed, a straightforward reflex of material incentives and class interests. Thus Stalin in *Marxism and Linguistic Questions*: "The base produces the superstructure so that it can serve the base."[3]

History can be viewed at three levels: at the level of the struggling individual soul; at the level of the institution such as family or church or corporation or government; and at the level, finally, overarching, to use the ancient way of saying it, of God's will in the world, what Hegel called the World Spirit.[4] I myself, as a believing Christian, do not sneer at the third possibility (and I pray that you do not either). If you doubt such spooky stuff, think it possible you may be mistaken. But I—as also a Samuelsonian economist lately influenced by the Austrians in the line of Mises, Hayek, Kirzner, Lavoie, Rizzo, Vaughn, White, Boettke, Boudreaux, Klein, Storr, and Chamlee-Wright— can in secular fashion name the overarching level "the Spontaneous Order," or "the Invisible Hand" of the Christian-lite Adam Smith, or the "Natural Selection" of the disappointed Anglican Charles Darwin. All impart a shape to history.

It need not be shaped by the Anglican Designer whom I suspect is at work. Nor does it have to possess an end or purpose or *telos*, at any rate not one that we humans can easily discern. True, the Abrahamic religions also favor a shaped history with an End. The self-described social Darwinists insisted in the nineteenth century that evolution was progress, in which they could discern the triumph of the present group of rich people and could discern also the sad backwardness of non-Aryan races—a doctrine with known results. The nationalists and imperialists and communists discerned similar *teloi*. "History tells us that races have a history and a *telos*," said the racist secularists influenced by their religious ancestry. (The phrase "history tells us that . . . ," it has been noted, is the modern analogue of "God tells us that . . . ," and can often be translated as "I propose to assert without evidence that . . .")

No purpose, or easy-to-spot *telos*, then, is discernible. I say merely that, on an overarching level, human history has a shape, which we can see sometimes in retrospect, a shape not easily inferred from the intentions of individuals or the character of institutions. The unintended consequences of bourgeois liberty and dignity made the modern world, which has by now a discernible shape: enrichment. No one rationally intended in 1700, by adopting broad-church doctrines and a respect for bourgeois inventiveness, to increase real national income per person by a factor of 30 or 100.

Innovative betterment is unpredictable. That's what makes it innovative betterment. Otherwise it is merely routine investment, a good thing, surely, but not, as I argued at length in *Bourgeois Dignity*, world-making. Ray Kroc did not in his wildest dreams of avarice, as we say, believe that his little franchising scheme in 1961 for expanding the hamburger joints of the McDonald brothers, which he had for some time been managing, would achieve by 2010 the selling of over 250 billion hamburgers. He did not make a rational plan based on Max U for such an end. When Orville Wright was asked in 1909 what uses one could make of his little machine for powered flight, he replied, "Sport, mainly. And scouting in war."[5] When Japanese manufacturers after World War II adopted W. Edwards Deming's methods of statistical quality control they had no idea that it would revolutionize world manufacturing. When Wilhelm von Humboldt founded in 1810 the University of Berlin he had no idea that his invention of the modern research university would spread to the masses.

What is strange about the modern world, in other words, is its utter economic unpredictability. As Nassim Nicholas Taleb puts it, the Great Enrichment was a "black-swan" event, deeply unpredictable, not to be reduced to a probability distribution with finite variance.[6] The *pre*modern world, by contrast, was highly predictable in economic shape. Dukes would go on collecting rents, merchants would go on making modest fortunes from trade, peasants would expect to earn what their fathers and grandfathers and great-grandfathers had earned—unless they could pull ahead a bit by tricking neighbor Nat, the fool, into selling the Nether Field for less than it was worth.

Institutions are conservative. They are routine, predictable, suitable for laying down the future in 1700. That, after all, is what makes them institutions, those beloved habits of the heart—in the phrase Tocqueville learned from Franz Lieber of Boston—and of the lip and of the law. Benedictine monasticism in the countryside grew fat for hundreds of years, and then the Franciscans and the Dominicans of the emerging Italian cities had another idea. If growth in spirit, not to speak of economy, depends on betterment, the growth cannot usually look to established institutions for inspiration. As Hayek put it:

> It is, in fact, desirable that the rules should be observed only in most instances and that the individual should be able to transgress them when it seems to him worthwhile to incur the odium this will cause. . . . It is this flexibility of voluntary

rules which in the field of morals makes gradual evolution and spontaneous growth possible, which allows further modifications and betterments.[7]

Betterments require *dis*obedience, creative *destruction*, an overturning or re-making or redirecting of what already exists, Steve Jobs and Bill Gates challenging Big Blue, autos replacing horses—not a bigger centralized computer or a faster horse. Unpredictability is characteristic of the major betterments.

Therefore betterments, I have said, depend on liberty. As the engineer and historian of technology John Lienhard puts it, "Inventing means violating some status quo. . . . All the great inventive epochs . . . have been marked by climates of increased personal liberty." He mentions the Hellenistic world of Archimedes, the Song dynasty in China, and of course the eighteenth century in Europe. He might have mentioned fifth-century Athens or Quattrocento Florence. "If we want to stimulate invention," Lienhard concludes, "then we need somehow to create an ambience of freedom."[8]

For example, the outcome of various revolts against hierarchy—from some versions of the Reformation in 1517 to some versions of the French Revolution in 1789—made people bold. Revolts happened elsewhere, frequently, in Japan and India and every other place. It is wrong to think that "Oriental despotism" made for utter passivity in ordinary Turks or Chinese. But in Europe, for contingent reasons having nothing to do with deep European virtue, the minor revolts against Habsburg taxes and Stuart stubbornness and Bourbon improvidence led, it happened, to full revolutions, the world turned upside down. Often enough, that is, they succeeded in making "a hitherto subaltern class capable of hegemony, believe in itself as a potential ruling class and be credible as such to other classes."

Some of the English in the 1640s, for example, in their impetuous, aristocratic, prebourgeois way, went about as far as you could go. The gentry-origin John Lilburne in *The Free Man's Freedom Vindicated* (1646) wrote about how "unnatural, irrational, sinful, wicked, unjust, devilish, and tyrannical it is for any man whatsoever, spiritual or temporal, clergyman or layman, to appropriate and assume unto himself a power, authority and jurisdiction, to rule, govern or reign over any sort of men in the world without their free consent."[9] It is difficult now to feel how insanely radical such a claim seemed to most Europeans in 1646. At the Putney Debates of the New Model Army in 1647, Colonel Thomas Rainborough declared, "I do think that the poorest man in England is not at all bound in a strict sense to that government that he has not had a voice to put himself under."[10] Shocking stuff. And Rainborough was, like Lilburne, a gentleman, a Puritan sea captain and army colonel, the son of a vice-admiral and ambassador. His enemy, Charles I, himself first used in print the word "leveller" to describe such notions, which seemed in 1647 to most English people quite mad—as one of Charles's supporters described it scornfully, that "every Jack shall vie with a gentleman and every gentleman be made a Jack."[11]

Until the eighteenth and especially the nineteenth century such views did not prevail, as against the position more usual at the time—that, as General Ireton, Cromwell's son-in-law, replied immediately to Rainborough at Putney, "No person has a right to this [voice] that has not a permanent fixed interest [namely, land] in this kingdom." To which Rainborough countered: "I do not find anything in the Law of God that a lord shall choose twenty burgesses [that is, the rulers of incorporated towns], and a [nonlordly] gentleman but two, or a poor man shall choose none." Fifteen months after Putney, Charles I, facing on January 30, 1649, the headman's block, succinctly asserted the royalist version of hierarchy: "A subject and a sovereign are clean different things." Render unto Caesar what is Caesar's. To which John Milton replied a month later, articulating the other strain in Abrahamic theology, "No man who knows aught can be so stupid to deny that all men naturally were born free, being the image and resemblance of God himself . . . unless the people must be thought created all for [the king], he not for them, and they all in one body inferior to him single, which were a kind of treason against the dignity of mankind to affirm."[12] Dignity.

What is novel in such assertions by radical English Puritans is the idea that every Jack should have political as against a vaguely spiritual dignity—having political and economic pie now, as against pie in the sky when you die. It emphasized secular rights, as did Locke, and was a turn peculiar to the seventeenth century. In the eighteenth century Rousseau brought the idea to the full attention of Europeans. The historian of the Enlightenment Margaret Jacob writes, "No more dangerous set of ideas [than 'a man's a man for a' that'] surfaced in the Enlightenment."[13] The radical position of the 1640s long haunted Europe. Though the Putney Debates were in practice won by the conservatives Cromwell and Ireton in favor of at least landed privilege, in the long run of centuries the radicals prevailed. The historian of the Levellers, David Wootton, notes that the Putney Debates, of 1647, were not actually published until the 1890s. For centuries the specter of radical democracy kept being pushed back into Hell. In 1765 Blackstone still takes it as obvious that "distinction of ranks and honors is necessary in every well-governed state," a sentiment one can still find among conservatives.[14]

The Levellers had secular predecessors, such as Wat Tyler, John Ball, and Jack Straw in 1381, or the Ciompi revolt of the wool carders in Florence in 1378, or for that matter Spartacus or the emigrating Jews under Moses, as Marxian scholars such as the historical sociologist Mielants note.[15] But Mielants is forgetting, as secular scholars tend to, the persistent egalitarian radicalism of the Church of Faith, as against the Church of Power, from the Desert Fathers of the third century down to the Liberation Theology of the twentieth.[16] The Dominican friar Girolamo Savonarola (1452–1498) brought the Florence of 1494 to radical democracy (in his case combined with conservative Christianity, a formula repeated among many Radical Reformers, such as the Anabaptists), which would terrify European elites for centuries—despicable "mob rule," they called it, until it became a universal political ideal.[17]

Yet such a tale of People in Revolt misses something happening among the elite too, a shift in ideas of what made for nobility. In the Middle Ages there was little need for a theory of nobility. You were the King of Sicily or the Duchess of Aquitaine by right of conquest or inheritance, and that was that. The historian of France Jonathan Dewald has shown that later the people at the top of the Great Chain of Being started trying to justify their position: "Seventeenth-century nobles [in France] became preoccupied with the na-ture of selfhood, . . . and they came at the same time to doubt many of the ethical underpinnings of their society. They came, in other words, to see the isolated self as real, important, and complicated, and they correspond-ingly doubted the value, even the reality, of the social conventions that sur-rounded it."[18]

The most spectacular example is the nobleman Montaigne, writing, "I do not care so much what I am to others as I care what I am to myself." "French noblemen," Dewald argues, "talked steadily more about lineage and descent after 1570 or so":

> Noble blood acquired greater importance in these years, increasingly obscuring
> other plausible justifications of privilege. The monarchy contributed to this en-
> hanced evaluation, by inspecting genealogies. . . . Concepts of lineage (*race* in the
> language of the seventeenth century) . . . provided ways for . . . the aristocracy as
> a whole to understand its relationship to the rest of society.

And yet, Dewald notes, the aristocracy thereby showed its anxiety about
its position—writing, for example, numerous autobiographies, which would
lack point in a society in which public role was the same as one's identity. "By
selling high positions and by intervening so often in matters of property, the
[French] state itself disrupted belief in a stable social order and forced nobles
to think carefully about money; in such circumstances, nobles came to view
their society as in some sense an artificial creation rather than an organic
hierarchy."[19] It was the first step to denaturalizing the Great Chain of Being,
leading to equality of personal rights (together with some bad news in social
engineering). The poet and political writer Sarah Skwire has noted in the
founding Quaker Margaret Fell's rhetoric a claim of equality even between
the sexes. Equality was in no way granted, said proudly humble Margaret to
Charles II, by the hierarchy.[20] Quaker and Leveller talk was merely the most
extreme evidence of a rising doubt that Blood Told.

The Great Chain of Being—that is to say, the material incentives and
ideological beliefs tending to produce entire obedience to the existing institutions—makes real conversation impossible, or at best pointless. Words
don't matter. We play our God-given role, as duchess or tavern wench, and
need no chatter, or charter, to justify it. In *Don Quixote*, for example, as I've
noted, the Don just *does* things. Sancho complains, but to no effect. The
comic point of the book is that the Don is invulnerable to conversation, or
rhetoric, or reason. Later novels, such as *Pamela* or *Shamela* or *Sense and
Sensibility*, consist of dialogue, reflection, real conversation. Moll Flanders
and Crusoe engage in real discussion, real internal dialogue, real decision
making. The conversation starts circa 1700. There were in Plato or *Utopia*
or *Il Cortegiano* many lovely discussions among the elite. But not across
classes. At Toyota there are a million betterments per year, most of them
coming from the shop floor—a hundred times as many per worker as at
General Motors, in which the suggestion box is said to be attached to the
wastebasket.[21]

The political revolutions of the seventeenth century were more important to more people than, say, the novelties of science. And indeed the success of business projectors, whether bourgeois or aristocratic, told people that they too could change things. Even scientific things. Even ecclesiastical things. Even political things.

"DEMOCRATIC" CHURCH GOVERNANCE EMBOLDENED PEOPLE

It was been usefully observed that history has taken sharp turns every half-millennium or so, a sharp unpredictability of the spirit.[1] God, and history, moves in mysterious ways. One of the half-millennium turns was the Reform of the Western church. The great turnings of creative destruction depend not on institutions, which serve routinely as drags on progress— another chronic flaw in neo-institutionalist theorizing—but on individual souls coming to move in harmony with God's new will in the world. Here I stand; I can do no other (in the words supplied by the first editor of Luther's collected works), not because I am willful or proud, and certainly not because I am following the routine of an existing institution, or of an existing dogma, but because the church has become corrupt, and to obey God I must try to cleanse it. Your will be done, on earth as it is in heaven.

The rhetoric of the Reformation criticized existing religious institutions and built up new ones, such as radical Anabaptism and later Quakerism, which gave men, and even women such as Margaret Fell, a voice denied by the old structures. In the end the theocrats from Calvin and Knox to Cromwell and Milton and Richelieu and Bossuet, who had won so many battles, lost the war. In England late in the seventeenth century, in reaction to such hard men, the Cambridge Platonists and others asserted a broad-church Anglicanism. It followed by a century the Arminianism of the regents of the Dutch Republic, in the same way that the English of the 1690s decided, after a century of stubborn resistance, to adopt Dutch economic institutions.

The surging Protestantism after 1517 did have something to do with all the good, fresh talk about the rights of man (and in Holland the reality even of some rights for women). True, anticlericals nowadays choke at taking religious viewpoints as anything but idiotic superstition, which science, you see, has obviated. But one can't understand the sixteenth and seventeenth centuries—or most European places in later centuries—without acknowledging that these are serious Christians we are construing.

The priesthood of all believers, and behind it the individualism of the Abrahamic religions generally, mattered to the beginnings of the strange notion that a plowman has in right as much to say on public affairs as a prince. Yet Martin Luther, appalled by the Peasants' Revolt in southern Germany of 1624–1625, was nothing like a radical in politics, and wished the plowmen to stick to their plows: "A worldly kingdom cannot stand unless there is in it an inequality of persons, so that some are lords, some subjects."[2] On the contrary, what made men and women bold in politics and the economy was not Luther's Magisterial Reformation (from *magister*, master) in Germany and Scandinavia, and also among high-church Anglicans, but the so-called Radical Reformation, ranging from some Calvinists to all Anabaptists and Quakers, and then even Anglicans in the form of Methodism, and finally a liberal Protestantism and even a liberal Catholicism supporting ordinary people having a go. In the first wave of the Radical Reformation in the Netherlands, ordinary people—comb-makers, bakers, cobblers, and others without inherited high standing—questioned whether the communion host was the body of Christ, suggesting in heretical jest that if the Virgin was holy then the donkey on which she rode was a holy ass, and comparing that same Queen of Heaven to the local madwoman.[3]

After the Industrial Revolution and the Great Enrichment had created an enormous pile of easily adopted betterments such as electricity and antibiotics, no specifically European pattern of religious faith was necessary, as is clear from the vigorous adoption recently of trade-tested betterment in non-Christian and indeed non-Abrahamic places such as China and India. In the event, however, in the sixteenth and seventeenth centuries in Europe the Reformation does seem to have strengthened economic betterment, on the basis of a spiritual individualism common to Judaism and Islam, or for that matter to some versions of Buddhism and Hinduism and Zoroastrianism. It just so happened, in other words, that a fuller dignity and liberty for economic actors grew out of some versions of a fuller dignity and liberty for *religious* actors. Before 1517 the very idea of a "religious actor" among ordinary people was foreign to the Church of Power. Religion was designed for churchmen and a few nuns, not for members of the flock-to-be-governed. Hegel's Northern-Eurocentric remark in 1822 still seems approximately true: "This is the essence of the Reformation: man is in his very nature destined to be free."[4]

Hegel meant that humans are collectively destined by God or the World Spirit or at any rate the patterned accidents of the European Four Rs to be free, not individually predestined. The inspiriting cause of economic change was not, *pace* Weber, anxiety over such predestined election. What made people bold in the practice of frenetic betterment—not merely defensive saving or hard work—was rather the participation of ordinary people in religious gatherings with weak or no governance from above. The Radical Reformation, as against the more hierarchical one of Luther or Zwingli or Henry VIII, in other words, was a delivery room for a democratic theory long a-borning. In particular, radical Protestant governance of congregations gave standing to any member—thus the governance-by-resistance-to-the-king's-bishops among German Pietists and English Methodists; governance-by-elders among Scottish Presbyterians and Moravian Hutterites; governance-by-local-community among Anabaptists (called now Mennonites), Independents (called now Congregationalists), and Baptists (called now Baptists); and, after a while, governance-by-no-one-in-particular among, say, Quakers, or at last among New Age sects. The Methodist theologian Stanley Hauerwas (b. 1940), for example, long a professor at Notre Dame and now at Duke, describes himself as a "high-church Mennonite" and his church as having "Catholic practices of Eucharist" (that is, of the mass) but "a free church ecclesiology" (ecclesiology, from Greek "calling out," concerns church governance; "free" in "free church" means "free of hierarchy").[5] John Wesley (1703–1791)—whose struggle during his long life calling Anglicans to holiness resulted after his death in a separate and nonconforming Methodist church—emphasized (like others on the Radical side of the Reformation) consensus within a congregation, unordained preachers, independence from state interference, and even sometimes pacifism and tax resistance in the face of the state's proud projects. It sums up to a fierce priesthood of all believers.[6]

Yet on the Roman Catholic side, too, the medieval theory of natural rights, especially among the friars such as the Dominican Thomas of Aquino and the Franciscan William of Ockham, justified a right even of revolt against an ungodly Church of Power or its collaborating kings. Quentin Skinner argues that French, Dutch, and English theorists of politics in the early seventeenth century owed a good deal to the scholastic tradition, such as its late flowering in the Spanish Jesuits Francisco Suárez (1548–1617), an opponent of theories of divine right, and Juan de Mariana (1536–1624), another libertarian pioneer.[7] Seventeenth-century Jansenism in France, again, which counted Pascal among its followers, wrote a French historian of the movement, "owing to its fundamental individualism . . . threatened the authority of the state as conceived by Louis XIV."[8] In the 1820s the reactionary magazine *Le Mémorial Catholique* (founded by the priest and later revolutionary intellectual Robert de Lamennais) described Jansenism disapprovingly as consisting "essentially in granting to each individual church . . . and each individual the right to set limits to spiritual sovereignty on questions of faith, morality, and discipline."[9] Good Lord. It was radical Protestantism in Roman disguise. The point, however, is that Jansenism, though surviving as a fond memory in the thoughts of some Frenchmen, such as Tocqueville, was eventually crushed by the pope and the king, receiving a fatal blow as early as 1713. The political implications of the priesthood of all believers was confined for a long time to northern, Protestant Europe, and in radical form to subdivisions even of the north.

Whatever their actual debt to the scholastics, the Protestants in the sixteenth century challenged the monarchies and aristocracies of popes and bishops by imagining as their model the first- and second-century Christian church. As the Church of Faith had repeatedly done against the Church of Power—but in the Radical Reformation at last succeeded—they wished to omit twelve hundred years of church history, sometimes fourteen hundred years. The sociologist Malcolm H. MacKinnon, disputing the route by which Max Weber connected Protestantism to "capitalism," notes that "Puritan idealism was more concerned with ecclesiology than soteriology [the doctrines of salvation that Weber had emphasized], concerned with 'purifying' church government. . . . The Puritan Revolution of the 1640s . . . [therefore] established the *political* preconditions of modern capitalism."[10] "The thrust of Reform," Charles Taylor observes, "was to make a Church in which everyone should show the same degree of personal commitment and devotion which had hitherto been the stance of a dedicated [clerical] elite. . . . To carry through on this Reform required that one define a way of life open to everyone."[11]

In Europe the bishops had long been secular lords, the popes had marshaled armies, and the church had collected a fifth or more of all land rents. Even before the Wars of Religion, to repeat, religion *was* politics. In the Reformation the political theories shifted away from disputes between popes and emperors, and toward disputes between governments and individual consciences. The economic historian Jordi Vidal-Robert has documented in detail how the Spanish Inquisition, running from the late fifteenth to the early nineteenth centuries in a hundred thousand trials, was used by the Spanish crown to repress internal revolt when the crown was preoccupied with a foreign war and needed a quick fix for internal disaffection.[12] "Religion, in fact," observed Hugh Trevor-Roper in 1940, "was also an aspect of politics—the outward symbol, the shibboleth, by which parties were known. . . . Religion was not merely a set of personal beliefs about the economy of Heaven, but the outward sign of a social and political theory."[13] What seems to us secular moderns as absurd excess in Archbishop Laud's or Oliver Cromwell's interfering with individual consciences, he argues, is no more or less absurd than would be invading Poland in the name of *Lebensraum* or invading South Vietnam in the name of anti-Communism or invading Iraq in the name of suppressing world terrorism or any other of the more peculiar modern projects based upon a political theory.

In other words, it was a small step in logic, if not immediately in practice, from the priesthood of all believers to the citizenship of all indwellers and the entrepreneurship of all commoners. Taylor notes of the repeated splitting of Protestant churches that "in this recurrent activity of founding and refounding, we are witnessing more and more the creation of common agencies in secular time," that is, a school for liberal revolutionaries.[14] Arthur Herman claims that the Presbyterian Kirk in Scotland was from the time of John Knox "the single most democratic system of church government in Europe."[15] Herman may not be remembering that in the same 1560s and 1570s some of the Dutch were creating the same sort of church government, by contrast to the less radical Lutherans and Anglicans elsewhere around the German Ocean. "No bishops," said the *gereformeerde* Dutch, as decades earlier the Genevans inspired by Calvin had said too, and the Zurichers inspired by Zwingli. We shall have pastors chosen by the lay elders—in Greek, "presbyters." In remote and proud Virginia even the Anglicans, the established church of the colony, in fact ran their affairs through their parish vestries, not much under the guidance of their official bishops in faraway England.[16]

The well-named Independents/Congregationalists of England, who especially flourished in the seventeenth century in New England (where they constituted the established church, financed until 1833 out of taxes), went still further, officially denying regional or national assemblies of elders any authority over a congregation.

After such knowledge, in other words, it was a small further step to republicanism in secular matters. As MacCulloch declares of Zwingli's experiments in Switzerland and its neighborhood during the 1520s:

> Majority voting was a new idea in [Swiss] communities that had previously made decisions by reaching consensus. This was a precedent of huge significance, not just for Reformed Churches throughout the world but for the shape of western political life generally. Often the English point complacently at their "mother of parliaments" as the source of western political ideals. They forget that by modern standards there was nothing especially democratic about their parliamentary history for most of its history [for instance, before 1867]; whereas the synodical, representative form of government in the Reformed Church established hierarchy in society.[17]

Better: it established in church governance a "hierarchy" responsive to the people because elected by the people. In any case, it radically overturned earlier hierarchies of bishops appointed from above by kings or popes. MacCulloch writes elsewhere, "The [English civil] war altered everything. The whole structure of the prewar [Anglican] Church was dismantled, and with the end of government control people could begin to make religious decisions for themselves."[18] And so they did, from Ranters to Quakers.

MacCulloch warns us, however, not to think of the era of the Wars of Religion while they were going on as politically liberal in a modern sense. Far from it. Both Catholics and Protestants in the sixteenth and seventeenth centuries evinced "a powerful hankering for . . . a single God-given order":

> Some two to four million people died in France, out of a population of about nineteen million, in the religious wars, and a higher share in Germany. Europe became a newly intensively regulated society, as Catholics and Protestants [and among Protestants, both radicals and magisterials] vied with each other to show just how moral a society they could create.[19]

The relaxed Christianity of the medieval church, and the Erasmian strain that theorized the medieval church at its waning, was replaced by rigorism on all sides.

Yet when the smoke cleared in the early eighteenth century many places were left with strengthened ideologies of even a poor man's liberty to do as he wished, even theologically, even ecclesiastically, even economically.

The priesthood of all believers, and especially a church governance by congregation rather than by hierarchy, invited lay people to consider themselves and their daily activities as infused with the Holy Spirit. At the same time the turn to a new humanism—inspiriting in the Netherlands the old "chambers of rhetoric" (*rederijkerskamers*) and in France and England the new grammar schools—showed that burghers could be Latinists too.[20] The son of a glover, William Shakespeare, had small Latin and less Greek, but he got what he had in a grammar school in Stratford. The Dutch Revolt against Spain 1568–1648 and the English tumult 1642–1688, the French Huguenot struggle during the 1580s against Henri III and Henri IV and the Paris League, and the parliamentary and then the noble Fronde of 1648 to 1653, stirring up a political environment readied by printing presses difficult to censor, made ordinary men and women bold.[21] Christopher Hill, the historian of what he called the English *Revolution*, found astonishing "the attempts of various groups of the common people to impose their own solutions on the problems of the time, in opposition to the wishes of their betters."[22] As the historian of early Quakerism Rosemary Moore put it, "One result of the [English] Civil War was the abolition, for a period of some years, of controls on speech, printing, and ways of worship. Ideas could flourish unchecked."[23] From 1517 to 1776, and 1789, the shared discourse was revolutionized. What was thought justifiable, and who was worthy of rhetorical attention, shifted, permanently, opening the Bourgeois Era. The ideas and the conscious and unconscious rules for handling them—the rhetoric—had changed.

Therefore, and with the resulting economic success, I have said, the virtue of prudence rose greatly in prestige, as compared with the formerly most-honored virtues of religious faith or battlefield courage. As Charles Taylor put it in 1989, what came to "command our awe, respect, or admiration"— what *The Bourgeois Virtues* called the "virtues of the transcendent"—was no longer solely the high virtues of saint or soldier but now "an affirmation of ordinary life."[24] To be sure, saintliness and soldiery continued to be admired, causing what Taylor describes as "a tension between the affirmation of ordinary life, to which we moderns are strongly drawn, and some of the most important [and old] moral distinctions."[25] (*The Bourgeois Virtues* was written in culpable ignorance of Taylor's thinking, and therefore much of the book redid in 2006 what Taylor had already done nearly two decades earlier—describing the "tension" between bourgeois virtues and the older honored pair of aristocratic and peasant/Christian virtues.)

Ecclesiology, then, affected economic thinking by analogy, through the autonomy of congregations in Calvinist places such as Geneva, Scotland, Holland, France, and Hungary, and in still more radical places such as Poland and Transylvania, and in scattered communities of Anabaptists and Independents under pressure elsewhere in Zürich, Bern, Augsburg, Münster, and the Netherlands. The medieval/mercantilist/socialist/regulatory idea that a hierarchy is necessary for an economy to work ("a worldly kingdom cannot stand unless there is in it an inequality of persons") was challenged by a notion that God would provide guidance to individual believers—for example, through the novel practice of ordinary people reading the Bible without a priest in sight, or through the still more novel practice of attending silently to an Inner Light. (Protestants, however, did not invent nonanalytic Bible reading. *Lectio divina*, divine reading in community, was practiced by monks such as the Benedictines, and was first theorized in the third century by the heretical church father Origen.) The extreme case is again the Society of Friends ("Quakers" was a *geuzennaam* assigned by its enemies), which in its official name embodies the individualist and egalitarian notion of church governance. If you go to a Quaker meeting you will find that the congregation sits in a circle—facing each other without a minister—and waits for someone to deliver his or her reflection. His or her, note.

Is this, one may ask, a source of the idea that central, or for that matter local and lordly, planning is unnecessary for an economy? I do not claim to have shown it here beyond cavil. Yet the hypothesis seems plausible. Early moderns were alarmingly earnest about their religions, as the mutual slaughter shows. The earnestness reached all social strata, though it was also used cynically by some in all strata. It would be no surprise if individual or congregational governance of a church, as against the hierarchies of Roman or Lutheran or Anglican confessions, taught people to venture in business.

(Note again the divergence from Weber's hypothesis of a psychological change emerging from the doctrine of predestination. The Society of Friends entertained no such doctrine, for example, yet its members were famously successful in business, at any rate after the less radical Protestants stopped hanging them on Boston Common.) And in any case the autonomy of the Radical Reformation allowed for betterment. John Lienhard instances an early theorist of the steam engine, Denis Papin (1647–ca. 1712, cast out of France as a Huguenot), and the at-last-successful inventor of the engine, the Devonshire blacksmith Thomas Newcomen (1664–1729), a Baptist.[26] In the eighteenth century, Kant, the son of German Pietists with their self-governing congregations, elevated autonomy, that is self-governance, to the chief virtue of Enlightenment.[27] A free society is a do-it-yourself society, as the philosopher Stephen Hicks puts it, a society in which things are not done to or even for a free adult, but done *by* her. No bishops. And at length no lords and kings. And then no central planning or expert regulation. Laissez faire.

The move to self-creation of a child or a slave, or a subject of a despotic king or an all-encompassing state, requires private property and enterprise and—a new word in the eighteenth century—"responsibility." The American historian Thomas Haskell wrote in 1999 a startling essay chronicling the new prominence of the word in a commercial America in the eighteenth and nineteenth centuries. The *OED* gives 1787 as the earliest quotation of "responsibility" in one of its modern senses, as merely accepting factually that one has done such-and-such, by Hamilton in *The Federalist Papers*, and shortly thereafter by Edmund Burke. Haskell notes that it was used much earlier in law in the sense of being required to respond to a legal action. Such a "responsible" person, meaning "liable to be called to [legal] account" (sense 3a), occurs as early as 1643. The *OED*'s earliest quotation for the *favorable* ethical meaning, the dominant modern sense, "*morally* accountable for one's actions; capable of rational conduct" (sense 3b), is as late as 1836—which is Haskell's point, though he dates it a little earlier. The linking of "responsibility" with the marketlike word "accountability" occurs in the first instance of "accountability" detected by Haskell, in 1794 in Samuel Williams's *Natural and Civil History of Vermont*: "No mutual checks and balances, accountability and responsibility."

Haskell is wary of praising the new dignity for market participants: "My assumption is not that the market elevates morality." But then he takes it back: "The form of life fostered by the market may entail the heightened sense of agency."[28] Just so. Surely commerce, with seventeenth-century religion and church governance among the radicals, did heighten the sense of individual, responsible agency, especially when thunder and lightning stopped being attributed to God's active intervention. Earlier in the essay Haskell attributed to trading the "escalating" sense of agency, that is, "responsibility." So trading *does* elevate morality. What faded was "the devil made me do it," or "my lord commanded me to do it," or "I was obedient in doing it, having subordinated myself to my official duties and the obligations of war service or my oath of allegiance or my oath of office." Trade was a context for widespread *individual* responsibility, as against obedience to the hierarchy's commands.

Trading always existed and was vigorous in places like eighteenth-century Japan and tenth-century England. Some whole societies, and big parts of many societies, were dominated by mercantile values. One thinks of the Phoenicians or their offshoot Carthage; or the overseas Chinese; or the overseas Japanese before they were forbidden in 1635 to return; or Jews such as Jesus of Nazareth, with his parables of merchants and makers. The river and seaport of Sakai in Ōsaka Prefecture was once independent, like Genoa or Lübeck, but was subordinated to the central power by Oda Nobunaga in 1569. Nagasaki was similar. Both were places in which trade ruled.

Yet if so, why was there not always the sense of "responsibility"? Evidently the sense of responsibility in eighteenth-century Europe and its offshoot in North America came from somewhere other than the pervasiveness of trade by itself—perhaps, I am suggesting, from the melding of autonomous Christians with autonomous traders. It protected a new sense that it was all right to be a person dealing in voluntary exchange, entailing an acceptance of the outcomes of such exchange as just—and therefore of a piece with responsible accountability. It was a new idea in Holland circa 1600 and especially in England circa 1700 and Scotland and British North America circa 1750, and beyond. It was the Bourgeois Revaluation and the Bourgeois Deal.

40

THE THEOLOGY OF HAPPINESS
CHANGED CIRCA 1700

On a long view it is only recently that we have been guiltlessly obsessed with the idea of pleasure or happiness. Even in secular traditions, such as those of the philosophical Chinese or Greeks, a pleasuring version of happiness is usually downplayed, at any rate in high theory, in favor of spiritual enlightenment. It is true even of the school of Epicurus, often tagged by its enemies as mere pleasure seekers. In Christianity for many centuries the treasure, not pleasure, was to be stored up in heaven, not down here where thieves break in.

After all, as a pre–eighteenth-century theologian would put it—or as a modern and mathematical economist would, too, at the right interest rate—an infinite afterlife was infinitely to be preferred to any finite pleasure attainable in earthly life. Such a doctrine made it seem pointless to attempt to abolish poverty or slavery or wife-beating. A coin given to the beggar would reward the giver with a leg-up to heaven, a *mitzvah*, a *hasanat*. But the ancient praise for charity implied no plan to adopt big welfare programs or to grant rights of personal liberty or to favor a larger national income. A life of sitting by the West Gate with a bowl to beg was, after all, an infinitesimally small share of one's life to come. Stop complaining. During your life in this vale of tears, get used to it. It's your God-given place in the Great Chain of Being. What does it matter how miserable you are in *this* life?

Such fatalism in many religions—"God willing," we say, "*deo volente*," "*im yirtzeh hashem*," "*insh'Allah*"—precluded idle talk of earthly happiness. The historian Darrin McMahon has chronicled the change from fatalism to the modern obsession with happiness, noting, for example, that the radicals of the world turned upside down in the English Civil War advocated for the poor in *this* life. During the 1640s the "Digger" Gerrard Winstanley (1609–1676) asked, "Why may not we have our heaven *here* . . . and heaven hereafter, too?"[1] The Diggers wished to hold all land in common. Later Winstanley himself became a merchant, a Quaker, and a landowner, making his personal heaven *here* by way of trade-tested betterment. McMahon observes that "one can . . . trace the 'diminishing emphasis' afforded to the 'spiritual benefits' of pain over the course of the seventeenth century" (he is quoting Ann Thompson, *The Art of Suffering and the Impact of Seventeenth-Century Anti-Providential Thought* [2003], on a shift she dates to after the Civil War).

For example, almost no one except some heretical Catholic priests dealing with Spain and Portugal's conquests in the sixteenth century and finally some Quakers in the eighteenth century, thought that slavery was anything other than a misfortune applied by God to temper the slave's soul. *Robinson Crusoe* of 1719 relates how Crusoe sold into slavery a boy who had saved his life. Defoe had no antislavery irony in mind. After all, part of Crusoe's subsequent prosperity, after his sojourn on the island, came from the slave trade.[2]

Similarly, few at the time, and fewer in the previous century, thought that poverty was somehow objectionable on theological grounds. A French official in the seventeenth century declared that "writing should not be taught to those whom Providence caused to be born peasants. . . . Such children should be taught only to read."[3] Infinitely lived Christians have no justified complaint if their lot in this present life is a burden. Again: take up your cross. Quit whining.

Then, in the seventeenth century, reaching a crescendo in the eighteenth century, our earthly happiness became theoretically important to us—in some theorizing at first directed only to the "us" of high intellectual fashion. In 1732–1734 the Fourth Epistle of Pope's *An Essay on Man* opens with, "Oh happiness! our being's end and aim! / Good, pleasure, ease, content! whate'er thy name: / That something still which prompts th' eternal sigh, / For which we bear to live, or dare to die" (lines 1–4). Later in the poem Pope takes away the egalitarian flavor that the idea soon came to have: "But fortune's gifts if each alike possest, / And each were equal, must not all contest? / If then to all men happiness was meant, / God in externals could not place content" (that is, God arranges peace among us by giving beauty and position unequally, by an irrevocable rank that we cannot contest; lines 63–66). Pope was a Tory, and no egalitarian, declaring for example, in words that Voltaire would spoof, "Whatever is, is right" (line 145). Still in Pope one's happiness comes from above: "nature plants in man alone / Hope of known bliss, and faith in bliss unknown" (lines 345–346), which if pursued with piety has the happy (in another sense) result that "Self-love thus push'd to social, to divine, / Gives thee to make thy neighbor's blessing thine" (lines 353–354). Pope's is an invisible hand being praised in the 1730s: the poem ends, "That reason, passion, answer one great aim; / That true self-love and social are the same; / That virtue only makes our bliss below" (lines 395–397). Shades of Adam Smith. What is novel in the eighteenth century is that increasingly the talk of happiness did without the hypothesis of bliss *above*.

Of course even before the clerisy started talking in such a happiness-focused way, the average person very much valued happiness. And doubt-less the slaves themselves, and the cripples by the West Gate, had a less lofty idea of happiness and fortune's gifts than did poets and philosophers and theologians and the privileged, and had a less sanguine view of the system of slavery and the structures of poverty. In any case, by 1776, "life, liberty, and the pursuit of happiness" was an unoriginal formula among the liberal side of the clerisy. John Locke had taught, as early as 1677, that "the business of men [is] to be happy in this world by the enjoyment of the things of nature subservient to life, health, ease, and pleasure"—though he added piously, as Pope did later, "and by the comfortable [that is, comforting] hopes of an-other life when this is ended." In the historian David Wootton's review of the last book by the historian Keith Thomas, *The Ends of Life*, we read, "Even the Epicureans, who thought that the purpose of life was eudaimonia (felicity), thought that there was a right and a wrong way to go about obtaining it. Self-restraint, not self-indulgence, was the key. This great tradition was broken in the mid-seventeenth century, and a small linguistic change marks the break point: people stopped talking about felicity, and began to talk about happi-ness."[4] By 1738, the Comte de Mirabeau wrote to a friend, recommending simply, "what should be our only goal: happiness," that is, *bonheur*.[5]

"Our only goal." To see how strange such a remark is, ask whether it could have been uttered by a leader of opinion two centuries before. Calvin? Michelangelo? Charles V? No. They sought heavenly, artistic, or political glory—not something so domestic as happiness. Yet late in the seventeenth century even Anglican priests commenced preaching that God wanted us to be happy as much as holy, working on a principle of "eudaimonism," which would be "happyism" in the usual translations but is better rendered literally from the Greek, "the doctrine that one has a good spirit protecting one." Anglicans and, astonishingly, some New England Congregationalists turned against the old, harsh, Augustinian-Calvinist line. Taylor summarizes the shift so: "God's goodness thus consists in his bringing about our good. His beneficence is explained partly in terms of our happiness."[6] We are not, declared the eudaimonists, mere sinners in the hands of an angry God, worms unworthy of grace. We are God's beloved creatures, his pets.

Associated with eudaimonism was a genial Arminianism, such as in Methodism, in which all people, not merely the elect, could get into heaven. Did an Arminian confidence in salvation also make people *economically* bold? The reason to frame the question that way is that the economic improvers were usually devout Christians, whether Anglican or Catholic or Calvinist, and anyway the culture surrounding the early Age of Betterment was still massively Christian.

By 1800 in progressive circles in England and the United States the Calvinist otherworldliness had fallen away, replaced by an aggressively Evangelical movement quite determined to be its brother's keeper in this life. Soon the non-Evangelicals in, say, the Church of England came to a similar view. Such a social gospel during the nineteenth century served to animate abolition, missionaries, imperialism, anti-imperialism, prohibition, and Christian versions of socialism. All of them in one form or another are still with us, together with a mid-twentieth-century obsession with other people's activities in the bedroom. Radical Protestant theology became worldly.

Sometimes the worldly turn fit smoothly with bourgeois betterment. As the nineteenth-century liberal Episcopal bishop of Massachusetts, William Lawrence, argued in 1901, "While every word that can be quoted against the rich is . . . true . . . the parables of our Lord on the stewardship of wealth, His association with the wealthy, strike another note."[7] And sometimes the worldly turn decried the new economy. In 1919 Paul Tillich, then a thirty-three-year-old Protestant pastor in Germany, wrote with his friend Carl Richard Wegener an "Answer to an Inquiry of the Protestant Consistory of Brandenburg" (1919):

> The spirit of Christian love . . . accuses the deliberate egoism of an economy . . . in which each is the enemy of the other, because his advantage is conditioned by the disadvantage or ruin of the other, and it demands an economy of solidarity of all, and of joy in work rather than in profit.[8]

Tillich was mistaken. In common with many devout and modern Christians, his argument assumes that the economy is zero-sum. The pursuit of profit—if the profit is not achieved from protections and monopolies supported by the state's monopoly of violence, monopolies greatly strengthened in socialist or regulatory states—leads to betterment for all, a joy in work serving others, a form of solidarity that has proven superior to Great Leaps Forward or Stakhanovite campaigns organized by Party officials, or for that matter Christian charity.

But anyway radical Protestantism affirmed the significance of this-world life and by 1800, for example, was recommending missionary sainthood in aid of the ordinary lives of Africans or Chinese, even among Protestants (the Catholics in the Portuguese, Spanish, and French empires had been doing it for centuries). "I'm from Protestant Christianity, and I'm here to help you." It's little wonder that, as the economic historian Robert Fogel among others has emphasized, the "third Great Awakening" of American Progressivism around 1890 was disproportionately staffed by the sons and daughters of Protestant clergymen.[9] The premise of theology, after all, whether Christian or not, is deeply that people don't know what they really want.[10] In Abrahamic religions, for example, people, as fallen creatures, want the wrong things—golden calves and the like. Thus the busybody side of American Progressivism around 1910, and its still lively temptation to put the tools of state violence into the hands of (Progressive) experts.

The preaching had changed much earlier than the nineteenth century, and so after a while the way people talked about self-interest and pleasure changed. Every Sunday in the late seventeenth century English people listened to long sermons by liberal Anglicans and liberal nonconformists to the effect, putting it crudely, that Christ died precisely so that you can pursue your self-interest. Darrin McMahon notes, "It has long been a truism of modern historiography that this shift from the happiness of heaven to the happiness of Earth was a product of the Enlightenment, the consequence of its assault on revealed religion and its own validation of secular pleasure." But, he continues, "It is also the case that the shift toward happiness on Earth occurred within the Christian tradition as well as with out."[11] And it occurred before the Enlightenment. The Anglican preacher Thomas Taylor said late in the seventeenth century, in line with the new natural theology just emerging from Newtonian and other revelations of God's infinite wisdom, "Where an appetite is universally rooted in the nature of any kind of beings we can attribute so general an effect to nothing but the Maker of those beings."[12] Joyce Appleby has shown that during the seventeenth century in England the conviction grew among formerly self-denying Protestants that capitalist betterment and consuming delight were "characteristics of human nature in general," and were therefore excused—nay, encouraged—by the Maker.[13] Charles II, who was conventionally pious (though as far from Puritan as one could get: he fathered, for example, seventeen admitted illegitimate children) inadvertently anticipated the new theological point of eudaimonism: "God would not damn a man for a little irregular pleasure."[14]

In truth the Papists had always been more relaxed about such matters. A natural-law philosophy dating back to Aquinas affirmed that commerce itself was God's natural instrument, as was desire for Nature's bounty. John Milton's seducing Comus asks, "Wherefore did Nature pour her bounties forth / With such a full and unwithdrawing hand?" (Milton 1634 [1957]; Milton did not approve.) Spanish philosophers of the sixteenth century and French and Italian philosophers of the eighteenth century anticipated many elements of Scottish political economy. In a formulation hostile to such Catholicism, the Swedish Lutheran bishop Anders Nygren, in 1930/1936 wrote:

> Luther . . . seeks to destroy . . . that [Catholic] interpretation of Caritas, which fundamentally contains more Hellenistic eros-love than primitive Christian Agape-love. . . . In Catholicism . . . the idea of acquisitive love [viz., eros] is the bond which ultimately holds the whole together. . . . Self-love is at the center here. . . . On the other hand . . . in Luther . . . God is Agape [which is to say, love for His created world, which God's grace allows to penetrate human souls]. . . . So far from self-love being a natural ordinance of God in nature, it is a devilish perversion.[15]

Something had to bend in such a Protestant orthodoxy for the broad-church and bourgeois sensibility to take hold in Europe. (Yet, as I have noted several times, there is a startling parallel to European eudaimonism in the same era in Ōsaka in Japan, and similarly in that same commercial city the rise of merchant academies with teachers professing the dignity of the bourgeoisie.) The outbreak of eudaimonism among Anglican and even nonconformist preachers may be viewed, then, as a return to Catholic orthodoxy after a century and a half of experiments with the asceticism of mild or not-so-mild yokes, among which was the non-Arminianism of orthodox Magisterial and Reformed Protestantism.

Eudaimonism is still Catholic orthodoxy.[16] The Second Vatican Council declared in 1965 that "earthly goods and human institutions according to the plan of God the Creator are also disposed for man's salvation and therefore can contribute much to the building up of the body of Christ."[17] There was nothing novel about the declaration—modern popes have repeatedly articulated it, against the evil of socialism—and one is therefore not entirely surprised to find that liberal notions of economics arose first in scholastic Spain. "Glory be to God for dappled things" is a persistent theme in Catholic Christianity, against the budge doctors of the stoic fur among Protestants. In 1329 John XXII condemned the German mystic Meister Eckhart for claiming that "God is honored in those who do not pursue anything, neither honor nor advantage, neither inner revelation nor saintliness, nor reward, nor the Kingdom of Heaven itself, but who distance themselves from all these things, as well as from all that is theirs."[18] John burned a number of such communists and declared heretical the belief that Christ and the Apostles did not have possessions.

In any case, whether eudaimonism in Protestant circles around 1700 was quite as original as it sounded to its proponents, the consequence for economic rhetoric in England, and earlier in Holland, as Margaret Jacob has argued, was large. "The most historically significant contribution of the [Anglican] latitudinarians," she writes, "lies in their ability to synthesize the operations of a market society and the workings of nature in such a way as to render the market society natural."[19] It was Anglicans, note: the place for such ideas, at least in the opinion of the English, was England around 1700, with the Colonies. Anglicans have always tried to take a third way between rigorist Calvinists and relaxed Catholics. Despite an official adherence to Lutheran and even Calvinist doctrine, the Church of England found it easy to slip back into an orthodoxy of admiring the world, especially under the properly Protestant auspices of Newtonianism. The historical sociologist Jack Goldstone, following Jacob, argues that "only in England was the new science actively preached from the pulpit (where Anglican ministers found the orderly, law-ordained universe of Newton both a model for the order they wished for their country and a convenient club with which to beat the benighted Catholic Church), sponsored in the Royal Society, and spread through popular demonstrations of mechanical devices for craftsmen and industrialists."[20]

In Spain and Italy most of the clergy, as against a tiny group of their philosophers, held back their praise for a natural life in trade. Among the Roman Catholics the eudaimonism favorable to trade-tested betterment was regularly overcome by a strictly hierarchical church governance. Notoriously the Church of Power, with few exceptions such as Liberation Theology, has sided with the government of the day, as spectacularly in French history—in contrast with the struggle against governments in the Radical Reformation. The governments did not want creative destruction if the destruction had any chance of disturbing their powers. And so Christ stopped at Eboli, and did not continue to Lucania.

All Christian churches had taught that love of riches is dangerous, such love being an idolatry that draws you away from God. It is the reason you give to the poor with an open hand, to dispose of corrupting lucre—to treat it as valueless, the way Thomas More in *Utopia* proposed to make toilet seats out of gold. The poor in this world can look toward glory in the next, while the rich must worry about the camel getting through the eye of the needle. In the nineteenth century, by contrast, under the influence of eudaimonism and Arminianism and postmillennialism from the pulpit the new sense was that the poor were corrupted by their poverty, or even that they were being punished by their poverty for their lack of bourgeois virtues. What was required for their salvation was slum clearance, missions in the cities, and campaigns of bourgeois women for temperance among the working classes, in the style of Shaw's *Major Barbara*. "Doing something," an entirely new attitude of amelioration by state action, Anthony Waterman argues, arose in the 1830s during the second cholera epidemic (the first originated in India in 1817). In particular, there was a new conviction that "cleaning up" was how to do the something.

The eudaimonistic turn was a Very Good Thing, resulting in fresh projects to better our stay here on earth, some of them unhappy (Prohibition, for example) but others remarkably successful. Democracy was one. If you followed the new fashion for universal happiness it became impossible to go on insisting that what really mattered was the will and pleasure of the Marquis of Salisbury or the Lord Bishop of Salzburg. Enlightened despots of the era

claimed to seek the good of all. The claim had the unintended result of im-
planting in the populace the thought that perhaps they could seek the good
for themselves, without the kind assistance of Louis or Frederick or Catherine or Joseph. The shift resulted at last in a politically effective concern for
the good of all, here and now.

Theology, I say again, mattered. When Francis Bacon called for modern
science "for the glory of the Creator and the relief of man's estate," he was
not kidding. Nor was the Royal Society kidding when in 1663 it dedicated
itself to the glory of God the creator. The economist and theologian Paul
Oslington notes that "a project of reading God's nature from creation" was
the framework for British thought generally for a century and a half down
to 1830, "a project in which most of the major figures in what we would now
call British science participated, including Francis Bacon, John Ray, Robert
Boyle, and Isaac Newton."[21]

A "postmillennial" eschatology (eschatology being the study of the last
thing, the *eschaton*) is viewed as plain heresy by Roman Catholics and to this
day elicits smiles from European theologians. Dating to the Westminster
Confession of 1646, it emerged vigorously in the American colonies, most
prominently in a 1739 sermon by Jonathan Edwards. When the Antichrist
(viz., that same Roman Catholicism) falls, Edwards declared, "the principal
fulfillment of all the prophecies of the Old Testament [will take place] which
speak of the glorious times. . . . Then shall all the world be united in one
amiable society. . . . [It] will be a time of the greatest temporal prosperity. . . .
Even the days of Solomon were an [imperfect] image of those days, as to the
temporal prosperity which shall obtain in them."[22] The "millennial" term of
years was by then conventionally based on a text in Revelations (20:4): "they
lived and reigned with Christ a thousand years" (quoted in Edwards, p. 353,
with uncharacteristic diffidence: "On this I shall be brief"). In postmillennialism Christ does not judge the living and the dead until *after* (thus "post")
the thousand cleansing years of the Good Society.

MacCulloch remarks that postmillennialism "was an exhilarating idea,
which bound those in its grip to begin activist efforts to improve society, . . . and it suggested a special destiny for the thirteen colonies. . . . The
mood has never fully left America," the self-described City on the Hill.[23] The
enchanted sense which Christians (and Jews, especially the Hasidim) had
that at any moment the world might end—which yielded a fatalism that
St. Paul railed against in his letters—was replaced with a practical project to

do good now. The kingdom of God can be encouraged on earth. And after a thousand years of gradual perfection in a bourgeois, temperate, and responsible way, in contrast to medieval notions of a Land of Cockaigne suddenly bursting upon us, the world ends. Christ has died, Christ has risen, and—if we work hard on earth at being proper neo-Israelites, or in a later version at merely being good to each other—Christ will come again.

By the nineteenth and the early twentieth centuries in the United States the "social Christians," professing postmillennialism, dominated the mainline Protestant churches, in the figures of Harry Emerson Fosdick, Walter Rauschenbusch (the grandfather of the liberal philosopher Richard Rorty), the Niebuhr brothers, and at length, from Germany, Paul Tillich. They merged with earlier British Christian socialists and were able "to accept [the English Christian socialists after the 1830s], [F. D.] Maurice and [Frederick W.] Robertson, almost as their own," since "their ideas blended so well with the predominant postmillennialism of Protestant thinking in America."[24]

Politics itself came to care about the progress of ordinary people, as against eternal salvation or the prerogative of kings. Turgot's lecture on progress in 1750 was delivered from a *theological* chair, as *Prieur of the Maison de la Sorbonne*. Robert Nisbet called it the "the first . . . secular . . . statement of the 'modern' idea of progress."[25] A shockingly high percentage of the English betterers of machines and procedures were Unitarians, and of the businessmen, Quakers—shocking because both groups were extremely small. In such advanced and liberal Protestantism a theology of salvation is replaced by a theology of human betterment, as in the Lockean ideas of life, liberty, and the pursuit of happiness. Its early fruit is the abolition of slavery, from the Quaker John Newton's "Amazing Grace" to the progressive Presbyterian Julia Ward Howe's "Battle Hymn of the Republic."

The resulting notions of "natural" human, economic liberty of the French Physiocrats and Adam Smith took a long time to become the default logic of even the elite. Smith was anticipated in Spain, I have noted, and many of his ideas were invented independently by contemporaries such as the Swede Anders Chydenius (1729–1803) and less radically by Antonio Genovesi (1712–1769) in Naples and Cesare Beccaria (1738–1794) in Milan. The recent upwelling of protectionist and anti-immigrant passion in Europe and the United States shows that natural economic liberty has still not become entirely the default. Waterman has argued that until well into the nineteenth century even the policy wonks did not think in Smithian ways, even in "free-trade" Britain. The economic historian John Nye has argued persuasively, indeed, that France was more devoted to free trade than one might have thought. And decades ago I myself argued that the move to lower UK tariffs on imports had as much to do with accidents of public finance as with a free-trade ideology.[26]

Up to the present, Waterman notes, Christians and socialists and especially Christian socialists, rather than admiring what we economists think lovely, the delightful "spontaneous order" arising from a revaluation of autonomy, hold fast to an older and organic view of society—sadly embodied, for example, in a book that Waterman and I in most respects admire, the Anglican *Book of Common Prayer*.[27] "Take away all hatred and prejudice, and whatever else may hinder us from godly union," the 1662 version pleads in a Prayer for Unity, "as there is but one Body, and one Spirit . . . one God and Father of us all; so we may henceforth be all of one heart . . . and may with one mind and one mouth glorify thee," with Charles II at the head.[28] Such an illiberal vision, sweet though it has sounded to conservatives and socialists, had to be contradicted, and in some Christian circles it was.

41

PRINTING AND READING AND FRAGMENTATION SUSTAINED THE DIGNITY OF COMMONERS

Printing was invented in China, not by Gutenberg. We have numerous Chinese printed books from a thousand years ago on paper, when the backward Europeans were still copying out by hand on animal skins "twenty bookes, clad in blak or reed." True, the great number of Chinese characters rendered moveable type awkward, if just possible. (Koreans invented an alphabet in 1644, but the prestige of Chinese culture restrained its use.) The printing ordered by the Chinese emperor in 1725 of merely sixty-six copies of a 5,020-volume encyclopedia, the *Gujin Tushu Jicheng* (Complete Collection of Illustrations and Writings from the Earliest to Current Times) involved 250,000 movable type characters cast in bronze (or so the modern version of the French *Encyclopédie*, Wikipedia, claims). What is striking and is not in doubt, as Mokyr has stressed, is the shockingly small number of copies made—some twenty only, as Mokyr says, or sixty-six according to the savants at Wikipedia. Anyway the number is in startling contrast to the later (though much smaller) French *Encyclopédie, ou dictionnaire raisonné des sciences, des arts et des métiers* (1751–1772), whose initial print run was over four thousand and whose eventual circulation, up to the French Revolution, of about twenty-five thousand put a copy within reach of every fully literate person in Europe.[1]

The printing machine, then, was important. Europeans who pressed olives or grapes in fact had a good deal of helpful experience with a similar machine. True, most inventions that we once confidently claimed for Europe, such as stirrups, the mold-board plow, the blast furnace, have long been shown to be Chinese. But in one technology relevant to printing, optics, Europeans really did have an edge on other civilizations, as the later European excellence in telescopes and microscopes showed again. One of the handful of uniquely European inventions before 1600, eyeglasses, did matter mightily to the eventual spread of reading the print. David Landes pointed out in 1998 that eyeglasses extended the working life of detail crafts-men. The inevitable long-sightedness of humans after age forty or so was offset.[2] And therefore it allowed middle-aged people to go on reading the material that poured out of the presses of Europe after Gutenberg, some of which was impolite to the regulating powers and suggestive that ordinary folk could have a go.

The first use of a slightly free press was religious. Among the first profit-able texts to come from Gutenberg's press, ironically, were fill-in-the-blank forms for the very indulgences (that is, time off in Purgatory) whose pro-lific selling in the 1510s to finance the beginnings of Julius II's Basilica of St. Peter's in Rome, and Michelangelo's painting in the Sistine Chapel (irony upon irony), outraged Martin Luther, the success of whose Reformation depended on . . . the printing press.[3] The Church of Faith had earlier and repeatedly challenged the Church of Power—for example, the Henricians from the 1110s, the Cathars from the 1140s, the Waldensians from the 1170s, the Lollards from the 1380s—but failed in a Europe without printing and its widening of literacy. The economic historian Jared Rubin has shown a pow-erful effect on the Reformation of closeness to printing presses.[4]

Literacy was encouraged by the relatively if not absolutely free presses of northern Protestantism. On August 18, 1520, the press of Melchior Lotther at Wittenberg issued four thousand copies of, as Luther put it, a "broadside to [the Emperor] Charles and the nobility of Germany against the tyranny and baseness of the Roman curia," *To the Christian Nobility of the German Nation*. The next week the press issued over four thousand more of a longer version.[5] Between 1517 and 1520 were printed some *three hundred thousand* copies of Luther's work—not twenty or sixty-six.[6] Had Emperor Charles V or Pope Leo X been able to exercise the sort of control over the presses of Germany that the Qianlong emperor of China or Suleiman the Magnificent of the Otto-mans could, the outcome in Europe's economy would have been different.

By 1536 William Tyndale's vigorous translation of the New Testament into English (the King James Bible was based on his version of both testaments) was circulating in some sixteen thousand copies, one for every two thou-sand English people. A translation based on Tyndale was ordered in 1538 by Henry VIII to be placed in every parish church.[7] (Tyndale had been executed in Brussels two years earlier. Writing, translating, and printing were still dangerous trades.) The printing and especially the reading of bibles in the vernacular confirmed Tyndale's angry boast to an orthodox opponent: "I will cause the boy that drives the plow to know more of the scriptures than you." And it came to pass, leading on to secular writing and reading and printing, and revolution.

For such revolutionary effects, the press had to be adequately free. Before the printing press, what the few readers could read had not much attracted the attention of the authorities. Even afterward there was not much for the state to worry about if it was published in Latin. But with publication in German and English and French and the rest, the European state sprung to attention—though unable by international standards to dam the flood. Censorship in the Chinese Empire was routine and thorough, such as in the eighteenth century executing a man and enslaving his entire family for the crime of printing the character for the emperor's name. So late as 1834 a Japanese writer who issued a pamphlet recommending the opening of the country was arrested and forced to commit suicide.[8] For the Ottomans, as Metin Coşgel, Thomas Miceli, and Jared Rubin have noted, there was a nearly three-century delay after Gutenberg, until 1727, in allowing books to be printed in Turkish (in the Arabic alphabet), and a century longer till printing was permitted in Arabic itself. Yet the Ottomans adopted gunpowder with lightning speed.[9] That is, it was not sheer, stupid conservatism but successful state control that kept the presses shuttered. Revealingly, non-Turkish and non-Arabic groups in the Ottoman Empire were free to publish. The empire allowed Salonika to become a center for publishing in Hebrew, Aramaic, and Ladino a mere fifty years after Gutenberg. What did it matter, the Ottoman elite probably reflected, so long as the mass of Turkish- and Arabic-speaking subjects did not have access to novel ideas of governance?

European elites after Gutenberg well understood the value of restricting reading, if they could manage it. Until the seventeenth century, and even afterward to some degree, publishing was unfree even in England. In 1579 Queen Elizabeth, outraged by a pamphlet written by the Puritan John Stubbs attacking her negotiations for marriage into the (Catholic) French royal family, had his right hand struck off by a cleaver, the cleaver hammered through his wrist with a croquet mallet—after which he removed his hat with his left hand and shouted "God save the Queen!" In the Stubbs case the law invoked was an arguably obsolete one referring to the former Queen Mary's husband, not a claim to a routine right to censor all publications.[10] Grave matters of national survival, the historian Cyndia Clegg notes, hung on the long dalliance of Elizabeth with the heirs to the French and other thrones. The time was, after all, before the famous victory Elizabeth predicted over the forces of the Armada.

In England the censorship of the theater—easy to do until the age of electronic reproduction because a theater was in the public and in one place—waxed and waned from Elizabethan times, depending on epidemics in London and the fortunes of Puritanism. The morality plays of late medieval times, such as the York Cycle, had been suppressed under Elizabeth, as papist in tone.[11] Censorship of the English theater, episodic before 1642, after which Cromwell the Puritan closed the theaters entirely, did not survive the Restoration, yet was brought back for good in 1737 by Walpole indignant at a Fielding play. Censorship of the theater then held sway in the land of our first liberties, astonishingly, until 1968. Or consider, in the land of our second liberties, the Motion Picture Code, which constrained Hollywood from 1930 to 1968 to portray married couples as sleeping in twin beds and, if sleeping, doing so alone. Note the ending year in both cases: 1968 and liberty.

Yet Clegg has argued about this and other Elizabethan cases that English censorship was clumsily unsystematic, and anyway was necessarily a novelty, like the Chinese or Singapore governments nowadays trying to keep ahead of an evolving technology of the Internet.[12] The truth is that by comparison with effective censorships further east, the failure of the various projects of centralizing the European subcontinent, from Charlemagne through the medieval popes to Phillip II and at last Napoleon and Hitler, doomed European censorship to only sporadic success. From the Vatican's Index of Forbidden Books in 1559 down to British prosecutions under the Official Secrets Act, censorship was undermined by publication in other jurisdictions in fragmented Europe, first Venice and then Basel and Holland, and by smuggling the resulting product. Remember the *Chatterley* ban, or *The Tropic of Cancer*. In parts of Europe, beginning in Poland and the Netherlands, the censors therefore lost their power, if ever they had it. By 1600 the Dutch had taken over from the Venetians the role of unrestricted publishers of Europe, publishing the books of heretics like Baruch Spinoza in Latin, John Locke in English, and Pierre Bayle in French, not to mention pornography in whatever language would sell.

French censorship in the eighteenth century was increasingly hysterical, perhaps because the leaky French borders meant it never worked. Voltaire's *Philosophical Letters* were publicly burned in 1733, after which many of the *philosophes* felt the hand of state and church. Montesquieu's *Spirit of the Laws* was published in his old age in 1748 in Switzerland, and smuggled into France. After 1832 Louis Philippe enacted laws against cartoons making fun of his pearlike visage and the corruptions of his régime. The French instead purchased their cartoons abroad, continuing to make merry of the Bourgeois King, and at length toppled his throne.

The merchant was portrayed in early modern paintings with ink-stained fingers, since a merchant had to be literate in his account books and had to be a writer of letters giving and getting economically valuable information. The bourgeoisie had long used written letters as news, of price currents or whatever; and letter-carrying improved in the sixteenth and especially the seventeenth centuries. The improved post created a Republic of Letters, in which a remote Benjamin Franklin could enter into scientific correspondence with Julien-David LeRoy in France. It was combined with the grammar-school movement in places like England and France and Poland, which allowed the spread of Latin as a lingua franca beyond the high clergy.

The uncontrolled printing presses in Europe eventually made for "news," on the model of the merchant's letter. The periodical newspaper was invented early in the seventeenth century, first in fragmented Germany, then slowly spreading to more unified polities with stronger censors. The wide distribution of newspapers awaited the coffeehouse circa 1680. London had by 1700 several hundred coffeehouses.[13] English juries during the eighteenth century would not convict in prosecutions for "seditious libel," and so the English authorities gave up trying. In the age of letterpress printing confined to small press runs, however, the same authorities quickly devised a financial substitute for censorship. Daniel Defoe was *paid* to write his *Review* by the politicians, and Walpole bought up newspapers to transmit the party line. By 1792 the British government of the day owned secretly over half of the press.[14] So much for a Fourth Estate standing guard.

And yet in a nineteenth century of cheap paper and massive steam presses capable of hundred-thousand-copy runs, compliments of the Great Enrichment itself, the newspapers gave up their business plan of personal extortion and political corruption and began to rely on advertising. The newspaper became by commercial means something approximating the noble forum it had long claimed to be, or at least, as the communication scholars Kevin Barnhurst and John Narone put it, a department store of ideas.[15] The roiling ideas of the modern world were purchased at the store, and European governments couldn't do much to stop the sales.

The professor of English Blaine Greteman at the University of Iowa, analyzing the (often Latin) letters of John Milton in the 1630s and 1640s, contradicts the Romantic notion of Milton as a lonely poet in a garret writing merely to the starry heavens. On the contrary, Milton wrote for a large community bound by weak ties of letter-carrying and tract-printing, tightened by the cheapening of paper (as Greteman puts it, "Milton would not have written as many letters if he had to write on vellum," that is, on parchment from the skin of young animals[16]). Greteman is applying here the point the sociologist Mark Granovetter made in 1973, that if you speak only to your family and friends in an inner circle of strong ties, your speech will not reach far, since there is not much *news* among close friends—your mother has anyway heard the same item from your sister and your next-door neighbor, just now (*iam iam*, as Greteman notes in Milton's Latin). But if you have a wide circle of *weak* ties—say 1,063 "friends" on Facebook—then the news, less reliant on the same few sources, sustains its novelty, and therefore its information content, over a greater social distance.

What is obvious about the Gutenberg Galaxy is that it greatly multiplies the weak ties of book-reading, and eventually, in the very late seventeenth century, the widening of newspaper-reading. The strong ties of church and aristocracy and "nations" abroad (the Lombards, for example, of a street in London, or in Venice the house of the Germans by the Rialto Bridge) did not make for a complete network—its incompleteness being, for the maintenance of elite power, rather the point. Removing ties one by one will eventually result in a network collapsing entirely, in the precise sense that after collapse not all people can reach each other by, say, six degrees of separation—you can't get there from here. You won't be able in 1520 to read Luther's *Address to the Christian Nobility of the German Nation*. You won't be able in the early seventeenth century to get news of Galileo's findings. You won't be able in 1647 to hear by word of mouth of the radical democratic ideas articulated in the Putney Debates (which, I repeat, were not in fact published, so terrifying was the articulation of democratic ideas: links can be broken on purpose). Or to take a recent example, you won't be able to elude the riot police in Cairo early in the Arab Spring.

Recent mathematical modeling by a group of physicists and engineers applies the notion of weak ties to the spread of the Black Death across Europe.[17] If links are broken, then disease, trade, information, religious novelties, and political ideas spread more slowly. Their historical point, and mine, is that the spread began with improved trade and communication, and accelerated with each betterment—such as printing and its uncensored spread.

Are strong ties or weak ties the most important for maintaining a social network? According to a Finnish study, just as Granovetter argued in 1973, the weak ties are what matter most for maintaining a complete and therefore democratic network in which dignity is accorded to every link of gossip. In a simulation based on comprehensive data on 4.6 million cell-phone users in Finland over several months, removing *strong* ties results in a shrinkage of the whole network but not in sudden collapse. Yet removing the *weak* ties that bind one family or office (say) with another causes, at 60 percent removal, "a sudden, phase transition-driven collapse of the whole network."[18] The researchers remark that "this finding is somewhat unexpected, because in most technological and biological networks the strong ties are believed to play a more important structural role than the weak ties, and in such systems the removal of the strong ties leads to the network's collapse." If you remove one connecting gear in a watch it immediately stops. If you stab someone in the heart she immediately dies. The theory of strategic bombing is based on the watch or heart analogy. It has not worked well because numerous weak ties are characteristic of trading societies, and most societies are trading societies. Killing a network of human communication happens only with the blocking of 60 percent of the lightly traveled roads, the closing of 60 percent of the less popular printing presses—not by deadly censorship in, say, a strongly tied royal court, or shaming within a tightly knit family. It takes an artificial extension of strong ties by a strong state intent on censorship to suppress the rumors of a free society. The Tokugawa régime in seventeenth-century Japan had to destroy thousands of bridges if it was going to check passports effectively at the few remaining ones (it did). With perhaps a similar purpose in mind, it banned (of all things) wheeled vehicles. And it insisted on a Versailles-type centralization of the aristocracy in Edo to strengthen the ties to the shogun.

The claim is that literacy and printing resulted in a wide conversation of betterment in western Europe. "Books have always a secret influence on the understanding; we cannot at pleasure obliterate ideas," said Dr. Johnson.[19] Such is the theme of a book by the literary critic Stephen Greenblatt, *The Swerve: How the World Became Modern* (2011). Greenblatt argues that a book with a secret influence on the Renaissance and through it the modern world was Lucretius's philosophical poem of circa 54 BCE, *De Rerum Natura*, "on the nature of things." Rediscovered and printed, he claims it transformed European thinking. The books, the paper, the newspaper, the post, the coffeehouse, the salon, the discussion group, the royal academies created a society in Europe approximating Jürgen Habermas's "ideal speech situation" or Hayek's "utilization of knowledge which is and remains widely dispersed among individuals."[20] Talk made us modern, and rich.

Cooperation by conversation sprang up below the level of the high-level intellectuality of the Birmingham Lunar Society, such as the young Benjamin Franklin's junto of craftsmen in 1727, or a case in a village in Gloucestershire in the mid-eighteenth century in which Jonathan Hulls, a grammar-school graduate whose occupations included farmer, clock repairer, joiner, and mechanic, got together with a schoolmaster and a maltster to write handbooks such as *The Trader's Guide*. Hulls patented a paddleboat driven by steam, though it failed on trial.[21] The community of engineers and instrument makers in the eighteenth century communicated. It was largely open source, as the economic historian Robert Allen argued long ago and as Margaret Jacob has shown recently in detail.[22] Wedgwood opposed patents, and had only one patent himself. He was the first of many open-source inventors.[23] His grandson was Charles Darwin, whose other grandfather was Erasmus Darwin the naturalist, a member with Wedgwood of the Lunar Society. Out of open-source discussion the Great Enrichment and modern science came. The problem in making the atom bomb or in curing cancer is sustaining communication among scores of intellectual communities. The communication is obviously killed by secrecy—whether trade secrets or military secrets. That was the earlier mode. But it is also killed by hierarchy, pride, and bad techniques of physical communication (status differentials, high transport costs, bad mails).

Yet it is often claimed that a modern city, nourishing and nourished by the Great Enrichment, is fatally unable to form connections. The claim is part of the almost universal belief that trading somehow damages intimacy. Neither seems to be true, and both are versions of the pastoral. The leader of the Chicago School of urban sociology, Robert Park, offered with his colleagues the conventional antimodern analysis in 1925: "A newspaper cannot do for a community of 1,000,000 inhabitants what the village did spontaneously for itself [but wait: little American cow towns would have four newspapers] through the medium of gossip and personal contact."[24] Who says? The high velocity of time-space has in fact enriched locality and intimacy. By contrast with the Orwellian loudspeaker, the Internet is democratic, like the printing press and the improved post. Communication with its rhetoric is central to modernity. By 1650 Cromwell was writing to Walter Dundas, who had articulated the case against the resulting freedom of opinion, "Your pretended fear lest error should step in, is like the man that would keep all the wine out of the country lest men should be drunk. It will be found an unjust and unwise jealousy, to deny a man the liberty he hath by nature upon a supposition that he may abuse it."[25]

But China and the Ottoman Empire and the rest also had good communication. Why the difference in outcome? The answer has been suggested already: Europe's political fragmentation,

It has long been plausibly argued that in Europe the competing states, as William McNeill and many others such as Alan Macfarlane and Eric Jones and Jean Baechler have stressed, made for a certain intellectual and therefore economic freedom. "The expansion of capitalism," wrote Baechler in 1971, "owes its origins and raison d'être to political anarchy."[26] "The plurality of small states in Europe," Macfarlane argues, "autonomous but linked by a common history, religion, and elite language, almost incessantly at war and, when not at war, in fierce cultural and social competition, was the ideal context for rapid productive and ideological evolution."[27] "In purely dialectical fashion," wrote Mokyr in 2002, following a logic devised by Schumpeter, "technological progress creates [vested interests] that eventually destroy it. . . . For a set of fragmented and open economies . . . this result does not hold."[28] Think of the Reading of print, the Reformation, the glories of a Dutch Revolt beset on every side—three of the Four Rs. Open source.

In the way that American cities and states compete for corporate headquarters—the Tiebout Effect I've mentioned—the Spanish crown in the

1490s competed with France, Portugal, England, and the Dukedom of Medina Celi for the services of Christoforo Columbo, admittedly in a competition less than fierce. John Cabot the English explorer for Henry VII of England was Giovanni Caboti of Genoa and Venice. He had hawked his project for the Northwest Passage around Europe. Henry Hudson did two voyages for the English Muscovy Company, but his third for the Dutch East India Company, and his fourth and last, after being arrested for going over to the Dutch, for another English company. As McNeill observes, "The European state system was crucial in preventing the takeover of mercantile wealth by bureaucratic authority in the way Chinese, Mughal, and Ottoman officials were able to do as a matter of course."[29] I would add Tokugawa Japanese officials to the list of bureaucratic authorities, and would worry nowadays about European Community and American Federal officials, too.

In China and the Ottoman Empire an invention was secret and monopolized and under suspicion. An anarchic fragmentation makes kings eager to innovate in *military* technology.[30] "Innovate or die" in such a case is to be taken literally. A unified polity, on the other hand, can scorn such betterment—unless indeed the Mongols or the Turks armed with cannon are knocking, or shooting, at the door. In nonmilitary technology the sultan was as likely to jail an inventor as to reward him for his trouble. In 1603 the level of Japanese technology was equal to that of Western Europe, and in some matters—musket making, perhaps, and certainly carpentry—it was superior. Geoffrey Parker argues that the reason the Far Eastern powers were not victims in the sixteenth and seventeenth centuries of Europe's "military revolution"—cannon-proof fortifications and volley firing of muskets—is that they had already had the revolution—in Japan's case decades and in China's centuries before.[31] Yet by 1800 Japan, after nearly two centuries of artificial isolation, and despite a trickle of "Dutch learning" into the country, was a century behind. Around 1600 Western mathematics embarked on two centuries of betterment in the solution of actual physical problems, such as the pendulum or the arc of a cannonball, at the same time that Japanese mathematics became as ornamental as Western mathematics became after 1800.[32]

The negotiations 1646–1648 for the Peace of Westphalia bringing an end to the Thirty Years War involved fully 156 political entities, only 16 of which were nation-states of a usual and modern form. The treaty indeed gave force to the convention of "sovereignty" in international law, the principle that internal affairs of states were their own business—a principle that a century before would have been thought absurd.[33] The historian of China Kenneth Pomeranz asks in a forthcoming book why China is so big, answering the question with reference to ideas—public rhetoric, ideology. In the way the Roman Empire was held together for centuries by an ideology of *Civis Romanus sum*, and so too the Han Chinese insisted on their unity. The *Romance of the Three Kingdoms*, one of the four great novels of the Chinese tradition, was written during the fourteenth century about the painful remaking of China into one from three in 280 CE. Its opening line asserts, "It is a general truism of this world that anything long divided will surely unite, and anything long united will surely divide."

No one, as many historians have noted, and I have repeated, was able to impose such unity on Europe, from Charlemagne to Hitler—and the notion of European citizenship is viewed with alarm or contempt by many Europeans even in the twenty-first century. In the sixteenth century the Dutch, for example, forcibly opted out of Charles V's and Philip II's vision of a Habsburg Europe, in a way that, say, Shanghai (as Pomeranz points out), which was similarly milked for the support of the rest of the empire, never succeeded in doing.

The sociological historian and political scientist Erik Ringmar correctly insists, in accord with recent scholarship challenging nineteenth-century orientalizing clichés about the Mysterious East with its supposedly kowtowing populations and hydraulic civilizations, that "Chinese and European societies were always very similar to each other and this was still the case as comparatively late as in the early eighteenth century."[34] Still, the failures of Charlemagne and his successor-unifiers contrasts with the successes of long-lasting Chinese dynasties, with breakdowns startlingly rare by Europe's tumultuous standard, repeatedly unifying an area the size of Western Europe from the first emperor of 212 BCE. Europe was odd politically because of its incompetence in making and holding empires within Europe itself, as also was South Asia and Africa. China is the outlier here.

Ringmar's argument keeps coming back to the fragmentation of states in Europe, as against China's empire: "in Europe, by contrast, power was always divided"; "the existence of a plurality of [Europe] states who all called themselves sovereign placed some very real limits on their independence";

"a [Chinese] state monopoly on foreign trade was put in place as early as the
fourteenth century and from this time onward commerce has periodically
been halted"; "periods of chaos [in China] were periods of fragmentation
when it was impossible to impose a single political framework. . . . This allowed . . . more political, social and cultural experiments. . . . The Warring
States period [for example] . . . was an extraordinarily creative period in
Chinese history"; (in China) "the idea of *pluribus unum* was never properly
institutionalized. . . . The different [temporary] states . . . did not come to
interact in a mutually counter-balancing system of states. Instead hegemony
imposed itself."[35]

On a smaller scale the logic of small-is-beautiful-for-betterment works
too. The relative lack of national regulation in England and then Britain,
aside from external tariffs, and the exposure of individual cities to the competition of other cities, was good for toleration, I have noted, as it was for
betterment. When the Kingdom of the Netherlands was founded in 1815 the
intercity competition that had been so fruitful in liberties and betterments
began to be suppressed. No wonder the Netherlands was slow to industrialize. The newly unified country became infected with many hundreds of
national cartels enforceable at law, down to the present.

The logic applies recently, too. In the 1980s, early in the history of the
Common Market, the economist Victoria Curzon Price has pointed out,
"competition among regulators" worked well for consumer choice, forcing
producers to compete in the quality/cost space. After 1985, however, Europe-
wide standards (with "qualified majority voting") started the avalanche of
regulations emanating from Brussels, declaring, say, Cadbury's chocolate to
be "not chocolate" or unpasteurized Italian cheeses to be illegal. Industrial
lobbying by the "gold-plated" producers, as Curzon Price puts it, produced
by regulatory capture in the Common Market, as in the Netherlands after
1815 or in the United States after the Supreme Court decisions on regulation,
a "level playing field"—instead of Italian cheese made under Italian regulations competing freely with French cheese made under French regulations.
Curzon Price puts forward a diagram of Quality (which is a good, however
measured) versus Cost (a bad), and a frontier of opportunities therefore
sloping upward. When the playing field is not leveled by Europe-wide regulation, there are numerous combinations of Quality and Cost. Individual
consumers can choose what is best for each of them. By contrast, Brussels
forces *one* combination, good for the gold-plated companies and the richer

countries but making it impossible for Greece or Romania to compete by offering low Quality at a low Cost. Centralization against competition protects Germany and France. European industry has adapted to the Common Market regulations, frozen in old standards now hard to change, which has led to productive sclerosis. Free-flowing commerce had come after 1800 from Europe's fragmentation, when the blockage from local and then national mercantilism had been overcome.

A cheery confidence in the obvious and simple system of natural liberty through the free press and Europe's porous polities was utterly novel in early modern times, tried out tentatively in Poland and Holland in the sixteenth century, and in post–Civil War England and later in Scotland and the English colonies in North America. Astonishingly, it worked, for liberty and dignity and the Great Enrichment.

POLITICAL IDEAS MATTERED FOR
EQUAL LIBERTY AND DIGNITY

"One history of Western politics," writes the political philosopher Mika LaVaque-Manty, citing Charles Taylor and Peter Berger (he could have cited most European writers on the matter from Locke and Voltaire and Woll-stonecraft through Tocqueville and Arendt and Rawls), "has it that under modernity, equal dignity has replaced positional honor as the ground on which individuals' political status rests":

> Now, the story goes, the dignity which I have by virtue of nothing more than my humanity gives me both standing as a citizen vis-à-vis the state and a claim to respect from others. Earlier, my political status would have depended, first, on who I was (more respect for the well-born, less for the lower orders) and also on how well I acquitted myself as that sort of person. In rough outline, the story is correct.[1]

Article 3 of the Italian Constitution adopted in 1948 (and later much revised, but not in this article) is typical: "All the citizens have equal social dignity and are equal before the law, without distinctions of sex, of race, of language, of religion, of political opinion, of personal and social position."[2]

"But," LaVaque-Manty continues, "there are important complications to it." One important complication is that Europeans used their older and existing values to argue for new ones. Humans do. LaVaque-Manty observes that "aristocratic social practices and values themselves get used to ground and shape modernity"—he argues that the strange egalitarianism of early modern dueling by *non*-aristocrats was a case in point. Likewise a wholesale merchant in Ibsen's *Pillars of Society* (1877) clinches a deal by reference to his (noble) Viking ancestors: "It's settled, Bernick! A Norseman's word stands firm as a rock, you know that!"[3] An American businessman will use the myth of the cowboy for similar assurances. Likewise Christian social practices and values got used to ground and shape modernity, such as the amplification of Abrahamic individualism before God, then the social gospel and Catholic social teaching, then socialism out of religious doctrines of charity and environmentalism out of religious doctrines of stewardship. And European intellectual practices and values—in the medieval universities (imitated from the Arab world) and in the royal societies of the seventeenth century, and again in the Humboldtian modern university, all founded on principles of intellectual hierarchy—get used later to raise the dignity of any arguer. Witness the blogosphere.

The for-a-while uniquely European ideas of individual liberty for all free men—and at length, startlingly (and to the continuing distress of some conservatives) for slaves and women and young people and sexual minorities and handicapped people and immigrants—was generalized from much older bourgeois liberties granted town by town. Tom Paine wrote in *The Age of Reason*, "Give to every other human being every right that you claim for yourself—that is my doctrine." Such was not the doctrine of many other people when Paine articulated it in 1794 and 1807. Now it is universal, at any rate in declaration. Though North, Weingast, and Wallis are attached to what they regard as materialist explanations for it, they are wise to interpret the transition from what they call "limited access" to "open access" societies as a shift from personal power for the Duke of Norfolk to impersonal power for Tom, Dick, and Harriet: "The relations within the dominant coalition transform from person to particular to general." Think of the Magna Carta for all barons and charters for all citizens of a city, and finally "all men are created equal."

The doctrinal change might have happened earlier, and in other parts of the world. But it didn't. The narrow focus of North, Wallis, and Weingast on England, France, and the USA obscures the ubiquity of what they call "doorstep conditions"—the rule of law applied even to elites, perpetually lived institutions, and consolidation of the state's monopoly of violence. Such conditions characterize scores of societies, from ancient Israel to the Roman Republic, Song China, and Tokugawa Japan, none of which experienced a Great Enrichment.[4] Alfred Reckendree has pointed out that just such conditions characterized Weimar Germany, which failed for lack of ethics.[5] In a recent history with a wider scope than England, France, and the USA, the volume's editor Larry Neal nonetheless offers a definition of "capitalism" as (1) private property rights, (2) contracts enforceable by third parties, (3) markets with responsive prices, and (4) supportive governments.[6] He does not appear to realize that the first three conditions have applied to every human society. They can be found in pre-Columbian Mayan marketplaces and Aboriginal trade gatherings. "Capitalism" in this sense did not "rise." The fourth condition, "supportive governments," is precisely the doctrinal change to laissez faire unique to northwestern Europe. What did "rise" as a result was not trade itself but trade-tested betterment. The idea of equality of liberty and dignity for all humans caused, and then protected, a startling material and then spiritual progress. What was crucial in Europe and its offshoots was the new economic liberty and social dignity for the swelling bourgeois segment of commoners, encouraged after 1700 in England and especially after 1800 on a wider scale to perform massive betterments, the discovery of new ways of doing things tested by increasingly free trade.

The second element, universal dignity—the social honoring of all people—was necessary in the long run, to encourage people to enter new trades and to protect their economic liberty to do so. The testing countercase is European Jewry down to 1945, gradually liberated to have a go in Holland in the seventeenth century and Britain in the eighteenth century and Germany and the rest later. Legally speaking, from Ireland to the Austrian Empire by 1900 any Jew could enter any profession, take up any innovative idea. But in many parts of Europe he was never granted the other, sociological half of the encouragement to betterment, the dignity that protects the liberty. "Society, confronted with political, economic, and legal equality for Jews," wrote Arendt, "made it quite clear that none of its classes was prepared to grant them social equality.... Social pariahs the Jews did become wherever they had ceased to be political and civil outcasts."[7] True, Benjamin Disraeli became prime minister of the United Kingdom in 1868, Lewis Wormeer Harris was elected Lord Mayor of Dublin in 1876, and Louis Brandeis became an associate justice of the U.S. Supreme Court in 1916. Yet in Germany after 1933 few gentile doctors or professors resisted the expulsion of Jews from their ranks. The Jews were undignified. In much of Christendom—with partial exceptions in the United States and the United Kingdom, and in Denmark and Bulgaria—they were political and social outcasts.

Liberty and dignity for all commoners, to be sure, was a double-sided political and social ideal, and did not work without flaw. History has many cunning passages, contrived corridors. The liberty of the bourgeoisie to venture was matched by the liberty of the workers, when they got the vote, to adopt growth-killing regulations, with a socialist clerisy cheering them on. And the dignity of workers was overmatched by an arrogance among successful entrepreneurs and wealthy rentiers, with a fascist clerisy cheering them on. Such are the usual tensions of liberal democracy. And such are the often mischievous dogmas of the clerisy.

But for the first time, thank God—and thank the Levellers and then Locke in the seventeenth century, and Voltaire and Smith and Franklin and Paine and Wollstonecraft among other of the advanced thinkers in the eighteenth century—the ordinary people, the commoners, both workers and bosses, began to be released from the ancient notion of hierarchy, the naturalization of the noble gentleman's rule over *hoi polloi*. Aristotle had said that most people were born to be slaves. "From the hour of their birth, some are marked out for subjection, others for rule."[8] Bishop (and Saint) Isidore of Seville said in the early seventh century that "to those unsuitable for liberty, [God] has mercifully accorded servitude."[9] So it had been from the first times of settled agriculture and the ownership of land. Inherited wealth was long thought blameless compared with earned wealth, about which suspicion hung.[10] Consider South Asia with its ancient castes, the hardest workers at the bottom. And further east consider the Confucian tradition (if not in every detail the ideas of Kung the Teacher himself), which stressed the Five Relationships of ruler to subject, father to son, husband to wife, elder brother to younger, and—the only one of the five without hierarchy—friend to friend. The analogy of the king as father of the nation, and therefore "naturally" superior, ruled political thought in the West (and the East and North and South) right through Hobbes. King Charles I of England, of whom Hobbes approved, was articulating nothing but a universal and ancient notion when, as I've noted, he declared in his speech from the scaffold in 1649 that kings and subjects are categorically different.[11]

But the analogy of natural fathers to natural kings and natural aristocracies commenced about then, gradually, to seem to some of the bolder thinkers less obvious. Outpourings of egalitarian sentiment, such as that by Jesus of Nazareth around 30 CE ("Inasmuch as ye have done it unto one of the least of these my brethren, ye have done it unto me"), had shaken all agricultural societies from time to time. But from the seventeenth century onward the shaking became continuous, and then down to the present a rolling earthquake of equality for all humans.

In the nineteenth century in Europe (if not yet in Bollywood) the ancient comic plot of young lovers amusingly fooling the Old Man, or being tragically stymied by him, died out, because human capital embodied in and owned by young people replaced in economic dominance the landed capital owned by the old. Even patriarchy, therefore, the kingliness of fathers, began to tremble, until nowadays most American children defy their fathers with impunity. Four verses before the verse in Leviticus routinely hauled out to damn homosexuals, their putative author Moses commands that "every one that curseth his father or his mother shall surely be put to death" (20:9). The verse would condemn most American teenagers to stoning, along with the homosexuals and those who mix wool cloth with linen or fail to take a ceremonial bath after their periods.

In its long, laborious development, the loony notion of dignity for anyone coming into the world without a saddle on his back was taken up by radical Anabaptists and Quakers, abolitionists and spiritualists, revolutionaries and suffragettes, and American drag queens battling the police at Stonewall. By now in civilized countries the burden of proof has shifted decisively onto conservatives and Party hacks and Catholic bishops and country-club Colonel Blimps and anti-1960s reactionaries to defend hierarchy, the generous loyalty to rank and sex, as a thing lovely and in accord with Natural Law.

The Rumboldian idea of coming into the world without a saddle on one's back had expressed, too, a notion struggling for legitimacy, of a contract between king and people. As Rumbold put it in his speech from the scaffold: "the king having, as I conceive, power enough to make him great; the people also as much property as to make them happy; they being, as it were, contracted to one another." Note the "as it were, contracted," a bourgeois deal akin to Abram's land deal with the Lord, a rhetoric of "covenant" popular among Protestants after Zwingli.[12] The terms of such a monarchical deal became a routine trope in the seventeenth century, as in Hobbes and Locke, and then still more routine in the eighteenth century. Louis XIV declared that he was tied to his subjects "only by an exchange of reciprocal obligations. The deference . . . we receive . . . [is] but payment for the justice [the subjects] expect to receive."[13] Frederick the Great claimed to view himself as governed by a similar deal with his subjects, calling himself merely "the first servant of the state" (though not refraining from exercising autocracy when he felt like it).

Even in autocratic France and Prussia (if not in Russia), that is, the sovereign had to honor property rights. In the Putney Debates Richard Overton declared that "by natural birth all men are equally and alike born to like propriety [that is, equal rights to acquire and hold property], liberty and freedom." The deal by which the people as a group had as much property as to make them "happy" (a new concern I've observed in the late seventeenth century) was thought crucial among a handful of such progressives and then by more and more Europeans from the eighteenth century on. In the French Declaration of the Rights of Man and of the Citizen in 1793 the last article (number 17), speaks of property in notably warm terms: "property is an inviolable and sacred right." Article 2 in the Declaration had placed property among four rights, "natural and imprescribable" (*imprescriptibles*, that is, by law immovable): "liberty, property, security, and resistance to oppression."

An article in the Universal Declaration of Human Rights adopted by the United Nations in 1948 (by God's little joke also numbered 17) declares (though with rather less warmth in a socialist-leaning age), "(1) Everyone has the right to own property alone as well as in association with others; and (2) No one shall be arbitrarily deprived of his property." Article 42 in the new Italian Constitution, in force in the same year, is still less warm:

> Private property is recognized and guaranteed by the law, which prescribes the ways it is acquired, enjoyed and its limitations so as to ensure its social function and make it accessible to all. In the cases provided for by the law and with provisions for compensation, private property may be expropriated for reasons of general interest.[14]

The socialist tilt toward "social function," "accessib[ility] to all," and a "general interest" that could justify expropriation continued for a while down the twentieth century. In 1986 the Labor prime minister of Australia, Bob Hawke, proposed for his country a Bill of Rights. It made no mention of the right to property.[15]

In the twentieth century the rhetorical presumption of life, liberty, and the pursuit of happiness for all was echoed even in the rhetoric of its most determined enemies (as in "the Democratic Peoples' Republic of North Korea" and other communist or fascist countries). The collectivist counter-deal by which such régimes actually worked, born with Rousseau, as I've noted, was that the General Will would be discerned by the Party or the Führer. No need for private property, then. We in government will take care of all that, thanks.

Democratic pluralism was, I have also said, doubled-sided. Progressive redistributions, under the theories of Rousseau and Proudhon that property is anyway theft, could kill betterment. Recall, again, Argentina, joined recently by Venezuela. Such cases bring to mind Mencken's grim witticism in 1916 that democracy is "the theory that the common people know what they want and deserve to get it, good and hard."[16] He also said, "Democracy is the art and science of running the circus from the monkey cage."[17] (Yet on the other side of the balance, a populist commitment to modest redistribution— though understand that most benefits, such as free higher education, go to the voting middle class, just as minimum wages protect middle-class trade unionists, and are paid in substantial part to the children of the middle class working at the local bar—saved social-democratic countries from the chaos of revolution. Think of postwar Germany, or for that matter the American New Deal.[18])

What came under question in the world 1517 to 1848 and beyond, slowly, on account of the religious radicals of the sixteenth century and then the political radicals of the seventeenth and eighteenth centuries and then the abolitionist and black and feminist and gay and untouchable radicals of the nineteenth and twentieth centuries, was illiberty and indignity, the one political, the other social. The questioning had, I claim, dramatic consequences in encouraging trade-tested betterment. The English Levellers, who were not modern property-hating socialists, had demanded free trade. They were in this, by the standards of the time, terrifying innovators, as in manhood suffrage and annual parliaments.

What made us free and rich was the questioning of the notion that "a liberty" was a special privilege accorded to a guildsman of the town or to a nobleman of the robe, and the supporting notion that the only "dignity" was privilege inherited from such men and their charter-granting feudal lords, or graciously subgranted by them to you, their humble servant in the Great Chain of Being. Philip the Good, duke of the Burgundian Netherlands, forced in 1438 the proud city of Bruges to accede to his rising power. His tyranny took the form of taking away its "privileges." His granddaughter, Mary, Duchess of Burgundy, though, was forced to sign the *Groot Privilege*, the bourgeois

Magna Carta of the Low Countries, giving such liberties back to all of the cities.

It was not only dukes and duchesses who took, or granted, privileges denied to most people. Hierarchy was reworked by the bourgeoisie itself into commercial forms, even in the first northern home of bourgeois glory. A famous radical poem of Holland in the 1930s, written on a slow news day by Jan Gresshof (he was fired for printing the poem in the newspaper he edited), speaks of the conservative wing of his colleagues of the bourgeois clerisy, "*de dominee, de dokter, de notaris*," the minister, the doctor, the lawyer-notary, who together strolled complacently on Arnhem's town square of an evening. "There is nothing left on earth for them to learn, / They are perfect and complete, / Old liberals [in the European sense], distrustful and healthy."[19] The hierarchy to be broken down was not only of dukes and duchesses, kings and knights, but of the members of the bourgeoisie themselves remade as pseudo-neo-kings and -knights, when it could get away with it. Thus a trophy wife in Florida clinging to the arm of her rich husband declared to the TV cameras, on the subject of poor people, "We don't bother with *losers*." Thus the Medici started as doctors by way of routinely learned skills (as their name implies), then became bankers by entrepreneurship, and then grand dukes by violence, and at last kept their dukedom by the settled hierarchy of inheritance and the legitimate monopoly of violence.

Mokyr has noted that the Dutch became in the eighteenth century conservative and "played third fiddle in the Industrial Revolution," from which he concludes that there must be something amiss in McCloskey's emphasis on the new ideology of bourgeois liberty and dignity.[20] After all, the Dutch had them both, early. But I just said that the bourgeoisie is capable of reversing its betterment by making itself into an honorable hierarchy, which is what the Dutch regents did. And Mokyr is adopting the mistaken convention that the Dutch in the eighteenth century "failed." They did not. Like Londoners, and according to comparative advantage, they gave up some of their own industrial project in favor of becoming bankers and routine merchants. I am claiming only that the new ideology came to Britain from Holland, which remains true whether or not the Dutch did much with it later. In their Golden Age the Dutch certainly did a lot of bettering with the ideology. I agree that Dutch society later froze up, ruled by *de dominee, de dokter, de notaris*. But national borders do not always compute. If we are to blame the Dutch in the eighteenth century for conservatism we will also have to blame the Southern English, who also turned to specializing in mere trading and financing, giving up their industrial might, clipping coupons in the funds and sitting in great houses surrounded by parkland, and like the Dutch adhering to distinctions of rank that were less important in the industrial north of England or in the industrial south of Belgium.

And Mokyr's inertial lemma—that once initiated, a social change must be permanent or else it did not exist in the first place—raises graver problems for his own emphasis on science as the initiating event than for mine on a new appreciation for bourgeois liberty and dignity. After all the Dutch in the seventeenth century had invented the telescope and the microscope among numerous other scientific devices, such as the pendulum in clocks. Why did not inertia propel them, if science does it, into the Industrial Revolution and the Great Enrichment? The Dutch case argues better for bourgeois dignity, which has sustained Holland ever since as one of the richest countries in the world, but argues poorly for science, in which it faltered.

The ethical and rhetorical change that around 1700 began to break the ancient restraints on betterment, whether from the old knights or the new monopolists, was liberating and it was enlightened and it was liberal in the Scottish sense of putting first an equal liberty, not an equal outcome. And it was successful. As one of its more charming conservative enemies put it:

> Locke sank into a swoon;
> The Garden died;
> God took the spinning-jenny
> Out of his side.[21]

IDEAS MADE FOR A
BOURGEOIS REVALUATION

It is merely a materialist-economistic prejudice, I say yet again, to insist that such a rhetorical change from aristocratic-religious values to bourgeois values *must* have had economic or biological roots. John Mueller, the political scientist and historian at Ohio State whose thoughts on "pretty good" democracy and capitalism I have used, argues in another book that war, like slavery or the subordination of women, has become slowly less respectable in the past few centuries.[1] Important habits of the heart and of the lip change. In the seventeenth century a master could routinely beat his servant. Not now. Such changes are not *always* caused by interest or by considerations of efficiency or by the logic of class conflict. The Bourgeois Revaluation had also legal, political, personal, gender, religious, philosophical, historical, linguistic, journalistic, literary, artistic, and accidental causes.

The economist Deepak Lal, relying on the legal historian Harold Berman and echoing an old opinion of Henry Adams, sees a big change in the eleventh century, in Gregory VII's assertion of church supremacy.[2] Perhaps. The trouble with such earlier and broader origins is that modernity came from Holland and England, not, for example, from thoroughly Protestant Sweden or East Prussia (except Kant), or from thoroughly church-supremacist Spain or Naples (except Vico). It is better to locate the widespread taking up of the politically relevant attitudes later in European history—around 1700. Such a dating fits better with the new historical finding that until the eighteenth century places like China, say, did not look markedly less rich or even, in many respects, less free than Europe.[3] In Europe the scene was set by the affirmations of ordinary life, and ordinary death, in the upheavals of the Reformation of the sixteenth century, the long Dutch Revolt and the longer civil war between French Catholics and Huguenots, and the two English Revolutions of the seventeenth century. The economically relevant change in attitude that resulted occurred in the seventeenth and early eighteenth centuries with the novel ruminations around the North Sea—embodied literally, I have noted, in the novel as against the romance—affirming as the transcendent *telos* of an economy an ordinary instead of a heroic or holy life. It was, in another of Charles Taylor's labels for it, "the sanctification of ordinary life."[4]

Margaret Jacob argues that the 1680s was the hinge. The Anglo-Dutch reaction to absolutism was the "catalyst for what we call Enlightenment." Enlightenment comes, she is saying, from the reaction to Catholic absolutism in England under late Charles II and his brother James II, and in France under Louis XIV with the Revocation and his secret negotiations with Charles and James. Jack Goldstone observes that in England in the 1680s even the common law was under attack. It was the politics, not the economics. Absolutist and Catholic France and anti-absolutist and Protestant England were both mercantilist. And the Dutch, French, and English, not to speak of the Portuguese and Spanish, had long been imperialists. What changed was ideas, mainly, not economic interests.

The common set of ideas in the Enlightenment were ethical and political. One must settle matters by making open arguments, it came to be said, not by applying political force. It is Erasmian humanism, the ancient tradition of rhetoric. The Reformation finally evolved in an Erasmian direction, though only after a good deal of killing in the name of "whose reign it is, his religion holds," and became democratic, after more killing. The ideas were Western European, from Scotland to Poland. Without such ideas the modern world might have happened, after a while, but in a different way—a centralized, French version, perhaps. It would not have worked well economically (though the food would have been better).

The old bourgeoisie and the aristocracy had said that they disdained the dishonor of merely economic trade and betterment. The Medici bank lasted only about a century because its later governors were more interested in hobnobbing with the aristocracy than in making sensible loans to merchants.[5] The scholastic intellectuals, for all their admirable rhetorical seriousness, did not get their hands dirty in experimentation, with rare exceptions such as Roger Bacon. It was sixteenth-century Dutch and English merchants, following on their earlier merchant cousins in the Mediterranean, who developed the notion of an experimental and observing life. Enlightenment was a change in the attitude toward such ordinary life. The rare honor of kings and dukes and bishops was to be devalued. And such honor was to be extended to merchant bankers of London and American experimenters with electricity. The comparative devaluation of courts and politics followed, slowly.

The debate by the middle of the eighteenth century, the political theorist and intellectual historian John Danford notes, was "whether a free society is possible if commercial activities flourish."[6] The admired models on the anticommercial side of the debate, as Pocock and others have shown, were Republican Rome and especially, of all places, Greek Sparta. The commerce favored by Athens or Carthage or now Britain would introduce "luxury and voluptuousness," in Lord Kames's conventional phrase, as the debate reached its climax, which would "eradicate patriotism," and extinguish at least ancient freedom, the freedom to participate. As the Spartans vanquished Athens, so too some more vigorous nation would rise up and vanquish Britain, or at any rate stop a "progress so flourishing . . . when patriotism is the ruling passion of every member." One hears such arguments still, in nostalgic praise in the United States for the Greatest Generation (lynching, and income in today's dollars, circa 1945, $33 a head) as against the diminished glory of our latter days (civil rights, and income, circa 2016, $130 a head). The nationalist, sacrificial, antiluxury, classical republican view with its Spartan ideal persists in in the pages of the *Nation* and the *National Review*.

On the contrary, said Hume, in reply to arguments such as Kames's, commerce is good for us. Georgian mercantilism and overseas imperialism in aid of the political, he said, was *not* good for us. Hume opposed, writes Danford, "the primacy of the political." "In this denigration of political life. Hume [is] thoroughly modern and [seems] to agree in important respects with [the individualism of] Hobbes and Locke."[7] Hobbes, Danford argues, believed that the tranquility notably lacking in the Europe of his time could best be achieved "if the political order [is] understood as merely a means to security and prosperity rather than virtue (or salvation or empire)."[8] "This amounts," Danford notes, "to an enormous demotion of politics, now to be seen as merely instrumental," as against seeing it as an arena for the exercise of the highest virtues of a tiny group of The Best. We nowadays can't easily see how novel such a demotion was, since we now suppose without a sense of its historical oddness that to secure these rights, governments are instituted among men, deriving their just powers from the consent of the governed. Politics has stopped being exclusively the plaything of the aristocracy.

Hume spoke of the "opposition between the greatness of the state and the happiness of the subjects."[9] In an earlier time Machiavelli could easily adopt the greatness of the Prince as the purpose of a polity, at any rate when he was angling for a job with the Medici. The purpose of Sparta was not the "happiness" of the Spartan women, helots, allies, or even in any material sense the Spartanate itself. The entire point of Henry VIII's England was Henry's glory as by the Grace of God, King of England, France and Ireland, Defender of the Faith and of the Church of England and in Earth Supreme Head. What was original about Hobbes is that he adopts the premise, in Danford's words, that "all legitimate [note the word] governments are trying to do precisely the same things: to provide security and tranquility so that individuals can pursue their own private ends."[10] Danford argues that "perhaps it would be better to describe the change as the devaluation of politics and the political rather than the elevation of trade."[11] To devalue royal or aristocratic values is to leave the bourgeoisie in charge. Romantic people attached on the right to king and country and on the left to revolution sneered at the Enlightenment.[12] What was unique about the Enlightenment was precisely the elevation of ordinary peaceful people in ordinary peaceful life, an elevation of trade over the monopoly of violence.

Erik Ringmar's answer to the question Why was Europe first? begins from the simple and true triad of points that all change involves an initial reflection (namely, that change is possible), an entrepreneurial moment (putting the change into practice), and "pluralism" or "toleration" (I would call the toleration the ideology of the Bourgeois Era, namely, some way of counteracting the annoyance with which the naturally conservative majority of humans will view any moving of their cheese). "Contemporary Britain, the United States or Japan," Ringmar writes, "are not modern because they contain individuals who are uniquely reflective, entrepreneurial or tolerant."[13] That's correct: the psychological hypothesis one finds in Weber or in the psychologist David McClelland or in the historian David Landes does not stand up to the evidence, as for example the success of the overseas Chinese, or indeed the astonishingly quick turn from Maoist starvation in mainland

China to 9 or 10 percent rates of growth per year per person, or from the Hindu rate of growth and the License Raj in India after independence to growth rates per person since 1991 over 6 percent. Why would psychology change so quickly? And how could a rise in entrepreneurial spirit from, say, 5 percent of the population to 10 percent, which could have also characterized earlier efflorescences such as fifth-century Athens, cause after 1800 a uniquely Great Enrichment of a factor of thirty?

But then unhappily Ringmar contends in Northian style, "A modern society is a society in which change happens automatically and effortlessly because it is institutionalized."[14] The trouble with the claim of "institutions" is, as Ringmar himself noted earlier in another connection, that "it begs the question of the origin."[15] It also begs the question of enforcement, which depends on ethics and opinion absent from the neo-institutional tale. "The joker in the pack," writes Eric Jones in speaking of the decline of guild restrictions in England, "was the national shift in elite opinion, which the courts partly shared":

> The judges often declined to support the restrictiveness that the guilds sought to impose. . . . As early as the start of seventeenth century, towns had been losing cases they took to court with the aim of compelling new arrivals to join their craft guilds. . . . A key case concerned Newbury and Ipswich in 1616. The ruling in this instance became a common law precedent, to the effect that "foreigners," men from outside a borough, could not be compelled to enrol.[16]

Ringmar devotes 150 lucid and learned and literate pages to exploring the origins of European science, humanism, newspapers, universities, academies, theater, novels, corporations, property rights, insurance, Dutch finance, diversity, states, politeness, civil rights, political parties, and economics. But he is a true comparativist (he taught for some years in China)—this in sharp contrast to some of the other Northians, and especially the good North himself. So Ringmar does not suppose that the European facts speak for themselves. In the following 100 pages he takes back much of the implicit claim that Europe was anciently special, whether "institutionalized" or not, by going through for China the same triad of reflection, entrepreneurship, and pluralism/toleration, and finding them pretty good. "The Chinese were at least as intrepid [in the seas] as the Europeans"; "The [Chinese] imperial state constituted next to no threat to the property rights of merchants and investors"; "already by 400 BCE China produced as much cast iron as Europe would in 1750"; Confucianism was "a wonderfully flexible doctrine"; "China was far more thoroughly commercialized"; European "salons and coffee shops [were] . . . in some ways strikingly Chinese."[17] He knows, as the Northians appear not to, that China had banks and canals and large firms and private property many centuries before the Northian date for the acquisition of such modernities in England, the end of the seventeenth century. (So too on many counts did England itself, for that matter.)

Sheilagh Ogilvie criticizes the neo-institutionalists and their claims that efficiency ruled, arguing on the contrary for a "conflictual" point of view, in which power is taken seriously:

> Efficiency theorists do sometimes mention that institutions evoke conflict. But they seldom incorporate conflict into their explanations. Instead, conflict remains an incidental by-product of institutions portrayed as primarily existing to enhance efficiency. . . . Although serfdom [for example] was profoundly ineffective at increasing the size of the economic pie, it was highly effective at distributing large slices to overlords, with fiscal and military side-benefits to rulers and economic privileges for serf elites.[18]

The same can be said for the new political and social ideas that at length broke down an ideology that had been highly effective at justifying in ethical terms the distribution of large slices to overlords.

Why, then, a change in a system so profitable for the elite? Ringmar gets it right when he speaks of public opinion, which was a late and contingent development in Europe, and to which he recurs frequently.[19] The oldest newspaper still publishing in Europe is a Swedish one of 1645, *Post- och Inrikes Tidningar* (Foreign and Domestic Times), and the first daily one in England dates to 1702. Benjamin Franklin's older brother James quickly imitated in Boston in 1721 the idea of a newspaper and became, with the active help of adolescent Ben, a thorn in the side of the authorities. That is, the institutions that mattered the most were not the "incentives" beloved of the economists, such as patents (which have been shown to be insignificant, and anyway have been universal, as state-granted monopolies, from the first formation of states) or property rights (which were established in China and India and the Ottoman Empire, often much earlier than in Europe; and after all the Roman law was clear on property). The important "institutions" were ideas, words, rhetoric, ideology. And these did change on the eve of the Great Enrichment. What changed circa 1700 was a climate of persuasion, which led promptly to the amazing reflection, entrepreneurship, and pluralism called the modern world.

It is not always true, as Ringmar claims at one point, that "institutions are best explained in terms of the path through which they developed."[20] He contradicts himself on the page previous and there speaks truth: often "the institutions develop first and the needs come only later." It is not the case for example that the origins of English betterment, if not of individualism, are usefully traced to early medieval times. It is not the case that, say, English common law was essential for modernity. The historian David Le Bris has shown that within France before the Revolution the French north *was* a common-law area, while the south was a civil-law area, but with little or no discernible differences in economic outcome during the next century.[21] Places without such law, further, promptly developed alternatives, when the ideology turned, as it often did turn suddenly, in favor of betterment. Ideas, not institutions, made the modern world.

THE RHETORICAL CHANGE
WAS NECESSARY, AND
MAYBE SUFFICIENT

We humans live, that is, by words as much as by bread. Such a claim is "weak" in the mathematician's sense of being very general, like Chebyshev's inequality, and not the sharpest result one can imagine, yet hard to dispute. The claim that ideas are powerful asserts merely what few would deny, when reminded by common sense. The economist John Maynard Keynes remarked famously at the height of a material catastrophe in 1936 that "madmen in authority, who hear voices in the air, are distilling their frenzy from some academic scribbler of a few years back."[1] His scientific opponent the economist Ludwig von Mises made the same point after the Second World War's material catastrophe: "The history of mankind is the history of ideas. . . . The sensational events which stir the emotions and catch the interest of superficial observers are merely the consummation of ideological changes. . . . New ideologies, which had already long since superseded the old ones, throw off their last veil, and even the dullest people become aware of the changes they did not notice before."[2]

In the present case the claim is that an antibourgeois rhetoric, especially if combined with the logic of vested interests, has on many occasions damaged societies. Rhetoric against a bourgeois liberty, especially when backed by governmental violence, prevented betterment in Silver Age Rome and Tokugawa Japan. It stopped growth in twentieth-century Argentina and Mao's China. It suppressed speech in present-day North Korea and Saudi Arabia. Such words-with-swords-and-guns in 1750 could have stopped cold the modern world beginning in Holland and England. In the twentieth century the bad rhetoric of nationalism and socialism did in fact stop its later development, locally, as in Italy 1922–1943 or Russia 1917–1989. National-ism and socialism can to this day reverse the riches of modernity, with the help of other rhetorics such as populism or environmentalism or religious fundamentalism.

Yes, politics in the eighteenth century depended on material power, such as the material freeing of ordinary people from the idiocy of rural life. Yes, the imperial (if profitless) adventures of the Europeans depended on the revolution in military technology, such as drilled fusillades of muskets and drilled broadsides of naval guns. One can grant material causes that much. But eighteenth-century politics also depended heavily on rhetoric, the very words and ideas, such as the widespread translation of the manual for drilling infantrymen in massed gunfire written by Prince Maurice of the Netherlands, and the widespread use of Italian plans for cannon-resistant fortifications. And in sweeter ways, too. As Gabriel Almond and Sidney Verba put it in their classic study of political attitudes, the good "civic culture" to which they attribute the success of Western liberalism is "based on communication and persuasion."[3] It is a bourgeois rhetoric. "Civic," after all, is from Latin *cives*, citizen of a city-state, and "bourgeois" means at root merely such a citizen, standing in the *forum* or *agora* to argue his case among the piles of vegetables and amphoras of wine offered there for sale.

The stronger claim I have made, harder to demonstrate, tells a story of origins, a sufficiency as against a merely long-run necessity assigned to bour-geois rhetoric in making and keeping the modern world. The rhetorical change circa 1700, admittedly, was in its origins not entirely autonomous. The story is not a Hegelian one of the *Weltgeist* and the cunning of reason, though remember the five-hundred-year turnings in Christianity. In conces-sion to the material, remember too the guns (for which some people reach when they hear the word "culture"). Remember trade, internal and external. Remember sheer rising numbers of bourgeois.

Yet the mere idea of a free press, if permitted politically and if accompa-nied by cheap printing borrowed from China, will lead eventually to politi-cal pamphlets, independent newspapers, Puritan courtesy books, epistolary novels, and guides to young men climbing the social ladder. The mere idea of a steam engine with separate condenser, if permitted and if accompanied by skilled machinists trained in making precision scientific instruments and the boring of cannon, and the expiration in 1800 of Watt's monopoly, will lead eventually to the mere idea of a steamship and a steam locomotive, and then to the steam turbine and the generation of electric power for factories and for lighting. The mere idea of powered flight, made sterile in the United States until 1917 by a dispute between the Wright brothers and the Smithsonian Institution, left the United States with bad airplanes compared with those of France, Britain, and Germany, which used the Wrights' ideas under license—until the patent pool 1917 to 1975 gave the United States the best airplane industry in the world.[4] The mere idea of the Galilean-Newtonian calculation of forces, if permitted and commercial and accompanied by mathematically educated people, will lead eventually to the mere idea of methodical calculations of flows of water for the betterment of Bristol's port.[5] Above all, as Albert Hirschman suggested in 1977, the mere idea that "commercial, banking, and similar money-making pursuits [were] honorable . . . after having stood condemned or despised as greed . . . for centuries past" will lead to a Bourgeois Revaluation, though at first, Hirschman observes, "nowhere [in Europe was the idea] associated with the advocacy of a new bourgeois ethos."[6]

Si non, non. China invented paper and printing and clocks centuries before the dull Europeans caught up. For two thousand years the Chinese system of examinations encouraged humanistic learning, as European universities did only later, and haltingly. The extremely rigorous examinations, initiated by the Han dynasty after 206 BCE and still going strong under the Qing until the last emperor in 1911, yielded about eighteen thousand degree holders a year. In, say, 1600 the Chinese figure was roughly comparable to the number of graduates of universities in Europe, which had roughly the same population then as China (150 million in China and 100 million in Europe). The production of such human capital in China was hugely superior to that in Europe for at least fifteen centuries after it began. It remained comparable to or better than Europe's until the nineteenth century. Then the *humboldtische* reforms in Europe after 1810 and the explosion of population in China caused a great divergence in graduates proportionate to population. The Chinese eighteen thousand did not rise, but the number of graduates in Europe did, notably in chemistry and other physical sciences.[7]

The Chinese system of examinations, in which the son of a peasant or merchant could ascend to become the chief counselor to the emperor, contrasted sharply with the aristocratic sources of power in Japan or Europe or South Asia. The examination elite in China was secure, yet able therefore to impose scholarly rather than mercantile values on the society. As the historian Jonathan Daly argues, in explaining the stagnation of Chinese inventiveness during the past five centuries, just when Europe was waking up, "One could achieve no higher or more remunerative honor in society":

> Some brilliant men studied mathematics, astronomy, and law, but they received only scant official encouragement. Some brilliant literati-officials pursued research and reflection in non-literary fields, but without much institutional backing. The examination system was thus a unifying force in Chinese culture but at the cost of stifling much creative thinking.[8]

That is, liberal educations and civil service examinations (adopted by Europeans in the nineteenth century in explicit imitation, Daly points out, of the fabled system of China) can be conservative, in both a good sense and a bad. When the great and original economist John Maynard Keynes took the examination for the civil service in 1906 his grades were stellar. But his worst was in economics.

One must take factual care. Down to the eighteenth century, after all, many Europeans were burning witches and heretics with legal support, and still in the sixteenth century all of them were, against a long tradition of toleration in much of Islam (though a tradition the Ottomans overturned in response to political disorders).[9] I have noted that the clichés of Orientalism—which claim that the East was a region of utter slavery (if rather sexily Romantic), whereas the West was gloriously free from the time of the Greeks, or at latest from the time of the Germanic tribes of the Homeland (with the inconsequential exceptions, in both Greece and the Homeland, of the 90 percent of the population who were women and foreigners and unfree men)—are imperfect guides to the true facts of East and West.

Yet the quasi-free habits of Holland and England and Scotland around 1700 granted a permission to entertain mere ideas. By the early eighteenth century certain political ideas that a century before would have given their speaker an appointment with a Rhineland witch-burner or an English drawer-and-quarterer circulated reasonably freely in the North Sea lands, at any rate by the standards of the nervous autocracies in contemporary France or China or Russia (though France, like Sweden, opened up in the turbulent 1780s, as did China and Russia finally in the turbulent 1890s). "There is a mighty light," wrote Shaftesbury to a Dutch friend in 1706, "which spreads itself over the world especially in those two free nations of England and Holland, on whom the affairs of Europe now turn."[10]

What made the light unceasing, and made Europe wake up in particular to the sweetness of business affairs, were the unique changes in language, that is, a new way of talking about profit and business and invention. The alarming Bernard Mandeville argued the case in *The Fable of the Bees*, first published as verse in 1705 but later made into a full-scale defense of commercial life by the addition of lengthy remarks and dialogues, especially in its notorious edition of 1723. Admiring the enterprising man, Mandeville sneers at a cloistered virtue such as the "indolent man" exhibits—"indolent" defined as one who does not venture into the marketplace, though very willing to "work in a garret . . . with patience and assiduity."[11] The two characters, note, are drawn in his mental experiment from two sides of "the middling people . . . of low circumstances tolerably well educated."[12] A retiring man of letters would "run with joy to a rich nobleman that he is sure will receive him with kindness and humanity" but will not try his mettle against real opposition.[13] Thus a member of the modern clerisy will apply to a foundation he is confident will admire his politics, MacArthur on the left or Olin on the right, but such a one "will never serve his friend or his country at the expense of his quiet" by venturing into the despised world of business, and so lives quietly at public or foundation expense.[14]

Mandeville emphasized that the person with the opposite, enterprising temper, the striving, or at least stirring, man, the man of action, faces "a multitude of strong temptations to deviate from the rules of strict virtue, which hardly ever come in the other's way."[15] "A very little avarice will egg him on to pursue his aim with eagerness and assiduity: small scruples are no opposition to him—where sincerity will not serve, he uses artifice."[16] But Mandeville's point, starting to be heard more often in the seventeenth and early eighteenth centuries, is that such assiduity enriches and ennobles the nation. "Wealth and power, glory and worldly greatness . . . [are] not to be attained to without avarice, profuseness, pride, envy, ambition, and other vices."[17] You admit you want wealth and power. So stop criticizing its sources: "Thus vice nursed ingenuity, / Which joined with time and industry / Had carried life's conveniences, / Its real pleasure, comforts, ease, / To such a height, the very poor / Lived better than the rich before."[18] Mandeville was trying to give honor to a commercial civilization by putting forward his paradox that what aristocratic and Christian civilizations called "vice" was what now made them rich. "Thus every part was full of vice, / Yet the whole mass a paradise."[19] He was quite mistaken—economic paradise depends on ethics, not on vice. But you see his purpose, to devalue the holy or aristocratic or political life, in favor of the bourgeoisie.

Mokyr, I have noted, has called the commercial turn a third project of the French *philosophes* and the Scottish improvers, in his phrase the "Industrial Enlightenment."[20] I would rather call it the Bourgeois Revaluation. But Mokyr and I, we of the ideational movement in economic history, do not disagree on its importance. And we certainly do not think it needs be construed as "full of vice." The historian Roy Porter speaks of the old question "How can I be saved?" (to which one could add, "How can I be ennobled?") yielding to the new question "How can I be happy here below?"[21] The questions changed, and so did the rhetoric of the replies. "The displacement of Calvinism," writes Porter about the intolerant and world-denying reformed Christianity that still in 1706 had within living memory held power among the Dutch, Swiss, Scots, English, and New Englanders, "by a confidence in cosmic benevolism blessed the pursuit of happiness, and to this end Britons set about exploiting a commercial society.... Human nature was not flawed by the Fall; desire was desirable."[22] Remember the broad-church preachers in England in the 1690s.

In Fielding's *Tom Jones* (1749) the absurd figures of the philosopher Square and the clergyman Thwackum embody the debate between Nature and Revelation: "Square held human nature to be the perfection of all virtue, and that vice was a deviation from our nature, in the same manner as deformity of body is. Thwackum, on the contrary, maintained that the human mind, since the fall, was nothing but a sink of iniquity, till purified and redeemed by grace."[23] The same debate was rehearsed in more heavily censored France, as in Diderot's private *Supplement to the Bougainville Voyage* (1772; published only in the safely revolutionary year of 1796). The imagined Tahitian wise man, Oirou, who has offered to a French priest his wife and his daughters for his pleasures, replies to the priest's refusal, "I don't know what this thing is that you call 'religion,' but I can only have a low opinion of it because it forbids you to partake of an innocent pleasure to which Nature, the sovereign mistress of us all, invites everybody."[24] Compare King Charles's philosophy of pleasure.

During the bourgeois shift of ethical rhetoric, some decades earlier than Diderot, that wandering child of Puritans, Benjamin Franklin, had exclaimed "'Tis surprising to me that men who call themselves Christians . . . should say that a God of infinite perfections would make anything our duty that has not a natural tendency to our happiness; and if to our happiness, then it is agreeable to our nature, since a desire of happiness is a natural principle which all mankind are endured [endowed] with."[25] Remember Johnson in the 1770s on the innocence of getting money. By 1776, a few days before Jefferson's draft of the Declaration of Independence (which Franklin helped revise), George Mason wrote in the Virginia Declaration of Rights, of May 15, "that all men are by nature equally free and independent and have certain inherent rights, . . . namely the enjoyment of life and liberty, with the means of acquiring and possessing property, and pursuing and obtaining happiness and safety." God's law was replaced by natural rights (the rights to life, liberty, and the pursuit of happiness, to spiff up Mason's phrase—the idea itself, a Leveller standard, was by then over a century old).[26] Negotiated rights— deal making and at length voting—replaced the God-given laws of social position, at first in stirring declarations and at long last in fact.

To employ an old-fashioned but still useful vocabulary, devised in 1861 by Henry Maine, the northwest of Europe, and Britain in particular, changed from a society of status to a society of contract, at any rate in its theory about itself.[27] Thus in the modern civil-rights law of public accommodation, as soon as you open a business making contracts for pay you are disabled from discriminating by status of race, gender, affectional preference, or the rest. As Johnson had written of the Western Islands of Scotland, "Money confounds subordination, by overpowering the distinctions of rank and birth."[28] The historian Christopher Bayly has made a similar point about the confounding power of the cash nexus in the Islamic world at the time Johnson wrote.[29] In northwestern Europe inheritance gave way to self-creation—again, at least in theory. Honest invention and hopeful revolution came to be spoken of as honorable, as they had seldom been spoken of before. And the seven principal virtues of pagan and Christian Europe were recycled as bourgeois. The wave of gadgets, material and political, in short, came out of a bourgeois ethical and rhetorical tsunami around 1700 in the North Sea.

PART VII

Nowhere Before on a Large Scale Had Bourgeois or Other Commoners Been Honored

TALK HAD BEEN HOSTILE
TO BETTERMENT

A recent graduate of the liberal Francisco Marroquin University in Guatemala City, Oscar Chiquitó, tells his story. A Mayan born in the backcountry, at age five his father said to him, "It is time to work. School is for lazy people who don't want to work." For some years the little boy worked in the fields beside his father, reaffirming the father's identity as a poor but hardworking man, and therefore in the father's mind an honorable peasant, a real man. (Abraham Lincoln's father, too, sneered at his son's reading of the Bible and *Pilgrim's Progress*, avoiding Real Work.) When Oscar was eight, his mother finally persuaded his father to let the boy go to school, at which he excelled, all the way through to being the rare Mayan to graduate from university.[1] (With similar drive, without benefit of university, or much schooling at all, the rail-splitter became the writer of the First and Second Inaugurals and the Gettysburg Address.) How many children are confined by more than poverty itself to repeat the lives of their parents, the better to reaffirm the parents' identity and dignity? Such a self-justifying if self-limiting psychology, after all, works on the rich too—we are rich and privileged: no need to strive; don't read a book or earn a degree; carry on to the season at Cannes.

Similar conservatism explains cases of successful merchants and financiers who nonetheless did not innovate. The Old Believers in Russia, and still in colonies from Brazil to Alaska, were good at commerce but not good at the mechanical and institutional inventions that made for an industrial revolution.[2] Mokyr has noted that likewise the Jews were for a long time not involved much in trade-tested betterment (though vigorous in trade-tested routine supply), especially not in mechanical invention. Financial capitalists they were, spectacularly so in the case of the Rothschilds in the age of emancipation, but not improvers beyond the countinghouse.[3] Until their emancipations beginning in the eighteenth century, Mokyr argues (as a secular Israeli-American himself, tough on the orthodox), the Jews were too devoted to honoring the past and the Torah. "Jews are conspicuously underrepresented in the pantheon of great inventors before the modern industrial age. Jewish traditional culture was inherently backward-looking and conservative and thus did not encourage revolutionary ideas and thinking outside the box."[4] Well, except for Marx and Freud, David Ricardo and Georg Cantor, George Gershwin and Lenny Bruce—who nonetheless make Mokyr's point, having invented ideas, not machines.

A similar point can be made about the origins of the French Enlightenment in the debate between the ancients and the moderns, or of the Scottish Enlightenment in the ending of Calvinist rule. In the same 2011 paper, Mokyr points out in Judaism before *haskala* (enlightenment, biblical higher criticism) the "large amount of obedience and respect for tradition and the wisdom of the past generations." It long characterized China as well, filial piety being a much-praised Confucian virtue, and would apply even to the commercially if not mechanically ingenious overseas Chinese. The historian Kwee Hui Kian attributes the astonishing multicentury rise of Chinese to dominance of trade in Southeast Asia to their "organizations centered on deity and ancestral cults," which is one way of characterizing rabbinic Judaism too.[5] Mokyr continues, "There are . . . prominent orthodox Jewish scientists [but even] their number has remained smaller than one would expect given the qualities of human capital involved in a Jewish orthodox education," trilinguality, for example, in Hebrew, Yiddish, and Polish. Contrary to the models of capital-obsessed economists, in other words, human capital has often been a conservative force, as in the imperial Chinese examination system and in the gentiles-only policy of hiring in many American law firms before the 1960s.

The realm of exchange is a middling realm of human contact stuck between biology and violence at the bottom and rhetoric and gift-giving at the top, as illustrated in table 4. The lowest realm of biology inspires philosophical utilitarianism. The satisfactions of the organism are characteristic also of grass and rats. Associate Justice Holmes said in 1912 that "the law of the grub . . . is

TABLE 4. The hierarchy of human contacts

Realm	Instrument	Outcome	Virtues or vices
rhetoric	gift	grace, betterment	love, faith, hope, pride
exchange	good	efficiency	prudence, justice, greed envy
violence	blow	subordination	courage, temperance, wrath
biology	urge	pleasure, pain	gluttony, lust, sloth

also the law for man."[6] The remark is true, but radically partial, and alarming in a Supreme Court justice. In the next higher realm, of violence (which Holmes also honored: "Every society rests on the death of men"), your satisfaction is not at issue, merely your obedience. You will be distressed that the thief has robbed you or that the judge has sentenced you, but you understand the violence being applied. Next higher is the realm of exchange, tit for tat, to mutual advantage. No minds are changed. Given tastes are served. In the middling realm of exchange, you try to get what gain can be achieved by a deal about goods bought and sold. We libertarians, such as the young Robert Nozick, call them "capitalist acts between consenting adults."

And at the highest end of human relations, the realm of rhetoric, after the persuasive act you are pleased, as after an exchange—but without the bothersome necessity to give something in return. When someone persuades you to believe the Pythagorean theorem, or to believe in the mutual gains from trade, or to drive a Toyota, or to marry, or to worship, you are not anxious (buyer's remorse and the dark night of the soul aside). You have, as we say, "changed your mind." We humans are at our best (and our worst) in the realm of the gift, understood not, as the anthropologist Marcel Mauss did in the 1920s, as merely another, indirect act in the realm of exchange but as unrequited love or faith (or spite or envy) in action.

The extreme case of grace is that God so loved the world that he gave his only begotten son. But merely human gifts, without the givebacks of exchange, are routine. As the economist John D. Mueller (not the Ohio State political scientist and historian of almost the same name) and many other economists, such as Kenneth Boulding (1910–1993), have observed, grace is entirely ignored in the economics of exchange.[7] Boulding invented what he called, infelicitously, "grants economics." He might better have used the anthropologist's term "gift" or even the theologian's term "grace."[8] The grant or gift or grace is still about the economy, since what it transfers is a scarce good. The economy of *God's* grace, to speak of technical theology, differs from human grace precisely because it is unlimited, not scarce.[9] But the grant/gift/grace of a mother giving to her son or the tax/theft/threat of a thug extracting from his victim draws the attention of economists to exactly what they do *not* attend to when thinking of exchange alone.

You know you are in a part of the economy dealing with "grants" instead of exchanges when, as Boulding put it, "*A* gives *B* something and *B* does not give *A* anything in the way of an *economic* good."[10] In a parent's gift to her child or the state's extraction from a citizen (the citizen being viewed in Boulding's terms as Ms. *A*, the state Mr. *B*) "there must be some integrative relationship between them," some sociology or politics legitimating the matter (when it is legitimate), such as the Family or the Tax-and-IRS System, an economy of love or an economy of fear. For example, courtesies such as a man opening a door for a woman signal the existence of a certain kind of gender relationship, for good or ill. To get the whole of the society right we need both the heroic/holy gift and the sensible, purely economic exchange: "Without the heroic," Boulding wrote, "man has no meaning; without the economic, he has no sense."[11] The modern world has broadened the notion of the heroic to include some aspects of commerce. Yet again: sense and sensibility. The Catalans, those ancient traders, describe themselves as having *seny y rauxa*, good sense and great passion. Or as the earlier diagram of the seven principal virtues puts it, we humans deal in both the profane and the sacred, behavior and meaning.

The hostility to trade-tested betterment among aristocrats and peasants is ancient and usual. Still, the hostility even to trade-tested supply is odd, since trade itself is also ancient and usual. We all get our livings or our food and housing and books from it, whether or not we welcome its betterment. Most people nowadays, and for many centuries our ancestors too, have spent most of their lives doing trade. You sell your labor, you buy your bread. What's the beef?

Whatever our role in the realm of exchange we suspect that the other person in our penny- or pound-"capitalism" is cheating us. If "cheating" means "leaving us with less profit than we would have had if the other was idiotically imprudent or wonderfully charitable," then every exchange involves it.

We resent the non-gift (we also sometimes resent the gift: so complex are humans). Anxiety and irritation have always flowed from the gap between what you are willing to pay and what the seller is willing to accept. The gap characterizes all deals in the realm of exchange—wage deals, house deals, bread deals, marriage deals—because they are by definition voluntary. They only occur if both parties agree. If coerced, they are not deals, except in a Jack Benny sense: "Your money or your life." If both parties agree, both must be made better off, at any rate by their own lights. Both are better, yet each could be still more advantaged if only the other party would accede. That's the source of the resentment. (The economists call the situation "being on the contract curve," along which all mutually advantageous deals have been exhausted. Then is the time for charity or violence, to shift one's position on the contact curve.)

Both sides win in a deal, and both have profits. But in the nature of mutual advantage, you could have got *more* profits. There's always that annoying gap. The man in the street calls the gain by his suppliers of groceries and housing their "profit," and resents that he can't shift more of it to himself. He does not pause to reflect that he himself is earning a species of profit too—or else he would not have agreed to the sale in the first place. From a supplier's point of view, the demander is himself a profiteer. Both sides are. Marshallian economists call the gap between willingness to pay and willingness to accept "the sum of consumer's and producer's surplus." Marxists call it, more vividly, and with disapproval, "exploitation" or "surplus value." Anyway it is the social gain from trade—the value created by trade—to be divided somehow into your profit from the transaction and the other person's.

We grumble. Did I get the best deal I could? Has he made a fool of me? He's a vicious profiteer. Why doesn't he gracefully give me a gift? We don't feel so when we have, in Boulding's vocabulary, "some integrative relationship" with the other person. The anonymous, nonintegrative character of much of trade gigantically raises the gains from it. We don't have to be a member of the same hunter-gatherer band to trade. We buy vegetables from California, insurance from Iowa, books from Oxfordshire. We can buy an accordion made in the Czech Republic by people we will never meet. Without such gains from trade, we would have radically lower consumption. If we were denied trade from faraway and confined to the local monopolies and rent-earners, such as protectionism protects, we would be, and were,

radically poorer. The anonymity of trade strikes us, admittedly, as less natural than a mother's gift to her child or a friend's support in distress. Yet without it we would have long hours of work doing the little we could accomplish
in self-sufficiency, trying to make an accordion ourselves from scratch, say,
or growing tomatoes in December in Chicago hothouses.

The trouble is imagination, combined with an aversion to loss that tends
to be stronger psychologically than the pleasure of gain. The psychologists
call it "negativity bias." When I hand over the money for a new house to
some stranger like you with whom I have no integrative relation, I imagine
(more vividly than the gain) the loss you the seller have imposed on me,
twice. After all, you "took" my money for the house, and you also took the
larger net money gain for me that I can imagine you *could* have let me have
by charging me less for the house. You selfish rat.

The brain scientists observe that the amygdala, a primitive part of the
brain interested in fight or flight, gets first dibs on impressions. It's necessary
for quick moves for survival. Don't debate or think it through or consult
an academic theorist—just jump, *now*, away from the saber-toothed tiger's
claw. No wonder our more advanced prefrontal cortex, which would tell us
not to be so silly as to resent a mutually advantageous sale of a house, gets
overwhelmed by negativity.[12]

The Hebrew Bible is full of prophetic thundering against the cheating that
is assumed to characterize the trading life anciently central to the Middle
East. (One can reflect that cheating can characterize *non*trading life with
people, too, even if wholly "integrative"—family life and tribal life, for example, of which the Hebrew Bible also gives many nasty examples—but the
subject here is indignation about the trading life.) The prophet Amos (fl. 750
BCE), for example:

> Hear this, you who trample the needy
>   and do away with the poor of the land, . . .
> skimping on the measure,
>   boosting the price
>   and cheating with dishonest scales.[13]

So always. The anticapitalist anarchistic anthropologist David Graeber, an
Occupy maven, spends 534 pages in *Debt: The First 5,000 Years* (2011) grum-

bling that "arguments about who really owes what to whom have played a central role in shaping our basic vocabulary of right and wrong."[14] His sole intellectual tool is Amos-like indignation against sellers and bosses and owners and creditors. He does not notice that the poor buyers and employees and renters and debtors also gain from such transactions, which after all are undertaken by mutual consent. And on the matter of loans Graeber does not notice the obvious economic logic that if we forthwith cancel all debts, as he repeatedly advises, no creditor will ever lend again. Look at Argentina, cut off from international loans by its populist habit of not paying its creditors. A world of never lending again, or never offering an apartment for a rent set by unhindered deals, or never selling anything at all if the populist state has outlawed the seller's surplus, is not a good plan for helping the poor. Look at badly maintained housing stocks under rent control.

Jack in the English folktale sells his mother's cow for a silly handful of beans, and the mother is outraged by her son's gullibility. "Have you been such a fool, such a dolt, such an idiot, as to give away my Milky-White, the best milker in the parish, and prime beef to boot, for a set of paltry beans? [She beats him.] Take that! Take that! Take that!"[15] The beans prove to be magical, of course, resolving the tension aroused in listeners to the tale by the first act (imagine the story of Jack and the Beanstalk ending abruptly with the mother beating him). Jack himself proceeds to use the beanstalk to climb to the giant's lair, to cheat him, and eventually to kill him, and thereby to amass his own profit. The story exhibits a peasant's view of exchange—always cheating, cheating, cheating, taking every advantage, however small. No mutual gain about it. A trade is viewed as zero-sum, the giant's loss being Jack's gain. Compare Simon Eyre coming upon the wrecked Dutch ship. We are on the economist's contract curve. "Country life," reflects the academic narrator in a J. M. Coetzee novel of 1999 about rural South Africa, "has always been a matter of neighbors scheming against each other." The narrator's early impression of his neighbor Petrus, who tries to cheat him in every deal, is that the man, though admirably hardworking, was "a plotter and a schemer and no doubt a liar too, like peasants everywhere. Honest toil and honest cunning."[16]

Dealing is zero-sum in the opinion of the aristocrats too, or the wannabe aristocrats. In Jane Smiley's *The All-True Travels and Adventures of Lidie Newton* (1998) an honor-obsessed Southerner in Quincy, Illinois, in deep winter around 1840 threatens with his guns drawn a storekeeper and livestock dealer: "Horace Silk, you will cheat me no more! Those mules I sold you for a hundred dollars you turned around and sold to Jed Bindle for two fifty, and you ain't given me none of the profits!" Imagine that—buying low, selling high, and keeping the profit. The Southerner's Borderer-aristocratic code of honor demands violent satisfaction. "But then Horace's father," the narrator continues, "interposed and explained to the man . . . the role of the middleman in every mercantile transaction." It is the rhetoric of a Yankee and a bourgeois, which doubtless helped less than the narrator's mother, who "stepped forward and persuaded [the Southerner] to come farther into the store and get warm," with an implied invitation for peaceful, knightly gallantry toward women, which he accepts.[17] All this cheating magic of trade has long angered people. And it has delighted them too, when they themselves pull it off in their own deals—from that point of view it's a bargain, *een goedkoop*, say the plotting Dutch, a "good buy." I won and he lost.

Zero-sum is the default in thinking about my gain and thine. It is the chief error in economic thinking in the street and in politics. The journalistic rule of balance in TV and newspaper stories has intensified the error, because in every story of a projected betterment the journalist feels she must find someone who says he is hurt by it. The reception among conventional journalists of the taxi-competing Uber is a case in point. Unsurprisingly, it is not difficult to find owners of $300,000 taxi licenses willing to tell the journalist that Uber is an invention of the devil. The journalist slides easily into the role of defending the monopolist licensed by the state against the scandalous competition of a man with a car.

John D. Mueller (the Catholic economist, again) notes that until recently the zero-sum assumption in Aristotle and Aquinas, and now in Pope Francis I, was roughly correct—that is, until 1800.[18] Only briefly in recent European centuries did a coherent rhetoric arise to assuage the anger against the other side of a trade. It partly persuaded a portion of the people that trading is positive-sum. It's the Bourgeois Deal. By contrast, as Mokyr observes, "the obstacles to any kind of technological innovation for an artisan or farmer around 1700 are almost unimaginable to a reader in the twenty-first century."[19] The Bourgeois Deal is accepted on the whole by modern people, though subject to outbreaks of populist reversion to peasant or proletarian type—or if educated, reversion to an aristocratic disdain for trade; or if highly educated, and channeling Evangelical Christianity around 1830, a reversion to theoretical socialism.

The attitude toward trade and betterment is central. Imagine an ancient Rome in which most males were fascinated by gadgets, in which work by hand or abacus was viewed as honorable (*honestus*), in which the occupiers of aristocratic status and other nonworking positions were commonly portrayed as lazy and stupid, in which engineers and inventors were heroes, in which entrepreneurial millionaires had admiring biographies of wide circulation written about them—and you are imagining a Rome that would have had a Great Enrichment. Ditto, with a somewhat different list of counterfactuals, for Song China, say, or the Abbasid Caliphate. But on the contrary, the great Hellenistic engineer Archimedes (ca. 287 BCE–ca. 212 BCE) declared that "the work of an engineer and every art that ministers to needs of life is ignoble and vulgar."[20] It's more noble to devise military engines for the state.

One of the two main historians of the Industrial Enlightenment, Margaret Jacob (Mokyr being the other), attributes the lag of French betterments in the economy to the preponderance of religious opposition to Protestant Newton (and in favor of Catholic Descartes) during the period of Jesuit rule of secondary education before the order's expulsion in 1762, and by the "preponderance of the state and the army in the area of [advanced] technical and mechanical education," even late in the eighteenth century.[21] "When scientifically and mechanically trained engineers came out of schools [in France, as contrasted with bourgeois Britain], they were overwhelmingly aristocratic in background . . . [and] went on generally to become military servants of the state," à la Archimedes. One of them, for example, was a minor aristocrat from Corsica baptized Napoleone di Buonaparte, who graduated in 1784 from an *École des Cadets-gentilshommes* (note the word, *gentilshommes*, literally "high-born men") founded in 1750 for the less wealthy of the aristocrats bound for the army.

Yet Jacob wishes to dispute what she calls the "shibboleth in the historical literature about French industrialization in the eighteenth century" that the state was an obstacle, noting that "the pre-1789 French state should be seen as immensely interested in economic developments, in some cases eager to facilitate them."[22] "Interested" the state was, to be sure, but it was largely ineffective because it depended on expertise from above rather than trade-testing from below, where the people were. Jacob supplies evidence that the immense interest in choosing winners among proposed betterments sub-mitted for judgment and in rewarding inventors with fifty-year monopolies did not turn out well. Only the Revolution saw the dismissal, for example, of the "jury" of the Paris academy under the *ancien régime*, which, aston-ishingly, "had judged industrial innovations." The academies had "power to approve or reject projects as diverse as the installation of a pump on a river or a new method of weaving." Compare the regulative state nowadays in Europe. Such centralizing—though attractive to the rational and aristo-cratic side of the Enlightenment—worked poorly when compared with the liberating, bourgeois, evolutionary, laissez-faire, trade-testing ideology ex-ercised so enthusiastically at the time in Britain. Jacob reports that "when French engineers [those aristocratic military servants of the state] visited Britain in the 1780s they were shocked and impressed by the egalitarian ap-proach taken by [bourgeois] civilians toward engineers." In the end Jacob concedes that "we must include the symbols of birth and authority—the po-litical culture and value system of the *ancien régime*," however theoretically interested the state was in facilitating economic development. The cultural setting of France was in practice hostile to trade-tested betterment, at any rate on a scale of comparison in which a comparatively laissez-faire Britain was a success.[23] France's policy was like that of the numerous modern states immensely interested in the economic development of their citizens (and it may be a few of the rulers and their cousins) by regulating trade in detail and jailing the competitors of state-sponsored monopolies, such as Uber.

Perform a mental experiment on France in the eighteenth century. In a France counterfactually without the nearby and spectacular examples of bourgeois economic and political successes in Holland and then in England and Scotland and in far America (constituting together what the historian Walter Russell Mead calls "the Anglosphere"), modern economic growth would have been killed—even in a France blessed with such clever advo-cates of trade-tested betterment as Vauban, Cantillon (an Irishman living in France, despite his French-appearing name), de Gourney, Voltaire, Quesnay, Turgot, and Condillac.[24] And such men were themselves influenced by the embarrassingly successful Anglo-Saxons across La Manche. Consider how antibourgeois and antilibertarian most of France's elite was until the Rev-olution—or still is for, that matter, in the early twenty-first century. Henry

Kissinger jokes that France, with the highest percentage of government spending in the OECD, is "the only successful communist country." Analytic geometry, because of its military applications, was declared a state secret in early modern France. Turgot fell from his cabinet post of controller-general in 1776 because he proposed the elimination of privileges ranging from those of the guilds' monopoly over technique to the nobility's exemption from taxation. There was haut-bourgeois and aristocratic privilege in Holland and Britain too. But it was less extensive and more reformable by parts.

Among the French for two centuries after the unfinished revolution of 1789 reactionary parties prospered that were uninterested in economic growth if they could but impose a rigid form of Catholicism on the schools and keep the army free of Jews. The cultural struggle was what the French themselves have called the interminable "Franco-French War."[25] Even nowadays the privileged young engineers-in-training of the École Polytechnique in France *march* around in *uniforms*, under a banner inscribed with a motto that would strike students at such bourgeois and anti-aristocratic institutions as MIT or Cal Tech in the United States or the Delft University of Technology in Holland or even at the rather less bourgeois Imperial College in Britain as hilariously antique and unbusinesslike: *Pour la Patrie, les Sciences et la Gloire*. In Spain too, which was the European hegemon of the sixteenth century, economic growth was in fact killed until recently, for conservative reasons (though reasons that continue to trouble the country), despite the examples of the Dutch and British and then even the French.[26] But in the bourgeois and aristocratically dishonorable countries, which eventually included even France—and in the long run even, of all improbable developments, Spain—the circumstances made a new rhetoric, which made new circumstances, which then again made new rhetoric. And the Great Enrichment came.

The problem is to distinguish the specifically late Roman imperial or medieval Christian or French aristocratic-military hostility to trade from the background noise of such hostility in all societies, even in societies like ours in which sufficiently favorable attitudes have allowed the economy and polity to thrive. Such an inquiry, to be persuasive, needs a comparative standard—of which a good one for Britain is France before the Revolution (and to some degree after). The background noise arises from the conviction we all start with—until instructed to the contrary in university or in adult life—that there is a just price, determined perhaps by the labor theory of value or by full and just information on all sides. Our attitudes toward prices is governed by a primitive realism, that is, a philosophical conviction that the essence of a good exists independent of its naming and valuing by humans. As I've noted, Marx as an economist wrote too early to benefit from the discovery by economists in the 1870s that value is determined, as the senior Melamed put it, out "where the people are." Old Aristotle had given examples of the alleged justice of full information, and recent economic theorists such as Joseph Stiglitz have taken up Aristotle's ideal, without giving evidence that falling short of perfection leads the economy all that far astray, or far enough to justify massive interventions by the state.

Janet L. Abu-Lughod and Jack Goldstone, among others, argue that the West and especially northwest Europe won because the East, or even the European east, was temporarily in disarray.[27] True, the "temporary" went on for quite a long time. The historian Andronikos Falangas puts it well when he writes of "a Kafkaesque complexity within the Habsburg bureaucracy, reflecting a conservative, even a distorted, attitude which was astonishingly incompatible with the development of a modern industrial economy."[28]

But the argument from Eastern disarray raises the wider question of why the last few centuries were so ripe for betterment in the West. Imagine, for example, that Europe had succumbed to a crushing theocracy—as many Europeans in the sixteenth and seventeenth century did eagerly imagine. If in such circumstances the Qing dynasty had not been conservative, or the Tokugawa isolationist, or the Moghul Empire unsteady, or the Ottoman Empire beginning its descent into sickness, would one or all of them perhaps have commenced the frenetic betterment after 1700, or perhaps a century or two later, that in fact characterized the West after 1700? That is, was there something oddly conducive to betterment that would have made the years 1700 to, say, 2100 markedly innovative anyway, anywhere?

Think, to take an extreme mental experiment, of the New World high cultures of the Aztecs, Mayans, Incas, and even Mississippians, which were beginning literacy and urbanization long before 1492, and would presumably without the Columbian Catastrophe eventually have had airplanes and the Internet, if perhaps some millennia later. Suppose, for example, that all human populations except for the New World ones had died of a plague in 1491—it is not so extreme a supposition, considering that after 1492, in the other direction, by way of smallpox it nearly happened. Would the descendants eventually have had liberal democracy and human enrichment out of Mayan and Incan or Mississippian civilizations? I think so. Or was there something deeply unique and important about Europeanness? I don't think so. An alternative way of posing the question in the actual history of Europe is to ask whether the other advanced contemporary cultures of Baghdad, Istanbul, Delhi, Beijing, Edo (admitting that there are other candidates on the edges: Timbuktu, for example, or Teotihuacan) faced permanent and insurmountable obstacles to rapid betterment. On its face such a notion seems implausible. The civilization known eventually as Mayan, to take a hard case, was one of merely two to invent place value for numbers and one of merely three or four to invent syllabic or alphabetic, as against iconographic, writing. Why would not a variety of cultures—which cannot, I say again, be cast into a box labelled "Oriental Despotism" and then discarded—all be incapable of rapid betterment? We know that China invented most of our panoply up to 1492, or even 1700. We know that up to the first siege of Vienna in 1529 the Turks were restlessly innovative in warfare and administration. We know that Tokugawa Japan was ingenious in the arts, whether fine or applied, and in other ways (widespread literacy, for example) seemed ready in 1800 for an industrial revolution.

One can blame eastern interference by the state. But the Orient was not the only place where such interference thrived. In 1618 the making of glass declines abruptly in southern England, in favor of glassmaking up in coal-rich Newcastle. One is tempted to put it forward as an instance of the low price of coal causing shifting betterment, supposedly the very soul of economic incentives, as Robert Allen has argued stoutly (against all economic logic and most of the historical evidence).[29] Then one learns that the king had proclaimed in 1615 that *only* coal should be used to make glass, ostensibly to save lumber for the wooden walls of the navy, but in actuality because James I´s favorite, Admiral Sir Robert Mansell of coal-rich Newcastle, got to the king first.[30] Europe was merely lucky that such machinations by the elite were at length overcome by trade-tested, markedly positive-sum betterments.

46

THE HOSTILITY WAS ANCIENT

Trading and profit making and entrepreneurship and betterment have been more or less despised by the aristocracy in pastoral or agricultural societies, and by the neo-aristocratic clerisy in our industrial society. True, one needs to think through the ample evidence for the ancient Near East, which seems on its face to be an exception. Yet the usual routine is despising trade. The Bhagavad Gita, in a society dominated by Aryan aristocrats in the manner of the *Iliad*, admitted that "those who take shelter in Me [Krishna, God], though they be of lower birth [than the aristocracy]—women, *merchants*, workers—can attain the supreme destination."[1] Good. But the merchants were nonetheless of lower birth.

Likewise, the commercial Chinese have long been burdened by a Confucian disdain for the class of merchants, ranked in the hierarchy even below peasants. Until the 1990s the undoubted doctrinal fact was emphasized by historians of China. Now some of the historians doubt that the low ranking mattered much. By now the mainland Chinese seem to have got over their disdain, as their cousins overseas had managed to do for many centuries. The fact suggests strongly that what has kept China poor has not been somehow Confucianism or Chineseness, but the governance of the Central Kingdom, especially under the Ming and Qing and Mao. As Mokyr puts it, what the Confucian tradition disdained was new useful knowledge or, as I would add, new knowledge useful by a test in trade. Chinese "Communist" real income per person is still a fifth of what it is in the United States. There is plenty of time for the Chinese to revert to ancient Confucian ideology and to kill, or at least sicken, the golden goose, as Argentinians did in the twentieth century and as crony capitalism has in Japan and as the habit of regulation and not-in-my-back-yard threatens to do in the United States.

The Christians in their beginnings were among the most anticommercial people of faith, more so than Jews or Muslims or Hindus or Zoroastrians or even Buddhists.[2] Important theorizers about the economy in the first millennium of Christianity were monks and mystics and desert fathers, in the style of St. Augustine deprecating the mere City of Man. The desert fathers and their anticommercial ideals were a large influence on Muslim mysticism too, despite the Muslim admiration for a merchant capitalist of Mecca.[3] The main historical paradox of the present book is that, startlingly, it was a Christian Europe, slowly after 1300 and unstoppably after 1700, that redeemed the bourgeois life.

Braudel wrote in 1979 that "when Europe came to life again in the eleventh century, the market economy and monetary sophistication were 'scandalous' novelties. Civilization, standing for ancient tradition, was by definition hostile to betterment. So it said no to the market, no to profit making, no to capital. At best it was suspicious and reticent."[4] Braudel was wrong about the practicalities of life, which were immersed in markets. But he was right about the surrounding ideology, especially about economic success. Simmel had put it well in 1907: "The masses—from the Middle Ages right up to the nineteenth century—thought that there was something wrong with the origin of great fortunes. . . . Tales of horror spread about the origin of the Grinaldi, the Medici, and the Rothschild fortunes . . . as if a demonic spirit was at work."[5] Simmel is being precise here, as he usually is. It is the masses, the populists, *hoi polloi*, who hold such views most vividly. A jailer in the thirteenth century scorned a rich man's pleas for mercy: "Come, Master Arnaud Teisseire, you have wallowed in such opulence! . . . How could you be without sin?"[6] Echoing Jesus when he speaks of rich men and camels, another of Le Roy Ladurie's Albigensians declared that "those who have possessions in the present life can have only evil in the other world. Conversely, those who have evil in the present life will have only good in the future life."[7]

Such disdain for possessions in the present life, and the matched disdain by landed aristocrats for the vulgarity of trade-tested betterment, is even nowadays hard to ignore even among the elite, because it is built into European literary and religious traditions, providing the foundations for novels such as Sinclair Lewis's *Main Street* or Richard Power's *Gain*, and movies galore. The peasant woman envied profit makers—though she took profit on her sales of eggs. The proletarian man grumbled about his boss—though he changed his tune when he became one. The aristocratic baron disdained traders—though he engaged in profitable trade when he could get away with it without losing social position, as at Florence. The historian Michael McCormick notes that the "late Roman legacy of contempt for commerce," reinforced by the rhetoric of the modern clerisy ashamed of its own bourgeois origins, has occluded the evidence for a revival of European trade in the eighth and especially the ninth centuries (note: two or three centuries earlier than the Belgian economic historian Henri Pirenne in 1925 had put it, or Braudel following him). "Christian dislike of commerce—if not for its proceeds—allied with the new aristocratic ethos of a warrior life to produce a ruling class [and therefore surviving evidence written by or in praise of them] that was often indifferent and sometimes even hostile to the trading life."[8] It continued in another version the scorn for the bourgeoisie that aristocratic Greeks and senatorial Romans displayed.

The historian David Gilmour argues persuasively that the difficulty of absorbing Italy into the Holy Roman Empire of the north left the Italians of Lombardy and Tuscany as early as the eleventh century to their own devices: "The growth and prosperity of the cities gave their citizens the desire and self-confidence to run the affairs of their own communes."[9] Northern Italians never really got over being merchants, though merchants who periodically dreamed of martial glory. The English writer Tobias Smollett lived in Florence during the 1760s: "With all their pride, however, the nobles of Florence are humble enough to enter into partnership with shop-keepers, and even to sell wine by retail. It is an undoubted fact, that in every palace or great house in this city, there is a little window fronting the street, provided with an iron-knocker, and over it hangs an empty flask, by way of sign-post. Thither you send your servant to buy a bottle of wine. . . . It is pretty extraordinary, that it should not be deemed a disparagement in a nobleman to sell half a pound of figs, . . . or to take money for a flask of sour wine."[10] One would then wonder, if Smollett was correct, why the Florentines did not create an industrial revolution.

No one in Europe before the nineteenth century created a thoroughly business-respecting civilization on a large scale. Commercial Verona came to be ruled by *gentlemen* of Verona, as was a commercial England in Shakespeare's time ruled by men with swords and sonnet cycles and positions at court rather than by men with ledger books. Even Antwerp in the Spanish Netherlands, mistress of sixteenth-century European trade, was governed by an oligarchy of nontraders. But in Amsterdam and Rotterdam and Leiden, and especially in Birmingham and Manchester and Glasgow, and then in Philadelphia and New York and Boston, the economic rhetoric did change, permanently.

Even in commercial Italy the line between aristocrat and *borghese* was sharp—even when the aristocrats were, like the Medici, descended from the middle class. The storyteller Giovanni Boccaccio (1313–1375) was the son of an employee of the Bardi bank of Florence (the bank was soon to be brought down by the refusal of proud Edward III of England to honor his debts). Boccaccio was raised to be a banker. In his collection of tales, *The Decameron* (composed 1349–1351), he treats merchants respectfully—though, like his countryman Dante a half century before, he is hard on merchants who cheat.

Yet Boccaccio's story about Saladin disguised as a traveling merchant of Cyprus (in order to discover and outwit the European preparations for the Third Crusade, 1189–1192) depends on the irony of noblemen unable to conceal their nobility—though allegedly mere *mercanti*. The Italian host, Torello, a "gentleman" (*gentiluomo*) or "knight" (*cavaliere*), a member of the Lombard urban gentry and not of the aristocracy ("he was a private urban citizen and not a [rural] lord": *era cittadino e non signore*) exclaims of the three noble Saracens, before he has quite penetrated their merchantly disguise, "May it please God for our part of the world to produce gentlemen [*gentili uomini*] of the same quality I now find in Cypriot merchants!"[11] Nobility shines through. Torello "thought they were men of eminence [*magnifichi uomini*], of much higher rank than he had imagined at first." Note the placement by rank in a hierarchy, which was the first task on meeting a stranger in the premodern world. It is similar to the first task of placement by race in the United States or by U/non-U social class in South Britain. Torello gives them silk- and fur-lined robes, in Polanyi's style of reciprocal exchange. The Saracens, "seeing the nobility [*nobilità*] of the robes, non-merchant-like [*non mercatantesche*]," fear he has sniffed them out. Though Torello does not entirely realize the great eminence of his guests (in European literature even a century and a half after the Third Crusade, Saladin was treated routinely as the most noble of opponents), he exclaims on parting—one last insult for the *borghese* compared with *magnifichi uomini*—"Whoever you are, you can't make me believe for the present that you are [implied: mere] merchants!"[12]

The result in most of Europe diverged strikingly from the zest for both exchange and warfare one finds in the elite of the pagan, Germanic north. Such a melding continued to characterize, McCormick observes, the saga literature of the Christian thirteenth century looking back on Iceland's founding and Norway's kings.[13] Vikings were traders as much as raiders. The words in Irish for "market," "penny," and "shilling" all come from the Norse traders and enslavers, who founded Dublin, Wexford, Waterford, Limerick, and Cork. (Some of my Norwegian ancestors, then, enslaved for profit some of my Irish ancestors. I wonder therefore to whom to apply for reparations.) Similarly the Mongols of the Golden Horde in southern Russia kept busy raiding the Slavs/slaves, to be transported for sale in Constantinople, and extracting protection money from Muscovy 1242–1480 and its neighbors. In modern Russian the words for "money," "goods," and "exchequer" are all of Mongol origin.[14]

Such facts make strange one contrast between the cultures of the Mediterranean and of the German Ocean.[15] Germanic law codes of early times encourage cash compensation for dishonor. (At least for free men. The laws we have are only about them—using the words "free" and "man" strictly— that is, about aristocrats and other men of high status relative to a dishonorable if large majority class of slaves and women.) An eye for an eye is always possible and honorable in the German laws (and in the code of Hammurabi of Babylon, circa 1792–1750 BCE). But so is thus-and-such quantity of silver for the eye, which payment abruptly ends the blood feud. Tacitus is a not surprised that minor crimes are punished simply by a fine, in cattle or horses (in keeping with his implausible claim that the *Germani* knew not the use of even foreign-coined money). But the major and capital crimes he instances with amazement are not mere assault (on that eye, for example) but large matters like cowardice or treason. Among the Germans, Tacitus writes, "even homicide can be atoned for by a fixed number of cattle or sheep," and therefore "feuds do not continue forever unreconciled."[16] Tacitus (probably of Gaulish origin but thoroughly Mediterraneanized) is astonished that the Germans let profane cash into matters of sacred honor. The prudent answer to a crime, you see, is to demand *wergeld*, dissolving endless blood feuds in the solvent of cash. The hero Gunnar in the Icelandic *Njáls Saga* does so, as did every honorable Icelander in those heroic days around 990 CE, at any rate according to the sagas composed around 1290 CE.

By contrast, in the south, from Homer to El Cid to *The Godfather*, one's honor is absolute. What is strange is that the implacable southerners had long lived in a monetized and commercialized Mediterranean, heirs to a classical civilization based since the early first millennium BCE on seagoing trade from Sidon to Sicily. Yet they would not accept money for murder. The savages of the northern forests, by contrast, were making delicate calculations of monetary equivalences in a supposedly less commercial society. The honorable—that is, the aristocratic—part of the civilization of the classical Mediterranean had always been suspicious of getting money, though eager to have it and spend it. By contrast the Icelandic sagas (written well after their events, I repeat, and not reports from the scene) are about men unashamedly at the margin between commerce and piracy. Arriving at a new coast they had to decide whether to steal what they wanted or to trade for it. Great hoards of Byzantine coins are found in Norse settlements around the Baltic, and around the North and the Irish seas, evidence that the piratical and commercial ventures of the Vikings were not narrow in scope.[17] But all this merely enlarges the paradox, that the apparently advanced part of the Western world had from the beginning to the present a more primitive and anticommercial code of honor. At any rate they had a less bourgeois one from Monday through Friday, and on Sundays a more otherworldly one, than in the primitive north. It makes one think that perhaps the first-second-third-stage-evoking vocabulary of "advanced" and "primitive" doesn't quite capture human attitudes toward trade.

The pagan Viking attitude toward merchants did not win out. Mediterranean values did. In late fourteenth-century England, for example, Chaucer favorably characterizes the three most admired classes, "A KNIGHT there was, and that a worthy man. . . . A poor PARSON of a town / But rich he was of holy thought and work. . . . With him there was a PLOUGHMAN who was his brother / . . . Living in peace and perfect charity."[18] No merchants are among the three honored. Chaucer characterizes the two dozen other pilgrims mentioned in "The General Prologue" (1387) of *The Canterbury Tales* in notably less flattering terms. True, the owner of the Tabard, our host, is described genially ("a fairer burgher is there none at Cheapside"). The five urban craftsmen of the middling sort mentioned together as dressed in fraternal livery (haberdasher, carpenter, weaver, dyer, and tapestry maker) are described, too, as "fair burghers," worthy to "sit in a guildhall on a dais," or to be aldermen (for property they had enough, and rent), but such folk are not further characterized in the extant *Tales*—except that in his tale the bourgeois Miller makes merry of a carpenter.[19] The Sergeant of the Law was "cautious and prudent," of "high renown."[20]

But four of the five solidly middle-class figures, the Merchant, the Reeve (that is, steward of his master's estate), the Miller, and the Doctor of Physik, are described in the "General Prologue," unsurprisingly in medieval literature, as vain, cheating dealers: the Merchant "proclaiming always the increase of his winning"; and "full rich [the Reeve] had a-storèd privily," shorting his master; and "well could [the Miller] steal corn, and charge its toll thrice"; and the Doctor "kept the gold he won [that is, earned] in pestilence. / For gold in physik is a cordiàl [that is, in medicine, a cure]. / Therefore he lovèd gold in speciàl."

The test does not have much power, because with the exception of the three honored classes and a few hearty, harmless, or holy others, all classes are greedy in Chaucer. A nonbourgeois, religious figure, the avaricious seller of papal pardons, is said to be as eager "to win silver as he full well could." The begging Friar, likewise, deals only with rich people, and gladly hears confessions of men hard of heart who cannot truly feel sorrow for their sins (recall "Come, Master Arnaud Teisseire, you have wallowed in such opulence!"), and "therefore instead of weeping and prayers / Men must give silver to the poor friars."[21] And so forth. Throughout the *Tales* one class accuses another of greed and hypocrisy, supplemented by lust. That, after all, is the running joke.

Right down to the Reformation, and in anticlericalism down to the present, the merchant has replied to the charge of worldly corruption that, after all, the priest too, in his splendid robes, is indulging in the world's pleasures, as he should not. Pope Francis I in 2013 refused the fancy housing and fancy dress of the popes, startling the world. By contrast, Chaucer's Monk, who loved hunting, regards the rule of St. Benedict as "old and somewhat strict": "he was a lord [note: a lord] full fat and in good point."[22] The Merchant character in David Lindsay's *Satire of the Three Estates* in the Scots of 1542–1544, a century and a half after Chaucer, does not defend his own social usefulness directly—as two centuries after Lindsay in Scotland, in the time of Hume and Smith, he would have most vigorously—but spends most of his stage time complaining about the clerical characters and their multiple benefices (holding many parishes simultaneously without giving pastoral care to any of them) and simony (selling church offices).[23]

One must not get carried away with literary examples like these. As a leading student of early Italian commerce points out, Chaucer's or Boccaccio's or other imaginative "portrayals" of merchants are "organized by a complex system of stereotypes and rhetorical images often resulting from ancient cultural models."[24] For example, the Merchant's obsession in Lindsay's *Satire* with the sins of the clergy is a standard turn in medieval literature, one estate complaining about the other instead of answering the (presumably true) charges just mentioned against itself. These are literary works, with, as the professors of literature after Julia Kristeva say, an "intertextual" relation to Horace or Virgil or the reciters of the Upanishads with their complaints about the pursuit of riches (while sitting pretty, as Horace and Virgil, for example, did, on riches earned by their poetry and their pro-Augustus politics). Literary and other texts are not somehow "objective" reports from the cultural frontier. Yet the historian James Davis, after a wide-ranging examination of the medieval English evidence, concludes, "What is striking is there are virtually no positive references in the literary and religious sources to capital accumulation, middlemen and retailers, entrepreneurship, product development or even economic growth."[25]

A century after Chaucer the Flemish-English play *Everyman* turns on a repeated metaphor of life's account book, from which one might mistakenly infer that commerce and the middle class were admired. Everyman says to Death, "all unready is my book of reckoning," and later, when he believes that Kindred will save him, "I must give a reckoning straight."[26] His deeds on the credit side do not suffice, as the character named Good Deeds himself says: "If ye had perfectly cheered me, / Your book of count full ready had be." As Everyman goes to his grave he says, "I must be gone / To make my reckoning and my debts pay."

But the inference from all this talk of accounting to an admiration of trade is of course mistaken. The metaphor of life's balance sheet before God is routine in all religions, whether well disposed toward bourgeois profit or not. Christianity in particular, though hostile from the beginning to commerce, is based on a metaphor of redemption of debt through Christ's sacrifice. The Greek word used in the New Testament for redemption, *apolutrosis*, was a commercial one (though as the historian Luke Gardiner notes, "Marcion of Sinope's [ca. 85–160] depiction . . . of Christ's redemptive Passion as an act of exchange, 'purchasing mankind from the Creator,' elicited outrage well into late Antiquity"[27]). At the end of the play Everyman appeals to Jesus: "As thou me boughtest, so me defend." And the third of his earthly companions to betray him, after Fellowship and Kindred, is his much-beloved pal, Goods. Everyman laments "Alas, I have thee loved, and had great pleasure / All my life-days on goods and treasure." To which Goods replies, as in olden times the prophet Joel replied, and the Messiah Jesus replied, and anticonsumerist clerisy still do, "That is to thy damnation, without leasing / For my love is contrary to the love everlasting." "My condition is man's soul to kill." And this too is, anciently, routine literary stuff.

And yet. Elsa Strietman, in discussing the Dutch version of *Everyman*, sees in the text a pre-Reformation focus "on the individual's responsibility to live a just life," and quotes the theologian Alister McGrath on its similarity to Luther's doctrine of the priesthood of all believers.[28] The first and Dutch version was a product of the "chambers of rhetoric" in the little cities of the southern Low Counties 1450–1550, described by another student of the matter as being institutions where "the self-confidence of the wealthy citizens manifested itself," against the prestige of courtly literature at Brussels or the Hague. "At a social level the *rederijkers* [the rhetoricians] formed a [haut bourgeois] liberation movement" against the aristocracy.[29] "The material side of life," Strietman remarks, "is not condemned or belittled as unworthy per se, which would fit in well if the intended audience of the play were not a world-forsaking monastic audience, but [as was the case in Brugge and Leuven] an urban community actively engaged in trading and banking. . . . The complaint against Elckerlijc [the Dutch name for Everyman] is that he has amassed possessions and loved them *extravagantly*. . . . [It is] the *immoderate* use of God's creation which invokes the Creator's terrible wrath."

A rich man may enter the kingdom of heaven, if he is temperate in his pursuit and use of wealth. The economist and intellectual historian Jacob Viner asserted in 1959 that "the Renaissance, especially in its Italian manifestations, brought new attitudes with respect to the dignity of the merchant, his usefulness to society, and the general legitimacy of the moderate pursuit of wealth through commerce, provided the merchant who thus attained riches used it with taste, with liberality, and with concern for the welfare and the magnificence of his city."[30] The attitude in bourgeois towns has not in truth changed much since then. Nowadays, at least outside of the corrupting theories of Max U economists, most normal people judge it blameworthy in a merchant to pursue wealth immoderately, extravagantly, tastelessly, illiberally, and without concern for the welfare of the poor and the magnificence of the city. Talk about this to the Pritzkers of Chicago, heirs to the Hyatt fortune, such as Jennifer Pritzker, who has financed a center for military history and subsidized studies of gender. Or visit little Muscatine in southeast Iowa and find its millionaires giving and giving to the University of Iowa.

But Viner was mistaken in overlooking the *medieval* precedents for an ethical bourgeoisie, and therefore incorrect in attributing the change to the aristocracy-admiring Renaissance—though he was correct that the precedents did not until much later become large enough to be the thing itself, a large-scale bourgeois civilization mainly free from aristocratic or clerical disdain and interference. Viner's history was off by a couple of centuries, so far as some high theory and a lot of low practice was concerned. At the time he wrote, the Renaissance was still seen by scholars as utterly novel, a sharp beginning for the modern world. Viner wrote at the height of the scholarly conviction that a chasm divides us moderns from the Dark Ages of medieval times. Since then historians such as Quentin Skinner, Jacques Le Goff, Lynn White, Ambrose Raftis, and David Herlihy have looked back into the scholastic and medieval sources, finding even a natural right of revolution in the writings of Dominicans and a justification for trading work in the writings of Franciscans and widespread technical betterment in a Europe allegedly uninterested in success in this world.

Yet the words mattered. That merchants were not honored, and that the taking of interest was officially banned (but only officially), put hooks and chairs in the way of betterment. As Timur Kuran puts it in discussing the parallel "ban" on paying interest among Muslims, "by blocking honest public discussion of commercial, financial, and monetary matters, it hindered the development of the capitalist mentality."[31] It is the problem—honest public discussion—to which the seventeenth and eighteenth centuries in northwestern Europe provided the solution. We have a similar disinclination even nowadays to discuss the good of a commercial culture.

47

YET SOME CHRISTIANS ANTICIPATED
A RESPECTED BOURGEOISIE

In other words, the attitude of medieval Europe and its church toward the bourgeoisie was nothing like entirely hostile, especially in northern Italy and in some of the ports of Iberia and the Baltic, even if it did not result in the business-dominated civilization of the southern Low Countries after 1400, and more widely Holland after 1568, and England after 1688. Barcelona, for example, was from medieval times an exception to the antibourgeois character of the rest of Spain—as in some ways it still is, and as Basque Bilbao came to be in the nineteenth century.

In Portugal during the fourteenth and fifteenth centuries, for example, the merchants were respected. The Portuguese had reconquered their Iberian territories from the Muslims with less effort than the Castilians had, and one could argue therefore that they were less militarized and therefore less captured by aristocratic values. Albert Hirschman quotes, and applies to the antibourgeois Spaniards of Castile, the backward-looking opinion of the Marquis de Vauvenargues (1715–1747) that "a man of quality, by fighting, acquires wealth more honorably and quickly than a meaner man by work."[1] It was the antique sentiment of the nobility. According to Tacitus the ancient German warrior thought it "tame and spiritless to accumulate slowly by the sweat of his brow what can be got quickly by the loss of a little blood."[2] In such a society the incentives to zero-sum rent seeking, as the economists put it nowadays, are plain enough. By contrast the Portuguese merchant and the "merchant knight" (*cavaleiro-mercador*, an impossible juxtaposition in most of Europe at the time) encouraged by Prince Henry the Navigator (1396–1460) and others in its vigorous royal family gave little Portugal the third European empire of trade, after those three centuries earlier of Venice and Genoa. In assembling their empires quickly the knight merchants of all three were willing to lose a little blood too.

Even in ancient Rome, Emanuel Mayer has argued, a pro-bourgeois rhetoric had some space.[3] And in western Christianity from the thirteenth century even certain high theorists admitted trading and profit as ethical goals. Thomas Aquinas and Duns Scotus, among others, such as Sinibaldo de Fieschi (later Pope Innocent IV, reigned 1243–1254), worked out in the high Middle Ages an ethical life for merchants. The criterion was that profit was acceptable if at the level necessary to maintain one's (God-given) place in the Great Chain of Being. In the early sixteenth century the Italian theologian and disputant with Luther, Tomasso de Vio (Thomas Cajetan), widened the criterion to admit higher profit for those with unusual abilities—an early statement of a marginal productivity theory of ethics: "It is reasonable that those with particular natural virtues aspire to positions of supremacy or wish to accumulate money."[4] Robert Nozick could not have said it better.

We moderns are inclined on the contrary to imagine with Hume and Voltaire and other deists, atheists, anti-Papists, anticlericals, and Protestants nowadays that the Middle Ages always elevated "monkish virtues" over the trade that Hume and Voltaire found so very civilizing. Yet the urban monks of the thirteenth century in fact emphasized the dignity of work in a proto-bourgeois fashion that sat poorly with the aristocratic, antiwork values of the Roman Empire. St. Benedict, son of a nobleman, had said in 529, *Otiositas inimica est animæ* (Leisure the enemy is of the spirit; *Rule, caput*, xliv), and required his monks to work manually, as only slaves and women and the undignified freedmen proletariat or the lower bourgeoisie did in the ancient ideal. The theologian Max Stackhouse argues that in modern times the identification of God's work with the world's work has gone further and is characteristic of western Christianity. He quotes the Marxian historian of technology David Noble: "Technology had come to be identified with transcendence. . . . Christianity alone [even in the Middle Ages] blurred the distinction . . . between the human and the divine."[5]

In any case, the antitrading theme in radical monkishness, seen in the desert fathers from the third to the fifth century, culminating in St. Augustine's (qualified) disdain for the City of Man, and echoing down the centuries to follow, fit poorly with a Europe reviving commercially from the eighth century on. The Avignon pope I have mentioned, John XXII (reigned

1316–1334), who had studied law in Paris, was highly suspicious of some of the poverty-glorifying friars. In 1329 he argued that man's possession of property was parallel to God's possession of the universe, an instance, you see, of man being made in the image of God. Altogether, with many of the popes down to the recent ones bestowing papal aristocracy on Mafia bankers, John XXII was satisfied with private property, at least if it was used for Christian—or at any rate church—purposes.

Nor was disdain for work in God's world consistent, as the historian Giacomo Todeschini has recently observed in an important essay, with the task that popes and abbots faced, "the pragmatic need to manage the system of Church properties."[6] Yet the economic theorizing of the church was not solely a self-interested trick—though a church taxed by, say, Philip the Fair of France did need some self-interested arguments if it was to survive in the king's law courts and in courtly opinion. The medieval doctors of the church devised a justification for trade—and this against their heritage from old Aristotle the teacher of aristocrats or, as I say, their more spiritual heritage from work-and-world-disdaining desert fathers and Augustine—that emphasized the work involved in trade. (If you believe that buying low and selling high is not work, you need to read the anxious correspondence of the Tuscan merchant Francesco Datini, 1335–1410).[7] Thus, what everyone thinks she knows about the medieval economy, that interest was forbidden, was made false in practice. Work allowed the charging of interest, even if in veiled forms, such as by foreign exchange transactions and false sales. Said the theologians: as God had worked to make the universe, so the Italian merchants worked to earn their just rewards. Both rested on the seventh day. Admiration of work is the central characteristic of a modern bourgeoisie. Here it fits easily with Abrahamic theology, which after all from its beginnings in Abram's property deal with the Lord has admired a hardworking engagement with God's creation. And a little dealing on the side.

Todeschini argues that to understand the cultural identity of late medieval businessmen it won't do to adopt "a forced and timeless separation of the lay and religious rationalities or of the opposition between economics and moral codes."[8] I would only add to his formulation that to understand the cultural identity of *modern* businesspeople it won't do to adopt a forced and timeless (Todeschini means "time-and-placeless," that is, "allegedly universal") separation of the lay and religious rationalities or of the opposition between economics and moral codes.

The medieval Italian manufacturers and merchants whom Todeschini describes were not merely Easter-duty Christians. They worked at their faith as they worked at their trading. (But I repeat: they do so now too, unless some professor or novelist has persuaded them that economic activity is inconsistent with moral codes.) "The conceptual grammar utilized in medieval economic treatises . . . [was] strictly connected with the theological language of election, salvation, and spiritual profit."[9] In thirteenth- and fourteenth-century Italy the "body" of the commercial companies (*il corpo delle compagnie*) is imagined as "the mystic Body of the city as the double of Christ's Body."[10]

Really, it was. In an allegedly secular age we sophisticated and agnostic and even anticlerical intellectuals can't quite believe such talk, and suppose with a smirk that we are witnessing hypocrisy. "Aha, Senior Datini: caught again pretending to be motivated by love of God, or at least the fear of Hell!" But read the ample writings and confidential notebooks of Italian merchants of the time, Todeschini argues, and you have to abandon the cynical and materialist hypothesis. The Fourth Lateran Council of 1215 figures with his Italian businessmen as much or more than the merely present bottom line—as the Council of Trent in 1562–1563 figured in the motivations of their anti-Protestant descendants. In the thirteenth century even in bourgeois Italy "the notion of 'good reputation' (*fama*) . . . is deeply related to the theological and juridical discourse about the importance of Christians to carefully protect the purity of their civic and religious 'name.'"[11] As Father Augustine Thompson argues in a recent book on "the lost holiness of the Italian republics," the communes of northern and central Italy in their democratic heydays 1125–1328 "were simultaneously religious and political entities. . . . Even the most evocative appreciations of communal political theory obscure its Christian character. Ecclesiastical and civic institutions formed a single communal organism." He instances the construction of baptisteries, such as the Florentine one with Lorenzo Ghiberti's Gates of Paradise, used for the characteristic rite of popular religion in the Italian cities. "Baptism made the children citizens of both the commune and of heaven. . . . These rites came to be so closely associated with republican identity that they were among the first things to go as princes established seigniorial rule in the early 1300s," and at last even in Genoa and Florence, the eldest children of liberty.[12]

Todeschini agrees: the commune was a "sacred society," even among its merchants. "It would be easy," he writes, "to underestimate this attention . . .

to the reputation of the merchant and define it as the obvious result of an increasing market society, duly concerned about the economic trustworthiness of its members: but it would be an error, . . . [a] very reductive point of view."[13] Licentiousness or commercial unreliability was a sin against the Body of Christ. The proverb on men's lips was "Gain at the cost of a bad reputation ought rather to be called a loss."[14] Says Death to Everyman, "He that loveth riches I will strike with my dart, / His sight to blind, and from heaven to depart— / Except that alms be his good friend— / In hell for to dwell, world without end."[15] Again, "hell" was no figure of speech among such men. They trembled in terror of it. The merchants of Siena and Prato and Milan "had the duty to be rich and at the same time honorable men."[16] It is rather like the merchants of New York and Tokyo and Mumbai today. Donato Ferrario founded a divinity school in fifteenth-century Milan, the way again the Pritzkers of Chicago have financed hospitals and libraries and architecture prizes, and it would be "improper and anachronistic" to decode "this choice as [a] simple and clever social expedient"—for Donato Ferrario or Jennifer N. Pritzker.[17] The gospel of wealth of a medieval merchant was based on the literal gospels and on the interpretation of the gospels by doctors of the church. The problem in modern life is that the cynical doctors of economics and their populist opponents, both, undermine a gospel of wealth—an undermining powered by a forced and timeless separation of the lay and religious rationalities.

Greed in northern Italy was constrained by secular virtues too, dating in their theorizing back to classical times and to Aristotle. The manuals for Italian businessmen in the fifteenth century appropriated the qualities that civic humanism assigned to the leaders of the *polis*.[18] Benedetto Cotrugli advises the captain of a merchant ship to be sober, vigorous, temperate, eloquent, and well-renowned (*de extimatione predito*). The northern Italian bourgeoisie of the fourteenth and fifteenth centuries exercised the virtue of profit-seeking prudence, to be sure. But they balanced prudence with holy faith and love, and pagan courage and justice too.

Admittedly, Todeschini himself explicitly asserts that "the caution and vigilance concerning moral, civic, . . . [and] economic behaviors" in the fourteenth and fifteenth centuries "cannot be reduced to an early manifestation of [a] 'bourgeois' spirit."[19] In his complaint about coding honorable and charitable behavior of the Florentines as "anachronistic" he implies that such decoding is all right nowadays. Todeschini appears to mean by "bourgeois" the modern notion, after Rousseau and Marx and Sartre, of single-minded pursuit of the largest possible bottom line, the restless stirring for gain, the absolute desire for enrichment, the passionate hunt for value. And he appears to think that it is characteristic of the modern world. He too is trapped in the modern prejudice against the very word "bourgeois," and in its recent use as a term of contempt.

I would reply that early and late, nowadays as in the fourteenth century, the member of *la borghesia* believes that "the social *Corpus* only . . . can sanctify his economic activities and identify him as a trustworthy merchant."[20] Tim Parks takes a more cynical view, arguing that a rich Florentine such as Cosimo de Medici (the Elder, or his distant relation, the Grand Duke) "bought his place in paradise" and "seduced the clergy by financing major Church renovation," and the ravishing religious art of the Renaissance. Parks imagines a modern Italian bourgeois on the highly subsidized rapid train to Rome saying to himself, "I feel virtuous—wealthy and virtuous—like those old Renaissance bankers. Isn't this what it means to be bourgeois, after all? A state of mind invented in Florence in the fifteenth century: the virtuous, forgivably self-satisfied businessman."[21] But businesspeople in the *quattrocento* as much as now want to be good, no less than politicians or priests or professors do, and indeed the businesspeople have the moral luck to be in situations daily where good and bad are obvious and the results clear. A rotten order of fish served in his restaurant has a more immediate result for the bourgeois owner than a rotten set of ideas offered up by the thoughtlessly antibourgeois professor. True, the earnest businesspeople often fail in their ethical projects, as fallen humans do. Yet so do the politicians, priests, and professors. Contrary to the notion that medieval people were very different from you and me, the medieval church allowed the merchants to do their good work—but held them to a high standard, with the tortures of the *Inferno* awaiting those who failed in their Christian duty.

Leon Battista Alberti (1404–1472) is best known for his pioneering of art criticism, but he wrote also a dialogue about the family, in which the character Giannozzo declares that "it is, perhaps, a kind of slavery to be forced to plead and beg with other men in order to satisfy our necessity [instead of working and trading to do so]. That is why we do not scorn riches." In quoting the Alberti passage, Richard Pipes notes that "this positive view of property and wealth came to dominate Western thought in the seventeenth and eighteenth centuries."[22] True, and the theme here. Adam Smith echoes Alberti's logic when he writes in the butcher-brewer-baker passage, "Nobody but a beggar chooses to depend chiefly on the benevolence of his fellow-citizens."[23]

But even in commercial Florence such views did not flower into a fully bourgeois civilization. Perhaps it is because they took root in an antibourgeois Italy dominated by princes of the land and of the church. In Dante's time, as in many times, a trade—with more or less everything else about our sublunary life—was viewed as an occasion for sin, and profit was viewed as its sign. Holiness in 1300 was earned by prayers and charitable works, whereas buying low and selling high was deemed even by a citizen of commercial Florence such as Dante a great danger to the soul (not that the powerful churchmen in *The Divine Comedy* were much more likely to avoid the danger). As it was put a century before Dante by the holier-than-thou Albigensians in southern France, the truly holy people were the "poor of the faith," that is, rich people like St. Francis of Assisi who chose in 1205 "lady poverty, a fairer bride than any of you have seen."[24] And still in Shakespeare's time, three centuries after Dante, a claim of "virtue" for a merchant was seen as flatly ridiculous. "Let me have no lying," says the rogue Autolycus in *The Winter's Tale*, "It becomes none but a merchant."[25] Ulysses says in *Troilus and Cressida*, "Let us like merchants show our foulest wares / And think perchance, they'll sell."[26]

At the other end of the five centuries of the momentous turn from an antibusiness to a probusiness civilization, Dante to Adam Smith, stands a pious dyer of wool cloth in Leeds, Joseph Ryder. The historian Matthew Kadane has recently described Ryder's diary, kept from 1733 to 1768 in forty-odd volumes, amounting to two million words (my long book is merely one-eighth as long). Dissenters were known for such spiritual exercises, a genre out of which *Robinson Crusoe* grew. Ryder's diary is probably not an exception, though in the nature of the case we do not have a random sample of a hundred such works to scrutinize—merely the long tradition of Puritan scrupulosity and its literary effusions from bourgeois men and women accustomed by their daily work to keeping accounts.

The job was, as Kadane puts it, "to watch oneself for the smallest sign of deviation from the godly course."[27] Ryder watched himself with the intensity of a Woody Allen character under psychoanalysis, and for the same reason: his modern life in trade, he believed, might corrupt his soul. He wrote— Ryder could have been a writer of hymns—"The dangers numerous are which every saint surround / Each worldly pleasure has its snare if riches do abound."[28] It is an ancient theme, that one cannot serve both God and mammon. The sin of pride in possessions or in success leads away from God, as does pride in anything here below. As Ryder put the matter in another of his hymnlike lines: "If I'm concerned too much with things below / It makes my progress heavenward but slow."[29] "By daily striving for worldly achievements undertaken to honor God," Kadane writes, "Ryder risked transforming his successes into excesses and his achievements into vanity." The last temptation is spiritual pride. I am proud that I am not proud, and at the last moment Satan swoops in to claim my soul.

Kadane finds no evidence for the materialist claim that appropriate consumption was merely a demonstration of creditworthiness, the outward and visible sign of inward and economic grace. His man Ryder does not resemble the credit-obsessed man that Craig Muldrew and others (following Marx in this, as the clerisy does) find in England then and earlier, keeping up appearances to keep up the credit score.[30] In Ryder's diary any "social implications of failure to meet credit obligations were subordinate to his worry about God's perception of him."[31] Kadane concludes, "What in the first instance gave shape to Ryder's economic outlook, self-image, and the image he projected to others was a spiritual struggle he wages daily in the privacy of his journal to stay poised between damning extremes," that is, the extreme of denying the use of God's gifts in the world and the other extreme of worldly pride.[32] Kadane argues that Adam Smith took an amiable view of vanity (Kadane is mistaken, and needs to reread *The Theory of Moral Sentiments*, slowly.) He supposes it was an attempt to free such people from their worries. I'm all right, you're all right, commerce is all right. Though a misreading of Smith, the pop-psychology hypothesis does serve to reinforce Kadane's correct point that on the contrary the transcendent often matters. Right down to the present many businesspeople have insisted that God's work comes first. They are not always lying or self-deceiving.

In modern times a strictly materialist hypothesis, the "hermeneutics of suspicion" à la Marx or Freud or Samuelson that dominates modern social science, strips away any ethics except prudence only. "Oh, Mr. Moneybags, you can't fool the goldfish! I see through your phony sermonizing into your plot to accumulate, accumulate!" But such a stripping of ethics originates from the rhetorical habits of our social or literary sciences, not from the facts. The economists Peter Boettke and Virgil Storr, I have noted, complain that "economists discuss actors as if they have no families, are citizens of no countries, are members of no communities." In the language of sociology, "individuals, in the hands of economists, are typically undersocialized, isolated creatures."[33] By erroneously depicting businesspeople as creatures only of the restless stirring for gain we paradoxically take away the ethical limits on their greed. Go for it; greed is good, because after all you are merely a disgusting capitalist. A *vain*, disgusting capitalist. The modern clerisy, left and right—vainly scornful of the virtue of prudence, and attributing the corresponding sin of greed to anyone who watches his costs and considers his benefits—has returned to the anti-economic, antitrade, anticommercial, antibettering, antibourgeois ethic of the desert fathers.

A secular gentleman, who was allowed to wear a sword, earned his virtue by military nobility, not by commercial bargaining. He was "a soldier, / Full of strange oaths and bearded like the pard, / Jealous in honor, sudden and quick in quarrel, / Seeking the bubble reputation / Even in the cannon's mouth." The very title of "gentleman" in Elizabeth I's time meant someone who attended the Cadiz Raid or Hampton Court, engaging in nothing so demeaning as actual work. Anna Wierzbicka argues for a shift in meaning of the word "experience" (an unusually big word in English, as she shows by comparison with French, German, Polish, and Russian). "In Shakespeare's language "*experience* was linked . . . [more] with living in general than with doing any particular kind of work [as in later *experienced*, i.e., skilled] . . . no doubt linked with the emergence of work as a conceptual category in modern life. . . . Most of Shakespeare's heroes and heroines did not have work."[34] When Dutch soldiers, recalling the practice of the Roman legions, started carrying shovels for building ramparts or digging foxholes it was thought ignoble, though irritatingly effective. Yet among even the Dutch, as late as 1743 a report on the conditions in the tiny colony around Cape Town noted of its denizens that "having imported slaves [inexpensive in Africa itself, which had at the time a great many societies with slaves], every common or ordinary European becomes a gentleman [the word would have been *meneer*, from *mijne heer*, my lord: *De Heer* in Dutch is the Lord (God)] and prefers to be served rather than to serve."[35] The distinction haunted Afrikaner society down to the twentieth century, as Hermann Giliomee and Bernard Mbenga argue, and kept it for a long time nonbourgeois, and poor.[36]

AND BETTERMENT, THOUGH
LONG DISDAINED, DEVELOPED
ITS OWN VESTED INTERESTS

The former aristocratic or Christian or Confucian elites, then, had contempt for business, and taxed it or regulated it at every opportunity, keeping it within proper bounds. Such social regulation was the chief obstacle preventing the march to the modern, namely, the withholding of honor from betterment and of dignity from ordinary economic lives. Not that the bourgeoisie is to be trusted entirely to welcome betterment or novelty, then or now. Recently a major Swedish capitalist (Sweden, I repeat, *is* capitalist) invited to breakfast a professor of economic history, on the strength it seems of her alleged expertise in how trade-tested betterment works. It turned out that he wanted historico-economic tips from the professor on how to *stop* improving, the better to lead a quiet life. The professor replied, "I'm sorry, sir, but you are our servant. You need to run faster and faster to stay in the same place." The capitalist was depressed by the news from economic history, though not entirely surprised, and went back to improving.

True, a small society of businesspeople protected by the state could itself rather easily set up obstacles to betterment, by arranging for local monopolies. The Florentine Republic in its prime allowed an unusually high percentage of its population into politics, and yet, with the exception of brief outbursts of populism, as in the rule of Savonarola after 1494, the numerous men qualified for office were of course *borghese*, not mere workers.[1] If the dominant classes of great merchants (*popolo grosso*, as they were called, "big people") worked at it long enough, as the Venetians did, they could reproduce a society of strict rank and birth. The Great Council of Venice was in 1297 closed to all who did not have fathers or grandfathers who sat on the very council (it was not in fact entirely closed, but new members were a trickle). Diego Puga and Daniel Trefler document the decline of Venetian economic openness that came with the high bourgeoisie's assertion of permanent power.[2] "Venice became a hereditary aristocracy," Peter Ackroyd notes, and its rulers even became, like other European aristocrats, land-based, as Serenissima acquired more and more *terra firma*. The once-bourgeois lords withdrew from commerce and spent their summers in Palladian villas on the mainland. Four percent of the population ran the place, the Faliers and the Foscaris and the other one hundred favored Venetian families (by contrast with Florence 1280–1400, which had fully 1,350 politically enfranchised families).[3]

It was a government of old men, in sharp contrast to the tumultuous young men who ran, say, medieval England—think of Hotspur and Prince Hal: "O Harry, thou hast robb'd me of my youth." Venice developed the virtues of oldsters. "What it lacked in novelty [note the word] and excitement," Ackroyd remarks, "it made up for in prudence."[4] Venice, usually cited as the mother of the lamentable system of patents for inventions (1474 on), had over a hundred guilds to regulate the betterments of handworkers and their masters. "To reveal any of the secrets of Venetian glass-making was to incur the death penalty. Any workman who escaped to the mainland was hunted down and where possible forcibly retrieved," and horribly punished.[5] As Adam Smith said, even in Britain in the eighteenth century "people of the same trade seldom meet together, even for merriment and diversion, but the conversation ends in a conspiracy against the public."[6] The goal was bourgeois monopoly and capture of the state to protect it—the Venetian monopoly of trade with Constantinople, for example, or the Venetian near monopoly of mirrors, of organ building, or of printing—around 1500 a sixth of the books issued in Europe came from Venice. The Venetians in 1486 invented the monopoly even of ideas, the still more lamentable institution of copyright. Under such monopolies the astonishing specialization of Venice that caught everyone's eye did not necessarily lead to invention. As William Easterly puts it, "specialists often have the most to lose from new technologies that displace the old ones they know so well, and may want to block innovation. Perhaps this is why many breakthroughs come from creative outsiders who combine technologies generated by different specialties."[7] Or the historian William McNeill:

By 1600, if not before, the [Venetian] republic came to be governed by a small clique of rentiers, who drew their income mainly from land, and to a lesser degree from officeholding itself. Active management of industry and commerce passed into the hands of domiciled foreigners [compare the metics of ancient Athens, or the Germans of Russia, or the Jews of Poland]. . . . The men who ruled Venice were no longer active in business, but devoted a large part of their official attention to regulating business behavior.[8]

Or Harry Truman: "An expert is someone who doesn't want to learn anything new, because then he wouldn't be an expert."

Such killing of betterment by the bourgeoisie itself, *de dominee, de dokter, de notaris*, was made possible by economic localism enforced by the state. Europe was riven until the nineteenth century by toll gates within countries and at all manner of frontiers—this in sharp contrast to China at the time, I have noted, which constituted one enormous market, and had for centuries. The central government officials, as the economic historians Jean-Laurent Rosenthal and R. Bin Wong observe, "gave China a quasi-free-trade zone the size of Europe."[9] "Under the Spanish Crown . . . there were significant trade barriers between Catalonia and Castile, areas much smaller than the typical Chinese province."[10] Beginning in 1738 the Prussian tax collectors in Berlin, having torn down the old defensive city walls (no longer effective anyway against modern cannons), had erected instead a twenty-foot-tall excise wall (*Akzisemauer*), which itself was torn down only in the liberal 1860s. The Berlin *Akzisemauer* is a fitting symbol of the rise and fall of European's self-defeating experiment in mercantilism, which had attempted in early modern times to reproduce at a national level the cozy monopolies of guildsmen in the Middle Ages.[11] The third act of Puccini's *La Bohème* (1896, from a novel of 1849 referring to the 1830s) takes place at a toll gate into Paris. Such a gate would not seem odd in many countries such as India even now, nor would it have seemed odd in postwar Europe before the blooming of the Common Market. In 1968 you waited in your car for hours with scores of lorries to cross the high pass from Austria into Italy.

The Cameralists of the eighteenth-century German lands claimed to have created, in the words of an admiring historian, a "well-ordered police state," and were in the business of arguing from university chairs in the subject, in the words of a nonadmiring historian, that "a well-organized structure of human and natural sciences—police science, economy, chemistry, forestry, mineralogy, and so on—would yield prosperity."[12] It was an attractive idea, and continues to attract the man of system, without the slightest evidence for its truth. The nonapproving historian Andre Wakefield is "not convinced that there was any connection between eighteenth-century science [including Cameralist administrative science, or indeed the physical sciences that Mokyr thinks were starting to matter] and economic development."[13] The evidence of stagnation of German incomes at the time suggests that he is right.

But getting out of mercantilism has been hard, so attractive is the belief, down to the latest appeal to "plan," that, as Wakefield puts it, "systematic knowledge, carefully cultivated by good princes and their officials, would benefit the general welfare."[14] Thus Deventer, a hanse town in the eastern Netherlands, was in 1500 strictly bound by tariffs and protections for existing trades—though no city in the Netherlands at the time was bound as tight in such matters as the Italian or German cities were. Bounds on trade were the general illiberal equilibrium of Europe before the Industrial Revolution. Here I agree with the neo-institutional orthodoxy in recent historical economics, such as Acemoglu and Robinson in *How Nations Fail* (2012). True, Acemoglu and Robinson, with other neo-institutionalists, never say how such an equilibrium could change without changing minds. But they are correct in claiming that illiberal ideas hurt.

During the fourteenth and fifteenth centuries in Germany even the urban poets of each little town were organized into guilds, that of Wagner's *Die Meistersinger von Nürnberg*, for example, with their tunes and meters laid out in rule books in a most un-Romantic way. Even in Scotland the corporation of Glasgow, to avoid competition, denied a young James Watt license to set up a workshop—he was driven, happily, to apply to the university, and there invented the separate condenser.[15] Without permission from the guild you could not innovate in producing cloth and were unlikely to evade the monopoly unless you could set up your factory, as in England, out in the countryside. If you wish nowadays to set up a new pharmacy in Holland you must apply to a town committee—composed of other, local pharmacists. Guess how many pharmacies there are in Holland. Compare the way that enterprise in postwar America evaded regulations and rents downtown by proliferating strip malls in the suburbs. Strip malls are forbidden to this day in much of Europe, which therefore retains the old charm of city centers, at the cost of grossly inconveniencing women doing the shopping after work.

In the style of central planning and regulation—as against wild, self-organizing voluntary trade—people expected, and even wanted, their economy to be predictable. The French film maven Jean-Claude Carrièrre spoke in 2009 of a land-owning relative in the old days "who, in January, did his accounts for the *coming* year. Last year's results were a solid basis on which to predict. . . . Thing's didn't change."[16] The economist Stan du Plessis speaks of his Afrikaner great grandparents, and of their parents, and theirs, and theirs, back to his Huguenot ancestors of the seventeenth century: "For these couples, as for humankind generally for almost all of history, parents lived the same lives as their children." The children "grew rich, if at all, and rarely, by accumulating more land and more cattle, more labor. . . . It is the same model we read about in the Old Testament (Genesis 13:1–30; Genesis 30:25–43)."[17] The model was that your gain is my loss, zero-sum, right now, disregarding the future.

In 1600 England—even though it was by then a big society with a single price obtaining in many items, at any rate by the narrow standard of Deventer or Nürnberg—still affixed chains on enterprise, under the theory that trade was zero-sum. Many Englishmen believed, as one of them wrote around 1600, that "to add more persons to be Merchant Adventurers is to put more sheep into one and the same pasture which is to serve them all."[18] Let us have predictable lives.

It is what is behind the persistent modern revivals of mercantilism against international comparative advantage, as in Lou Dobbs on Fox News, or the books of Robert Reich and John Grey, or the French vintners demanding still more protection, or the Department of Trade and Industry in South Africa requiring hard-to-get licenses for all business, or the antiglobalization rioters at the meetings of the Group of Seven.[19] Oddly, people who would readily agree that attempting to lay down the future would be disastrous in, say, painting or rock music or journalism or most science and all writing of novels or of scholarly books, think that we already know how to organize a mere economy, and that the government knows best in central planning or regulation or nudging. In 2013 the liquor stores of Indiana campaigned against allowing grocery stores to offer cold beer on Sundays on the grounds, their spokesperson said, that half the liquor stores in the state would go out of business in the presence of such a competition so convenient for customers. A free-trader would reply: so be it; the people speak of their convenience in what they are willing to offer in trade. As Adam Smith put it in the opening sentences of the "Introduction and Plan of the Work" in *The Wealth of Nations*, "The annual labor of every nation is the fund which originally supplies it with all the necessaries and conveniencies of life which it annually consumes. . . . According therefore, as this produce . . . bears a greater or smaller proportion to the number of those who are to consume it, the nation will be better or worse supplied." The purpose of a nation's economy is consumption, not jobs, or the number of liquor stores.

After the change in rhetoric around 1707 a free-trade area as large as Britain's could develop sufficient material and intellectual interests in free trade to unbind Prometheus.[20] A balance of the interests against the passions, in other words, is not merely a modern liberal fancy. There grew up in Britain during the eighteenth century a group of interests which had by then a stake in *free* trading at home and abroad, and all the more so eighty-two years after 1707 in the expanding free-trade area of the United States. In the Constitution approved in 1789, the Commerce Clause (art. II, sec. 2, clause 3) assigns Congress the right to "regulate commerce" between the states and was immediately interpreted to prevent interstate tariffs (reinforced it would seem by article I, sec. 10, making any tariff, whether on foreign goods or another state's goods, a congressional prerogative). The key event is that, until the rise of the modern and omnicompetent state, the powers lost control of trading, which went spinning (literally) off by itself in unpredictable ways. It would account for the failure of earlier and small and therefore easily monopolized merchant republics to achieve what Holland almost achieved, and then England and then Scotland and then the English colonies in North America did achieve. Scale mattered. What mattered, too, was refraining from (regularly idiotic) central control. Unlike the Bourbon state, the Hanoverian state did have control of the fisc. But when in the eighteenth century the remnants of mercantilism lost their charm, it decided it had no urgent desire to stop people from spinning cotton to their hearts' and their pocketbooks' content.

When the new rhetoric gave license for new businesses, the businesses could enrich enough people to create their own vested interests for opposing a mercantilist plan for local greatness through monopoly. If the Indiana blue laws were relaxed, the grocery stores would in a while form an interest group preventing the reimposition of the law about cold-beer sales that had artificially favored liquor stores. Such new interests in the past few centuries have bred toleration for creative destruction, and for unpredictable lives, and for most children having much more than their grandparents. For this reason it is unlikely that India will return to overregulation and protection- ism even after the liberals responsible for 1991 have left the scene (Singh's role is exaggerated, and in the 2010s he caved in to mercantilist-socialist forces), or that any future government of China will reverse the trade-tested reforms. As North, Wallis, and Weingast put it recently, "Creative economic destruction produces a constantly shifting distribution of economic in- terests, making it difficult for political officials to solidify their advantage through rent-creation."[21]

In 1720 the wool, silk, and linen manufacturers of Europe constituted an interest against the importing of Indian cotton goods. Yet the importing and then (to the horror of the woolen interests) even the European manufactur- ing of cotton evaded the fierce prohibitions of law and eventually created an interest in cotton manufacturing that could demand its own laws. We call the interests "vested," but the term is not quite right, since a vested interest is absolute and guaranteed in law, such as a vested inheritance to a property. The word "vested" comes from the metaphor of putting on the clothes of a priest. It is permanent and unconditional. Even the English manufacturers of wool, though holding on for a long time to the exclusive right to make winding sheets for clothing the dead (speaking of literal vesting), could not prevent on other counts the removal of the vestments. Betterment over- whelmed the old profits *pro tempore*, as the lawyers might say, creating new, quasi-vested interests, stronger and stronger in their own defense. In 1774 the former barber Richard Arkwright—anxious to protect the profits from his introduction of a machine for making strong cotton yarn—bribed and persuaded his way to getting Parliament to repeal the former prohibition of all-cotton cloth, and a year later got it even to remove the import tariff on raw cotton. Europe nourished, so to speak, a party of betterment, by a happy accident of ideas and circumstances.

The danger now is that a sclerosis of vested interests, as the economist Mancur Olson once argued, will clog the arteries of progress.[22] But voice and ideology matter. Consider nowadays the rising free-market complaints, especially among computer folk, against the growing monopolies of pat- ent and copyright. The economists Michele Boldrin and David K. Levine have complained the loudest, detailing how evading patents in, say, early automobiles or airplanes made the two technologies commercially possible. They ask ominously, "Where, today, is a software improver to find safe haven from Microsoft's lawyers?"[23] Or Coca-Cola's or Disney's or Pfizer's? When the French decided in 1791 to imitate the British law of patents they imitated also its high costs (this in contrast to American patents, authorized by the constitution of 1789)—for fifteen years of a state-protected monopoly the fee was fully 1,500 livres, many years wages for a workingman.[24]

Or compare now again the free-market complaints by American farmers against anti-Hispanic conservatives. The farmers complain because without immigrants, legal or illegal, they are unable to harvest their crops. Openness to immigration was, indeed, an important part of the liberal rope, as against the xenophobia we see from time to time even in a liberal Europe and United States. (The comedian Steven Colbert testified to a congressional hearing on immigration reform on September 24, 2010, that "My grandfather did not travel across four thousand miles of the Atlantic Ocean to see this country overrun by immigrants. He did it because he killed a man back in Ireland.") The journalist Álvaro Vargas Llosa notes that because of Milton Friedman and others making the Smithian-liberal case in the twentieth century, "arguing for tariffs against competition for the sake of protecting an industry has lost its prestige and comes at a price for those who dare speak openly in such terms." "The battle for the free movement of goods, services, capital, and ideas has been won in principle"—but not the battle for the free movement of people. On the contrary, he says, "calling for the expulsion of one's neighbors or fellow workers because they come in from another country is respectable."[25] (An economist would add a pro-immigration technical point, that free movement of goods has the same economic effects on wages and prices as free movement of people. They are substitutes. You can buy a TV imported from China or you can buy a TV from immigrant Chinese workers in Chicago: it's the same TV. Therefore at least on economic grounds it is illogical to advocate free imports of goods yet oppose free imports of people.)

Ideas and conditions intertwined into a uniquely modern and liberal rope. The first task of Napoleon's conquering armies was to abolish guilds—in accord with the preamble to the French Constitution of 1791: "Neither confraternities nor corporations of professions, arts, and crafts any longer exist." True, French commercial interests, and not merely ideological enthusiasms, were served by France's conquering armies.[26] Prudence matters, even though ideas matter too. Yet the abolition was lasting. For example, in Germany a new equilibrium was attained with new vested interests for nonguild manufacturing, though keeping a medieval tradition down to the present of craft education. The result of abolishing confraternities and corporations of professions, arts, and crafts was the unprecedentedly rich societies of Europe and the world. Before the First World War provided an accidental boost to protectionisms such as racist quotas and national passports—previously only [the numerous] illiberal countries had required passports—shipping companies in Britain and Germany, with J. P. Morgan in tow, had repeatedly persuaded American politicians to resist restrictions on immigration to the United States.[27] In the first great climax of globalization in July of 1914 what was good for passenger shipping lines was also good for the free movement of people. The new vested interests of a bourgeois civilization sufficiently overbalanced the old vested interests of traditional clergy, peasants, aristocrats, and local bourgeois monopolists.

AND THEN TURNED

The word "betterment," which I have preferred to "innovation" for its suggestion of a profit test, acquired that very sense early. It is a Norman French word meaning at first (ca. 1320), "the turning of a thing to profit." Betterment never lost its virtuous and financial connotations, though later applied narrowly to betterment of agricultural land. By contrast, "innovation," a derivation from Medieval Latin, was disreputable into the nineteenth century. The *Oxford English Dictionary* attributes its first use in sense 5, "introducing a new product into the market," to Joseph Schumpeter in 1939, which seems implausibly late (the *OED* is conservative in such dating). And one can quarrel, too, with the lexicographer's understanding of what Schumpeter was up to in the book quoted, *Business Cycles*. In the word "innovation" Schumpeter included, as all economists do when they use it, betterments in making products too, and in financing them and in trading them and in inventing them *de novo*, not merely the introducing of a new product. Betterment is any new good or service or any new way to do an old one.

But anyway, the quotations from earlier times the *OED* uses to illustrate how "innovation" was employed are almost always censorious. The 1561 English translation of Calvin's *Institutes* declares that "It is the duty of private men to obey, and not to make innovations of states after their own will." (Note: this is the Calvin of the allegedly disruptive Protestant ethic.) The Anglican theologian Richard Hooker writes in 1597 about "suspicious innovations." The high-church archbishop Laud's proceedings in 1641 are said to be "notorious" "in bringing innovations into the Church." Edmund Burke was annoyed in 1796 by a "revolt of innovation," which results in "the very elements of society [being] confounded and dissipated." But remember Johnson decades earlier, with "the age is running mad after innovation," of which he with a certain irony approved. Unsurprisingly, one finds the radical Jeremy Bentham in the vanguard in 1817 praising "a proposition so daring, so innovational." But only by 1862 could Henry Buckle, the optimistic English positivist, sneer conventionally at people for whom "every betterment is a dangerous innovation"—and even then he was playing off the conservative use of the word.

The word "novelty" seems older and more common (its *OED* entry is much longer), a Middle French *nouveauté*. But it too, the *OED* notes dryly, was "Freq. with negative connotations in early use," as in Wycliffe's Bible circa 1385 concerning "cursed novelties of voices" (from Latin *profanas vocum novitates* in the Vulgate that Wycliffe relied on; or more accurately in the original Greek, "profane babblings," that is, heresies already evident to St. Paul). "Novelty" always connoted something verging on silly and trivial (regularly so, for example, in sense 1e), the way James VI/I wrote in his *Counterblast to Tobacco* in 1604 that the noxious weed was "an inconsiderate and childish affectation of novelty." (*New Yorker* cartoon: two men dressed like Sir Walter Raleigh sit around smoking clay pipes, and one says, "Well, if turns out to be unhealthy it'll be easy to quit.") Compare another old word, "newfangled," which has retained a vivid air of silliness. Yet novelties can be sober threats when the word is elegant variation for the dangerous "innovations," found in 1496 in the *OED* for example "in purchasing and inringing novelties and innovations in the Church." "Novelties" acquires strongly favorable connotations only late in the *OED*'s quotations, as when certain critics in 1921 complain of a short story that "it lacks novelty and vitality," or when E. H. Gombrich's *The Story of Art* (1950) tells of an artist's paintings that "must have shocked the Egyptians of his day by their novelty."

Something changed in elite talk about betterment or trade-tested innovation or novelty from 1300 to 1600 in bits of northern Italy and the southern Low Countries and the Hanse towns, then more broadly and decisively down to 1648 in North Holland, then after 1689 in England and after 1707 in Scotland, and broadly always in Britain's North American colonies, gathering force and population, and still more broadly and still more decisively down to 1848 all over northwestern Europe and its offshoots. In England the change in rhetoric about the economy happened during a concentrated and startling period 1600 to 1776, and especially during an even more concentrated and even more startling period from 1689 to 1719. The heralds in England gave up trying to enforce the rule that only a gentleman could wear a sword.[1] Betterment tested by trade, a system of property rights coordinated by prices, and the bourgeois speech-work in support of it came to be regarded as, of all crazy things, virtuous. In some ways—though not all— trade betterment and other bourgeois work did in fact become virtuous.

It was a close call, because good or bad rhetoric from journalists and professors and novelists also matters for how the rulers rule, whether the rulers are the kings or the people. The close call happened after 1700 or so, and it was largely a rhetorical and ethical change. Material and legal constraints on the economy and society of Europe, I have said, did not change much in the run-up to 1800, that is, from 1689 to 1789, at any rate not on the scale of the material and legal change from 1789 to 1914, or still more the change from 1914 to the present. People traveled in carriages and sailing ships in 1789 as they had in 1689; they dealt with a common or civil law clotted then for centuries, though good at protecting old property. Just as they had in 1689, in 1789 most people ate grain raised mainly locally, and if well-off they ate some spices raised entirely in the East Indies. Except in a few places long urbanized, such as the provinces of Holland and Utrecht in the Netherlands, or Paris and London, they lived in villages as before. They expected, in 1789 as in 1689, to live the same lives as their parents. They worked for masters with whom they were personally acquainted. If they misbehaved they were routinely beaten, by their masters if they were hired servants or by their husbands if married women or by their fathers if minor children. They died at high rates from waterborne diseases. They could not vote. They could not read. The laws under which they lived favored the rich, from the game laws to naval impressment. But in the century after 1789 in northwestern Europe, all these changed, and radically. Not before.

That is, not a great deal of a narrowly economic or political or legal sort changed in the eighteenth century. Therefore narrowly economic or political or legal changes, if we pay attention to a chronology in which causes come before their results, cannot be the cause of an Industrial Revolution, which everyone agrees was stirring in the eighteenth century. The instinctive materialism of economists and other professional cynics looks inadequate to the task of explaining the Great Enrichment of the modern world. We must look to ideas, which did change at the right time in the right places, and greatly.

The rhetorical change was a necessity, a not-to-be-done-without, of the first Industrial Revolution, and especially of its astounding continuation into the nineteenth and twentieth centuries. The goldsmith John Tuite's patent of 1742 modifying Newcomen's steam engine was, according to Margaret Jacob, the first British patent to be granted that says boldly in the application that it will put people out of work, saving labor. Before that time all patents needed to claim in a medieval and then mercantilist rhetoric that employment would be increased. In 1744 the British Newtonian, Freemason, and chaplain to the Prince of Wales, Jean Desaguliers, of Huguenot origin, was the first person to emphasize in print, Jacob continues, the labor-saving character of steam engines.[2] Mokyr concludes that "the British government was by and large unsupportive of reactionary forces that tried to slow down the Industrial Revolution."[3] It was a rhetorical change with big consequences, a change, as the classical rhetoricians put it, in stasis (Greek "standing, position"), the initial framing of the question of how one should view betterments. Betterments were for the first time recognized as factually important in civilian life. They were for the first time defined as good, and not subject to interference. (Thus the four categories of stasis as the Roman rhetorician Quintilian gave them: fact, definition, quality, and policy or jurisdiction). The new stasis shifted the burden of proof, to use another rhetorical concept, from those who advocated creation to those who opposed destruction. Ideas and rhetoric in northwestern Europe had begun to change in favor of creative destruction.

One can admire, appropriately, the entrepreneurial vigor of heroic figures, as in 1958, for example, the Austrian sociologist and anthropologist Helmut Schoeck did: "We tend to forget that mankind's emergence from stereotyped and stagnating ways of life, on low subsistence, has exclusively depended on the emergence of independent and enterprising individuals, . . . who had enough resistance to escape from social controls . . . imposed in the name and interest of 'the whole society'."[4] Yes, and all credit to them.

But the question is, why then, and why them? The social suppression of betterment had to change, or else the emergence that Schoeck admires would have been spread smoothly over history. It was not. That is what is mistaken in Matt Ridley's attractive notion that trade produced ideas that had sex with each other; and then their grandchildren ideas had sex; and so in geometric progression. Until 1800 new ideas had not achieved anything like a geometric progression, though trade was then already tens of millennia old. The number of people disposed by nature to enact betterments did not leap up after 1800. Human inventiveness viewed as a certain share of any population with unusual combinations of prudence, courage, and hope is a background condition, available at any time from the first clear evidence of art among *Homo sapiens* race on the eve of the migrations out of Africa. The social hostility to the man of business and the rulers' hostility to hierarchy-disturbing creative destruction was suppressing betterment. The ancient problem was, as Schoeck put it, "social controls . . . imposed in the name and interest of 'the whole society.'"

Andrew Coulson of the Cato Institute, among others, has suggested to me that there has to be in the story a threshold of people with good ideas. I don't think so. More entrepreneurs yields more betterment, to be sure. But, as Coulson himself notes, a psychological change could increase the percentage of entrepreneurs only a little bit—by 30 percent, say—but not, surely, by a *factor* of thirty. It is another reason why Weberian claims about a changing psychology of entrepreneurs cannot be right.

My argument is not, that is, about a Weberian rise in the percentage of improvers, as though a genetic modification of the breeding stock (contra Gregory Clark 2007b), or a spiritual modification of anxiety about salvation (contra Weber 1905). The argument is that there was a sharp rise in the society's receptiveness to improvers. It was social memes, socially inheritable ideas, that changed—not individual genetics or psychological dispositions or physical strength or ability to read. Liberty and dignity meant that the society was receptive to trade-tested betterment, agreeing (if sometimes with bad grace) with the Bourgeois Deal. Society came to agree, that is, with frenetic betterment.

The argument is not, I say again, about the percentage of the population exhibiting, let us say, worldly asceticism. It is sociological, a change in the way society views such people. It's odd that Max Weber, one of the founders of sociology, relies on a nonsocial, psychological force, and a force, furthermore, unable to explain what it sets out to explain. In a recent paper Luca Nunziata and Lorenzo Rocco exploit some data in Switzerland to conclude that Protestantism has a "statistically significant" effect on entrepreneurship. They fail to grasp the old point that such "significance" has nothing to do with importance. Fortunately, they also report the size of the coefficient, "Protestants being 2.3 to 4.4 percentage points more likely than Catholics to be entrepreneurs."[5] A 2.3 to 4.4 percentage-point advantage does not an industrial revolution, much less a great enrichment, make.

An impressive paper by Kelly, Ó Gráda, and Mokyr in 2013 has the same problem. It attributes the Industrial Revolution to the higher quality of human capital in Britain.[6] Mokyr here strays from his commitment to ideas as causes. Yet the paper is persuasive in marshalling evidence that British workers were more productive than French (and therefore not, as Robert Allen has argued, more expensive per unit of product than French workers). But if two Frenchman equal one Briton, so what? The goal is not to explain a 20 or 40 percent betterment per person, which might well be explained by taller Britons with a better apprenticeship system, but a *1,900 percent* betterment, at the lowest, arising from an entirely new way for the society to work as a whole. The per person skill or energy level is irrelevant, since France, say, could merely assign two men to do the work that one man does in Britain, at no loss, *ex hypothesi*. Kelly, Ó Gráda, and Mokyr, with many others, take us back to a one-person-at-a-time Weberian psychological story—or here a physiological story with the same plot. But to explain the Great Enrichment, and probably the Industrial Revolution, we need sociological causes, economy-wide causes capable of explaining a truly gigantic rise in ingenuity.

The core model, in other words, should not be nuclear fission, the reaching of a threshold—at which, with the creative people bouncing against each other, the reaction becomes self-sustaining. It was more like a forest fire. The kindling for a creative conflagration lay about for millennia, carefully prevented from burning by traditional societies and governing elites with watering cans. Then the historically unique rise of liberty and dignity for ordinary people disabled the watering cans and put the whole forest to the torch.

In the little neoclassical church of San Bárnaba in Venice there was in 2012 an exhibition of tiny wooden models of Leonardo da Vinci's mechanisms of war and flight and the differential gearing of cart wheels. The captions on the models were not much informed by the history of science and did not, for example, answer the first question that comes to mind: Was Leonardo wholly original with, say, differential gearing to make a cart turn a corner smoothly? (He was not.) Did the Chinese imagine many of the same inventions many centuries before, such as wagons with sails? (They did, actually using them, as did the highly inventive Simon Stevin of Bruges a hundred years after Leonardo, without knowledge of Leonardo's then-undiscovered *Notebook*.) Or indeed, did Leonardo learn from contemporaries and earlier figures? (Yes, such as the mathematician Luca Pacioli, a personal friend and teacher, and the engineer Mariano Taccola [1382–ca. 1453], an inspiration and model, as for the diving mask.)

But the second question, more relevant here, also unanswered by the exhibition, was Why was there no uptake of Leonardo's proliferation of practical and semipractical ideas, as there was at a slow pace in China from the early first millennium BCE on, or indeed, as there was in the uptake of Stevin's land yacht around 1600, encouraged by Prince Maurice of the Dutch Republic and his friends, sailing on the hard beach sand of Scheveningen? Leonardo in 1500, like the Franciscan Roger Bacon (imprisoned from 1277 to 1292 for "suspected novelties") or the Arabs earlier or the Chinese much earlier, was an instance of the scientific and engineering intellect, largely repressed before its greatest time—which was after 1700 and especially after 1800. The conditions for uptake in 1500 must have been defective. After 1700 the conditions for uptake must have been suddenly and radically improved.

The estimable writer Malcolm Gladwell talks about "outliers," people whom we usually call "geniuses" of art and science and sport and business. He argues that "what truly distinguishes their histories is not their extraordinary talent but their extraordinary opportunities."[7] A society with opportunities makes a Bill Gates or a Ted Williams or a W. E. B. De Bois or a Jane Austen. No change in human nature is required. What is required is social admiration and social permission for the occupations of a tough computer geek or a superb baseball batter or a pioneering sociologist of the African-Americans or a much-better-than-gothic writer of romances—in order to charm a young person into entering and practicing, practicing, practicing— and the freedom to do so. Gates as a precocious adolescent had access to the computer facilities at the University of Washington in Seattle. Gladwell continues: "We pretend that success is exclusively a matter of individual merit. . . . [My] stories [are], instead, about people who were given a special opportunity to work really hard and seized it, and who happened to come of age at a time when that extraordinary effort was rewarded by the rest of the society."[8] He gives examples, quoting the words of the sociologist C. Wright Mills, of "the poor boy ambitious for high business success . . . [born] around the year 1835"—Rockefeller, Carnegie, Morgan, Pullman, Armour, Gould,

Weyerhaeuser, and seven more men, among the most successful business-men in human history, able to take advantage of the Gilded Age.[9] By con-trast, "if you were born in the 1840s," says Gladwell, "you missed it." If a Watt or a Krupp or an Edison was born in the fifteenth or the thirteenth century, like da Vinci and Bacon, he missed it too. "Full many a flower is born to blush unseen / And waste its sweetness on the desert air."

50

ON THE WHOLE, HOWEVER, THE BOURGEOISIES AND THEIR BETTERING PROJECTS HAVE BEEN PRECARIOUS

Yet before the Revaluation of the eighteenth century, talk against betterment for profit was nearly universal. The Confucian thinker, Wang Fuzhi (1619–1692), whose work became influential in China centuries after his death, right down to Mao, declared in *Comprehensive Mirror* (1691) that "the merchants are the clever members of the class of mean [another translation is 'small'] men, and their destruction of man's nature and ruin of men's lives have already become extremely serious. . . . They are so deeply sunk in profit they cannot be made to move into the stream of gentlemen and Chinese."[1] English rhetoric at the time was similar, though about to change.

So the bourgeoisie is always with us, but bourgeoisies have usually been precarious. Braudel again chronicled the reluctant triumph of a business civilization: "As the years passed, the demands and pressures of everyday life [in Europe in early modern times] became more urgent. . . . So with a bad grace, it allowed change to force the gates. And the experience was not peculiar to the West."[2] Even during the momentous turn 1300–1776 in Europe there were de-embourgeoisements, retreats back into the rhetoric of aristocracy or church. The English economist Edwin Cannan looking back from 1926 wrote:

> We are apt to forget that the idea that a wage-earner, a trader, or an investor may be, and indeed generally is, a very respectable person is very modern. From Homer we learn that people whom Odysseus visited on his travels thought it all the same whether he was a trader or a piratical murderous marauder. Primitive people are said to have regarded exchange as a kind of robbery rather than a

mutual giving. Greek philosophers thought wage-earners incapable of virtue, and money-lenders have been objects of antipathy throughout the ages. In Smith's own time Dr. Johnson and Postlethwayt very seriously considered whether a trader could be a gentleman.[3]

The knight-merchants of venturing Portugal lost their influence at court, and did not create a bourgeois nation, though the nation was repeatedly allied from 1386 with what at length became an even more bourgeois England, arrayed against a fiercely aristocratic and increasingly antibourgeois Spain. Immanuel Wallerstein noted that in Portugal in the fourteenth and fifteenth centuries "there seemed to be advantage in the 'discovery business' for . . . the nobility, for the commercial bourgeoisie . . . [and] even for the semi-proletariat."[4] But except for obsessed figures like Prince Henry the Navigator himself, the heirs settled down to routine exploitation.[5] Costa, Palma, and Reis have argued recently on the basis of some econometric correlations that Portugal benefited greatly by 1800 from its empire. Yet nonetheless they conclude that its great relative poverty by then "must be sought primarily in domestic conditions."[6] Yes.

The regulations could kill betterment. It happened in Florence in the sixteenth century, preventing an early Great Enrichment there, though afterward the Florentines continued down to the present with their tradition of being manufacturers with markets worldwide. It happened, too, in the Netherlands in the eighteenth century, which also continues down to the present to be an economic power far out of proportion to its population. In the Dutch Republic before 1795 a tiny oligarchy—some two thousand men, perhaps a smaller group in proportion to the whole even than in Venice, ran the country.[7] Yet it left Amsterdam a leading center for finance well into the nineteenth century, and Holland is still a great bank and European entrepôt. I have noted that some historians of Britain even claim—on little evidence, considering that the place has ranked among the thoroughbreds in GDP for two and a half centuries—that a loss of the bourgeois spirit of entrepreneurship happened in Britain itself (of all unlikely places) in the nineteenth century (of all unlikely periods).[8]

But that's what is strange about northwestern Europe. The decisive, and let us pray irreversible, turn to a bourgeois civilization, despite ongoing signs down to the present of reluctance and bad grace, with occasional reversions to mercantilism in opposition to free-trade agreements and in the supposition that every part of the economy needs conscious regulation, happened there and didn't happen elsewhere. The making of the German Ocean into a bourgeois lake circa 1453–1700, to be followed in the eighteenth century by the making of the North Atlantic into a larger one, and in the nineteenth century the world's seas into the largest one of all, constitutes only the most recent case of urban trade. But it was strangely decisive, even in places like Holland that slipped back into a proud oligarchy. Aristocratic elites even in northwestern Europe held power into the twentieth century, and the haute bourgeoisie kept remaking itself into gentry or, if especially lucky, aristocracy—*Baron* Rothschild, of all things, as an anti-Semite would complain in 1885; or, still more unsettling, *Sir* James Paul McCartney (MBE 1965, KBE 1997), as an elitist would have complained in 1997. Yet a bourgeois, business-dominated civilization kept a-building. It was in some places not much retarded even by repeated experiments in motivation-damaging socialism or by repeated adventures in treasure-exhausting nationalism.

Why irreversible? It is not absolutely so, as the half-successful experiment in reversing it in the Soviet Union 1917–1991 shows. If the state is powerful and antibourgeois, as under Stalin or Mao or Castro, it can kill the goose—though the dead goose has a Lazarus goose waiting inside him. The reversal from bourgeois prosperity need not even be tyrannical. Populist sentiment against traders or corporations or careers in business, if skillfully aroused, can return us to the material and spiritual conditions of 1800 and $2 or $3 a day. Governments cannot do much to nurture human creativity. Free and even government-provided schools can nurture creativity, if not corrupted into sinecures for bad teachers and worse bureaucrats, and not teaching merely traditional or clerisy-approved attitudes. Courts of law can protect it, if not corrupted into protections for the rentier elite. But governments have in addition many, many tools for killing creativity. Majority voting, as much as it is to be encouraged, is not the same thing as dignity and liberty for the betterers who make us rich and free, unless the parallel democracy of the marketplace is encouraged.

If a democracy honoring ordinary people, including the bourgeoisie, is combined with a respect for law and liberty allowing the bourgeoisie to innovate under the Bourgeois Deal, then the results are satisfactory. The history of northwestern Europe and then of other places exhibits a mechanism of weak irreversibility, a ratchet in free trading and bourgeois dignity that seems at length to have prevailed. Let us again pray that the comparable and opposite ratchet, of government taxing and spending, such as Robert Higgs discerns, does not overwhelm betterment.[9]

Why northwestern Europe? It is not racial or eugenic, a hardy tradition of scientific racism after 1870 to the contrary, revived nowadays by some economists and evolutionary psychologists forgetful of the history.[10] Nor is it the traditions of the Germanic tribes of the north, as the Romantic Europeans have been claiming now for two centuries. Consider the explosive economic successes of highly non-European and non-Germanic places such as India and China, and before them Korea and Japan, and for a long time the economic successes of overseas versions of all kinds of ethnic groups, from Jews in North Africa to Parsees in England to Old Believers in Sydney.

Yet it is an open question, a mystery, why China, for example, did not originate modern economic growth on the scale of the Great Enrichment— which by now you know I claim is one of the chief outcomes of a bourgeois civilization. China had enormous cities and millions of merchants and security of property and a gigantic free-trade area when bourgeois northern Europeans were still hiding out in clusters of a few thousand behind their tiny city walls, with barriers to trade laid on in all directions. Internal barriers to trade in China existed but were centrally and uniformly imposed, and nothing like the chaos of local tariffs in Europe.[11] China for centuries had village schools, and high rates of literacy and numeracy by early modern standards. Until the fall of the Ming (1644), it "undoubtedly had the highest level of literacy in the world."[12] Chinese junks gigantically larger than anything the Europeans could build until the coming of iron hulls in the nineteenth century were making occasional trips to the east coast of Africa before the Portuguese managed by a much shorter route to get there in their pathetic caravels.

Yet, as the Chinese did not, the Portuguese persisted, at least for a long while, naming, for example, the southeast African province of KwaZulu-Natal, far around the Cape of Good Hope, for the festival of Christ's Nativity of 1497 on which they first got there, inspiring other Europeans to a scramble for empire and trade. "We must sail," sang Luis Camões, the Portuguese Virgil, in 1572. Gnaeus Pompey's ancient declaration *Navigare necesse est; vivere non est necesse* (sailing is necessary; living is not) was adopted all over Europe, in Bremen and Rotterdam. And so they did, sail, whatever the risks.

What is odd, and needs historical inquiry, is that no one else did, even the Arabs who dominated the Indian Ocean trade, at least not with the loony passion of the Europeans. Especially the technologically brilliant Chinese did not sail, except for a vigorous commerce, mainly on non-Chinese ships, with the Indian Ocean and Japan. The historian Joseph McKay notes that "Chinese society and politics denigrated seagoing pursuits, emphasizing instead agricultural development and the expansion of an inland empire."[13] The superiority of junks compared with European ships suggests that if they had honored instead of denigrating seagoing pursuits, present-day North and South America would be speaking a version of Cantonese.

Perhaps the problem was precisely China's unity, as against the scramble of Europe at the time, Genoa against Venice, Portugal against Spain, England against Holland. Any comparison of Europe and China keeps coming back to the point. For example, China was rhetorically unified, the way any large, one-boss organization, such as a modern university, thinks it is. A "memorandum culture," such as Confucian China (or rather more paradoxically the modern university) has no space for rational discussion, because the monarch does not have to pay attention.[14] Consider (I say to my colleagues in the mushrooming "administrative university") your local dean or provost, immune to reason in an institution officially devoted to reason, blocking an appointment in a world-renowned Department of English, closing entirely a famously original Department of Economics, all in favor of mediocrity. "Rational discussion is likely to flourish most," Barrington Moore has noted, "where it is least needed: where political [and religious] passions are minimal" (which would not describe the modern university).[15] Tuan-Hwee Sng and Chiaki Moriguchi have recently argued that the Chinese state, because it was so large (larger, of course, than Japan's even when Japan was unified under the Tokugawa, for example, with which they compare it) had to keep taxes low to keep distant bureaucrats on a corruption-leash, and was not as able as Meiji Japan therefore to spring into action when it became obvious in the mid-nineteenth century that it needed to.[16]

Goldstone is worth quoting at length on the matter:

> China and India had great concentrations of capital in the hands of merchants; both had substantial accomplishments in science and technology; both had extensive markets. In the eighteenth-century China and Japan had agricultural productivity and standards of living equal or greater than that of contemporary European nations. . . . Government regulation and interference in the economy was modest in Asia, for the simple reason that most economic activity took place

in free markets run by merchants and local communities, and was beyond the reach of the limited government bureaucracies of advanced organic societies to regulate in detail. Cultural conservatism did keep economic activities in these societies on familiar paths, but those paths allowed of considerable incremental innovation and long-term economic growth.[17]

Well, yes, Smithian "long-term economic growth"—but nothing like the explosion of the Great Enrichment. And that's the puzzle.

In explaining China's failure to converge on the Western standard in the nineteenth century, the historian Kenneth Pomeranz, with many of his colleagues in sinology, explicitly rejects the claim that the low status of merchants in Confucian theory was a crux. But wait. Until China began seriously to honor and protect entrepreneurs—namely, under the neo-pseudo-Communists of the 1980s, at any rate in the coastal provinces—China's growth was modest indeed. F. W. Mote argues that "it is a commonplace mistake to equate . . . China's new thought currents . . . in the sixteenth to eighteenth centuries with the bourgeois enlightenment . . . in eighteenth-century Europe. . . . Chinese merchants took their place in the leading social stratum and strengthened it."[18] That is, they were conservative, in the way that many European closed societies of merchant princes became so—Venice, again, or guild-dominated Europe generally.

The contrast of Japan with northwestern Europe presents an even deeper mystery. In the eighteenth century Japan looked rather similar to England in literacy, city life, bourgeois intellectual traditions, widespread craftsmanship, a lively internal trade. The historian Donald Keene notes that from the hand of Saikaku (1642–1693; his family name was Ihara) there came "a *Treasury of Japan*, a collection of stories on the theme of how to make (or lose) a fortune. The heroes of these stories are men who permit themselves no extravagance, realizing that the way to wealth lies in meticulous care of the smallest details." Keene and the storytellers themselves may be adopting a Horatio Alger–quasi-Weberian belief that thrift—as against the vastly more powerful trade-tested betterment—is what makes for enrichment. In any case Saikaku's heroes are all merchants, *chōnin*, that is, townsmen of the middle class. Daniel Defoe a little later couldn't have done better in their praise. As I have argued, the Japanese as early as the late seventeenth century were starting to make the adjustment even to a pro-bourgeois social theory, at any rate in merchant circles.[19]

True, Tokugawa Japan had isolated itself from foreigners and was hostile to many sorts of betterment—in guns, for example, which were successfully controlled by the Tokugawa régime after it came to power through their skillful use. The retreat from the gun kept sword fighting going strong into the nineteenth century, providing later opportunities for samurai movies and militaristic propaganda. And guns were only part of the authoritarian control of consumption and production by the Tokugawa shogunate. I have noted that it outlawed *wheels*, except for the few carriages of nobles voyaging to Edo, and rigorously enforced the law. As late as the 1850s in Hiroshige's "One Hundred Famous Views of [the City of] Edo" you will view many pack men and packhorses, but no carts.[20]

At length, under the Meiji restoration of 1868 the Japanese—still a century before the Chinese—began to honor and protect entrepreneurs, albeit with a heavy governmental hand. And so Japanese growth in the nineteenth century exploded. The Japanese converged smartly in the nineteenth century, though poor in coal and colonies—that is, until they commenced conquering places like Manchuria. They undertook such conquests on the grounds of just such a resources theory of international relations as historians such as Pomeranz favor. The chief Japanese war museum was still declaring in 2002 that Roosevelt "forced resource-poor Japan" to wage war.[21] When after World War II the Japanese were literally forced to abandon their militaristic and resource-based dreams of glory, they attained in short order a European standard of living through peaceful trading for coal and iron ore and soybeans.

So elsewhere, mysteries. Early Islam was by no means hostile to trade and betterment. Cairo, Baghdad, and Cordoba were all green-field creations, stunning the few backward Europeans who visited them. It is routine to note that Western Christian culture circa 1000 CE—setting aside the then still formidable rump of the Eastern Greeks around Constantinople—looked comically primitive by the standard of the Abbasid Caliphate. Muslims innovated in all fields of the intellect and of the economy, from philosophy to horticulture.[22] The Mediterranean came to be dominated by Islamic fleets. Yet as a leading student of the matter, Timur Kuran, remarks, "That this economic dominance withered away forms a major puzzle in economic history."[23] In any case, as the economic historian Jared Rubin put it, "arguments appealing to 'the conservative nature' of Islam often overlook (or ignore) . . . [that] from the seventh to the tenth centuries Islamic contract law, finance, and provision of public goods . . . were consistently modified in reaction of the exigencies of the day."[24] For example, "Early Islamic *hiyal* were closer to open lending at interest than any type of transaction allowed by the [Western] Church until the fifteenth century."

Kuran argues that Islam chose early a mixed religious-commercial law that made the taking of interest costly (though as Rubin notes it was a cost attached also to transactions in Christian Europe, or for that matter Judaism; and it was evaded in identical ways), and especially, he continues, made the corporation inconceivable.[25] The notion of a partnership or corporation as a legal person was part of the Roman law inherited by Europe. In Europe an incorporated town or guild or charitable foundation could sue and be sued. But not, it is claimed, in Islam. Even great cities in Islam did not have the legal standing routine in Europe by the twelfth century. And for some reason still to be discovered, Kuran observes, in the Middle East "the local merchant community did not see any reason to pressure local courts to create fundamentally new laws," such as town charters giving the merchants collectively a legal standing.[26]

Although the partnership form was more flexible in Christendom than in Islam, the literal modern corporation for business was a very late flower, not really used in the West for much of anything important to the economy until the late in nineteenth century, except for a few exotic trading companies and then canals and railways.[27] And in the Middle East, contrary to Kuran's attribution of deep history as the cause for present Arabic or Muslim backwardness, French corporate law was adopted in the nineteenth century with alacrity, and yet in economic growth there was no upsurge, as Kuran's account might lead one to expect.

Rubin argues rather that "the differential persistence of economically inhibitive laws is a consequence of the greater degree to which Islamic political authorities are dependent on conforming to the dictates of religious authorities for legitimacy."[28] Metin Coşgel and Thomas Miceli (2013) show that the point is widely applicable. That is, the secular makers of laws of commerce could not risk offending the religious authorities, for which see recent Iranian history. Christianity arose in the shell of the Roman Empire, which had no great need for priestly approval. By contrast, writes Rubin, "Islam was formed at a time of weak centralized power and tribal feuding in the Middle East." The tribalism deep in Middle Eastern history, as in many other histories such as Highland Scotland's, has persisted down to the tribalism of, say, present-day Jordanian politics. Therefore in Islam and much less so in Christendom the secular depended on the sacred to survive.[29] True, in 1077 Emperor Henry IV was forced to walk in a hair shirt through the snow of Canossa to beg forgiveness from Pope Gregory VII. But later European monarchs, not. King Gustav Vasa of Sweden in 1527, Henry VIII of England in 1534, and Elector Johann Friedrich I of Saxony in 1541 felt no such dependence on the sacred powers when they decided to pillage the pope's monasteries. And from Ivan the Terrible to Vladmir Putin the Russian tsars have used Orthodox Christianity when it suited them, and crushed it when it didn't.

In the ancient Mediterranean, I have noted, the economic rhetoric was notably hostile to commerce even though the place was soaked in it. And the ancient Near East around 1500 BCE, with ample commercial records, would be a place to start testing whether the approval of bourgeois values such as we now understand them had precedents four millennia ago. Some think they do. But precedents that die out in an elevation of the bourgeoisie to the aristocracy or that are killed by kingly extractions, such as Ivan's destruction of Novgorod, do not make a successful bourgeois world.

One would like to know about South Asian cities. Again, like China's, they were large and busy when Europe was somnolent, though under the Mughals the biggest cities were transient, because dependent on the mobility of the Mughal court. Perhaps caste mattered. In South Asia it usually does.

A study of world bourgeoisies would be a good idea, and especially a study of the attitudes of the surrounding societies to the betterments each proposed, to understand why the ultimately successful one has a conventional genealogy something like that in figure 5. The conventional genealogy, with its notable lean toward Europe, and its musty smell of scholarship current in the year 1950 or so, needs to be tested now with serious comparative study. It will not suffice to go on repeating the clichés of 1950s modernization theory, or Polanyi, or Weber, or Marx, or even the Blessed Smith. The economic historian Maarten Prak provides a test, for example, of the conventional notion that urban citizenship was more vigorous in Europe than elsewhere in Eurasia. Perhaps not, he found. China, for example, at any rate in Ming and Qing times, had "an urban society with substantial autonomy,

Roman commercial law to 476 CE

Byzantine and Muslim trade   Viking commerce 500-900

Revival of European town life 800-1100   Jewish, Lombard, Frisian commerce

Venice, Genoa, Barcelona circa 1300

Florence, Portugal circa 1500   Hanseatic towns circa 1150-1669

The Northern Lowlands 1585-1689

English, Scottish, American eighteenth century

Japanese parallels

The Rhineland, northern France, Belgium circa 1820

Political triumph of liberal and bourgeois values
in Europe

[theoretical reaction: nineteenth century] [political reaction: twentieth century]

Japan, Latin America, Asia late twentieth century: spread to world

FIGURE 5. The conventional genealogy of the Western European and world bourgeoisie.

a robust civil society, significant levels of citizen organization with active craft and merchant guilds, as well as social welfare provisions cutting across lineage solidarities." The one difference from Europe was "few traces . . . [in China] of military forms of citizenship." It does not sound like an unmixed disadvantage.[30]

PART VIII

Words and Ideas Caused the Modern World

51

SWEET TALK RULES THE ECONOMY

There is something strange in modern economics. Nobody talks—except to say yes/no to offers expressed in numbers of dollars, or to "convey" information, as though through a conduit. Economist in their theories ignore persuasion, stories, metaphors, all the chatter of the office and the marketplace in which, as Smith said, "everyone is practicing oratory on others through the whole of his life."[1] The modern economist allows only cold information, not hot persuasion. "Toyota Avalon in good condition: $9,600." "No," replies the customer. The customer might feel moved to add, "Because I can get the same for $8,500 down the street, you jerk. Shame on you for charging more than he does!" The seller might be similarly moved to reply with something like, "My good man, that would be a mistake. The seller down the street is a nasty case." But especially in Marxian or Samuelsonian economics such insults and additional remarks are assumed to lack point. Again, cheap talk. They do not signal anything of import, precisely because they are cheap. If they worked, everyone would use them, and therefore they would stop working, though still cheap.

It might not be a scientific problem that Marxian and Samuelsonian economics and their mathematics of social entities has no room for persuasive talk, of which humans do so much. That some people are left-handed is not something that economics needs to acknowledge, unless the economist is studying the scissors trade.[2] Institutional economists of an older variety often claim that Samuelsonian economics is, say, bourgeois, and therefore suitable only to the Bourgeois Era. You will hear them claiming that an African economics suits Africa and an Indian economics India. The Samuelsonian economist merely smiles and carries on taking her first partial derivative. And the Marxian economist merely scowls and carries on searching for contradictions.

But if a certain activity bulked large in the economy—larger than most measures of foreign trade, say, or larger than expenditure on investment—then a scientific suspicion would be aroused. And so it is with persuasive talk. Nothing happens voluntarily in an economy, or a society, unless someone changes her mind. Behavior can be changed by compulsion, but minds cannot.[3] The economist's all-purpose tool of incentives does change Mr. Max U's *behavior*. But as to mind, he hasn't got one to change. The fact is that persuasion beyond mere transmittal of offers and information is a startlingly large item in a modern economy. We economists might have to stop ignoring the fact.

David Lodge's novel *Nice Work* shows an English professor, Robyn Penrose, realizing that the managing director she was assigned to "shadow" was first and last a persuader:

> It did strike [her] sometimes that Vic Wilcox stood to his subordinates in the relation of teacher to pupils. . . . She could see that he was trying to *teach* the other men, to coax and persuade them to look at the factory's operations in a new way. He would have been surprised to be told it, but he used the Socratic method: he prompted the other directors and middle managers and even the foremen to identify the problems themselves and to reach by their own reasoning the solutions he had himself already determined upon. It was so deftly done that she had sometimes to temper her admiration by reminding herself that it was all directed by the profit-motive.[4]

Or as the German poet Rose Äuslander (1901–1988) put it, "In the beginning was the word, and the word was with God. And God gave us the word, and we lived in the word. And the word is our dream, and the dream is our life."[5]

What's the aggregate evidence? Roughly a quarter of national income, to be statistical about it, is earned from merely bourgeois and feminine persuasion—not orders or information but persuasion, changing minds. And not merely changing some behavior, but "sweet talk," you might say. One thinks immediately of advertising, but advertising is a tiny part of the total.

Advertising, which is commercial free speech, enrages the clerisy because the clerisy doesn't like the tasteless stuff bought by *hoi polloi*, not one bit. It has been saying since Veblen that the Many are in the grips of a tiny group of advertisers, who fool them into buying. So the purchases of Coke and gas grills and automobiles are the result of hidden persuasion or, to use a favorite word of the clerisy, an amazingly efficacious "manipulation."

To a Marshallian/Austrian economist the peculiarly American attribution of gigantic power to thirty-second television spots is puzzling. If advertising had the powers attributed to it by the clerisy, unlimited fortunes could be had for the mere writing. Yet advertising is less than 2 percent of gross domestic product, and much of it is uncontroversially informative: shop signs, entries on web pages, ads in trade magazines aimed at highly sophisticated buyers.[6] When Vance Packard in 1957 published his attack on advertising, *The Hidden Persuaders*, he thought he would lose his friends on Madison Avenue. But they were delighted. An account-executive friend would come up and say, "Vance, before your book I had a hard time convincing my clients that advertising worked. Now they think it's magic."

How big is sweet talk, and its evil twin, veiled threats of dismissal? Take a list of detailed categories of employment and make a guess as to the percentage of the time in each that is spent on persuasion. For example, read down the roughly 250 occupations listed in "Employed Civilians by Occupation" (table 602) in the *Statistical Abstract of the U.S.* (2007) looking for the jobs that involve a good deal of sweet-talking, or on the contrary the jobs without any.[7] The 125,000 "appraisers and assessors of real estate" are not, in an honest economy, open to human persuasion, as any American knows who has had a house appraised recently. The 243,000 firefighters also just do their jobs, with little talk—although one sees here the depth of sweet talk in a modern economy, or for that matter a nonmodern economy, because a firefighter in a burning building does actually a good deal of talking, and sometimes engages in urgent persuasion. The 121,000 aircraft pilots and flight engineers persuade us to keep our seat belts fastened until the plane arrives at the gate and the seat-belt sign is turned off. That's a small part of their job, but think of the supervisory roles they often assume as captains, and the sweet talk needed to keep the crew cooperating, and the disasters attributable to cultural differences in talking persuasively to the control tower. The straight talk common to the West is often seen as impolite in the East, and there are documented cases of crashes caused by squeamishness about appearing to be too abrupt in speech. The 1,491,000 construction laborers are not known for persuasive language, except in the old days when a pretty girl walked by, such as Dil in the movie *The Crying Game*. But anyone who has actually worked in such a job knows the necessity of getting cooperation from your work mates, persuading the boss that all is well, being a regular guy or gal. It's sweet talk. But set such jobs aside.

Out of the 142 million civilians employed in 2005 it seems reasonable to assign 100 percent of the time of the 1,031,000 lawyers and judges to persuading, preparing to persuade, or being an audience for persuasion; and likewise that of the 154,000 public relations specialists and the large number of "social, recreational, and religious workers," such as counselors, social workers, clergy—a total of 2,138,000 of them persuading people how to live. All right: as low as 90 percent—but high.

Managers and supervisors of various sorts are the biggest category to which it seems reasonable to assign a lower but still high figure, say, 75 percent of income earned from sweet talk. In a free society the workers cannot be peremptorily ordered about and beaten with knouts if they do not respond. They need to be persuaded. What the U.S. Census Bureau styles "managerial occupations," such as George Halvorson, once chairman and CEO of Kaiser Permanente, or Daniel R. McCloskey, once senior national accounts manager for Illy Coffee North America, are a massive 14.7 million, fully 10 percent of the labor force. The "first-line supervisors" scattered over all sectors (construction, personal services, gambling)—whom I suppose similarly to be earning 75 percent of their income from persuasion—add another 5.5 million. Add a further 380,000 for personal financial advisors, plus the 150,000 editors and (merely) 89,000 news analysts, reporters, and correspondents—bearing in mind the explosion, since 2007 and thus not included in these figures, of bloggers and other self-employed *journalistas* vying for attention with their own sweet talk. Journalists mostly imagine themselves to be doing straight reporting, but it doesn't take much rhetorical education to realize that they must select their facts persuasively and report them interestingly in sweet words. Likewise the enormous category of salespeople (13.4 million, which excludes the 3.1 million cashiers), though also present to prevent shoplifting, can reasonably be accounted as 75-percent sweet talkers. "The dress is *you*, dear." It may even be true. In my experience, actually, it usually is. With our strange suspicions about rhetoric we exaggerate the amount of lying that salespeople engage in, at any rate in a society that values ethical behavior in such matters.

Among 50-percent persuaders we can count loan councilors and officers (429,000: as with judges in courts of law, they are professional audiences for persuasion, saying yes or no after listening to your sweet talk and gathering your information); human resources, training, and labor relations occupations (660,000: "Mr. Babbitt, I just don't think you have much of a future at Acme"); writers and authors (we are merely 178,000, but again think of the tens of thousands of people who work at it in blogs and writers' groups without publication, though also without payment figuring in national income); claims adjusters and investigators (303,000); and, a big category, the 8,114,000 educational, training, and library occupations, such as college professors (we are 1.2 million alone) and nursery-school teachers.

Perhaps a mere quarter of the effort of the 1,313,000 police and sheriff's patrol officers, detectives and criminal investigators, correctional officers, and private detectives is spent on persuasion, though the ones I've talked to put the figure higher. Look at the difference from one night to the next in the persuasiveness in 2014 of the police in Ferguson, Missouri.

In health care, as anyone who has worked in it knows, sweet talk is important—advocating for the patient, getting him to stay on his blood-pressure medicine, talking sweetly with other caregivers, dealing with insurance companies and hospital administrators (some of whom are included above in the managerial category). In the large category "health care practitioners and technical occupations," we can remove from the realm of persuasion the technical occupations—x-ray technicians, medical records technicians, and so forth—although even these can't merely silently work, if they work well. The technician at the eye doctor keeps saying to you, "Good, that's right. Turn your head up a little. Good." Sweet talk. For the physicians, dentists, nurses, speech pathologists, and so forth who actually talk to patients and to each other—a total of 7,600,000 health-care talkers—it seems reasonable to say that persuading accounts for a quarter of their economic value. Perform a mental experiment: try to imagine a speech pathologist—an occupation I know well—with no persuasive skills whatever, a mere transmitter of the information that, say, a child need not be ashamed of being a stutterer when Winston Churchill and Margaret Drabble and Marilyn Monroe were stutterers too, and imagine how much less valuable she or he would be without sweet talk. The 353,000 paralegals and legal assistants count in the one-quarter category, too. A quarter sounds low.

The occupations mentioned alone, without hunting in putatively non-persuasive categories such as mail carriers or bus drivers or "life, physical, and social science occupations" (within which are classed many of the persuasive economists and law professors themselves), amount to 36,100,000 equivalent workers (that is, the number of 90-percent persuaders multiplied by 0.9, 75-percenters by 0.75, 50-percenters by 0.5, and one-quarter folks by 0.25, all added up). For 2007 (to which I am applying the 2005 categories), that's an astonishing quarter of the income-earning private employees in the United States. It would be higher if weighted instead by dollar incomes, considering the big number of managers and supervisors (about 20 million, remember, out of the 142 million workers). Managers are of course highly paid compared to the people they persuade to work hard.

In short, a quarter of our incomes attributed to sweet talk is a lower bound. Similar calculations for 1988 and 1992, using the slightly different categories available for those years, yielded similar results.[8] Somewhat surprisingly the weight of sweet talk in the economy does not seem to have much risen since then—though if police and health-care workers were put in the 50-percent category, and educators in the 75 percent, as the 1988/1992 calculations assumed, the share of persuasive work in 2005 would nudge up to 28.4 percent of the total. The Australian economist Gerry Antioch has redone the figures, and for 2009 arrives at 30 percent.[9]

The calculation could be improved with more factual and economic detail. For instance, as I just said, the workers could be weighted by salaries. The marginal product of persuasion could be considered in more detail. The occupational categories could be subdivided. The premium for better persuasion could be estimated from sales commissions or promotions. One way of backing the estimates from the detailed occupational categories would be to do in-depth interviews, probing in each job for sweet talk—as against mere information or coercion or physical activity—by riding along in squad cars and listening and watching. The managers likewise could be shadowed. It is what Ronald Coase, in economics, did during the 1930s to discover transaction costs and what Robyn Penrose, in fiction, did during the 1980s to discover managerial teaching.

Coercion, as against persuasion, is in most rich places less prevalent now, in some ways, than it was in the same places in the eighteenth century. True, coercion in taxation is much higher—try persuading the IRS to make a special exception for you. Slaves or some servants in husbandry were once coerced. Yet in olden days a self-employed yeoman farmer or even a farmhand, categories that together would describe in, say, 1800 most free people, was not much coerced or supervised. Silas in Frost's poem "Death of the Hired Man" makes his hay load skillfully the way he wants, and "He's come to help you ditch the meadow. / He has a plan. You mustn't laugh at him." So it's not clear how the long-run balance of compulsion and autonomy has changed. Yet even within the modern state bureaucracies financed by the compulsion of taxes, sweet talk figures large, and orders and compulsion are correspondingly lower.

On balance the sweet-talking share of national income was probably smaller before the Great Enrichment. More often a manager did not have to be a David Lodge teacher. He or she could simply be a tyrant. Commanding Lieutenant (not yet Captain) William Bligh of the *Bounty* is supposed to have been a case in point, "that *Bounty* bastard," as the sailors later called him in extenuation of their mutiny. (His actual fault appears to have been a discipline-wrecking indulgence toward his crew's desire to linger in Tahiti.) The captain even of a merchantman, and still more of His Majesty's ship, expected instant obedience, necessary when rounding the Horn in a gale. The monastic Rule of Benedict required immediate, pride-fighting obedience. Occupations that depended on sweet talk were fewer in olden days. In future days they will be more and more numerous.

The result can be checked against other measures. Douglass North and John Wallis reckoned that 50 percent of American national income was Coasean transaction costs, the costs of persuasion being part of these. Expenditures to negotiate and enforce contracts—the Wallis-North definition of transaction costs—rose from a quarter of national income in 1870 to over half in 1970.[10] Their measure is not precisely the one wanted here. Their transactions costs also include, for example, "protective services," such as police and prisons, some of whose income (I am claiming three-quarters of it remaining after sweet talk) is "talk" only in an inappropriately extended and sometimes physically violent sense. Literal talk is special—in particular it is cheap, as guns and locks and walls are not—in a way that makes it analytically separate from the rest of transaction costs. We say, "A word to the wise is sufficient." Sweet talk is the carefully chosen but to a large degree opportunity-cost-free words of persuasion, and a quarter of our income comes from it.

The same point can be made from the other side of the national accounts, the product side. The more obviously talky parts of production amount to a good share of the total, and much of it is persuasion rather than information or command. Out of an American domestic product of $11,734 billion in 2004 one can sort through the categories of value added at the level of fifty or so industries, assigning rough guesses as to the percentage of sweet talk produced by each—80 percent for "management of companies," 20 percent for "real estate rental and leasing," 40 percent for "art and entertainment," for example—and get up to about 17 percent of the total. The figure squares with the income side, crudely. Anyway, persuasion is big.[11]

Not all the half of American workers who are white-collar do sweet talk for a living, but many do, and more do as office work gets less physical. Office work in the age of word processing has moved far from physical typing and filing and copying done by women, not to speak of the earlier transition from Bartleby the Scrivener or Bob Cratchit on a high stool. So, for that matter, have many blue-collar jobs come to involve sweet talk, such as warehousemen persuading each other to handle the cargo just so, as have pink-collar jobs, such as waitresses dealing all day with talking people. Debra Ginsberg in her memoir *Waiting: The True Confessions of a Waitress* (2000) shows that the first minute of contact with the customers is a little stage show, and determines the tip. It's not "mere" talk. A good percentage of such talkers are persuaders. The secretary shepherding a document through the company bureaucracy is often called upon to exercise sweet talk and veiled threats. If she can't use talk, sweet or not-so-sweet, to bend the official institutions of her bureaucracy she's not doing her job. The bureaucrats and professionals who constitute most of the white-collar workforce are not themselves merchants, but they do a merchant's business of persuasion inside and outside their companies.

A thorough survey of seven thousand workers in the United States by Daniel Pink confirms the result, as reported in *To Sell Is Human: The Surprising Truth about Moving Others* (2012). "Across a range of professions," he writes, "we are devoting roughly 24 minutes of every hour to moving others" in nonsales sweet talk, that is, without a purchase.[12] He asked, "What percentage of your work involves convincing or persuading people to give up something they value for something you have?" and got the reply of 41 percent. "The capacity to sell isn't some unnatural adaption to the merciless world of commerce. . . . Selling is fundamentally human."[13] Humans have always made decisions on where to go next to hunt and gather, or to which port to take the olive-oil-filled amphoras. The decisions are not always those of a tyrant in a centralized bureaucracy who won't take counsel, such as a university provost or a military general. In free societies, whether during our long past as hunter-gatherers before agriculture or during our manufacturing-and-services present, sweet talk rules.

Economists should stop ignoring sweet talk, then, because it is big, and because it is going to get bigger, and because it is of a radically different category than the making of shoes and ships. Earning by making shoes and ships "by hand" (literally "manu-facture") is disappearing into automation by computer and production by robot, in the way that growing food and fiber by hand disappeared into gene-altered crops and combine harvesters with air-conditioned cabs. In 1840, 68 percent of the labor force in the United States was in agriculture, in 1900 still 40 percent, but now less than 2 percent. The percentage of the American labor force in manufacturing was 36 percent in 1950 and has been declining ever since, in the face of mechanization. It is now 20 percent, which was agriculture's share in 1940, before diesel tractors and hybrid crops really took hold. In early films of the Ford factories one is startled by the throngs of men around the assembly line, replaced first by power tools and then by robots.

The repeated alarms against robots, I have suggested, are silly, since robots are merely mechanical slaves for our benefit. As Matt Ridley puts it, "We can build a civilisation in which everybody lives the life of the Sun King, because everybody is served by (and serves) a thousand servants, each of whose service is amplified by extraordinary amounts of inanimate energy and each of whom is also living like the Sun King."[14] Better. When goods (especially) and many services no longer require workers (think of the maddening phone trees, which have disemployed human operators), will we all be unemployed? Of course not. If the theory of technological unemployment espoused by the man in the street (and, startlingly, as I have noted, by some of the economists in the study) were true, almost *all* of us would be unemployed. Easily four-fifths of the employments of 1850 no longer exist—doing laundry by hand at the river, or climbing the rigging like his daddy used to do—or are radically smaller and radically more productive—household servants with Hoovers (that "can't get in the corners. / You might as well give up") or teamsters understood as drivers of wagons pulled by animals. Yet we are not four-fifth unemployed.

Unlike the old jobs eliminated by the coming of new tools, however, sweet talk's share in the economy does not go down, no matter what technological form it takes. In future we will be left mainly in sweet-talking occupations. The question of what is to be done will bulk larger and larger as actual doing fades from our busyness. Deciding what to do cannot in the end be mechanized—the dream of social engineering to the contrary—because the argument about what to do is never ended. If one side gains an advantage from a new persuasive device, the other side realizes the problem and adopts the device itself. Look at the technologies of electing a president in the United States, which grow in sophistication without end. Good. We decide on the height of road crowns to properly drain roads in rainy Scotland. Then we have to decide whether similar crowns are needed in Saudi Arabia. Then we need to change people's minds about how many roads to build. Then we have to persuade them to adopt road pricing. And on and on. The work we do will be more and more about decisions and persuading others to agree, changing minds, and less and less about implementation by hand. The reason so many intelligent economists have feared technological unemployment is that they do not put persuasion in the national product. But the economy does.

52

AND ITS RHETORIC CAN
CHANGE QUICKLY

What of it? This:

Fernand Braudel's trilogy *Civilisation Matérielle, Économie et Capitalisme, XVe–XVIIIe Siècle* (1967–1979) argued that rich people were irritatingly rich and inclined to monopoly, and that cultural habits often persisted and usually mattered. All this is true. Where he and I disagree is that I believe the rich get competed against when ideas persuade and that cultural habits have on occasion, and for the same reason, been malleable.

Sweet talk, for which the ancient word is rhetoric, is a part of culture. But it is the superficial part. "Superficial" is not here another word for "stupid" or "unimportant" or "the sort of talk those idiotic opponents of my ideas indulge in." Nor is it the unchanging background that we can leave out of a story of change. Analyses that turn on a human nature inherited from imagined African savannahs or an English character inherited from imagined Anglo-Saxon liberties don't really explain why men rape or why England has more cargo. The rhetoric of men's sexual dominance over women ("But she wants it"; "I am a man, and women are made for my lusts") or the rhetoric of a business civilization ("That government is best that governs least") do explain such things, and both of the rhetorics can and have changed. Not easily or often. But sometimes surprisingly quickly.

Attributing to deeper culture or personality a behavior that in fact arises from present rhetoric or circumstances is called by social psychologists the "fundamental attribution error."[1] Seemingly profound and permanent differences in cultural dispositions to which we attribute influence on behavior can disappear in a generation or two. The grandchildren of Hmong immigrants to the United States differ in many of their values-in-action only a little from the grandchildren of British immigrants. (If you are not persuaded, add a "great" to "grandchildren," or another "great.") What persists and yet develops and in the end does influence us are spoken ethical valuations, that is to say, rhetoric, through exposition at a mother's knee or through stories told in literature high and low, or through the rumors of the newspapers and the chatter on the web—a climate of opinion and party politics new in England in the 1690s, for example.[2] We put value on others, and on ourselves and on the transcendent, in our talk. Such talk changed.

Consider for example the high rhetorical valuation of prudence and hope and courage in American civilization. It keeps faith with a spoken identity of unrootedness. Arjo Klamer once called America a "caravan" society, as against the "citadel" society of Europe. The caravan is seen in the American frontier myth or the Hollywood road movie, an expression of the American folk religion that "you can be anything you want to be." It wiped out in a couple of generations a northern European ethic of temperance and egalitarian justice (consult Garrison Keillor) or an East Asian ethic of prudence and family faithfulness (consult Amy Tan).

Before 1991 many people said that India would never develop economically, that Hindu culture was hopelessly otherworldly and would always be hostile to betterment. True, some wise heads, such as the professor of English literature Nirad Chaudhuri, demurred. In 1959 Chaudhuri pointed out that Christian England was actually less profit-oriented in its prayer for daily bread than was the daily Hindu prayer to Durga, the Mother Goddess: "Give me longevity, fame, good fortune, O Goddess, give me sons, wealth, and all things desirable."[3] Gurcharan Das notes that the second stage of a worthy Hindu life is that of the householder. "The dharma texts recognize the value of the second stage, which was the indispensable material basis of civilization."[4] Among the successive goals for a flourishing life in Hinduism is "a second goal . . . *artha*, 'material well-being,' which makes sense, for how can one be happy in conditions of extreme deprivation?"[5] How indeed?

But most social scientists looking at Holy India saw only vicious circles of poverty. During the forty years after independence such a rhetoric of a Gandhi-cum–London School of Economics socialism held the "Hindu rate of growth" to 3.2 percent per year, implying a miserable 1 percent a year per person as the population grew. Nehru wrote with satisfaction in 1962 that "the West also brings an antidote to the evils of cut-throat civilization—the principle of socialism. . . . This is not so unlike the old Brahmin idea of service."[6] At last, however, such anticommerce rhetoric derived from the Europeans of the 1930s and "the old Brahmin idea of service" faded. A profiting and bettering rhetoric took root in India, partially upending the License Raj.[7] A third of a million Indians subscribe to the fortnightly Indian magazine *Business Today*, founded in 1992, which contains breathless articles praising enterprise. And so India commenced, after liberal economists took charge in 1991, increasing the production of goods and services at rates shockingly higher than in the days of five-year plans and corrupt regulation and socialist governments led by students of Harold Laski. By 2008 Indian national income was growing at fully 7 percent a year per person (7.6 in 2005 and 2006). Birth rates fell, as they do when people get better off.

After 1991 and Singh's liberal allies, much of the culture didn't change, and probably won't change much in future. Economic growth, as the Japanese have long shown, does not entail becoming identical to Europeans. Unlike the British, the Indians in 2030 will probably still give offerings to Lakshmi and the son of Gauri, as they did in 1947 and 1991. Unlike the Germans, they will still play cricket, rather well. And in 2050, after merely two generations at the rates of growth possible for economies launching on the Bourgeois Deal, average income will have risen by a factor of fully 16 over what it was in 2008. The level will then be well over what is was in the United States in 2003. Even by 2050 in much of their talk and action the Indians will not have the slightest temptation to become like Chicagoans or Parisians, any more than once very poor southern Italians have taken on an American style of driving or a British style of food, though they are now by international standards rich. The Italians even of the *Mezzogiorno* did adopt in part a northwestern European rhetoric about the economy, as the Indians have largely now. They entered the modern world, and the modern word, of a bourgeois civilization, and were made the better for it, materially and spiritually.

What changed in Europe, and then the world, was the rhetoric of trade and production and betterment—that is, the talk about earning a living among influential people, such as Defoe, Voltaire, Montesquieu, Hume, Turgot, Franklin, Smith, Paine, Wilkes, Condorcet, Pitt, Sieyes, Napoleon, Godwin, Humboldt, Wollstonecraft, Bastiat, Martineau, Mill, Manzoni, Macaulay, Peel, and Emerson. And then almost everyone commenced talking so, with the exception of an initially tiny group of antibourgeois clerisy gathering strength after 1848, such as Carlyle, List, Carey, Flaubert, Ruskin, Marx, and Thoreau. The bourgeois talk was challenged mainly by appeal to traditional values, aristocratic or religious ("the old Brahmin idea of service"), which morphed into utopian visions of nationalism, socialism, fascism, and radical environmentalism.

Before the great change around 1700, Europe had little by way of pro-betterment ideology, and a great deal against anything so frightfully bourgeois. Castiglione's *Il Libro del Cortegiano*, "The Book of the Courtier," was written in 1508–1516 about an imagined conversation at the court of Guidobaldo and Francesco Maria, Dukes of Urbino, the cream of Renaissance princes. In 1528 at Venice a first edition in the number of 1,031 copies in Italian was published, and in subsequent decades it was translated into every major European language, in twenty different cities, to become one of the most popular books of the age. It praises the very best ladies and gentlemen, among whom it emphatically does not count the bourgeoisie. Ladies who use too many cosmetics are "like wily merchants who display their cloths in a dark place." A true gentleman is motivated by glory to hazardous deeds of war, "and whoever is moved by gain or other motives . . . deserves not to be called a gentleman [*gentiluomo*], but a most base merchant" [*vilissimo mercante*]. One gentleman in the imagined conversation is portrayed as deflecting praise—his praiser, he protests modestly, in offering superficially plausible praise for such a flawed person as the gentleman in question, is like "some merchants . . . who put a false coin among many good ones."[8]

But in truth the bourgeoisie figures hardly at all in the book, although the splendor of the Italian Renaissance rested on its activity. Without the coming after 1700 of a bourgeois civilization—different from the civilization recommended by Castiglione's gentlefolk living courtly lives off taxes and rents from a commercial society they disdained—the profit from commercial invention continued even in northern Italy to be seen as ignoble, and betterment as inglorious. Let us innovate for noble war, by all means. But not by printing cloth and by building engines to print them that run on falling water—such are the base concerns of the mere bourgeois. Buying low and selling high continued to be seen as suspect. Institutionalized theft in rents and taxes, and honorably restrained betterment in warfare, continued to be seen as noble and aristocratic, the way alms and tithes continued to be seen as holy.

∞

A wise economist, who did not entirely agree with my celebration of bourgeois virtues, said in 1991 that from a study of "surface phenomena: discourse, arguments, rhetoric, historically and analytically considered"
emerges a finding that "discourse is shaped, not so much by fundamental
personality traits [*pace* Weber and Landes], but simply by the imperatives
of argument, almost regardless of the desires, character, or convictions of
the participants."[9] Modern betterment is not about the rise of greed or of
"self-interest properly understood" or of some other fundamental personality trait or deep cultural characteristic. These did not "rise." Human nature
did not (much) change after 1700.

What did change were the articulated ideas *about* the economy—talk
and ideas about the sources of wealth, about positive-sum as against zero-
sum economic games, about progress and invention, about the sweet talk
supporting them, and above all about what sort of calling in an occupation
is admirable. A professor of English, Michael McKeon, put the point well
in 1987: "Capitalist ideology entails, most fundamentally, the attribution of
value to capitalist activity: minimally, as valuable to ends greater than itself
as significant of virtue; perhaps as valuable in its own right; finally, even as
value-creating."[10] The last phrase, "value-creating," means in his mind the
encouragement of values, that is, the virtues—not in the economist's sense
the gain from exchange (though not, I suppose, excluding it). McKeon shows
that 1600–1740 (the period to which he attributes the origin of the English
novel) witnessed the rise of such a valorized betterment.[11]

The big change happened in what Karl Popper called World Three, above
material traits (World One) and psychological traits (World Two), up at the
level of recorded, spoken, bruited-about ideas concerning the material and
psychological and cultural traits. And therefore fresh versions of the lower
worlds One and Two were born too. The danger is, considering the force of
ideas, that they can be killed off by utopian or reactionary rhetoric of the
left or the right—and quickly, especially when backed by guns. The true believers wielding the guns are persuadable to some very nasty enthusiasms,
such as the Shining Path in Peru, led by a professor of philosophy, or the
Khmer Rouge in Cambodia, intent on reviving the medieval glories of the
Khmer Empire. The liberal ideas about the economy were killed off in 1914
and 1917 and 1933, locally. They can be again, globally. Let's not.

Another wise economist, who also might not have found my views altogether congenial, said in 1936 that "the ideas of economists and political philosophers, both when they are right and when they are wrong, are more powerful than is commonly understood. . . . I am sure the power of vested interests is vastly exaggerated compared with the gradual encroachment of ideas."[12] So here.

IT WAS NOT A DEEP
CULTURAL CHANGE

The Industrial Revolution and the Great Enrichment and the modern world did not arise in the first instance from the Scientific Revolution, imperialistic venturing, exploitation of the periphery, a rise in the savings rate, an enforcement of property rights, a quickening of the capitalist spirit, an original accumulation of capital, a higher birth rate of the gifted people, a rise of manufacturing as compared with commercial activity, or from any of the mainly materialist machinery beloved of economists and calculators left and right. The machines weren't necessary. There were substitutes for each of them, as Alexander Gerschenkron argued long ago.[1]

Take science, which Mokyr puts at the center. The achievements of science relevant to technology and therefore to economic activity were modest until around 1900, did not come to influence large swathes of the economy until after the Second World War, and were not transformative of human fate until about now. To say so is not to attack physical and biological science but to exercise sober economic science. Mokyr's most persuasive argument anyway is not Science in Action but *Belief* in Science. His argument at the level of ideologies is agreeable with mine, because the early successes of high science, the softening of a belief in an active God (that is, of providentialism) and, especially, the new belief in equality of rights did lead people to take charge. The word "belief," indeed, cognate with "love," means in religion before natural theology not propositional belief in, say, $F = ma$, as Karen Armstrong has pointed out, but rather a loyalty to a way of life, the following of what Jesus would do, for example, or the 613 laws of Orthodox Judaism.

Mokyr puts weight on Baconianism, the passionate, quasi-religious be-lief that a new day was coming by way of Science—whose claims to much practical fruit he does admit as an economist were not plausible until rather recently, and especially, against the gloomsters, now. He is right, then, that the very idea of science mattered. Francis Bacon, in Mokyr's account, was John the Baptist to the various messiahs of Science, above all Newton. But the messiahs, and even Newton, performed few practical miracles until late in the game—when, for example, in the 1960s we wanted to navigate our way to the moon. The earlier, technologically relevant miracles happened at the lower level among ordinary religionists of a liberal society and therefore of a liberated technology. The Bourgeois Revaluation liberated and dignified ordinary people making betterments. The egalitarian liberalism against the Great Chain of Being so characteristic of Holland, Britain, and most of all the United States encouraged technology more than it encouraged elite sci-ence. The methodical passion of a figure like John Harrison, the carpenter of Lincolnshire making one excellent clock after another until he achieved the marine chronometer, is typical. So, too, Franklin the candle-maker's ap-prentice. Wedgwood the potter's apprentice. Edison the railway telegrapher.

That is, the belief in (that is, loyalty to) science, progress, equality, indi-vidual liberty, social dignity, having a go, were all of a piece. The belief in a new day came to be especially strong in the United States, congruent with the bizarre American theology of postmillennialism. But the mover is the belief, not the actual, modest achievements of high science in celestial me-chanics or even in a few earth-bound electrical and chemical experiments. And in any case, without the "liberal plan of equality," as Smith put it, elite science would not itself have flourished and would therefore never have come to matter to the economy, as it certainly did in the long run. It would have been crushed by monopolies, special interests, protectionism, mercan-tilism, Luddism, denial of education, and local complaints against distant competition, the way, for example, the Irish economy was crushed, forbid-den to benefit from the Act of Union after 1707 as Scotland did, and the way seventy years later the American colonials, with less justice than the Irish, said that they were being crushed economically.[2]

Surprisingly, what seem at first the most exiguous of things—words, met-aphors, narratives—were the most necessary. In the first Industrial Revolu-tion there were no substitutes for bourgeois talk. Followership *after* the first revolution, to be sure, has been another matter. With techniques borrowed from bourgeois societies a Stalin could rigorously suppress bourgeois talk and yet make a lot of steel. In 1700, however, the absence of the new dignity for merchants and inventors in Britain would have led to the crushing of enterprise, as it had always been crushed before. Governments would have blocked invention *de novo* or reuses of older technologies in order to protect the vested interests, as they always had done. Gifted people would have opted for careers as soldiers or priests or courtiers, as always. The hobby of scientific inquiry that swept Britain in the early eighteenth century would have remained in the parlor and never transitioned to the mill. In France and Italy that is what happened—and it would have gone on happening had there not been the stimulus of the Dutch and then the British example.

The talk mattered, whether or not the talk had exactly its intended effect. In the eighteenth-century a male and female public that eagerly read Hannah More and William Cowper created middle-class values from hymns and novels and books of ethics, "an expanding literate public seeking not only diversion but instruction."[3] Similarly, the Abbé Sieyes's essay *What Is the Third Estate?* (1789) had a lasting impact on French politics. In *A Rhetoric of Bourgeois Revolution* (1994) the intellectual historian William Sewell argues that "the literary devices that characterized Sieyes's rhetoric of social revolution quickly became standard elements in a revolutionary rhetorical lexicon. His language, it seems fair to say, had . . . enduring and powerful effects on French political culture."[4] As Tocqueville put it in 1856, "Our men of letters did not merely impart their revolutionary ideas to the French nation; they also shaped the national temperament and outlook on life. In the long process of molding men's minds to their ideal pattern their task was all the easier since the French had had no training in the field of politics, and thus they had a clear field."[5] Even in the North-American British colonies from Vermont to Georgia and in the new nation made out of them—places with a good deal of local training in the field of politics—the rhetoric of the American Declaration of Independence, or the Gettysburg Address, or the Four Freedoms speech, or the I Have a Dream speech, have had enduring effects in molding people's minds.[6] The word's the thing.

Modernity did not arise, I say yet again, from the deep psychosocial changes that Max Weber posited in 1904–1905. Weber's evidence was the talk of people. He believed he was probing deeper, into the core of their psychosocial being. Yet it was not a Protestant ethic or a change in acquisitive desires or a rise of national feeling or an "industrious revolution" or a new experimental attitude or any other change in people's deep behavior as *individuals* that initiated the new life of trade-tested betterment. These were not trivial, and were surely the flourishing branches of a new bourgeois civilization. They were branches, however, not the root. People have always been proud, hardworking, acquisitive, and curious, when circumstances warranted it. From the beginning, for example, greed has been a sin, prudent self-interest a virtue. There's nothing early modern about them. As for the pride of nationalism, Italian cities in the thirteenth century, or for that matter Italian parishes anywhere until yesterday, evinced a nationalism— the Italians still call the local version *campanilismo*, from *campanile*, the church bell tower from which the neighborhood takes its daily rhythms— that would do proud a patriotic Frenchman of 1914.

Yet Weber's instinct to take religious doctrine seriously in explaining the change deserves respect, though not exactly in the form of his triumphalism about reformed Protestantism. Only fragments remain of his original notion that Calvinists were especially enterprising. In 1995 Jacques Delacroix summarized a few of the more striking counterexamples: "Amsterdam's wealth was centered on Catholic families; the economically advanced German Rhineland is more Catholic than Protestant; all-Catholic Belgium was the second country to industrialize."[7] One could mention, too, the earlier evidence of capitalist vigor in Catholic Venice, Florence, Barcelona, Lisbon— unless one were precommitted to the mistaken notion (not, it should be emphasized, Weber's) that no "capitalism" could possibly exist before 1600. And in the first couple of centuries of the priesthood of all believers, Sweden, Prussia, and Scotland, fiercely Protestant all, showed few signs of economic dynamism.[8]

Weber was correct, I have affirmed, however, that cultures and societies and economies require an animating spirit, a *Geist*, an earnest rhetoric of the transcendent, and that such rhetoric matters to economic performance.[9] Weber's word *Geist* is less incense-smelling in German than its English translation of "spirit." Yet the *Geist* of betterment was not deep. It was superficial, located in the way people talked. Such a rhetoric could be changed, and often was. For example, conservatives in the United States during the 1980s and 1990s attacked the maternal metaphor of the New Deal and the Great Society, replacing it with a paternal metaphor of discipline.[10] In China the talk (and admittedly also the police action) of the Communist Party down to 1978 stopped all good economic betterment in favor of collective farms. Afterward the régime gradually allowed betterment, and now China buzzes with talk of this or that opportunity to turn a *yuan*. India did likewise. Sometimes, as around the North Sea 1517 to 1719, the rhetoric can change even after it has been frozen for millennia in aristocratic and religious frames of antibourgeois talk. Rhetoric-as-cause lacks a charmingly Romantic depth and *profundité*. But it is more encouraging, less racist, less nationalistic, less deterministic.

Consider twentieth-century history in Britain and the United States. Look at how quickly under McKinley, then Teddy Roosevelt, and then Woodrow Wilson a previously isolationist United States came to carry a big stick in the world, to the disgust of libertarian critics such as H. L. Mencken and Robert Higgs.[11] Look at how quickly the rhetoric of working-class politics changed in Britain between the elections of 1918 and 1922, crushing the great Liberal Party. Look at how quickly the rhetoric of free speech changed in the United States after 1919, through the dissenting opinions of Holmes and Brandeis.[12] Look at how legal prohibitions in Britain directed at advertisements for jobs or housing saying "Europeans only," commonplace in the 1960s, changed the conversation. (As late as 1991 such a rhetoric was still allowed in Germany: a pub in Frankfurt had a notice on the door, *Kein Zutritt für Hunde und Türken*: "No entry for dogs and Turks."[13]) Look at how quickly American apartheid changed under the pressure of the freedom riders and the Voting Rights Act. Racist talk and racist behavior, to be sure, didn't vanish overnight in any of the countries. But the racist talk could no longer claim the dignity of law and custom, and the behavior itself was on the run. Witness Barack Obama.

Look, again, at how quickly employment for married women became routine. Simone de Beauvoir, Betty Friedan, and other rhetoricians of feminism mattered.[14] Look at how quickly under New Labour the nationalizing Clause IV of the British Labour Party fell out of favor. Tony Blair and his rhetoric of realism mattered. Look at the change in American and European attitudes toward GLBT folk and their marriages. One can reasonably assert some material causes for parts of all these, surely. But rhetoric mattered too and was subject to startlingly rapid change.

The historian David Landes asserted in 1999 that "if we learn anything from the history of economic development, it is that culture makes all the difference. (Here Max Weber was right on.)"[15] He is mistaken, if "culture" here means, as Landes did intend it to mean, historically deep national characteristics. We learn instead that superficial rhetoric makes all the difference, potentially refigured in any generation that cares to do so. *Spain*, after all, was among the first European countries to allow gay marriage. It is a more cheerful conclusion, I repeat, than that the fault that we are underlings is not in our present speech but indelible in our ancient stars or race or class or nationality. The political economist Gérard Roland makes a good case that ideology persists for a long time, as in Russia's affection for tsars and secret police.[16] But he would agree that the evidence is mixed. As the economists William Baumol, Robert Litan, and Carl Schramm put it in 2007, "There are too many examples of countries turning their economies around in a relatively short period of time, a generation or less [Korea, Singapore, Thailand, Ireland, Spain]. . . . These successes cannot be squared with the culture-is-everything view."[17] The same could be said of countries turning their politics around in a short period of time, with little change in deep culture, such as defeated Germany, Franco-less Spain, Russia-freed Poland, enriched Taiwan. Culture is not much to the point, it would seem— unless, indeed, "culture" is understood as "the rhetoric people presently find persuasive." In which case, yes, right on.

The argument here is, contrary to a notion of essences derived from a Romantic theory of personality—and contrary to the other side of the Romantic coin, a notion of preknown preferences derived from a utilitarian theory of decision-without-rhetorical-reflection—that what we do is to some large degree determined by how we talk to others and to ourselves. As the French political theorist Bernard Manin put it, "The free individual is not one who already knows absolutely what he wants, but one who has incomplete preferences and is trying by means of interior deliberation and dialogue with others to determine precisely what he does want."[18] Manin points out that *avant les lettres*, in 1755, Rousseau mixed the Romantic and the utilitarian hostilities to such a democratic rhetoric into a nasty and influential concoction, which precisely denied deliberation and rhetoric. Just vote. Or better, let the Party discern the General Will, without voting.

YES, IT WAS *IDEAS*, NOT INTERESTS OR INSTITUTIONS, THAT CHANGED, SUDDENLY, IN NORTHWESTERN EUROPE

Better ideological conditions for uptake—people permitted by their society's prevailing rhetoric and its legal and customary results to experiment, to have a go, and, especially, to talk to each other in an open-source fashion about their experiments and their goings, rather than hiding them in posthumously decoded mirror writing out of fear of theological and political disapproval—awaited a change in the conditions of talk.[1] They awaited after 1700, as Mokyr would say, the Industrial Enlightenment: "Economic change in all periods depends, more than most economists think, on what people believe."[2] Or more precisely, as he has also written, "Intellectual innovation could only occur in the kind of tolerant societies in which sometimes outrageous ideas proposed by highly eccentric men [and women, *lieverd*] would not entail a violent response against 'heresy' and 'apostasy.'"[3] Or, as I would say, to put the same thought in a political and rhetorical way, they awaited in the Dutch Republic after 1600 or in England after 1688 or in New England after 1697 or in Scotland after 1707 or in France after 1789 the changes in the character of the conversation of northwestern Europe that propelled the French and Scottish Enlightenments among other marvels, such as science, Freemasonry, newspapers, concertos, and the economic and political dignity of ordinary people.[4] The change did not instantly result in perfectly open societies. But by earlier standards, such as the politico-religious slaughters in Tudor-Stuart England, or late-Valois France, or the German lands 1618–1648, they were pretty good.

By the nineteenth century the resulting handful of open and liberal societies were not met, alas, with universal applause—for example from the hierarchy of the Roman church. In 1864 Pope Pius IX condemned in number 80 of his Syllabus of Errors the absurd proposition that "the Roman Pontiff can, and ought to, reconcile himself, and come to terms with, progress, liberalism and modern civilization." Yet already in the pope's hearing, as his blast itself shows, ideas had changed many of the economies. Betterocracy became usual. By the late nineteenth century even the popes commenced favoring "capitalism" over, at least, socialism. Social life without private property is impossible, they affirmed, at any rate in large groups. So said Pope Leo XIII in 1891 in *Rerum Novarum*, reechoed by Pius XI in 1931, John XXIII in 1961 and 1963, Paul VI in 1967 and 1971, and John Paul II in 1981 and 1991.[5] These men were not nineteenth-century liberals—especially, as Michael Novak explains, they were not, in the harsh Continental sense, the "old liberals" of Jan Gresshof's satiric poem. But they celebrated private property, when used with regard to soul and community.

Two steps forward, though, one step back. I have noted that in 2013 Pope Francis I reverted, as many earnest Christians do, and among them many popes, to a medieval theory of the zero-sum society, two centuries after the economy and its ideology had created progress, liberalism, positive-sum, and modern civilization. As the libertarian economist Peter Bauer noted of Paul VI's *Populorum Progressio* (1967) and *Octogesima Adveniens* (1971):

> The spirit of these documents is contrary to the most durable and best elements in Catholic tradition. They are indeed even un-Christian. Their Utopian, chiliastic ideology, combined with an overriding preoccupation with economic differences, is an amalgam of the ideas of millenarian sects, of the extravagant claims of the early American advocates of foreign aid, and of the Messianic component of Marxism-Leninism.[6]

The intellectual historian Sophus Reinert argues that the translations of John Cary's 1695 *Essay on the State of England* into French, Italian, and German developed an anti–free trade case—of which Reinert approves, in business-school style (Reinert teaches at the Harvard Business School). Business schools, which focus naturally on the fortunes of the individual firm, teach that "competitiveness" is all. They believe it follows that governments, not price signals from the world economy, should choose winners. The economists in the business schools have a hard time persuading their colleagues that the pattern of trade and specialization is determined, on the contrary, by "*comparative* advantage," which has nothing to do with absolute advantage, and which professors of management and of history regularly mistake it for. Pakistan exports clothing to the United States, the economists preach (without much effect on editorial boards and politicians), not because it is better per hour at making socks and sweaters but because it is *comparatively* better at them than at making jet airplanes and farm tractors. If Pakistan is going to do anything, it had better focus on knitted clothing, not high-tech machines.

The Continentals in the nineteenth century, Reinert notes, believed that England's great success in trade was the product of the sort of policy that Europeans had always thought necessary, mercantilism: an "exceedingly conscious [industrial and commercial] policy" favoring, they imagined, industrialization. Mercantilism was a denial of comparative advantage in the pursuit of treasure by foreign trade. The Continentals therefore carried on as before, but more so, seeking to "codify and promote the ideas and policies responsible for the economic development of states locked in ruthless international competition."[7] Mercantilism is the theory that trade is a hockey game rather than a square dance, zero-sum not positive-sum. Thus, with Reinert's approval, came Friedrich List of Germany and a century later "dependency theory" and still later the "industrial policy" of a wise state picking winners. The trouble is that the "success" we are talking about down to 1815 was a zero-sum extension of trading by way of empire and military victories. If a conscious industrial policy had ever been able to achieve a great enrichment, it would have happened before—mercantilism in the small would have sharply enriched ordinary people by a factor of 30 or 100 in an imperialist Venice or a protectionist Augsburg or a centralizing Edo. It didn't. Latin American countries under the spell of List and dependency theory therefore have stagnated.

My theme—that ideas and circumstances are intertwined in making the modern world—is also the theme of a school of historians of European political thought, such as Peter Laslett, J. G. A. Pocock, Quentin Skinner, John Dunn, Richard Tuck, and Mark Goldie. The Cambridge/Johns Hopkins methodological point is that you may not omit ideas, nor even their internal logic or their political contexts pushing them to extremes. A good example is Carlos Eduardo Suprinyak's recent study of the way a dogma of the balance of trade became the default reasoning of early English mercantilists.[8] Robert Higgs argues that such case studies are the only way forward in thinking about ideological change. "In the context of human creativity and free will," he concludes, "no theory of ideological change can be fully deterministic."[9] Surely. The ideology is sometimes—the materialist would mistakenly say "always"—crudely self-interested. Schumpeter took a more nuanced view:

> Ideologies are not simply lies; they are truthful statements about what a man thinks he sees. Just as the medieval knight saw himself as he wished to see himself and just as the modern bureaucrat does the same and just as both failed and fail to see whatever may be adduced against their seeing themselves as the defenders of the weak and innocent and the sponsors of the Common Good, so every other social group develops a protective ideology which is nothing if not sincere.[10]

Not just people at the time, Schumpeter continued, but historians looking back have ideologies about what they think they see. "The source of ideology is our pre- and extrascientific vision of the economic process and of what is—causally or teleologically—important in it and since normally this vision is then subjected to scientific treatment, it is being either verified or destroyed by analysis and in either case should vanish qua ideology."[11] I am not so confident as Schumpeter was, at the height of twentieth-century positivism, that verification and analysis will be the end of ideology. But an ideological change is also my project, to change the prescientific vision of my colleagues.

Leo Tolstoy, in contrast to his somewhat older contemporaries Karl Marx or Henry Thomas Buckle, was no materialist but rather what might be called a society-ist. "The less connected with the activity of others our activity is," he wrote in 1869, "the more free it is; and on the contrary, the more our activity is connected with other people the less free it is."[12] We can raise our arm at will, but for half a million men to invade Russia, Tolstoy argues, more than the individual will of Napoleon was required. The notion is familiar to economists reflecting on the summed wills of suppliers and demanders. But in Tolstoy's passion to reject the great-man theory of history he made fun of the force of ideas: "A locomotive is moving. Someone asks: What moves it? Some see it as a force directly inherent in heroes, as the peasant sees the devil in the locomotive; others as a force resulting from several other forces, like the movement of the wheels; others again as an intellectual influence, like the smoke that is blown away."[13] Yet, my dear Count, you will admit that if the smoke gets in the eyes of the engineer, or if an idea of putting a high-pressure steam engine on rails inspires the provincial British artisans Richard Trevithick and George Stephenson, then ideas can matter mightily.

One can make merry of an ideational history that does not give a serious account of how exactly ideas moved people and where exactly the ideas came from. Wrote Tolstoy: "Certain men wrote certain books at the time. At the end of the eighteenth century there were a couple of dozen men in Paris who began to talk about all men being free and equal. This caused people all over France to begin to slash at and drown one another."[14] Or Sellar and Yeatman's explanation of the Industrial Revolution in *1066 and All That*: "Many remarkable discoveries and inventions were made [in the early nineteenth century]. Most remarkable among these was the discovery (made by all the rich men in England at once) that women and children could work for 25 hours a day . . . without many of them dying or becoming excessively deformed. This was known as the Industrial Revelation."[15]

But consider the analogy with religion. The monotheistic, universalist religions of what Karl Jaspers called the Axial Age, 600 BCE to 200 BCE, arose it seems from the conversation of ideas between different civilizations, made possible by the material condition of improved trade.[16] No one would deny that monotheism thereafter had gigantic material effects on politics and the economy. But monotheism after all is an idea, not a means of production, spreading for example from Temple Judaism (or it may be, as Freud dubiously claimed, from the pharaoh Akhenaten in the fourteenth century BCE) to Christianity to Islam, with remoter contacts in Zoroastrianism (providing the notion of reincarnation at the end of history) and even perhaps ideas from some versions of sophisticated Hinduism and Buddhism. Monotheism is a meme. When given a chance by trade or even by one holy man speaking to another—pre-Socratic philosophers in Ionia, for example, mulling Persian ideas—the intellectual prestige of a search for the One turns out to compete rather well in people's minds with the vulgar particularism of tree worship and witchcraft and Olympian gods.

Even the great Marxian historian Gordon Childe declared in 1943, "Without going in for any metaphysical subtleties, socially approved and sustained ideas that inspire such action"

> must be treated by history as just as real as those which stand for the more substantial objects of archaeological study. In practice ideas form as effective an element in the environment of any human society as do mountains, trees, animals, the weather and the rest of external nature. Societies, that is, behave as if they were reacting to a spiritual environment as well as to a material environment.[17]

Yet I do not want to be understood as ignoring constraints, prices, incomes, geography, climate, class, demography, interests, and all the other nonideational forces elevated to single causes during the age of intellectual materialism, 1890–1980. After about 1980 in departments of history something like the opposite error was committed. Departments that once harbored quantitative historians of the ilk of William Aydelotte on the British Parliament, Richard Hellie on Muscovy, and Daniel Scott Smith on colonial America somewhat absentmindedly dropped numbers, except page numbers, and with them dropped material causes. Cultural studies came to reign, and the students seldom asked "How much?" Certain historical scholars I admire greatly sometimes write as if ideas *alone* mattered: on the French Revolution, Lynn Hunt and—both of these are friends and former colleagues—Keith Baker and Bill Sewell; on the American Revolution, Gordon Wood (whose writing on Franklin I have already quoted extensively); on American history generally, Jill Lapore (whom I came to admire in the pages of the *New Yorker*) and Tom Haskell (the slayer of Fogel, whose writing on "responsibility" I have used here).[18]

Material circumstances mattered, of course. The Little Ice Age was long thought to have put pressure on régimes from Ming China to the Spanish Netherlands (though a recent paper by Kelly and Ó Gráda calls into question the statistical basis for such a history).[19] And rising population worldwide in the sixteenth century set one elite against another.[20] The rapid adoption in the West of a gunpowder technology invented in the East put the final nail in the coffin—or rather the final bullet hole in the armor—of the mounted knight and his Norman castle walls and, with a long lag, his aristocratic values. As late as the sixteenth century the mounted knight, or for that matter a

Spanish commoner similarly equipped, could sometimes prevail, but only if faced with Aztecs and Incas deathly ill from imported smallpox and measles, and lacking iron and guns and horses.[21]

And speaking of Mexico and Peru, the voyages of discovery and the resulting empires were perhaps useful if not essential contexts for an industrial revolution. Trade inside Europe *was* essential, as was the long-established security of property. Yet these were only contexts, available from Nagasaki to Norwich, not vital and uniquely northwestern European causes. If Europeans had not ventured in their startlingly violent way to Africa and India and the New World, and had not acquired empires by intent or by inadvertence, yet had nurtured the idea of all men being free and equal, the Great Enrichment would have nonetheless occurred.

Demographic history, as Richard Easterlin has argued, is a good place to watch the dance between ideas and conditions.[22] The Great Fall in Mortality is as important to a (literally) full human life as the Great Enrichment. Easterlin argues that ideas led the fall in mortality—this against the prevailing orthodoxy dating from the 1940s and Thomas McKeown that nutrition, not medicine, is what drove it. The demographer Sheila Johansson argues persuasively from the excellent records since the late Middle Ages on elite families—presumably not suffering from malnutrition, at any rate in the amounts they ate—that useful ideas such as quinine for malaria, inoculation for smallpox, and orangeries providing wintertime cures for scurvy brought death rates down for the rich. When ideas pioneered by the privileged yielded cheap versions, the poor eventually benefited. "Ignorance, not hunger, is the villain of mortality history."[23] Yet one can admit on the material side that the poor eventually benefited, too, from eating better, in potatoes and tomatoes from the Columbian Exchange. The betterment was a dance between ideational and material causes. As I have argued against my allies Mokyr and Jacob, though, ideas from high science were not casual until late in the story. None of the early medical advances that Johansson speaks of had anything to do with theoretical breakthroughs. They were empirical, yes, but not deductions from biological laws, such as the germ theory of disease (itself among the earliest practical fruits of high science, yet accepted only late in the nineteenth century.)

That a material base can have an influence, in other words, does not at all require that we reduce mind to matter, or indulge our tough-guy affection for realism in international relations and declare that economic growth comes out of the barrel of a gun. John Stuart Mill, writing in the 1840s on the sources of the new sympathy for the working class, noted that "ideas, unless outward circumstances conspire with them, have in general no very rapid or immediate efficacy in human affairs; and the most favorable outward circumstances may pass by, or remain inoperative, for want of ideas suitable to the conjuncture. But when the right circumstances and the right ideas meet, the effect is seldom slow in manifesting itself."[24] The Industrial Revolution and especially the Great Enrichment and its rhetoric of respect for ordinary people, for example, given the quasi-free market for ideas, made possible the rise of mass democracies. Mill speaks especially of the British Reform Bill of 1832. The Bill was admittedly a modest extension of the franchise (unlike the fuller democratizations of 1867, 1884, 1918, and 1928). But if the specifically rhetorical change had not happened as it did—a change on the lips of influential people about political representation—modern economic growth and therefore modern democracy in Britain would have been throttled in its cradle, or at any rate malnourished well before its maturity.

Economic growth and democracy had been routinely throttled or malnourished in earlier times. North, Wallis, and Weingast want to be seen as tough-guy materialists, but when they seek explanations of the "transition proper" to "open access societies," they fall naturally into speaking of a rhetorical change. Two crucial pages of their 2009 book speak of "the transformation in thinking," "a new understanding," "the language of rights," and "the commitment to open access."[25] Though they appear to believe that they have a material explanation of "open access to political and economic organizations," in fact their explanation for why Britain, France, and the United States tipped into open access is ideational.[26] Ideas change through sweet talk as much as through material interests.

An interest-only theory of the economist Steven N. S. Cheung inspired North, Wallis, and Weingast. Cheung, though a naturalized American and a capitalist-roader of the purist kind, was by his own account a teacher of the Communist Party grandees who allowed China to experiment after 1978 with trade-tested betterment. In 1982 he explained to a Western audience that such an institutional change comes from accumulated information combined with interest.[27] It is a mere matter of calculation. A part of the elite somehow acquires information about better institutions, "better" being defined as "better for the interests of the elite." And then the better-informed party spends resources to compel the others, against the interests of the nonelite others.

There is, in the simplest version of Cheung's theory, no sweet talk, no ideological persuasion, no fundamental changing of minds, no mutual gain in the realm of ideas—merely cost and benefit defined as material interest. Acemoglu and Robinson have an identical theory, expressed in a more nuanced and mathematical form.[28]

The Cheung theory does fit some of China's turn to "capitalism." Party officials making their first trips to the West after Mao's death were mortified by the riches they saw—which was their new information.[29] Let us have some of that, they thought, and some Swiss bank accounts for leading Party officials as well. The political struggle of Deng Xiaoping to put "socialist modernization" into practice had costs, which figured in the Cheungian calculation. And yet a great deal is missing from such a prudence-only account of benefit and cost. The favorite book of a recent premier of China, Wen Jiaobao, is Adam Smith's *The Theory of Moral Sentiments*, which, as I have noted, famously begins, "How selfish soever man may be supposed, there are evidently some principles in his nature, which interest him in the fortune of others."[30] That's not the premise of the Max U theory from Cheung, North, Wallis, Weingast, Acemoglu, or Robinson. As the economists Ning Wang and Ronald Coase argued recently about the political prospects for China, "multiparty competition does not work unless it is cultivated and disciplined by a free market for ideas, without which democracy can be easily hijacked by interest groups and undermined by the tyranny of the majority. The performance of democracy critically depends on the market for ideas, just like privatization depends on the market for capital assets."[31] Coase and Wang pay attention to the way the ideas of the elite and the people changed for reasons beyond sheer interest. Without the power of words our liberties and our central heating would have been denied.

ELSEWHERE IDEAS ABOUT THE
BOURGEOISIE DID NOT CHANGE

I was a student in the 1960s of the economic historian Alexander Gerschenkron (1904–1978) and am therefore vividly aware of the hazards of
propounding necessary conditions derived from an inadequately comparative and cosmopolitan perspective. Gerschenkron's economistic metaphor,
that a thing can "substitute" for another, he said, puts Britain itself as much
as other countries under a cosmopolitan scrutiny so far as the applicability of theories is concerned (there is some doubt from later research, actually, concerning the applicability of Gerschenkron's own theory to the
other countries[1]). Gerschenkron gave examples from the industrialization of
Germany, Italy, and Russia that exhibited, he believed, substitutes for what
looked from the British history like prerequisites. The big banks in Germany
in the 1870s, for example, and state enterprises in Russia in the 1890s substituted for a vigor in entrepreneurship and a bourgeois honesty in trade that
were by 1750 taken for granted in Britain.

In other words, Gerschenkron, an economist as much as a historian, believed that there is more than one way to skin a cat. If foreign trade or entrepreneurship or saving had been lacking, the economist's argument goes,
other impulses to growth could have taken their place. The replacement entails a loss, but usually a modest one. A vigorous domestic trade or a single-
minded government or a forced saving from the taxation of agriculture
could take the place of the British ideal of the merchant left alone by government to reinvest his profits in a bettering cotton factory.

Albert Hirschman (1915–2012, another great economic scientist overlooked in favor of spinners of nonfacts by the committee for the Sveriges

Riksbank Prize in Economic Sciences in Memory of Alfred Nobel) was much influenced by a lecture in 1951 by Gerschenkron, on "Prerequistes," and wrote:

> When it was increasingly realized that economic backwardness cannot be explained in terms of any outright absence or scarcity of this or that human type or factor of production, attention turned to the attitudes and value systems that may favor or inhibit the emergence of the required activities and personalities. . . . But whenever any theory was propounded that considered a given value system a *prerequisite* of development, it could usually be effectively contradicted on empirical grounds: development had actually taken place somewhere without the benefit of the "prerequisite."[2]

Yes.

Historians or economists focused on one locale, such as Britain, are liable to miss similar conditions elsewhere that belie their celebration of, say, the English common law (but oddly not the Scottish civil law, considering that Scotland, too, had an Industrial Revolution) or the British empire (but oddly not also the French empire, whose trade with France grew faster in the eighteenth century than Britain's imperial trade with Britain). A wide angle of view disciplines speculation. The North, Wallis, and Weingast book I have mentioned from time to time is modestly subtitled *A Conceptual Framework for Interpreting Recorded Human History*. Yet it omits recorded human history except England's, France's, and the United States', and treats the trinity partially and often erroneously. The framework for interpreting recorded human history has no mention in the index or the text of Africa, Arabia, China, Germany, Greece, Iran, Italy, Japan, Sweden, the Ottoman Empire, the Mughals, the Netherlands, or Russia except for a few pages on the USSR.[3] One province of the world, it must be said, does not constitute a believable human history. One must, as Gerschenkron and Hirschman were affirming, be seriously comparative and cosmopolitan.

But what one is seriously comparative and cosmopolitan about can include ideas too. In the evolutionary terms that the British sociologist W. G. Runciman would use, I am arguing that the meme "trade-tested-betterments are good" had reproductive success, and further, that on the success of the idea depended the material success of the modern world.[4] The thought was father to the wish. Evolution in biology and in an economy, both, depend on variation and a mechanism of selection from the variation, and then on heritability to fix the selected variation. Legal liberty and sociological dignity for ordinary people provided variation, in the form of cooperation, such as the multiple solutions in Europe for the reverse engineering of formerly exclusively Chinese stoneware and porcelain, among which three survived. Josiah Wedgwood, up from apprenticeship to a potter when he was eleven, and whose motto was "Everything yields to experiment," performed fully five thousand experiments to find in 1775 Jasper blue.[5]

A parallel point, made among the French *philosophes*, is that democracy and free speech, too, give the society wider variation of possibilities. It is a form of cooperation, a conversation notably enlivened in the eighteenth century. Betterment was encouraged by coffeehouses and newspapers, by clubs unique to Europe such as the Europe-wide Freemasonry movement, by better means of communication such as the much-improved mails (though here the comparison with China would not be so favorable: Europe was merely catching up), and by groups such as the Lunar Society, whose discussions ranged reasonably freely over theology and natural philosophy (at a time when unified polities in Russia, China, Japan, and the Ottoman Empire made it easier for the elite to suppress discussion). The betterments were political, such as in the late eighteenth century the successful American and then the unsuccessful Dutch revolution of 1787 and the partially successful French revolutions; or betterments in religion, as they imagined them to be, such as Methodism and Pietism; or betterments in music from the free cities of Europe; or betterments in science; or, to come to the main theme, betterments in technology from the hands of academically uneducated craftsmen talking with each other and experimenting thousands of times to get Jasper blue or thousands of times to get a filament for a lightbulb.

The new liberty and dignity in the Anglosphere then provided the selection, in the form of competition. (But if the forces of conservation are too strong, as they often are, the variation-cum-selection has no chance of achieving heritability—the third condition for evolution being—and thus of altering matters.[6]) If betterments did not meet a profit test, they died. And it was for the good of poor people that they should, because otherwise the surviving "betterments" are boondoggles for well-connected chaps, or monuments for the already rich. They are Baconian research projects of doubtful worth, destructive creation rather than creative destruction. That is what is wrong with Thorstein Veblen's notion that engineers, not the price system, should rule. Engineers are full of bad ideas too, such as high-speed trains constructed at great expense on little-used lines—unless central-planning rationalism is indeed the ticket, which outside of wartime it usually is not. Trade-tested cooperation, competition, and conservation in the right mix is the ticket for rapid economic evolution

The economic and historical question, confronted here and in *Bourgeois Dignity*, is Why in Britain and why then? Many people still believe, without much evidence, that ideas were not important. Yet it seems clear, for example, that without the ideas and pen of Adam Smith the rhetoric of betterment would have developed in different ways, if at all. He himself wrote eloquently in 1776 against the notion that only material interests matter. After all, the polemical point of *The Wealth of Nations* was to assault what he called the "commercial system," that is, mercantilism, a system of ideas popular down to the present in protectionist tariffs, industrial policy, and subsidization of trade-rejected proposals. Slowly—very slowly, as Anthony Waterman and Emma Rothschild and John Nye note—his special eloquence came to matter.[7]

Smith would not have wasted his breath if he had thought ideas were mere reflexes of the interests. No writer urging better economic or political policy can support without self-contradiction the cynical, amoral theory of prudence-only materialism. If materialist economism is true, put down your pen. Let the short-run self-interest of the poor and of the powerful grind on and on to wreck betterment, in the style of East Germany. Let us accept our fate. As Mokyr remarks in favor of an ideational element, "It would be wrong to believe that ideologies were simply a reflection of economic interests and that persuasion itself did not matter at all. Many influential intellectuals in history were traitors to their class, none more so than that great believer in historical materialism, Friedrich Engels."[8] Maybe it is mistaken to assert that rhetoric in favor of trade-tested betterment and the acceptance of profit—a new neural pathway in the brain laid down by practice—was sufficient to initiate prosperity and liberty. But at least such an assertion is not a performative self-contradiction, such as journalistic and scholarly persuaders trying to persuade us that persuasion is a nullity.

The world-making setting-aside of the theistic hypothesis by Hobbes and Spinoza in the seventeenth century, for example, was not a consequence of the relations of production. Philosophically speaking the materialist preju-dice is that in the first place real interests and incomes happen, then words are fashioned to refer to them. The prejudice only makes sense if one has assumed implicitly a reference theory of language, the notion that words are merely labels for preexisting things in the world. Yon sheep is to be named by God's will "sheep." But one of the main discoveries of the humanities in the twentieth century is that the reference theory of language, while helpful for learning Italian or Afrikaans ("Bread is *pane* or *brood*"), is nothing like a complete theory of how we do things with words. Since Heine, Saussure, Wittgenstein (Mark II), Kenneth Burke, J. L. Austin, Michel Foucault, John Searle, and the rest, we have known that language speaks us as much as we speak language. We construct a world with it, or the world is constructed for us.

Consider "speech acts," as the philosopher John L. Austin dubbed them, that drive our personal and national histories: "I thee wed"; "I ask that the Congress declare that . . . a state of war exists between the United States and the Japanese Empire." There is nothing weird or scary or unscientific or self-contradictory about claiming that rhetoric matters.[9] It is the ancient findings of the sciences of language, first articulated in Greek rhetoric and Jewish Talmud and Sanskrit grammar, and rediscovered in the twentieth century after a long love affair in the West with Platonic realism and Comt-ean positivism.

But the numerous vulgar Marxians of the left and the right claim to be-lieve that the Interests and Reality rule every time. Thus the great American economist George Stigler (1911–1991) asserted in *The Economist as Preacher* (1982) that "we live in a world that is full of mistaken policies, but they are not mistaken for their followers. . . . Individuals always know their true self-interest. . . . Each sector of the public will therefore demand services from intellectuals favorable to the interests of that sector."[10] That part of the argu-ment is identical to Antonio Gramsci's on the role of the intellectual: "Every social group . . . creates together with itself, organically, one or more strata of intellectuals."[11] But Gramsci the Italian Marxist (1891–1937) was less of a his-torical materialist than was Stigler the Chicago School economist. Gramsci believed in a role for rhetoric and the Party, as Lenin did too, and was op-posed to an "economism" such as Stigler advocated in his old age, the cynical half-truth that the interests will always win out.

The European Civil War of 1914–1989 showed how nineteenth-century theories hatched by the clerisy could kill off liberty and prosperity, and tens of millions of people to the bargain. If you doubt that ideas matter, consider the importance of idea-besotted leaders in that pitiful history, when the right circumstances and the right ideas met. The ideational literature in recent political science calls the vital few "carriers," "capable of persuading others to reconsider the ways they think and act."[12] No Lenin, with his pen, no October/November 1917. No Hitler, with his voice, no January 1933. Ideas, for good or ill, matter.

The Bourgeois Revaluation leading to frenetic betterment was a probing, as loyalty to rank weakened, as the holy, catholic, and apostolic church fragmented, and as gender roles began to alter in character, of what people believed they ought to believe about ordinary life. It altered the way influential people (the elite that Mokyr and Jacob emphasize) offered warrantable beliefs to each other about exports of cotton textiles or the dignity of inventors or the basis of legitimate power. In the metaphor about metaphors of the linguist George Lakoff, it altered the mental frames that people used to speak of the economy, by laying down, so to speak, new neural pathways in their brains.[13] It altered the stasis with which people defended what they did, after 1700 radically and for the good.

The Revaluation was completed by 1776 in the brains of elite intellectuals such as Turgot, Smith, Hume, Franklin, and Kant. The more plebeian Sentimental Revolution of the 1770s was an aspect of its spread, a bringing down into the bourgeoisie of the stories of the experiences-worthy-to-be-recorded formerly limited to kings and queens. The separation of spheres between bourgeois men and women was another aspect of the spread of the Revaluation.[14] By 1848 the idealism of ordinary life, though incomplete and always under challenge from older rhetorics of king, nobility, and God, had become the rhetoric of the times in which we still live, the Bourgeois Era.

FOURTH QUESTION
What Are the Dangers?

PART IX

The History and Economics Have Been Misunderstood

56

THE CHANGE IN IDEAS CONTRADICTS
MANY IDEAS FROM THE POLITICAL
MIDDLE, 1890–1980

The rhetorical and ethical change around 1700, I say, contrary to the materialist persuasions of many of my colleagues, caused modern economic growth, which at length freed us from ancient poverty. As Jane Jacobs put it, the ethical code for commerce slowly replaced the ethical code for guardianship.[1] Hierarchy seemed less natural, though given a second life around 1890 by scientific racism. Modern economic growth did not corrupt our souls, contrary to the antibourgeois rhetoric of the modern clerisy since 1848, and contrary also to an older line of aristocratic and priestly sneering at bourgeois life.

The rhetorical and ethical change at the national level was necessary for the first Industrial Revolution and then for the Great Enrichment. It was even perhaps jointly sufficient—with property rights standing as a supersaturated solution established in Europe many centuries earlier, and anyway characteristic of most societies worldwide, into which the crystal of the dignity of ordinary life was dropped.[2] The new enlargement of liberty and dignity for the innovative bourgeoisie, as Charles Tilly would have put it, faced in northwestern Europe an "opportunity structure" that made growth possible, although he would not have acknowledged that the same structures faced Japan and China and the rest.

It was sudden, in a long view. Douglass North and Robert Thomas declared to the contrary in 1973 that "the industrial revolution was not the source of economic growth."[3] You must, they claimed, start much earlier.

One wonders why. Why must all causes be deep in history? Only if you stop the story of Europe in 1800 CE or even, at a stretch, in 1870 can you persuade yourself that the run-up to the Great Enrichment is best viewed as being a thousand years, or five hundred, during which England saw, as Thomas and North asserted (they did not have the advantage of the recent research on magnitudes), a "sustained economic growth." It was "sustained," we have since discovered, at about one-tenth of 1 percent per year. Two-tenths at the most. Good for the medieval and early modern English. But if you carry on to the present you realize that the greatest fact of secular history is not the run-up of 1348–1750—if "run-up" it was, as though to a high jump, and not merely an irrelevant jog in the other direction along the track. Nor is the greatest fact the impressive Industrial Revolution, 1750–1848. It is the amazingly enriching follow-on, the Great Enrichment, not so amazing in 1867 when the mature Marx wrote, though becoming amazing in 1883 when the young Toynbee spoke. It was not a mere factor of 2 over many centuries (as the "run-up" was), or even of 2 over one century (as the classic Industrial Revolution was, 1760–1860), but of 100 over two centuries, if allowing for improved quality. It was a sustained economic growth of 5.87 percent per year—higher than the medieval and early modern rate by a factor of sixty, and an acceleration well above even the admirable British Industrial Revolution.

Some of my fellow economic historians, such as Stephen Broadberry and Bishnupriya Gupta and Jan Luiten van Zanden, make much of the slow doubling or tripling of incomes in Europe before the Industrial Revolution (in Maddison's reckoning, definitely tripling), and quarrel learnedly in the journals about its exact dimensions. As Jutta Bolt and van Zanden put it, North-and-Thomas style, "The Industrial Revolution that began in the UK (and quickly spread to Western Europe and North America) was therefore not a sudden break in economic performance, but a continuation of the growth record since the Middle Ages."[4] In a similar way, Jean-Laurent Rosenthal and B. Bin Wong spend much of *Before and Beyond Divergence: The Politics of Economic Change in China and Europe* (2011) arguing persuasively about comparisons between the two ends of Eurasia between 1500 and 1800. But they admit that "our explanation of why modern economic growth began in Europe rather than China has stopped around 1800."[5] They believe, without showing, and contrary to the evidence on income per head or on the small size of the sectors affected by modernization in Britain by

1800, that "the great divergence in technological change . . . was completed by 1800." Nothing like it is true. The enormous bulk of technological change arose from conditions after 1800. At best, 1800 was the end of the beginning, not the beginning of the end.

Stopping at 1800 is an error of historical judgment, committed by economic and historical scientists whom I admire extravagantly, and many of whose works I depend on here. It would be better for them, I suggest diffidently, to turn attention to the real source of our present condition—the Great Enrichment—and to stop debating whether England before 1800 experienced betterment at 0.1 per year or at 0.2 percent per year. True, a rise by a factor of two or three per person in the ability to get food or shelter or education, even if dragged on over five centuries, is a good thing. I recommend it, at any rate by comparison with zero or negative growth. There is some doubt, to be sure, that the factor or two or three actually happened, as Gregory Clark points out in a fierce review of Angus Maddison's book, *Contours of the World Economy, 1–2030 AD: Essays in Macro-Economic History* (2007), and less fiercely in a paper with Joseph Cummins and Brock Smith.[6] Others will just as fiercely dispute with Clark. I suggest we stop the fierceness and start asking why betterment was so much better after 1800 than before.

In the story we may dub "Continuist," beginning in the remote mists of European history, the Industrial Revolution is seen as a mysterious continuation of allegedly and very modestly rising incomes in Europe, 1100–1800, or northwestern Europe, 1600–1820. But growth would have had the same astounding follow-on in Rome or China if its essence and consequence was merely an initial doubling or tripling of incomes—whether slowly, as the Continuists favor, or in a spurt of a century or so, as the Industrial Revolutionists favor. Such commercial or industrial revolutions, I have noted, have been by no means uncommon in history—the "industrial revolution" of the coming of windmills to Europe, say, or of the coming of silk cultivation in China. Eric Jones argues persuasively that "China under the Song, and probably under the preceding late Tang, dynasty underwent a transformation that included many 'industrial revolution' features. There was enormous monetization and industrialization, presupposing structural change on a scale usually associated with modern growth, and reflected in the swelling of Song cities."[7]

The Continuists assert that the growth in northwestern Europe "continues," by a process not revealed, yet for some reason, also not revealed, growth in other areas—in Rome or China or Mesopotamia or Greece or the Ottoman Empire, or for that matter ancient Guatemala or fourteenth-century Hawaii—does not. It will not suffice to solve the puzzle by appealing to the Scientific Revolution, which did not matter a great deal, I have noted, for average income until later. In any case, with similar liberty and dignity for commoners, China or Japan, or for that matter India, might well have developed a similar science. They had a notably superior one to begin with. Nor is the economist's growth theory a solution to why growth continues. It supposes that economies of scale in knowledge suddenly dropped in, per-haps delivered to the north of England by aliens, around 1800, and for some reason did not drop similarly into a dozen other times and places similarly graced with big cities or good geography or literate populations or all of them together.

The economic historian Paolo Malanima argues that a bad response in Italy to a general European crisis of the eighteenth century provided the first signs of English superiority, fully in line with the conventional dating of the Industrial Revolution in England, and goes on to chart a quadru-pling of the real wages of building craftsmen in southern England during the first century of the Great Enrichment. Zero growth, or even doubling, is less startling for human history than such a factor of four—well before science mattered much, but after the spread in the relevant nations of northwestern Europe of liberal ideas. And in the twentieth century another factor of four occurred, conventionally measured.[8] To focus without good scientific rea-son on Europe's deep history, on the earliest and slowest growth of one of the trees, is to miss the forest, growing explosively only after 1800.

Eric Jones eloquently dismissed in 2010 the view of many others of my fellow economic historians, such as Pomeranz, Mokyr, and Goldstone, that nothing revolutionary on the scale of the Great Enrichment happened until roughly 1800. I've noted that he had already instanced in his book *Growth Recurring* (1988) such "major growth phases" as early Song China and early Tokugawa Japan.[9] But the phases were rises without follow-ons, the sorts of doubling that might have "continued" if China or Japan had acquired what northwestern Europe had in the eighteenth and especially the nineteenth century—a seriously betterment-admiring society without crushing re-straints from government. And the "failed takeoffs," as Acemoglu and Zili-botti call them, of Amsterdam, Florence, and Genoa, were indeed failures as to follow-on. (Yet putting Amsterdam in the category of failure is a scientific mistake: I have noted that the place merely changed, as London did, from being chiefly manufacturing and merchanting to being chiefly banking and merchanting; and Florence is to this day a substantial industrial city; and Genoa is still the port of northern Italian industrialization.)

Jones opines that "what kept growth episodes so few was mainly excessive rent-seeking on the part of the holders of political power."[10] Probably. The economic historian Sheilagh Ogilvie, for instance, presents evidence that medieval guilds of merchants were growth-killers—not the growth-makers that some recent theorists and historians of the neo-institutionalist school have posited. She writes:

> The "conflict" view [as against the rosy neo-institutional view of guilds] would agree that there is a good economic reason why guild-like merchant associations existed so widely from the twelfth to—in some societies—the nineteenth century. But it was not because they increased aggregate output by guaranteeing commercial security or contract enforcement. Rather, they limited competition and reduced exchange by excluding craftsmen, peasants, women, Jews, foreigners, and the urban proletariat from most profitable branches of commerce. Merchant guilds and associations were so widespread and so tenacious not because they efficiently solved economic problems, making everyone better off, but because they efficiently distributed resources to a powerful urban elite, with side benefits for rulers.[11]

People in the poorest countries nowadays, who assume not unreasonably that their economies are zero-sum, reckon that they can best advance by theft, graft, influence, corruption, rent-seeking. People in rich countries reckon, on the contrary, that the best way to advance is invention and betterment, which is why such countries became wealthy, at any rate until government expenditures got large enough to encourage rent-seeking to take over again.[12] But anyway the "major growth phases" were periods in which income per person rose by factors of 2 or at most 3, not factors of 10 or 30 or 100. Economic history needs, in other words, to deemphasize, as Jones sometimes does not, in deference to the Continuists, the manufacturing-cum-regional-specialization that we call loosely "industrialization." The demographer and economic historian Anthony Wrigley noted in 1988 that such a startling change as the Great Enrichment could not have been a mere "continuation" of events dating back to the Middle Ages, considering that such wise heads as Hume, Smith, Malthus, Ricardo, and Mill missed entirely what began, slowly, to happen in the eighteenth century and early nineteenth centuries.[13] The protean Jones himself puts the point well:

> Had the Enlightenment idea of progress not influenced practical affairs, England might have become a normal country, in the terms of the period, content with a quietly prosperous but not forcefully progressive economy—like the United Provinces or Tokugawa Japan or Venice. Living standards would have been well ahead of Stone Age affluence but stalled on a plateau of bucolic prosperity, the potential for growth meandering away in a Venetian twilight.[14]

Precisely. The problem, as Mokyr has noted, is to explain why meandering in the twilight did not occur, as it so often had in earlier efflorescences, as Goldstone named the earlier industrial revolutions.

The Age of Enlightenment conceived as French cannot be the explanation, since the French, absent a British commercial irritation, would have gone on talking charmingly in salons about utopias, and would have continued to invent military devices of doubtful civilian utility, such as the hot-air balloon. As a French businesswoman remarked recently—though invoking, too, the usual understanding of French glory in the *Siècle des Lumières*—the French "are good at inventing things, but once they've made the invention they don't know what to do with it."[15] Similarly, in the late seventeenth century, the suddenly practical and commercial English, absent a Dutch irritation, would probably have stayed nonnaval and nonfinancial and nonbourgeois, and poor. The explosion of ideas started in Holland, irritating its neighbors to action.

To explain what we are trying to explain we have to think of its roots as first a relatively recent Dutch growth of betterments tested by trade, and then a recent British, or even in particular a Scottish, greater growth, or an Industrial Enlightenment. The roots, however, would have shriveled, as they so often had for earlier industrial revolutions, if they had not been accompanied this one time by a dramatic change in ideology. The British enrichment—out of Holland—came above all from a particular kind of bourgeois-admiring ideology. Ogilvie again provides a crucial fact, that rent-seeking guilds were unusually weak in Holland and Britain after 1500 by comparison to Italy or Germany or Spain.[16] In London or Amsterdam you could set up in business with a relatively free hand, which is the crucial condition of entry that the Peruvian economist Hernando de Soto has brought to attention.[17] In France from the sixteenth century onward, by contrast, *L'État* closely regulated the betterments of the bourgeoisie, and tempted it with offers to acquire for ready cash a tax-free nobility of the robe.

The Dutch and eventually the British ideology came gradually to be one of betterment free from monopolizing guilds or interfering autocrats. The new ideology made wholly honorable the fiddling by ordinary folk with air pumps and steam engines and looms and pottery. It pushed the French to recommend a British and an earlier Dutch respect for individual initiative, at least among a liberal minority of French thinkers. They were suspicious of the *intendents* sent out from Versailles to regulate the details of factory openings equipped with rolls of red or, nowadays, green tape. Lawrence Wylie reported the attitude of a French bureaucrat in the 1950s: "If the public speaks evil of me I serenely shit on it. The complaint merely goes to show the value of my office and of my methods. The more the public is shat upon, the better the State is served."[18] The Dutch and then the British bourgeoisies, or the craftsmen such as Watt or Wedgwood or Arkwright climbing into the haute bourgeoisie, were liberated from earlier constraints, some self-imposed, to discuss their progressive projects with a new rhetoric. They got to be dignified in the bargain. They were for the first time named as betterers beneficial to the nation as a whole. And light blue plaques eventually adorned the houses where they had lived and worked.

Thank God, then, for the Bourgeois Deal, and its democratic test by consumer satisfaction, and the private profit that so lucidly signals its success. And thank God too for the social gain from reasoning by commercial cost and benefit rather than by first-act equality or national glory or the interests of the *aristoi* or cute novelties in engineering or the number of souls entering heaven.

The "thank God" here is not entirely ornamental. The spirit that infuses this book, as my friend and fellow Episcopalian the philosopher Robert Sessions has pointed out to me, is one of thankfulness. Every day I am thankful that I was born in the twentieth century in the United States—for all my country's admitted faults—and not in some alternative time and place in which chance might have put me. Or as Sessions and I, as believing Christians, might express it, in which God might have put me: seventeenth century Spain, for example, or 6000 BCE Germany. (To the more vehe-mently atheist of my friends I apologize in advance for the theology here—it will cease in a moment. But consider the possibility that theology at least brings important matters to the table. The communion table.)

As a Christian I am committed to believing that a starving orphan in Calcutta has just as valuable a soul as an elderly professor in Chicago. That was Mother Teresa's core belief, and therefore, according to some hostile accounts, she felt justified in neglecting the merely physical health of her charges—all that mattered, after all, was the souls' path to eternal life. It was a medieval theology. Mother Teresa's orphanage and hospices were said in some unfriendly discussions, such as those of Christopher Hitchens, Tariq Ali, and perhaps more believably those of the editor of the *Lancet*, the lead-ing British medical journal, to have had a notably higher death rate than oth-ers. The Teresa orphanages resounded with screams of pain resulting from the denying of opiates, backed by a "theology of suffering."[19] Sessions and I, as progressive Christians, have a quite different attitude toward suffering in this sublunary world.

Mother Teresa, like some on the left and right, in other words, didn't believe that economic growth mattered. What mattered to her—and here we do not need to rely on hostile accounts—and what still matters to many on the left and the right, are *only* transcendents, such as eternal life or secular utopia or the environment or the British Empire. Eric Hobsbawm, the his-torian and British communist, was asked on a television show by the liberal Michael Ignatieff in 1994 whether "the murder of 15, 20 million people [in the USSR under Stalin] might have been justified" in light of its contribu-tion to founding a communist society (one might ask the same about Mao's famine, 1958–1962, with forty-five million deaths).[20] Hobsbawm promptly answered, as Mother Teresa, in another key, would have too, "Yes." By con-trast, the transcendent beloved by Sessions and me includes God's desire for actual humans to flourish in the once, the now, and the future. We are thankful (to keep with the theological talk) for God's grace in heaven, but here below too.

Yet many progressive Christians, sadly, join their atheist cousins on the left and right in not believing in the good of the Bourgeois Deal, claiming on the contrary that it has been bad for the poor. Yet in the long run, in the third act, the Bourgeois Deal permitted the poor to raise themselves up—if you care about raising them up, as Mother Teresa and many other religious conservatives, I repeat, do not; and as Hobsbawm and many other opponents of Western liberalism profess to care about in the far utopian future, believing that it's quite all right to break a few scores of millions of eggs meanwhile on the way to the Perfect Omelet.

In one of Adam Smith's formulations, by contrast, the Bourgeois Deal leads the bourgeoisie by pursuing profit to promote an end that is no part of its intention. Such a version of the invisible hand, by the way, is not altogether fair to the entrepreneurial or goods-supplying bourgeois. He often *does* have in mind the betterment of the lives of his customers. Ask him. Or watch him closely. Look at the behavior of the staff at Hobgoblin Music or a Trader Joe's grocery store. Lives spent trying to figure out what customers want and how to get the item to them in a nonruinous way and how to improve service and quality at a lower cost, one could argue, lead the bourgeoisie to ethical attitudes superior in some ways to those of a haughty aristocracy or an envious peasantry or a proud clerisy. Or at least so Smith argued.

Gustavus Franklin Swift of Chicago was not the first to try shipping slaughtered rather than live cattle eastward in refrigerated cars. But he was the first to succeed, in 1880. The major railways balked. They were making too much money shipping live cattle. Had the railways been able to appeal to the government to regulate Swift's betterment out of existence in the first act, to "protect jobs" on the railways, or to "guard public safety," they would have done so, and creative destruction would have been smothered in the cradle. Swift persuaded a minor railway running between Chicago and Detroit, the Grand Trunk, to take on his new cold cars. Then he shipped the meat to Boston, through Canada, beyond the reach of a corrupt U.S. Congress. His Chicago competitors the Armour brothers in 1883 copied his success, and performed the drama of trade and betterment even better. The price of meat for poor people in Boston was held down, in the third act of a drama of betterment tested in trade. (The drama didn't depend on there being hundreds of competitors, note, as the conventional economic argument has it; in order to hold prices down, two sufficed.)

Similar dramas have been playing continuously at your local market-theater since 1800. Thus steel and autos and air conditioners and computers, in terms of hours of work to get them, have all become much cheaper, and commonly better. The Swifts and the Armours for a while profited, true, spending their profits on the Art Institute, on Grace Church on the near south side of Chicago, and on Jane Addams's charitable activities over on Halsted Street—but also on diamond baubles and on the Pinkertons to beat up trade unionists. But millions of ordinary people profited from cheaper meat. Thank God that competition, cooperation, and the price system, not the regulators or the engineers, ruled.

European people came to think of themselves as endowed by their businesslike Creator—not by their secular lord or their state bureaucrat—with inalienable rights, especially to liberty and property. It was a rhetoric of betterment. As Tom Paine declared in 1776 in *Common Sense*, "We have it in our power to begin the world over again." We get to decide what to do with our landed property and can set up a distillery or a cotton mill on it if we wish. Or rather, you as an individual can, without the gracious permission of the sovereign, even if the sovereign is a democratic and protectionist "we"—Paine also supported free-trade policies and a restrained republican government, for, as he noted in the same pamphlet, "government even in its best state is but a necessary evil, in its worst state an intolerable one." In the nineteenth century such rhetoric paid back the Europeans, surprisingly, with partially freed slaves and partially freed women. People in the late twentieth century from the Philippines to Ukraine came to expect to have a say in their governments expressed through votes, as they had in their trading a say expressed by dollars. The polity, too, paid them back, with democratic liberalism, a free press, the Iowa caucuses, the South African constitution, and all our joy.

We need to guard the resulting success against both cynicism and utopianism. One might well worry about the "cultural contradictions of capitalism" articulated with horror or glee by Daniel Bell, Karl Polanyi, Joseph Schumpeter, and Max Weber, and by Lenin and Marx before them, and by many of Lenin's and Marx's liberal enemies, too. The trouble with a liberal society is that it has few defenses against the worst of left or right dogma, because its leading principle is pluralistic nondogmatism. It gives an opening for monist critics, who would be instantly martyred or jailed in an illiberal polity, such as Russia or Singapore.

Traditional Judaism, though not always progressive, is internally liberal, with its incessant disputes between the schools of Shammai and Hillel. The Soviet premier Nikita Khrushchev complained about Jews from the perspective of a state-sponsored faith. His own faith had a monistic answer for everything, and therefore no need for discussion. It had perfect defenses against criticism, in the gulag or the mental hospital. Khrushchev therefore complained that the Jews "are all individualists and all intellectuals. They want to talk about everything . . . and they come to totally different conclusions!"[21] Imagine that: different conclusions—variations to be selected in an evolutionary fashion by the test of profit, whether intellectual or monetary. How silly, Khrushchev implied: we already know. Leszek Kołakowski wrote as a young and disillusioned Pole in 1956, when Polish communism had shown its hand, in his long list of "what [true, honest] socialism is not," that socialism is not "a state that is convinced that no one could invent anything better" or "a state that always knows better than its citizens where the happiness of every one of its citizens lies."[22]

Betterment can indeed, in the way of cultural contradiction, raise up its own grave diggers. "Is it possible," asked the early liberal Macaulay in 1829, "that in the bosom of civilization itself may be engendered the malady which shall destroy it? Is it possible that, in two or three hundred years, a few lean and half-naked fishermen may divide with owls and foxes the ruins of the greatest European cities—may wash their nets amidst the relics of her gigantic docks?"[23] As he noted, under democracy such an unhappy outcome might come from the strictly short-run, prudence-only, interest-rules, people-know-which-side-of-their-bread-is-buttered-without-ethics theory of the act-utilitarians among us.

But we do not have to admit the act-utilitarian, prudence-only theory. It hasn't worked well as a descriptive theory outside of studies of rats and pigeons and certain narrowly economic contexts—it has failed, for example, in realist studies of international relations. It encourages an unethical, because inhuman, ethics, which you can study, for example, in the tapes of President Nixon in the Oval Office. On the contrary, ideologies matter to humans, and they can change and the better ones can be selected. People are in fact open to learning that using the IRS to persecute radicals is bad, or that bourgeois life might be virtuous, or that bankers should be wise rather than clever. The Swedish professor of accounting Sten Jönsson has led a group of PhD students at the University of Gothenburg in an inquiry into the ethics of accounting in banking. The group argues for "the appropriate banker."[24] "Appropriateness [in classical rhetoric it was called 'decorum,' as in Hariman (2001)] is a moral and ethical concept . . . that refers to values in context." Ideology, for better or for worse, teaches ethics.

AND MANY POLANYISH IDEAS
FROM THE LEFT

Some perceptive scholars have believed that "capitalism" is recent, and they believe so because they have read, or at least believed, Karl Polanyi's book of 1944, *The Great Transformation*. They defend Polanyi still, many decades after he, an inspired amateur, ventured into an economic history that was hardly then explored scientifically. Perhaps they defend him now because a big part of what he said—that ideology and rhetoric matter—is so obviously true and important. Therefore they believe the rest of what he said—principally, that societies were not organized by trade until the nineteenth century, a belief which to economic historians seems obviously false.

More likely it is their politics. The emotional pattern seems to be something like, "Polanyi, a person of the left like me, says many true things, beautifully. Therefore his tales about what happened in economic history must be true." Marx before him got similar treatment. Lately the more eloquent of the environmentalists, such as Wendell Berry, get it too. People want to believe that beauty is truth. A supporting emotional frame on the left arises from the very idea of historical progress: "We must be able to do *so* much better than this wretched capitalism." It is not true, but it motivates.

Likewise on the other side of the political spectrum, which is also hostile to, and ignorant of, the Great Enrichment, conservatives react in the same way to their own honored ancestors, such as Thomas Carlyle: "Carlyle is a person of the right like me, and speaks in an engaging and idea-filled, if not exactly beautiful, style. Therefore his tales about the warmth of the relationship between master and slave in Jamaica, or lord and peasant in merry old England, must be true." The supporting emotional frame on the right arises from the very idea of historical roots: "There must be some noble reason that hierarchy exists, contradicting this vulgar capitalism." It is not true either, but it also motivates.

Enthusiasts for both the left and the right detest "the market" and are alarmed by betterment—on the left because they see trade-tested betterment taking jobs from poor people in the first act, on the right because they see it as upsetting natural hierarchies in the third act. Both therefore adopt the premise that trading is a exploitative novelty, and that (so-called) betterment has done nothing but ruin solidarity. When people on the left or the right find an especially eloquent expression of their distaste for trading and betterment they are liable to stop reading.

The political scientist Sheri Berman, for example, acknowledges her debt to Polanyi in the first page of her book of 2006, and goes on to retail the story so comforting to the left, that "only in the eighteenth century [Polanyi actually said the early nineteenth] did economies in which markets were the primary force in the production and distribution of goods begin to emerge." She follows Polanyi in claiming that before modern times "decisions about the production and distribution of goods were made not by markets but by those with social and political power."[1] Her historical assertions are factually mistaken. If they were true, real wages would not have doubled after the Black Death killed a third of the laborers in Eurasia.[2]

Yet Berman says more correctly, citing Polanyi and a paper Santhi Hejeebu and I wrote in 1999 detailing the large factual errors in Polanyi's economic history, that "capitalism meant an end to a world where one's position and livelihood were defined primarily by membership in a particular group"—the society of status as against the society of contract.[3] And still more correctly she says that "perceived failures . . . of the reigning intellectual paradigms create a demand for new ideologies."[4] Yes, and quite disturbing to "many Marxists, rational-choice theorists, and realists, . . . [for whom] ideologies are best understood as mere tools or 'cover.'"[5] It is at the level of ideas that society changed, out of a demand for the replacement of institutions perceived to have failed. They had "failed" only relative to a utopian version of progress that took over the social imaginary of the West after 1848, despite the enormous actual improvement going on at the time. We can (always) do better, the left declares. We should (always) pass more laws. Any problem (always) requires more regulation. We should (always) pursue a fanciful ideal, proven wrong repeatedly in socialist experiments, making an imagined perfect the enemy of the actual pretty good. The erroneous perception of failed capitalism in the 1890s and the 1930s therefore inspired, as Berman goes on to relate, the move to social democracy in Sweden and Holland and England and France.

Walter McDougall's handsome popular history of the United States (2004), to give another recent example, begins with Polanyi's picture of an England in the sixteenth century as an "embryonic market society." "At *no time and place*" other than in England, declares McDougall (whose use of italics is elsewhere more restrained), "in the century preceding England's overseas expansion [that is, the sixteenth century] was an entire society organized by market exchange." His warrant for such a startlingly outdated assertion is a book from the Monthly Review Press by Ellen Meiksins Wood, whom McDougall describes as a "renegade Marxist." "She in turn," he reports, "praises the insights of Karl Polanyi's classic *The Great Transformation*."[6]

Yet in fact Egypt, Babylon, China, Greece, Rome, Gaul, Italy, the Arab world, the Ottoman Empire, the Toltecs, Japan, the Viking lands, Germany, Poland, and England, from ancient to early modern times, were entire societies heavily influenced by commercial exchange (which does not mean that other institutions, such as families or kinship or kingship or religion or hierarchy, had no influence on how the society worked, even in economic life, even now). In the *Meno*, Socrates around 410 BCE is arguing, as he often was, against payment in cash for teaching virtue, in this case the virtue of prudence. But he has no doubt that the trade test is appropriate for cobblers and seamstresses: "Those who mend old sandals and restore clothes would be found out within the month if they returned the clothes and sandals in a worse state than they received them; if they did this they would soon die of starvation."[7] Athens was a commercial society.

Polanyi didn't believe that markets mattered in olden times, such as Plato's. But the evidence accumulated since 1944 tells a story of economies rich in markets in Europe and China and South Asia and the Muslim lands and Africa and America—though the markets were routinely disdained in the rhetoric of many military or priestly elites, and regulated by the guild rhetoric of the haute bourgeoisie, keeping trammels on the rest of the commoners and their betterment.

Even historians whose detailed scientific findings contradict the Polanyist vision are liable to slip into Polanyism when they are not paying strict attention. Because the modern world is shockingly rich (which is true) it must be the case, the historian Joyce Appleby concluded, that "capitalist practices represented a radical departure from ancient usages *when they appeared upon the scene in the seventeenth century*."[8] This despite evidence for trade dating from the caves onward, and for urban wholesaling dating from Jericho onward, and for banking from Israel and Athens onward. The English seventeenth century is Appleby's field of scientific specialty, and long ago she discovered that an "intellectual engagement with the meaning of economic change"—an astonishing three hundred English pamphlets debating the logic of monetary reform in the 1690s, for example—"blocked a reversion to the old ways of thinking."[9] That's right, and accords in fact with Polanyi's ancillary (if nonmaterialist and therefore somewhat self-contradicting) idea that ideological change in England around 1800 was what supported the modern and distasteful world. (Appleby and I show that the ideological change happened a century and a half before Polanyi thought it did. But change it did.)

Yet when Appleby talks a little about earlier economies, outside her specialty, she turns frankly Polanyist. People tend to. Polanyi gives expression to the nineteenth-century Romantic story on which we all were raised in school and at the movies. When we get beyond what we actually know, we understandably revert to fairy tales, especially when the tales support what we believe to be politically true. It's human nature, or social psychology, or ideology, or rhetoric. We adopt stereotypes about women or black people or medieval peasants or robber barons just when we don't actually know much about them.

"Capitalism," defined by Appleby elsewhere in her book merely as "a system based on individual investments in production of marketable goods" (which would describe any society starting from women in the caves making pierced shells for sale for necklaces), "slowly replaced the traditional ways of meeting the material needs of a society" (but there was no "way" from 100,000 BCE on that did not use marketable goods, that is, trade; and the Industrial Revolution was not slow, not by historical standards). The assertions are scientifically false, unless "traditional ways" in the sentence are defined to be ways before 1700, which would make it a tautology. The traditional ways were not "replaced," if investment in "marketable goods" is what one means, because there was no Polanyan, pretrading time.

Appleby then reverts to straight Polanyism. In olden times, she declares, "custom, not incentives, prompted action and dictated the flow of work throughout the year." Custom mattered, as it does now in the offices of

Google and General Motors. But it did not exclusively "prompt action" or "dictate the flow of work." Markets, profitability, and the slow preindustrial pattern of betterment did. Look at the open fields of medieval England.[10] "People did not assign themselves parts in the social order," she continues. "Tasks were allocated through the inherited statuses of landlord, tenant, father, husband, son, laborer, wife, mother, daughter, and servant."[11] Yes, so we have been told in our sweet tales of Olden Times by, say, Carlyle. But that's also how tasks are "allocated" now, if one means the social roles that people traditionally start with. The task of child-minding is traditionally "allocated" to the mother, and only by a reallocation does it move elsewhere, in an exchange for money earned outside the home, under a feminist ideological impulse and a change in the provision of traded alternatives for food preparation and child care. Appleby (b. 1929), who started her professional career after having three children, knows this. Similarly, in all eras the task of hiring labor is "allocated" to landlords (or to their big capitalist tenants). But prices established by trading, then as now, partially determine how such social roles were reallocated—a prosperous serf in 1300 hiring laborers to harvest his big holding becomes for the nonce a "capitalist," or a father in 1400 surrendering the farm to his son, or a daughter in 1550 shifting from field work to dairy when the price was right.

Redistribution was Polanyi's third category, as against householding and reciprocity. Redistribution occurs sometimes even in large economies. Look at the welfare state after Bismarck. But Polanyi wanted it to be the main story, before the rise of wretched capitalism. "Redistribution obtains within a group," he declared, "to the extent that in the allocation of goods (including land and natural resources) they are collected in one hand and distributed by virtue of custom, law, or ad hoc central decision."[12] The examples in Polanyi's work are kingship and socialism, but the deeper model is the family, in which the mother redistributes food. Polanyi asserted that ancient Greece, China, and India, the empire of the Incas, the New Kingdom of Egypt, the Dahomey Kingdom of West Africa, and in particular Hammurabi's Babylonia, were all organized on the principle of redistribution. He rejected the economistic vision of trade and markets governing such things at the large scale, writing in 1944, in advance of scientific work on the matter, that "broadly, the proposition holds that all economic systems known to us up to the end of feudalism in Western Europe were organized either on the principles of reciprocity or redistribution, or householding, or some combination of the three."[13]

Not, for God's sake, the recent and detestable markets. Polanyi later grouped householding as a special case of redistribution and included "market" as a third type of "economic integration." He claimed always that so-called market prices are nothing of the sort, but merely "equivalences" determined by, say, the code of Hammurabi, not by supply and demand. And he claimed that so-called merchants in such societies, in particular in the ancient Near East, were in fact temple or governmental officials, not anything like the bourgeois merchants of modern betterment. The eighteenth-century-BCE *mentalité*, said Polanyi, was not capitalist.

Polanyist notions of this sort have found their way secondhand into such works as Diamond's *Guns, Germs, and Steel* (1997): "The Mesopotamian temple was the center not only of religion but of economic redistribution," "large societies can function economically only if they have a redistributive economy," and so forth.[14] But the tale of ancient anti-economism, as I and many other students of the matter say, appears to be mistaken. The evidence is less embarrassingly overwhelming for distant times than it is for the importance of markets in England and other European and non-European countries for the centuries leading up to 1800, since we do not have so overwhelming a tide of evidence for 1800–1200 BCE as we have for 1200–1800 CE. Still, from the time of Sargon we have quite a lot of evidence for Mesopotamia, and less but still ample for Egypt, and then for Greece and Rome. And recently we have begun to get more evidence from China and South Asia and Africa and America too, much of it collected after Polanyi's ideas were innocently formed, and sometimes indeed in critical response to his eloquent advocacy.[15]

Occasionally the evidence does work in favor of a redistributive model. Michael McCormick has argued that shipments of wheat in payment of taxes for the *annona*—which was indubitably a redistribution, the annual distribution of bread, with circuses, to the populace of Rome and, later, Constantinople, ending in Constantinople at last in 618 CE—came to dominate trade in the western Mediterranean when the more commercial trade declined. "On the eve of its destruction [that is, the eastern empire's], more and more of the eggs of [very] late Roman shipping had come to rest in the basket of the *annona*. So it was that, comparatively speaking, commercial shipping lessened to its lowest point in centuries in the second half of the seventh century."[16] This way of putting it, however, emphasizes McCormick's larger theme: that in the time before and after the "destruction," as late as the sixth century and as early as the eighth century, private merchants were dashing about Europe north and south of the Alps in search of private profit, entirely without a state assignment to their task.

But mostly the evidence works against a dominance of redistribution outside the household, that is, against the alleged lack of real price-directed trade and an alleged presence of socialized distribution. From the earliest times the distribution of goods among households was made not by the visible hand of the prince or priest but by the invisible hand of price and property. For daily life we now know the most about ancient Mesopotamia, centered in what is now Iraq, because the people of the region wrote on cheap and tough clay rather than on expensively carved stone or on papyrus that rapidly rotted in a humid climate. In 1920, unfortunately, early in the history of Assyriology (as the study of ancient Mesopotamia is called), a German economist of the historical school named Anna Schneider wrote an influential book, *Die Anfänge der Kulturwirtschaft: Die sumerische Tempelstadt* (The Origin of Cultural Economy: The Sumerian Temple City), claiming that the economy of the city of Lagash in southern Iraq was run on the basis of redistribution by the priests of the local temple. Since Lagash was the only city then excavated, and a big one by the standards of the third millennium BCE, her book had an impact. Schneider based her interpretation on articles by the Assyriologist Anton Deimel, who finally in 1931 put forward his full theory in his own book, *Sumerische Tempelwirtschaft zur Zeit Urukaginas und seiner Vorgänger* (Sumerian Temple Economy at the Time of Urukagina [the ruler of Sumerian Lagash ca. 2400 BCE] and His Predecessors). For "a period of many years," wrote the historical geographer Robert M. Adams in 1966, "the existence of a so-called *Tempelwirtschaft* was taken for granted on the basis of the pioneering but somewhat misconstrued and overgeneralized work of Father Anton Deimel (Schneider 1920; Deimel 1931)."[17]

Some Assyriologists continue to doubt that landholding and use was independent of the temple. The ideological heat the issue generates can be measured in a passage about the controversy from 1979 by the Assyriologist Johannes Renger at the Free University of Berlin. When his colleagues found "large numbers of legal documents [that] attest private ownership of fields. . . . this meant [Renger is being sarcastic] that it finally could be demonstrated that also in antiquity private enterprise and initiative and the maximization of profits represented the highest and most mature form of socio-economic development of the human race!"[18] The exclamation point assures that Renger's sneering, antibourgeois tone will not be missed.

The problem was that Deimel in 1931 had relied on the clay-written evidence collected from the very temple, which as another Assyriologist, Daniel Snell, remarked recently, "quite reasonably showed the concerns of the temple leaders and staff members."[19] If four thousand years from now an archaeologist were to uncover the records of Chicago's Department of Streets and Sanitation, but not the records of the commercial society that surrounded it, she might well conclude that Chicago worked mainly through orders to road crews to fix potholes in the Third Ward. If she got deeper into the records, and saw through their surface rhetoric of legality, she might conclude that Chicago's economy was chiefly a matter of payoffs to aldermen from road contractors, tax lawyers, and property developers. Her conclusion about the sector she had examined with such insight would not be wrong. But the further inference would be mistaken—that the city's entire economy worked mainly by reciprocity and redistribution ("Where's mine?" *Ubi est mea*). Chicago is overwhelmingly a commercial economy, for all its redistributive corruption in regulation and government purchases.

"Traces of the temple theory persist in textbooks," Snell notes, and influenced Polanyi and his followers. But in 1969 Ignace Gelb, in 1972 Klaas Veenhof, and in 1981 Benjamin Foster, questioned even the traces.[20] Veenhof showed that Mesopotamian merchants were mostly independent of state or temple, that is, that they were traders, "bourgeois" if you will. Foster showed that it is doubtful the records Deimel used were even those of a temple. "We cannot any longer maintain," wrote the Assyriologist J. N. Postgate in 1992, "that because the temple collected commodities and distributed them to its dependents the entire economy operated through [Polanyan] 'redistribution,' or that the priests controlled all agricultural production and commercial activity."[21] The economist Morris Silver has been arguing persuasively for a long time that the evidence of the Hebrew Bible fits with the anti-Polanyi evidence.[22]

Polanyi lives on in the work of a few in Assyriology. For example, in his 2003 PhD dissertation from the UCLA Department of Near Eastern Languages and Cultures the Danish Assyriologist Jacob Dahl repeats Polanyi's assumption of "marketless trade," by which Polanyi and his followers, like the Marxian classicist Moses Finley, meant, somewhat surprisingly to an economist, "lacking market-*places*."[23] No economist would suppose that the lack of a physical *agora* or *forum* shows that an economy was not organized by markets. Orders by mail from Sears, Roebuck in 1914 or from Amazon in 2014 would by such an account be "nonmarket." And to this day many a Middle Eastern city lacks a marketplace of a European sort (called a *souq*, sometimes; though Arabic speakers do not seem to have the trouble the Polanyans have in applying the word to the abstract notion of a market without a central location). Yet trade goes on vigorously in the mazes of streets (which the Arabic speakers label a "fabric *souq*," or *suq*, meaning sometimes a narrow lane lined with fabric shops, not an open place on the European plan of a *mercato centrale*). And indeed the very word *souq*, now sometimes also applied to the open spaces that European Polanyists are in search of, derives from Akkadian "street, a narrow place."

And Polanyi lives on, I have noted, in the writings of enthusiasts from the political left, his natural home. A recent example is Fred Block and Margaret Somers's resuscitation of his political program in *The Power of Market Fundamentalism: Karl Polanyi's Critique* (2014), whose publisher's description claims boldly that markets "cannot be self-regulating because they require ongoing state action. Furthermore, they cannot by themselves provide such necessities of social existence as education, health care, social and personal security, and the right to earn a livelihood."[24] Yet the requisite "ongoing state action" does not so obviously require the 40 percent of national income spent by states on average in the OECD. To enforce laws against force and fraud it requires courts (some of them entirely private, such as prearranged facilities for mediation, or in the Middle Ages courts merchant). The "right to earn a livelihood" is routine in trading societies, though regularly obstructed by states favoring, or "protecting," this or that group—plumbers, for example, or doctors. To claim that voluntary dealing in trade cannot provide education, health care, and social and personal security is to show a startling lack of awareness. Such services were so provided, in many places and times, such as education in Sweden from the 1990s, or Catholic education in the United States. How such necessities of social existence are *financed* is a separate matter. Many who disagree with the left and Polanyi in their enthusiasm for state *provision*, which is to say schools run by state bureaucracies, agree with them on the desirability of taxing people like Fred Block, Margaret Somers, and me to *pay* for the services.

The main problem with Block and Somers is that they nowhere ask How much?—how much of a state, how much the market can achieve, how much "ongoing state action" is necessary as against voluntary trades. Yet Block and Somers are hardly alone. On left and right both, economic systems are accused of "failures," which neither side troubles to measure. Economists collect Nobel Prizes for imagining in existence theorems of this or that "market failure," which they never show are important enough to justify utopian schemes of state intervention or reversions to traditional societies. Enemies of the market overturn governments on the promise of a change in the nature of man under socialism. The debate is interminable because it is never brought to quantitative test.

YET POLANYI WAS RIGHT
ABOUT EMBEDDEDNESS

The failure of Polanyi's search for an earlier society entirely free of the damned economists' and capitalists' markets does not imply, however, that his more fundamental point was mistaken. His qualitative point, which might be tested quantitatively, was that even anonymous markets are, as the modern sociologists express it, "embedded," which is merely to say that marketeers are people too and care about being so. As I have noted, what is similarly correct in Max Weber's otherwise flawed *Protestant Ethic* is that "capitalism" was embedded in a spiritual life. It was a point that Adam Smith devoted his life to making, though many of his followers have managed to forget it. Smith fiercely opposed, as I have also noted, the characterization in Bernard Mandeville (and before him in Hobbes and before him in the Machiavelli of *The Prince*) of people as disembedded, Max U calculators of prudence only. Weber's notion of *verstehen*, the understanding of meanings in societies, is just as "scientific" as materialist causal analysis of the Danish Sound Tolls and medieval shipping, and just as necessary for a wholly scientific sociology or history or economics. We are construing humans, after all, not atomic particles or lab rats, and we are the humans, with access to human moral sentiments.

Across cultures and for all of human history, Polanyi argued, material exchange had meaning far beyond individual want-satisfaction. That's right. Think of your taste in furniture, reupholstering your great-great-grandfather's chair, uncomfortable though it is, because it means Family. Polanyi argued that trade affirmed and strengthened the social values of the larger community.

Yes. Think of your gas grill for neighborhood cookouts in Winnetka, Illinois, or your plasma TV for the Superbowl party in Riverside, California. As Adam Smith two centuries before him had said repeatedly, Polanyi said that trade occurs with a meaning.

Polanyi was, in this matter, on to something—I say so as an economist who was for decades hostile to such views, and hadn't read Polanyi with much care, or even Adam Smith beyond a few snippets. I am still, I think, justified in rejecting the anti-exchange burden of Polanyi's work, and especially the anti-exchange theme in the otherwise distinguished work of his followers such as the classicist Moses I. Finley or the political scientist James C. Scott or the economic historian Douglass North or, on a lower scholarly level, the numerous Polanyi-influenced people who have not read beyond *The Great Transformation*, or at any rate some rumors of it. None of them gets the facts right. They think trade "arose" recently. Trade had in fact already arisen anciently, in the twentieth and nineteenth centuries BCE, as Baechler put it, or for that matter in the eightieth century BCE outside the caves of our remote ancestors in Africa speaking full language.

Yet Polanyi's extra something—that markets are embedded—humbles even the proud economist. It is, for example, the main point of the present book, and indeed of all three books in "The Bourgeois Era." Headline: Longtime Anti-Polanyist Admits Polanyi Had Basic Idea Right. Arjo Klamer has developed a context for markets rather similar to Polanyi's, but free from Polanyi's passionate and evidence-violating distaste for trading at mutually advantageous prices.[1] The marketplace, the *agora*, as Klamer puts it, where mutually advantageous trades take place, is prominent in all societies. It is flanked by the private *oikos*, the household where children are raised, and the *polis*, the government where the monopoly of violence is exercised. Klamer points also to what he calls the Third Sphere—that is, a third public sphere, in addition to the public spheres of *agora* and *polis*, a cultural commons in which "people realize social values like community, a sense of identity, solidarity, neighborhood, country, security, conviviality, friendship and so on."[2] They realize their identities as Ajax Football Club fans, or as good friends from high school, or as loyal Dutch people. But they realize such values in a society with many markets. Gerald Gaus, citing numerous empirical studies, concludes that "we should, I think, resist this conception of markets as simply treating others 'instrumentally'":

Market relations are embedded in a system of norms, which relies on our innate ability to be guided by norms and imperatives. To treat people purely instrumentally would be to prefer to play "snatch" [as chimps in fact do] rather than "exchange" with them—I would prefer to snatch and run rather than exchange my good for theirs.[3]

It's embedding—the barbeque, the Superbowl party, the *Kaffeeklatsch* in which women tell the story of their tribe, meaningfully. But embedding in social relations happens also in the marketplace. You, being a human, form a relationship with your auto repair man, or your building contractor, or the local Starbucks barista. You could also call it, and Klamer does, the "conversation" of the culture. In other words, the Third Sphere depends (as the other spheres also do) on Klamer's master concept, the conversation—the conversation about being an American woman or a Dutch merchant or a person who values modern art or an executive developing trust in a business relationship. Akira Okazaki of Japan Airlines played cards for months with fisherman from Prince Edward Island in Canada during the 1970s in order to develop a backhaul business in bluefin-tuna-on-ice for the sushi market back home.[4] Talk, talk, talk. Realize social values. Okazaki made friends. And did a little business on the side.

Note that nothing that Klamer or I say implies that all conversations will be sweet, or uninfluenced by power. The standard critical remark from the left against the German sociologist/philosopher Jürgen Habermas is "But he has forgotten power." (Admittedly, this being always the remark from the left, about any topic whatever, tells against its air of knowingness.) The reply is that supposing all conversations are merely window dressing for Material Power is itself an unscientific dogma. Sometimes it's true, as for example in the administrative university when the dean pretends to listen to the faculty. But sometimes human conversations matter.

The anthropologist Alan Page Fiske has developed still another balanced version of embeddedness, which can be partially matched to Polanyi's and Klamer's categories—as all of them, I would point out, can be matched to the much older tradition in Europe of the seven principal virtues, or to the four sprouts of ethical character in Confucianism. In his *Structures of Social Life* Fiske speaks of "market pricing" as one of four "elementary forms." The other three—communal sharing (you get meat because you belong to Our

TABLE 5. Fiske, Polanyi, Klamer, and the virtues

Polanyi's categories	Klamer's spheres	Fiske's forms	The question	The seven principal virtues
provisioning	*oikos*	communal sharing	"Who are 'we'?"	love, temperance
redistribution	*polis*	authority ranking	"Who's in charge?"	courage, faith
reciprocity	not a perfect correspondence with Klamer's Third Sphere	equality ranking	"Who or what counts as equal?"	justice, faith, hope
modern market	*agora*	market pricing	"What are the ratios of exchange?"	prudence

Source: Fiske (1991 [1993]), pp. 46–47; Polanyi 1944; Klamer 2011; McCloskey 2006, chap. 26, and in the present book chap. 20, fig. 3.

Crowd), authority ranking (I am the chief, so I get more meat), and equality matching (we're all in this together, so let's make the amounts of meat exactly equal for everyone)—do not involve prices, that is, exchange rates between two different kinds, meat for milk, arrow points for cave paintings. The society must somehow decide on the prices, "the ratios of exchange." Fiske accepts, contrary to Polanyi, that in any society with markets—and as an economic historian I attest that most societies have them, and Fiske the cultural anthropologist and Klamer the cultural economist think so too—the "market decides, governed by supply and demand."[5] Fiske cleverly points out that the succession of the four—communal, authority, equality, market—correspond to stages of human maturity up to about age eight, when kids finally get beyond item-by-item equality and accept exchange and its pricing, your frog for my jackknife.[6] Even more cleverly he points out that the succession also corresponds in the theory of scaling to categorical scales (in/out), ordinal scales (higher/lower), interval scales (same amounts), and ratio scales (such as Fahrenheit temperature).

Table 5 shows how the various groupings lie down together.

Trade-and-its-bourgeoisie is supported by much more than prudence only, though obviously prudence is its central virtue, just as courage is the central virtue of warfare in an ideal aristocratic society, and faith/love that of worship in an ideal Christian one. But anyway the categories of Klamer, Fiske, and the seven principal virtues firmly reject the Polanyan notion that trade is corrosive of all human values, being a merely modern pathology to be cured by using the state's monopoly of violence to outlaw or heavily regulate property and trade. The categories reject Polanyi Mark I by accepting Polanyi Mark II, which embeds economic life in human life generally. Aquinas and the other urban monks of the thirteenth century, I have noted, were busy with such embedding. The medievalist James Davis discusses the historiography of the much-misunderstood just price, observing that "the ideal espoused by Aquinas was that of an open market, where [here comes the embedding] participants were aware of their social and moral obligations."[7] For modern life, too, just so—trade being a field of moral obligation, unless some misled economist has persuaded us otherwise.

Polanyi himself wanted to re-embed trade, minus the detestably bourgeois bits. Yet all actual bourgeois people have nontrading relations in their lives, and the trading itself is embedded. Analyzing the economic consequences is the scientific program of humanomics. Only stick-figure parodies like Marx's Mister Moneybags or Dickens's Paul Dombey (until the end of the book, when he realizes his humanity) or Sinclair Lewis's George Babbitt (ditto), and the endless movie sneers at corporate conformity organized by Hollywood producers devoted to corporate conformity, do not see the embedding.[8] It is considered clever to sneer at businesspeople as prudence-only stick figures. Nor do actual bourgeois themselves often see the embedding of their lives, at least when they are misled by the rhetoric of "greed is good" and "he who dies with the most toys wins."

Perhaps the better word for the embedding is "entangling," because the different spheres talk to each other and parody each other in endlessly complicated ways. Such is *Homo loquens*, the speaking person since language took hold. In *The Purchase of Intimacy* (2005) and other books, the sociologist Viviana Zelizer has detailed the entanglement of commercial matters with the third and other spheres. The bourgeois man, after all, belongs to a religion or tribe or clan, and always to a family and usually to the Third Sphere of his town. The economists Peter Boettke and Virgil Storr have recently written about such "sophisticated embeddedness," and their master Ludwig von Mises wrote to similar effect.[9] These noncommercial relations often radically alter the deals the bourgeois makes. As the novelist of the modern bourgeoisie, Thomas Mann, speaks of the protagonist of *Buddenbrooks* entangling the sacred and the profane: "Sometimes, entirely by accident, perhaps on a walk with the family, [Tom Buddenbrook] would go into a mill for a chat with the miller, who would feel himself much honored by the visit [thus the uses of ancient hierarchy]; and quite en passant, in the best of moods, he could conclude a good bargain."[10] Good for both.

The community of believing Muslims, the *umma*, was for hundreds of years after the death of the Prophet a minority in the various Arab conquests outside the Arabian peninsula.[11] You dealt differently with a fellow resident of the House of Islam—he paid lower taxes, he could not be your slave, he could not charge you interest. Such theories, unsurprisingly, became with the use of centuries a bit tattered around their edges, for example, in the matter of charging interest or enslavement. But the sacred mattered.

True, trading tends to be prudent, and on that count, if not on all counts, tends to be radically egalitarian in the matter of whom one deals with. A beggar's dollar commands as much bread as a millionaire's. In contrast to allocation by beauty or social class or party membership or racial preference or bureaucratic edict, the baker doesn't care to whom he sells the loaf. This feature of trading has recommended it to the egalitarians among true liberals in a long line from David Hume and Adam Smith to Milton Friedman and Robert Nozick and Deirdre McCloskey. Prudence is indeed, as I said, the central virtue of the *agora*, as courage is of the *polis* and love is of the *oikos*. But, I repeat, trading can be influenced by motives other than prudence only, as embedding/entangling declares. An elderly mother buys a second house for the warm months close to her children, but worries whether it is prudent and quarrels with her beloved daughter over the mix of cash and affection in the matter. Love and prudence are entangled. Merchants and inventors and corporate executives are people, too, with professionalized identities by no means always contemptible. So even, as Paul du Gay has argued, are their much-maligned bureaucratic regulators—bourgeois all.[12]

Money prices seem to non-economists highly partial. The glorious lamp of heaven the sun is not paid for in money, housework is unpaid, the workers who make the marketed stuff we live on do not get all the income, and many parts of the Third Sphere get no money rewards at all. But economists showed in the late nineteenth century that paying according to "marginal productivity" directs the many things that do have opportunity costs in a market the correct way—paid labor, for example. To substitute a monopoly patent for an intellectual property that has no opportunity cost in its use, or for the National Bureau of Economic Research (of all institutions) to charge for its publications by average, not marginal, cost, or for the state to block by protection or central planning the paying by marginal productivity, has bad results. Output is squeezed. Directions are inefficient.

Yet the non-economists are correct to complain that the cynical economists know the price of everything but the value of nothing. We want as humans to honor the sacred. True, what is sacred changes from time to time. Raising up the poor has become, for example, a sacred duty in the modern, liberal world, since about the time when the ethic of taking up your cross began to fade. My left-wing friends are, I believe, mistaken to think that the state is a sweet and good instrument to raise up the poor. On the other hand, some of my conservative and libertarian friends are equally mistaken to believe that trading suffices. At a conference of many hundreds of libertarians in Barbados a while ago I said to a man I had not formerly met, by way of expressing in casual conversation a sacred duty we libertarians of course all acknowledged, "We must help the poor." He instantly shot back—it was like being punched in the stomach—"Only if they help me." His libertarianism was fatherly. But there is a motherly version available, in which children are instructed to be ethical human beings in both the trading and nontrading parts of their lives.

A bourgeois life, I say yet again, does involve and should involve noncommercial realms, as a fully human life must involve the sacred too. That is what Polanyi got right. But markets play their entangled part, and in a great city the trades and the bourgeoisie running them have always played a great part, recently with dramatic results in enriching the poor. That is what Polanyi got wrong.

59

TRADE-TESTED BETTERMENT IS DEMOCRATIC IN CONSUMPTION

Why, though, a profit test for betterment? What's the good of profit? It's worth pausing to consider the economic theory and the historical facts.

Trade-tested supply earns only "normal" profits, as the economists put it. Betterment, by contrast, earns "supernormal" profits. But both profits, I claim, contrary to the customary doubts, are sweet in their effects, if accompanied by the liberty to compete and the dignity to cooperate that inspired the betterment in the first place.

Economic betterment counts as honorable only in the Bourgeois Era. Or to be precise, the honorable activity in the Aristocratic Era was "betterment" *without* a money-profit test. As I have observed, no one asked if a better machine of war or an improved crusade against the Muslims was profitable by a test of what ordinary people would pay for it (well: except for the bourgeois Venetians, who were faithful but also prudent, as in the Fourth Crusade). If Greek fire or a siege engine won the battle for the present elite, or if the Teutonic Knights converted the Balts to Christianity by force of expensive arms, that was test enough. Cost be damned.

The test of economic cost was supposed to be remote from aristocratic concerns. At the beginning of Tolstoy's *War and Peace*, published in 1869 about fictional 1806, the noblewoman Anna Palovna Scherer notes with approval that mere monetary profitability was dishonored in aristocratic Russia: "England with her commercial spirit will not and cannot understand the Emperor Alexander's loftiness of spirit."[1] England was regularly after 1700 the vulgarly bourgeois example to be cited in contrast to lofty aristocratic or religious spirits, as Venice had been the example after 1200 and

Holland had been after 1600 (and both were the bad, bourgeois examples cited by a lofty, aristocratic England, not yet in those early days embourgeoisfied). When Russia's Catherine the Great in 1767 continued to enjoy the revenues from church lands seized by her late-lamented husband, Peter III, the Metropolitan Matseevich scolded her by declaring that "with us it is not like in England that one is to live and make one's way by money alone."[2] For saying this about Catherine, German-born and therefore in Russia commercially suspect, he was imprisoned for life.

But what is so wonderful about England in 1806 with her commercial spirit? In summary, this: sharply contrary to modern anticommercial opinion among non-economists, the trade test and the profit that announces its fulfillment are democratic and benefit poor people.[3] Michael Walzer taught a course in 1970–1971 with the libertarian philosopher Robert Nozick, and though a communitarian he admitted in his book arising from the encounter that "the market is radically pluralistic in its operations and its outcomes, infinitely sensitive to the meanings that individuals attach to goods."[4] Yes. The sociologist Howard S. Becker wrote in an e-mail exchange with a French sociologist in 2005 that Becker's notion of a "world" is to be contrasted with the nasty power plays characteristic of Pierre Bourdieu's "fields" or of any other social theory that focuses on mechanical striving without socialization, such as pre-Gramsci Marxian thought or the economist's illiberal theory of games:

> The metaphor of "world"—which does not seem to be at all true of the metaphor of "field"—contains people, all sorts of people, who are in the middle of doing something which requires them to pay attention to each other, to take account consciously of the existence of others and to shape what they do in the light of what others do. In such a world, people . . . develop their lines of activity gradually, seeing how others respond to what they do and adjusting what they do next in a way that meshes with what others have done and will probably do next. . . . The resulting collective activity is something that perhaps no one wanted, but is the best everyone could get out of this situation and therefore what they all, in effect, agreed to.[5]

It is the vision of liberal economics since Adam Smith.

The case is most easily seen on the side of consumption (an economy is a circular flow, so there is another side, of production and employment). In an actual market for bus trips or hamburgers the tastes of at least a profitably large number of ordinary people, rich or poor, are imagined before a firm will venture to supply its product. The decline of the Greyhound model for buses created an opening for Stagecoach Group (a company that has operated no-frills buses in Britain since 2003) to introduce its chain into the United States in 2006, as Megabus. It's doing well with college students and the actual poor. White Castle, the first American fast-food chain, beginning in 1912, made profits from the start. Ordinary people loved the crummy little hamburgers. Like the much-maligned McDonald's long afterward, White Castle provided a cheap and nourishing meal to ordinary people.[6] Popeye's hefty friend in the old cartoons, J. Wellington Wimpy, consumed White Castle hamburgers by the dozen, and in the 1930s lent his surname to what would become the first UK hamburger chain.

I have noted that the profit-in-trade test parallels the intellectual test of an "open society," in Karl Popper's vocabulary. As the philosophers David Schmidtz and Jason Brennan say, "Perhaps free speech and free trade are usefully viewed as members of the same family. They may turn out to have a history of going hand in hand, even though they are logically separable."[7] Art and science and politics advance by the same testing in a marketplace—sometimes in a literal, cash marketplace, sometimes in an analogical marketplace of prestige without money reward. An open artistic or scientific society creates novelties, such as the modern symphony orchestra or the modern university, both products of the early stages of the Great Enrichment. The only alternative to a marketplace of ideas is a socialism of ideas, along Plato's lines, centrally planned by wise heads, and at any rate by violent hands able to compel people to adopt the plan: We already know the truth, we Genuine Philosophers, and therefore we should banish the misleading poets and rhetoricians and democratic politicians.[8]

My friend and colleague the anthropologist, English professor, and left-leaning social critic Ralph Cintron was walking with his wife, my friend Jane Nicholson, in a fishing town in Croatia and noted an attractive island connected to the mainland by a causeway. They walked out, but at the gate were turned away by a guard, who explained (Jane is exceptionally good at languages and probably could have addressed him in his own) that the island was an exclusive resort for the very rich. You're not welcome. Walking back, Cintron noted the contrast with the proliferation of advertising they now saw on the causeway facing *outward*, toward the island, welcoming them

to various restaurants and hotels in the town, open for the business of ordinary people and of the rich people from the island too, should they deign to
come into town. It struck him that trade-tested betterment and profit was
a gigantic machine of cooperation to provide for the rest of us, a Howard
Beckerian world.

The rich, or the aristocracy, or the princes of the church, have always
had their unadvertised resorts on closed islands. The rest of us, though, now
have millions of businesses standing eager to serve us. I am told that when
an academic from the Soviet Union was allowed for the first time to attend
a conference in Switzerland, he wandered out of his hotel and into a local
pharmacy—and burst into bitter tears. Only then did he fully realize the size
of the cornucopia stopped up by the rule of communism at home, a cornucopia infinitely sensitive to the meanings that individuals attach to goods.

A commercial test for supplying consumption is signaled by money profit.
When something tested in trade is popular, it earns money for someone.
(And in the analogous marketplace of ideas in art, science, and politics a
tested notion earns a similar profit of fame or power.) Trade and profit are
mutually implied, since both sides get mutual benefit from a trade, a benefit
called profit. If many people love Post-Its or *Star Wars*, then 3M Corporation
or 20th Century Fox earns profits. According to *Forbes* magazine's list of
the very rich, George Lucas was worth in 2013 $3.9 billion, chiefly from *Star
Wars*, which is a measure of how much his movies pleased people. You therefore can't advocate "people, not profits" if you want the democratic advantage
of betterment tested by the willingness of a sufficient number of ordinary
people to pay for it, getting other people to do things that will assist them, as
Becker says, "in the middle of doing something which requires them to pay
attention to each other": getting bus rides, hamburgers, movies, plastic, airplanes, groceries, power saws, anesthesia, light switches, cheap wood screws,
commercial satellites, and economists with common sense.

The six heirs of Sam and Jim Walton were worth in 2013 a combined total
of $107.3 billion (which put them half again above Bill Gates); in 2014 *Forbes*
reckoned the Waltons' net wealth was still higher, $150 billion. Gates's wealth
was earned from software retailing, in which profit margins are high. But the
Waltons' wealth was earned in soft goods and especially groceries, which
Walmart now leads, in which profit margins are low, for Walmart around
3.5 percent of gross.[9] Walmart is doing something right—not, as anti-
Walmart folk claim, by underpaying its staff, which the lively forces of entry

and exit in the offers and acceptances of work prevent Walmart from doing, even if it wanted to (as Becker put it, Walmart has to "take account consciously of the existence of others and to shape what they do in the light of what others do"; and early in 2015 Walmart increased its entry-level wage above that of its competitors). Walmart did right by pioneering controls on inventory using bar codes and by pioneering mass but negotiated buying, for the benefit of its shoppers, with a small margin left over for the Walton heirs. A proposed innovation such as a new machine or a reorganization of supply that does *not* pass the test of the dollar votes of people is merely a cute trick—an engineer's impractical fantasy or the clerisy's imposed taste or a politician's heavily-subsidized pet project, a bridge to nowhere.

All this is not to say that enormous inherited wealth, or ludicrous executive compensation, is blameless if it is earned by corrupt deals or is used to buy stupid yachts and political power. As Warren Buffett declares, "The idea that you turn over huge positions in society simply because someone came from the right womb . . . [is] almost un-American."[10] Adam Smith, the advocate of equal personal dignity, rejected the worship of profit, or the worship of rich people getting it, even if they actually earned the profit by selling to customers and didn't merely inherit a bond portfolio or stock ownership from Daddy. He rails against such worship for an entire chapter of *The Theory of Moral Sentiments*.[11] Thus, too, the Psalmist, railing against "they that trust in their wealth, and boast themselves in the multitude of their riches" (49:5). Worshipping people who earn profit (profit that merely tells us what activities are or are not democratically popular) would be like worshipping the predictions of the weatherman (which merely tell us what tomorrows are likely to be aesthetically pleasing). That the Waltons are rich does not make them admirable people, despite the undoubted commercial savvy of Sam and his brother Jim. The men on Wall Street with Adam Smith ties who worship rich people like Buffett or the Waltons, and who defend high compensation for Great Men of Management such as Jack Welch, formerly of General Electric, whose payout in 2001 was $417 million, are not getting the ethical point of old Warren, or old Smith, or the old Psalmist.[12]

But if a profit occurs—at any rate, if the profit does not come from political favors, as it does to the sugar industry or the wind-farm industry—the economy is articulating something worth attending to. It is saying, "Do more of this. People want it strongly enough to pay for it." If a loss occurs it is saying, "Don't do that. People won't pay for it." The articulation comes from the dollar votes of ordinary people, a democracy of what people in aggregate are willing to pay. It's not one person, one vote, and the rich do get more votes. And so for some purposes—voting for representatives especially— dollar voting would be objectionable, though in cynical truth it happens. But in markets under dollar voting, at least the rich do not get to tell the poor what to buy; whereas under personhood suffrage the tyranny of the majority, sometimes purchased by the rich, can indeed force the poor to buy a war, say, or a subsidy to the rich. Dollar votes are in any case better than the will of the raj or even most plans of the bureaucrat. A trading society will not, unless compelled by state power, build a pyramid or a Taj Mahal, because ordinary people are not willing to pay for such items. The trading economy will pay Jack Welch crazy sums, but essentially for the same reason that nontrading societies pay their kings and Communist Party officials crazy sums—not the dollar votes of the people but the clubbiness of compensation committees. National glory, or more exactly the glory of kings and politicians and their wives, does not get supplied by a profit-making firm except by governmental purchase—itself untested by cash bids from the actual citizens, because the wherewithal for the governmental purchase is compulsory taxation. The test of governmental purchase is at best the result of a majority vote overriding the preferences of the minority, at worst the result of an elite's self-interested will. The test of the corporate compensation committee is at best a sober evaluation of Welch's value added, at worst the result of an elite's self-glorifying and self-interested hero worship.

By contrast, a profit-making firm's criterion is, Will a large enough number of merely common people pay more for the stuff in question than it costs to make? If a society regularly makes stuff that costs *more* than people are willing to pay, it is moving backward, and getting poorer. The exception to the backward-motion theorem occurs when some government or some charitable person or some firm for its own benefit provides unprofitable stuff with powerful and desirable spillovers that cannot be captured by a market. The standard examples justifying government provision are supposed to be vaccination (though in eighteenth-century India "variolators" would wander India infecting villages with smallpox, and villages paid for the service) or lighthouses (though in nineteenth-century Britain a fee for such services would be collected at the nearest port).[13] A more familiar example is the spillover from one shop generating foot traffic for other shops, which was the socially profitable model of the shopping mall. Its newer form, shopping on the Internet (which is creatively destroying the malls), is another example, each new person or firm joining it for private reasons, yielding a spillover of a more complete and therefore more commercially valuable network. It's the opposite of the bad spillovers of one more car joining a traffic jam.

The man in the street, and many an academic not an economist, understands correctly that the economy is a circular flow of goods and services. She understands "supply chains," as they are called in business, and can appreciate Adam Smith's remark about a coat:

> The woolen-coat . . . is the produce of the joint labor of a great multitude of workmen. The shepherd, the sorter of the wool, the wool-comber or carder, the dyer, the scribbler, the spinner, the weaver, the fuller, the dresser, with many others, must all join their different arts. . . . Let us consider only what a variety of labor is requisite in order to form that very simple machine, the shears with which the shepherd clips the wool. The miner, the builder of the furnace for smelting the ore, the feller of the timber, the burner of the charcoal. . . .[14]

It is a conventional thought. A hundred years before Smith the French Jansenist theologian Pierre Nicole (1625–1695) wrote that it

> is thus a wonderful invention that men have found to provide everyone with commodities that the greatest kings could not enjoy, no matter how many officials they had or how much wealth, if this [civil] society [*l'ordre politique*] did not exist. Without this invention, how much wealth, how many servants would a man need merely to enjoy the advantages that a Parisian bourgeois enjoys with 4,000 livres income? . . . He can truthfully say that he has a million men working for him . . . , since they are all ready to serve him and he need only command them, adding an agreed-on recompense.[15]

But only economists after Smith and their fellow travelers understand the function of the opposite and exactly balancing direction of flow—the money payments for the goods and services, yielding profits. The money payments signal *what is to be done*. If such payments don't flow in adequate amounts, the economy shifts its attention to some other activity. Contrary to what most people think, profit is not a gigantic share of national income—usually below about 15 percent if you do not mix up routine payment of interest with the rewards to minor or major creative destruction. But its signaling function is worth the price. The shift of attention caused by the varying profits on capital invested in oil wells or furniture stores is democratically good, because it is responsive to what people rich and poor are really willing to pay, infinitely sensitive, again, to the meanings that individuals attach to goods. The economist Thomas Sowell performs a slam dunk on the point, comparing "capitalist" profits with socialist inefficiency:

> While capitalism has a visible cost—profit—that does not exist under socialism, socialism has an invisible cost—inefficiency—that gets weeded out by losses and bankruptcy under capitalism. The fact that most goods are more widely affordable in a capitalist economy implies that profit is less costly than inefficiency. Put differently, profit is a price paid for efficiency.[16]

People often think of profit earned by a business as an arbitrary exaction, like a tax on restaurant meals collected by the government, or like theft. Get rid of the tax, or the theft, they say. Give it instead to the workers, who after all made the meals. The economist replies: all right, give the profit to the workers if you can, as in a cooperative restaurant or a mutual insurance company or a partnership of doctors or lawyers. There's no law against it. Feel free. But, the economist will add, *calculate* anyway the profit, whoever gets it. If a co-op restaurant is not earning a profit, then the opportunity cost of its inputs of cooks and ranges and fish drawn away from other restaurants to make the meals exceeds the cash value that its customers put on the meals. Imagine a restaurant making bad food, which when the word gets out earns little revenue, an "Italian" restaurant that uses canned spaghetti sauce, say, or a "fish" restaurant that uses frozen fish sticks. The unprofitable restaurant should close down, and let other restaurateurs use the inputs. We as a society are made better off by such a rule of positive profit. The only reasonable exception to following the rule for ordinary goods, I repeat, is when there is some other source of value to add to the scales—"an externality," the economists have said since the 1950s, or more lucidly, the virtuous "spillover," a good that cannot be provided by a voluntary deal or by a positive spillover from a voluntary deal. Factually speaking, such exceptions seems to be rare—or to be precise, no economist has shown that they bulk large in the economy, though many have asserted confidently that they do, and that the present economist knows just where they are.

Some people, to be sure, are hurt by the application of the rule of profit, in particular the restaurateur who thought it was a good idea to open the bad-food place that, unhappily, turned out to be a bad idea, socially speaking. Yet there's justice in such a test (which is one reply to the belief that all enterprises should be worker-owned cooperatives, and none should be making profit for a single boss). She, who put her money where her mouth was, should in justice pay the price for her mistake of misallocating the society's cooks and fish. If she does not pay, because the state keeps her in business with protection derived by taxing or regulating other people, she survives to misallocate another day. By the trade test she is induced to go out of business, and do something else with her days. It is, I have noted, a hard rule, but obviously necessary if we are to have a fair and prosperous economy. The cook dismissed from the unprofitable restaurant finds employment at a profitable one. The wholesale fish are sold instead to Legal Seafood, and end up being wisely used from the entire society's point of view—that is, used profitably.

The customers then literally get what they pay for. Or more exactly, they get *more* than what they pay for. In every voluntary deal they get the "consumer's surplus" I have mentioned, the gain from trade on the consumer's side of the bargain—enterprise profit being the "*producer's* surplus" on the other side. When in 2013 the Spanish appliance maker Fagor, a branch of the immense Mondragón group, a worker-run cooperative beloved of moderate leftists the world around, was closed, it owed over a billion euros—a measure of how much more its costs were than its prospective stream of revenues, and also a measure of its failure to generate enough consumer's and producer's surplus, and also a measure of how urgently it needed to close, democratically speaking.

The big and little tragedies of a profit-directed economy are necessary for it to get better. The same is true in science and art, though not about *money* profit. Many experiments fail, and we get the benefit from the better ideas for surgeries and paintings and fish restaurants that succeed because resources have been reallocated to them instead.

Trade-tested betterment is the most altruistic of economic systems, because everything is directed toward satisfying ordinary customers. As Pogo the Possum almost said long ago, "We has met the customer, and he is us."

60

AND LIBERATING IN PRODUCTION

The same is true, the economist observes, with wage work. (Now we are speaking of the production side of the economy, the other side of the exactly balanced wheel of wealth.)

Consider "wage slavery," one of the left's economic dogmas. (The right's economic dogmas are commonly no better. Dogma is the problem, which is to say passionate beliefs held uncritically.) A choice to work for a wage at a terrible job—rather than, say, starve—is nothing like "slavery." A slave does not get paid what other people are willing to pay for her labors. A washerwoman does. A shoe-factory worker also gets paid what others are willing to pay, indirectly, because the owner of the factory who buys his labor then sells the shoes to consumers. Under slavery, by contrast, the slave's owner gets all the pay, all the time.

It is true that "traditional" societies, such as England's in the sixteenth century, attempted to restrict the mobility of labor—a worker's mobility being crucial to his liberty. It was no surprise, since landlords made the laws. Wholly free labor did have to be invented, as Robert Steinfeld has argued, and came to be so especially in the eighteenth and nineteenth centuries.[1] In legal theory, Polanyi was correct in saying that fully free labor didn't exist until late. Legal forms such as being a "servant in husbandry" allowed farmers to seek out and punish a worker who left before his yearly contract was finished. Violence against apprentices was common. Yet there *was* a contract, and at the hiring fair the agricultural workers could leave a bad master. More deeply, it has long been known that in medieval England even people nominally enserfed could and did move.[2]

A free laborer may be poor, the unhappy result of the economy in which she works being underdeveloped, or a result of her being too debilitated by malaria to work. The cure is to develop the economy or to give her a guaranteed income out of taxes on you and me or, even better, to cure malaria. Nothing is served, though, by merging the idea of "poverty" with the idea of "slavery." The paid laborer, like the factory owner, is no slave, since he is paid in proportion to how well he serves other people. Slaves are not. A slave is "paid" in subsistence, if the owner reckons that it's not good business to let him starve, but *not* in proportion to productivity. Paid employment is the satisfying of other people in exchange for a wage. Slavery by contrast is a violent extraction, not an exchange, and has nothing to do with pleasing anyone except the owner-by-violence of the product of another human being.

Slavery, pogroms, race riots, and indeed state compulsion enforced by the police and army clearly make people worse off, at any rate in the people's own judgment. Take taxes (please). Robert Higgs, who is an expert on both the history of slavery and the history of taxes, notes that the arguments in defense of slavery have run parallel with the arguments for taxes.[3] No one volunteers for slavery, just as no one pays taxes voluntarily.[4] Taxes are paid, it may be, willingly, proudly, patriotically, but not as a voluntary, un-coerced contributions to the noble projects of the state. Imagine the government coming hat in hand and requesting that you give up 20 percent of your income to help run an invasion of Iraq. The proceeds from taxes might, or might not, be used for purposes that we on reflection approve of. By contrast, in a voluntary purchase every dime goes to such a purpose, at any rate according to our judgment in spending the dimes (we may mistake our purposes; but a state using our money is still more likely to do so). Yet the taxing side of the state's activity always makes us worse off, at any rate (again) considered individually and therefore considered as a system of incentives to comply. If there were no penalties backed by the monopoly of violence, you would not pay your taxes.

No one, that is, chooses to be compelled by the army or the police or the IRS to pay U.S. taxes in 2016 or to be impressed into the Royal Navy in 1806, Hobbesian fantasies of a freely chosen Leviathan aside. No one lines up voluntarily to be waterboarded by the CIA or to be spied on by the NSA. Yet people do line up to get paid work. Workers in Indonesia line up by the thousands to make Converse shoes for Nike. The wages paid make even the terribly poor—in the terribly poor's judgment—better off than they would be with under the even more terrible alternatives, such as begging in the street. The wages are paid and accepted voluntarily for what they are worth in satisfying paying customers. It's too bad that the Indonesian economy has been so badly run in the past that such a job looks to the very poor Indonesians to be a satisfactory deal (solution: let trade-tested betterment work for a generation or two, as in Singapore or in Hong Kong, which were in 1950 Indonesian-poor but now have average real incomes a little below and far above that of the United States).[5]

Both Marx from the left and Carlyle from the right, among many others suspicious of the Great Enrichment before it was so obviously great, called paid work "slavery." It was part of Carlyle's argument, echoed in the American South under slavery, that compared with the horrors of northern American and northern British "free" wage labor the actual slavery in the British Empire, beginning to be terminated in 1833, had been in fact a good thing, not bad—darkies playing banjos in happy subservience. In *Uncle Tom's Cabin*, the literary critic Walter Benn Michaels argues, Harriet Beecher Stowe regarded the susceptibility of slaves to commercial forces outside the control of even a loving master (as when the master goes bankrupt or dies) as the worst of the institution. Michaels remarks, "Insofar as [Stowe's] critique of slavery came to be a critique of the 'Southern market' it had inevitably to constitute a repudiation of free labor as well. What Stowe most feared was the notion of a market in human attributes."[6] It is what the left clerisy has always feared, and much of the right clerisy too. They in effect fear the human dignity, and the corresponding risk, of free labor. They want society to be a caring, stable, predictable family with Daddy earning and Mommy allocating. Stowe wanted everyone to be protected in a loving family, which is the root of one's youthful attachment to socialism. Let us, a guilty because privileged clerisy, take care of you, you sadly childlike darkies or poor folk or Indonesian shoe-factory workers.

If poverty were slavery, there would be identifiable people responsible for such a terrible condition, namely, the slave owners—as there are in the surviving cases of, say, sexual slavery of Southeast Asian and Eastern European girls. Then we could all join in stopping the slavery and making the former wage slaves thirty to one hundred times better off if they were set free in the United States or the Netherlands. But for mutually advantageous wage deals there is no such class of evil slave drivers to be punished and expropriated, at any rate if we care about the welfare of the poor who lose the jobs.

Stopping people from taking terrible jobs—through prohibitions or protections or minimums, justified by the warm if mistaken feeling over one's
second cappuccino that one is thereby being generous to the poor (at gratifyingly little expense to oneself)—takes away from the poor what the poor
themselves regard as a bettering option. It is theft of deals the poor want
to make. "Sweatshops" in the New York garment trade, for example, such
as those in which the freedom-loving economist Milton Friedman's parents
briefly worked, lead in the third act to college-educated children and grandchildren. They did so, for example, in Friedman's parents' case. The "third
act" metaphor I have used so often, or Bastiat's metaphor of "the seen and
the unseen," carries the philosophical point. It is made for example by the
political philosopher John Tomasi—that we should in ethics care about not
merely the people on the scene in the first act (supposing that the faux policies do benefit them, which is a mistaken supposition) but future generations too.[7] Yet of course even in the first act the sweatshops of New York were
better than leaving Friedman's parents to dig for food in the city dump, or to
sit back in Russia waiting for the next pogrom. That's why people lined up to
get the sweatshop jobs.

The leftish usage and its politics echo down to the present, as in *The
Concise Oxford Dictionary* of 1999, in which "wage slave" is defined coolly as
"a person who is wholly dependent on income from employment," with the
notation "informal"—but not "ironic" or "jocular" or, better, "economically
illiterate."[8] Thus Judy Pearsall, the editor of the *Concise Oxford*, who lives, it
may be, in a nice semidetached in London NW6 and drives an old Volvo,
is a "slave." You yourself are probably a slave. I certainly am a slave. We are
all "slaves"—though all of us are paid in proportion to the traded value of
goods and services we produce for others and none of us owes *unpaid* service to any boss (except, as Higgs and I would observe, to the state through
taxation or draft, an actual slavery admired by most of the left and much of
the right). Such progressive or conservative terminology of "wage slavery"
is like calling an exchange of harsh words "verbal rape." We need terms for
the physical violence entailed in actual slavery and in actual rape, or for that
matter in actual taxation backed by the wide powers of the IRS to do violence. We should not cheapen them by applying them to our middle-class
guilt in NW6 or Morningside Heights.

One finds Oscar Wilde in 1891 declaring that "socialism [about which
he knew only the contents of a lecture he had just heard by George Bernard

Shaw] would relieve us from that sordid necessity of living for others," by which he means charity but also paid work: "An individual who has to make things for the use of others, and with reference to their wants and their wishes, does not work with interest, and consequently cannot put into his work what is best in him."[9] Even the owner of property is not exempt, Wilde continues, because property "involves endless claims upon one, endless attention to business, endless bother." Think of it. Worker or capitalist or landlords, we are all "slaves" to supplying things for others. Frightful.

In that highly metaphorical and imprecise sense, we are indeed "enslaved," and to our mutual good. After Hegel, many intellectuals have declared that capitalism makes people work for others, and makes the worker therefore an "object," not a "subject." So it was said by Marx and Heidegger and Sartre, since "being for others" is "inauthentic." If I adopt a social role, such as selling you a deep-fried Mars bar from my fish-and-chips shop in Edinburgh, I am treating you as an object, and you, when you hand over your money, are treating me the same. As the philosopher Roger Scruton puts it, to follow such a Kantian obedience to ethical law with respect to others "launches us down that path towards the 'bourgeois' order on which finicky intellectuals are so reluctant to tread."[10]

Though the road ends in trade-tested betterment.

61

AND THEREFORE BOURGEOIS RHETORIC
WAS BETTER FOR THE POOR

The Bourgeois Revaluation was an ethical event. Northwestern Europe came to honor the outcome of trade, in both senses of "honor." It accorded dignity to the creators, and it gave the outcomes the liberty to happen, as in "honoring" a contract. But laissez faire was ethical in another sense too.[1] It was a decision to treat trade as ethically privileged, which meant even in economic life to stop according privilege to hierarchy ("Stand aside, knave") and start according privilege to exchange ("The price is the price"). When goods are scarce they need to be allocated somehow, and hierarchy is usually a nasty way of doing it. The loyalty to one's master that characterizes feudal or clan or client societies was to be set aside. Love or loyalty was now to have nothing to do with it, rhetorically speaking.

Such fundamental human behaviors as love and loyalty continued strongly in a Bourgeois Era whose less reflective rhetoric claimed to set them aside "for business." "Friends" were normally construed in Shakespeare's time, say, or in Quattrocento Florence as allies in a struggle to preserve status in a hierarchy. The modern bourgeois society is more, not less, devoted to a secular and disinterested version of the virtue of love.[2] But in any case it is the rhetoric we are talking about, the sociologically justified way of life, not the sometime inconsistent behavior, such as Ben Franklin's. The doomed hero Stringer Bell on the TV series *The Wire* always says, in his bourgeois way, "Business is business." As Marx and Engels put it in the *Manifesto*, "the bourgeoisie . . . has pitilessly torn asunder the motley feudal ties that bound man to his 'natural superiors.'" Such an alleged rhetoric of alienated, unentangled trade was what French and British conservatives such as Balzac,

Carlyle, Disraeli, Flaubert, Dickens, and Ruskin detested about the bourgeoisie and all its works—though it was not how the bourgeoisie actually behaved. As their enemy Macaulay put it, the conservatives such as Carlyle talked instead "of the reign of Queen Elizabeth as the time when England was truly merry England, when all classes were bound together by brotherly sympathy."[3]

Hierarchy, though less and less justified in theory, did not actually disappear, even late in the game. Men, elders, union plumbers, millionaires, officials, whites, Americans, middle-aged people, citizens, bosses, and privileged burghers of the town to this day lord it over women, minors, non-union workers, paupers, subjects, blacks, foreigners, the young, illegals, workers, and rednecks. Hierarchy is nasty indeed, leading, for example, to protection for the jobs of middle-class and middle-aged people, and therefore to massive unemployment among young people in Spain and South Africa. We of the Chicago School of economics in the 1970s agreed with the New Left historians of the time in noting, and detesting, the Bad Old Golden Rule: Those who have the gold rule.

But after the Bourgeois Revaluation such hierarchy less commonly trumped the outcome of trade, and especially the hierarchy did not in the crucial matter of betterment. The rhetoric mattered. The new rhetoric justified letting trade-tested progress have a go. Marxians call the acceptance of such betterment "false consciousness," a con job. Ideologies are indeed con jobs, whether good cons or bad. In psychiatry, false consciousness is called "lack of insight." If you as the patient don't agree with the psychiatrist's ideology you are said to exhibit such a lack.[4] But unless the masses in a democracy accept betterment they can be led by populists or Bolsheviks or fascists to rise up and kill the goose. That's another con job, with worse consequences. Killing the golden goose has never been good for the poor.

The leftish sociologist Charles Lemert argued, for example, that false consciousness among workers is an instance of what the great leftish sociologist C. Wright Mills called a lack of the "sociological imagination." Lemert asks, "Why does it happen that oppressed people, who clearly possess the ability to understand their situations, so often fail to do so?"[5] What he means is that if you as a poor person do not understand society—by not understanding, for example, the Marxian axiom that employment is inherently exploitative—then you will accept deals that are not fair. You will falsely believe that you are paid so badly because that is all you ethically deserve or, as economists started saying in the late nineteenth century, because your low pay corresponds to your actual, low marginal product. You will not understand the left's sweetly erroneous claim that you are paid $8.50 an hour rather than $15.00 an hour because trade in labor is inherently exploitative, and the bosses are stealing the difference as surplus value, which you can seize back from the system if you will but organize.

The workers in such an account are thus—falsely, with lack of insight—persuaded by the Bourgeois Deal. The boss says, Let me, oh workers, engage in betterment, with a profitability test, which may result in closing this or that plant and, I regret to say, may result in a spell of unemployment for some of you. I deeply sympathize. In exchange, in the long run I will make you all rich. (Up his sleeve, to himself, according to Marxian lore: Ha, ha, *suckers!*) Workers, the left says, mistakenly accept a false claim of creative destruction. Wake up, you workers! Arise, you prisoners of starvation!

But suppose the Bourgeois Deal is sound. Then the falsity in consciousness is attributable not to the misled proletarians lacking sociological imagination but rather to the leftish sociologists themselves, lacking economic imagination. The politics is reversed. Workers of the world, unite: demand trade-tested progress under a régime of private property and profit making. Still better, become bourgeois, as large groups of workers in rich countries do believe themselves to have become, approaching 100 percent in the United States, measured by self-identification as "middle class." It would then seem at least odd to call "false" a consciousness that has raised the income of poor workers in real terms by a factor of 30 or 100, as from 1800 to the present it has. That is why it is scientifically crucial to grasp the size of the Great Enrichment, and why I keep repeating it. If you grasp the scientific truth, and inscribe it on your heart, your attitude toward the economy and its history will shift.

If workers have been "fooled" by accepting the Deal, then for such a way of being fooled let us give two and a half cheers—the deduction of half a cheer being because it's not dignified to be "fooled" by anything. Two and a half cheers for the new dominance since 1800 of a bourgeois ideology and the spreading acceptance of the Bourgeois Deal.

Taxing the rich, who get their income from the profitability test, to help the poor, who do the work, seems in the first act a fine idea. When a bourgeois child first realizes how very poor the people are in the next neighborhood, she naturally wishes to open her wallet, or still better Daddy's wallet. It is at such an age—fourteen or sixteen—that we form political identities, which we seldom then revise in the face of later evidence. In an ancient society of slaves the slave-owning child had no such guilt, because the poor were fated to be slavish. But once the naturalness of hierarchy is questioned, as it was in the eighteenth century in northwestern Europe, it seems obvious to adopt socialism. Our families, I have noted, are little socialist economies, with Mom as central planner. Let's remake society, the generous adolescent proposes, as one big family of 320 million people. Surely the remaking will solve the problem of poverty, raising up the poor by big amounts, such as the 15 or 20 percent of income now stolen annually by the bosses.

The equality is natural in a home, having one source of income—the father or, lately, the mother—and a task of "distributing" the proceeds. Papa might ethically get more food if he is a hewer in a mine and needs the extra calories to get through a ten-hour shift at the coal face, but otherwise the distribution is naturally, and ethically, equal. The Swedish political motto from the 1920s on was "a national home."

But a nation is not a home. In the Great Society—as Hayek called it in advance of President Johnson, meaning a big society governed by trade as against a little band or family governed by equal distribution. The source of income is not merely the father's pay packet descending like manna on the child but the myriad specialized exchanges with strangers that we make every day, Nicole's million men working to make Smith's woolen coat. Equality of "distribution" is not natural to such a society, not a society of 9 million Swedes, and certainly not one of 320 million Americans.

And in some important respects equality is *improved* by an ethic of trading. Free entry erodes monopolies that in traditional societies keep one tribe rich and the rest poor. Unfettered ability of workers to offer themselves for employment erodes differentials among equally productive workers in cotton textiles. And it erodes differentials, as I noted in mentioning Robert Frost's wavering between teaching and farming, between a professor who teaches with the same scant equipment that Socrates used—a place to draw diagrams, a stretch of sand in Athens, Greece, or a whiteboard in Athens, Georgia, and a crowd of students—and an airline pilot working with the finest fruits of a technological civilization. The pilot produces thousands of times more value of travel services per hour than a Greek steersman in

400 BCE. The professor produces, if she is very lucky, the same insight per student hour as Socrates. But equality of physical productivity doesn't matter in a free, great (that is big and trading and mobile) society. Entry and exit to occupations is what matters. Some few of the professors could have become airline pilots, and some few of the pilots professors, which is enough to give even workers like the professors who have not increased in productivity in the past twenty-five hundred years an equal share of the finest fruits.

Having noted this highly egalitarian result of a society of trade-tested betterment, though, what about subsequent "distribution" of the fruits? Why shouldn't we—one might ask mildly, who "we"?—seize the high incomes of the professor and the airline pilot and distribute them to dustmen and cleaners? The reply is that a wage is not merely an arbitrary tax imposed on the rest of us. Such a tax is what an inequality within the household would be, Cinderella getting less to eat than her sisters out of sheer spite. Differential wages in a great trading society, by contrast, direct an astonishingly complicated, if largely unplanned and spontaneous, division of labor, whose next move is determined by the differentials—that is, by the profit in a trade or in an occupation. If medical doctors make ten times more than cleaners, the rest of the society, which pays voluntarily for the doctors and cleaners is saying loudly, If some of the cleaners can become doctors, for Lord's sake shift them into doctoring!

If we reduce the Great Society to a family by rigorously taxing high earnings we destroy the signaling. People wander between cleaning and doctoring without such signals about the value people put on the next hour of the services. Neither doctoring nor cleaning gets done well if we run the society on the family plan of "from each according to her ability, to each according to her need." We become the unspecialized society of a household and lose the massive gain from specialization and the accumulated ingenuity transmitted by education to a trade and by the steadily bettered robots applied to each, the nail guns and computers that make master carpenters and master schoolteachers better and better at providing houses and educations to others.

Efficiency, therefore, requires differentials in wages. Yet the startling betterment coming from post-1800 ingenuity, not efficiency, is the heart of the matter—though, to be sure, enterprise profits and wage differentials encouraged the entry and exit that constitutes the test. The 900 to 9,900 percent increase in the pie, a roughly constant share of it going to the poor, dwarfs the benefits to the poor of any redistribution of a given pie. Redistribution, though it assuages bourgeois guilt, has not been the chief advantage to the poor. Economic growth has.

The social arithmetic shows why. If the 15 percent or so of profits (excluding interest payments and land rents) in the American economy were forthwith handed over to the workers, earning 60 or so percent of income, the workers (including some amazingly highly paid "workers," such as sports and singing stars, and big-company CEOs) would be about 25 percent or so better off, right now. But one time only. The expropriation is not a 25 percent gain every year forever, but merely this one time, since you can't expropriate the same people year after year and expect them to come forward with the same sums ready to be expropriated again and again. A onetime expropriation raises the income of the workers by 25 percent, and then their income reverts to the previous level—or at best (if the profits can simply be taken over by the state without damage to their level, miraculously, and then distributed to the rest of us by saintly and all-wise bureaucrats without sticky fingers and without favored friends) continues with whatever rate of growth the economy was experiencing (supposing again, unnaturally and contrary to the evidence of communist experiments from New Harmony, Indiana, to Stalinist Russia, that the expropriation of the income of capital will not reduce the rate of growth of the pie).

Or, to speak of expropriation by regulation, were an act of Congress to mandate ten hours' pay for eight hours' work, the incomes of the portion of the working class that got it would rise, again, one time, by 25 percent. So it would be in the first act, under the same, unnatural supposition that the pie was not thereby reduced, when the managers and entrepreneurs exit the now unprofitable activity. Such a redistribution sounds like a good idea, unless you reflect that at such rates the profit-earning bosses would be less willing to employ people in the first place.

Here's another idea for income transfers, then: If we took away the alarmingly high share of U.S. income earned by the top 1 percent, which was in 2010 about 22 percent of national income, and gave it to all the rest of us, we as the Rest would be 22/78, or a little over 28 percent, better off.

Or put it still another way. Suppose the 15 percent of national income that is profit was allowed to be earned by the people directing the economy, by the owner of the little convenience store in your neighborhood as much as by the malefactors of great wealth. But suppose the profit earners, out of a gospel of wealth, and following Catholic social teaching, decided that they themselves should live modestly and then give all their surplus to the poor. The economist David Colander declares that "a world in which all rich individuals . . . [believed] that it us the duty of all to give away the majority of their wealth before they die," the world "would be quite different from . . . our world."[6] But wait. The entire 15 percent would raise the incomes of the rest—and a privileged few of the rest would be university professors getting Guggenheim fellowships, or left-wing folk getting Macarthur "genius" awards—but nothing like the extent to which they've been raised by modern economic growth. And even the gospel-of-wealth calculation supposes that all profits go to "rich individuals." The owner of the Ma-and-Pa convenience store earns profits, but is not rich.

The point is that the 25 or 28 percent increases to be had through one-time redistributions are two orders of magnitude smaller—and much less effective in helping the poor—than the 900 or 2,900 or 9,900 percent gains from greater productivity since 1800. The very poor, in other words, could be made a tiny bit better off, one time, their incomes increased by a factor of 1.25 or so in one year, by expropriating the expropriators, or persuading them to give all their money to the poor. But they and their ancestors have been made *much* better off—real wages 1800 to the present having risen by a *factor* of 10 or 30 or 100—by living in a radically more productive economy. If we want to make the nonbosses or the poor better off by a significant amount, the accumulating benefit of the Great Enrichment beats a onetime redistribution every time.

Chairman Mao's emphasis on class warfare spoiled what gains his Chinese Revolution had at first achieved by overturning the landlord system and giving women some liberty. When his heirs shifted in 1978 to "socialist modernization" they (inadvertently) adopted trade-tested betterment and achieved in thirty years a rise of Chinese per-person real income by a factor of 20—not a mere 25 percent gain, but 1,900 percent.[7] Deng Xiaoping's anti-equalizing motto was, "Let some people get rich first." It's the Bourgeois Deal, the profit-guided betterment in the first act that makes for gigantic gains for the poor in the third act.

Socialist expropriation or Christian charity, when their onetime character is properly acknowledged, are startlingly less efficacious than they seem at first. Continuing even with the unreasonable supposition that an expropriation would have no effect on the size of the pie, they are anyway only onetime enrichments. A more prudent way of distributing the spoils would be to invest the expropriation or the charity in a fund to be drawn on perpetually for the benefit of the exploited workers. Suppose that the onetime sum was as much as 30 percent of national income, a land reform, say. Suppose that as a rough approximation the whole population goes on earning by non-expropriation the 70 percent remaining. We are assuming that, contrary to socialist fantasies of costless expropriation, the 30 percent earned by the bosses goes away permanently, because the bosses don't show up any more for entrepreneurial or managerial duty—the checking for social profitability, the deciding what is to be done that plays a larger and larger role as we get better at making goods and services with less hand labor. But we are accepting the socialist fantasy, repeatedly demonstrated in historical experiments to be fantastic, that setting the reward to physical or landed capital at zero does *not* reduce the productivity of labor. (It does in fact reduce it, as it did in the USSR, by grossly misallocating such capital. And what does one do, I ask my beloved socialist fantasists, with capital returns to now *peasant-*owned land or worker-owned *human* capital?) Suppose that the rate of return on the Expropriation Fund was 5 percent per year. The poor people's income (which is to say the 70 percent, magically not reduced by socialist measures) would be raised above what it would have been by (30 × .05) divided by 70, or 2.1 percent. Good, and not one-time-only. But it is still far below the 7 to 10 percent achieved every year in India and China nowadays by letting profits be earned. And, being a fixed sum of return on a onetime sum invested, its significance would fall and fall as a share of the workers' income in a more and more productive economy.

To step beyond fantasy, the expropriation of profits would kill progress entirely. It has done so, I repeat, historically. True, as Thomas Piketty observes, the United States and the United Kingdom for many decades after the 1920s had very high marginal rates of taxation.[8] It is a scientific question whether taking the 30 percent of national income I have imagined in a land reform would reduce the 70 percent earned by the rest of us. In extreme cases, such as centrally planned socialism, it seems to, if not in the (few) well administered land reforms. Maybe we could get away with reinstating 90 percent marginal tax rates—in order, Piketty argues, to reduce high executive compensation that takes now a tiny portion of GDP. Maybe not. In fact the rich have tax lawyers and accountants devoted to avoiding taxes. Indeed, in Marxian and some Samuelsonian theory (which all depend on capital accumulation), if the bosses do *not* keep their ill-gotten gains the machinery of accumulation stops.

But there are less damaging ways of reducing an executive compensation we find offensive, or are envious of, than disposing of the profits that guide betterment and then handing the proceeds over to philosopher kings and queens in Paris or Washington to redistribute them fairly to the Muslims in Paris suburbs or to the homeless sleeping on heating grates in Washington. Note that in truth such sweet redistribution is not what most governments spend most of their tax revenues doing. National defense is not poor-friendly. Australia and New Zealand approach a redistributive ideal. But the United States, with its lush undergrowth of corporate welfare and tax deals for our dear friends the very rich, costing according to the conservative Heritage foundation some $100 billion per year, does not. True, "social security," as old-age pensions are called in the United States, are a large portion of what the U.S. Federal government spends, but even such pensions supported by tax dollars go to the well-off more than to the poor.

Supposing our mutual purpose, then, is to help the poor—as in ethics it certainly should be—and considering that the learned cadres of the clerisy are supposed to have sociological imagination, their advocacy for equalizing restrictions and redistributions, and their spurning of growth-inducing liberty can be viewed at best as thoughtless. Perhaps, considering what economic historians now know about the Great Enrichment, but which the left clerisy, and many of the right clerisy, resists acknowledging, it can even be considered unethical. Members of the left clerisy, such as Tony Judt or Paul Krugman or Thomas Piketty, who are quite sure that they themselves are taking the ethical high road against the wicked selfishness of Tories or Republicans or La Union pour un Mouvement Populaire, might on such evidence be considered dubiously ethical. They are obsessed with first-act changes that cannot much help the poor, and often can be shown to damage them grievously, and are obsessed with an angry envy at the consumption of the very rich. They are willing to stifle, through taxing the earners of high wages or profits, the trade-tested betterments that in the long run have gigantically helped the poor. It's an intellectual crime. Galileo in Bertolt Brecht's play puts it this way: "I say to you: he who does not know the truth is merely an idiot. But he who knows it and calls it a lie, is a criminal. Get out of my house!"[9]

The productivity of the economy in 1900 was low, and in 1800 lower. The only way that the bulk of the people, and the poorest among them, were going to be made seriously better off was by making the economy much more productive. The share going to the workers was roughly constant (in one respect during the nineteenth and early twentieth century labor's share was rising, because land rent, once a third of national income, fell steadily in its share). The share was determined, as economists such as the American J. B. Clark and the Swede Knut Wicksell put it in the late nineteenth century, by the marginal productivity of workers. And so, according to the economist's argument, even the poorest workers could be expected to share in the rising productivity—by those factors or 10 or 30 or 100. And they did. The descendants of the horribly poor of the 1930s, for instance, are doing much better than their ancestors. Radically creative destruction piled up ideas, such as the railways creatively destroying walking and the stagecoaches, or electricity creatively destroying kerosene lighting and the hand-washing of clothes, or universities creatively destroying literary ignorance and low productivity in agriculture. The Great Enrichment—in the third act—requires not accumulation of capital or the exploitation of workers but the Bourgeois Deal.

Jared Diamond, in a recent book, praises the "restorative" justice practiced in Papua New Guinea when a little boy, after descending from a bus, dashed across the street into the path of a company's truck and was killed.[10] The formal law charged with carelessness the truck driver, whom after great delays the formal, Western-style law of the country found to be entirely innocent. The actual carelessness by adults on the scene was the carelessness of the bus driver, who knew the boy was meeting his uncle across the busy street, or of the uncle himself, who did not bother to cross the street to meet the bus on the safe side. A Western law of tort properly applied would have charged the bus driver or the uncle, which would have had the characteristically bourgeois outcome of providing future incentives for people who can actually affect outcomes to take care—unlike the truck driver who suddenly found a little boy in front of his truck in second gear. The formal common law, like economics itself, is forward-looking.

In the event, the informal law of the Papua New Guinea community, which is backward-looking, held the (in Western terms, wholly innocent) truck company and truck driver liable for "sorry talk" and "sorry money," as the expressive Tok Pisin phrases put it. Diamond recounts the scene of restoration in which the owner of the company paid sorry money out of his supposedly deep pockets, saying to the parents, "This money is nothing compared to your son's life, but I give it to show how sorry we are."

Diamond understandably admires the way the ceremony restores relations broken by the accident, cooling hot heads in the boy's family who would otherwise have turned to violence. (The Papua New Guinea society whose ethics Diamond admires is an unusually violent one.) But restoring relations is an egalitarian ideal, characteristic of societies suspicious of the Bourgeois Deal and suspicious of the forward-looking creative destruction it implements. In the actual case, the cost of the restoration fell on the wrong parties, "wrong" considering the rule of liability that would do well for the prosperity of a future society. In traditional and in socialist societies the focus is on the past. Acemoglu and Robinson note that when the auto was introduced into Somalia the tribes commenced extracting compensation— in blood—if an accident involved a member of another tribe, regardless of bourgeois incentives to avoid future accidents.[11] In South Asia when someone in an extended family does well in business, his remoter relatives show up at his house and expect to be supported. Even in a thoroughly bourgeois society the entrepreneur would expect to be so used by his brother, say, or would at least feel a responsibility to find him a job somewhere. But in a nonbourgeois, traditional society we are speaking of very remote relatives, very numerous. "We are your fourth cousins, from your great-great-great grandmother of blessed memory. The past, not the future, rules." The entrepreneur's compelled generosity to all his first-through-fourth cousins puts a tax on bourgeois enterprise, as does his compelled generosity to the subsidy-and-redistribution schemes of the state, not to speak of less worthy projects.

Such an egalitarian principle animates left-wing thought, with its favored rhetoric of share, restore, insure, equalize, smooth out, mollify, compensate. These are good words, surely. We would want to hear them routinely used in a small family or a small office or other places of love and solidarity, where the means of progress are already discovered. True, we would *not* want to hear the *bad* words associated with solidarity in traditional society: ancestral practices such as female circumcision, obedience to the headman, honor killing, family violence, sexual availability of women for rape: in 2013, 62 percent of a sample of men in Bougainville in Papua New Guinea "admitted to having committed rape, more than a quarter of them in the past year."[12] Nor would we like to hear the comparably bad words that have in fact been associated with thoroughgoing socialist societies, and some tyrannical capitalist ones: obedience to the Party, suppression of mobility, lack of discovery, murder of journalists.

In any event, the good rhetoric of solidarity differs from the rhetoric characteristically admired in the marketplaces of a bourgeois society, marked by such words as prudence, try, deal, enrich, venture, incentive, win-win, the trade test, ingenuity, betterment, progress. The Bourgeois Era is egalitarian, I have noted, admiring a justice of equal dignity and liberty accorded to commoners. If the rhetoric of backward-looking solidarity in tradition or utopia-imagining solidarity in socialism dominates over the rhetoric of forward-looking prudence, the Bourgeois Deal can be stopped. Papua New Guineans will remain proudly traditional. British miners will remain proudly working class, and will persuade the government to keep mining coal that costs more than it can sell for. In consequence they and the rest of the society will remain poor, and with each payment of sorry money or each ton of unprofitable coal the people will as a society get poorer. If we insist on staying at Fiske's stage of "equality ranking," we will never get to the later stage of "market pricing," with its remarkable ability to yield, when aristocratic hierarchy and expert central planning and bourgeois monopoly are disabled, a Great Enrichment. Enforcing equality in the first act of the economic drama stops the productivity gains of the third act, and the uplifting of the poor. In other words, *laissez faire, laissez passer* comes with the Bourgeois Deal.

In 2012 the American ambassador to the United Nation's International Telecommunication Union suggested that letting trade alone might be best for the Internet and for its participants: "The natural path we're on is pretty good," he said to reporters. "Does that mean there aren't things that could improve? Absolutely. . . . But the best thing to do, if you could pick two options, . . . to get prescriptive . . . versus leaving things open, we're much better [off] by leaving things open."[13] So it has seemed, 1800 to the present, uniquely.

PART X

That Is, Rhetoric Made Us, but Can Readily Unmake Us

AFTER 1848 THE CLERISY CONVERTED
TO ANTIBETTERMENT

In the early 1990s I was standing in an Evanston, Illinois, bookstore charmingly called Great Expectations, talking to the owner, Truman Metzel. It was a wonderful store, exhibiting I thought bourgeois virtue. Through the combined virtues of prudence and courage called enterprise Metzel kept obscure university-press books in stock. Mine, for instance. It was a policy that a decade later, under a new owner, led to the shop's shuttering, under pressure from the big-box stores and especially from Amazon (where all my books, dear friends, stand ready to be purchased). On second thought, maybe Metzel was not all that prudent.

Anyway, I was saying to him, "You know, there are only two well-known European novels since 1848 that have portrayed businessmen on the job in anything like a sympathetic way. The first is Thomas Mann's tale of his north-German merchant family, *Buddenbrooks* [1901]. And the second . . ." Here I paused, or rather stuttered, which people sometimes interpret as pausing for effect. Another customer standing there piped up, "And the second is David Lodge's story of love between a university lecturer and a managing director, *Nice Work* [1988]."

Bingo. Those two alone, at any rate among the canon of the best that has been thought and known in the world, were the only books I could think of at the time with businessmen heroes. Perhaps there are others, but they are not well known. Well, Willa Cather, whom I later came to admire, is good on businesspeople. And I later learned from the economist Robert Lucas of V. S. Naipaul's *A House for Mr. Biswas*, whose hero, a journalist, at least rejects the traditional custom in Trinidad of fourth cousins showing up for handouts,

and wants above all to own a house he has earned. European literature, including American and Australian and English Indian literature and other
offshoots, talks about businessmen, incidentally. The share of such talk,
though, is startlingly lower than the share of life taken up in business. Carol
Shields was among the few novelists declaring that "a novelist must give her
characters work to do." She cited the critic Emma Allen, who "believes that
the great joy of detective fiction is watching the working hero being busy
every minute." Shields complained, "I've read novels about professors who
never step into a classroom. They are always on sabbatical or off to a conference in Hawaii."[1] She had in mind, for example, David Lodge's earlier academic novels, such as *Changing Places* (1975) and *Small World* (1985). Love at
home, or lust in Hawaii, gets more attention in fiction than does prudence or
justice at work. Courage on the battlefield figures more in art and literature
than enterprise in the market. Henry James's characters in *The Ambassadors*
(1903) are financed in their dalliances abroad by some sort of manufacturing back in New England. But James pointedly refuses to tell us what the
undoubtedly frightfully vulgar manufacturing was.

Among painters the same is true, and most strikingly after industrialization had become important in our lives. Most of the Impressionists showed
men and women at leisure, even if working men and women, as in Renoir's
At the Moulin de la Galette of 1876. They seldom showed people at work. In
the Caillebotte painting I mentioned of a street junction in Paris, almost all of
the figures hurrying about in the drizzle are bourgeois, none of them at work.
A working woman is vaguely figured, seen just to the right of the pearl earring
of the foregrounded bourgeoise approaching under the protection of her
husband's umbrella. Yet Caillebotte, a wealthy man, was in fact attuned to the
subject of work, as in *The Floor Planers*, shown at the second Impressionist
exhibition in 1876. Zola, who approved of the Impressionists, nonetheless
said of Caillebotte's painting that a "painting that is so accurate . . . makes it
bourgeois," which was not intended as a compliment. A systematic exception
among the Impressionists is Degas who, though from a rich family, recurred
again and again in his enormous output to people of all classes at work. His
ballet dancers—half of his works (note the word)—are not little bourgeois
girls in a class, but professionals working for pay. His famous statue of one,
from 1881, was more an anthropological exhibit than a conventional sculpture. The model was in fact one of the "rats," the paid, working-class adolescent dancers of the corps de ballet. The work is nothing like sculpture's usual

homage to the sacred. Contrast at the time Rodin's *The Thinker* (1879–1889), or even his *Burghers of Calais* (1884–1889), a group of six bourgeois figures engaged in offering themselves as hostages to aristocratic warriors.

And when the scene in painting or novels and later the movies does occasionally shift to men at work the bourgeois man of the past century and a half is pilloried. The bourgeois marketplace was once looked upon with favor by novelists. I mentioned Alessandro Manzoni's *The Betrothed* (second edition, 1842) as a case in point. The middle of the nineteenth century was the sunset of sympathy for the businessman and his commercial forces, a sun which had first risen in Netherlandish painting three centuries before. *Moby Dick* (1851), at least in the first mate Starbuck, can be read as taking a liberal view of business. But *The Confidence Man* (1857), also by Melville, cannot. Charles Dickens converted to an antibourgeois novelist in *Dombey and Son* (1848) and to a political novelist in *Hard Times* (1854), never to return to his earlier geniality about turning a little profit. Since 1848, from the very moment the businessman came into his own, the novelists have not let up. Mark Twain, though himself a businessman, thought of bourgeois men as thieves (admittedly, he thought of more or less everyone that way, as comical liars, fools, and con men). Zola's *Germinal* (1880) and *Ladies' Paradise* (1883) exhibit the owners of coal mines and of soft-goods stores as villains. The theme reaches its height in Booth Tarkington's *The Magnificent Ambersons* (1918), Sinclair Lewis's *Main Street* (1920), and above all Lewis's *Babbitt* (1922), which still provides some of the clerisy their only close acquaintance with the American man of business. And so it continued through the *Wall Street* movies (1987, 2010).

It was similar in the other arts and the other writings. In 1910 George Bernard Shaw looked back to a Great Conversion around 1848:

> The first half [of the nineteenth century] despised and pitied the Middle Ages. . . . The second half saw no hope for mankind except in the recovery of the faith, the art, the humanity of the Middle Ages. . . . For that was how men felt, and how some of them spoke, in the early days of the Great Conversion, which produced, first, such books as the *Latter Day Pamphlets* of Carlyle, Dickens' *Hard Times*, . . . and later on the Socialist movement.[2]

Painting in seventeenth-century Holland, by contrast, I have noted, celebrated bourgeois virtue, a celebration that cannot be found much by the time of Picasso and Diego Rivera—though consider Norman Rockwell, despised by the elite of the clerisy. The British Arts and Crafts movement stirring in the 1860s celebrated workmen and their skills, not bosses and their machines. John Ruskin praised the Gothic in architecture as proletarian work—rather than the elite play he disparaged in the architecture of the Renaissance. He wrote in 1866, "Let us, then, inquire together what sort of games the playing class in England spend their lives in playing at. The first of all English games is making money."[3] He never grasped that one "makes money" only by making goods and services that other people are willing to give up their money for.

There is scarcely an English or French intellectual in the nineteenth century who was not simultaneously the son of a bourgeois and sternly hostile to everything bourgeois. Ruskin's father was a wine importer; one grandfather was a successful wholesale merchant, the other ran a pub. Though the son of a cotton merchant of Charleston, South Carolina, the poet Arthur Hugh Clough felt he could sneer at what he called the businessman's decalogue (1862): "Thou shalt not steal; an empty feat, / When it's so lucrative to cheat.... / Thou shalt not covet, but tradition / Approves all forms of competition."[4] In Addison, Steele, Defoe, and Lillo a century and a half before, or in Ben Franklin and Samuel Johnson a century before, or in Jane Austen a half century before, we have seen, or even in the early Dickens of the *Pickwick Papers* (1836–1837), the tone is different, genially tolerant of bourgeois projecting.

Something strange has happened in the minds of the clerisy since the Great Conversion, something worth understanding. As a Marxian might put it, the cultural superstructure since 1848 has contradicted the material base. Whether an inevitable tendency to contradict itself or some less neat explanation is appropriate, the loss of faith in the bourgeoisie at its hour of triumph had grave consequences in politics beyond the economy.

Fathers and sons were at war, Clough against his father, Turgenev against his. As Franco Moretti observes, in early Victorian literature (he instances novels of the 1840s and 1850s by Dickens, Disraeli, Gaskell, and Dinah Craik's *John Halifax, Gentleman*, 1856), "As the two generations are pitted against each other, the older one turns out to be more bourgeois than the younger":

> I cannot think of any other genre, short of ancient tragedy, where such a bitter curse binds together two consecutive generations. And the message of the plot is

unmistakable: there has been only *one* bourgeois generation—and now it's disappearing, perverted or betrayed by its own children. Its moment is over.[5]

The message is the same even in *Buddenbrooks*. Hanno, the son of the ethically bourgeois dealer in grain, and a town councilor, carries an artistic gift inherited from his mother (paradoxically, herself transplanted to Lübeck from thoroughly bourgeois Holland), which dooms him.

The sociologist Graham Peterson offers a plausible explanation, which seems to fit the facts in detail. "In the first act of ideological revolution," he writes,

> the new promotion of heresy and deviance attacked routine, convention, and aristocratic elites. In the second act of ideological revolution, that very same impulse toward heresy and deviance attacked the first generation of heretics. And this cycle has continued—heretics becoming conventional and getting attacked by their teenage children.[6]

That is to say, since the cake of custom was broken in the early nineteenth century, a cycle of one avant-garde after another has prevailed, in all matters from music to politics.

In this (and in certain other matters) I have changed my mind. I began in economic history age twenty-four, freshly trained as a Samuelsonian economist, arguing against the historian David Landes that in my mature opinion the culture was trivial beside "given" technology and tastes. In that year of 1966, recently converted by the study of economics away from a Joan Baez, folk-singing brand of Marxism, I was nonetheless determined in Marxian/Samuelsonian style to emphasize the material rather than the spiritual, the Samuelsonian forces of price and prudence as against what I called sociology, about which it must be said I knew very little.

I take back none of my calculations in economic history during those days, calculations that still seem to me handsome and true. It is still true that Victorian Britain did not fail and that medieval peasants were not imprudent. I have no more patience now than I did half a century ago with the supposition that people ignore gigantic, obvious opportunities for profit. As a matter of historical fact and economic logic, they don't. Supposing without evidence that they do seems to me to adopt an impious attitude toward the towering dead, with their nightingales and psalms, treating them in retrospect as idiots. It's even bad sociology.

The resolution of the tension between prudence-only and culture-only lies in the notion of "bourgeois virtue," and especially the sociology of how people feel about it. When I first planned to speak about the subject in the early 1990s, to the Institute for Advanced Study at Princeton, the secretary called me up in far Iowa to get the exact title. When she heard the title, she laughed, and exclaimed "'Bourgeois virtue'! That's an oxymoron, isn't it?" Her reaction puts the problem well. It will seem disorienting to talk about ethics to economic historians and economists and other instinctive materialists, or to conventionally anticapitalist folk on the left. But we're not going to see the economy rightly until we face its actual virtues and its actual vices, and especially the actual ethical theories with which the society speaks about the economy. (And likewise, I remind my progressive Christian friends, we're not going to see the virtues rightly until we face the actual economy. Even for the church, one of the great virtues is prudence, leading to an enrichment of the poor and a sound balance sheet for the diocese.)

"By the late nineteenth century," notes the historian Jürgen Kocka, "capitalism was no longer thought to be a carrier of progress."[7] The ethical case against "capitalism" was summarized early by the Reverend H. H. Williams of Oxford, writing on "Ethics" in the eleventh edition of the *Encyclopædia Britannica* in 1910: "The failure of 'laissez-faire' individualism in politics to produce that common prosperity and happiness which its advocates hoped for caused men to question the egoistic basis upon which its ethical counterpart was constructed." Even in 1910 the Reverend Williams's mistake was factual. Trade-tested betterment had by then begun to yield common prosperity and happiness. Yet the clerisy, such as Williams, had long since, as Shaw noted, turned against the bourgeoisie. "How beastly the bourgeois is / especially the male of the species," sang D. H. Lawrence in 1929.[8] As Auden put it a decade later:

He [the bourgeois] never won complete support;
However many votes he bought, . . .
But at the very noon and arch
Of his immense triumphal march
Stood prophets pelting him with curses

And sermons and satiric verses. . . .
BLAKE shouted insults, ROUSSEAU wept. . . .
While BAUDELAIRE went mad protesting
That progress is not interesting.[9]

The literary historian Catherine Gallagher notes that "the ideology most often associated with the industrial bourgeoisie, laissez-faire entrepreneurialism, [was] on the defensive . . . from its inception."[10]

Anticapitalism arrived for many reasons. Oddly, photography is one, conveyed with inexpensive newspaper printing of photos. It gave us, for example, the Lewis Hine photo of the little girl standing for work in the cotton mill. As the activist Sarah Cleghorn put it in 1915: "The golf links lie so near the mill / That almost every day / The laboring children can look out / And see the men at play." A diverted Christianity was another cause, apparent, for example, in the numerous children of Protestant ministers filling the ranks of American Progressivism. And a new prestige for social science and the making of statistical surveys led to the conviction that people could be engineered, with results that would be better than profit-driven trade.

But anticapitalism came in part also because trade-testing disturbed the society without at first enriching ordinary people greatly. It did enrich them eventually, and spectacularly, but too late in the nineteenth century to scotch the feeling in the clerisy that laissez-faire individualism in politics had failed. When trade unionism, the Bismarckian welfare state, Progressivism, and socialism arrived, they corresponded with the big rise in real wages, and gave the impression of causing it—when it was in fact caused by rising productivity from trade-tested betterment. To this day progressives believe that without minimum wages and trade unions our wages would fall to $2 an hour. Their bit of anti-economic illogic is that without state-enforced minimums there would occur "a race to the bottom." The argument ignores the competition among bosses that yields wages equal to what employees produce at the margin.

Real wages in Britain rose as shown in table 6. The problem was that the sharp payoff was at first delayed—note the acceleration only during 1850–1880, then a slowdown, and then the greater accelerations in the twentieth century. The late nineteenth-century slowdown, though moderate, gave birth to the idea of socialism. History "Gives too late / What's not believed in, or if still believed, / In memory only, reconsidered passion."

TABLE 6. Annual real earnings of UK workers per person rose sharply, but with a slowdown

	Factor of increase				
in 30 years		in 90 years		in 180 years	
1820–1850	1.37				
1850–1880	1.53	1820–1910	2.73		
1880–1910	1.30			1820–2000	10.5
1910–1940	1.40				
1940–1970	1.65	1910–2000	3.84		
1970–2000	1.67				

Source: Gregory Clark's estimate reported in *Measuring Worth*, http://measuringworth.com /datasets/ukearncpi/result2.php.

The historian Mike Rapport summarizes the tragedy of 1848: "In the long term," he writes "it is true that capitalism dramatically improved the overall standards of living in Europe. With the benefit of hindsight, therefore . . . [the] chastisement of radical impatience with the limitations of the emerging liberal order in 1848 seems entirely justified." It's again the Bourgeois Deal and the third act. "With more forbearance in 1848 . . . the liberal order [on the Continent] would have survived, and within a generation . . . {Continental] Europeans would have enjoyed both constitutional government and the wealth created by maturing industrial economies." Yet he quotes Alexander Herzen, in Paris during the revolution of 1848: "How will you persuade a workman to endure hunger and want while the social order changes by insensible degrees?"[11] As one would expect, then, in the rich regions of new settlement—Australia, Canada, Argentina, and above all the United States—the turn against bourgeois virtues was less sharp than in Old Europe.

THE CLERISY BETRAYED THE BOURGEOIS DEAL, AND APPROVED THE BOLSHEVIK AND BISMARCKIAN DEALS

Stanley Fish, the student of Milton's poetry and the public intellectual I've mentioned, shocks his colleagues by bragging about being the highest-paid humanist in the world, and drives his Jaguar smartly into the parking lot of the Summer School of Criticism and Theory, to the scandal of the anticonsumerist professors of literature in elbow-patched Harris tweeds. Fish delights in sharing the stage with his friend David Lodge, to be exhibited as the original for Lodge's creation, Morris Zapp, the highly bourgeois American professor of literature in Lodge's early academic novels. Fish proves by the scandal of his exception the prevalence of the rule, "No commerce, please: we're members of the clerisy."

The clerisy is an appendage of the bourgeoisie. The treason of the clerisy in France and England, I have noted, was a treason against their fathers, uniformly bourgeois. So it was in Germany, as with Marx the son of a lawyer and Engels the son of a factory owner, though the excellence of the German higher education system provided more routes for sons of saddle-makers and ribbon weavers to become professors than universities did in France or England. And later the American progressives, advocating a secularized but nonetheless Christian ideal for public policy, were out of all proportion, I just said, the sons and daughters of Protestant ministers, themselves from bourgeois roots—grandsons and granddaughter arrayed against their bourgeois grandfathers.[1]

It's a puzzle. In his *Bohemian versus Bourgeois: French Society and the French Man of Letters in the Nineteenth Century* (1964) César Graña asked,

"What is it in the spiritual scene of modern society that may account for such intellectual touchiness, willfulness, and bitterness" among the clerisy against the bourgeoisie?[2] His answer was what has since been called the "aporia of the Enlightenment project," namely, the conflict between liberty and rationalism in modern life. The bourgeoisie is seen by members of the clerisy such as Balzac, Dickens, Lawrence, and Sartre as the embodiment of rationalism. And rationalism, the clerisy declares, is bad.

Graña was probably correct. An impatience with calculation, I've noted, has been the mark of the Romantic looking back to medieval virtues since the ironies of Cervantes. The modern men Graña writes about, however, have been mistaken. They mistook bourgeois life in just the way a rebellious son mistakes the life of his father. Mark Twain: "When I was a boy of 14, my father was so ignorant I could hardly stand to have the old man around. But when I got to be 21, I was astonished at how much the old man had learned in seven years." The life of the bourgeois father is not always routine. It is often creative. What has raised income per person in the rich countries by a factor of at least ten and more likely one hundred since the eighteenth century is ingenuity backed by commercial courage, not rational science. Dickens was mistaken to think that facts alone are wanted in the life of manufacturing. Manufacturing depends on enterprise and single-mindedness far from coolly rational. Weber was mistaken to think that the modern state embodies principles of rationality in bureaucracy. Anyone who thinks that a large modern bureaucracy runs "like an army" cannot have had much experience in either a large modern bureaucracy or an army. Armies do not run like machines, and large modern bureaucracies call on loyalties far from mechanically rational. Freud was mistaken to claim that modern life forces a choice between the reality principle and eroticism. A businessperson without an erotic drive, suitably sublimated, achieves little.

The lack of insight by the clerisy into business life is odd. In the European novel late in its history the businessman, unless he proves in the end to evince aristocratic or Christian virtues, is almost always a cardboard fool. "Man must labor, / Man must work. / The executive is / A dynamic jerk," chanted Ogden Nash late in this tradition. Intellectuals in the West have had a tin ear for business and its values.

Economics, as the science of business, has been similarly spurned, leading to additional adolescent sneering at what the lad doesn't quite grasp. Early in the nineteenth century writers like Macaulay or Manzoni read and understood the new political economy, and acknowledged the force of co-operation, entry, arbitrage, scarcity, and creative destruction. But later intellectuals construed economics as the faculty of reason, arrayed against the freedom they so loved, a misunderstanding encouraged by the talk among classical economists of "iron laws." Or else they portrayed businesspeople as merely seekers of special favors from Congress (thus Twain and Warner in *The Gilded Age*, 1873). By the late nineteenth century economics had dropped out of the conversation entirely. No intellectual since 1890 has been ashamed to be wholly ignorant about the economy or economics, especially about the bourgeois economics that Marx admired and used and misused. It is a rare intellectual or novelist—David Lodge, I repeat, or Willa Cather—who can see the businessperson as anything other than the Other, to be compelled by state violence under the supervision of the clerisy to cough up their ill-gotten gains to the proletariat, with suitable diversions to university professors and foundation fellows.

A change is overdue. To admire the bourgeois virtues is not to buy into Reaganism or the Me Decade. We must encourage trade-tested betterment and then trade-tested supply, it being the hope for the poor of the world and being in any case a substantial part of what we are, even if we are professors of literature. Such bourgeois work need not be selfish or unjust or in other ways unethical. An aristocratic, country-club capitalism, well satisfied with itself, or a peasant, grasping capitalism, despising itself, are both lacking in the virtues. Neither works. They lead to monopoly and economic failure, alienation and revolution. We need a democratic, trade-tested betterment of the Whole Foods sort, that nurtures communities of good townsfolk in South Central LA as much as in Iowa City. We need, after the betterments have been invented, a democratic, trade-tested routine supply. We encourage such good things by beginning a conversation about the bourgeois virtues, or at any rate by stopping the trite and ignorant conversation that assumes without reflection or evidence that the economy is corrupting.

One can think of men and women to stand as models. Considering the distaste with which imaginative literature since around 1830 has viewed the businessperson, the models had better be nonfictional. Benjamin Franklin, I have said, is a good case—or so the enemies of "capitalism" have thought. Graña recounts the venom I have noted against Franklin in the writings of D. H. Lawrence, Stendhal, and Baudelaire: "a knave in Franklin's style," writes Lawrence, "the rising bourgeoisie come to replace the faltering aristocracy."[3]

Being ashamed of being bourgeois has for two centuries amounted to being ashamed of being American. The sneerers at Franklin like Baudelaire and Lawrence were notorious as antidemocrats and anti-Americans. Dickens hated the United States as much as he hated businessmen. Heidegger opposed *Amerikanismus*, and his master Adolf said, "My feelings against Americanism are feelings of hatred and deep repugnance." America, Ian Buruma and Avishai Margalit explain, is seen in what they call "Occidentalism" as "rootless, cosmopolitan, superficial, trivial, materialistic, racially mixed, fashion-addicted," all the usual complaints against the bourgeoisie, and many of the complaints against the Jews.[4]

But America is not the only bourgeois society. Germany is too, though one that in its intellectual circles wishes it was not. Italians are famous townsfolk. And China, having had for centuries the largest cities, must have buried in its history a bourgeois tradition counter to the traditions of the peasant/landlord or of the scholar/bureaucrat. A myth of recency has made the virtues arising from urban trading seem those of a shameful parvenu. It is time we recognized the actual economic history and start assessing the class of traders and inventors without prejudice.

The Bourgeois Deal, I say, was triumphing down to 1848. As the Australian economist Jason Potts summarizes my case:

> McCloskey's point is that the words we use about economic activities matter because they carry ethical valuations. Her point is that a shift in these ethical valuations, in the rhetoric, was the cause of the rise of modern prosperity—of the modern world no less—but that this can also reverse, by the same process, by a re-imposition of the dishonor tax [a phrase Potts borrows from Donald Boudreaux] associated with intolerance of commercial activity, or a sense of its indignity.[5]

After 1848 the Bourgeois Deal and its ethical supports came under attack from two alternatives. The Bolshevik Deal, that is, central-planning socialism and state ownership of property, was first imagined in the 1830s and 1840s and then implemented heavily after 1917 and especially after 1945. The notion of Saint-Simon, Fourier, Marx, Engels, Bernstein, Kautsky, Shaw, the Webbs, Lenin, Trotsky, Stalin, Gramsci, Lukács, Mao, and the rest was that the "nature of Man under socialism" would change, according to the utopian vision of the French Enlightenment, guided by us in the Party, or by us of the expert clerisy. The notion was contrary to the idea of the Scottish Enlightenment that human nature is stable and that humans are equally if imperfectly rational and should be allowed as free and dignified adults to make their own decisions.[6]

The Bolshevik Deal came substantially to an end in 1989. In 1974, before the end, Leszek Kołakowski observed, in an open letter responding to a hundred-page open letter sent to him by the British Marxian historian E. P. Thompson, that the Bolshevik solution to *all* problems was state ownership of the means of production—thereby getting rid of the nasty concentrations of power in property owned by the bourgeoisie. To quote again the far-sighted Macaulay in 1830, against Robert Southey's protosocialism, Southey, and later Thompson, would suggest that "the calamities arising from the collection of wealth in the hands of a few capitalists are to be remedied by collecting it in the hands of one great capitalist, who has no conceivable motive to use it better than other capitalists, the all-devouring state."[7] Even the Western Marxians such as C. L. R. James eventually claimed, in extenuation of the evident sins of the USSR and of Maoist China, that eastern "communism" was actually a "state capitalism," and admittedly all-devouring.

But in truth communism as practiced in Eastern Europe and in China and a few other sad places was not a "capitalism." It was *not* a system of trade-tested betterment, with its great variety of human projects, each with its own field of honor—best retail banker in Chicago, cleanest bean fields in Johnson County, most profitable auto dealership in Berlin. The socialist state reduces society to one great project, which is why socialism does make sense in a war for survival, such as the Great Patriotic War. In a one-project society your honor is achieved only by applying to the Central Bureau, in the style of absolute monarchs or university presidents. John Tomasi has observed that a special merit of trade-tested betterment is that it gives people many projects and many fields of honor.[8] A tyrannical or even a democratic but centralized economy devours all in one.

Kołakowski was making a subtler point about socialism, too. Even conceptually, the one instrument—the abolition of private property—could not accomplish all that we as free humans want, except in "a leftist heaven [in which] everything is compatible and everything settled, lamb and lion sleep[ing] in the same bed. . . . We want technological progress and we want perfect security for people; [but] let us look closer how both could be combined."[9] We want, Kołakowski notes, all three: equality, liberty, and efficiency. I would say rather we want dignity, liberty, and betterment. The point remains—an economist's point—that any three goals "limit each other and can be implemented only through compromises. . . . Attempts to consider any one of these values as absolute . . . are bound to destroy the other two." For example, "absolute equality can be established only within a despotic system," a point that since 1880 has often eluded High Liberals fond of excusing their fondness for state violence in regulation and compulsion by saying that in a democratic age, after all, *we* as voters are the state. For example, "we" carried on the War on Drugs, destroying the families and neighborhoods of poor people, without complaint from the left by High Liberals, or from the right by Black churchmen. Or, Kołakowski continues, "Efficiency as a supreme value calls again for despotism [in central planning], and despotism is inefficient above a certain level of technology," another point that has eluded the enthusiasts for regulation and planning.[10] Thomas Balogh, the Hungarian-origin British economist who advised the Labour politicians after Sputnik, predicted confidently that "Russian output per head will surpass that of Britain in the early 1960s and that of the U.S. in the mid-1970s."[11] Paul Samuelson's (and later also William Nordhaus's) textbook in economics gave a chart in every editions from the 1950s on, far into the 1980s, making the identical claim that (according to every edition, using the same chart) in the *next* fifteen years the Soviet system would result in technological betterment surpassing that of the United States.[12]

Kołakowski's subtlety about trade-offs can be expressed in the way the Dutch economist Jan Tinbergen (1903–1994) thought about economic policy. Tinbergen's was a mathematical proposition. For each goal (the three goals, say, of dignity, liberty, and betterment) the social engineer needs a separate lever or tool (Tinbergen called the goal a target and the lever an instrument). Only by miraculous accident would pulling one lever (for instance, abolishing private property) accomplish all three optimally. You can see the mathematical character of Tinbergen's theorem. Each lever may have a calculable effect of this or that magnitude on each of the three separate goals. But there must be at least three levers with *differing* effects if each of the goals is to be attained. The requirement that the effects differ is implied by the mathematics of vector multiplication, and is anyway common sense. Thus dignity for entrepreneurs can support progress, as it did, and can also in the political sphere protect liberty, at any rate for entrepreneurs. But, to speak of the goal most admired on the left, it is said to leave equality in question. Likewise, liberty understood as the equal application of law can undermine unequal privilege (think of how such a liberty would affect the university-bound children of China, say, whose prospects now depend on whether or not they are children of Party officials), which is good for equality but might possibly not be the best route to betterment, at any rate in the short run.

Making the socialization of all private property the single, all-purpose lever will not do the best job for the three goals, except in a leftist heaven of lamb and lion sleeping in the same bed. (We are assuming that the communist governments of Eastern Europe and of China did in fact want to achieve dignity, liberty, and betterment for ordinary people, setting aside the ample evidence that they did not.) "Most of what we learn in life," Kołakowski patiently explains to Thompson, "is about which values are compatible and which mutually exclusive." Perfect national security, as Americans found once again in the news of 2013 about the National Security Administration, excludes maximum liberty. But "most utopians," Kołakowski continues, "are simply incapable of learning that there are incompatible values."[13] The Good must be one, said Plato (his graduate student Aristotle disagreed), and so said Burke about tradition and Bentham about utility and Marx about the abolition of private property.

The Kołakowski-Tinbergen theorem is what another Slavic-origin liberal, Isaiah Berlin, often emphasized. In 1955–1956 Berlin noted of *égalité*, even in so single-minded an advocate as the Marquis de Condorcet—jailed, ironically, in 1794 by the Revolution he inspired in a jail renamed *Bourg-l-'Égalité*, a name recently changed from Bourg-la-Reine [Queen City], were he shortly died—that it is almost always accompanied by other goals, which modify it in practice. Berlin instances "happiness, virtue, justice, progress in the arts and sciences, the satisfaction of various moral and spiritual values of which equality, of whatever kind, is only one":

> Condorcet does not himself seem to be troubled by the problem of whether the quest for equality will clash with the need to seek these other ends, for in common with many thinkers of his day, he took it for granted all too easily that all

good things were certainly compatible. . . . It was left to others to emphasize the fact that in life as normally lived the ideals . . . come into conflict [even] within the same society and, often enough, with the moral experience of a single individual.[14]

Likewise one learns from virtue ethics: virtues are not fungible, and not reducible to one. Humans face tragic choices.

The other and anti-Bolshevik alternative to the Bourgeois Deal is the Bismarckian Deal, inaugurated in 1881 and triumphant after 1889, the first year of old-age pensions in the German Empire. Bismarck's scheme to steal the thunder of his enemies—that is, of the soon-to-be literally Bolshevik Dealers and of the left generally—is the origin of the modern welfare state. (Alexander Herzen in 1855 perhaps had the charitable precursors of such conservative end-runs around the workers' politics in mind when he spoke of "the almshouse of reaction."[15]) In Britain its triumph dates from the establishment, in 1911, of compulsory unemployment insurance (which Bismarck had contemplated but was unable to get the Reichstag to take seriously), or more thoroughly from 1942 with the Beveridge Report. In the United States it dates from 1933 and the New Deal. The deal is that the welfare state will substitute for your own or your family's voluntary provision for old age or unemployment or medical care, and you will come to view the present state as your noble and benevolent lord.

The "substitution for voluntary provision" was in fact significant, and not only in unemployment insurance. As the university administrator Terence Kealey argues, it has been so for universities in Britain, which before the First World War were independent of the state. Not until the inflation of the war and then the postwar taxes, Kealey argues, did private contributions to British universities dry up. "I gave at the office," became the cry: that is, "I paid for the universities through state taxes, and do not wish therefore to contribute privately." Kealey's point suggests why Continental universities, all state funded, have got since their foundings so little help from millionaires or alumni, in sharp contrast to Japan or the United States with their private universities, and now private endowments even for public universities. After 1919 the universities in Britain "were increasingly understood to be a government responsibility," as they always had been in France and Germany and Italy.[16]

And so too with other extensions of the welfare state. On the eve of the British National (Unemployment) Insurance Act of 1911, of the twelve million then covered by the act fully nine million already had voluntary arrangements, especially through "friendly societies."[17] To this day much of the provision for old age, child raising, unemployment, and medical care comes from the nongovernmental insurance scheme called the family. Consider the Millennial Generation living with their parents. And some of the rest of provisioning is from neighbors and local governments and voluntary charities Bismarckian provision from the taxpayer crowds out. The net gain can be small.

Likewise the government's support for minimum wages, licensing laws, building codes, trade-union exclusivity, a war on drugs, inflation, and military adventures drives people out of employment and undermines provision by families or local authorities or charities. The economist Thomas C. Leonard reports on the nasty origins of the minimum wage a century ago, in a eugenic program to expel women, immigrant, and blacks from the labor force. "The progressive economists . . . believed that the job loss induced by minimum wages was a social benefit, as it performed the eugenic service of ridding the labor force of the 'unemployable.'"[18] Unlike giving the poor additional *income* to bring them up to a dignified standard (by the earned income tax credit, for example), which true liberals and compassionate conservatives advocate, the minimum *wage* was specifically designed to make the poor poorer. By the Bismarckian Deal, then, the state, having caused the social problem, solves it by making many of the poor, and the professors, into wards of the state, and—the politicians hope—making them also into reliable voters and vocal advocates for whichever political party gets the credit.

In 1867 both Bismarck in Prussia and Disraeli in the UK played the Conservative card to trump the left by extending the franchise to many working-class men. The economist Frederik Toscani has persuasively argued that conservative governments wanted to undermine the influence of the irritatingly liberal and uncooperative clerisy, whose human capital was swiftly becoming a secure means of support, by appealing over its head to the workers.[19] The notion was that eventually—though not, as it happened, in the first election Disraeli faced under the new rules—the workers would vote Conservative and nationalistically, as "angels in marble," against their apparent class interest. As early as 1871 Bismarck articulated the socioeconomic corollary of the trick played on the left: "The action of the state is the only means of arresting the Socialist movement. We must carry out what seems justified in the Socialist program and can be realized within the present framework of state and society."[20]

A modern case is South Africa, in which high wages for trade unionists are protected by a high, state-enforced minimum wage and the state-enforced impossibility of dismissing anyone once they have somehow got a job. The system discourages substitution of the pool of cheap and now unemployed labor for unionized and now employed labor, which secures for the government the affection of the unions. The South African union of unions, COSATU, though frankly communist (though with an honorable history fighting apartheid), has for example opposed a scheme for the government to subsidize employment for youths. The resulting high unemployment (officially 25 percent, 70 percent for youths) is assuaged by small income subsidies to those without jobs sitting in huts in the backcountry of the East Cape or KwaZulu-Natal. Out of gratitude the jobless people vote regularly for the party that signs their checks—thus far since democracy the party has been the African National Congress (speaking of honorable histories), though with a slowly declining majority.

As Bismarck in retirement told the pro-German British journalist, historian, and civil servant William H. Dawson, "My idea was to bribe the working classes—or shall I say, to win them over?—to regard the state as a social institution, existing for their sake and interested in their welfare."[21] And as he put it in a speech in 1889, "I will consider it a great advantage when we have 700,000 small pensioners [then nearly the entire population over age 60 in the German Empire] drawing their annuities from the state, especially if they belong to those classes who otherwise do not have much to lose by an upheaval," for example, an upheaval against monarchy or in favor of the Social Democrats or against Bismarck's plans for peace in Europe.[22] The historian A. J. P. Taylor wrote in 1955 that "social security has certainly made the masses less independent everywhere; yet even the most fanatic apostle of independence would hesitate to dismantle the system which Bismarck invented and which all other democratic countries have copied. . . . Three-quarters of a century later even educated men put security before freedom."[23] Though the welfare state has been subject recently to fiscal strain, it is still highly popular in most rich and some poor countries. The Bismarckian Deal seems secure.

The non-Bourgeois Deals leftish and rightish look good in the first act of the drama, thanks to Comrade Lenin and Count Bismarck. But by the third act they look less good. The Conservative prime minster in the United Kingdom from 1957 to 1963, Harold Macmillan, accomplished a Bismarckian trumping of Labour by building a good deal of public housing—which twenty years later another Conservative, Margaret Thatcher, during her flirtation with libertarian and anti-Bismarckian ideas, sold off at bargain prices to the poor who inhabited it.

ANTICONSUMERISM AND PRO-
BOHEMIANISM WERE FRUITS OF THE
ANTIBETTERMENT REACTION

When around 1848 the clerisy first encountered the Great Enrichment, it supposed, quite naturally, that the new riches must have been generated in the old-fashioned way—by present-day stealing or by inheritance from ancient stealing. The unprecedented size of the Great Enrichment was not apparent in the 1830s and 1840s, and did not yet overwhelm the old story of zero-sum. Real wages in Britain or France were rising—but not surging upward, as they did finally in the third quarter of the nineteenth century.

And so it was to be expected that the novelists of the period thought of rich people as clever thieves or obsessed misers or lucky inheritors, or the elicit lovers of the wives of such people. Productivity, win-win, the Great Enrichment, mutual advantage, and the Bourgeois Deal could have nothing to do with it. Thus in Dickens every hero starts poor, ending rich from inheritance, not from buying ideas low and selling them high in the tiresome bourgeois way that in the third act benefits us all. Balzac's bourgeois character in 1835, Père Goriot, sells a product bound to evoke superior smiles in his readers, vermicelli (a kind of spaghetti, but funnier-sounding in Italian and French, since *verme* and *ver* are the words for "worm"), and is idiotically devoted to his perfidious daughters. Balzac himself, like Mark Twain later, was a failed businessman who scorned businessmen. Eugène de Rastignac, the ambitious lad from the South of France (as Balzac's father was), is corrupted in the series of novels in which he appears by the high-fashion game of adultery in Paris under the Restoration and the July Monarchy. It's how an ambitious but poor lad gets ahead in a zero-sum economy assumed by left and right in 1835.

The historian Peter Gay, in the fifth volume of his astonishing portrait of the sexual and cultural history of the European bourgeoisie, noted that from 1800 onward:

> Artists in all genres increasingly made society itself the target of their scorn. . . . Did not the nineteenth-century bourgeoisie love money and hate art? Was it not so different from the old honorable, public-spirited patriciate as to be in effect a new class? . . . Hence creative spirits felt duty-bound to detest the bourgeoisie and to adopt an aggressive stance that gave them pleasure as they mobilized to rescue the sacred cause of honest art, honest music, and honest literature. . . . This is the modernist myth that has continued to shape our perception of the Victorian middle classes' attitude toward the higher things.[1]

What is more dangerous than such early myths from the clerisy is their persistence and elaboration long after 1848. Early on, for example, the clerisy began to declare that ordinary people are misled in trading, and so require expert protection and supervision—a feeling characteristically "modernist," as Gay puts in his personal vocabulary. The feeling persisted, as one among a string of worry beads about "market failures" handled obsessively by left and right since 1848. None of the worrisome possibilities has been shown to have much oomph by comparison with the Great Enrichment out of liberty and dignity.

Look at the theory of "consumerism." Émile Zola and numerous other novelists expressed eloquent alarm at consumerism before the letter. Later analyses of consumerism became less and less sympathetic with what the lady or the gentleman wants, and more apocalyptic. The American clerisy in particular has long thought that "capitalist" spending is just awful. In 1985 the historian Daniel Horowitz argued that the clerisy in the United States has been since the 1920s in the grip of a "modern moralism" about spending. The traditional moralism of the nineteenth century looked down with alarm from the middle class onto the workers and immigrants drinking beer and obeying Irish priests and in other ways showing their loss of virtue. But traditional moralists such as the U.S. Commissioner of Labor, Carroll D. Wright, "had no basic reservations," Horowitz writes, "about the justice and efficacy of the economic system—their questions had to do with the values of workers and immigrants, not the value of capitalism."[2]

By contrast, the modern moralist in the age of socialism after 1917, in the style of Thorstein Veblen and Sinclair Lewis, looks down from the clerisy onto the *middle* class. Therefore, Horowitz observes, "At the heart of most versions of modern moralism is a critique, sometimes radical and always adversarial, of the economy," which the middle class specializes in running. Horowitz is polite to his fellow members of the American clerisy—Veblen, Lewis, Booth Tarkington, Stuart Chase, the Lynds, Galbraith, Riesman, Marcuse, Lasch, Bell, Chomsky, Berry, Schor—and does not say outright that their critique is simply mistaken. He does observe, however, that "denouncing other people for their profligacy and lack of Culture is a way of reaffirming one's own commitment."[3] That seems about right.

Such antibourgeois, antimarket, antidemocratic, antiprogress theories haunt us still, for example in the image of the bohemian Artist or the pure-minded Philosopher. Giacomo Puccini's opera *La Bohème* was a piece of so-called realism in music, *verismo*, poised against the mythic themes of Verdi and Wagner. But it was a "true-ism" that romanticized—compare *Les Misérables* (1862). Premiered at Turin in 1896 under a young Arturo Toscanini to great acclaim, and in the coming months produced worldwide from Buenos Aires to Los Angeles, it was based on Henri Murger's serialized novel five decades earlier (*Scenes de la Vie de Bohème*, 1846–1848), which was rewritten (with a coauthor) in 1849 as a successful stage play (*La Vie de Bohème*), published as a book in 1851. The setting is the life of Left Bank artists (for instance, Murger himself in his youth) in the 1830s. The opera, then, is a reprise of the bohemian myth late in its history. It is Romanticism in realistic drag, as are *Tosca* (1900) and *Madame Butterfly* (1904) and a good deal of modern art from the Ash Can School to *Bonnie and Clyde*.

In the 1920s, as reported by Archy the poet reincarnated as a literary cockroach (he types by throwing himself headlong down on the keys, but weighs too little to use the shift key), Mehitabel the alley cat declares:

i am living on
condensed milk and
synthetic gin hoopla
for the vie de boheme
exclamation point

there s nothing bourgeois
about those people
that have taken
me in archy i
have been there
a week and have
not yet seen them
go to bed
except in the daytime[4]

The word "bohemian" derives from the French word for Roma, who drifted in mysteriously from Eastern Europe—Bohemia, say. By the nineteenth century it had in French and English its modern meaning of a ragtag social rebel, a hippy as we later came to say. The bohemian ideal, according to Puccini's librettists Luigi Illica and Giuseppe Giacosa, with whom he also wrote *Tosca* and *Butterfly*, is to live poorly but like a prince—that is, idly, not producing anything the world is actually willing to pay for, merely collecting rents, or at least scraps from the tables of those who do collect rents or who work for a living. What makes you worthwhile is not what you do for others but what you do in shaping yourself—as an artist or a duke, and nothing like a vulgar bourgeois maker of goods and services for the benefit of others. Recall Wilde: "An individual who has to make things for the use of others . . . cannot put into his work what is best in him." The theory is the aristocratic and Romantic one of the modern artist, as in the notorious program some decades ago of the Dutch welfare state buying warehousefuls of unsellable paintings made by self-proclaimed artists.

The four youthful bohemians in the opera are a playwright/poet (tenor: flightiness *con brio*), a musician (baritone), a painter (baritone), and a philosopher (basso profundo). In the pointedly comic setup to the last act, before Mimi in her final illness arrives, the bohemian boys honor the aristocratic conventions by sending them up in turn: the fancy meal ("yesterday's dinner" of cheap bread with a little herring), the imagined call to the king's side (*Il Re mi chiama al minster*, spoofed in some productions as Colline rising to relieve himself into a chamber pot), the formal dances of the court (Rodolfo takes Marcello for his lady in the quadrille), and that emblem of aristocracy from the time of its first self-doubts, which by 1896 was still seriously practiced mainly in Slavic lands, the duel:

SCHAUNARD. What manners of a lackey!

COLLINE [seizing the stove tongs, as a sword]. If you do not admit the outrage to me, unsheathe your steel!

SCHAUNARD [seizing Marcello's palette, as a shield]. All right: a challenge [putting himself in position for dueling]. It's your blood I wish to drink!

COLLINE. One of us will be disemboweled.

SCHAUNARD. Prepare a stretcher.

COLLINE. Prepare a graveyard.[5]

Rodolfo and Marcello meanwhile dance together merrily, singing, "While the combat proceeds / Spin and bounce the peasant dance." Enter Musetta with reality in tow.

Most audiences take all this as Just Fun. But read as drama, it fails. For all the lovely music and the attempts at witticisms, the bohemian life is exhibited as having no ethical core, at any rate no adult one. It's a child's life, Peter Pan and the lost boys translated to adult standards of drinking and whoring. It's Rip Van Winkle's passing over the adult responsibilities of keeping a farm and children and above all a wife, the Romantic dream of lighting out for the territories and being boys together always, the dream of the buddy movie, the road movie, the marriageless males *sur la route*. Thus René Clair's film *À Nous la Liberté* (1931) or the parody of *La Bohème* by the Three Stooges, *Wee, Wee, Monsieur* (1937).

None of the young bohemians in *La Bohème* works at a job, or even at his declared art except fitfully and unsuccessfully. This from a youngish musician already commercially successful, who had just beaten a rival in the quick and businesslike construction of an opera out of a novel. (When Murger himself wrote the novel, by the way, he had already turned to bourgeois respectability and away from the boyish life of penniless high jinks.) As Isaiah Berlin observed, "Work in Romanticism is sacred as such, not because of its social function, but because it is the imposition of the individual or collective personality, that is, activity, upon inert stuff."[6] The work is Art— identity, not mere bourgeois service to others.

The two bourgeois figures in the opera, Benoit the landlord and Alcindoro, a rich councilor of state, exist to be cheated. Any artist, an ostentatious beggar, is permitted to get free lodging and free food by cheating those who work for a living. How droll! Working for what ordinary people are willing to pay you is a sucker's game. Rodolfo and his boyish friends live like the Dharma Bums, cutting up chairs for fuel and selling coats to pawn-brokers, or sharing handouts and windfalls. Rodolfo says merrily in act 2, "I have a millionaire uncle: If he goes to the good Lord / I want to buy [you, Mimi,] a much more beautiful necklace."[7] In the same act the incongruous figure of Parpignol—the librettists' version of profundity, one fears—sells toys to the children on one side of the stage while on the other the restaurant sells delicacies to the young deadbeat hippies, their bourgeois victim in tow. The mothers in the end will buy the toys. And the victim of the bohemians' prank will be left with the bill for the food. A little boy whimpers loudly, "Want the trumpet, the horsie!" At which Rodolfo asks: "And you, Mimi, what do *you* want?" Mimi: "The pudding."[8] Free toys; free pudding. That's what life's about, eh, guys? Hey, where's the Miller Lite? Let's rock. The plot of *La Bohème* is life as a fraternity party.

Which is how to rescue the ethical standing of the tale. If Rodolfo and Marcello and their pals and girlfriends are thought of as being about twenty years old, the frat-party plot makes sense, and we indulge it, in honor of our own misspent youths.[9] The nineteenth century's Most Famous Bohemian (and second-best French poet) was Arthur Rimbaud, who spent his late adolescence (1870–1873) imitating the by-then fictional role of dissolute bohemian—engaging, though, in nonfictional drinking of absinthe, smoking of opium, and fist fighting with Verlaine down and out in Paris and London, and writing poetry, such as, around his sixteenth birthday, precisely a poem named "Ma Bohème": "I went off with my hands in my torn pockets / . . . I traveled beneath the sky, Muse! And I was your vassal."[10] *C'est charmant*, as long as we see the poem as that of a sixteen-year-old. A poet vaporizing about huge cloudy symbols of a high romance into his seventh decade would not get our sympathy. We indulge a twenty-two-year-old Keats, especially as we know he will die in a few years. In the opera the problem is that a thirty-five-year-old singer cast as Rodolfo and behaving like a twenty-year-old is hard to sympathize with. It's the problem in opera of casting for voice and casting for appearance. A twenty-year-old tenor can't fill the hall at the Lyric Opera, either with his voice or with eager fans.

Characteristically, Puccini's bohemians sneer at exchange or payment as a basis for living. In the uproar of vendors in act 2, the bohemian boy-bass philosopher Colline intones *Odio il profano volgo*, "I hate the vulgar crowd," which an audience of educated if bustling and bourgeois Piedmontese men in 1896 would have instantly recognized as a reference to Horace's ode against commerce: *Odi profanum vulgus*—and if they were a trifle vague about their Horace, Colline helpfully provides the citation (*al par d'Orazio*).[11] In act 3 Rodolfo is about to abandon dying Mimi because . . . well, she's dying, which leaves the fraternity boy very, very frightened (*Ma ho paura, / Ma ho paura*: "But I fear, but I fear").[12] The parallel episode in the original novel is treated as a criticism of the boys. Not in the opera. Rodolfo explains lamely, "My room is a squalid den," bad for her health. So it's, See you around, Mimi— we're off to play a con game on an innkeeper. Love alone will not revive her: *Non basta amor, non basta amor.*

This sort of "love," achieved from first introductions to rapturous *Te amos* in a few minutes of stage time in act 1, doesn't cure tuberculosis. What does not enter Rodolpho's boyish head is that getting a job—doing something for others in exchange for money that the others earned by doing something else for other others—would make possible a warm hearth, and medicine, for his "beloved." Men have been doing such jobs since Adam's Curse. And boys have been avoiding them just as long. Right to the end, the opera presents Rodolfo as ethically empty and boyishly fun-loving. Mimi on her deathbed gently extracts a partial confession that Rodolfo played a little trick on her in the first act by hiding the room key. But as usual she's the one who does the ethical work. Even as she dies, he cannot bring himself to treat her as an adult would. In his world of fantasy he's a little boy (as Mimi puts it, *mio bel signorino*, "my handsome little gentleman"). Her last request, for a muff to warm her hands, is fulfilled not by the bohemian lover Rodolfo but by the other sensible woman in the opera, Musetta, who has already pawned her earrings to get a doctor. It is she, not Rodolfo, who had gone out to locate and retrieve Mimi dying on the street. Mimi is allowed to credit Rodolfo for the gift, mistakenly ("You! Spendthrift! Thank you. But it was costly").[13] In the bohemian myth since 1848 it is manly responsibility that is shirked. The women do what work is to be done. The guys sit around talking about the latest bullfight and smoking. Every once in a while they dash off a still-life painting or write a free-verse poem or a short story about fishing.

La Bohème has been wildly popular among bourgeois operagoers ever since. That's the point: the libretto encapsulates a bourgeois line against the bourgeoisie that has been popular since 1848. The popularity of *La Bohème* drove the music critic of an earlier generation, Joseph Kerman (1924–2014), to distraction. He regarded Puccini (*Tosca*, *La Bohème*, *Madame Butterfly*, and his masterwork *Turandot*) and his contemporary Richard Strauss (*Der*

Rosenkavalier, and his masterwork, *Salome*) as disastrous cheapeners of the traditions of Verdi and Wagner, as having "a firm common ground of insensitivity . . . false through and through, . . . undramatic [the worst slur in a Kermanian vocabulary], for their imaginative realm is a realm of emotional cant." In 1952 he predicted "that works like *Turandot* and *Salome* will fade from the operatic scene," leaving Verdi and Wagner unsullied by their midget followers.[14]

By now, looking down from his operatic Valhalla, Kerman must be vexed beyond endurance. Puccini and Strauss, with their ethically false stories, prosper. The spectacle still brings row upon row of Chicago's haute bourgeoisie, buying out the Lyric's productions of *La Bohème* every night, attired as befits their rank. "I'm sorry, ma'am," the coat-check woman says, "we can't take mink coats." The bourgeois and bourgeoises clap ecstatically at the tenor's high C in *Che gelida manina*. And they pass over the lyrics and their antibourgeois ethics without tiresome censoriousness. "Who am I, who am I?" is answered with "I am a poet. What do I do? / Write. And how do I live? / I live."[15] If the sons of the bankers and bureaucrats in attendance made such declarations they would be hustled off to a psychiatric examination, or to law school. Rimbaud's mother in fact kept hustling him back home to Charleville to dry out.

The libretto itself does occasionally invite criticism of *la vie bohème* (again, more so the novel). But the opera audiences are not encouraged to take up the invitation. Puccini and his librettists could have frankly celebrated the bohemians, forcing the bourgeoisie in the stalls to think again about their boring choice of a life of doing good by doing well. Throw it over and move to Tahiti, you cowards. Or they could have frankly attacked the artistic/literary layabouts, congratulating the bourgeois choice of adulthood and commerce. Thus Rimbaud before his twenty-first birthday abruptly abandoned the life of art and became, startlingly, a supervisor of building projects, a trader in hides, coffee, and musk, an arms dealer, and a slave trader, albeit in exotic locations in the Middle East and Africa rather than back in bourgeois Charleville. He was not, it seems, much of a businessman. But that was the occupation on his calling card until his death at age thirty-seven, and he was not ashamed of it.

Puccini's libretto wanders between. The film *Moulin Rouge* (2001) has the same plot as *La Bohème* and the same ethical confusion. The hero is a layabout with pretensions to literary art, the heroine a whore. Mimi in the opera is not that kind of working girl, but anyway she is gainfully employed. The bourgeois businessman in *Moulin Rouge* is at one time threatening, the next endearing. Even Jim Broadbent, the best actor in sight, can't entirely pull it off. The ethical vacuity is what Kerman meant when he skewered a scene in Strauss as having "all the solidity of a fifty-cent valentine"; or on the libretto of *Tosca*, Puccini's "shabby little shocker": "If Joyce Kilmer [of 'Poems are made by fools like me. / But only God can make a tree'] or Alfred Noyes ['The highwayman came riding, riding up to the old inn door'] had taken it into his head to do a grand poetic drama on Tosca, that would have been something analogous in the medium of language."

When Kerman said Puccini is "undramatic" he meant that his work has no ethical content and therefore no ability to engage people in their real lives—at any rate to engage people with day jobs and some seriousness about life. As Roger Ebert and Gene Siskel used to put it, we don't care for Rodolfo and so can't enter into the plot of *La Bohème*. (The music is another matter.) We do care for Mimi. Like Madame Butterfly she works for a living and is merely the victim of the cowardly boys. Similarly the heroine/prostitute in *Moulin Rouge* has at least the integrity of skill in the courtesan's trade. The male writer/hero in *Moulin Rouge*, by contrast, is, natch, a man of leisure, because blocked, unpublished, with no ideas. So much for bourgeois deadlines and a professional attitude toward writing.

Kerman said of Puccini that his dramas are "depraved." Full marks for making such an ethical criticism in 1952, at the height of an Oscar Wilde–esque belief that "there is no such thing as a moral or an immoral book. Books are well written, or badly written. That is all." The English poet and critic Matthew Arnold, by contrast, had declared in 1880 that "in poetry [of Arnold's lofty sort, that is, No Jokes] . . . the spirit of our race will find . . . as time goes by and as other helps [namely, the sea of Faith] fail, its consolation and stay."[16] The ethical problem with the *La Bohème* story, retold in *Moulin Rouge* or *The Dharma Bums* or numerous other fruits of late bourgeois culture, is not the naughtiness, which is mild, but its lack of ethical point beyond the greeting card. *The Story of O* (1964) is horribly pornographic but anti-ethically pointed, and therefore chillingly dramatic. It stays with the reader, as the music of Musetta's waltz stays with the listener. But nothing in the story of the opera matters, or stays.

Most observers of grand opera will reply to Kerman and his eager student McCloskey, "Small wonder: you don't actually expect *drama*, do you?

The singing of the music is miracle enough, yes?" Bourgeois audiences since 1896 have been uncritically yet unengagedly charmed, as they would *not* be if an actual Rodolfo presented himself for employment (unlikely prospect) in their candy factory or accounting firm.

Around 10:00 p.m. they gather up their fur coats and opera glasses, after lengthy applause, well satisfied. They have watched at play the boys who refuse a bourgeois life, and nothing in the opera touches them for longer than the holding of that high C.[17]

65

DESPITE THE CLERISY'S DOUBTS

Neither the traditionalist right nor the progressive left are happy with the modern world. They look with a jaundiced eye on the Great Enrichment. They doubt that people's lives are actually much better than in olden days, especially in the second, spiritual sense of the word "enrichment." The right wing, for example, regrets that people are no longer as connected as they were in traditional villages (a regret that the traditional villagers, who now live in Shanghai, Johannesburg, and Los Angeles, do not share).

Some of the left's and the right's doubts originate in nostalgia (Greek: "homecoming-ache"). Not that there is nothing in the past we might regret losing and ache to come home to. After all, "gales of creative destruction" (to use the vivid if alarming phrase describing trade-tested betterment that Schumpeter popularized from a 1913 book by Sombart) involves destruction. Modern wireless telephones, for example, are irritating to us oldsters. We keep turning them off accidentally by bumping some mysterious switch with our ears, and we indulge therefore in nostalgia for the now-destroyed, heavy 1940s phones, with a proper dial. Yet modern telephones and telephoning are radically cheaper than in 1940 or even 1990, as can be seen in the way poor countries, by leaping to cell phones, have been able to skip an infrastructure of copper cables. When the horseless carriage on modern roads paved with asphalt or concrete took over, we lost the satisfactions of having a real horse, a breathing, sweating fellow mammal that humans could love. Yet the now-destroyed horse entailed greater expense per mile and greater pollution of cities than an automobile. (Still, some humans, especially male ones, seem to love their horseless carriages in Top Gear as much as their great-great grandfathers loved their horses.) The upstate New York wilderness portrayed in the nineteenth century by the Hudson River School of painters is now wrecked by summer homes and McDonald's, and criss-crossed by interstate highways. Yet such vulgar modernities do give more city dwellers access to the countryside than they once had. ("How do you get to the Catskills?" "Stop practicing.")

Many find it alarming that the cities themselves are now enormously larger and more numerous. Yet the cities use radically less carbon fuel per person than suburban or rural housing, and the alarmed clerisy are often themselves perched in high-rise buildings downtown. In 2008 for the first time more than 50 percent of humans lived in urban areas, in the startling nineteen cities with populations over ten million and the fully four hundred cities over one million and on down.[1] We can look with nostalgia back on the rose-covered cottages and Maypole dancing of the countryside, but people vote with their feet worldwide in favor of cities. Villages sound swell until you live in one and find that everyone knows your business and often enough wants to interfere with it. At $3 a day and less the villages are intolerable. The left's old claim that people are pushed from the countryside into the cities has been shown repeatedly by economic historians to be a myth.[2] The people are not pushed but pulled: as recorded by Nora Bayes (1919), Eddie Cantor (1923), et al., "How you gonna keep 'em down on the farm / After they've seen Paree?" The scientific grounds for the clerisy's nostalgia, that is, can be doubted, item by item. The old Kentucky home we ache for was miserable, unless you were the slave *owner*.

And if the creative destruction producing its irritating novelties is tested commercially we can at least be assured that on balance the mass of the people prefer it, in their vulgar, massy ways. One suspects that the conservatives of left and right don't much like the "mass" and its badly informed preferences. Let us take care of you, they cry. Let tradition celebrated by wise elders, or planning implemented by wise experts, guide you, oh you sadly misled mass. And offstage the ancient lords and the cosy monopolists look on such conservative theorizing by the clerisy with delight, assured by it that their rents will be preserved.

Or the clerisy calls on us to "protect producers' jobs," disregarding the dollar votes of the much more numerous consumers. Such job protectionism is one of the numerous mistaken themes in the hatred of Walmart by the left. The historian Geoffrey Blainey speaks of the coming of the railway to towns in the Australian bush in the nineteenth century: "The owners of the town's little breweries—with three employees—suddenly realized that barrels of beer arriving cheaply on the new railway from a big city brewery outsold the local barrels and might soon shut them down." The two-thirds rule of economies of scale in mass beer and bread processing more or less assured such an outcome. Likewise "the drivers and owners of the bullock carts and horse-drawn mail coaches often cursed the railways." Yet "for every citizen who cursed ten cheered."[3] That's the point: creative destruction is good for the society as a whole, viewed democratically.

Sympathetically considered, the right and left unhappiness with the rich modern world can be viewed, too, as an understandable present-mindedness. A focus on our present woes is accompanied by a vague nostalgia about the past. It's like standing too close to a pointillist painting, such as Georges Seurat's *A Sunday Afternoon on the Island of La Grande Jatte* in its room at the Art Institute. At close range we see the dots as dots only and lament the disorder. We ache for the real telephones and beloved horses in our homeland. If we stand back, however, the disorder resolves into an attractive scene, with many, many humans now having lives of wide scope. The ongoing history, so lamentably destructive of the dots of remembered hours of gladness, lost, alas, like a youth too soon, reveals its attractions when seen in longer perspective. The attractions are masses of people much better off now than two centuries ago, and a massy democracy. The global Northerners on the left who view the Great Recession as the last crisis of capitalism (if, to repeat, one forgets all the previous diagnoses of a last crisis) or who decry the allegedly slow growth of real wages in the rich countries since 1980 (if, to repeat, one does the economic science erroneously, ignoring, for example, the sharply improving quality of goods), and who therefore advocate more and more and more regulation of markets, are standing too close to the picture.

Yet—and now I will irritate my right-wing friends—in places like Sweden or the United States the too-close perspective of the global Northerners, and the mistaken policies it leads to, is no big concern. Inefficiency is not the main problem. Failure to allow the zooming out of marginal product curves in trade-tested betterment is. If you are rich already, go ahead and stand as close to the painting as you wish. I will not worry overmuch about you. Post–Great Enrichment countries can be pretty careless with exact economic effiency, because they will nonetheless remain pretty rich, and will adopt most of the better betterments, almost no matter how badly they arrange their affairs. Look at Italy's inefficiencies as against New Zealand's honesty, and note their very similar incomes per head.

That is, a clumsily designed social safety net, or rich-kid-enriching free higher education, or further regulation of overregulated industries such as food or banking or housing, or any of the socialism-lite measures so popular in essentially capitalist countries such as Sweden or the United States, are not greatly impoverishing. The extreme case was central planning and complete state ownership, which *did* greatly diminish communist incomes. Yet even Polish income down to 1989 did not actually fall. Poles had (wretched) automobiles and (one-channel) TVs, thanks to spillovers of trade-tested betterment from "capitalist" countries. I have already shown that the exact efficiency achieved by equalizing marginal product to marginal opportunity cost is not the formula for the Great Enrichment. Warmly welcoming trade-tested betterments is, and causes the marginal product curves to zoom out by factor of ten or thirty or one hundred.

The Norwegians passed in 1917 a "braking law" that expressed in plain form the conservative-left-and-right worry about "capitalism" that social democrats and political reactionaries had then and still have: "Every head-long development is dangerous. . . . The many new factory centers need to have time to settle down peacefully and learn to lead and develop their private conduct and the conduct of the local communities."[4] Such a law *can* stop the zooming out. It would have been impossible in 1917 in the wild United States. Yet by now environmental objections to development such as the Keystone XL Pipeline have created braking laws even in the second home of *laissez faire*. The left and right join in opposing the future—the one because it is not a planned future and the other because it is not identical to the past.

In 2013, for example, some companies in the United States had taken brilliantly bettering advantage of smart phones. The Uber X company offered rides in ordinary cars to smart-phone users (as did Lyft and SideCar). The Square company offered merchants a means of processing credit cards on their phones. Airbnb offered New Yorkers access to private homes as hotels. And Aereo allowed mobile devices to pick up local TV signals. Yet all four were prompty attacked by American regulators, those heroes of the progressive and conservative enemies of progress. Unsurprisingly, the regulators,

well paid with your tax dollars, and many of them proud to be protecting
consumers, were concerned that the electronic revolution would disturb
the profits of conventional taxis, of banks with credit cards, of hotels, and
of copyright holders of TV programs.[5] The regulators did not ask whether
creative destruction was better for the mass of people, or whether as regulators they were, sometimes unintentionally, carrying water for monopolies of
taxis, credit cards, hotels, and TV stations.

The point is that nonetheless, and despite the shrill warning of a Road
to Serfdom from the right, Norway and the United States let the zooming
pretty much happen, and are as a result now among the highest-income
countries in the world, and are pretty happy about it. The per-person incomes of high-income countries cluster at historically bizarre levels—the
Washing Line or even the Drying Line. They do so despite the great variation in how well or how badly the countries arrange their governmental affairs. The incremental gains to merely more efficient arrangements are not
proportionate. The quantitative fact is another piece of evidence for the
argument in *Bourgeois Dignity* that the Great Enrichment was about ideas
and betterment, dignity and liberty, not about the economist's beloved exact
equilibrium of supply and demand—which, for example, "good institutions"
are supposed to deliver.

As the economist Salim Rashid puts it:

> To speak of maintaining law and order among a free people through the use of re-
> wards and punishments is facile. Bishop Warburton pointed out long ago that one
> simply could not raise a fund large enough to reward all citizens every time they
> spoke the truth; by the same token, if the police force is of a size small enough to
> be maintained by voluntary taxation, then there will be significant probability of
> escaping detection, and every "rational" individual, . . . will turn criminal every
> so often.[6]

But on the whole they don't. He quotes Hume: "'Tis certain, that self-love,
when it acts at its liberty, instead of engaging us to honest actions, is the
source of all injustice and violence; nor can a man ever correct those vices,
without correcting and restraining the *natural* movements of that appetite."[7]
We need moral sentiments, arising from the instinctive sympathy denied
to sociopaths and Max U. Rashid notes that Hayek "is so convinced that a
maximizing calculus would not preserve the system of private property that

he has gone so far as to assert that modern civilization 'is wholly the result of the religions teaching a moral of property, honesty and the family.'"[8] Ethics, not institutions, changed.

Swedish, Dutch, and some American people of good will reach for their socialism when they hear the words "pollution" or "corporation" or even "market." About the hardihood of the regulatory reflex Milton Friedman complained in 1989:

> Major premise: Socialism is a failure. Even lifelong Communists now accept this proposition. . . . Minor premise: Capitalism is a success. Economies that have used capitalism—free private markets—as their principal means of organizing economic activity have proved capable of combining widely shared prosperity and a high measure of human freedom. . . . Conclusion: The U.S. needs more socialism.[9]

Startlingly, the American left-wing economist Robert Heilbroner (1919–2005), in his old age, came to agree in part with Friedman. Heilbroner wrote in that same 1989 year of turning points that "less than 75 years after it officially began, the contest between capitalism and socialism is over: capitalism has won. . . . Capitalism organizes the material affairs of humankind more satisfactorily than socialism."[10] He was not enthusiastic about such an outcome, and his praise for "capitalism" was heavily ironic. Yet there it is: more stuff.

Getting from $1 or $3 a day to the Washing Line, and especially to the Drying Line, does require a commitment to liberal values. Rigorously applied neo-mercantilism or neocameralism or neopopulism or neo-antibourgeoisism or any of the other illiberal alternatives kills betterment. Such political ideas are notably inferior in outcome to neoliberalism and the Bourgeois Deal. And scientifically speaking the Deal captures better than any other account what actually happened 1800 to the present.

The left has long believed the contrary. Bakunin wrote in 1869, "As soon as [the bourgeois] had conquered the source of power," in 1830 in France, for example,

> they began to understand that their bourgeois interests had nothing in common with the interests of the masses, that, on the contrary, the two were radically opposed, and that the power and exclusive prosperity of the possessing class

had to be supported by the misery and social and political dependence of the proletariat.[11]

The outcome of the conquest of power by the bourgeoisie was in fact the opposite of what Bakunin expected. The Bourgeois Deal resulted in the end of the misery and of the social and political dependence of the proletariat. Great numbers of us became bourgeois, and even those who didn't came to earn in real terms ten or hundred times more. The interests of the bourgeoisie and the masses were, in the third act, the same. When the late nineteenth-century American labor leader Samuel Gompers was asked what his philosophy was, he replied not "planning" or "regulation" or "socialism," or "equality," but the bourgeois promise: "more."

Killing betterment, "more," with idiotically high tariffs and horribly corrupt regulation and nitwitted central planning or envy-driven taxation does indeed impoverish a country, blocking the alleviation of misery and social dependence. But what makes bad institutions bad are not the formal rules but their ethical or unethical implementations, the spirit, *die Geist*. If central planners were all incorruptible geniuses of good will, even central planning might work pretty well—in a household, I say once more, it often does, which is the instinctive basis of its appeal. And a company is a site of planning, as though a lump of conscious control, as the economist Dennis Robertson once put it, floating in a buttermilk of unplanned markets. If regulations and braking laws, even though onerous, were enforced with justice and temperance alloyed with love, the loss to average income would not be great.

It's a matter of diminishing returns to ethical behavior. At low levels of ethical behavior, as in Malawi now or in the USSR once, the loss of income from the evil is large. But at high levels of ethical behavior, such as in Minnesota now, the marginal gain from additional ethical behavior is small. The Italian case shows, indeed, that the level of unethical behavior and corruption has to be quite high to do significant damage to forces of entry and exit and betterment in the private sector, if the private sector is large enough. Italy, as I said, and as the Italians say, is rich *despite* its government. An Italian commentator remarked that his country was like the *Costa Concordia*, run aground in 2012 by Captain Francesco Schettino, a beautiful ship with an irresponsible idiot in charge.

In India before 1991 under the License Raj the level of imprudence, intemperance, and injustice was so high that the country was kept impoverished, at \$1 or \$2 a day, as against Italy's \$80 a day. The Indian owner of a factory who wanted to move a machine *inside* his factory had to get planning permission, and pay a bribe to the planner. A city-planning friend of mine in Chicago notes that even in the United States such a move might require permission from the city, on account of the building code. So much the worse for building codes, dictated by plumbers and electricians as schemes of job protection, making it impossible, I have noted, to build cheap housing for the poor. But the problem in India under the License Raj or Chicago under the old city machine was that the officials who gave permission extracted bribes.

Or look again at Venezuela, which in 2013, after many years of unrelenting idiocracy under Chavez-Maduro populism, such as gasoline supplied by the state at half a U.S. cent per gallon, required emergency food supplies from Colombia, which has recently come out of its own economic idiocracy. In 2014 Venezuela was still subsidizing hundreds of agricultural communes, given out to reliably left-party voters whether or not they knew anything about agriculture. A similar agricultural policy, with similarly impoverishing results, was pursued by Mugabe in Zimbabwe.

In the twentieth century the global South's clerisy, as in India and Venezuela and Zimbabwe, borrowed the too-close, nostalgic perspective on modern economic growth from its sibling-clerisy of the global North, ranging from Rousseau through Marx and Bakunin down to Harold Laski and David Harvey, and came to think, like them, that the Problem was markets and profit and property and trade-tested betterment (economic secret: they are the Solution). The excellent communist poet Pablo Neruda in Chile did so, as did the not so excellent founder of Arab fascism in its Ba'athist form, the philosopher and sociologist Michel Aflaq.

Such borrowing of socialist or fascist or sweetly regulatory braking laws from the North has been damaging to the really poor of the world, who are mainly in the South. The North's careless post–Great Enrichment social policies, such as subsidizing unprofitable post offices, nationalizing pharmacies, opposing Walmart, enforcing minimum wages, instituting industrial planning, or giving tariff protections for local industry, were taken over by the South's clerisy as fine ideas for initiating socialism in India or decreasing Latin American inequality or improving Arab connectedness. They didn't work as advertised. Meanwhile, when applied rigorously they locked the really poor countries into the miseries of 1800-style incomes. Ghana's enthusiastic embrace of Western socialism under Kwame Nkrumah (1909–1972), the "African Lenin" and a figure still admired by the Western left, drove its income down. Ghana, once one of the richest economies in Africa, became one of the poorest. Now, under more rational government, it's doing a tiny bit better, though still merely 148th out of 185 countries in average real income, above Bangladesh but below India.

Indignantly opposing optimism about the economic and cultural possibilities for our grandchildren have been seven old pessimisms, and now an eighth new one.

The old pessimism of 1848 said that the poor were fated by Malthusian logic to stay poor. The pessimism of 1916 said that only Europeans were genetically capable of getting out of $3-a-day poverty. That of 1933 said that anyway the getting out was finished because the final crisis of capitalism was at hand. That of 1945 said that betterment was finished and stagnation was at hand, with excess savings inevitably dragging income down. That of 1968 said that anyway, when we got out of the (nonfinal) crisis and found that technological stagnation didn't in fact happen, we fell into a consumerism corrupting of our souls.[12] The old pessimism of 1980 said that the consumerism in the core countries, though it had apparently not corrupted or immiserized the proletariat there, depended on an army of exploited people in the Southern periphery. And the not-so-old pessimism of the 1990s—it had been articulated in Britain as early as the 1890s in the face of the "German [Commercial] Invasion"—said that Old Europe and the (dis)United States were doomed to fall down the league table, and Lo, all our pomp of yesterday / Is one with Nineveh and Tyre.

The seven old pessimisms, still dusted off for blog posts and newspaper editorials from both left and right, and built into most alert minds as obvious truths, immune to factual amendment, and justifying if challenged a hot indignation unaccompanied by scientific evidence, have proven mistaken. None of them ever had much evidence for it, 1800 to the present. Their invulnerability to scientific evidence suggests that they arise from a prior, fixed, and emotional conviction that market-tested betterment is significantly imperfect. The only task is to spot the imperfection, and then turn the state loose to repair it.

The pessimisms remain wildly popular, flat-earth versions of economic history. Most people, for example, take Charles Dickens, of all people, as a good historian of the Industrial Revolution (about which dear Charles was ignorantly hostile). They repeat knowingly the cliché that Balzac knew more than any sociologist about French society, though he knew nothing at all about its economy, or about economics. If more sophisticated they seize on *The Communist Manifesto* of 1848, which for all its verve is mostly historical and economic error—though its errors are understandable, considering that it was written so early in the professionalization of scientific history and of scientific economics.

Similarly on the right, gray-beard chatter among historians since the Greeks and Edward Gibbon concerning the rise and fall of empires is taken as the Very Voice of History. Recent versions of the Voice ignore or deny the transformative character of the Great Enrichment, and declare that "like Rome" we (white people) are doomed to decline. Spooky fears about a Numero-Uno China haunt the West (the same way as not long ago spooky fears about a Numero-Uno Japan did. Anti-oriental racism? Surely not.) Yet such movements up and down the league tables do not detract a cent from the Enrichment. They never have. The rich countries like Austria or Australia cluster with the thoroughbreds far ahead of the field, and stay there whether or not they jostle for a literal "lead" of a mere 10 percent above others—to be set beside a Great Enrichment of 2,900 percent or more.

The right wing has worries about national power rankings the way the left wing has worries about individual income rankings. But in uplifting the poor, rank is not the point. Level is. Modern economic growth is not about seventh-pessimism rankings, and was not caused by exceptional national power to do violence. After all, backward Russia in 1812 and 1941–1944 turned back invasions from a technologically advanced and militarily powerful Western Europe, as it had done in the Great Northern War against Sweden in 1709. The Great Enrichment is about an irreversible arrival of the poor at the Washing Line and then the Drying Line, caused by their own efforts made productive by accepting the Bourgeois Deal of letting the bourgeoisie innovate for the long-run good of us all. Not national rank.

The new, eighth pessimism of our own times is that environmental decay is irreversible. It is usually accompanied by a revival of the first, that limited resources make population growth impoverishing. The new/old pair will probably prove mistaken too. In the 1960s and 1970s the environmentalists

assured us that Lake Erie was dead, passed on, bereft of life, metabolic pro-
cesses now history, joined the bleedin' choir invisible, in short an ex-lake.
They said that its polluted decline had become irreversible. Now people
swim in it.

The associated revival of the first, Malthusian pessimism is well illustrated by the strange career of the butterfly biologist Paul Ehrlich (b. 1932).
In 1968 on the first page of *The Population Bomb* he declared, "The battle to
feed all of humanity is over":

> In the 1970s and 1980s hundreds of millions of people will starve to death. . . . At
> this late date [of 1968] nothing can prevent a substantial increase in the world
> death rate. . . . Nothing could be more misleading to our children than our pres-
> ent affluent society. They will inherit a totally different world. . . . We are today
> involved in the events leading to famine and ecocatastrophe.[13]

None of Ehrlich's scientific predictions has proven even approximately correct. India is now a net exporter of grain. The world death rate from the
1960s to the 2000s declined by a third. Birth rates worldwide are falling to
a half or a third of the old levels. In Bangladesh the average number of children per wife, I have noted, has fallen to 2.2, from 6 thirty years ago, and so
worldwide.[14] Many more people than in 1968 live in affluent societies, and
are themselves affluent. World population growth has accompanied sharply
rising per-person income. Inequality has dramatically *fallen* worldwide. Extreme poverty has sharply *declined*. Famines have become rare. And to recur
to the eighth, environmental pessimism, great amounts are now being spent
to avoid ecocatastrophe, with some gratifying successes, if more to do.

Yet nearly half a century after making some of the worst scientific predictions of his generation—outdoing in this respect even the proud physicists missing dark matter and the proud economists missing the Great
Recession—people still heed what Ehrlich says, inviting him, for example,
to NPR's *Science Friday* and hanging on his words. It is a remarkable performance, worth bottling and selling. Ehrlich has been selling over and over
since the 1960s the same erroneous prediction, which all of the eight pessimisms voice: the sky is falling, the sky is falling. Such is our delight in pessimistic tales that we are still listening, thrilled to be In The Know.

You can get a sample of the tenacity of even the oldest, Malthusian pessimism, Ehrlich's favorite, by looking into the anonymous one-star reviews

recently on Amazon.com of books by the optimistic economist and scientific torturer of Ehrlich, Julian Simon (1932–1998). For their hostility toward Simon the authors of the reviews—often it would appear self-confident physical and biological scientists innocent of economics or economic history— depend on Malthus, on noncomputational mathematics, and on indignantly asserted factual error or irrelevancy. For example: "Julian Simon is an idiot: As a biologist, I have to point out that mister Simon's ideas are ridiculous. . . . The simple fact of the matter is that ANY level of growth in a closed system is unsustainable." The emphasis in "ANY level of growth" signals an appeal to mathematics as logic, unfalsifiable but not thereby true as economic or any other sort of science. At its present 7.2 billion people, or its predicted peak of 10 billion, I have noted, the global population is an order of magnitude below the carrying capacity of the earth. And the angry biologist needs to be reminded that life itself is a local exception to the Second Law of Thermodynamics, precisely because it is *not* a closed system. Or again, an angry remark by another apparent scientist: "Thomas Malthus was always logical, just subject to delays for his worst-case scenarios. . . . It's unclear if Simon understood [in 1971 at the first edition of his pathbreaking book *The Ultimate Resource* (executive summary: not oil, but human creativity)] that U.S. oil production had already peaked in 1970."[15] But Malthus's scenarios were not "worst-case." They were supposed to be the average, and they proved after 1798 to be false. True, United States oil production and reserves did seem to peak in 1970. Yet what is the relevance of one part of world production in a unified market? And now in the United States the production of oil, thanks to fracking, is drifting toward its old record. In 2015 U.S. oil production exceeded that of Saudi Arabia. Even setting aside the main American energy source, coal, total energy extracted from oil and gas produced in the United States has long exceeded previous peaks.

Worldwide a "peak oil" has yet to happen, decades after it was confidently predicted by physical and biological scientists contemptuous of economic science. World crude-oil production has increased since 1970 by over 40 percent. The paleontologist Niles Eldridge, for example, as late as 1995 quoted with approval a geologist at Columbia who had predicted in the 1960s on the basis of "simple measures of the volumes of the great sedimentary basins" that the world would run out of recoverable petroleum in the mid-1990s.[16] Ah, yes, simple measures. In fact after the 1960s worldwide the "proven oil reserves" grew—a miracle unless you realize that "proving" is itself an economic activity. And the price of oil corrected for general inflation did not rise. Yet Eldridge in 1995 failed to draw the appropriate lesson in economics from his errors, or from Ehrlich's or the Club of Rome's similar errors, which Eldridge also quoted with approval.

Pessimism on the basis of the most alarming of today's trends is jolly good fun, I know. But since 1800 it has been a poor predictor.

66

WHAT MATTERS ETHICALLY IS NOT
EQUALITY OF OUTCOME, BUT THE
CONDITION OF THE WORKING CLASS

The left progressives and the right conservatives protest. "But in those dear, dead olden days we were equal." No, we were not, not since the invention of farming, after which the stationary bandits called priests and aristocrats took command. The literature of hunter-gatherers, with its Coyote tales and surreal adventures of ordinary aboriginals, is egalitarian, at least when set beside the agriculturists' aristocratic gods apparently intent on torturing humans. Maybe the agriculturalist-theologians were saying something about their landlords. And the equality we ordinary peasants had was one of utter, terrified misery, walking through a pond with water up to our chins. It was an equality of the two St. Elizabeth's Day Floods in the Netherlands, of 1404 and 1421, in which whole villages disappeared overnight under the avenging sea, or of the Bengal Famine of 1943, in which a million and a half equal souls died.

"But we were happy." Well. It was a "happiness" of constant terror, of disease at all ages, of dead children, of violent hierarchy, of women enslaved and silenced, of 5-percent literacy. And anyway the main purpose of a human life is not happiness of a catlike sort, relishing a fish dinner on a sunny windowsill in late June, nice though such pleasures are from time to time.[1] Nor is its main purpose the happiness of a collective sort in the *festa* or *tamasha* of a traditional day of celebration, or in the Super Bowl, or in the Nuremburg Rallies, nice (or nasty) though they are to attend from time to time. The point is that $3 a day affords no scope for the exercise of vital powers along lines of excellence, a flourishing human life. The exercise of vital powers includes opening a shop for clothing as much as opening a book of literary fiction. It is an erroneous prejudice of the clerisy that only nonmarket and especially nonprofit activities are truly creative. Most people cannot write Frost's poems or assemble Chagall's stained glass, but to repeat the Tomasi point, in the economy the freedom to exercise vital powers is open to a much wider range of folk.[2] The liberal Isaiah Berlin defined his admired "negative freedom" as "the number of paths down which a man can walk, whether or not he chooses to do so."[3] Mark Twain noted, to be sure, that a man who won't read, or open a shop, has no advantage over a man who can't. But at least the literate and liberated one has an alternative path available if he ever wakes up enough to take it. At $3 in a traditional or totalitarian society the number of paths are two only, conformity or brigandage.

The left believes that it matters greatly that inequality has, it claims, increased recently. It believes that over the long run the poor of the world have been getting poorer. It is mistaken on both counts. (About the same alleged facts the right is sometimes distressingly gleeful: "I've got mine." But such a reaction is also mistaken, both factually and ethically.)

True, the rich have got richer. But so have the poor, and it matters more to them. Millionaires, not to speak of billionaires, have limits on how much they can use their immense wealth for anything. Mainly, the wealth sits there, like pleasure yachts at the marina. And the income earned from the financial, physical, and human capital of the rich cannot yield greatly unequal *consumption*—of, say, trousers, which after all have to be put on one leg at a time, or tutoring in French, which for that hour at least precludes coaching in cricket. Therefore economic growth, however unequally it is accumulated as wealth or earned as income, is radically more egalitarian in its consumption.

By now in rich countries, and increasingly in poor countries, equality in consumption has been achieved. As the American economist John Bates Clark predicted in 1901, "The typical laborer will increase his wages from one dollar a day to two, from two to four and from four to eight [which has been accurate in real terms of per-person income down to the present, though not allowing for radically improved quality of goods and services]. Such gains will mean infinitely more to him than any possible increase of capital can mean to the rich. . . . This very change will bring with it a continual approach to equality of genuine comfort."[4] "Equality of genuine comfort" happened, for example in the United States, and kept happening, and now worldwide in fact and in prospect. Donald Boudreaux lists the items that in 1965 only the few Americans like Howard Hughes (his representative for the billionaires of those days) could have that by now every middle-class American has—overnight package delivery, cars doors automatically opened, long international telephone calls, large-screen viewing facilities in the home, international cuisine, a car for everyone in the household over fifteen, foreign vacations, a dishwasher, quickly developed photos (now instantaneous, and e-mailable), central air conditioning, not to speak of items unavailable even to rich but sad Howard in 1965—soft contact lenses, Viagra ("to romp more robustly through Cupid's grove," says Boudreaux), or, more relevant to Hughes, Lexapro and Paxil for depression.[5]

The equality of genuine comfort has risen remarkably, and has continued to rise even recently. Think, to be quite serious about it, of betterments in medicine and the much wider access to higher education and the approach to equal rights, if nothing like perfect, for gays, women, African-Americans, the handicapped, and now even for gender crossers. The rise in life expectancy since 1970 among rich and poor, for example, when translated into dollar equivalencies amounts to a quite large rise in virtual income.[6] Robert Fogel argued persuasively in 1999 that the inequality that matters mainly in a rich country like the United States now is not that of material consumption but of cultural advantage.[7] A modest American family such as Michelle Obama's parents, if they have laserlike focus on education, can see their children through college and even law school. Let us have, then, rich countries that can give such advantages to their children.

The left, however, instead of focusing on the raising of the absolute level of the poor, suggests that we take riches from the well-off, even if the productivity of the quite well-off doctor or the fantastically well-off oil man in fact helps the present poor by giving them hip replacements or gas heating. Foreign aid has this ethically dubious rationale. The left will cite opinion polls showing (as though it were not obvious, though unethical) that people are envious, and would after all prefer taking from millionaires over raising all incomes. Don't tax him. / Don't tax me. / Tax that boss / Behind the tree. The envy, as I've noted, has a long history. In traditional societies no one except the chief or the lofty lord of the manor stuck much above the rest of the poppies for long, which supported an ethical imperative among tribesmen and peasants not to be seen to excel even if you could, and to be suspicious of the witchcraft of those who did. It was a mechanism of envy helping drag people down, down to $3 a day.

The egalitarianism we *Homines sapientes* learned so well in the hundreds of thousands of years of worldwide hunter-gathering is part of our humanity, and surely not a disgraceful part. Among friends, or within a family, we are well justified in admiring it. Remember Jared Diamond and his New Guineans. But when it is extended to the wider society, a rule of No Tall Poppies kills off trade-tested betterment, especially when it assumes that tallness in one poppy *causes* lowness in another. The Indian epic the *Mahabharata*, given its final form about the time of Christ, declared that the behavior "by which one person profits, grieves another."[8] No it doesn't, not now in the positive-sum Bourgeois Era. Yet one find echoes of such zero-sum talk still. It leads to a small pie, and to misery among the poor.

The social-democratic historian Tony Judt asked in his last book, "What of those goods which humans have always valued but do not lend themselves to quantification? What of well-being? What of fairness or equity? What of exclusions, opportunity—or its absence—or lost hope?"[9] What indeed. But to overcome all his worries, the ethical object should be the level of the poor person's situation, not her rank. A dignified level of income, which has been achieved mainly by economic growth rather than by subsidy and redistribution, matters to personal dignity. It lends itself to quantification and to sensible public policy. Adam Smith pointed out that in his day a poor man in England would be ashamed to appear in public without leather shoes.[10] Such a level of income was needful at the time for social presence. It is why a pleasuring definition of happiness does not keep pace with the scope of a dignified human life. Richer people are not necessarily much "happier"(though they are in fact a little: wouldn't you like $500,000 a year?). In the modern United States, lack of a car or truck seems undignified. Viewed internationally, the many poor people driving clunkers in the U.S. are rich. When the Soviet authorities exhibited the 1940 Hollywood adaptation of *The Grapes of Wrath* as evidence of how miserable the poor were in "capitalist" America, it backfired. What amazed the Soviet audiences was that the Joad family fled starvation not on foot, but *by truck*.

The left long predicted that "capitalism" would impoverish people. Once it became obvious that such an attack on how we live now was not persuasive, in view of the evident enrichment of poor people, even in the Third World, the left moved to lamenting instead that "capitalism" damages people spiritually. When that theme too was worn out, it shifted to environmental-ism. Recently it has insisted on the evil of any difference in personal or re-gional income whatever. The left, in other words, wants to find "capitalism" nasty, independent of the evidence. I have a dear Marxian friend who says to me, "I *hate* the market." "But Jack," I say, "you *love* to shop for antiques . . . in the market." "I don't care. I *hate* the market."

All right, step beyond the calculable income of people, their scope in merely material terms. Observe however that "those goods which humans have always valued but do not lend themselves to quantification" have been made abundant in rich modern economies. Exclusions are lowered when a rich society can spend a good deal on, say, higher education, as modern Britain does on a massive scale. Confucius said, "Make people rich first, then educate them," because you can't educate them if they are trapped in stomach-aching poverty.[11] In 1900 a boy or girl went to work at fourteen (or on farms at a lower age), was lucky to get an apprenticeship, and died in har-ness, or in service. Experiencing the immanence of Nature is more available in a society with automobiles and the leisure to drive them into the national parks than it was in poor societies threatened by Nature red in tooth and claw, by Natural mud and Natural freezing and Natural packs of wolves. Wolf packs roamed out in Nature until the nineteenth century even in the urban-ized Netherlands.

You can imagine along with Judt many lovely and unconstrained uto-pias, perfectly equal yet somehow also perfectly free and perfectly creative and perfectly productive, too. You can thereby make an unattainable best the enemy of an attainable pretty good. But observe that most of the world wants merely the pretty-good hope that Britain or the United States or more widely a European or now an East Asian level of productivity offers. Hopeful immigrants haunt the entrance to the Chunnel on the Continental side or the Rio Grande on the Mexican side or the Mediterranean Sea on the Tunisian side, waiting for their chance to go over into an attainable future of material well-being at levels ten or thirty times greater than those in their homelands—into the rough equality in trousers put on one leg at a time and into the attractive if not guaranteed opportunity to acquire in the end thirty trousers in the best wool. The anticolonialist professor, judge, and Egyptian grand mufti Muhammad Abdu (1849–1905) remarked of the contrast be-tween the then relatively rich and liberal France and his desperately poor and undemocratic Egypt, "In Paris, I saw Islam but no Muslims." That is, he saw there an attainable approximation to the society of justice and equality recommended in the Koran, yet few followers of the Prophet lived then in Paris. "In Egypt," by contrast, "I see Muslims but no Islam."[12]

Gaus points out that our ancestors the hunter-gatherer bands were egalitarian in a way we have only in the past few centuries in the richer countries reestablished through equality of genuine comfort, such as dramatic rises in life expectancy for rich and poor. Settled agriculture during the Neolithic Revolution brought towns and eventually a little literacy. Beginning around 9000 BCE in Turkey, for example, the proto–Indo European language was spread west and east and north by the new farmers.[13] But agricultural societies did *not* accord dignity to all. Farming brought a harsh social hierarchy of priests, warriors, merchants/bureaucrats, peasants, and untouchables—in Sanskrit, *brahmin, kshatriya, vaishya, s[h]udra, pariah.* "Equality" is properly about equal dignity, attributing to people twice-born-ness, say, or giving them the vote, or arranging for an economy in which even the poor can buy leather shoes or an old pickup truck. Equal dignity for ordinary people, which is to say, autonomy—no inherited overlords, and bosses only voluntarily—is by English people first taken somewhat seriously in the seventeenth century, as against various sorts of "heteronomy"(rule by others), such as theonomy (rule by God, such as in the seventeenth century Milton wished) or stasonomy (rule by status, such as in the nineteenth century Balzac, Dickens, and Carlyle wished). Earlier, in Elizabethan England, "masterless men" had been a terror. In the eighteenth century by contrast the idea of autonomy triumphed, at any rate among the progressive clerisy, and then became a leading Romantic idea, à la Victor Hugo, a still popular version being "I am the master of my fate: / I am the captain of my soul," reprised by Frank Sinatra and Sid Vicious as "I did it my way." Though end-state egalitarians would argue that markets "enslave" people and therefore the people can be saved only by forced-march liberation, helpfully provided by the brahmins now in power, laissez faire lets you run your own life.

Equality in a small group is a tool against domination, "normative resistance to bullying," as Gaus puts it. Stone throwing makes a group of tribesmen, or for that matter tribeswomen, equal to any chief, in the way a .38 revolver equalizes the use of force. There will be no retribution from relatives if his brother is assigned to kill the bully, or if we all get together to shoot arrows or toss rocks.[14] Humans are unusually skilled by comparison with other great apes in throwing accurately, as one can see in a sling-equipped David versus Goliath, or a non-Cubs outfielder hitting the cutoff man. The throwing of stones in a hunting-and-gathering band makes for equality of dignity. As it was put by the archaeologist Christopher Boehm (on whom Gaus is relying), "A decisive system of political egalitarianism needed to be imposed if earlier humans were to regularly eat large-game meat . . . [and] to do so without undue conflict when lethal weapons were available to all. . . . That is my moral origins hypothesis."[15] The "lethal weapons" were, for example, among late Stone Age people the newly invented bow and arrow, or hundreds of thousands of years earlier the Acheulean hand "axes," used for butchering the very meat, or throwing at scavengers, and at arrogant would-be bosses.[16]

Gaus doesn't worry overmuch about Hayek's Worry—that anciently evolved distributive sentiments of equality will undermine the highly productive Bourgeois Deal.[17] I agree. Agricultural societies were highly bossed, even centrally, and were unproductive for the poor because the bosses took the surplus by compulsion. Yet when compelled hierarchy started to creak in the seventeenth century, reinstating a pre-agricultural equality, the societies of northwestern Europe began to allow what turned out to be an extremely productive equal dignity in a modern, arms-length form. People want dignity, even more than they say they want income equality. And in a modern economy they achieve it. If we insist on ignoring the equality of genuine comfort, and if we marshal populist politics against a first-act inequality of income that yields enrichment for the poor as much as it yields baubles for the rich, we can kill dignity and material comfort for the rest of us. It's happened, repeatedly.

Envy is an associated danger. Being insatiable, and destructive of cooperation, it had better not be indulged. You can, if you wish to wreck your soul, becoming envious of others, "Wishing me like to one more rich in hope, / Featured like him, like him with friends possessed, / Desiring this man's art, and that man's scope." Envy-driven left populism, *ochlocracy* in Greek, the rule of the mob, Hayek's Worry, can do grievous damage if indulged. A folktale from the Czech lands tells of Jesus and St. Peter traveling in disguise, asking peasant families for food and shelter for the night. At last a generous peasant couple provides. The next morning the travelers reveal their identities, and Jesus says, "To reward your blessed charity, you may receive anything you want." The husband and wife consult in whispers for a moment, and the husband turns to Jesus, saying, "Our neighbor has a goat, which provides milk for his family . . ." Jesus anticipates: "And so you want a goat for yourselves?" "No. We want you to kill the neighbor's goat."

Cut down those tall poppies. Don't think you are someone special. Thus the modern Law of Jante I mentioned (ask any Scandinavian). The intellectual historian Henry C. Clark has observed that cutting down the tall poppies is an "unsocial passion," as Adam Smith put it, the uncooperative conviction that my rank in advance of yours is more important than the annoying and probably self-enriching project for our alleged mutual betterment that you keep offering.[18] A right-wing version of zero-sum also maintains hierarchy, and was well understood in Czech and other lands before 1800. At all costs we must keep the distribution of income we started with. No disturbing betterment is to be tolerated, even if [John Rawls–style] the standard of genuine comfort of the poorest is thereby greatly improved. The Spanish proverb is "*mal de muchos, consuelo de tontos*," that is, widespread evil is a comfort to fools, making them feel that after all they are equal, and have no one to envy.

The indulging of the vice of envy shows in many arguments on the left. Judt, for example, justifies taxing the rich explicitly as "diminishing social tensions born of envy."[19] Perhaps it would be better—as Henry Clark and I would suggest—to earnestly counsel people not to indulge the vice of envy. Envy results in a lot of dead goats and dead souls and dead economies. And after all the same sort of argument from "social tensions born of" the other's vice is used to justify in conservative countries the sequestration of women—not only in conservative Islam; Spain was long such a country. Orthodox Judaism partakes in the same save-the-guys logic of women's shame. Cover up, dear, lest some man gets aroused by seeing your bare arm. We should clothe women in the chador to diminish male tensions, born of the vice of lust. We should lop off the incomes of even the deserving rich to diminish social tensions, born of the vice of envy.

The uplifting during the Great Enrichment of real income to more than ten or thirty times or one hundred the world's pre-1800 level per person gives every sign of spreading in the next fifty years to the rest of humanity. Our cousins the poor will inherit the earth. They will have enough for genuine comfort and full participation in the community. For almost all of us recently it's been getting better and better, and doing so in more and more places. Within a few generations almost all the world's poor will have lifted themselves up, a house for Mr. Biswas.

All that can stop it is the tying up of betterments in, say, corrupted red tape or environmental green tape or egalitarian white tape. Or, more directly, if we take the advice of some on the right, we can bring out the black tape, and commence shooting ourselves in the feet, and in the heads—the way the wise and realistic and genetically special and instrumentally rational and so very modern-minded and disenchanted Europeans did early in August 1914, dragging the rest of us into the quarrel and setting back for decades the first enrichment. Let's not.

67

A CHANGE IN RHETORIC MADE
MODERNITY, AND CAN SPREAD IT

Ruminate, if you please, on where we've arrived.

Once upon a time a great change occurred, unique for a while to Europe, especially after 1600 in the lands around the North Sea, and most especially in Holland in the seventeenth century and then in Britain in the eighteenth and especially the nineteenth century. The economist Robert E. Lucas Jr. puts it this way: "For the first time in history, the living standards of masses of ordinary people have begun to undergo sustained growth. The novelty of the discovery that a human society has this potential for generating sustained improvement in the material aspects of the lives of all of its members, not just of a ruling elite, cannot be overstressed."[1]

Realizing the potential depended on a bourgeois ideology adopted by whole societies, not merely by the bourgeoisie itself. The ideology had been foreshadowed in the Hanse towns such as Lübeck and Bergen and Danzig, and in some trading towns of southern Germany, and in the prosperous little cities of Flanders and Brabant, in Barcelona, in the Huguenot strongholds of France, and especially in the northern Italian cities such as Venice, Florence, Genoa, and the rest. It had been tried out a bit in non-European places, too—such as to a limited extent in late seventeenth-century CE Ōsaka, or it seems in second-century BCE Carthage, or "Tyre, the city of battlements, / whose merchants were princes / and her traders the most honored men on earth" (Isaiah 23: 8). But the new ideology persisted over wider areas after the Province of Holland and after the eighteenth century and after north Britain—meaning, to be precise about each place, "Holland" in the exact sense of the northwestern Low Countries, and northern and midland

England and parts of Lowland Scotland, with Amsterdam and London providing financial and trading services to the manufacturing places such as
Westphalia and Lancashire. Then it spread to the world.

The change, the Bourgeois Revaluation, was the coming of a business-
respecting civilization, an acceptance of the Bourgeois Deal. Much of the
elite, and then also much of the non-elite of northwestern Europe and its
offshoots, came to accept or even admire the values of exchange and betterment. Or at the least the polity did not attempt to block such values, as it
had done so energetically in earlier times. Especially it did not do so in the
new United States. Then likewise, the elites and then the common people
in more of the world followed, including now, startlingly, China and India.
They undertook to respect—or at least not to utterly despise and overtax and
regulate—the bourgeoisie.

Not everyone accepted the Bourgeois Deal, even in the United States.
There's the rub, and the worry: it's not complete, and it can be undermined
by hostile attitudes and clumsy regulations. In Chicago you need a $300
business license to start a little repair service for sewing machines, but you
can't do it in your home because of zoning, arranged politically by big retailers. Antibourgeois attitudes survive even in bourgeois cities like London
and New York and Milan, expressed around neo-aristocratic dinner tables
and in neo-priestly editorial meetings. A journalist in Sweden noted recently that when the Swedish government recommended two centimeters of
toothpaste on one's brush no journalist complained:

> [The] journalists . . . take great professional pride in treating with the utmost
> skepticism a press release or some new report from any commercial entity. And
> rightly so. But the big mystery is why similar output is treated differently just
> because it is from a government organization. It's not hard to imagine the media's
> response if Colgate put out a press release telling the general public to use at least
> two centimeters of toothpaste twice every day.[2]

The bourgeoisie is far from ethically blameless. The newly tolerated bourgeoisie has regularly, I say once again, tried to set itself up as a new aristocracy to be protected by the state, as Adam Smith and Karl Marx predicted
it would. And anyway even in the embourgeoisfying lands on the shores
of the North Sea, the old hierarchy based on birth or clerical rank did not
simply disappear on January 1, 1700. In 1773 Oliver Goldsmith attacked the

new sentimental comedies on the London stage as too much concerned with mere tradesmen (*The London Merchant* being an earlier, tragic version), whom he found dreary from a faux-aristocratic height, later characteristic of the clerisy (he himself was the dissolute son of an Irish clergyman).[3] He thought it more satisfactory to display to an audience of tradesmen and their wives the foibles of aristocrats, or at least of the gentry and their servants, as in *The Marriage of Figaro*. Tales of pre- or antibourgeois life strangely dominated the high and low art of the Bourgeois Era. Flaubert's and Hemingway's novels, D'Annunzio's and Eliot's poetry, Eisenstein's and Pasolini's films, not to speak of a rich undergrowth of cowboy movies and spy novels, all celebrate peasant/proletariat or aristocratic values. A hard coming we bourgeois have had of it.

The hardness was not mainly material. It was ideological and rhetorical. Or so at least some historians and sociologists have argued, and even a few economists—Adam Smith and John Stuart Mill and Joseph Schumpeter and Albert Hirschman, to name four. What made the modern world, as many economic historians are realizing, was not trade or empire or the exploitation of the periphery. These were exactly peripheral. Patrick O'Brien reckoned that even in 1790 only 4 percent of European production was exported, and in 1590 it would have been much smaller.[4] Imperialism had been routine in the Athenian or Song or Mughal or Spanish empires, yet the empires, which were commercial empires too, did not make a modern world. Nor was the maker a class struggle, though Marx and Engels were wise to emphasize the leading role of the bourgeoisie.

Yet neither did the Great Enrichment come from the engine of accumulation analyzed by the Marxian and Samuelsonian economists. The analyses are worth having, because in their own scientific realms they reveal a little—and by their shortfalls they reveal, too, how much of human life depends on ideas and rhetoric. Some modern Marxian economists, for example, say that betterment of the Great Enrichment came from a cynical struggle for power in the workplace, and that steam-driven looms and the like were merely what bosses devised to break proto-unions and to discipline the workforce.[5] There's something in it. But not much. And modern Samuelsonian economists say that the Enrichment came from the prudent division of labor or the accumulation of capital or increasing returns to scale or the expansion of international trade or the downward march of transaction costs or Malthusian pressures on behavior. There's something in all of these too. But not much. The limits of the prudence-only arguments of the Marxians and the Samuelsonians show how important are the virtues other than prudence. Expressed as a summary for economists: What happened in the Industrial Revolution, 1750 to 1860, and especially in the Great Enrichment after 1800 or 1848, was neither Karl Marx nor Paul Samuelson in the main, but Smith and Mill and Schumpeter and Hirschman. And expressed as a summary for everyone else: Not matter, mainly, but ideas.

The makers of the modern world of computers and frozen pizza were the new ideas for machines and organizations—especially those of the eighteenth century and afterward, such as the spinning jenny and the insurance company and the autobahn, and the new ideas in politics and society, such as the American Constitution and the British middle class. The new ideas arose to some modest degree from material causes such as educational investment and the division of labor, and even from the beloved of Samuelsonian "growth theorists" in economics nowadays, economies of scale and investment in human capital, renamings of the proposition that nothing succeeds like success. All right. But the pioneering betterments of the eighteenth and nineteenth centuries in Europe and its offshoots arose mainly from a change in what Smith in 1759 had called "moral sentiments." A unique liberalism was what freed the betterment of equals, starting in Holland in 1585, and in England and New England a century later. Betterment came largely out of a change in the ethical rhetoric of the economy, especially about the bourgeoisie and its projects.

You can see that "bourgeois" does not have to mean what conservatives and progressives mean by it, namely, "having a thoroughly corrupted human spirit." The typical bourgeois was viewed by the Romantic conservative Thomas Carlyle in 1843 as an atheist with "a deadened soul, seared with the brute Idolatry of Sense, to whom going to Hell is equivalent to not making money."[6] Or from the other side, in 1996 Charles Sellers, the influential leftist historian of the United States, viewed the new respect for the bourgeoisie in America as a plague that would, between 1815 and 1846, "wrench a commodified humanity to relentless competitive effort and poison the more affective and altruistic relations of social reproduction that outweigh material accumulation for most human beings."[7] Contrary to Carlyle and Sellers, however, bourgeois life is in fact mainly cooperative and altruistic, and when competitive it is good for the poorest among us. We should have more of it. I join in this the philosopher Richard Rorty, who viewed himself as a "post-modern bourgeois liberal."[8]

That does not imply, however, that one needs to be fond of the vice of greed, or needs to think that greed suffices for an economic ethic. Such a Machiavellian and Mandevillean theory has undermined ethical thinking about the Bourgeois Era. It has especially done so during the past three decades in smart-aleck hangouts such as Wall Street or the Department of Economics. Prudence is a great virtue among the seven principal virtues. But greed is the sin of prudence *only*—namely, the admitted virtue of prudence when it is not balanced by the other six, becoming therefore a vice. That is the central point of McCloskey, *The Bourgeois Virtues*, of 2006, or for that matter of Smith, *The Theory of Moral Sentiments*, of 1759 (so original and up-to-date is McCloskey).

Nor has the Bourgeois Era led in fact to a poisoning of the virtues. In a recent collection of mini-essays asking "Does the Free Market Corrode Moral Character?" Michael Walzer replied "Of course it does." But then he wisely adds that *any* social system corrodes one or another virtue. (Compare Montesquieu in 1748 noting that "Commercial laws, it may be said, improve manners for the same reason that they destroy them. They corrupt the *purest* morals. This was the subject of Plato's complaints; and we every day see that they *polish and refine the most barbarous.*"[9] Both, though I have some doubts about "the purest.") That the Bourgeois Era surely has tempted people into thinking that greed is good, wrote Walzer, "isn't itself an argument against the free market. Think about the ways democratic politics also corrodes moral character. Competition for political power puts people under great pressure . . . to shout lies at public meeting, to make promises they can't keep."[10] Or think about the ways even a mild socialism puts people under great pressure to commit the sins of envy or state-enforced greed or violence or environmental imprudence. Or think about the ways the alleged affective and altruistic relations of social reproduction in America before the alleged commercial revolution put people under great pressure to obey their husbands in all things and to hang troublesome Quakers and Anabaptists.

That is to say, any social system, if it is not to dissolve into a war of all against all, needs ethics internalized by its participants. It must have some device—preaching, movies, the press, child raising, the state—to slow down the corrosion of moral character, at any rate by the standard the society sets.

The Bourgeois Era has set a higher social standard than others, abolishing slavery and giving votes to women and the poor. For further progress Walzer the communitarian puts his trust in an old conservative argument, an ethical education arising from good-intentioned laws. One might doubt that a state strong enough to enforce such laws would remain uncorrupted for long. In any case, contrary to a common opinion since 1848 the arrival of a bourgeois, business-respecting civilization did not corrupt the human spirit, despite temptations. Mostly in fact it elevated the human spirit. Walzer is right to complain that "the arrogance of the economic elite these last few decades has been astonishing."[11] So it has. But the arrogance comes from the smart-aleck theory that greed is good, not from the moralized economy of exchange that Smith and Mill and Marshall saw around them, and which continues even now to spread.

The Bourgeois Era did not thrust aside, as Sellers the historian elsewhere claims in rhapsodizing about the world we have lost, lives "of enduring human values of family, trust, cooperation, love, and equality."[12] Good lives such as these can be and actually are lived on a gigantic scale in the modern, bourgeois town, freed from chill penury and the little tyrants of the fields. In Alan Paton's *Cry, the Beloved Country*, John Kumalo, from a village in Natal, and now a big man in Johannesburg, says, "I do not say we are free here." A black man under apartheid in South Africa in 1948 could hardly say so. "But at least I am free of the chief. At least I am free of an old and ignorant man."[13]

Christianity and socialism, both, are mistaken to contrast a rural Eden to a corrupted City of Man. The popular poet of the Sentimental Revolution, William Cowper, expressed in 1785, as I've noted, a cliché dating back to Hellenistic poetry: "The town has tinged the country; and the stain / Appears a spot upon a vestal's robe, / The worse for what it soils." No. This urban, bourgeois world we live in here below is not a utopia. But neither is it a hell. In Christianity the doctrine that the world is a hell is a Neoplatonic heresy, the Gnostic one of Marcion, against which the Apostles' Creed was directed. At any rate our specifically bourgeois world should not be judged a hell by the mere force of a sneering and historically uninformed definition of "bourgeois." The judgment should depend on factual inquiry, not on the most ignorant clichés of politics left and right and middle in Europe, 1848 to the present.

∞

That is, rhetoric is what we have for altering our beliefs, short of reaching for our guns or acting on impulse (or, what amounts to the same thing, acting on our always-already-known utility functions). The American rhetorician and philosopher Richard McKeon (1900–1985; a teacher of Rorty and of the great editor Douglas Mitchell, among others) distinguished lower rhetoric, as a persuasion expositing an already known position, from the higher rhetoric, that explored positions in a real conversation. Though it is surely not evil to try to persuade someone by sweet words of a position already known—after all, it is better than shouting them down or shooting them or forcing them into bantustans—the creativity of the West in the eighteenth and nineteenth centuries arose from the other, higher, good-conversation rhetoric. "Austrian" economists such as Israel Kirzner or Friedrich Hayek (both of whom provoke snorts of disdain among the Samuelsonians) call it "discovery." George Shackle, another economist snorted at by the Samuelsonian orthodoxy (which does a lot of uninformed snorting), remarked wisely, "What does not yet exist cannot now be known. . . . [We] cannot claim Knowledge, so long as we acknowledge Novelty."[14] Unknown knowns, as someone put it.

The discovery will on occasion involve money payments, in which the two parties discover a mutually advantageous deal. Smith argued that "the offering of a shilling, which to us appears to have so plain and simple a meaning, is in reality offering an argument to persuade one to do so and so, as it is for his interest."[15] But discovery involves other forms of nonviolent persuasion as well. Schumpeter (who was Austrian merely in an ethnic sense, and no ally of Mises) called it entrepreneurship, which requires deals and sweet talk and discovery at every juncture. Examine the business section on the racks at the airport bookstall and you will discover that fully a third of the books are about rhetoric, that is, how to persuade employees, bankers, customers, yourself.

As the American literary critic Wayne Booth expressed it, rhetoric is "the art of probing what men believe they ought to believe," "the art of discovering good reasons, finding what really warrants assent, because any reasonable person ought to be persuaded," the "art of discovering warrantable beliefs and improving those beliefs in shared discourse."[16] Or as Bernard Manin put it, "Between the rational object of universal agreement [such as the Pythagorean theorem on a Euclidian plane] and the arbitrary [such as that vanilla is better than chocolate] lies the domain of the reasonable and the justifiable, that is, the domain of propositions that are likely to convince [such as the success of trade-tested progress], by means of arguments whose conclusion is not incontestable, the greater part of an audience made up of all the citizens."[17] It is logically true that at a higher level an economic law, such as "demand curves slope down," is disjoint with a high-level ethical law such as "do unto others as you would have others do unto you." At such a level you cannot derive ought from is, or for that matter is from ought.[18] But we live in science and in ordinary life mostly at a middling level in which positive and normative overlap. When an economist affirms that free trade is good for the nation she is combining lower-level economic propositions ("laws," if you wish) about the shape of the production possibility curve, on the one hand, with clearly ethical propositions on the other (the ethical law, for example, known to economists as the Hicks-Kaldor criterion, saying that actual losses to protected industries are to be ignored if they could at least in theory be offset in cash amount financed from the gains to someone else). That is, we live in science and ordinary life by warrantable beliefs, the not-incontestable—in a word, by rhetoric.

We Europeans have for some centuries now been strangely ashamed of rhetoric. Therefore we have devised numerous euphemisms for it (because one cannot live thoughtfully without it, even if in some disguised form), such as "method" in Descartes's definition, or "ideology" in Marx's, or "deconstruction" in Jacques Derrida's, or "frames" in Erving Goffman's, or the "social imaginary" as Jacques Lacan and Charles Taylor define it—"what makes sense of our practices," writes Taylor, "a kind of repertory."[19] The English professor Gerald Graff's "templates" and the physicist David Bohm's "dialogue" are still other reinventions, among literally dozens, of the wheel of ancient rhetoric.[20] Such reinventions were needed because in the seventeenth century philosophers such as Bacon, Descartes, Spinoza, and Hobbes had revived with their own persuasive rhetoric the Platonic, antirhetorical notion that clear and distinct ideas are somehow achievable without human rhetoric. (It was contradicted by Plato himself by the strength of his rhetoric asserting his unattainable ideal of an antirhetoric of Truth, and by Bacon, Descartes, Spinoza, and Hobbes in their own eloquence against eloquence.)

A fully agreeing, Truth-possessing, predictable, stagnant, utopian, slave-owning, tyrannical, ant-colony, hierarchical, utterly equal, zombie-populated, gene-dominated, or centrally planned society wouldn't need rhetoric, since the issues would already have been settled. Merely act, following your DNA, the traditions of the Spartanate, the Baconian method, the *volonté générale*, the

Party line (*Partiinost'*), the views of Thabo Mbeki about AIDS, or whatever else your lord or your utility function says. The rule is: Don't reflect. Don't discuss. Heh, just do it. No rhetoric.

For many purposes it is not a crazy rule. Indeed an innovative society depends on tacit knowledge scattered over the economy, and the economy depends on allowing such tacit and habitual knowledge to be combined by invisible hands. As Hayek put it, "Civilization enables us constantly to profit from knowledge we individually do not possess. . . . These 'tools' which man has evolved . . . consist in a large measure of forms of conduct which we habitually follow without knowing why."[21] You type on your computer without understanding machine language or what a "registry" is. You drive your auto to the dry cleaners without knowing precisely how its engine works or what a "supercharger" is. "Civilization advances," wrote Alfred North Whitehead in 1911, "by extending the number of important operations which we can perform without thinking about them."[22]

But in the absence of *fresh* persuasions, the rules, habits, operations, knowledge, institutions—in a word, the tools of enrichment, material and spiritual—would never change. The computer would be frozen in the state it achieved in 1965. Autos would never shift to hydrogen fuel. Financial markets would never innovate. Mill called the exhaustion of productive persuasion "the stationary state," which he rather admired, as ending the sick hurry of modern life: "The richest and most prosperous countries would very soon attain the stationary state," he wrote, "if no further betterments were made in the productive arts."[23] In his day the productive arts were exploding with betterment (which Mill did not notice; he did not make a habit of wandering in northern factories, as did in the 1870s the young economist Alfred Marshall). The productive explosion depended on Mill's other main delight, liberty of discussion—rhetoric all the way down. As he tended to, sweet Mill was contradicting himself (somewhat in the manner that radical environmentalists do nowadays) when he admired the stationary state, yet admired, too, a free rhetoric that was fated always to disrupt it.

It is precisely the enormous change in such productive arts 1700 to the present, accelerating late in the nineteenth century, that has made us modern. It is not merely, as I have shown, a matter of science and the frontiers of knowledge. It was not until well after British electricity and then the telegraph in the 1840s, or German organic chemistry and then the artificial dyes and the medicines in the 1890s, and Italian radio and the communication with the masses in the 1920s, that Science started to pay back seriously its debt to Technology. Merely "started." Not a great deal of the economy was involved until late in the twentieth century.[24] Until well into the nineteenth century the most important changes in technique had little to do with scientific theory. Railways. Interchangeable parts. Sewerage in cities. Iron hulls of ships. Assembly lines. Bituminous pavement. The classic case is the steam engine. Although the discovery of the atmosphere clearly played a role in the early steam engine, most of its betterments were matters of tinkering, and high and low skills of machine-making. Eastern science perhaps could just as well have formed the basis for an industrial revolution, and until the late seventeenth century it was clearly better than the European. The European tinkering was informed, true, by a scientific method of obsessive calculation and experimentation. But until lately the bulk of technological change was not applied science, with rare exceptions such as Franklin's lightning rods on church steeples or Humphrey Davy's and George Stephenson's safety lamps in coal mining.

Well after the theorizing of the steam engine by Carnot, as Lawrence Joseph Henderson put it in 1917, the science of thermodynamics owed more to the steam engine than the steam engine owed to science. Margaret Jacob argues plausibly for an ideal cause working earlier through a material one. The steam engine, itself a material consequence of seventeenth-century ideas about the "weight of air," inspired new ideas in the 1740s about machinery generally. Yet it is doubtful that the inventor of the "atmospheric" steam engine, Newcomen, an artisan familiar with pumps, knew much about high science.

Science didn't make the modern world. Technology did, in the hands of newly liberated and honored instrument makers and tinkerers.[25] (Jacob hates the word "tinkerers." She wants high science to be the hero.) Superheating in compound marine engines and mainline locomotives, practical finally very late in the nineteenth century, might be attributed to theory—but its basic principle is that of a pressure cooker. The historian of technology David Edgerton speaks of the "shock of the old," that is, the unpredictable and creative use, often by humble consumers, of *old* technologies, such as the use of galvanized iron in the roofs of huts in *favelas*.[26] It's tinkering, almost literally.

The routine of trade or accumulation or exploitation does not explain such creativity in bettering workshops, the tinkering, the shock of the old. We need to focus on how habits change, how people imagine new

technologies, improving them in response to economic pressures and especially in response to a new culture of honor, and devising new uses out
of old technologies. What changed with accelerating mass from 1600 and
1800 was how people talked about each other, yielding a change in how they
thought about technical and then social problems. In other words, a society
of open inquiry depends on rhetoric in its politics and in its science and in
its economy, whether or not the word "rhetoric" is honored.[27] And because
such societies are rhetorically open they become intellectually creative and
politically free. To the bargain, I have argued, they become astonishingly
rich. The story cannot be principally about institutions, which did not much
change before 1789 or 1832. It is about social ethics, which did. A rhetorical-
ethical Revaluation is what began to happen on the path to a business-
respecting—but not therefore virtue-ignoring—civilization, first in some
scattered cities of Europe in the Middle Ages, then in northwestern Europe
and its offshoots, but at last in fully modern form, potentially, everywhere.

The Revaluation, in short, came out of a rhetoric that would, and will,
enrich the world.

NOTES

EXORDIUM

1. I owe the phrase to Alberto Mingardi of the Istituto Bruno Leoni.

2. Inoue 1991, 2001. For additional reflections on Inoue's work, see McCloskey 2006b, pp. 296–297.

3. Mokyr, forthcoming (2016). Mokyr's name, which will come up frequently, is pronounced "moh-KEER."

4. "Having a go" is a British idiom, used in this application in the 1970s by the economic historian Peter Mathias (1972 [1979], p. 66). I remember Peter using the expression at a dinner discussion I attended at Oxford then, and I remember with embarrassment my callow scorn at its lack of (irrelevant) mathematics. Now I agree with him.

5. Conze and Kocka, eds. 1985.

6. Flaubert (May 10, 1867), in *Oeuvres complètes et Annexes: Correspondance*, p. 5883.

7. Huizinga 1935 (1968), p. 112.

8. Leoni 1965 (2009), p. 83.

9. "Samuelsonian" is historically more accurate than the more usual word, "neoclassical," which includes for example Austrian and Marshallian economists who do not think much of modeling exclusively with constrained maximization and are more concerned with entry and evolution. It is a term of affection, not of dismissal. During the 1960s I myself was trained at Harvard in Samuelsonian economics, and during the 1970s I taught at the University of Chicago, which was at the time turning away from Marshall and Knight and toward Samuelson and Arrow. Samuelsonian economics was invented in the 1940s and 1950s by the brilliant and amiable Paul Anthony Samuelson (1915–2009)—long my mother's mixed-doubles tennis partner—together with his equally brilliant and equally amiable brother in law, Kenneth Arrow (1921–)—long a distantly friendly colleague of mine. Startlingly, they are joint uncles of the crown prince of Samuelsonian economics, Lawrence Summers.

10. Haidt 2006; Epley 2014.

11. For example, Wilson 2010, which is the only substantive use in economics of Wittgenstein's *Philosophical Investigations*. Wilson coined the word "humanomics."

12. Herb Gintis, listen up.

13. Ibsen 1877 (1965), p. 112.

14. I am using the word "Marxian" for "influenced by Marx," as against "Marxist," that is, following the Master in more orthodox and often violent fashion. A Marxian such as Donna Haraway, for example, might argue in her books that social class is a crucial element in history. A Marxist such as Antonio Negri might assist in the kidnapping and murder of businesspeople.

15. Edwards (2013, 2014) makes a brave attempt, though one can criticize his methods. More grounded is Deng 2013.

16. Berndt and Berndt 1964, pp. 302–305. On forming property rights in beaver, see Demsetz 1967. But see Carlos and Lewis 1999, pp. 709, 726. Colin Turnbull's *The Mountain People* (1972) is the classic, if vigorously disputed, picture of a war of all against all, among the Ik of Uganda.

17. In speaking of "alertness" I refer to Israel Kirzner's Austrian economics of the entrepreneur, as in Kirzner 1979, 1989.

18. A discussion of the matter by Donald Boudreaux, John Nye, Joel Mokyr, and me, in which I concede some ground to the neo-institutionalists, is Hart and Richman, eds. 2014. See also McCloskey 2014.

19. Kurzban, DeScioli, and O'Brien 2007.

20. Jacob D. Rendtorff of Roskilde University of Copenhagen pointed out to me the friend-to-friend "corruption" in Scandinavia. But its order of magnitude is not the same as it is in more normal parts of the world.

21. The point comes from Bart Wilson.

22. Ostrom 1990, 2010; Ostrom, Gardner, and Walker 1994.

23. Once again, McCloskey 2011a. On children's games, see Piaget 1932 (1965), pp. 13, 25; Tomasello 2014.

24. White 1984, citing Thucydides, bk. 3, 3.82–[4].

25. North 1990; Acemoglu and Robinson 2012.

26. Allen 2009. Against his skewed logic and evidence, see Humphries 2011; Hudson 2010; Kelly, Ó Gradá, and Mokyr 2013; McCloskey 2010a, pp. 188–189.

27. Smith 2007. The Chinese economist Ning Wang has observed to me that constructivist economics fails because it relies on theorems subject to a fundamental arbitrariness, which I have called the A-Prime-C-Prime Theorem (McCloskey 1994). Evolution, such as that experienced in China after 1978, on the other hand, explores without prejudice and judges by results.

28. Kelly, Ó Gráda, and Mokyr 2013, p. 1.

29. Meisenzahl and Mokyr 2012, p. 447.

30. Bowden, Karpovich, and Usher 1937, p. 311. It was Usher who wrote the technological history in the book.

31. Jacob 2014, p. 148.

32. Sobel 1995.

33. Van der Beek 2013, p. 1.

34. Piketty 2014, p. 418.

35. Boudreaux 2014, personal correspondence.

36. Ibsen 1879 (1965), pp. 132.

37. Peart and Levy 2005; Levy 2001; Peart and Levy, eds. 2008. Kim Priemel of Humboldt University of Berlin suggests to me that "equity" would be a better word for the Scottish concept. But I do not want to surrender so easily an essentially contested concept such as French *égalité*, which indeed in its original bourgeois-revolutionary meaning was more Scottish than what I am here calling "French."

38. Smith 1776, 4.9, p. 664. Following, for example, the editors of the Oxford Shakespeare, when quoting earlier English, even so recent as Smith (by which time English spelling had pretty much settled down), I regularly modernize the spelling and punctuation. The past is a foreign country, but the foreignness should be exhibited in its strange behavior and strange ideas, not in its conventions of printing.

39. Waterman 2014b, pt. 1.

40. Waterman 2014b, pt. 2; Smith 1759 (1790), 4.1.10. Waterman also notes the dissipation of such rents causing waste. It is a balance.

41. Arendt 1951 (1985), p. 54. It is unclear in the passage whether Arendt means "equality in the opinion of others," as I do, or "equality of material outcome," as conventional socialists do. Probably the latter.

42. Mill 1859 (2001), pp. 86–87.

43. MacLeod 1998, 2007. The statue ended up in St. Paul's.

44. Kelly and Ó Gráda (2014) seem to have put paid to one of the older claims about the sources of the turmoil, China to Europe: the Little Ice Age. "Black swan" refers to Nassim Nicholas Taleb's notion of a highly improbable, and unpredictable, event (Taleb 2007).

45. On perspective, see the astonishing book by Lepenies 2013.

ACKNOWLEDGMENTS

1. Cavell 2002, p. xvii.

CHAPTER 1

1. When I use the phrase "pretty good" here, as I will often do again, I am referring to the Ohio State political scientist John Mueller's important book *Capitalism, Democracy, and Ralph's Pretty Good Grocery* (1999), which in turn refers to the comically modest marketing in Garrison Keillor's hometown of Lake Wobegon. For example, "If you can't find it at Ralph's Pretty Good Grocery, you can probably get along without it."

2. The figures are Angus Maddison's estimate of world income before 1800 in 1990 prices, brought up by me to the prices of 2010 or so. Maddison 2001, appendix B, table 21, p. 264.

3. I use throughout for recent times the readily available figures of real income per person in U.S.-equivalent prices from the World Bank, the International Monetary Fund, and the so-called Penn Tables (devised by Alan Heston and colleagues at the University of Pennsylvania). The Penn Tables are conceptually the best, but in truth there is little at stake in the choice among the three. Roughly speaking—which suffices for present purposes—they tell the same story. For example, for 2012 the World Bank and for 2010 the IMF both put Brazilian real GDP at about $33 a head per day, 24 percent of the U.S. level in the corresponding year (and equal, as I have noted, to the average for the world). For 2010 the Penn Tables put it at $27 a head, or 21 percent of the their estimate of the U.S. level. A difference between 24 and 21 percent does not

change any conclusion here or elsewhere in the book. We are dealing throughout with rough figures of how much people make, earn, and consume. The three sets of estimates (and a fourth, from the CIA, giving much the same results) are conveniently gathered (for 2011/2012) at http://en.wikipedia.org/wiki/List_of_countries_by_GDP_(PPP)_per_capita, and for the Penn Tables https://www.google.com/webhp?hl=en#hl=en&q=Penn+Tables.

4. "Make, earn, and consume" because in a correct accounting (but see note 6) the figures would show that what an economy produces is the same to the last cent as what its people earn as income and what they consume, whether in the marketplace, in homework, or in leisure. The figures are from the IMF and World Bank, in 2010. Gregory Clark (2009) argues that Maddison's figure of a little over a dollar a day in 1800 is too low for subsistence.

5. "World," *CIA World Factbook* (accessed April 10, 2013).

6. The economic historian Stefano Fenoaltea and the economist Philipp Lepenies have both pointed out to me recently that for short-run reasons of policy at the time, the concept of national product used by Simon Kuznets, the deviser of the modern program of income measurement, and eventually by Maddison, did not go beyond trading figures, that is, what people could buy. Homework is mostly ignored. It is a major error for the long run (as Kuznets and other students of the matter realized), since production in the home of, say, made clothing and processed food was a large part of consumption in earlier times, as was at all times the care industry for children, husbands, and parents (as the economist Nancy Folbre has persuasively argued). The money value of sheer leisure—the merry beggar singing careless by the highway—is ignored as well. That last item at least might be equal in ancient and in modern times, and its value would rise along with the opportunity cost in making goods and services (but see de Vries 2008; Voth 1998). On the other hand, much of modern consumption is *understated* in the same figures—the quality point I make below. Let us hope the errors offset. But not to worry, and if to worry not to worry too much: errors at such magnitudes do not matter for anything I say here, because we are concerned with orders of (very great) magnitude. Any factor of 10 or 30 or 100 will do, and some such factor is justifiable by all manner of evidence.

7. http://en.wikipedia.org/wiki/Organisation_for_Economic_Co-operation_and_Development Indicators.

8. In Maddison's tables, which seem best for the purpose, Brazilian GDP per person in 2001, deflated to 1990 international Geary-Khamis dollars, was $5,570 (Maddison 2007, table 4c, p. 522). From Index Mundi, which collected its numbers from the annual CIA Factbook (http://www.indexmundi.com/brazil/gdp_real_growth_rate.html), one can reckon from the ratio of Brazil's real per-capita income in 2010 to that in 2000/2002 that the Maddisonian figure for 2010 would have been about $8,021. One looks through Maddison's tables, then, for the United Kingdom (table 1c, p. 441) and for the United States (table 2c, p. 466) to find the years in which they achieved the 2010 Brazilian level. Other methods I have tried do not yield believable results. Having visited Brazil four times briefly over the past few decades (though wholly ignorant of Portuguese), I am an Expert on Brazil; and having lived in England for a few months as a teenager in 1959 (Woodbine cigarettes, pints and quarts of Ludlow beer), and having been a small child in the United States in the 1940s (radio drama, penny candy), I can attest that the present result seems about right.

9. For example, the OECD's instruments, overlapping with mine, agree. See van Zanden et al., eds. 2014.

10. Gilmour 2011, p. 20.

11. Quoted in Robb 2007, p. 84.

12. Robb 2007, p. 78.

13. For recent expositions, see Fogel 2004; Floud et al. 2011. But on Fogel, see de Vries 2008, pp. 117–120. A judicious survey is Kelly and Ó Gráda 2012.

14. Quoted from Moburg's memoir in Brown 2008, pp. 9–10.

15. Examine Wikipedia's astonishing "List of Tuberculosis Cases" at http://en.wikipedia.org/wiki/List_of_tuberculosis_cases (the editors, to be sure, plead for "citations to reliable sources"). Beyond those mentioned in the text there were, for example, Burns, Schiller, Scott, Balzac, Chopin, John C. Calhoun, nearly the entire Brontë family, Delacroix, Thoreau, Napoleon II, Robert Louis Stevenson, John Ruskin, Chekhov, and Orwell.

16. James 2007, pp. 350, 352.

17. Brown 2008, p. 16, the year corrected by Myllyntaus and Tarnaala 1998, p. 36.

18. Levi 1945.

19. Poznik et al. 2013, p. 565.

20. Mithen 2003, p. 60.

21. Parkin 1992.

22. Goldstone 2009 is an excellent guide to the recent scholarship, for example pp. 80–81. I have depended on Goldstone's little book, and look forward to a big one he is writing.

23. Connelly 2008, chap. 4.

24. Hamashita 2007; Bayly 2004.

25. Broadberry and Gupta 2012, Table 12.

26. Li 2011.

27. Li and van Zanden 2012.

28. Drelichman and V'

29. Gilmour '

30. Le'

CHAPTER

1. Lepenies ... levation of the logic to a "natural law," was taken from anoth ... Townsend thirteen years earlier.

2. Ross Emme ... .e straight on the differences between Malthus Mark I and Mal

3. Quoted in Lepei ... 50.

4. Voigtländer and V

5. Galor 2005.

6. On the excellence of potatoes with milk, see Cook 2013.

7. Startlingly, Townsend articulated exactly such a model in 1786 (Lepenies 2014).

8. Mokyr 1983 and Ó Gráda 2010.

9. Waterman 2012, p. 425.

10. G. Clark 2007a, table 4 and figure 10.

11. G. Clark 2007a, figure 8.

12. Malthus 1798, chapter 2, end.

13. Attenborough 1998.

14. McGuire and Coelho 2011 is an excellent recent treatment of a large literature using such an argument.

15. Haensch et al. 2010. In 2015 it was claimed by students of the matter that the Plague was spread from Central Asia not by flea-bearing rats but by, of all things, (flea-bearing) gerbils.

16. Alfani 2013, for example on p. 427.

17. Ross Emmett emphasizes Malthus's notions here, Emmett n.d., p. 3.

18. Sahlins 1972 (2004).

19. Gaus 2013, p. 13.

20. Olson 1993 is the seminal paper. Thus Scott 2009, and for a West African example, from my beloved colleague the late James Searing, Searing 2002.

21. Mayshar, Moav, and Neeman 2011.

22. Weatherford 2004; Perdue 2005, Hellie 2003, McNeill 1964, Lattimore 1940.

CHAPTER 3

1. Gerschenkron 1971.

2. Nordhaus 2004.

3. Gaus 2013, p. 8. Richerson and Boyd 2004.

4. Ó Gráda 2010.

5. McCloskey 1976, 1989.

6. Appleby 1980, p. 643 for Britain and France.

7. For present-day figures (the "Penn Tables"), see Heston, Summers, and Aten 2012 and updatings such as https://www.google.com/webhp?hl=en#hl=en&q=Penn+Tables. For 1800, see Maddison. Luxembourg's half million folk earn on average $252 a day, the highest (Maddison 2007).

8. Fallows 2010, p. 72.

9. Leon 2012, p. 171.

10. As Czarniawska 2013 shows.

11. Sandberg 1979.

12. I am indebted to the philosopher Kenneth Stikkers at Southern Illinois University for stressing to me this quasi-pun in the phrase the "Great Enrichment."

13. Coase and Wang 2013b, p. 207.

14. Harcourt 1994, p. 207; Röpke 1958 (1960), p. 8.

15. http://unesco.org/education/GMR2006/full/chapt8_eng.pdf; https://efareport.wordpress.com/2012/05/31/literacy-rates-are-rising-but-not-fast-enough/.

16. http://hyperallergic.com/68051/2012-museum-attendance-numbers-show-a-diverse-global-art-scene/; http://worldometers.info/books/.

17. Rosling 2013.

18. Levi 1945, p. 30.

19. Hanawalt 1976.

20. Unger 2007, p. 132. Actually in 2009 Belgium ranked only twenty-second worldwide, half as avid as the Czech Republic or Venezuela.

21. Nelson 2015, p. 15. See Nelson 2013a, 2013b, 2010.

22. F. Smith n.d.

CHAPTER 4

1. Ridley 2010, p. 8.

2. Adrian Bowyer of the RepRap Project suggested the survival point to me.

3. Smith 1776, 1.2.

4. The factor of 100 is argued in a little more detail in *Bourgeois Dignity*, pp. 54–59, using Nordhaus on lighting and his suggested extrapolations (Nordhaus 1996). Fouquet and Pearson (2011) confirm Nordhaus on lighting.

5. Macaulay 1848, end of chap. 3. Tom G. Palmer drew my attention to the passage.

6. Braudel 1967 (1973), p. 235. And yet rich Romans had floor heating from hot water, denied to rich Europeans until recently.

7. Bailey 1999.

8. See, for example, Kenny 2011, Kenny n.d.

9. Simon 1981 (1996).

CHAPTER 5

1. Schumpeter 1942 (1950), pp. 67–68.

2. Boudreaux 2013.

3. Smith 1776, 1.1.11.

4. The figure of 9,900 percent derives from the fifth-grade arithmetic I mentioned earlier. A factor of 100, if expressed as a percentage change over the base, is calculated as 100 minus the base of 1 (in the year 1800), which is by the subtraction 99, divided by the same base, 1, but then multiplied by 100 to get it into per hundred terms, that is, $[(100 - 1)/1] \times 100$ percent, or 9,900 percent.

5. Professor Eduard Bonet of Escuela Superior de Administración y Dirección de Empresas, Barcelona, drew my attention to Follett's point about democracy.

6. Here I diverge, reluctantly, from Margaret Jacob's view (for instance in Jacob 2014), which Mokyr follows.

7. Ó Gráda 2014, p. 8.

8. I am indebted to Marlies Mueller for reminding me of Popper's usage.

9. See the lucid treatment in Wagner 1994. The capitalization and italicization of *ORDO* refers to the title of a yearbook published from 1948 by the Freiburg (Germany) School of economists recommending *Ordnungspolitik*, "order policy."

10. Bell 2014; and Boldrin and Levine 2008.

11. Smith 1759 (1790), 4.1.11, para. 9.

12. Reich 2014.

13. Gobry 2014.

14. That was the point of my early supply-side essay about British economic growth in the late nineteenth century, McCloskey 1970.

15. See for example Lawrence 2015; and for Canada Grubel 2015, making the point that a person's mobility through the quintiles over her life changes the picture dramatically.

16. Whitford 2005.

17. Boudreaux and Perry 2013.

18. Deaton 2013, p. 231.

19. Fogel 1999, p. 190.

20. Horwitz 2013, p. 11 of the working paper, now published as Horwitz 2015.

21. Horwitz 2013, p. 2 of the working paper.

22. Horwitz's table 4 reports the percentage of poor households with various appliances: in 1971, 32 percent of such households had air conditioners; in 2005, 86 percent did.

23. Klinenberg 2002.

24. Barreca et al. 2013 show the large effect in the United States of air conditioning in reducing excess mortality during heat waves.

CHAPTER 6

1. Reich 2014.

2. Isaacs 2007, quoted in Horwitz 2013, p. 7.

3. Saunders 2013, p. 214.

4. Frankfurt 1987, pp. 23–24.

5. ilga.gov/commission/lrb/conent.htm.

6. Sen 1985; Nussbaum and Sen 1993.

7. Trollope 1867–1868, vol. 1, pp. 126, 128.

8. Gazeley and Newell 2010, abstract, p. 19, chart 2 (p. 17).

9. Frankfurt 1987, p. 34; my italics.

10. Margo 1993, pp. 68, 65, 69.

11. Brennan, Menzies, and Munger 2013.

12. Smith 1776, 1.1.10, p. 22.

13. Nozick 1974, p. 164.

14. Benjamin 1936.

15. Boudreaux 2001.

16. Saunders 2013, pp. 213, 215.

CHAPTER 7

1. See S. Williamson, http://www.measuringworth.com/.

2. Short 2012, especially his chart "Real GDP per Capita Percent Off High," extrapolated into 2013; and for international comparisons, 2008–2012, http://data.worldbank.org/indicator /NY.GDP.PCAP.CD.

3. Hobsbawm 2011, p. 419 (the last page). I knew Hobsbawm a little when we were colleagues in the Department of History at Birkbeck College back in 1975–1976, and I have long admired his historical scholarship, without always agreeing with it.

4. Hobsbawm 2011, p. 417.

5. Mishra 2011, p. 12.

6. Reich 2014.

7. Reich 2014.

8. Ibsen 1877 (1965), p. 43.

9. Ibsen 1877 (1965), p. 117.

10. Postrel has written the book on glamour (2013).

11. Zola 1882–1883 (1992), pp. 68–70.

12. Quoted in Kristin Ross's introduction to Zola 1882–1883 (1992), pp. xi–xii; the italics are Zola's.

13. Simmel 1908 (1955), pp. 61–62; his italics.

CHAPTER 8

1. Robert Gordon 2012; Summers 2014; Brynjolfsson and McFee 2014; Phelps 2013; Edward Gordon 2013; Sachs and Kotlikoff 2012; Cowen 2011, 2013.

2. Fogel 2005.

3. *National Review*, May 19, 2014.

4. Cowen 2013, pp. 4, 6.

5. Cowen 2013, p.20.

6. Cowen 2013, p. 39.

7. Cowen 2013, p. 3.

8. Mokyr 2013, 2014.

9. Pagano and Sbracia 2014; compare again Fogel 2005.

10. Macaulay 1830 (1881), pp. 186, 187.

11. Macaulay 1830 (1881), p. 185.

12. Phelps 2013, pp. viii, x, 14, 15, 21, and throughout.

13. Population shares from Maddison 2007, p. 378.

14. I realize that a Rule of 69 would be a little more accurate for continuous as against periodic (that is, annual or quarterly) compounding, and that perfectly accurate continuous compounding would involve $e = 2.718281 \ldots$ But 72 has lots of integer divisors, is pretty accurate except at very high (for example, 30 percent) interest rates, and is honored by history.

15. *Wall Street Journal*, October 7, 2013, p. A14.

16. Quoted in Brandt, Ma, and Rawski 2014, p. 99.

17. Simon 1981 (1996).

18. Wuetherick, personal communication, January 26, 2014.

19. *Independent*, June 17, 2014, p. 9.

20. Troesken 2014.

21. Barreca, Clay, and Tarr 2014, p. 5, table 1 (p. 37). I can remember my father shoveling coal in the basement of our apartment in Cambridge, Massachusetts, in 1947, and my mother can remember trying to keep clothing and windowsills clean in the face of coal heating and coal smoke outside in winter.

22. The Danish philosopher of science Hans Siggaard Jensen tells me in a personal communication that windmills are designed with three vanes mainly because farmers have always used three vanes—*one* vane is from an engineering point of view more efficient.

23. Chapman 2014.

24. Stone 2013.

25. Denyer 2014.

26. Stone 2013, quoting studies following Chernobyl. One student of the matter concludes that "losses arising from Chernobyl were not of sufficient magnitude and the event was so long ago that the accident should not be definitive in decisions about investment in new reactors" (Simmons 2011, p. 12). Cleanup workers at Fukushima have no discernible rise in disease. See Rivkin 2013.

27. Maddison 2007, p. 383. I am aware that China and India should be removed from the 1973–2003 rate to make the hypothetical exact, which would make it a trifle lower—say, 4 percent. But 4 percent is still, as I say, unprecedented.

28. Mencken 1917 (2006), p. 63.

29. Knight 1923 (1997), p. 137.

30. For example, "The migration of modern humans out of Africa resulted in a population bottleneck [in the small bands of humans migrating] and a concomitant loss of genetic diversity"(Campbell and Tishkoff 2008); "all systems show greater gene diversity in Africans than in either Europeans or Asians" (Jorde et al. 2000, abstract). There is, they say, "a marked founder effect associated with the expansion out of Africa."

31. Pritchard et al. 1999, pp. 1795, 1797.

32. Personal communication at HedgePo's Global CIO Summit, Gleneagles, Scotland, October 23, 2014.

CHAPTER 9

1. Klein 2007. For another view from the left, this time based on facts, see Mirowski 2013 and Mirowski and Plehwe, eds. 2009.

2. Collier 2007.

3. World Bank, "Remarkable Decline in Global Poverty, But Major Challenges Remain," April 17, 2013. I join you in being puzzled by the divergence between such figures and the one-out-of-seven estimate by Collier. I think it is because Collier was speaking of the distribution by country instead of by individual. But the statistical methods strongly converge. Extreme poverty, however you measure it, has fallen dramatically during the era of "neoliberalism."

4. "China Experiments with Free Trade Zone," *Chicago Tribune*, October 1, 2013, sect. 2, p. 6. That such news was buried on the last page of the business section shows how routine the liberalization of China and India has become. Even Cuba promises a free port: "Former Exit Port for a Wave of Cubans Hopes to Attract Global Shipping," *New York Times*, January 27, 2014.

5. McCloskey 2006a.

6. Friedman 2005.

7. World Bank, "Economy Ratings," http://www.doingbusiness.org/rankings.

8. Doingbusiness.org.

9. "GNI per capita, PPP (current international $)," http://data.worldbank.org/indicator /NY.GNP.PCAP.PP.CD/countries?display=graph.

10. Pomeranz 2000.

11. Needham 1954–2008.

12. Gwei-djen and Needham 1980, p. 231; Mokyr 2008, p. 257.

13. Comin and Mestieri 2013, table 1.

14. Klíma 2002, p. 52.

15. Mabhubani 2013.

16. Prados de la Escosura 2014, figure 4.

17. Maddison 2007, p. 303.

18. Sala-i-Martin and Pinovsky 2010; Sala-i-Martin 2002, 2006.

CHAPTER 10

1. O'Brien and Hunt 1993.

2. Voigtländer and Voth 2013.

3. McCloskey 2010a, pp. 313–315; Peter Murrell 2009 shows that there is no break in trend in 1688.

4. Pollock and Maitland 1895. As early as 1171 Henry II imposed an already flourishing English common law on the Pale of his newly conquered Irish properties.

5. Boswell 1791 (1984), vol. 2, p. 203 (April 14, 1778). For a fuller argument see McCloskey 2010b.

6. Douglas 1972 (1979); Sahlins 1972 (2004).

7. Ferguson 2011, pp. 12–14; "dominate," pp. 3, 5, and throughout.

8. For similar views of dominance and decline see Kindleberger 1996.

9. Ferguson 2011, pp. 9, 11.

10. Ferguson 2011, p. 8.

11. Mishra 2011.

12. Quoted in Martin 2014, p. 38.

13. The contumely of the MCC toward Indian cricket is documented in Astill 2013.

14. Davis and Huttenback 1993 and works cited there.

15. Davis and Huttenback 1993, p. 28.

16. See Maurer 2013; Schlesinger and Kinzer 1982.

17. Quoted in Palmer 2014, p. 70.

18. Notwithstanding O'Brien 2011, and again Reinert 2011.

19. Parker 1989, pp. 84 (quoting Tojo), 280–285 (reviewing mortality statistics).

20. Morris 2010, 2014. True, headlines are not written by professors but by headline writers, and so Morris is not to be blamed directly for the assertion in the headline. But the body of the text supports the headline.

21. Einaudi 1908–1946 (2000), p. 273.

22. Kealey 2001, p. 243.

23. Frank 1998, pp. xxv, 282.

24. For additional evidence, see McCloskey 2010a, chaps. 26, 27.

CHAPTER 11

1. Easterly 2001.

2. The exact item in the website alananthony.com, from which I retrieved the quotation, does not work anymore.

3. Clayton, Dal Borgo, and Hasekl 2009, p. 22.

4. Walzer 1983, p. 11.

5. Einaudi 1943, p. 42.

6. Wallerstein 1983, p. 13. So, since the first part of the word "astrology" is derived from the Latin for "star," it would be legitimate to presume that stars are a key element in human fate.

7. Marx 1867, chap. 24, sect. 3.

8. Acemoglu and Robinson 2012, p. 471.

9. Toynbee 1884 (1887), p. 87.

10. Goldstone 2002, abstract.

11. Clapham 1926, p. 74. Compare Pollard 1981, pp. 24–25; Tunzelmann 1978; Kanevsky 1979.

12. Musson 1978, pp. 8, 61, 167–168.

13. Acemoglu and Robinson 2012, pp. 471–472.

14. Findlay and O'Rourke 2007, pp. 318–319.

15. Quoted in Kenyon 1983, p. 272. We can only hope that the result will not be, as she continues, that they are "replaced not by new, better and truthful fables, but by furious arguments."

16. Friedman 1970.

17. Friedman 1970, p 33; emphasis added, as Daniel G. Arce M takes care to do when quoting this passage (Arce M 2004, p. 263).

CHAPTER 12

1. Keynes 1936, p. 16, sec. 4; chap. 24, sec. 2 ("depriving capital of its scarcity-value within one or two generations").

2. J. Williamson 1993, p. 15.

3. Quoted in Das 2009, p. 295.

4. Augustine, Tractate 7 (John 1:34–51).

5. Diamond 1997, p. 258.

6. Ward-Perkins 2005, pp. 102, 112, 117, 118, 146. He notes, in Ward-Perkins 2000, that the loss of Roman techniques was true even in the wide areas that remained for a long time afterward populated by Celtic (Welsh, that is) people, formerly thoroughly Romanized, and explains it with the prestige of the Germanic overlords of the other parts of the island.

7. Acemoglu, Gallego, and Robinson (2014) point out the biases in cross-time measures of the return to *human* capital, noting that they are alleged to be dramatically higher, for no good reason, than the estimates by Jacob Mincer and followers based on cross sections. McCloskey 2010a also made this point. It seems to me a decisive argument against accumulation of *human* capital as an exogenous explanation of the Great Enrichment.

8. Prak 2011, p. 10.

9. Weber 1923 (1981), p. 355.

10. Weber 1904–1905 (1958), p. 17.

11. Ridley 2010, p. 5.

12. Though see the recent work by Bessen and Nuvolari (2012).

13. Ridley 2010, p. 8.

14. A clarion call is Sutch 1991.

15. Chamberlain 1959 (1976), pp. 10–11.

16. See again Grafe 2012.

17. Bartlett 2010, pp. 43, 49–50.

18. Mithen 2003, pp. 68, 84, and throughout.

19. Berndt and Berndt 1964, p. 113.

20. See McBrearty 2007 and other essays in Mellars et al., eds. 2007.

21. Braudel, 1967 (1973), pp. 620–621.

22. On Athens, see Cohen 1992.

23. Mielants 2008, p. 15.

24. The evidence for this surprising fact is examined in McCloskey 2010a, pp. 131–137.

25. Engerman and Sokoloff 2012.

26. Steele 2001.

27. Marx 1867 (1887), pp. 170–171; my italics.

28. Karl Marx–Friedrich Engels–Werke, Band 23, S. 11–802, Dietz Verlag, Berlin/DDR 1962, p. 168, http://mlwerke.de/me23/me23_161.htm.

29. Megill 2002, p. 262.

30. Maurizio Viroli (2014, p. 3)would argue that Guicciardini is the better choice for a "realist" *origine*.

31. Hardy 1886, chap. 14.

CHAPTER 13

1. Weatherford 2004, p. 69.

2. Weatherford 2004, p. 224.

3. Brennu-Njáls Saga, 70 kalfi. Njál is speaking to Mord at the Althing, the Icelandic gathering for trade and law reading and dispute settling. In the translation in the Gutenberg Project it is in chapter 69, not 70.

4. All the learning here is extracted from http://forum.wordreference.com/threads/icelandic-proverb.788627.

5. Compare Robert Higgs's argument (2012, introduction) that families and neighborhoods could enforce most laws better than a remote state.

6. James VI of Scotland 1598 (1996), p. 69.

7. Kimbrough, Smith, and Wilson 2010; Wilson, Jaworski, Schurter, and Smyth 2012.

8. Kimbrough, Smith, and Wilson 2010, p. 208.

9. Mokyr 2010, p. 378 and following.

10. Yoffee 2005, p. 112.

11. Parks 2013, pp. 8–9, 18, 143–144.

12. Davis 2012, pp. 453–455.

13. Rossi and Spagano 2014.

14. Fish 1980; Fish 2001, e.g., pp. 47, 57, 92.

15. The neo-institutionalist tale told by people such as North, Greif, Acemoglu, Robinson, and others is treated more fully in McCloskey 2010a, chaps. 33–37.

16. Mokyr 2010, p. 1.

17. McCloskey 2008.

18. Carlos and Lewis 1999, p. 726.

19. Adams 1994.

20. I learned to add the *L* to the analysis by speaking to the Bruno Levi Institute in Milan and the WIPCAD Lecture series at the University of Potsdam, Germany.

CHAPTER 14

1. Coate 2010, p. 15.

2. Chamlee-Wright and Storr, eds. 2010.

3. O. Williamson 1999, p. 322.

4. O. Williamson 1999, p. 324.

5. McCloskey 2001. Compare Cowan (1983), who makes a similar point: ideology, not vacuum cleaners or washing machines relieving them of home duties (with a net yield, she argues, merely of cleaner homes and clothing), led women into paid work.

6. Bourdieu and Wacquant 1992, p. 126.

7. As Donald Boudreaux has persuaded me to admit, and as Joel Mokyr and John Nye have helped me to see more clearly (Hart and Richman, eds. 2014).

8. Again, Mueller 1999.

9. A referee for the *Journal of Institutional Economics* pointed this out to me in January 2015.

10. Bostrom 2014, p. viii.

11. Lepenies 2006, p. 16.

12. Kelling and Wilson 1982.

13. Searle 2010, p. 95.

14. Searle 2010, pp. 95–96; my italics.

15. Searle 2010, p. 115.

16. Searle 2010, p. 113.

17. Searle 2010, p. 122.

18. For a fuller discussion of "conjective," see McCloskey 1994. I recently discovered that Charles Taylor was making the same point as early as 1971, under the label of "intersubjectivity" (in "Interpretation and the Sciences of Man," *Review of Metaphysics* 25 [September]: 3–51). Again, I should have been reading Taylor thirty years ago, when John Nelson of the University of Iowa first suggested I do so.

19. Searle 2010, p. 10.

20. The example is due to my officemate in the late 1960s, the economist Steven N. S. Cheung.

21. Tallis 2011.

22. Searle 2010, p. 8.

23. Wilson 2010.

24. Quoted in Hodes 1972, pp. 71–72.

25. Searle 2010, p. 121.

26. All this in Tomasello 2014, pp. ix, 3, 5, and following.

27. Searle 2010, p. 7.

28. Searle 2010, p. 9.

29. Searle 2010, p. 106.

CHAPTER 15

1. Zamagni 2010, p. 63.

2. Das 2009, pp. xxxiii–xxxiv.

3. The stunning corruption of the federal government in the nineteenth century is detailed in Cost 2015.

4. For detailed justifications for what follows, see McCloskey 1985b, chaps. 22–25.

5. Spaulding 2014.

6. Dutton 1984; MacLeod 1988; MacLeod and Nuvolari 2006; Mokyr 2009; Boldrin and Levine 2008.

7. Smith 1776, 4.9, p. 664.

8. "Corruption Perceptions Index 2012," http://transparency.org/cpi2012/results.

9. World Bank, "Doing Business," doingbusiness.org/rankings (real income, Penn Tables for 2010).

10. I owe this remark to Pal Sandvik of the University of Berlin.

11. Lebergott 1984, p. 61. Donald Boudreaux reminded me of the passage. It is rather in contradiction to what Lebergott says on the previous page, that inputs accounted for all output.

12. Razafindrakoto, Roubaud, and Wachsberger 2013, English abstract.

13. Acemoglu and Robinson 2012, p. 450.

14. Epstein 2009, p. xii.

15. Parks 2013, p. 51.

CHAPTER 16

1. Easterly 2001, pp. 27–28.

2. "Corruption Perceptions Index 2013," http://transparency.org/cpi2013/results.

3. "Corruption Perceptions Index 2013."

4. The four states are the worst as reported in Liu and Mikesell 2014.

5. A gripping summary of the evidence worldwide, starting with Afghanistan, is Chayes 2015. Both Chayes and Cost (2015) are optimistic that better institutions without ethical reformation can save us. One doubts it.

6. Madison in *The Federalist Papers*, no. 51, 1787.

7. Ó Gráda 2014, personal conversation.

8. Kiesling 2008, 2012.

9. Phillips and Zecher 1993.

10. Editorial, *Washington Post*, October 8, 2014.

11. Higgs 2012, p. 12.

12. Kolko 1965.

13. De Soto 2000.

14. McCloskey 1972, 1975.

15. Todorov 2000 (2003), p. 83.

16. Frost 1946, p. 118 ("Christmas Trees: A Christmas Circular Letter," 1916). Frost is the most economistic of major poets.

17. McCloskey 2012b.

18. Zamora 2014.

19. Again, Ridley 2010.

CHAPTER 17

1. Boswell 1791 (1949), vol. 2, p. 191 (April 10, 1778).

2. Johnson 1775 (1984), p. 141.

3. Johnson 1775 (1984), p. 99; punctuation modernized.

4. Boswell 1791 (1949), vol. 1, pp. 155–157 (1755).

5. Boswell 1791 (1949), vol. 2, p. 16 (April 5, 1776). On which Boswell commented, "Numerous instances to refute this will occur to all who are versed in the history of literature."

6. Boswell 1791 (1949), vol. 1, p. 532 (March 27, 1775).

7. Boswell 1791 (1949), vol. 1, p. 273 (July 20, 1763). And Joan Rivers: "People say that money is not the key to happiness, but I always figured if you have enough money, you can have a key made."

8. Boswell 1791 (1949), vol. 2, p. 447 (1783).

9. Johnson 1753, pp. 238–223.

10. Quoted in Wood 2004, p. 66.

11. That was the problem, a sociological and political one, not the psychological one that Weber posited.

12. The discussion of Austen has benefited in many ways from comments by Anthony Waterman.

13. Hughes-Hallett 1991, p. 118.

14. Austen 1813, vol. 2, chap. 6. So many are the editions of Austen's novels, and so short are her chapters, and so easily searched, and so healthful is it at any time to pause to reread a few of her pages, that I give only chapter citations.

15. Davidoff and Hall 1987, p. 30.

16. Quoted in Moretti 2013, p. 11.

17. Thompson 1963.

18. Hollander 1994.

19. See Terry 1988.

20. Woolf 1925, p. 142.

21. Ellis 2005, p. 416.

22. Austen 1815, chap. 4. "Country" here means "county" or "region."

23. Wood 2004, p. 38. I cannot resist the musician's definition of a "gentleman": someone who knows how to play the accordion, but doesn't.

24. Trollope 1874, vol. 1, pp. 226, 155. The theme persists throughout the novel, e.g., vol. 1, pp. 149, 183, 214, 269.

25. Wahrman 1995.

26. Austen 1813, vol. 2, chap. 2, I thank Jan Osborn of Chapman University for drawing my attention to the passage.

27. Butler 1975, p. 298.

28. Cowper, 1785 (1997), bk. 4, lines 671–682.

29. Ellis 2005, p. 416.

30. Ellis 2005, p. 417.

31. Wiltshire 2009, p. 167.

32. As Jason Douglas pointed out to me.

33. Auden 1936 (1976), p. 79.

CHAPTER 18

1. Ellis (2005, p. 423) applies it to the slave trade, and implies that Austen took the slave trade as a synecdoche for bourgeois life. Since the people who, as Ellis notes, "have some recent losses" on their West Indian estates are the Bertrams of Mansfield Park, the epitome of the gentry, not the bourgeoisie, Ellis's figure does not seem to compute.

2. Copeland 1986, 1997, 2005.

3. MacDonagh 1993, p. 44.

4. Chapman, ed. 1955 (1985), p. 175–176.

5. Le Faye 2011, p. 205 (letter 77 to Martha Lloyd, November29–30, 1812).

6. Butler 1985, p. xxvi.

7. Waterman 1991.

8. Chwe 2013.

9. As Chris Findeisen pointed out to me.

10. As Don Boudreaux pointed out to me.

11. Haidt 2006; March 1971; Nye 1991; Akerlof and Shiller 2009.

12. Austen 1787–1790. She continues in the crazy humor of her juvenilia, "Their children were too numerous to be particularly described; it is sufficient to say that in general they were virtuously inclined & not given to any wicked ways. Their family being too large to accompany them in every visit, they took nine with them alternately."

13. Einaudi 1919 (1961), p. 272. Alberto Mingardi directed me to the passage.

14. Ibsen 1892 (1965), act 1, p. 800.

15. Austen 1811, vol. 2, chap. 14.

16. Austen 1813, vol. 1, chap. 19.

17. Sun Tzu, *The Art of War*, trans. 1910, chap. 4, at http://chinapage.com/ sunzi-e.html. A few paragraphs here are taken from *The Bourgeois Virtues*.

18. Jullien 1996, p. 197.

19. Earle 1989, p, 73.

20. Parker 1989, p. 66.

21. Parker 1989, p. 76.

22. Michie 2000, p. 6. Compare Michie 2011.

23. Wheeler 2005, p. 409.

24. No. 108 (November 18, 1814), in R. W. Chapman, ed., 1955 (1985), p. 174.

25. Wheeler 2005, p. 412.

26. Waterman, personal correspondence.

27. Austen 2004, p. 143 (to Cassandra, December 27, 1808).

CHAPTER 19

1. Hume 1741–1742 (1987), p. 546.

2. Smith 1759 (1790), 1.1.1.

3. Smith 1776, 1.11.

4. Smith 1977, p. 188.

5. Smith 1776, 1.10.

6. Joy 1877.

7. Hovenkamp 1990.

8. Boldrin and Levine 2008; Lienhard 2006, p. 101.

9. Walton 1993, pp. 146–148.

10. Smith 1776, 4.2.44.

11. Dupré 2004, p. 337.

12. Smith 1776, 4.5.55.

13. Smith 1776, 4.5.55.

14. Smith 1776, 1.10.118.

15. Fleischacker 1999, 2014. Compare Gordon Brown, then chancellor of the exchequer, and later prime minister, in a speech at the University of Edinburgh, claiming Smith for the center left (Brown 2002).

16. Berry 1992, p. 84.

17. Stewart 1793 (1980), p. 266.

18. Stewart 1793 (1980), p. 326.

19. Stewart 1793 (1980), p. 307; my italics.

20. John Kirby (1990) is my source for allotting the Greek *eros, bia, peitho* in the diagram.

21. Hursthouse 1999, pp. 102–103, 107, 111.

22. Canetti 1973 (1985), p. 26.

23. Smith 1980, p. 262.

24. Stewart 1793 (1980), p. 300.

25. Kuehn 2001, pp. 153–163.

CHAPTER 20

1. Rothschild 2002.

2. Leo Strauss 1953; John Finnis 1980. Compare Hont and Ignatieff 1983; but then see Fleischacker 2004, pp. 221–226.

3. Buchanan and Tullock 1962; Rawls 1971; Nussbaum 2006; and criticism in McCloskey 2011a.

4. Anscombe 1958, MacIntyre 1981; Nussbaum herself again 1986; Hursthouse 1999.

5. Knight 1923 (1977), p. 62.

6. Canetti 1973 (1985), p. 218.

7. Leopardi 1845 (1985), p. 28.

8. Smith 1776, 4.2.

9. See Brown 1994, pp. 165–166 and footnotes, for a discussion of such an "overly economistic" readings of *The Wealth of Nations*; and Evensky 2005, chap. 10, on the "Chicago Smith" versus the "Kirkaldy Smith."

10. Taylor (1989) makes much of the rise of individualism. It would be unwise to dismiss the argument of so wise a scholar that individuality is novel. But one wonders. From the docu-

ments we have, Israelites and Romans and the English peasants of *Piers Ploughman* or the people of *The Canterbury Tales*, or for that matter the blessed of *Il Paradiso*, do not look collectivist or communitarian or whatever alternative to "individualist" people have in mind when they make the argument.

11. Das 2009, chap. 1.

12. Frank 2005, p. 141. Frank claims the losses are "large and avoidable" but does not inquire into how large and avoidable the losses would be from having the government help us to avoid them.

13. Frank 2005, pp. 140–141.

14. Das 2009, p. 11.

15. For the Dalai Lama's opinion of the matter, see Brooks 2014.

16. Das 2009, p. 73.

17. Cicero 44 BCE, 32.

18. And compare Nygren 1930/1936 (1982).

19. Prestona and de Waal 2002.

20. Again, McCloskey 2011a.

21. Aquinas 1269–1272, art. 1, p. 112.

22. Brown 1994, pp. 7, 53, 177.

23. Fleischacker 2004, pp. 34–35, 97, 99. See also Peart and Levy 2005; Peart and Levy, eds. 2008.

24. McCloskey 2007, 2011b.

25. Simmel 1907 (2004), p. 240.

26. Smith 1759 (1790), 7.2.1.6–7.2.110, pp. 268–270. I will also give page numbers, to the Glasgow edition.

27. Smith 1759 (1790), 7.2.1.28, p. 282.

28. Smith 1759 (1790), 6.concl.1, p. 262.

29. Smith 1759 (1790), 6.concl.1, p. 262.

30. Smith 1759 (1790), 3.3.35, p. 152.

31. Smith 1759 (1790), 3.3.34, p. 152.

CHAPTER 21

1. Smith 1759 (1790), 1.1.2.1, pp. 13–14.

2. Shaftesbury 1699, 1732 (2001), Vol. 2, p. 135.

3. Klamer, like Mokyr, figures heavily in my writings, and so you might as well know that his first name is pronounced "ARE-yoh," and his last "KLAH-mer."

4. Anscombe 1958 (1997), p. 34.

5. Smith 1759 (1790), 7.2.2.14, p. 299.

6. Peterson and Seligman 2004, p. 30.

7. Hooker 1594 (1888), bk. 1, 40, 4.

8. Smith 1759 (1790), 3.3.43, p. 156.

9. Taylor 1989, p. 503. I am leaning here also on the lucid commentary on Taylor by Anna Wierzbicka (2006, pp. 80–82).

10. Taylor 1989, p. 242.

11. Porpora, *Landscapes of the Soul: The Loss of Moral Meaning in American Life* (Oxford, 2001), pp. 71–72, quoted in Wierzbicka 2006, p. 81.

12. Fleischacker 2004, pp. 61, 63.

CHAPTER 22

1. Smith 1776, 4.7, pt. 3.

2. Smith 1977, pp. 196–197 (June 3, 1776).

3. Hume 1741–1742 (1987), p. 548.

4. Smith, "Letter to Gilbert Elliot," October 10, 1759, in Smith 1977, p. 54.

5. Smith 1977, p. 54.

6. Smith 1977, p. 55.

7. *Gratia non tollit naturam sed perfecit*, Aquinas 1251–1273 (*Summa Theologica*), 1, Q8, ad 2.

8. Epictetus 8, 14, 17.

9. Epictetus 1.

10. Smith 1977, p. 52.

11. The same letter to Elliott, in Smith 1977, p. 53.

12. Hayek 1979, vol. 3, p. 76.

13. Again, Hayek 1979, vol. 3, p. 76. I refer to Peart and Levy 2005; Peart and Levy, eds. 2008.

14. I am indebted Peter Calcagno for a conversation that discovered what follows.

15. Smith 1776, 4.2.9, p. 456.

16. Smith 1776, 2.3.36, p.346.

17. Smith 1776, 4.2.9, p. 456.

18. Examples of the error from two economists whom I greatly admire are Boettke in Boettke, Caceres, and Martin 2013, p. 91, top line; and Gintis 2013, p. 119, top paragraph. Neither can be imagined *not* to have read *The Wealth of Nations*, as most people who commit the error can, and so I cannot explain it.

19. Fleischacker 2004, pp. 90–91.

20. Schumpeter 1949, p. 353.

21. Again, Peart and Levy 2005.

22. Smith 1762–1766, (A) 6.56, p. 352.

23. Montesquieu 1748, bk. 20, 1. See Henry Clark 2007.

24. Smith 1759 (1790), 2.1.3, p. 111.

25. Boettke 2011. Lynne Kiesling kindly set me straight on all this (see Kiesling 2011).

26. Schumpeter 1912 (1934); Kirzner 1973, 1989.

27. Field 2011.

28. Epstein 2009, p. xi.

29. I thank Graham Peterson for this insight.

30. Smith 1776, 4.9.51, p. 687.

31. Skinner 1969, reprinted in Tully, ed. 1989, p. 55; Austin is discussed on p. 61.

32. Kagan 2006, p. 133.

33. Smith 1759 (1790), 4.2.2.17, pp. 233–234.

34. Skinner 1969, in Tully, ed. 1989, p. 62.

CHAPTER 23

1. Huang 1998, p. 246.

2. Auden, "New Year Letter (January 1, 1940)," pt. 3, p. 184.

3. Anton Howes of King's College London set me straight on an ungenerous and inaccurate interpretation of Weber.

4. Lawrence 1923 (2003), p. 30.

5. Baudelaire 1857 (1986), p. 101.

6. Moretti 2013, p. 47.

7. Wood 2004, pp. 5–6.

8. Baudelaire 1857 (1986), p. 99.

9. MacIntyre 1981, pp. 171, 185.

10. Franklin, p. 143.

11. Wood 2004, p. 36.

12. Wood 2004, p. 12 and chap. 1, "Becoming a Gentleman."

13. Franklin, p. 115.

14. Franklin, p. 115.

15. Franklin, p. 113.

16. Wood 2004, p. 27.

17. Franklin, chap. 4.

18. Franklin, p. 106; my italics.

19. Franklin, p. 166.

20. Kant 1785 (2002), p. 10 (AK 4:395).

21. Franklin, p. 159. The Lopez remark is from a television interview I saw many years ago.

22. Franklin, p. 190.

23. Lawrence 1923, chap. 2.

24. Franklin, p. 114; his italics suppressed, mine added.

25. Franklin, p. 158.

26. Franklin, p. 54.

27. Franklin, p. 58.

28. Franklin, pp. 153 (Proverbs 3:16), 144 (Proverbs 22:29); Weber 1904–1905 (1958), p. 53.

29. Franklin, pp. 92, 83.

30. Field 2002.

31. Smith 1759 (1790), 1.3.2.7, p. 57.

32. Juvenal 4:86–93. Polonius was not so lucky.

33. Smith 1977, p. 121.

34. Smith 1977, p. 44 (Hume to Smith, July 28, 1759,).

35. Smith 1980, p. 243.

36. Herman 2001, p. 59.

CHAPTER 24

1. Andrew 1980, p. 432.

2. Fischer 1989; Grosjean 2014.

3. McCloskey 2006c, pp. 219–221.

4. Davidoff and Hall 1987, p. 21.

5. Andrew 1980, p. 429, n97.

6. Wahrman 1995.

7. Davidoff and Hall 1987, p. 152.

8. MacCulloch 2010, p. 754.

9. Davidoff and Hall 1987, p. 450.

10. MacCulloch 2010, p. 754.

11. Crystal and Crystal 2002, p. xx.

12. Austen 1815, chap.25.

13. Quoted to this effect in Moretti 2013, p. 135n.

14. Smiles 1859 (1958), p. 368.

15. McKeon 1987 (2002), p. 191.

16. Maine 1861 (1905), chap. 9, pp. 297–298.

17. Miller, 1957, p. 170.

18. Bismarck quoted in Taylor 1955, p. 101.

19. Temple 1673, IV, p. 83.

20. Hirschman 1977, p. 58.

21. Trump 1987.

22. Mann 1901 (1952), p. 200.

23. For a persuasive call to think again, see Lauck 2013.

24. Mann 1901 (1952), pp. 42, 380, 209, 320, 144, 370, 34, 400.

25. Mann 1901 (1952), pp. 124, 57, 215.

26. Mann 1901 (1952), p. 243.

27. Mann 1901 (1952), p. 215.

28. Mokyr 2009, p. 8.

CHAPTER 25

1. James 2007, p. 217.

2. Taylor 2007, p. 171.

3. Thomas 2009, pp. 122, 114.

4. Waterman 1994, p. 48.

5. Armstrong 2009 (2010), pp. 167, 171, and throughout. It is her main point, and is derived from the theologian Wilfred Cantwell Smith in *Belief in History* (1977) and *Faith and Belief* (1979).

6. Armstrong 2009 (2010), p. 187.

7. Luther, Sermon 25:7, quoted in Armstrong 2009 (2010), p. 171.

8. For a fuller discussion of "honest" in the play see McCloskey 2006b, pp. 294–295; and Empson 1951 (1989), p. 218.

9. Moynahan 2002, p. 402.

10. *Paradise Lost*, 2nd ed. (1674), 4:313f.

11. *2 Henry IV*, 5.1.

12. Quoted in Thomas 2009, p. 52.

13. Shaftesbury 1713, vol. 4, p. 4.

14. "The Putney Debates," Online Library of Liberty, http://oll.libertyfund.org/pages /1647-the-putney-debates.

15. Quoted in Johnson 1779–1781, "Addison."

16. Searches from the Bibliomania version of *Tom Jones*, http://bibliomania.com/0/0/22/49 /frameset.html.

17. Smith 1759 (1790), 3.3.6, p. 138.

18. Smith 1759 (1790), 7.4.28, p. 337.

19. Project Guttenberg text, as also for the counting of "honest" and compounds. Anthony Trollope, *Phineas Finn*, http://gutenberg.org/files/18000/.

20. https://www.google.com/webhp?hl=en#hl=en&q=:Jane+Austen%22+searchable+works.

21. Trollope 1867–1868, vol. 1, pp. 322, 323, 325.

22. Compare Moretti 2013, p. 173: "Honesty is for this [bourgeois] class what honor had been for the aristocracy; etymologically, it even derives from honor. . . . The word of the merchant is as good as gold."

23. The searchable Italian text is available at http://www.classicitaliani.it.

24. Machiavelli 1513 (1964), 9, para. 2, pp. 76, 77 (El principato); 19, para. 6, pp. 160, 161 (Da queste); 21, 5, pp. 188, 189 (E sempre interverrà).

25. Huppert 1999, pp. 99–102.

26. Moliere 1670, act 3, scene 12.

27. Balzac 1835 (1946), pp. 26, 64.

28. Stendhal 1830, pp. 44 (*Maintenant, monsieur, car d'après mes ordres . . .*), 47 (*Cette scène valut à Julien le titre de monsieur . . .*). Moretti (2013, p. 151) recounts a similar struggle over the honorific *Don* and the sarcastic *Mastro-Don* (craftsman-"Don") in Giovanni Verga's novel of a *borghese* in Sicily, *Mastro-Don Gesualdo* (1889; translated into English in 1923 by, of all people, D. H. Lawrence).

29. Devoto and Oli 1990, p. 1279.

30. Ragazzini. ed. 1993, p. 443.

CHAPTER 26

1. Pleij 1994, p. 64.

2. *OED*, "honest," sense 3c.

3. Mandeville 1714 ed., lines 409–410; "honest" in various forms occurs at lines 118, 225, 233, 257, 295, 334, as the silly virtue of a hive of bees who are therefore neither prosperous in economy nor great in power.

4. I am under the impression, perhaps false—I cannot get my Slavic-speaking and Spanish-speaking friends to set me straight, and therefore if I am wrong they are, you see, to blame—that the Slavic languages in modern times, like Spanish, appear *not* to have separated the two meanings as sharply. In Czech, for example, *čestný* means both "honorable" and "honest," as does the Polish Latin-imported *honorowy*, meaning both "noble" and "truth-telling." On the other hand, the non-imported Polish word for "noble" is *czcigodny*, cognate from the same root *cześć* with the Czech word, and *uczciwy* (note the u-) is now "that will not cheat."

5. Bybelgenootskap van Suid-Afrika, *Die Nuwe Testament en Psalms*. Capetown: CTP Boekdrukkers, 1983.

6. For all this, see the astonishing website *The Unbound Bible*, http://unbound.biola.edu/index.cfm.

7. Elias 1939 (2000), p. 88.

8. Rose 2002, p. 35.

9. Quoted in Thomas 2009, p. 55.

10. Emmanuel van Meteren (1535–1612). The quote is given in many places, such as Paxman 1998, p. 35.

11. Paxman 1998, p. 63.

12. Heal and Holmes 1994, pp. 39–42.

13. Holmes, personal correspondence, July 2014.

14. Clark et al. 2014.

15. Adhia 2013, p. 106.

CHAPTER 27

1. As J. Paul Hunter (1990) argues.

2. Coetzee 1986, p. 18. I might as well share with you my hard-won knowledge of how his name is pronounced: "kuut-SEE." No extra charge.

3. Watt 1957, p. 65.

4. Coetzee 2001, p. 24.

5. Hippolyte Taine 1866–1878, *Histoire de la Littérature Anglaise*, quoted in Coetzee 2001, p. 25.

6. Defoe 1719 (1993), pp. 41–42.

7. Defoe 1719 (1993), p. 41.

8. Defoe 1719 (1993), p. 68.

9. Austen 1818b, p. 1.

10. Coetzee 1994 in 2001, p. 227.

11. Langford 1992, pp. 5, 61, 105.

12. Langford 1992, pp. 5, 30, 107.

13. Willey 1964, pp. 221, 223, 228; italics suppressed.

14. Sturkenboom 2004.

15. See McCloskey 2006b, chaps. 17–18.

16. Addison 1713 (2004), act 1, scene 4, lines 33–38.

17. Addison and Steele 1711–1712 (1926), *Spectator*, no. 287 (Tuesday, January 29, 1712).

18. Addison 1713, act 4, scene 4, line 81.

19. Wright 1935, p. 656.

CHAPTER 28

1. Loftis 1959.

2. Viner 1970, p. 316.

3. Taylor 2007, pp. 178–179.

4. See the discussion in McCloskey 2006b, pp. 121–122.

5. Stone and Stone 1984, p. 192.

6. Addison and Steele 1711–1712 (1926), *Spectator*, no. 55 (Thursday, May 3, 1711).

7. Steele 1722, act 4, scene 2, as also the next quotation.

8. Voltaire 1733, 1734, p. 19.

9. Emerson 1844, 3rd paragraph.

10. My learning here comes from the literary historian Beatrice Schuchardt, who informed me of the work of Fuentes (1999) and García Garrosa (1999).

11. Child 1860.

12. Nettleton, Case, and Stone 1969, p. 595.

13. Lillo 1731 (1952), act 1, scene 1, p. 293. Act, scene, and page references are to the Modern Library edition, edited by Quintana.

14. Lillo 1731 (1952), p. 294.

15. Lillo 1731 (1952), 3.1.3–9. Laurent Volkmann of the Friedrich Schiller University of Jena reminded me of the passage. Notice that the word "science" has not yet been specialized, as it was in English in the middle of the next century, to "physical and biological science."

16. Cumberland 1771, act 1, scene 1, lines 3–5, in Nettleton, Case, and Stone 1969, p. 715.

17. Lillo 1731 (1952),I 1.1, p. 295.

18. Lillo 1731 (1952), 5.2, p. 331.

19. Lillo 1731 (1952), prologue and prose preface.

20. Quoted in Nettleton, Case, and Stone 1969, p. 596.

21. Fields 1999, p. 2.

22. Lillo 1731 (1952), 1.2, p. 296.

23. Lillo 1731 (1952), 4.2, p. 329.

CHAPTER 29

1. Sombart 1913 (1915), p. 115.

2. "Stevinus," *Encyclopaedia Britannica*, 11th ed., 1910–1911.

3. Temple 1673 (1972), 4, p. 87.

4. Knighton 2013, for example chap. 7, "Creating a Standard."

5. Petty 1690 (1890), preface.

6. Nye 2007, p. 153.

7. Nye 2007, p. 153.

8. Nye 2007, p. 52: "the Portugal trade furnishes us with some dying Commodities." Spelling and punctuation modernized.

9. Moretti 2013, p. 88.

10. See Ziliak and McCloskey 2008.

CHAPTER 30

1. Tocqueville 1840 (1945), vol. 1, pt. 2, chap. 9.

2. Nee and Swedberg 2007, pp. 4–5.

3. On Whorf, see McWhorter 2008, pp. 137–169, and especially his vexation on p. 144.

4. Storr 2013, p. 59.

5. Storr 2013, pp. 66–69.

6. Letter to Francisque de Corcelle, quoted in Swedberg 2009, p. 280.

7. Weber 1904–1905 (1958), p. 53.

8. Weber 1904–1905 (1958), p. 53.

9. Weber 1904–1905 (1958), p. 31. Again I thank Anton Howes of King's College, London for making me think this through again.

10. Swedberg 2009, p. 279.

11. Jones 2010, p. 8.

12. The late David Landes's writings provide cases in point of the Weberian mistake, from Landes 1949 onward.

13. Jones 2010, pp. 2, 4.

14. Jones 2010, p. 36.

15. This and the two quotations following, Niebuhr 1952, chap. 3, sec. 1.

16. Mote 1999, p. 391.

17. So, about China, Kenneth Pomeranz tells me.

18. Professor Françoise Lavocat of Université Paris 3 tells me this.

19. Simmel 1907 (2004), p. 444. Compare Shils (1957, p. 599), who brackets Simmel with Tönnies and early Sombart (and I would add, though I think Shils would not have, Weber) as "German sociological romanticism."

20. Oschinky 1971.

21. Kimbrough, Smith, and Wilson 2008; Kimbrough, Smith, and Wilson 2010; Wilson, Jaworski, Schurter, and Smyth 2012.

22. Quoted in Wood 1999, p. 262.

23. Pipes 1999 (2000), p. 25.

CHAPTER 31

1. Guttman 2014. I thank Lynn Greenhough for drawing my attention to the piece.

2. Berg 1985, 2004; Berg and Hudson 1992.

3. De Vries 2008.

4. McCloskey 1970.

5. Mokyr 2010, p. 35.

6. Mackenzie 1771, chap. 28, 127.

7. Temple 1672, chap. 6.

8. Montesquieu 1748 (1777), bk. 20, sect. 7.

9. Coase and Wang 2013a, p. 10.

10. Coase and Wang 2013a, p. 9.

11. Quoted in Phillipson 2010, p. 35.

12. Pat Hudson (1992, pp. 218–225) gives a brief but penetrating introduction to the issue.

13. Hume 1741–1742 (1987), "Of Civil Liberty," p. 93.

14. Coleman 1973.

15. See the factual doubts concerning "failure" expressed in McCloskey 1970, 1973; Edgerton 1996, 2007.

16. Heston, Summers, and Aten 2012, http://siteresources.worldbank.org/ICPINT/Resources/ICP_final-results.pdf.

17. As is argued in detail in Edgerton 1996, 2007.

18. Kennedy 1976, p. 59, which is the source for the popular verse quoted as well.

19. Kadane 2008. Kadane's research is fine, as is his writing. But, remarkably, he reads Smith as "demoralizing" (that is, allowing in an amoral sense such behaviors as worldly vanity, pp. 253–254). It is the left's and the right's misreading, both, that Smith was about justifying the worst of greed. Kadane makes Smith into Mandeville, claiming that "for Smith, 'vanity' augmented national wealth" (p. 259). One can find a *little* textual justification for such a claim, I admit. But Smith is fierce against vanity.

20. Kindleberger 1996, p. 93, quoting Letwin, *Josiah Child, Merchant Economy* (1969).

21. Sprat 1667 (1958), p. 88.

22. Dryden 1672, 2.1.391–393. Compare Van der Welle 1962, p. 140. I am indebted for the Dryden scholarship here to Kevin Vanden Daelen.

23. Child 1668 (1698), pp. 148, 68.

24. The Swedish historian Erik Thomson (2005) has shown that the English were not the only Europeans startled by the economic success of the United Provinces and ready, with some reluctance, to imitate them.

CHAPTER 32

1. "2015 Index of Economic Freedom," http://heritage.org/index/ranking. In his reworking of the statistics of (negative) market liberty, Leandro Prados de la Escosura wisely excludes the share of government expenditure (2014, pp. 8–10). He quotes Hayek writing in 1960: "A government that is comparatively inactive but does the wrong things may do much more to cripple the forces of the market economy than one that is more concern with economic affairs but confines itself to actions which assist the spontaneous forces of the economy."

2. Edgerton 1996. For a heavy use of the biological metaphor of birth, growth, maturity, and decline, see Kindleberger 1996.

3. Smith 1776, 4.9, p. 664.

4. Quoted in Brailsford 1961, p. 624. Thomas Jefferson, the driver of slaves, had the temerity to use Rumbold's words. Compare Jefferson's behavior, unto death, with John Lilburne's charge in 1646 that the upper house of Parliament was now acting as the king had: "All you intended . . . was merely to unhorse and dismount our old riders and tyrants, that so you might get up, and ride us in their stead" (Brailsford 1961, p. 93).

5. Maus 2002, p. 1837.

6. More 1516 (2010), p. 179.

7. I give the English translation of the Scots original. Lindsay 1542–1544 (2000), lines 4070–4075; the next quotations are 4082–4083 and 4085–4087. I thank my *vriendinnetje* Margaret Raftery of the University of the Free State for the reference.

8. Lindsay 1542–1544 (2000), lines 4187–4189 (bakers), 4194–4195 (cordiners).

9. Quoted in Marcus, Mueller, and Rose, eds. (2000), p. 328.

10. Filling 2009, p. 9.

11. *Coriolanus*, 1.1.158–167.

12. A point the English historian David Cannadine makes (Cannadine 1990).

13. Quoted in Wilson 1965, pp. 155–156.

14. Jardine and Stewart 1999, p. 433.

15. Burton 1621, pp. 352–361.

16. Akerlof 1970.

17. Davis 2012, p. 136.

18. Storr, personal correspondence, 2008.

CHAPTER 33

1. Marlowe 1592, 1.1.113, 2.2.56.

2. Bevington 2002, p. 483.

3. On the joke, sense 2b in the *OED*.

4. McNeir 1938.

5. Bevington 2002, p. 485.

6. It was a convention not always exploited. In Massinger's *A New Way to Pay Old Debts* (mid-1620s) everyone, high and low, speaks in blank verse.

7. Thus: "For *he* to*day* that *sheds* his *blood* with *me*," iambic pentameter.

8. Magnusson 1999, p. 120: the lower orders "lack the mastery to assimilate the prestige forms successfully to their actual performance."

9. Google Books scan of the reprinted 1698 edition, p. 117. The first public edition had been 1664, well after Mun's death. Bizarrely, this famous remark (and "One man's necessity becomes another man's opportunity," p. 116) is in aid of showing that expenditure on a suit at law is a good thing, because at least the money "is still in the kingdom," and so foreign trade is unaffected, and so all is well in the crucial matter of acquiring bullion from abroad. It is the usual trickle-down or trickle-up economics of "keeping the money at home," which nowadays lies behind, say, schemes to subsidize new sports stadiums.

10. Quoted in Waterman 2014b.

11. Cf. Bevington 2002, p. 484: "his ship literally comes in."

12. Deloney 1597, quoted in Stevenson 1976, p. 13.

13. Stevenson 1976, p. 14.

14. Mortenson 1976, p. 252.

15. Bevington 2002, p. 484.

16. McBurney 1965, pp. xi–xiii.

17. 17:38–49. The "gentlemanlike" is a little odd, though attested in the *OED* from 1557 to 1882. Perhaps it is a Dutchism from *meneerlijk*.

18. Stevenson 1976, pp. 8, 7.

19. Quoted in Stevenson 1976, pp. 3–4; my italics.

20. Stevenson 1976, p. 5.

21. Frey 2012.

22. Stevenson 1976, p. 18.

23. Alger 1868, p. 1.

24. Alger 1868, chap. 24; in chap. 20 the overslick salesman Coleman is called a "capitalist," in the earlier meaning of a substantial wealth holder. Alger was no enthusiast for trade-tested improvement, though he is routinely cited as one.

25. Multatuli 1860 (1988), p. 15. By the way, the real name of "Multatuli" (Latin for "many things have I borne") was in fact Dekker (which means "roofer"), like the Elizabethan dramatist.

26. Quoted in Watt 1957, p. 210.

CHAPTER 34

1. Sombart 1913, p. 17.

2. Sombart 1913, pp. 118, 128.

3. A'Hearn, Baten, and Crayen 2009; Dore 1965; Rawski 1979.

4. *1 Henry IV*, 2.5.160–199, condensed.

5. Boswell 1791 (1949), 2, 1783, p. 456.

6. Boswell 1791 (1949), 2, p. 458.

7. G. Clark 2007b, pp. 175–180.

8. Maynial 1911, pp. 7, 10.

9. Johnson 1775 (1984), p. 139.

10. Johnson 1775 (1984), p. 104.

11. Quoted in Mathias 1979, p. 312.

12. Davidoff and Hall 1987, p. 26.

13. Goethe 1796, chap. 10, para. 13.

14. Quoted in Mathias 1979, p. 296.

15. Tufte 1982, pp. 28, 32f, 44ff.

16. Bryson 2003, p. 57.

17. See, for example, Lane 1973, p. 142.

18. Wardley 1993.

19. Fussell, ed. 1936.

20. Jones 2010, p. 22.

21. Titow 1972.

22. I owe this idea to Professor Shan Chun of the Chinese University of Politics and Law, Beijing.

23. Keegan 1976, p. 90.

CHAPTER 35

1. McCormick 2001, pp. 14, 671–672.

2. I use throughout the Mattingly and Handford translation (Penguin, 1970), compared occasionally with the Stuart 1916 Latin. Tacitus, sect. 5, p. 105.

3. Tacitus, sect. 16, p. 114.

4. Tacitus, sect. 29, p. 125.

5. Huizinga 1935 (1968), p. 25.

6. Huizinga 1935 (1968), pp. 110–112.

7. Hohenberg and Lees 1985; Mann and de Vries 1984.

8. Schama 1987, pp. 47, 420.

9. Pleij 1994, p. 74.

10. Pleij 1994, p. 63.

11. Pleij 1994, p. 67.

12. Pleij (1994, p. 64) makes this point in quoting the printed edition of Heinric en Margriete.

13. Alpers 1983.

14. Fuchs 1978, p. 8.

15. Fuchs 1978, p. 115.

16. Sluijter 1991, p. 184.

17. Cicero nowhere gives the tag in so many words, but it is implied in several places, for instance *de Oratore* 27.115.

18. Brettell manual to accompany Brettell 2002, p. 14.

19. Kiers and Tissink 2000, p. 173.

20. My colleague long ago at the University of Iowa, the political philosopher John Nelson, taught me this.

21. Deursen 1999, p. 173.

22. For the interesting textual rise and fall of "earnest," see Moretti 2013, pp. 131–133.

23. Larkin 1970 (1983), p. 297.

24. Schama 1987, pp. 452–453.

25. Fuchs 1978, p. 147.

CHAPTER 36

1. Churchill, 1764 (1997), lines 185–196.

2. Temple 1673 (1972), 4, p. 88.

3. Wilson 1968, p. 55.

4. Jaume 2008 (2013), p. 147.

5. All this, McCants 1997, pp. 2, 4, 5.

6. McCants 1997, p. 201.

7. Hobbes 1640 (1650), chap. 9, para. 10. I admit that he might be anticipating moral sentiments. It is unwise to read Hobbes uncharitably, as Michael Oakeshott once noted, calling *Leviathan*, "the greatest, perhaps the sole, masterpiece of political philosophy written in the English language" (Oakeshott, "Introduction to *Leviathan*" [1946], http://oll.libertyfund.org /pages/hobbes-oakeshott-s-introduction-to-leviathan).

8. Israel 1995, p. 352.

9. Israel 1995, p. 355.

10. Simmel 1908 (1955), p. 154. Simmel continues, "so as to make their reduced energies more productive," and then finally in a eugenic gesture typical of his times, "so as to prevent the degeneration of their progeny."

11. Israel 1995, p. 358.

12. Langford 1992, p. 136.

13. But see the proposals for social insurance from businessmen in Aachen decades earlier (Reckendrees 2014b).

14. Israel 1995, p. 360.

15. De Vries and der Woude 1997, pp. 659, 661.

16. Parker 1985, p. 25.

17. Zagorin 2003, p. 259.

18. Huizinga 1935 (1968), p. 53.

19. Israel 1995, p. 673.

20. Wilson 1968, p. 18.

21. Wilson 1968, p. 17.

CHAPTER 37

    1. MacCulloch 2010, p. 686.

    2. Herman 2001, pp. 2-10.

    3. Union of Utrecht, art. 13.

    4. Nadler 1999, p. 11.

    5. MacCulloch 2010, p. 640.

    6. MacCulloch 2010, p. 677; his italics.

    7. Zamoyski 1987, pp. 90-91.

    8. MacCulloch 2004, p. 187.

    9. Zamoyski 1987, p. 144. The declarations by Erasmus and Grotius are mottoes for Zamoyski's chap. 7, "The Kingdom of Erasmus," and chap. 5, "God and Caesar."

    10. Zamoyski 1987, p. 75.

    11. Zamoyski 1987, p. 149.

    12. Toulmin 1992, p. 53.

    13. Vondel 1632, line 2: "*lekker burgerbloed.*"

    14. Zeeman 2004.

    15. Israel 1995, pp. 640, 638, 535.

    16. I am following here Stephen Toulmin's interpretation in Toulmin 1992, pp. 47-55.

    17. Israel 1995, p. 536.

    18. Quoted in Zagorin 2003, p. 149.

    19. Temple 1673 (1972), chap. 6.

    20. 1670 figures from Maddison 2001, p. 77, with a rough guess for countries not covered.

    21. Israel 1995, p. 639.

    22. Hansen 2014.

    23. Butler 1725, p. 349.

    24. Smith 1759 (1790), 7.2.4.12, p. 312.

    25. Rotter 1966.

    26. Khurana 2007.

    27. Israel 1995, p. 504.

    28. Stark 2001 (2003), p. 25.

    29. Trevor-Roper 1940 (1962), p. 3.

    30. The Italian historian Antonino de Stefano, quoted in Stark 2003, p. 61.

    31. Niebuhr, *The Social Sources of Denominationism* (1929), p. 12, quoted in Stark 2001 (2003), p. 25.

    32. Bakunin 1869, Third Letter.

    33. Stark 2001 (2003), p. 61. Compare pp. 24, 27, 55, and throughout.

    34. Butterfield 1980.

    35. Zagorin 2003, pp. 10, 12.

CHAPTER 38

    1. Hobsbawm 2011, p. 324.

    2. Bakunin 1869, Second Letter.

    3. Quoted in Sinyavsky 1959 (1960), p.159.

4. Rev. Brian Hastings helped me see this.

5. On the army's Ft. Myer, Virginia. tests of 1909, see Kenneth Chafee McIntosh, "Sudden Greatness," *Atlantic Monthly*, September 1921, http://theatlantic.com/magazine/archive/1921/09/sudden-greatness/306536/.

6. Taleb 2007.

7. Hayek 1960, p. 62.

8. Lienhard 2006, p. 118.

9. "Leveller Principles," section 8 of "Supplementary Documents" in *Puritanism and Liberty, Being the Army Debates (1647–9) from the Clarke Manuscripts* (Chicago: University of Chicago Press, 1951); accessed in Online Library of Liberty, http://files.libertyfund.org/files/2183/Clarke_1346_EBk_v6.0.pdf.

10. "The Putney Debates," Online Library of Liberty, http://oll.libertyfund.org/pages/1647-the-putney-debates. The Jack quotation is from Mercurius Pragmaticus, 9–16 November 1647.

11. Marchamont Nedham, quoted in Brailsford 1961, p. 309.

12. Milton 1649 (1957), pp. 255, 257.

13. Jacob 2001, p. 57.

14. Blackstone 1765–1769, 1, p. 153.

15. Mielants 2008, p. 40.

16. I take the vocabulary of the Church of Faith versus the Church of Power from Rodney Stark's sociological histories, such as Stark 2001 (2003).

17. MacCulloch 2010, p. 592.

18. Dewald 1993, p. xii.

19. Dewald 1993, p. 15.

20. Skwire 2013.

21. Surowiecki 2008.

CHAPTER 39

1. Rev. Brian Hastings in conversation; Tickle 2008; inspired by the ideas of the Episcopal bishop Mark Dyer.

2. Luther, ca. 1525, Point 48 ("On the Third Article").

3. Shorto 2013, p. 42.

4. Hegel 1821–1831 (1953), p. 122.

5. Quoted in Rasmusson 1995, p. 24.

6. Rasmusson 1995, p. 26.

7. Grice-Hutchinson 1952; Fernandez 2010.

8. René Taveneaux, writing in 1965, quoted in Jaume 2008 (2013), p. 149.

9. Jaume 2008 (2013), p. 166.

10. MacKinnon 1987, p. 242–243.

11. Taylor 2007, p. 735.

12. Vidal-Robert 2013.

13. Trevor-Roper 1940, pp. 2, 4.

14. Taylor 2004, p. 106.

15. Herman 2001, p. 19.

16. MacCulloch 2010, p. 718.

17. MacCulloch 2004, p. 171.

18. MacCulloch 2004, p. 508.

19. MacCulloch 2010, p. 685.

20. Huppert 1977.

21. On the dramatic fall in the cost of printing, see Baten and van Zanden 2008; Plopeanu et al. 2012.

22. Hill 1972, p. 11.

23. Moore 2000, p. 3.

24. Taylor 1989, pp. 20, 13, and throughout; McCloskey 2006b, chaps. 10–13, esp. p. 151.

25. Taylor 1989, p. 23.

26. Lienhard 2006, p. 57.

27. I owe this point to Marcel Becker of Radboud University.

28. Haskell 1999, p. 10.

CHAPTER 40

1. McMahon, p. 176, from Christopher Hill. As many do, McMahon retains Hill's interpolation, "that is, a comfortable livelihood in the earth," as though Winstanley had written it.

2. See for the analysis Watt 1957, p. 209.

3. Quoted by Huppert 1999, p. 101.

4. Wootton 2005.

5. Quoted in Bruckner 2000 (2010), p. 1.

6. Taylor 1989, p. 267.

7. Lawrence 1901. For an elaboration of the argument, see McCloskey 2010a, pp. 446–450.

8. Quoted in Sherman 1976.

9. As Robert Sessions reminded me.

10. As Anthony Waterman reminded me.

11. McMahon 2005, p. 15.

12. Taylor, "A Sermon Preached," quoted in McKeon 1987 (2002), p. 203.

13. Appleby 1978, p. 9. Elsewhere she has frequently used the phrase "rooted in human nature," noting the use of the idea by Locke and Jefferson.

14. Morrill 2001, p. 380. In this form the source is an acquaintance of King Charles, Bishop Gilbert Burnet (Burnet, *A History of His Own Times*, 1850 ed., p. 236).

15. Nygren 1930/1936 (1982), pp. 739–740.

16. Greeley 2000, p. 7 and chap. 2, "Sacred Desire." And Pope Benedict XVI's first encyclical, *Deus Caritas Est* (2005): "Eros and agape—ascending love and descending love—can never be completely separated. . . . Man cannot live by oblative, descending love alone. He cannot always give, he must also receive" (para. 7).

17. Second Vatican Council, "Decree Concerning the Pastoral Office of Bishops in the Church," Rome, October 28, 1965 http://www.vatican.va/archive/hist_councils/ii_vatican_council /documents/vat-ii_decree_19651028_christus-dominus_en.html.

18. John XXII's bull is *In the Lord's Field*, item 8: *In agro dominico*, translated from Meister Eckehart, *Deutsche Predigten und Traktate* (Zurich: Diogenes Verlag AG, 1979), p. 449 ff, http://www.geocities.ws/hugovanwoerkom/bullxxii_o.html.

19. Jacob 1976, p. 51.

20. Goldstone 2002, citing Jacob 1988.

21. Oslington 2008, p. 63.

22. Edwards 1739, pt. 2, period 3, pp. 347, 351, 353.

23. MacCulloch 2010, p. 759.

24. Phillips 1996, p. 5.

25. Nisbet 1980, p. 180.

26. Nye 2007; McCloskey 1980.

27. Waterman 2004, chap. 3; Waterman 2008.

28. *Book of Common Prayer* 1662 (1999), p. 539.

CHAPTER 41

1. Jacob 2014, p. 148. Jack Goldstone challenges me with the counterexample of what he supposes are the small number of copies of *The Encyclopedia of the Social Sciences* (2nd ed., 1967) "in private libraries." Yet it is surely an order of magnitude, maybe two, more than twenty or sixty-six.

2. Landes 1998, chap. 4.

3. Moynahan 2002, p. 140.

4. Rubin 2014.

5. Lehmann 1970, p. 4.

6. Rietbergen 1998, p. 230.

7. MacCulloch 2010, p. 617.

8. Fairbank, Reischauer, and Craig 1989, pp. 234, 486.

9. Coşgel, Miceli, and Rubin 2012.

10. Clegg 1997, chap. 6.

11. In the opinion of Hutton (1567), writing to the mayor and council of York, "See I many things that I cannot allow, because they be disagreeing with the sincerity of the Gospel," that is, with the Protestant reading of it. Compare Walker's introduction to Hutton 1567, p. ix.

12. Milton 1644 (1957).

13. Cowan 2005, p. 30.

14. Pettegree 2014, pp. 11, 368.

15. Barnhurst and Narone 2001, pp. 20, 190.

16. Greteman in discussion at the Newberry Library Milton Seminar. See Greteman 2012.

17. Marvel and others 2013. I am indebted to Graham Peterson for the citation.

18. Onela et al. 2007, p. 7334.

19. Johnson 1754, *Adventurer*, No. 137, 1754.

20. Hayek 1960, p. 15.

21. Jones 2010, pp. 96–97.

22. Allen 1983; Jacob 2014.

23. Dodgson and Gann 2010, p. 7.

24. Park, Burgess, and McKenzie 1925, pp. 83–84.

25. Neal 1817, vol. 4, chap. 1, p. 49.

26. Baechler 1971 (1975), p. 113.

27. Macfarlane 2000, p. 274.

28. Mokyr 2002, p. 278.

29. McNeill 1980, p. 63.

30. As William Ruger points out to me.

31. Parker 1988 (1996), pp. 140, 143.

32. On the ornamental character of modern mathematics, see Kline 1982.

33. The Euratlas Periodis Web shows a picture of the chaos of sovereignties and dependencies in Europe, and especially in what is now Germany. It gives detailed maps at every century mark from 1 to 2000 CE. If you want more detail, and 8,000 percent zoomability, you can acquire for 55 euros the Euratlas Periodis Expert English Version 1.1 by Marc-Antoine Nüssli and Christos Nüssli.

34. Ringmar 2007, p. 227.

35. Ringmar 2007, pp. 18, 160, 252, 270, 289.

CHAPTER 42

1. LaVaque-Manty 2006, pp. 715–716.

2. Compare the only slightly less sweeping language of the French Declaration of the Rights of Man and of the Citizen, art. 1: "Men are born and remain free and equal in rights. Social distinctions may be founded only upon the general good."

3. Ibsen 1877 (1965), p. 30.

4. North, Wallis, and Weingast 2009, p. 26. I disagree, that is, with their claim that "the *first* societies to reach the doorstep conditions were Britain, France, the Dutch, and the United States" (p. 166; my italics). None of their evidence comes from societies such as China or Japan or the Ottoman Empire that might test their claim. Nor for that matter do they study the Dutch case.

5. Reckendrees 2014a. He does not use the word "ethics," but that is what was the cause in the breakdown of civility in German politics in the late 1920s.

6. Neal and Williamson, eds. 2014, vol. 1, p. 2.

7. Arendt 1951 (1985), pp. 56, 62.

8. Aristotle, *Politics*, Bk. 1, 1254a.

9. Moynahan 2002, p. 541.

10. David Friedman made the point in a blog reacting to *Bourgeois Dignity*, July 15, 2013, http://daviddfriedman.blogspot.com.

11. Charles's speech is given at Project Canterbury ("Printed by *Peter Cole*, at the sign of the Printing-Press in Cornhil, near the Royal Exchange"), http://anglicanhistory.org/charles/charles1.html. In the document the year is given as 1648, because in the Julian calendar the year did not begin until March. So it is a Julian date in a New Style year.

12. MacCulloch 2004, p. 174.

13. Quoted in Taylor 2007, p. 178.

14. Senato.it has the Italian and the English translation.

15. Blainey 2009, p. 272.

16. Mencken 1916, p. 000.

17. Mencken 1949, p. 622.

18. As, among others, Sheri Berman (2006) has argued, as I've noted.

19. Reprinted and translated in Horst 1996, p. 142. The poem was called *Liefdesverklaring*, or "Love-Declaration."

20. Personal correspondence, 2014.

21. Yeats 1928 (1992), p. 260.

CHAPTER 43

1. Mueller 2011, pt. 1.

2. Lal 1998; summarized in Lal 2006, pp. 5, 155.

3. Needham, 1954–2008; Pomeranz 2000; and others.

4. Taylor 1989, p. 23; Taylor 2007, p. 179.

5. Parks 2005, p. 180.

6. Danford 2006, p. 319. The quotation from Lord Kames (1774) is Danford's.

7. Danford 2006, p. 324.

8. Danford 2006, p. 331.

9. Hume, 1741–1742 (1987), "Of Commerce."

10. Danford 2006, p. 332.

11. Danford 2006, p. 330.

12. See Palmer 2014.

13. Ringmar 2007, p. 31.

14. Ringmar 2007, p. 32.

15. Ringmar 2007, p. 24. Ringmar's remarkable literacy in an English not his native tongue, by the way, shows in his accurate use of the phrase "begs the question," which is widely used to mean "suggests the question."

16. Jones 2010, pp. 102–103.

17. Ringmar 2007, pp. 250, 254, 274, 279, 280, 281–282.

18. Ogilvie 2007, p. 662–663.

19. Ringmar 2007, pp. 72, 178, 286.

20. Ringmar 2007, p. 37.

21. Le Bris 2013.

CHAPTER 44

1. Keynes 1936, chap. 24, pp. 383–384.

2. Mises 1951, p. 566–567.

3. Almond and Verba 1963, p. 8.

4. I owe the fact to Terence Kealey of the University of Buckingham.

5. Jacob 2014, p. 124.

6. Hirschman 1977, pp. 9, 12.

7. The Chinese figure is from Fairbank et al. 1989, p. 228. The much less definite European reckoning comes from W. Clark 2003, pp. 214–215, and in more detail Simone 2003. The European figures do not include seminaries and merchant academies, which were not small. On the other hand, the examinees in China were older.

8. Daly 2013, p. xii.

9. I want to say plainly, in case it is not already plain, how much my thinking has depended on Goldstone's, summarized in Goldstone 2009.

10. Quoted in Porter 2000, p. 3. Jacob (2001, p. 13) quotes it as "a new light." The "affairs of Europe" that Shaftesbury mentions, though, concerned war (of the Spanish Succession), not the economy. Shaftesbury was an earl, not a merchant.

11. Mandeville 1733, 2, p. 116.

12. Mandeville 1733, 2, p. 110.

13. Mandeville 1733, 2, p. 118.

14. Mandeville 1733, 2, pp. 117, 119.

15. Mandeville 1733, 2, p. 117.

16. Mandeville 1733, 2, p. 111.

17. Mandeville 1733, 2, p. 106.

18. Mandeville 1733, 2, p. 26.

19. Mandeville 1733, 1, p. 24.

20. Mokyr 2002.

21. Porter 2000, p. 22.

22. Porter 2000, p. 15.

23. Fielding 1749 (1915), bk. 3, chap. 3.

24. Diderot 1772 (1796), quoted in Jacob 2001, p. 166; cf. p. 169: "Is there anything so senseless as a precept that forbids us to heed the changing impulses that are inherent in our being?"

25. Quoted in Campbell 1999, p. 99, from vol. 2 of *The Papers of Benjamin Franklin* (January 1, 1735–December 31, 1744; ed. L. W. Labaree, 1960]). Against my general practice, I have kept some of Franklin's Capitalization, in order to point to the master Conflict in the eighteenth century between principles of Revelation and principles of Nature.

26. Taylor 1989, p. 11.

27. As Maine said at the end of chapter 5 of *Ancient Law* (1861 [1905]). My usage here is anachronistic, because Maine was arguing about the transition from patriarchal law, such as Roman law, to English law circa 1861, in which more people than the paterfamilias (though not yet married women) were able to make "free agreements of individuals."

28. Johnson 1775 (1984), p. 115.

29. Bayly 1989, p. 34.

CHAPTER 45

1. https://ita.ufm.edu/es/ita-stories/oscar/.

2. Gerschenkron 1970; Raskov and Kufenko 2014; personal conversation with Raskov.

3. Or so I infer from reading in Ferguson 2000 and Wormell n.d.

4. Mokyr 2011, abstract.

5. Kian 2013, p. 8.

6. Quoted in Menand 2002, p. 45; the next, more famous, quotation is given on p. 51.

7. John D. Mueller 2010, p. 358. Mueller claims (Mueller 2010, p. 392n33) that in *The Bourgeois Virtues* I ignore love as a gift, which suggests that in looking over the book he omitted chapter 5.

8. D. Klemm 2004. On Boulding's framework of gifts, see McCloskey 2013a.

9. Tanner 2005.

10. Boulding 1973, p. I; my italics.

11. Boulding 1958, p. 186.

12. Haidt 2006, p. 29. The argument about house buying would be testable with brain scans, I suppose.

13. Amos 8:4–5.

14. Graeber 2011, p. 8.

15. Joseph Jacobs version, 1860, at D. L. Ashliman's website, http://pitt.edu/~dash/type 0328jack.html.

16. Coetzee 1999, p. 117.

17. Smiley 1998, p. 128.

18. John D. Mueller 2010, pp. 34–35.

19. Mokyr 2009, p. 23.

20. In F. Klemm, *A History of Western Technology* (1964), quoted in Leinhard 2006, p. 43.

21. Jacob 2014, pp. 147–150. Compare Mokyr 2008, p. 111.

22. Jacob 2014, pp. 140, 141.

23. Jacob 2014, pp. 142, 150.

24. Mead 2007, p. 114.

25. *La guerre franco-française* was first coined in 1950 in a book about Vichy France, but has been taken up to describe left versus right from 1789 to the present (Williams 2014, p. 2).

26. See Grafe (2012), the book of the economic historian of Spain I keep mentioning, which argues that Spain's problem was the power of regions—not the sort of centralism that France has practiced from the sixteenth century to the present.

27. Abu-Lughod 1989 (1991), p. 354.

28. Falangas 2006 p. 250.

29. Allen 2009.

30. Jones 2010, p. 119.

CHAPTER 46

1. Bhagavad Gita 9.32.

2. For more evidence on the point, see McCloskey 2006b, pp. 442–446.

3. Hourani 1991 (2005), pp. 72–73.

4. Braudel 1979 (1982), p. 555.

5. Simmel 1907 (2004), p. 245.

6. Le Roy Ladurie 1978 (1980), p. 332.

7. Le Roy Ladurie 1978 (1980), p. 336.

8. McCormick 2001, p. 13.

9. Gilmour 2011, pp. 57, 70.

10. Smollett 1766, p. 753.

11. Boccaccio 1349–1351 (2000), Tenth Day, Tale 9, p. 213; "he was a private citizen . . . ," p. 217.

12. Boccaccio 1349–1351 (2000), p. 219.

13. McCormick 2001, p. 13.

14. Neville 1990, p. 22.

15. I thank my colleague in Hispanic Studies at the University of California at Riverside, James Parr, for conversations on this point.

16. Tacitus, sect. 21, p. 119; sect. 12, p. 111.

17. Sawyer 1962 (1971).

18. Chaucer 1387 (1958), Prologue, lines 43, 478, 529.

19. Chaucer 1387 (1958), lines 361–373.

20. Chaucer 1387 (1958), lines 309–316.

21. Chaucer 1387 (1958), lines 231–232, 245–248.

22. Chaucer 1387 (1958), lines 173–174, 200.

23. The editions have differing line numbers, depending on the manuscript sources used; here I refer to Lindsay 1542–1544 (2000), lines 2892–2893, 2852–2863, 2941–2949, 3047–3061, and 3753–3756, as against merely 2810–2849 recommending a predictable tax system, and 2542–2549 of puzzling blather. In the 1879 edition available electronically the lines are roughly 4045–4073, pages 197–198 in the online text. I again thank Professor Margaret Raftery of the University of the Free State, South Africa, for leading me into the text.

24. Todeschini 2008, p. 23.

25. Davis 2012, p. 134.

26. *Everyman*, ca. 1480, lines 134, 333; subsequent quotations are lines 501–502, 232, 882, 428–430, 442.

27. Gardiner, personal correspondence, 2013. From prospectus for "'What Price God's People?' The Cathedral and the Bazaar in Late Antiquity."

28. Strietman 1996, p. 107.

29. Dijk 1996, p. 113. The italics in the Strietman quotation that follows are mine.

30. Viner 1959, p. 43.

31. Kuran 2003, p. 310.

CHAPTER 47

1. Hirschman 1977, p. 58.

2. Tacitus, sect. 14, p. 114.

3. Mayer 2012, p. 5.

4. *Commentary on the Summa Theologica of the Divine Doctor Thomas Aquinas* (1507–1522), quoted in Barbieri 1940 (2013), p. 2n3.

5. Stackhouse and Stratton 2002, p. 37.

6. Todeschini 2008, p. 19.

7. Origo 1957 (1986).

8. Todeschini 2008, p. 18.

9. Todeschini 2008, p. 18.

10. Todeschini 2008, p. 24.

11. Todeschini 2008 p. 26.

12. Thompson 2005, "Introduction."

13. Todeschini 2008, p. 26.

14. Todeschini 2008, p. 27, in Latin.

15. *Everyman*, ca. 1480, lines 76–79.

16. Todeschini 2008, p. 34.

17. Todeschini 2008, p. 33.

18. Todeschini 2008, p. 18 and throughout.

19. Todeschini 2008, p. 29.

20. Todeschini 2008, pp. 31–32.

21. Parks 2013, pp. 119, 134.

22. Pipes 1999 (2000), p. 27.

23. Smith 1776, 1.2.2.

24. Le Roy Ladurie 1978 (1980), p. 337.

25. *Winter's Tale* 4.4.702.

26. *Troilus and Cressida* 2.1.352–353.

27. Kadane 2008, p. 257.

28. Kadane 2008, p. 258.

29. Kadane 2008, p. 260; well, not so gifted a hymn writer.

30. Muldrew 1998; Marx 1867 (1887), chap. 24, sect. 3, p. 651.

31. Kadane 2008, p. 262.

32. Kadane 2008, p. 263.

33. Boettke and Storr 2002, p. 165.

34. Wierzbicka 2010, p. 36.

35. Report of Baron van Imhoff, governor-general of the East Indies, to the Dutch Indian Company, quoted in Feinstein 2005, p. 50. (Also quoted in Gilomee and Mbenga 2007, p. 67: the quotation is well known.) The quotation is the English translation, that of the van Riebeeck Society, 1918, the original Dutch of which I have not consulted. Therefore I am not certain that *meneer* was in fact the word used.

36. Giliomee and Mbenga, eds. 2007.

CHAPTER 48

1. Gilmour 2011, pp. 79, 82.

2. Puga and Trefler 2013.

3. Gilmour 2011, p. 79.

4. Ackroyd 2009, pp. 139–140.

5. Ackroyd 2009, p. 32.

6. Smith 1776, 1.10, pt. 2, p.152.

7. Easterly 2010.

8. McNeill 1974, p. 147.

9. Rosenthal and Wong 2011, p. 99.

10. Rosenthal and Wong, 2011, p. 93; compare pp. 79, 82, 90, 94, 97, 99.

11. Härtel 2006, pp. 13, 18.

12. Wakefield 2009, p. 142.

13. Wakefield 2009, p. 139.

14. Wakefield 2009, p. 144.

15. Chamberlain 1959 (1976), p. 29.

16. Carrièrre and Eco 2011, p. 58; my italics.

17. Du Plessis 2008.

18. Quoted in Wrightson 2000, p. 191.

19. On South Africa's sad licensing system, see the Zapiro cartoon for April 30, 2013, in the *Mail and Guardian* newspaper, quoting the famous Escher picture of stairs ever climbing.

20. David Landes 1969, 1965. This is a good place to acknowledge that I spent the first half of my historical career disagreeing with David on the role of the entrepreneur. I seem to be doomed to spend the second half agreeing with him. *En partie seulement.*

21. North, Wallis, and Weingast 2009, p. 25.

22. Olson 1993.

23. Boldrin and Levine 2008, p. 264.

24. Jacob 2014, p. 151.

25. Vargas Llosa 2013, p. 302.

26. I owe this insight to Dr. Stefan Gorißen of the University of Bielefeld.

27. Per Kristian Sebak, personal communication, 2012.

CHAPTER 49

1. Earle 1989, p. 5.

2. Jacob 2014, p. 78.

3. Mokyr 1990, p. 241.

4. Schoeck 1958 (1977), p. 156.

5. Nunziata and Rocco 2014, p. 19.

6. Kelly, Ó Gráda, and Mokyr 2013.

7. Gladwell 2009, p. 55.

8. Gladwell 2009, p. 67; my italics.

9. Gladwell 2009, p. 63n.

CHAPTER 50

1. Wang Fuzhi 1691 (2000), pp. 33–34.

2. Braudel 1967 (1973), p. 555.

3. Cannan 1926 (1927), p. 424. I am indebted to Donald Bourdeaux for the reference.

4. Wallerstein 1974, p. 51.

5. Elbl 2001.

6. Costa, Palma, and Reis 2013, abstract.

7. Parker 1985, p. 244.

8. Landes 1965, 1969; Coleman 1973; Wiener 1981.

9. Higgs 1987.

10. I mean G. Clark 2007b.

11. Mote 1999, p. 362, on the Southern Song—but, he notes, only beginning then.

12. Mote 1999, pp.373, 775.

13. McKay 2013, p. 556.

14. Barrington Moore 1998, pp. 148, 151. For an instance in China, see Mote 1999, p. 335, on the career of the philosopher Chen Liang (1143–1194) in the Southern Song.

15. Moore 1998, p. 156.

16. Sng and Moriguchi 2014.

17. Goldstone 1998, p. 276.

18. Mote 1999, p. 765.

19. McCloskey 2006b, p. 122, on Najita 1987.

20. http://brooklynmuseum.org/exhibitions/online/edo/.

21. Bookbinder 2010, p. 496.

22. Watson 1983.

23. Kuran 2003, p. 309.

24. Rubin 2008, p. 7, and subsequent quotation.

25. Kuran 2005, 2010.

26. Kuran 2003, p. 312.

27. Shilts 1999, 2004, 2007.

28. Rubin 2008, p. 3.

29. Rubin 2008, p. 11.

30. Prak 2011, p. 19.

CHAPTER 51

1. Smith 1762–1766, (A) 6.57.

2. An economist at Brown University, Herschel Grossman, used to claim that no one who was right-handed could be an economist.

3. A little video making the point is McCloskey 2013b.

4. Lodge 1988/1990, p. 219.

5. Äuslander, "Am Anfang war das Wort" (1981), http://deanita.de/buecher19.htm.

6. For advertising and for nominal income, see http://data360.org/dataset.aspx?Data_Set _Id=352.

7. *Statistical Abstract of the United States 2007*, http://census.gov/compendia/statab/2007 /2007edition.html.

8. McCloskey and Klamer 1995.

9. Antioch 2013, table 3.

10. Wallis and North 1986, table 3.13.

11. *Statistical Abstract of the United State 2006*, table 650, p. 430; Louis D. Johnston, "History Lessons: Understanding the Decline in Manufacturing," http://minnpost.com/macro-micro -minnesota/2012/02/history-lessons-understanding-decline-manufacturing.

12. Pink 2012, p. 21.

13. Pink 2012, p. 6.

14. Ridley 2011, p. 217.

CHAPTER 52

1. Jones and Harris 1967.

2. For example, the study of children's literature in support of the "need for achievement" in McClelland 1961.

3. Chaudhuri 1959, p. 178; see also his chap. 5, "Money and the Englishman." Chaudhuri was a professor English literature who made his first trip to England after the Second World War.

4. Das 2009, p. xxxiv. See also Das 2000, which he regards as his sympathetic treatment of the "householder" stage.

5. Das 2009, p. xxxviii.

6. Quoted in Lal 2006, p. 166. One is reminded of the old and vulgar joke in which the farmer says, "When I hear the word 'service,' I wonder who is getting screwed."

7. Adhia 2010, 2013.

8. Castiglione 1528 (1901), bk. 1, sect. 40, p. 54; 1.43, p. 57; and 2.65, p. 138.

9. Hirschman 1991, p. x; my italics.

10. McKeon 1987 (2002), p. 201; and p. 202: "Self-orienting activity, . . . the very fount of modern honor . . . creates values, and this is the criterion of virtue. . . . [It is also] in some real sense value-creating . . . that is, of exchange value."

11. Alan Macfarlane (1978, pp. 202–203) disagrees, and puts it much earlier in English history: "When Jefferson wrote, . . . 'all men are created equal and independent,' . . . he was putting into words a view of the individual and society which had its roots in thirteenth-century England or earlier. It is not . . . a view that emerged by chance in Tudor or Stuart England."

12. Keynes 1936, p. 383.

CHAPTER 53

1. Gerschenkron 1957 (1962).

2. Beckett 1965 (2008), p. 157.

3. Davidoff and Hall 1987, p. 162.

4. Sewell 1994, p. 198.

5. Tocqueville 1856 (1955), p. 146–147. I owe this citation to Clifford Deaton.

6. Wills 1992.

7. Delacroix 1995, p. 126.

8. Compare Goldstone 2009, p. 45.

9. Virgil Storr 2006 makes this point in the context of the economy of Barbados.

10. Lakoff 1996 (2002), 2008.

11. Higgs 1987, 2012.

12. *Whitney v. California*, 274 U.S. 357 (1927).

13. Ardagh 1991, p. 297.

14. McCloskey 2001.

15. Landes 1998, p. 516.

16. For example in Roland 2010.

17. Baumol, Litan, and Schramm 2007, p. 122.

18. Manin 1985 (1987), p. 364.

CHAPTER 54

1. Allen 1983; Nuvolari 2004. For a historical survey, see Bessen and Nuvolari 2012.

2. Mokyr 2010, p. 1, the opening sentence of the book.

3. Mokyr 2010, chap. 2.

4. On Freemasonry and the associated "radical enlightenment" (a concept that Margaret Jacob, not Jonathan Israel, devised), see Jacob 1981 (2006). Bakunin declared that during the eighteenth century "the bourgeoisie too had created an international association, a universal and formidable one, Freemasonry. It was the International of the bourgeoisie" (Bakunin 1869, First Letter).

5. These are Pius, *Quadragesimo Anno*; John, *Mater et Magistra* and *Pacem in Terris*; Paul, *Populorum Progressio* and *Octogesima adveniens*; and John Paul, *Laborem Exercens* and *Centesimus Annus*. Michael Novak is my guide here; Novak 1984, chaps. 6–8.

6. Bauer 2004, p. 107.

7. Reinert 2011, pp. 202, 269.

8. Suprinyak 2011.

9. Higgs 2008.

10. Schumpeter 1949, p. 349.

11. Schumpeter 1949. p. 351.

12. Tolstoy 1868–1869 (1933), p. 548.

13. Tolstoy 1868–1869 (1933), Second Epilogue, p. 499.

14. Tolstoy 1868–1869 1933), Second Epilogue, p. 491.

15. Sellar and Yeatman 1931 (1932), chap. 44, pp. 92–93.

16. Goldstone 2009, p. 36.

17. Childe 1943, p.14–15.

18. I am indebted to Jack Goldstone for reminding me of the fact and providing this way of saying it.

19. De Vries 1976, 2009; Kelly and Ó Gráda 2014.

20. Goldstone 1991.

21. McNeill 1976; Diamond 1997, chap. 3.

22. Easterlin 1995 (2004).

23. Johansson 2010, p. 6.

24. Mill 1845 (1967), p. 370.

25. North, Wallis, and Weingast 2009, pp. 192–193.

26. North, Wallis, and Weingast 2009, p. 194.

27. Cheung 1982.

28. Acemoglu and Robinson 2006. Ning Wang has suggested to me that Cheung allows for ideas.

29. Coase and Wang 2013b, pp. 32–35.

30. Smith 1759 (1790), first page; Coase and Wang 2013b, p. 205.

31. Coase and Wang 2013a, p. 10. And yet at one point in their book, they praise Cheung and his eager American students North, Weingast, and Wallis (Coase and Wang 2013b, pp. 163–164).

CHAPTER 55

1. Sylla and Toniolo 1992.

2. Hirschman 1958 (1988), p. 4; his italics.

3. North, Wallis, and Weingast 2009, pp. 295–308. Art Carden charitably suggests that they were expecting others to take up their hypothesis for other times and places. My point, though, is that if one is not sufficiently comparative from the outset, the hypotheses are wrong at the outset.

4. Runciman 2009.

5. Dodgson and Gann 2010, pp. 1, 3.

6. Sten Jönsson of the University of Gothenburg reminds me that heritability is the third element, and that too much of it can be bad, breeding too true.

7. Waterman 1991; Rothschild 2001; Nye 2007.

8. Mokyr 2009, p. 2.

9. McCloskey 1994 is a philosophical treatment, with cases in McCloskey 1990 and McCloskey 1985a.

10. Stigler 1982, pp. 10, 60.

11. Gramsci entry for 1932, in Forgacs, ed. 2000, p. 301.

12. Berman 2006, p. 11, referring to Mark Blyth, James Kloppenberg, Judith Goldstein, G. John Inenberry, Robert Keohane, and William Sewell Jr. The phrase "the vital few" is from the economic historian Jonathan Hughes, writing in praise of American economic entrepreneurs (1966).

13. Lakoff 2008. The sociologist Erving Goffman had devised the concept in 1974.

14. Davidoff and Hall 1987.

CHAPTER 56

1. Jacobs 1992. Ronald Mawby of Kentucky State University led me to the book.

2. I owe the image to the legal economist and economic historian David Haddock.

3. North and Thomas 1973, p. 157.

4. Bolt and Van Zanden 2013, p. 12; my italics. A lucid review of the estimates, especially in the matter of calorie consumption, and an attempt at an "ecumenical" overall judgment is Kelly and Ó Gráda 2013.

5. Rosenthal and Wong 2011, p. 232; compare p. 47, where they speak of "economic growth in Europe" as though its striking aspect was not technological betterment after 1800 but an increase in capital per worker 1348–1800.

6. Clark 2009; Clark, Cummins, and Smith 2010.

7. Jones 1988, p. 35.

8. Malanima 2013, p. 64.

9. Jones 2010, pp. 27–29.

10. Jones 2010, p. 29.

11. Ogilvie 2014, p. 471.

12. John Nye has made this point to me.

13. Wrigley 1988, p. 46.

14. Jones 2010, p. 245.

15. Willsher 2014. Anyone who has owned a French automobile, such as a Peugeot 504 station wagon, vintage 1975, feels it on her pulse.

16. Ogilvie 2011, pp. 413, 433; see also Ogilvie and Carus 2014

17. De Soto 2000; Shorto 2013, p. 94.

18. Wylie 1957 (1964). I am unable to find the page.

19. My sister Laura McCloskey, a professor of public health, set me straight on Mother Teresa.

20. Ignatieff 1994.

21. Quoted in Sinyavsky 1959 (1960), p. 176.

22. Kołakowski 2004, pp. 64–65.

23. Macaulay 1829; Bartleby bartleby.com/209/1088.html.

24. Jönsson 2012, pp. 17, 19, 20.

CHAPTER 57

1. Berman 2006, p. 2.

2. Pfister, Riedel, and Uebele 2012.

3. Berman 2006, p. 3.

4. Berman 2006, p. 10.

5. Berman 2006, p. 9.

6. McDougall 2004, p. 22, 18, 516n1.

7. Plato, *Meno*, 91d–e.

8. Appleby 2010, p. 26; italics supplied.

9. Appleby 2010, p. 13; for the 300 pamphlets p. 109. Her "long ago" book is Appleby 1978.

10. McCloskey 1975 1976.

11. Appleby 2010, p. 5.

12. Polanyi 1977, p. 40.

13. Polanyi 1944, pp. 54–55.

14. Diamond 1997, pp. 280, 287.

15. For a contrary, pro-Polanyi view see Renger 2003.

16. McCormick 2001, p. 783.

17. Adams 1966, p. 81.

18. Renger 1979, p, 250.

19. Snell 1997, p. 149.

20. Gelb 1969; Veenhof 1972.

21. J. N. Postgate 1992, p. 109.

22. Silver 1983a, 1983b, 1994.

23. Dahl 2003, p. 14n25.

24. Harvard University Press catalogue, Spring 2014.

CHAPTER 58

1. Klamer 2011; Klamer and Zuidhof 1998; Staveren 2001.

2. Klamer 2011, p. 154.

3. Gaus 2013, p. 25.

4. Issenberg 2007.

5. Fiske 1991 (1993), pp. 47, 45. I am indebted to Dr. Rick Wicks of the University of Gothenburg for putting me onto Fiske's astonishing work.

6. Fiske 1991 (1993), pp. 48–49.

7. Davis 2012, p. 60.

8. Compare Bell 2008.

9. Boettke and Storr 2002.

10. Mann 1901 (1952), p. 210.

11. Hourani 1991 (2005), p. 96.

12. du Gay 2000.

CHAPTER 59

1. Tolstoy 1868–1869, bk. 1, p. 5.

2. Neville 1990, p. 106.

3. Compare Mises 1951, "Preface to Second German Edition (1932)," p. 21.

4. Walzer 1983, p. 21.

5. Becker and Pessin 2005.

6. I am indebted to my brother John McCloskey for drawing my attention to this point.

7. Schmidtz and Brennan 2010, p. 2.

8. In *Knowledge and Persuasion in Economics* (1994), I make the case at length for an open society of science, even economic science.

9. Walmart's margin is higher than the grocery industry average of 1.9 percent, because the soft goods have higher margins. http://ycharts.com/companies/WMT/profit_margin; http://yourbusiness.azcentral.com/profit-margin-supermarket-17711.html.

10. Interview with Warren Buffett, *American Association of Retired Persons* (magazine), August–September 2013, p. 60.

11. Smith 1759 (1790), 1.3.

12. Koehn 2014.

13. Greenough 1980; Coase 1974.

14. Smith 1776, 1.1.11, pp. 22–23.

15. Quoted in Danford 2006.

16. Sowell 2015, p. 114. Donald Boudreaux drew my attention to the passage.

CHAPTER 60

1. Steinfeld 1991, for example p. 106.

2. Raftis 1964.

3. Higgs 2012, chap. 2.

4. The historical exceptions, such as starving Russians selling themselves into slavery in early modern times, are rare, about as rare as people signing a social contract with Leviathan.

5. By the Penn Tables; Heston, Summers, and Aten 2012. By the other measures (the World Bank, for example), Hong Kong is also ahead of the United States.

6. Michaels 1987, p. 111.

7. Tomasi 2012, pp. 254, 257.

8. Oxford 1999, p. 1610.

9. Wilde 1891 (1930), pp. 257, 270. The next quotation is from p. 259. The editor, Hesketh Pearson, remarks that Wilde had been inspired by Shaw's lecture, "without bothering himself much about economics" (p. xii). The astoundingly scholarly Wikipedia entry for "wage slavery," by the way, gives arguments from people like Noam Chomsky against my views, and those by people like Robert Nozick in favor of them.

10. Scruton 1994, p. 468.

CHAPTER 61

1. The discussion here benefited from reading on three successive days three illuminating papers, Demsetz 2010, Khalil 2010, and Ogilvie 2007.

2. McCloskey 2006b, pp. 156–159.

3. Macaulay 1848, end of chap. 3.

4. I explain the idea of psychiatric "insight," with illustrations from personal experience, in McCloskey 1999, pp. 96–131.

5. Lemert 2012, p. 21.

6. Colander 2013, p. xi.

7. On 1978, see Coase and Wang 2013b, p. 37.

8. Piketty 2014, chap. 14.

9. Brecht 1937–1939/1943, scene 8.

10. Diamond 2012, chap. 2.

11. Acemoglu and Robinson 2012, p. 240.

12. "Nearly a quarter of men in Asia-Pacific admit to committing rape: Survey shows extent of sexual violence in region where 70% of men report facing no legal consequences." *Manchester Guardian*, 9 September 2013.

13. Terry Kramer, head of the U.S. delegation, reported in the *Chicago Tribune*, October 9, 2012.

CHAPTER 62

1. Shields 2002, p. 264.

2. Shaw 1912.

3. Ruskin 1866, p. 41.

4. Clough 1862 (posthumous), at http://www.potw.org/archive/potw238.html.

5. Moretti 2013, p. 113.

6. Peterson 2014.

7. Personal communication, November 2014.

8. Lawrence 1929.

9. Auden 1936(1976), pt. 3, p. 185.

10. Gallagher 1985, p. xv.

11. Rapport 2008, pp. 406–407.

CHAPTER 63

1. Crunden 1982, p. 17; Himmelfarb 1991.

2. Graña 1964, p. 186.

3. Graña 1964, p. 172.

4. Buruma and Margalit 2004, p. 5.

5. Potts 2014.

6. The contrast is highlighted in Levy 2001, Levy and Peart 2001, Peart and Levy 2005, Peart and Levy, eds. 2008, and Sowell 1987 (2007)

7. Macaulay 1830, p. 183.

8. Tomasi 2012.

9. Kołakowski 2004, p. 14.

10. Kołakowski 2004, pp. 25–26.

11. Quoted in Kealey 2001, p, 240. There is a joke from the time of the Brezhnev-Reagan negotiations in Iceland in 1986 that imagines the famous economists Nicholas Kaldor and Thomas Balogh—academic Labourites both and naturalized Britons, Hungarian by birth (though nothing like antidemocratic, it should be understood, and certainly not communists)—packed in a wooden box and used by Brezhnev as a bargaining tool for extracting concessions: "If you don't concede, I will let out Hungarian economists to destroy your economy!"

12. Levy and Peart 2011.

13. Kołakowski 2004, p. 28.

14. Berlin 1955–1956 (2013), pp. 125–126.

15. Rapport 2008, p. 400.

16. Kealey 2001, p. 238.

17. Green 1993, p. 26.

18. Leonard 2005, pp. 212–213.

19. Toscani 2013.

20. Quoted in Taylor 1955 (1967), p. 162.

21. Dawson 1894, p. 347, in chap. 46, "Prince Bismarck's Home Life."

22. Quoted in Palmer 2012, p. 35.

23. Taylor 1955 (1967), pp. 203, 206.

CHAPTER 64

1. Gay 1998, Vol. 5, chap. 1.

2. Horowitz 1985, p. 166f.

3. Horowitz 1985, p. 168. I have taken this paragraph from *The Bourgeois Virtues*. The point bears repetition.

4. Marquis 1916–1935 (1943), p. 70.

5. Puccini, Illica, and Giacosa 1896 (1954), p. 29. The translation is sometimes odd. I have corrected it to be more literal.

6. Berlin 1966 (2001), p. 203.

7. Puccini, Illica, and Giacosa 1896 (1954), p. 13.

8. Puccini, Illica, and Giacosa 1896 (1954), p. 14.

9. The classicist John T. Kirby of the University of Miami suggested this to me.

10. Rimbaud 1874 (1914, 1962), p. 111.

11. Puccini, Illica, and Giacosa 1896 (1954), p. 13.

12. Puccini, Illica, and Giacosa 1896 (1954), p. 24.

13. Puccini, Illica, and Giacosa 1896 (1954), p. 32.

14. Kerman 1952, pp. 258, 262, 264.

15. Puccini, Illica, and Giacosa 1896 (1954), p. 9.

16. Arnold 1880.

17. Kerman 1952, pp. 260 (valentine), 254 (little shocker, depraved), 20 (Joyce Kilmer).

CHAPTER 65

1. UNFPA (United Nations Population Fund), *State of World Population 2007*, http://www .unfpa.org/swp/2007/english/introduction.html.

2. Williamson 1993, p. 14.

3. Blainey 2009, p. 95.

4. Sejersted 2011, p. 29.

5. Sachdev 2013, sect. 2, pp. 1, 4.

6. Rashid 2005, p. 11.

7. Hume 1738, 1740 (1893), bk. 3, p. 125.

8. Rashid 2005, p. 11.

9. Friedman 1989. I thank Fred Smith of the Competitive Enterprise Institute for this citation.

10. Heilbroner 1989. Vladimir Popov (2014) offers hope for socialism, though admitting at length what Heilbroner concluded.

11. Bakunin 1869, Second Letter.

12. Shils 1957, p. 490: the ex-Marxists "criticize the aesthetic qualities of a society which has realized so much of what socialists once claimed was of central importance, which has, in other words, overcome poverty and long arduous labor."

13. Ehrlich 1968 (1975), p. xi.

14. If you disbelieve it, you need to listen to Hans Rosling's astonishing video for the BBC, I say again: "Don't Panic—The Facts about Population," http://www.gapminder.org/videos/dont -panic-the-facts-about-population/.

15. Amazon.com reviews of Simon, *The Ultimate Resource 2*, accessed July 2013.

16. Eldridge 1995, p. 9. Such mistaken science comes from the English-language notion that the only "sciences" are physical and biological. Eldridge believed a geologist but did not consult an economist or a historian, because they are not (English-definition, *OED* sense 5b) "scientists." And so he got the scientific facts wrong.

CHAPTER 66

1. McCloskey 2012a.

2. Tomasi 2012.

3. Berlin 1999, p. 59.

4. Clark 1901 (1949).

5. Boudreaux 2014.

6. Kevin Murphy and Robert Topol reckon that rising life expectancy in the United States from 1970 to 2000 added a national health-capital value: people value their lives. In 2000 the

gain of $61 trillion in 2004 prices (net of the additional cost of health care for the older folk) was valued, Murphy and Topol reckon, at fully 10 to 50 percent of annual national income, varying with the year chosen. The benefits were fairly equally spread by individual income: rich and poor benefited. Murphy and Topol 2006, p. 902.

7. Fogel 1999.

8. Das 2009, p. 294.

9. Judt 2010, p. 169.

10. Smith 1776, 5.2.k.5, pp. 869–870.

11. Quoted in Coase and Wang 2013b, p. 206.

12. Armstrong 2009 (2010), p. 296.

13. Bouckaert et al. 2012.

14. Gaus is depending on Boehm 2001.

15. Boehm 2012, p. 161.

16. For Boehm's evidence from Spanish cave art, see Boehm 2012, p. 158; second italics mine.

17. Gaus 2013, throughout, for example, p. 18.

18. Clark forthcoming.

19. Judt 2010, p. 170.

CHAPTER 67

1. Lucas 2002, p. 109.

2. Tedin 2012; my italics.

3. Goldsmith 1773.

4. O'Brien 1982.

5. Lazonick 1981, 1991; Marglin 1974.

6. Carlyle 1843 (1899), bk. 3, chap. 2, p. 147.

7. Sellers 1996. He used similar formulations in many writings.

8. Rorty 1983 (1990). Admittedly the word "liberal" didn't mean to him quite what it means to me.

9. Montesquieu 1748, bk. 20, para. 1; my italics. Smith said much the same in *Theory of the Moral Sentiments*.

10. Walzer 2008.

11. Walzer 2008.

12. Sellers 1991, p. 6.

13. Paton 1948, p. 34.

14. Shackle 1972 (1992), pp. 3, 26. The sentence is hard to read, which is one reason Shackle has had little influence. That, and his non-Samuelsonian method.

15. Smith 1762–1766, p. 352.

16. Booth 1974, pp. xiii, xiv, 59.

17. Manin 1985 (1987), p. 363. Booth and Manin both acknowledged the influence of the Belgian law professor and rhetorician Chaim Perelman (1912–1984), and Booth that of the American literary critic Kenneth Burke (1897–1993) and of the American professor of philosophy I mentioned, Richard McKeon.

18. As, for example, Alejandro Chafuen 2003, p. 24, as cited in Casey 2006, p. 72n7. The assertion has been widely touted since Hume.

19. Taylor 2004, p. 115.

20. Graff and Birkenstein 2005; Bohm 1996 (2004).

21. Hayek 1960, pp. 25, 27.

22. Whitehead 1911, preface.

23. Mill 1848, 1871 (1970), bk. 4, chap. 6, para. 1.

24. McCloskey 2010a, chap. 38.

25. If you still doubt it, consult chapter 38 in *Bourgeois Dignity*.

26. Edgerton 2007, p. 41.

27. You may find persuasion about persuasion in the books of McCloskey 1985 (1998), 1990, 1994. If you are truly eager you can adjourn to deirdremccloskey.org and call up numerous persuasive articles arguing in much more detail for the views on rhetoric sketched here.

WORKS CITED

A'Hearn, Brian, Jörg Baten, and Dorothee Crayen. 2009. "Quantifying Quantitative Literacy: Age Heaping and the History of Human Capital." *Journal of Economic History* 69:783–808.

Abu-Lughod, Janet. 1989. *Before European Hegemony: The World System A.D. 1250–1350*. New York: Oxford University Press. Paperback 1991.

Acemoglu, Daron, and James A. Robinson. 2006. *Economic Origins of Dictatorship and Democracy*. Cambridge: Cambridge University Press.

Acemoglu, Daron, and James A. Robinson. 2012. *Why Nations Fail: The Origins of Power, Prosperity, and Poverty*. New York: Crown Business.

Acemoglu, Daron, Francisco A. Gallego, and James A. Robinson. 2014. "Institutions, Human Capital, and Development." Annual Review of Economics. *Annual Reviews* 6 (1): 875–912.

Ackroyd, Peter. 2009. *Venice: Pure City*. London: Chatto & Windus.

Adams, John. 1994. "Economy as Instituted Process: Change, Transformation, and Progress." *Journal of Economic Issues* 28 (June): 331–355.

Adams, Robert M. 1966. *The Evolution of Urban Society: Early Mesopotamia and Prehispanic Mexico*. New Brunswick, NJ: Aldine Transaction.

Addison, Joseph, and Richard Steele. 1711–1712 (1926). *The Spectator*. 4 vols. London: J. M. Dent, Everyman's Library.

Addison. Joseph. 1713 (2004). *Cato: A Tragedy, and Selected Essays*. Christine Dunn Henderson and Mark E. Yellin, eds. Indianapolis: Liberty Fund.

Adhia, Nimish. 2010. "Do Ideas Matter for Economics Policy? Evidence from Newspaper Coverage of Balance of Payments Crises in India." https://uic.academia.edu/Departments /Economics/Documents.

Adhia, Nimish. 2013. "The Role of Ideological Change in India's Economic Liberalization." *Journal of Socioeconomics* 44:103–111.

Akerlof, George Λ. 1970. "The Market for 'Lemons': Quality Uncertainty and the Market Mechanism." *Quarterly Journal of Economics* 84:488–500.

Akerlof, George A., and Robert J. Shiller. 2009. *Animal Spirits: How Human Psychology Drives the Economy, and Why It Matters for Global Capitalism*. Princeton, NJ: Princeton University Press.

Alfani, Guido. 2013. "Plague in Seventeenth-Century Europe and the Decline of Italy: An Epidemiological Hypothesis." *European Review of Economic History* 17:408–430.

Alger, Horatio, Jr. 1867. *Ragged Dick; or, Street Life in New York with the Boot-Blacks*. http://www.gutenberg.org/ebooks/5348.

Alger, Horatio, Jr. 1868. *Struggling Upward; or, Luke Larkin's Luck*. Reprint, Kessinger Publishing, n.d. http://www.gutenberg.org/cache/epub/5117/pg5417.html.

Allen, Robert C. 1983. "Collective Invention." *Journal of Economic Behavior and Organization* 4:1–24.

Allen, Robert C. 2009. *The British Industrial Revolution in Global Perspective*. Cambridge: Cambridge University Press.

Almond, Gabriel A., and Sidney Verba. 1963. *The Civic Culture: Political Attitudes and Democracy in Five Nations*. Princeton, NJ: Princeton University Press, 1963.

Alpers, Svetlana. 1983. *The Art of Describing: Dutch Art in the Seventeenth Century*. Chicago: University of Chicago Press.

Andrew, Donna. 1980. "The Code of Honour and Its Critics: The Opposition to Duelling in England, 1700–1850." *Social History* 5:409–434.

Anscombe, G. Elizabeth M. 1958 (1997). "Modern Moral Philosophy." *Philosophy* 33:1–19. Reprinted in Roger Crisp and Michael Slote, eds., *Virtue Ethics*, pp. 26–44. Cambridge: Cambridge University Press.

Antioch, Gerry. 2013. "Persuasion Is Now 30 Per Cent of US GDP: Revising McCloskey and Klamer after a Quarter of a Century." *Economic Roundup*, vol. 1 (April). Australian Treasury. https://ideas.repec.org/a/tsy/journl/journl_tsy_er_2013_1_1.html.

Appleby, Andrew B. 1980. "Epidemics and Famine in the Little Ice Age." *Journal of Interdisciplinary History* 10 (Spring): 643–663.

Appleby, Joyce Oldham. 1978. *Economic Thought and Ideology in Seventeenth-Century England*. Princeton, NJ: Princeton University Press.

Appleby, Joyce Oldham. 2010. *The Relentless Revolution: A History of Capitalism*. New York: Norton.

Aquinas, St. Thomas. Ca. 1269–1272. *Disputed Questions on Virtue* [*Quaestio disputata de vertibus in commune and Quaestio . . . cardinalibus*]. Trans. R. McInerny. South Bend, Indiana: St. Augustine's Press, 1999.

Arce M, Daniel G. 2004. "Conspicuous by Its Absence." *Business Ethics* 54:261–277.

Ardagh, John. 1991. *Germany and the Germans*. Revised ed. London: Penguin.

Arendt, Hannah. 1951 (1985). *The Origins of Modern Totalitarianism*. New ed. New York: Harcourt.

Aristotle. Ca. 330 BCE. *Politics*. Trans. Earnest Barker. Oxford: Oxford University Press, 1946 (1968).

Armstrong, Karen. 2009 (2010). *The Case for God*. New York: Knopf/Anchor Books.

Astill, James. 2013. *The Great Tamasha: Cricket, Corruption, and the Spectacular Rise of Modern India*. New York: Bloomsbury.

Attenborough, David. 1998. Episode 9 in *The Life of Birds*. BBC television series.

Auden, W. H. 1936 (1976). "Letter to Lord Byron." In Auden 1976.

Auden, W. H. 1940 (1976). "New Year Letter (January 1, 1940)." In Auden 1976.

Auden, W. H. 1976. *W. H. Auden: Collected Poems.* Ed. E. Mendelson. New York: Random House.

Austen, Jane. 1787–1790. "Edgar and Emma" in *Volume the First.* http://everything2.com/user /JudyT/writeups/Edgar+and+Emma.

Austen, Jane. 1811. *Sense and Sensibility.*

Austen, Jane. 1813. *Pride and Prejudice.*

Austen, Jane. 1814. *Mansfield Park.*

Austen, Jane. 1815. *Emma.*

Austen, Jane. 1818a. *Northanger Abbey.*

Austen, Jane. 1818b. *Persuasion.*

Austen, Jane. N.d. *Sanditon.*

Austen, Jane. 2004. *The Letters of Jane Austen.* Digireads.com Publishing.

Baechler, Jean. 1971 (1975). *Les Origines du Capitalisme.* Paris: Gallimard. Trans. as *The Evolution of Capitalism.* Oxford: Basil Blackwell.

Baechler, Jean. 2002. *Equisse d'une Histoire Universelle.* Paris: Gallimard.

Bailey, Steve. 1999. "Of Gomi and Gaijin." In D. W. George and Amy G. Carlson, eds. *Japan: True Stories of Life on the Road,* pp. 147–149. San Francisco: Travelers' Tales.

Bakunin, Mikhail. 1869. *To The Comrades of the International Workingmen's Association of Locle and Chaux-de-Fonds.* Geneva. https://www.marxists.org/reference/archive/bakunin/works /1869/program-letters.htm.

Balzac, Honoré de. 1835 (1946). *Père Goriot* [*Le Père Goriot*]. Trans. E. K. Brown, Dorothea Walter, and J. Watkins. New York: Random House/Modern Library.

Barbieri, Gino. 1940 (2013). *Decline and Economic Ideals in Italy in the Early Modern Era* [*Gli Economici degli Italiani all'inizio dell'era Moderna*]. Trans. S. Noto and Marian Christina Gatti. Firenze: Leo S. Olschki Editore.

Barreca, Alan, Karen Clay, Olivier Deschenes, Michael Greenstone, and Joseph S. Shapiro. 2013. "Adapting to Climate Change: The Remarkable Decline in the U.S. Temperature-Mortality Relationship over the 20th Century." Closed access paper, National Bureau of Economic Research paper 18692.

Barreca, Alan, Karen Clay, and Joel Tarr. 2014. "Coal, Smoke, and Death: Bituminous Coal and American Home Heating." Forschungsinstitut zur Zukunft der Arbeit. Discussion paper 7987.

Bartlett, Thomas, 2010. *Ireland: A History.* Cambridge: Cambridge University Press.

Baten, Jörg, and Jan Luiten van Zanden. 2008. "Book Production and the Onset of Modern Economic Growth." *Journal of Economic Growth* 13 (3): 217–235.

Baudelaire, Charles. 1857 (1986). "New Notes on Edgar Poe." In *The Painter of Modern Life and Other Essays.* Trans. and ed. 1964, Jonathon Mayne. New York: Da Capo.

Bauer, P. T. 2004. *From Subsistence to Exchange and Other Essays.* Princeton, NJ: Princeton University Press.

Baumol, William, Robert E. Litan, and Carl J. Schramm. 2007. *Good Capitalism, Bad Capitalism, and the Economics of Growth and Prosperity.* New Haven, CT: Yale University Press.

Bayly, Christopher. 1989. *Imperial Meridian: The British Empire and the World, 1780–1830.* London: Longman.

Bayly, Christopher. 2004. *The Birth of the Modern World: Global Connections and Comparisons, 1780–1914*. Oxford: Blackwell.

Becker, Howard S., and Alain Pessin. 2005. "A Dialogue on the Ideas of 'World' and 'Field.' " Ed. Harvey Molotch. French version in *Sociologie de l'art*, English trans. in *Sociological Forum* 21 (2006). Manuscript version at http://nyu.edu/classes/bkg/objects/becker.doc.

Beckett, J. C. 1965 (2008). *The Making of Modern Ireland, 1603–1923*. London: Faber and Faber.

Bell, Emma. 2008. *Reading Management and Organisation in Film*. Hampshire: Palgrave Macmillan.

Bell, Tom W. 2014. *Intellectual Privilege: Copyright, Common Law, and the Common Good*. Fairfax, VA: Mercatus Center, George Mason University.

Bentham, Jeremy. 1789 (1948). *A Fragment on Government, with an Introduction to the Principles of Morals and Legislation*. Ed. W. Harrison. Oxford: Basil Blackwell.

Berg, Maxine. 1985. *The Age of Manufactures: Industry, Innovation and Work in Britain 1700–1820*. Oxford: Blackwell.

Berg, Maxine. 2004. "In Pursuit of Luxury: Global History and British Consumer Goods in the Eighteenth Century." *Past and Present* 182:85–142.

Berg, Maxine, and Pat Hudson. 1992. "Rehabilitating the Industrial Revolution." *Economic History Review* 45:24–50.

Berlin, Isaiah. 1955–1956 (2013). "Equality." *Proceedings of the Aristotelian Society* 56:301–326. Reprinted in Henry Hardy, ed., *Concepts and Categories: Philosophical Essays*, pp. 106–134. 2nd ed. Princeton, NJ: Princeton University Press.

Berlin, Isaiah. 1966 (2001). "The Essence of European Romanticism." Reprinted in Berlin, *The Power of Ideas*, ed. Henry Hardy. London: Pimlico,

Berlin, Isaiah. 1999. *The First and the Last*. New York: New York Review Press.

Berman, Sheri. 2006. *The Primacy of Politics: Social Democracy and the Making of Europe's Twentieth Century*. Cambridge: Cambridge University Press.

Berndt, Ronald M., and Catherine H. Berndt. 1964. *The World of the First Australians*. Sydney: Ure Smith.

Berry, Christopher J. 1992. "Adam Smith and the Virtues of Commerce." In J. W. Chapman and W. W. Galston, eds., *Virtue: Nomos XXXIV*, pp. 69–88. Yearbook of the American Society for Political and Legal Philosophy. New York: New York University Press.

Bessen, James, and Alessandro Nuvolari. 2012. "Knowledge Sharing among Inventors: Some Historical Perspectives." In *Revolutionizing Innovation: Users, Communities and Open Innovation*, ed. D. Harhoff and K. Lakhani. Cambridge, MA: MIT Press.

Bevington, David. 2002. Introduction to Thomas Dekker's *The Shoemaker's Holiday*. In Bevington et al., eds. 2002, pp. 483–487.

Bevington, David, Lars Engle, Katherine Eiseman Maus, and Eric Rasmussen, eds. 2002. *English Renaissance Drama: A Norton Anthology*. New York: Norton.

Bhagavad-Gita as It Is. 2001. Ed. and trans. A. C. Bhaktivedanta Swami Prabhupada. Bkaktivedanta Book Trust.

Blackstone, William. 1765–1769. *Commentaries on the Laws of England*. Facsimile edition. Chicago: University of Chicago Press, 1979.

Blainey, Geoffrey. 2009. *A Shorter History of Australia*. North Sydney, NSW: Random House Australia.

Block, Fred, and Margaret R. Somers. 2014. *The Power of Market Fundamentalism: Karl Polanyi's Critique*. Cambridge, MA: Harvard University Press.

Boccaccio, Giovanni. 1349–1351 (2000). *Decameron*. Ed. and trans. Stanley Appelbaum. Italian and English text. Mineola, New York: Dover.

Boehm, Christopher. 2001. *Hierarchy in the Forest: The Evolution of Egalitarian Behavior*. Cambridge, MA: Harvard University Press.

Boehm, Christopher. 2012. *Moral Origins: The Evolution of Virtue, Altruism, and Shame*. New York: Basic Books.

Boettke, Peter. 2011. "Why *The Great Stagnation* Thesis Is the Most Subversive Libertarian Argument of Our Age" (blog post). *The Coordination Problem*, July 15. http://www.coordination problem.org/2011/07.

Boettke, Peter J., and Virgil Henry Storr. 2002. "Post-Classical Political Economy: Polity, Society and Economy in Weber, Mises and Hayek." *American Journal of Economics and Sociology* 61 (January): 161–191.

Bohm, David. 1996 (2004). *On Dialogue*. Routledge Classics. Oxford: Routledge.

Boldrin, Michele, and David K. Levine. 2008. *Against Intellectual Monopoly*. Cambridge: Cambridge University Press.

Bolt, Jutta, and Jan Luiten van Zanden. 2013. "The First Update of the Maddison Project: Re-Estimating Growth before 1820." http://www.ggdc.net/maddison/maddison-project /publications/wp4.pdf.

Book of Common Prayer. 1662 (1999). With an introduction by Diarmaid MacCulloch. London: Everyman.

Bookbinder, Paul. 2010. "'Wie es Eigentlich Gewesen' or Manufactured Historical Memory." *Journal of the Historical Society* 10:475–506.

Booth, Wayne C. 1974. *Modern Dogma and the Rhetoric of Assent*. Chicago: University of Chicago Press.

Bostrom, Nick. 2014. *Superintelligence: Paths, Dangers, Strategies*. Oxford: Oxford University Press.

Boswell, James. 1785 (1984), *The Journal of a Tour to the Hebrides with Samuel Johnson, LL.D.* Reprinted with Johnson's *A Journey to the Western Isles* (1775). Harmondsworth: Penguin.

Boswell, James. 1791 (1949). *The Life of Samuel Johnson, LL.D.* 2 vols. Everyman's Library. London: Dent.

Bouckaert, Remco, et al. 2012. "Mapping the Origins and Expansion of the Indo-European Language Family." *Science* August: 957–960.

Boudreaux, Donald J. 2001. "Can You Spot the Billionaire?" *The Freeman*, January 1.

Boudreaux, Donald J. 2014. "The Consumption Gap Between the Rich and the Rest of Us" (blog post). *Café Hayek*, January 21. http://cafehayek.com/2014/01/the-consumption-gap -between-the-rich-and-the-rest-of-us.html.

Boudreaux, Donald J. 2013. "No Time Like the Present." *Barron's*, September 14.

Boudreaux, Donald J., and Mark Perry. 2013. "The Myth of a Stagnant Middle Class." *Wall Street Journal*, January 23.

Boulding, Kenneth E. 1958. *The Skills of the Economist*. London: Hamish Hamilton.

Boulding, Kenneth E. 1973. *The Economy of Love and Fear*. Belmont, CA: Wadsworth.

Bourdieu, Pierre, and Loic J. D. Wacquant. 1992. *An Invitation to Reflexive Sociology*. Chicago: University of Chicago Press.

Bowden, Witt, Michael Karpovich, and Abbott Payson Usher. 1937. *An Economic History of Europe since 1750*. New York: American Book.

Brailsford, Henry Noel. 1961. *The Levellers and the English Revolution*. Stanford. CA: Stanford University Press.

Brandt, Loren, Debin Ma, and Thomas G. Rawski. 2014. "From Divergence to Convergence: Re-evaluating the History Behind China's Economic Boom." *Journal of Economic Literature* 52:45–123.

Braudel, Fernand. 1967 (1973). *Civilisation Matérielle, Économie et Capitalisme, XVe–XVIIIe*. Vol. 1, *Les structures du quotidien*. Trans. S. Reynolds, as *Capitalism and Material Life 1400–1800*. New York: Harpercollins.

Braudel, Fernand. 1979 (1982). *Civilisation Matérielle, Économie et Capitalisme, XVe–XVIIIe*, vol. 2, *Les jeux de l'échange*. Trans. S. Reynolds, as *The Wheels of Commerce 15th–18th Century*. New York: Harper and Row.

Brecht, Bertolt. 1937–1939/1943. *Galileo* [English trans. of *Leben des Galilei*]. http://arvindgupta toys.com/arvindgupta/lifeofgalileo.pdf.

Brennan, Geoffrey, Gordon Menzies, and Michael Munger. 2013. "A Brief History of Inquality." Unpublished paper, Australian National University, Canberra; University of Technology, Sydney.

Brettell, Richard. 2002. *From Monet to Van Gogh: A History of Impressionism*. Great Courses. Course nos. 7185, 7186. Teaching Company Lectures.

Broadberry, Stephen, and Bishnupriya Gupta. 2012. "India and the Great Divergence: An Anglo-Indian Comparison of GDP per Capita, 1600–1871." Department of Economics, University of Warwick Centre for Competitive Advantage in the Global Economy.

Brooks, Arthur C. 2014. "Capitalism and the Dalai Lama." *New York Times*, April 27, Opinion Pages.

Brown, Andrew. 2008. *Fishing in Utopia: Sweden and the Future That Disappeared*. London: Granta.

Brown, Gordon. 2002. "Can Both the Left and Right Claim Adam Smith?" Enlightenment Lecture, University of Edinburgh, April 25.

Brown, Vivienne. 1994. *Adam Smith's Discourse: Canonicity, Commerce, and Conscience*. London: Routledge.

Bruckner, Pascal. 2000 (2010). *Perpetual Euphoria: On the Duty to Be Happy*. Trans. Steven Rendall. Princeton, NJ: Princeton University Press.

Brynjolfsson, Erik, and Andrew McFee. 2014. *The Second Machine Age: Work, Progress, and Prosperity in a Time of Brilliant Technologies*. New York: Norton.

Bryson, Bill. 2003. *A Short History of Nearly Everything*. New York: Broadway Books.

Buber, Martin. 1909 (1923). *I and Thou*. Trans. Ronald Gregory Smith. Edinburgh: T. & T. Clark.

Buchanan, James, and Gordon Tullock. 1962. *The Calculus of Consent*. Ann Arbor: University of Michigan Press.

Burton, Richard. 1621. *Anatomy of Melancholy*. http://www.gutenberg.org/ebooks/10800.

Buruma, Ian, and Avishai Margalit. 2004. *Occidentalism: The West in the Eyes of Its Enemies*. New York: Penguin.

Butler, Joseph, Bishop. 1725. *Fifteen Sermons*. In *The Analogy of Religion and Fifteen Sermons* (1736), pp. 335–528. Reprint, London: Religious Tract Society, n.d.

Butler, Marilyn. 1975. *Jane Austen and the War of Ideas*. Oxford: Clarendon Press.

Butler, Marilyn. 1985. Introduction to reissue of Chapman, ed. 1955 (1985).

Butterfield, Herbert. 1980. *Toleration in Religion and Politics*. Ed. Adam Watson. New York: Council on Religion and International Affairs.

Campbell, James. 1999. *Recovering Benjamin Franklin*. Chicago: Open Court.

Campbell, Michael C., and Sarah A. Tishkoff. 2008. "African Genetic Diversity: Implications for Human Demographic History, Modern Human Origins, and Complex Disease Mapping." *Annual Review of Genomics and Human Genetics* 9:403–433.

Canetti, Elias. 1973 (1985). *The Human Province*. London: Andre Deutsch.

Cannadine, David. 1990. *The Decline and Fall of the British Aristocracy*. New Haven, CT: Yale University Press.

Cannan, Edwin. 1926. "The Gospel of Mutual Service." *Economica* 5 (June): 123–134. Reprinted in Cannan, *An Economist's Protest* (London: P. S. King, 1927).

Cantoni, Davide. 2015. "The Economic Effects of the Protestant Reformation: Testing the Weber Hypothesis in the German Lands." *Journal of the European Economic Association* 13 (August): 561–598.

Carlos, Ann M., and Frank D. Lewis. 1999. "Property Rights, Competition, and Depletion in the Eighteenth-Century Canadian Fur Trade: The Role of the European Market." *Canadian Journal of Economics/Revue canadienne d'Economique* 32:705–728.

Carlyle, Thomas. 1843 (1899). *Past and Present*. London: Chapman and Hall.

Carrièrre, Jean-Claude, and Umberto Eco. 2011. *This Is Not the End of the Book*. London: Harvill Secker.

Casey, Gerard. 2006. "Scholastic Economics." *Yearbook of the Irish Philosophical Society*. Pp. 70–83.

Castiglione, Baldasarre. 1528 (1901). *Il Libro del Cortegiano (The Book of the Courtier)*. Trans. and ed. L. E. Opdyke. New York: Liveright. Reprint, New York: Dover, 2003. Searchable Italian text at http://www.classicitaliani.it/index061.htm.

Cavell, Stanley. 2002. *Must We Mean What We Say?* Updated ed. Cambridge: Cambridge University Press.

Chafuen, Alejandro A. 2003. *Faith and Liberty: The Economic Thought of the Late Scholastics*. Lanham, MD: Lexington Books

Chamberlain, John. 1959 (1976). *The Roots of Capitalism*. Jersey City: Van Nostrand. Reprint, Indianapolis: Liberty Fund.

Chamlee-Wright, Emily, and Virgil Henry Storr, eds. 2010. *The Political Economy of Hurricane Katrina and Community Rebound*. Cheltenham, UK: Edward Elgar.

Chapman, R. W., ed. 1955 (1985). *Jane Austen: Selected Letters*. 2nd ed. Oxford: Oxford University Press.

Chapman, Steve. 2014. "Capitalism and Climate Change." *Chicago Tribune*, Sept 25, p. 21 only.

Chaucer, Geoffrey. 1387 (1958). "General Prologue" to *The Canterbury Tales*. Ed. A. C. Cawley. London: Dent.

Chaudhuri, Nirad C. 1959. *A Passage to England*. London: Macmillan.

Chayes, Sarah. 2015. *Thieves of State: Why Corruption Threatens Global Security*. New York and London: Norton.

Cheung, Steven N. S. 1982. "Will China Go Capitalist?" Hobart Papers. London: Institute of Economic Affairs.

Child, Francis James. 1860. *English and Scottish Ballads*. Vol. 8. Boston: Little, Brown. https://books.google.com/books?id=XgRbgUIIo54C.

Child, Josiah. 1668 (1698). *A New Discourse of Trade*. University of Michigan Library. https://books.google.com/books?id=b_hBAAAAYAAJ.

Childe, Gordon. 1943. *What Happened in History*. London: Pelican.

Churchill, Charles. 1764 (1997). "The Times." In Katherine Turner, ed., *Selected Poems of Thomas Gray, Charles Churchill, and William Cowper*, pp.72–91. London: Penguin.

Chwe, Michael. 2013. *Jane Austen, Game Theorist*. Princeton, NJ: Princeton University Press.

Cicero, Marcus Tullius. 44 BCE. *Laelius De Amicitia*. Trans. W. A. Falconer. Loeb ed. Cambridge, MA: Harvard University Press, 1923.

Cicero, Marcus Tullius. 55 BCE. *De Oratore*. Loeb ed. https://archive.org/stream/cicerodeorato reo1ciceuoft/cicerodeoratoreo1ciceuoft_djvu.txt.

Clapham, J. H. 1926. *An Economic History of Modern Britain*. Vol. 1, *The Early Railway Age, 1820–1850*. Cambridge: Cambridge University Press.

Clark, Gregory. 2007a. "The Long March of History: Farm Laborers' Wages in England 1208–1850." *Economic History Review* 60 (February): 97–135.

Clark, Gregory. 2007b. *A Farewell to Alms: A Brief Economic History of the World*. , NJ: Princeton University Press.

Clark, Gregory. 2009. Review of Angus Maddison, *Contours of the World Economy, 1–2030 AD: Essays in Macro-Economic History*. *Journal of Economic History* 69:1156–1160.

Clark, Gregory, Joseph Cummins, and Brock Smith. 2010. "The Surprising Wealth of Preindustrial England." University of California, Davis, Department of Economics.

Clark, Gregory, Neil Cummins, Yu Hao, and Daniel Diaz Vidal. 2014. *The Son Also Rises: Surnames and the History of Social Mobility*. Princeton, NJ: Princeton University Press.

Clark, Henry C. 2007. *Compass of Society: Commerce and Absolutism in Old-Regime France*. Lanham, Maryland: Lexington Books.

Clark, Henry C. Forthcoming. *Honor Management: The Unsocial Passions and the Untold Story of Modernity*.

Clark, John Bates. 1901 (1949). "The Society of the Future." *Independent* 53 (July 18): 1649–1651. Reprinted in Gail Kennedy, ed., *Democracy and the Gospel of Wealth*, pp. 77–80. Boston: Heath.

Clayton, Tony, Mariela Dal Borgo, and Jonathan Haskel. 2009. "An Innovation Index Based on Knowledge Capital Investment: Definition and Results for the UK Market Sector." Working Paper, Forschungsinstitut zur Zukunft der Arbeit (Institute for the Study of Labor). IZA DP No. 4021. Bonn.

Clegg, Cyndia Susan. 1997. *Press Censorship in Elizabethan England*. Cambridge: Cambridge University Press.

Coase, Ronald H. 1974. "The Lighthouse in Economics." *Journal of Law and Economics* 17: 357–376.

Coase, Ronald H., and Ning Wang. 2013a. "How China Became Capitalist." *Cato Policy Report* 35 (1): 1, 8–10.

Coase, Ronald H., and Ning Wang. 2013b. *How China Became Capitalist*. Basingstoke, UK: Palgrave-Macmillan.

Coate, Douglas. 2010. "Disaster and Recovery: The Public and Private Sectors in the Aftermath of the 1906 Earthquake in San Francisco." Department of Economics, Rutgers University, working paper.

Coetzee, J. M. 1986. *Foe*. London: Martin Secker & Warburg; and London: Penguin, 1987.

Coetzee, J. M. 1999. *Disgrace*. London: Martin Secker & Warburg.

Coetzee, J. M. 2001. *Stranger Shores: Essays 1986–1999*. London: Vintage, 2002.

Cohen, Edward. 1992. *Athenian Economy and Society: A Banking Perspective*. Princeton, NJ: Princeton University Press.

Colander, David. 2013. "Introduction." To Gino Barbieri. 1940. *Decline and Economic Ideals in Italy in the Early Modern Era* [*Gli Economici degli Italiani all'inizio dell'era Moderna*]. Trans. S. Noto and Marian Christina Gatti. Firenze: Leo S. Olschki Editore, 2013.

Coleman, Donald C. 1973. "Gentlemen and Players." *Economic History Review* 26:92–116.

Collier, Paul. 2007. *The Bottom Billion: Why the Poorest Countries Are Failing and What Can Be Done about It*. Oxford: Oxford University Press.

Connelly, Matthew. 2008. *Fatal Misconception: The Struggle to Control World Population*. Cambridge, MA: Harvard University Press.

Conze, Werner, and Jürgen Kocka, eds. 1985. *Bildungssystem und Professionalisierung in Internationalen Vergleichen*. Stuttgart: Klett-Cotta.

Cook, C. Justin. 2013. "Potatoes, Milk, and the Old World Population Boom." http://mpra.ub .uni-muenchen.de/51885/.

Copeland, Edward. 1986. "Money." In J. David Grey, ed., *The Jane Austen Companion*. New York: Macmillan.

Copeland, Edward. 1997. "Money." In Copeland and Juliet McMaster, eds., *The Cambridge Companion to Jane Austen*, pp. 127–143. Cambridge: Cambridge University Press.

Copeland, Edward. 2005. "Money." In Janet Todd, ed., *Jane Austen in Context*, pp. 317–326. Cambridge: Cambridge University Press.

Coşgel, Metin M., Thomas J. Miceli, and Jared Rubin. 2012. "Political Legitimacy and Technology Adoption." *Journal of Institutional and Theoretical Economics* 168:339–361.

Cost, Jay. 2015. *A Republic No More: Big Government and the Rise of American Political Corruption*. New York: Encounter Books.

Costa, Leonor Freire, Nuno Palma, and Jaime Reis. 2013. "The Great Escape? The Contribution of the Empire to Portugal's Economic Growth, 1500–1800." Universidad Carlos III de Madrid, Working Papers in Economic History, no. 13-7.

Cowan, Brian. 2005. *The Social Life of Coffee: The Emergence of the British Coffeehouse*. New Haven, CT: Yale University Press.

Cowan, Ruth Schwartz. 1983. *More Work for Mother: The Ironies of Household Technology from the Open Hearth to the Microwave*. New York: Basic.

Cowen, Tyler. 2011. *The Great Stagnation: How America Ate All the Low-Hanging Fruit of Modern History, Got Sick, and Will (Eventually) Feel Better*. New York: Dutton.

Cowen, Tyler. 2013. *Average Is Over: Powering American beyond the Age of Stagnation*. New York: Dutton.

Cowper, William. 1785 (1997). *The Task*. In Katherine Turner, ed., *Selected Poems of Thomas Gray, Charles Churchill, and William Cowper*. London: Penguin.

Cox, W. Michael, and Richard Alm. 1999. *Myths of Rich and Poor: Why We're Better Off Than We Think*. New York: Basic Books.

Crunden, R. M. 1982. *Ministers of Reform: The Progressives' Achievement in American Civilization, 1889–1920*. New York: Basic Books.

Crystal, David, and Ben Crystal. 2002. *Shakespeare's Words: A Glossary and Language Companion*. London: Penguin.

Czarniawska, Barbara. 2013. "Corruption or *Nineteen Eighty-Four*?" Unpublished paper, GRI, School of Business, University of Gothenburg.

Dahl, Jacob Lebovitch. 2003. *The Ruling Family of Ur III*. PhD thesis, Department of Near Eastern Languages and Cultures. University of California Los Angeles.

Daly, Jonathan. 2013. *The Rise of Western Power*. London: Bloomsbury.

Danford, John W. 2006. " 'Riches Valuable at All Times and to All Men': Hume and the Eighteenth-Century Debate on Commerce and Liberty." In David Womersley, ed., *Liberty and American Experience in the Eighteenth Century*, pp. 319–347. Indianapolis: Liberty Fund.

Das, Gurcharan. 2000. *India Unbound: From Independence to Global Information Age*. New York: Anchor Books/Random House.

Das, Gurcharan. 2009. *The Difficulty of Being Good: On the Subtle Art of Dharma*. Oxford: Oxford University Press.

Davidoff, Leonore, and Catherine Hall. 1987. *Family Fortunes: Men and Women of the English Middle Class, 1780–1850*. Chicago: University of Chicago Press.

Davis, James. 2012. *Medieval Market Morality: Life, Law and Ethics in the English Marketplace, 1200–1500*. Cambridge: Cambridge University Press.

Davis, Lance E., and Robert A. Huttenback. 1993. "Do Imperial Powers Get Rich Off Their Colonies?" In McCloskey, ed. 1993, pp. 26–33.

Dawson, William H. 1894. *Germany and the Germans*. Vol. 2. New York: Appleton.

Deaton, Angus. 2013. *The Great Escape: Health, Wealth, and the Origins of Inequality*. Princeton, NJ: Princeton University Press.

Defoe, Daniel. 1719 (1993). *Robinson Crusoe*. Norton Critical Edition. Ed. M. Shinagel. New York: Norton.

Defoe, Daniel. 1726 (1841). *The Complete English Tradesman*. Vol. 17 in *The Novels and Miscellaneous Works of Daniel De Foe*. Oxford. https://archive.org/details/novelsmiscellane17defo.

Deimel, Fr. Anton. 1931. *Sumerische Tempelwirtschaft zur Zeit Urukaginas und seiner Vorgänger*. Roma : Pontificio Istituto Biblico.

Dekker, Thomas. 1599 (2002). *The Shoemaker's Holiday*. In Bevington et al., eds. 2002.

Delacroix, Jacques. 1995. "Religion and Economic Action: The Protestant Ethic, the Rise of Capitalism, and the Abuses of Scholarship." *Journal for the Scientific Study of Religion* 34: 126–127.

Demsetz, Harold. 1967. `"Toward a Theory of Property Rights." *American Economic Review, Papers and Proceedings* 57:347–359.

Demsetz, Harold. 2010. "The Problem of Social Cost: What Problem? A Critique of the Reasoning of A. C. Pigou and R. H. Coase." Unpublished paper, Department of Economics, UCLA.

Deng, Kent G. 2013. "Demystifying Growth and Development in North Song China, 960–1127." Department of Economic History, London School of Economics, Working Paper 178/13.

Denyer, Simon. 2014. "In China's War on Bad Air, Government's Decision to Release Data Gives Hope." *Washington Post*, February 2.

Deursen, A. T. van. 1999. "The Dutch Republic." In J. C. H. Blom and E. Lamberts, eds., *History of the Low Countries*, pp. 143–218. New York: Berghahn Books.

Devoto, Giancomo, and Gian Carlo Oli. 1990. *Il Dizionario della Lingua Italiano*. Firenze: Le Monnier.

De Vries, Jan. 1976. *The Economy of Europe in an Age of Crisis, 1600–1750*. Cambridge: Cambridge University Press.

De Vries, Jan. 2009. "The Economic Crisis of the Seventeenth Century after Fifty Years." *Journal of Interdisciplinary History* 40:151–194.

De Vries, Jan. 2008. *The Industrious Revolution: Consumer Behavior and the Household Economy, 1650 to the Present*. Cambridge: Cambridge University Press.

De Vries, Jan. 2009. "The Economic Crisis of the Seventeenth Century after Fifty Years," *Journal of Interdisciplinary History* 40:151–194.

De Vries, Jan, and Ad van der Woude.1997. *The First Modern Economy: Success, Failure, and Perseverance of the Dutch Economy, 1500–1815*. Cambridge: Cambridge University Press.

Dewald, Jonathan. 1993. *Aristocratic Experience and the Origins of Modern Culture: France, 1570–1715*. Berkeley: University of California Press.

Diamond, Jared. 1997. *Guns, Germs, and Steel: The Fates of Human Societies*. New York: Random House.

Diamond, Jared. 2012. *The World until Yesterday: What We Can Learn from Traditional Societies*. New York: Viking Penguin.

Dijk, Hans van. 1996. "Structure as Means to Audience Identification in the Dutch *Rederijker* Drama." In Martin Gosman and Rina Walthaus, eds., *European Theatre 1470–1600: Traditions and Transformations*, pp. 113–117. Groningen: Egbert Forsten.

Dodgson, Mark, and David Gann. 2010. *Innovation: A Very Short Introduction*. Oxford: Oxford University Press.

Dore, Ronald P. 1965. *Education in Tokugawa, Japan*. Berkeley: University of California Press.

Douglas, Mary. 1972 (1979). "Deciphering a Meal." In Douglas, *Implicit Meanings*, pp. 249–275. London: Routledge and Kegan Paul.

Drelichman, Mauricio, and Hans-Joachim Voth. 2014. *Lending to the Borrower from Hell: Debt, Taxes and Default in the Age of Philip II*. Princeton, NJ: Princeton University Press.

Dryden, John. 1994. *The Works of John Dryden*. Vol. 12, ed. Vinton A. Dearing. Berkeley: University of California Press.

du Gay, Paul. 2000. *In Defense of Bureaucracy: Weber, Organisation, Ethics*. London: Sage.

Du Plessis, Stan. 2008. "Economic Growth in South Africa: A Story of Working Smarter, Not Harder." Unpublished presentation (May 20) to a conference at the Faculty of Theology,

University of Stellenbosch on Religion and the Eradication of Poverty in the Context of Economic Globalization. Department of Economics, University of Stellenbosch.

Dupré, Louis. 2004. *The Enlightenment and the Intellectual Foundations of Modern Culture*. New Haven, CT: Yale University Press.

Dutton, Harry I. 1984. *The Patent System and Inventive Activity during the Industrial Revolution*. Manchester: Manchester University Press.

Earle, Peter. 1989. *The Making of the English Middle Class: Business, Society and Family Life in London, 1660–1730*. London: Methuen.

Easterlin, Richard A. 1995 (2004). "Industrial Revolution and Mortality Revolution: Two of a Kind?" *Journal of Evolutionary Economics* 5:393–408. Reprinted in Easterlin, *The Reluctant Economist: Perspectives on Economics, Economic History and Demography*. Cambridge: Cambridge University Press.

Easterly, William. 2001. *The Elusive Quest for Growth: Economists' Adventures and Misadventures in the Tropics*. Cambridge, MA: MIT Press.

Easterly, William. 2010. Review of Matt Ridley, *The Rational Optimist*. *New York Times*, June 11.

Edgerton, David. 1996. *Science, Technology and the British Industrial "Decline," 1870–1970*. Cambridge: Cambridge University Press.

Edgerton, David. 2007. *The Shock of the Old: Technology and Global History since 1900*. Oxford: Oxford University Press.

Edwards, Jonathan. 1739. "Sinners in the Hands of an Angry God." Electronic Texts in American Studies. Ed. Reiner Smolinski. http://digitalcommons.unl.edu/cgi/viewcontent.cgi?article=1053&context=etas.

Edwards, Ronald A. 2013. "Redefining Industrial Revolution: Song China and England." Unpublished essay, Tamkang University.

Edwards, Ronald A. 2014. "Economic Revolution: Song China and England." Unpublished paper, Tamkang University.

Ehrlich, Paul R. 1968 (1975). *The Population Bomb*. New York: Ballantine Books. Cited as "Revised" in reprint of 1975 by Jackson Heights, New York: Rivercity Press.

Einaudi, Luigi. 1908–1946 (2000). *From Our Italian Correspondent: Luigi Einaudi's Articles in* The Economist *1908–1946*. Ed. Roberto Marchionatti. Firenze: Olschki Editore.

Einaudi, Luigi. 1919 (1961). "La Lotta Contro il Caro Vivere. Controllo e Libertà di Commercio." *Corriere della Sera*, 2 July. Reprinted in Einaudi, *Cronache Economiche e Cronache Politiche di un Trentennio (1893–1925)*, vol. 5. Torino: Einaudi, 1961.

Einaudi, Luigi. 1943. "Economia di Mercato e Capitalista Servo Sciocco." (Review of Turroni, *Introduzione all pilitica economia*.) *Rivista di Storia Economica* 8 (no. 1–2): 38–46.

Elbl, Ivana. 2001. "The State of Research: Henry 'the Navigator'." *Journal of Medieval History* 27:279–299.

Eldridge, Niles. 1995. *Dominion*. New York: Henry Holt.

Elias, Norbert. 1939 (2000). *The Civilizing Process*. Trans. E. Jephcott. Oxford: Blackwell.

Ellis, Markman. 2005. "Trade." In Janet Todd, ed., *Jane Austen in Context*, pp. 415–424. New York: Cambridge University Press.

Emerson, Ralph Waldo. 1844. "Character." In *Essays: Second Series*. http://emersoncentral.com/character.htm.

Emmett, Ross B. n.d. "Malthus *with* Institutions: A Comparative Analysis of Prudential Restraint." Unpublished paper, James Madison College, Michigan State University.

Empson, William. 1951 (1989). *The Structure of Complex Words*. London: Chatto & Windus. Reprint, Cambridge, MA: Harvard University Press.

Engerman, Stanley L., and Kenneth L. Sokoloff. 2012. *Economic Development in the Americas since 1500: Endowments and Institutions*. Cambridge: Cambridge University Press.

Epley, Nicholas. 2104. *Mindwise: Why We Misunderstand What Others Think, Believe, Feel, and Want*. Chicago: University of Chicago Press.

Epstein, Richard. 2009. "Introduction" to Bruno Leoni, *Law, Liberty and the Competitive Market*. Ed. Carlo Lottieri. Trans. Gian Turci and Anne MacDiarmid. New Brunswick, NJ: Transaction Publishers.

Evensky. Jerry. 2005. *Adam Smith's Moral Philosophy*. Cambridge: Cambridge University Press.

Fairbank, John K., E. O. Reischauer, and A. M Craig. 1989. *East Asia: Tradition and Transformation*. Revised ed. Boston: Houghton Mifflin.

Falangas, Andronikos. 2006. Review of Olga Katsiardi-Hering, *Artisans and Practices of Dying Yarns*. *Modern Greek Studies Yearbook* 22/23:246–250.

Feinstein, Charles H. 2005. *An Economic History of South Africa: Conquest, Discrimination and Development*. Cambridge: Cambridge University Press.

Ferguson, Niall. 2000. *The World's Banker: A History of the House of Rothschild*. London: Weidenfeld & Nicolson.

Ferguson, Niall. 2011. *Civilization: The West and the Rest*. London: Penguin.

Fernandez, Angel. 2010. "Derechos de propiedad y derechos subjetivos en Juan de Pariana" (Property and subjective rights in Juan de Mariana). Complutense University of Madrid, working paper. http://mpra.ub.uni-muenchen.de/25591/1/MPRA_paper_25591.pdf.

Field, Alexander J. 2002. *Altruistically Inclined? The Behavioral Sciences, Evolutionary Theory, and the Origins of Reciprocity*. Ann Arbor: University of Michigan Press.

Field, Alexander J. 2011. *A Great Leap Forward: 1930s Depression and US Economic Growth*. New Haven, CT: Yale University Press,

Fielding, Henry. 1749 (1915). *Tom Jones, A Foundling*. London: Bell.

Fields, Polly Stevens.1999. "George Lillo and the Victims of Economic Theory." In *English Drama 1650–1760: A Critical Miscellany* 32 (2, Fall). Department of English, Georgia State University.

Filling, John. 2009. "The Body, the Belly and Blood in *Coriolanus*." Philosophy of Science Association conference, April 2009. https://psa.ac.uk/2009/pps/Filling.pdf.

Findlay, Ronald, and Kevin H. O'Rourke. 2007. *Power and Plenty: Trade, War, and the World Economy in the Second Millennium*. Princeton, NJ: Princeton University Press.

Finnis, John M. 1980. *Natural Law and Natural Rights*. Oxford: Clarendon Press.

Fish, Stanley. 1980. *Is There a Text in This Class? The Authority of Interpretive Communities*. Cambridge, MA: Harvard University Press.

Fish, Stanley. 2001. *How Milton Works*. Cambridge, MA: Harvard University Press.

Fiske, Alan Page. 1991 (1993). *The Structures of Social Life: The Forms of Elementary Human Relations: Communal Sharing, Authority Ranking, Equality Matching, Market Pricing*. New York: Free Press.

Flaubert, Gustave. 2014. *Oeuvres complètes et Annexes. Correspondance.* Arvensa.com.

Fleischacker, Samuel. 1999. *A Third Concept of Liberty: Judgment and Freedom in Kant and Adam Smith.* Princeton, NJ: Princeton University Press.

Fleischacker, Samuel. 2004. *On Adam Smith's "Wealth of Nations": A Philosophical Companion.* Princeton, NJ: Princeton University Press.

Fleischacker, Samuel. 2014. "Adam Smith and the Left." In Ryan Hanley, ed., *Adam Smith: A Princeton Guide.* Princeton, NJ: Princeton University Press.

Floud, Roderick C., Bernard Harris, Robert W. Fogel, and Sok Chul Hong. 2011. *The Changing Body: Health, Nutrition, and Human Development in the Western World since 1700.* For the NBER. Cambridge: Cambridge University Press.

Fogel, Robert William. 1999. *The Fourth Great Awakening and the Future of Egalitarianism.* Chicago: University of Chicago Press.

Fogel, Robert William. 2004. *The Escape from Hunger and Premature Death, 1700–2100: Europe, America, and the Third World.* Cambridge: Cambridge University Press.

Fogel, Robert William. 2005. "Reconsidering Expectations of Economic Growth after World War II from the Perspective of 2004." *IMF Staff Papers* 52:6–14.

Folbre, Nancy. 2001. *The Invisible Heart: Economics and Family Values.* New York: The New Press.

Forgacs, David, ed. 2000. *The Antonio Gramsci Reader: Selected Writings 1916–1935.* New York: New York University Press.

Fouquet, Roger, and Peter J. G. Pearson. 2011. "The Long Run Demand for Lighting: Elasticities and Rebound Effects in Different Phases of Economic Development." Basque Centre for Climate Change (BC3), Working Paper no. 6.

Frank, Andre Gunder. 1998. *ReOrient: Global Economy in the Asian Age.* Berkeley: University of California Press.

Frank, Robert. 1999. *Luxury Fever.* New York: Free Press.

Frank, Robert. 2005. "Positional Externalities Cause Large and Preventable Welfare Losses." *American Economic Review* 95(2): 137–141.

Frankfurt, Harry. 1987. "Equality as a Moral Ideal." *Ethics* 98 (October): 21–43 .

Frankfurt, Harry. 2004. *The Reasons of Love.* Princeton, NJ: Princeton University Press.

Frey, Donald F. 2012. Review of Olivier Zunz, *Philanthropy in America: A History.* EH.net (January). http://eh.net/book_reviews/philanthropy-in-america-a-history/

Friedman, Benjamin M. 2005. *The Moral Consequences of Economic Growth.* New York: Knopf.

Friedman, Milton. 1970. "The Social Responsibility of Business is to Increase Its Profits." *New York Times Magazine,* September 13.

Friedman, Milton. 1989. "We Have Socialism. Q.E.D." *New York Times,* December 31. http://www.nytimes.com/2008/10/19/opinion/19opclassic.html.

Frost, Robert. 1946. *The Poems of Robert Frost.* New York: Modern Library.

Fuchs, R. H. 1978. *Dutch Painting.* London: Thames and Hudson.

Fuentes, Yvonne. 1999. *El triángulo sentimental en el drama del Dieciocho (Inglaterra, Francia, España).* Kassel: Edition Reichenberger.

Fussell, G. E., ed. 1936. *Robert Loder's Farm Accounts, 1610–1620.* Third series, vol. 53. Camden Society.

Gallagher, Catherine. 1985. *The Industrial Reformation of English Fiction, 1832–1867*. Chicago: University of Chicago Press.

Galor, Oded. 2005. "From Stagnation to Growth: Unified Growth Theory." In Philippe Aghion and Steven Durlauf, eds., *Handbook of Economic Growth*. Amsterdam: Elsevier.

García Garrosa, María Jesús. 1999. "*El comerciante inglés* y *El fabricante de paños*: de la traducción a la adaptación." In *Anales de Literatura Española 7*.

Gaus, Gerald F. 2006. "The Evolution of Society and Mind: Hayek's System of Ideas." In Ed. Feser, ed., *The Cambridge Companion to Hayek*. Cambridge: Cambridge University Press. Manuscript version at http://gaus.biz/HayekOnEvolution.pdf.

Gaus, Gerald F. 2013. "The Egalitarian Species." Unpublished paper, Department of Philosophy, University of Arizona, presented to the George Washington Forum in American Ideas, Ohio University, November 16, "Equality and Public Policy."

Gay, Peter. 1998. *Pleasure Wars: The Bourgeois Experience: Victoria to Freud*. Vol. 5. New York: Norton.

Gazeley, Ian, and Andrew Newell. 2010. "The End of Destitution: Evidence from British Working Households 1904–1937." University of Sussex, Economic Department working papers, no. 2.

Gelb, Ignace J. 1969. "On the Alleged Temple and State Economies in Ancient Mesopotamia." *Studi in onore di Edoardo Volterra* (Milano) 6:132–156.

Gerschenkron, Alexander. 1957 (1962). "Reflections on the Concept of 'Prerequisites' of Modern Industrialization." *L'industria* 2. Reprinted as pp. 31–51 in Gerschenkron, *Economic Backwardness in Historical Perspective: A Book of Essays*. Cambridge, MA: Harvard University Press.

Gerschenkron, Alexander. 1970. *Europe in the Russian Mirror*. Cambridge: Cambridge University Press.

Gerschenkron, Alexander. 1971. "Mercator Gloriosus: Review of John Hicks' *Theory of Economic History*." *Economic History Review* 24:653–666.

Giliomee, Hermann, and Bernard Mbenga, eds. 2007. *New History of South Africa*. Cape Town: Tafelberg.

Gilmour, David. 2011. *The Pursuit of Italy: A History of a Land, its Regions and their Peoples*. London: Allen Lane Penguin.

Ginsberg, Deborah. 2000. *Waiting: The True Confessions of a Waitress*. New York: HarperCollins.

Gladwell, Malcolm. 2009. *Outliers: The Story of Success*. London: Penguin.

Gobry, Pascal-Emmanuel. 2014. "This Is the Fundamental Thing That Most People, Including Paul Krugman, Don't Get about Economics." *Forbes*, May 19. http://www.forbes.com/sites/pascalemmanuelgobry/2014/05/19/economics-explained/.

Goethe, J. W, von. 1796 (1917). *Wilhelm Meister's Apprenticeship*. Harvard Classics, 1917. Cambridge, MA: Harvard University Press.

Goffman, Erving. 1974. *Frame Analysis: An Essay on the Organization of Experience*. Cambridge, MA: Harvard University Press.

Goldsmith, Oliver. 1773. "An Essay on the Theatre; or, a Comparison between Laughing and Sentimental Comedy." http://www.theatredatabase.com/18th_century/essay_on_the_theatre_001.html.

Goldstone, Jack A. 1991. *Revolution and Rebellion in the Early Modern World*. Berkeley: University of California Press.

Goldstone, Jack A. 1998. "The Problem of the 'Early Modern' World." *Journal of the Economic and Social History of the Orient* 41:249–284.

Goldstone, Jack A. 2002. "Efflorescences and Economic Growth in World History: Rethinking the 'Rise of the West' and the Industrial Revolution." *Journal of World History* 13:323–389.

Goldstone, Jack A. 2009. *Why Europe? The Rise of the West in World History, 1500–1850*. New York: McGraw-Hill.

Gordon, Edward E. 2013. *Future Jobs: Solving the Employment and Skills Crisis*. Santa Barbara, CA: Praeger, ABC-CLIO.

Gordon, Robert J. 2012. " Is U.S. Economic Growth Over? Faltering Innovation Confronts the Six Headwinds." Closed access paper, National Bureau of Economics Research Working Paper no. 18315.

Graeber, David. 2011. *Debt: The First 5,000 Years*. Brooklyn: Melville House.

Grafe, Regina. 2012. *Distant Tyranny: Markets, Power and Backwardness in Spain, 1650–1800*. Princeton, NJ: Princeton University Press.

Graff, Gerald, and Cathy Birkenstein. 2005. *They Say/I Say: The Moves That Matter in Academic Writing*. New York: Norton.

Gramsci, Antonio. 2000. *Prison Notebooks*. In *The Antonio Gramsci Reader: Selected Writings 1916–1935*, ed. David Forgacs. New York: New York University Press.

Graña, César. 1964. *Bohemian versus Bourgeois: French Society and the French Man of Letters in the Nineteenth Century*. New York: Basic.

Greeley, Andrew. 2000. *The Catholic Imagination*. Berkeley: University of California Press.

Green, David G. 1993. *Reinventing Civil Society: The Rediscovery of Welfare without Politics*. London: Civitas.

Greenough, Paul G. 1980. "Variolation and Vaccination in South Asia, c. 1700–1865: A Preliminary Note." *Social Science and Medicine* 14:345–347.

Grice-Hutchinson, Marjorie. 1952. *The School of Salamanca: Readings in Spanish Monetary Theory*. Oxford: Clarendon Press.

Griswold, Charles L., Jr. 1999. *Adam Smith and the Virtues of Enlightenment*. Cambridge: Cambridge University Press.

Grosjean, Pauline. 2014. "A History of Violence: The Culture of Honor and Homicide in the US South." *Journal of the European Economic Association* 12:1285–1316.

Grubel, Herbert. 2015. "Income Distribution, Income Mobility and the Rich in Canada: Or, All Canadians Are Getting Richer, the Poor More So Than the Rich." Fraser Institute preliminary paper.

Guttman, Nathan. 2014. "Leo Melamed Retraces Path of Escape From Nazis to Japanese Port." *Jewish Daily Forward*, June 27. http://forward.com/news/200802/leo-melamed-retraces-path-of-escape-from-nazis-to/.

Gwei-djen, Lu, and Joseph Needham. 1980. *Celestial Lancets: A History and Rationale of Acupuncture and Moxa*. Cambridge: Cambridge University Press.

Haakonssen, Knut. 1981. *The Science of a Legislator: The Natural Jurisprudence of David Hume and Adam Smith*. Cambridge: Cambridge University Press.

Haensch, S., R. Bianucci, et al. 2010. "Distinct Clones of *Yersinia pestis* Caused the Black Death." *PloS [Public Library of Science] Pathogens* 6(10).

Haidt, Jonathan. 2006. *The Happiness Hypothesis: Finding Modern Truth in Ancient Wisdom*. New York: Basic Books.

Hamashita, Takeshi. 2008. *China, East Asia, and the Global Economy: Regional and Historical Perspectives*. New York: Routledge.

Hanawalt, Barbara A. 1976. "Violent Death in Fourteenth- and Fifteenth-Century England." *Comparative Studies in Society and History* 18:297–320.

Hansen, Kristoffen Mousten. 2014. "Harmonization vs. Regulatory Competition—Which Way for Liberty and Progress?" Paper delivered at the Tenth Mises Seminar of the Istituto Bruno Levi conference at Sestri Levante, September.

Harcourt, Geoffrey C. 1994. "Comment." In H. Geoffrey Brennan and A. M. C. Waterman, eds., *Economics and Religion: Are They Distinct?*, pp. 205–212. Dordrecht: Kluwer.

Hardy, Thomas. 1886. *The Mayor of Casterbridge*.

Hariman, Robert. 2001. "Decorum." In *Encyclopedia of Rhetoric*. New York: Oxford University Press.

Hart, David M., and Sheldon Richman, eds. 2014. Discussion with Joel Mokyr, John Nye, and McCloskey of "Donald J. Boudreaux's 'Deirdre McCloskey and Economist's Idea about Ideas.'" *Liberty Matters* website, July. Indianapolis: Liberty Fund. http://oll.libertyfund.org/titles/boudreaux-liberty-matters-deirdre-mccloskey-and-economists-ideas-about-ideas-july-2014.

Härtel, Christian. 2006. *Berlin: A Short History*. Berlin: Auflag.

Haskell, Thomas L. 1999. "Responsibility, Convention, and the Role of Ideas in History." In P. A. Coclanis and S. Bruchey, eds., *Ideas, Ideologies, and Social Movements: The United States Experience since 1800*, pp. 1–27. Columbia: University of South Carolina Press.

Hayek, Friedrich. 1960. *The Constitution of Liberty*. Chicago: University of Chicago Press.

Hayek, Friedrich. 1979. *Law, Legislation, and Liberty*. Vol. 3, *The Political Order of a Free People*. Chicago: University of Chicago Press.

Heal, Felicity, and Clive Holmes. 1994. *The Gentry in England and Wales, 1500–1700*. Stanford. CA: Stanford University Press.

Hegel, Georg Wilhelm. 1821–1831 (1953). *Lectures on the Philosophy of History*. Trans. C. J and P. W. Friedrich. In C. J. Friedrich, ed., *The Philosophy of Hegel*. New York: Modern Library.

Heilbronner, Robert. 1989. "The Triumph of Capitalism." *New Yorker*, January 23, p. 93.

Hellie, Richard. 2003. "Russia: Early Modern Period." In Mokyr, ed. 2003.

Herman, Arthur. 2001. *How the Scots Invented the Modern World*. New York: Three Rivers Press/Random House.

Heston, Alan, Robert Summers, and Bettina Aten. 2012. *Penn World Table Version 7.1*. Center for International Comparisons of Production, Income and Prices at the University of Pennsylvania, July.

Higgs, Robert H. 1987. *Crisis and Leviathan: Critical Episodes in the Growth of American Government.* Pacific Research Institute for Public Policy. New York: Oxford University Press.

Higgs, Robert, 2008. "The Complex Course of Ideological Change." *American Journal of Economics and Sociology* 67:547–566.

Higgs, Robert H. 2012. *Delusions of Power: New Explorations of the State, War, and Economy.* Oakland, CA: Independent Institute.

Hill, Christopher. 1972. *The World Turned Upside Down: Radical Ideas during the English Revolution.* London: Maurice Temple Smith.

Himmelfarb, Gertrude. 1991. *Poverty and Compassion: The Moral Imagination of the Late Victorians.* New York: Knopf.

Hirschman, Albert O. 1958 (1988). *The Strategy of Economic Development.* New Haven, CT: Yale University Press.

Hirschman, Albert O. 1977. *The Passions and the Interests: Political Arguments for Capitalism before Its Triumph.* Princeton, NJ: Princeton University Press.

Hirschman, Albert O. 1991. *The Rhetoric of Reaction: Perversity, Futility, Jeopardy.* Cambridge, MA: Harvard University Press.

Hobbes, Thomas. 1640 (1650). *The Elements of Law Natural and Politic.* http://www.constitution.org/th/elements.htm.

Hobsbawm, Eric. 2003. *Interesting Times: A Twentieth-Century Life.* London: Allen Lane, Penguin.

Hobsbawm, Eric. 2011. *How to Change the World: Reflections on Marx and Marxism 1840–2011.* New Haven, CT: Yale University Press.

Hodes, Aubrey. 1972. *Encounter with Martin Buber.* London: Penguin.

Hohenberg, Paul M., and Lynn H. Lees. 1985. *The Making of Urban Europe: 1000–1952.* Cambridge, MA: Harvard University Press.

Hollander, Anne. 1994. *Sex and Suits: The Evolution of Modern Dress.* New York: Knopf.

Hont, Istvan, and Michael Ignatieff. 1983. "Needs and Justice in the *Wealth of Nations.*" In Hont and Ignatieff, eds., *Wealth and Virtue.* Cambridge: Cambridge University Press.

Hooker, Richard. 1594 (1888). *The Works of Richard Hooker.* Vol. 1, ed. John Keble. http://oll.libertyfund.org/titles/921.

Horowitz, Daniel. 1985. *The Morality of Spending: Attitudes toward the Consumer Society in America, 1875–1940.* Baltimore: Johns Hopkins University Press.

Horst, Han van der. 1996. *The Low Sky: Understanding the Dutch.* Schiedam: Scriptum.

Horwitz, Steve. 2013. "Inequality, Mobility, and Being Poor in America." *Social Philosophy and Policy* 31:70–91.

Hourani, Albert. 1991 (2005). *A History of the Arab Peoples.* London: Faber and Faber.

Hovenkamp, Herbert. 1990. "The First Great Law & Economics Movement." *Stanford Law Review* 42:993–1058.

Hudson, Pat. 1992. *The Industrial Revolution.* London: Edward Arnold.

Hudson, Pat. 2010. Review of *The British Industrial Revolution in Global Perspective. Economic History Review* 63:242–245.

Hughes, Jonathan R. T. 1966. *Vital Few: The Entrepreneur and American Economic Progress.* New York: Houghton Mifflin.

Hughes-Hallett, Penelope, ed., 1991. *The Illustrated Letters of Jane Austen*. New York: Clarkson Potter.

Huizinga, Johan H. 1935 (1968). *Dutch Civilization in the Seventeenth Century and Other Essays*. Ed. Pieter Geyl and F. W. N. Hugenholtz. Trans. A. J. Pomerans. London: Collins.

Hume, David. 1738, 1740 (1893). *Hume's Treatise of Morals: And Selections from the Treatise of the Passions*. Book 3 of *Treatise of Human Nature*. Google Books, from Ginn and Company edition (1893).

Hume, David. 1741–1742 (1987). *Essays, Moral, Political and Literary*. Ed. Eugene F. Miller. Indianapolis: Liberty Fund.

Humphries, Jane. 2011. *Childhood and Child Labour in the British Industrial Revolution*. Cambridge: Cambridge University Press.

Hunter, J. Paul. 1990. *Before Novels: The Cultural Contexts of Eighteenth-Century English Fiction*. New York: Norton.

Huppert, George. 1977. *Les Bourgeois Gentilhommes: An Essay on the Definition of Elites in Renaissance France*. Chicago: University of Chicago Press.

Huppert, George. 1999. *The Style of Paris: Renaissance Origins of the French Enlightenment*. Bloomington: Indiana University Press.

Hursthouse, Rosalind. 1999. *On Virtue Ethics*. Oxford: Oxford University Press.

Hutton, Matthew. 1567. "Letter to the Mayor and Council of York." In Greg Walker, ed., *Medieval Drama: An Anthology*, p. 206. Oxford: Blackwell, 2000.

Ibsen, Henrik. 1877 (1965). *Pillars of Society*. In Ibsen 1965, pp. 13–122.

Ibsen, Henrik. 1879 (1965). *A Doll House*. In Ibsen 1965, pp. 123–196.

Ibsen, Henrik. 1892 (1965). *The Master Builder*. In Ibsen 1965, pp. 779–860.

Ibsen, Henrik. 1965. *Ibsen: The Complete Major Prose and Plays*. Trans. and ed. R. Fjelde. New York: Penguin.

Ignatieff, Michael. 1994. "Interview with Eric Hobsbawm." Show Special, 24 October, on Hobsbawm's *The Age of Extremes*.

Inoue, Kyoko. 1991. *MacArthur's Japanese Constitution: A Linguistic and Cultural Study of Its Making*. Chicago: University of Chicago Press.

Inoue, Kyoko. 2001. *Individual Dignity in Modern Japanese Thought: The Evolution of the Concept of Jinkaku in Moral and Educational Discourse*. Ann Arbor: Center for Japanese Studies/University of Michigan Press.

Isaacs, Julia B. 2007. *Economic Mobility of Families across Generations*. Brookings Institution, http://brookings.edu/~/media/research/files/papers/2007/11/generations%20isaacs/11 _generations_isaacs.

Israel, Jonathan. 1995. *The Dutch Republic: Its Greatness, Rise, and Fall, 1477–1806*. Oxford: Clarendon Press.

Issenberg, Sasha. 2007. *The Sushi Economy*. New York: Gotham Books.

Jacob, Margaret C. 1981 (2006). *The Radical Enlightenment: Pantheists, Freemasons and Republicans*. London: Allen and Unwin. 2nd rev. ed., Lafayette, LA: Cornerstone.

Jacob, Margaret C. 1988. *The Cultural Meaning of the Scientific Revolution*. Philadelphia: Temple University Press.

Jacob, Margaret C. 2001. *The Enlightenment: A Brief History*. Boston: Bedford/St. Martin's.

Jacob, Margaret C., and Catherine Secretan, eds. 2008. *The Self-Perception of Early Modern Capitalists*. New York: Palgrave Macmillan

Jacob, Margaret S. 1976. *Newtonians and the English Revolution 1689–1720*. Ithaca, NY: Cornell University Press.

Jacob, Margaret S. 2014. *The First Knowledge Economy: Human Capital and the European Economy, 1750–1850*. Cambridge: Cambridge University Press.

Jacobs, Jane. 1992. *Systems of Survival: A Dialogue on the Moral Foundations of Commerce and Politics*. New York: Random House.

James, Clive. 2007. *Cultural Amnesia: Notes in the Margin of My Time*. London: Picador.

James VI of Scotland. 1598 (1996). *The True Law of Free Monarchies; and, Basilikon doron*. Ed. Daniel Fischlin and Marl Fortier. Toronto: Centre for Reformation and Renaissance Studies.

Jardine, Lisa, and Alan Stewart. 1999. *Hostage to Fortune: The Troubled Life of Francis Bacon*. New York: Farrar Straus & Giroux/Hill and Wang.

Jaume, Lucien. 2008 (2013). *Tocqueville: The Aristocrat Sources of Liberty*. Trans. A. Goldhammer. Princeton, NJ: Princeton University Press.

Johansson, Sheila R. 2010. "Medics, Monarchs and Mortality, 1600–1800: Origins of the Knowledge-Driven Health Transition in Europe." University of Oxford, Discussion Papers in Economic and Social History, no. 85.

Johnson, Samuel. 1753. "The Merit of Actions Is Not to Be Judged by Their Event." In William Page, ed., *The Life and Writings of Samuel Johnson* (1840), pp. 234–245.

Johnson, Samuel. 1754. *Adventurer*, no. 134, February 26. http://samueljohnson.com/adv137 .html.

Johnson, Samuel. 1775 (1984). *A Journey to the Western Isles*. Reprinted with Boswell's 1785 *The Journal of a Tour to the Hebrides with Samuel Johnson, LL.D.* Harmondsworth: Penguin.

Johnson, Samuel. 1779–1781. *Lives of the Most Eminent English Poets: Addison, Savage, and Swift*. http://www.gutenberg.org/files/4679/4679-h/4679-h.htm.

Jones, E. E., and V. A. Harris. 1967. "The Attribution of Attitudes." *Journal of Experimental Social Psychology* 3:1–24.

Jones, Eric L. 1988. *Growth Recurring: Economic Change in World History*. New York: Oxford University Press.

Jones, Eric L. 2010. *Locating the Industrial Revolution: Inducement and Response*. London: World Scientific.

Jönsson, Sten. 2012. "The Appropriate Banker and the Need for Ontological Re-positioning." Gothenburg Research Institute, Report 2012:4. University of Gothenburg, Sweden.

Jorde, L. B., W. S. Watkins, et al. 2000. "The Distribution of Human Genetic Diversity: A Comparison of Mitochondrial, Autosomal, and Y-Chromosome Data." *American Journal of Human Genetics* 66 (March): 979–988.

Joy, Charles A. 1877. "Papin's Steam Engine." *Scientific American* 36.

Judt, Tony. 2010. *Ill Fares the Land*. London: Penguin.

Julien, François. 1996. *A Treatise on Efficacy: Between Western and Chinese Thinking*. Trans. Janet Lloyd. Honolulu: University of Hawaii Press.

Juvenal. Ca. 100 CE. *The Satires of Juvenal and Persius*. Trans. G. G. Ramsay. New York: G. P. Putnam, 1924.

Kadane, Matthew. 2008. "Success and Self-Loathing in the Life of an Eighteenth-Century Entrepreneur." In Jacob and Secretan, eds. 2008.

Kagan, Jerome. 2006. *An Argument for Mind*. New Haven, CT: Yale University Press.

Kanefsky, John. 1979. "Motive Power in British Industry and the Accuracy of the 1870 Factory Returns." *Economic History Review* 32:360–375.

Kant, Immanuel. 1785 (2002). *Groundwork for the Metaphysics of Morals*. Trans. and ed. Allen W. Wood. New Haven, CT: Yale University Press.

Kealey, Terence. 2001. "Back to the Future." In James Tooley, ed., *Buckingham at 25: Freeing Universities from State Control*, pp. 228–246. London: Institute for Economic Affairs.

Keegan, John. 1976. *The Face of Battle: A Study of Agincourt, Waterloo, and the Somme*. London: Jonathan Cape.

Kelling, George L., and James Q. Wilson. 1982. "Broken Windows: The Police and Neighborhood Safety." *Atlantic* 249 (March): 29–38.

Kelly, Morgan, and Cormac Ó Gráda. 2011. "The Economic Impact of the Little Ice Age." University College Dublin, UCD Centre for Economic Research working paper series, no. 14.

Kelly, Morgan, and Cormac Ó Gráda. 2014. "Change Points and Temporal Dependence in Reconstructions of Annual Temperatures: Did Europe Experience a Little Ice Age?" *Annals of Applied Statistics* 8:1372–1394.

Kelly, Morgan, and Cormac Ó Gráda. 2013. "*Numerare Est Errare*: Agricultural Output and Food Supply in England before and during the Industrial Revolution." *Journal of Economic History* 73:1132–1163

Kelly, Morgan, Cormac Ó Gráda, and Joel Mokyr. 2013. "Precocious Albion: A New Interpretation of the British Industrial Revolution." School of Economics, University College Dublin. For the *Annual Reviews of Economics*, July 2013.

Kennedy, Paul M. 1976. *The Rise and Fall of British Naval Mastery*. New York: Scribner's.

Kenny, Charles. 2011. *Getting Better: Why Global Development Is Succeeding*. New York: Basic Books.

Kenny, Charles. n.d. (ca. 2014). "Is Anywhere Stuck in a Malthusian Trap?" Washington: World Bank. At http://charleskenny.blogs.com.

Kenyon, John. 1883. *The History Men*. London: Weidenfeld and Nicolson.

Kerman, Joseph. 1952. *Opera as Drama*. New York: Vintage 1952.

Keynes, John Maynard. 1936. *The General Theory of Employment, Interest and Money*. London: Macmillan.

Khalil, Elias L. 2010. "Institutions, Power, History and Optimization." Unpublished paper, Department of Economics, Monash University.

Khurana, Rakesh. 2007. *From Higher Aims to Hired Hands: The Social Transformation of American Business Schools and the Unfulfilled Promise of Management as a Profession*. Princeton, NJ: Princeton University Press.

Kian, Kwee Hui. 2013. "Chinese Economic Dominance in Southeast Asia: A *Longue Durée* Perspective." *Comparative Studies in Society and History* 55 (January): 5–34.

Kiers, Judikje, and Fieke Tissink, with others. 2000. *The Glory of the Golden Age: Dutch Art of the 17th Century*. Amsterdam: Waanders Publishers.

Kiesling, Lynne. 2008. *Deregulation, Innovation, and Market Liberalization: Electricity Regulation in a Continually Evolving Environment*. London: Routledge.

Kiesling, Lynne. 2011. "Boettke on Cowen, Smith, Schumpeter, and Stupidity" (blog post). *Knowledge Problem*, http://knowledgeproblem.com/.

Kiesling, Lynne. 2012. "Regulation's Effect on Experimentation in Retail Electricity Markets." In Emily Chamlee-Wright, ed., *The Wealth and Well-Being of Nations*, vol. 4, *Self-Governance, Polycentrism, and the Social Order*, pp. 89–113. Beloit, WI: Beloit College Press.

Kimbrough, Erik O., Vernon L. Smith, and Bart J. Wilson. 2008. "Historical Property Rights, Sociality, and the Emergence of Impersonal Exchange in Long-Distance Trade." *American Economic Review* 98:1009–1039.

Kimbrough, Erik O., Vernon L. Smith, and Bart J. Wilson. 2010. "Exchange, Theft, and the Social Formation of Property." *Journal of Economic Behavior and Organization* 74:206–229.

Kindleberger, Charles P. 1996. *World Economic Primacy: 1500–1990*. New York: Oxford University Press.

Kirby, John T. 1990. "The "Great Triangle" in Early Greek Rhetoric and Poetics." *Rhetorica: A Journal of the History of Rhetoric* 8:213–228.

Kirzner, Israel. 1973. *Competition and Entrepreneurship*. Chicago: University of Chicago Press.

Kirzner, Israel. 1979. *Perception, Opportunity and Profit*. Chicago: University of Chicago Press.

Kirzner, Israel. 1989. *Discovery, Capitalism, and Distributive Justice*. Oxford.

Klamer, Arjo. 2011. "Cultural Entrepreneurship." *Review of Austrian Economics* 24:141–156.

Klamer, Arjo, and Peter-Wim Zuidhof. 1998. "The Role of the Third Sphere in the World of the Arts." Paper presented at the Association of Cultural Economics International (ACEI), Barcelona.

Klein, Noami. 2007. *The Shock Doctrine: The Rise of Disaster Capitalism*. New York: Metropolitan Books.

Klemm, David. 2004. "Material Grace: The Paradox of Property and Possession." In *Having: Property and Possession in Religious and Social Life*, ed. William Schweiker and Charles Mathewes, pp. 222–245. Grand Rapids, MI: Eerdmans.

Klemm, F. 1964. *A History of Western Technology*. Cambridge, MA: MIT Press.

Klíma, Ivan. 2002. "What Do We Think of America?" *Granta*, no. 77, pp. 50–53.

Kline, Morris. 1982. *Mathematics: The Loss of Certainty*. New York: Oxford University Press.

Klinenberg, Eric. 2002. *Heat Wave: A Social Autopsy of Disaster in Chicago*. Chicago: University of Chicago Press.

Knight, Frank. 1923 (1977). "The Ethics of Competition." *Quarterly Journal of Economics*. Reprinted in Knight, *The Ethics of Competition*, 33–67 (1935; reprint, New Brunswick, NJ: Transaction Publishers, 1977).

Knighton, C. S. 2013. *Pepys and the Navy*. Stroud, Gloucestershire: History Press.

Koehn, Nancy F. 2014. "Great Men, Great Pay? Why CEO Compensation Is Sky High." *Washington Post*, June 15.

Kołakowski, Leszek. 2004. *My Correct Views on Everything*. Ed. Z. Janowki. South Bend, IN: St. Augustine's Press.

Kolko, Gabriel. 1965. *Railroads and Regulation, 1877–1916.* Princeton, NJ: Princeton University Press.

Kuehn, Manfred. 2001. *Kant: A Biography.* Cambridge: Cambridge University Press.

Kuran, Timur. 2003. "Levant: Islamic Rule." In Mokyr, ed. 2003, vol. 3, pp. 309–314.

Kuran, Timur. 2005. "The Absence of the Corporation in Islamic Law: Origins and Persistence." *American Journal of Comparative Law* 53:785–834.

Kuran, Timur. 2010. *The Long Divergence: How Islamic Law Held Back the Middle East.* Princeton, NJ: Princeton University Press.

Kurzban, R., P. DeScioli, and E. O'Brien, E. 2007. "Audience Effects on Moralistic Punishment." *Evolution and Human Behavior* 28:75–84.

Lakoff, George. 1996 (2002). *Moral Politics: How Liberals and Conservatives Think.* 2nd ed. Chicago: University of Chicago Press.

Lakoff, George. 2008. *The Political Mind: Why You Can't Understand 21st-Century American Politics with an 18th-Century Brain.* New York: Penguin.

Lal, Depak. 1998. *Unintended Consequences: The Impact of Factor Endowments, Culture, and Politics on Long-Run Economic Performance.* Cambridge, MA: MIT Press.

Lal, Depak. 2006. *Reviving the Invisible Hand: The Case for Classical Liberalism in the Twentieth Century.* Princeton, NJ: Princeton University Press.

Landes, David S. 1949. "French Entrepreneurship and Industrial Growth in the Nineteenth Century." *Journal of Economic History* 9:45–61.

Landes, David S. 1965. "Technological Change and Industrial Development in Western Europe, 1750–1914." In H. J. Habakkuk and M. M. Postan, eds., *Cambridge Economic History of Europe,* vol. 6. Cambridge: Cambridge University Press.

Landes, David S. 1969. *The Unbound Prometheus: Technological Change and Industrial Development in Western Europe from 1750 to the Present.* Cambridge: Cambridge University Press.

Landes, David S. 1998. *The Wealth and Poverty of Nations: Why Some Are So Rich and Some So Poor.* New York: Norton.

Lane, Frederic C. 1973. *Venice: A Maritime Republic.* Baltimore: Johns Hopkins University Press.

Langford, Paul. 1992. *A Polite and Commercial People.* Oxford History of Britain. Vol. 4, *The Eighteenth Century and the Age of Industry.* Oxford: Oxford University Press.

Larkin, Philip. 1970 (1983). "Introduction to *All What Jazz: A Record Diary, 1961–1971.*" Reprinted in *Required Writing: Miscellaneous Pieces 1955–1982.* London: Faber and Faber.

Lattimore, Owen. 1940. *Inner Asian Frontiers of China.* New York: American Geographical Society.

Lauck, Jon K. 2013. *The Lost Region: Toward a Revival of Midwestern History.* Iowa City: University of Iowa Press.

LaVaque-Manty, Mika. 2006. "Dueling for Equality: Masculine Honor and the Modern Politics of Dignity." *Political Theory* 34:715–740.

Lawrence, D. H. 1923. *Studies in Classic American Literature.* http://xroads.virginia.edu/~HYPER/LAWRENCE/lawrence.html.

Lawrence, D. H. 1929. "How Beastly the Bourgeois Is." In Lawrence, *Pansies.* London: Martin Secker.

Lawrence, Robert Z. 2015. "The Growing Gap between Wages and Labor Productivity." *Real Time Economic Issues Watch*, Peterson Institute for International Economics, July 21. http://www.capx.co/external/why-are-wages-lagging-productivity-in-the-us/.

Lawrence, William. 1901. "The Relation of Wealth to Morals." *The World's Work* 1 (January).

Lazonick, William. 1981. "Production Relations, Labor Productivity and Choice of Technique: British and US Cotton Spinning." *Journal of Economic History* 41:491–516.

Lazonick, William. 1991. *Business Organization and the Myth of the Market Economy.* New York: Cambridge University Press.

Lebergott, Stanley. 1984. *The Americans: An Economic Record.* New York: Norton.

Le Bris, David. 2013. "Customary versus Civil Law within Old Regime France." Unpublished paper, KEDGE Business School. http://mpra.ub.uni-muenchen.de/52123/1/MPRA_paper_52123.pdf.

Le Faye, Deirdre. 2011. *Jane Austen's Letters.* Oxford: Oxford University Press.

Lehmann, Helmut T. 1970. "Introduction." *Three Treatises.* 2nd ed. Philadelphia: Fortress Press.

Lemert, Charles. 2012. *Social Things: An Introduction to the Sociological Life.* 5th ed. Lanham, MD: Rowman & Littlefield.

Leon, Donna. 2012. *Beastly Things.* London: Arrow Books.

Leonard, Thomas C. 2005. "Eugenics and Economics in the Progressive Era." *Journal of Economic Perspectives* 19:207–224.

Leoni, Bruno. 1965 (2009). "Myths and Realities of Monopoly." In Leoni, *Law, Liberty and the Competitive Market.* Ed. Carlo Lottieri. Trans. Gian Turci and Anne MacDiarmid. New Brunswick, NJ: Transaction Publishers.

Leopardi, Giacomo. 1845 (1985). *Pensieri: A Bilingual Edition.* Trans. W. S. Di Piero. New York: Oxford University Press.

Lepenies, Philipp H. 2013. *A Matter of Perspective Art, Enlightenment, and the Emergence of the Development Mindset.* Philadelphia: Temple University Press.

Lepenies, Philipp H. 2014. "Of Goats and Dogs: Joseph Townsend and the Idealisation of Markets—A Decisive Episode in the History of Economics." *Cambridge Journal of Economics* 38:447–457.

Lepenies, Wolf. 2006. *The Seduction of Culture in German History.* Princeton, NJ: Princeton University Press.

Le Roy Ladurie, Emmanuel. 1978 (1980). *Montaillou: Cathars and Catholics in a French Village, 1295–1324.* Trans. Barbara Bray. London: Penguin.

Levi, Carlo. 1945. *Christ Stopped at Eboli: The Story of a Year.* Trans. Frances Frenaye. New York: Farrar, Straus, and Company. http://archive.org/stream/christstoppedateo13078mbp/christstoppedateo13078mbp_djvu.txt.

Levy, David M. 2001. *How the Dismal Science Got Its Name: Classical Economics and the Ur-Text of Racial Politics.* Ann Arbor: University of Michigan Press.

Levy, David M. and Sandra J. Peart. 2001. "The Secret History of the Dismal Science: Economics, Religion and Race in the 19th Century." Economics Forum. http://econlib.org/Library/Columns/LevyPeartdismal.html.

Levy, David, and Sandra Peart. 2011. "Soviet Growth and American Textbooks: An Endogenous Past." *Journal of Economic Behavior and Organization* 78:110–125.

Li, Bozhong. 2011. "An Early Modern Economy in China: A Study of the GDP of the Huating-Lou Area, 1823–29." University of Utrecht, Centre for Global Economic History, Working Paper no. 18.

Li, Bozhong, and Jan Luiten van Zanden. 2012. "Before the Great Divergence? Comparing the Yangzi Delta and the Netherlands at the Beginning of the Nineteenth Century." *Journal of Economic History* 72:956–989.

Lienhard, John H. 2006. *How Invention Begins: Echoes of Old Voices in the Rise of New Machines.* New York: Oxford University Press.

Lillo, George. 1731 (1952). "The London Merchant." In Ricardo Quintana, ed., *Eighteenth-Century Plays.* New York: Modern Library.

Lindsay, Sir David. 1552–1554 (1879). "Ane Pleasant Satyre of the thrie Estaitis." In *The Poetical Works of Sir David Lyndsay*, vol. 2. Ed. David Laing. Edinburgh. https://archive.org/stream/poeticalworkswitoolinduoft/poeticalworkswitoolinduoft_djvu.txt.

Lindsay, Sir David. 1552–1554 (2000). "Ane Satyre of the Thrie Estaitis." In Greg Walker, ed., *Medieval Drama: An Anthology*, pp. 541–623. Oxford: Blackwell.

Liu, Cheol, and John L. Mikesell. 2014. "The Impact of Public Officials' Corruption on the Size and Allocation of U.S. State Spending." *Public Administration Review* 74:346–359.

Lodge, David. 1988 (1990). *Nice Work.* London: Penguin.

Loftis, John Clyde. 1959. *Comedy and Society from Congreve to Fielding.* Stanford, CA: Stanford University Press.

Lucas, Robert E., Jr. 2002. *Lectures on Economic Growth.* Cambridge, MA Harvard University Press.

Luther, Martin. Ca. 1525. *Admonition to Peace: A Reply to the Twelve Articles of the Peasants in Swabia.* http://projects.ecfs.org/eih/documents/LutherAdmon.html.

Macaulay, Thomas Babbington. 1829. "Mill on Government." *Edinburgh Review*, March. http://www.gutenberg.org/files/2168/2168-h/2168-h.htm#link2H_4_0007

Macaulay, Thomas Babbington. 1830. "Southey's Colloquies on Society." *Edinburgh Review*, Jan. Reprinted in *Critical, Historical, and Miscellaneous Essays by Lord Macaulay*, vol. 2, pp. 132–187. Boston, 1860 (1881).

Macaulay, Thomas Babington. 1848. *The History of England from the Accession of James II.* Vol. 1. http://www.gutenberg.org/ebooks/1468.

MacCulloch, Diarmaid. 2004. *The Reformation.* London: Penguin.

MacCulloch, Diarmaid. 2010. *Christianity: The First Three Thousand Years.* New York: Viking Penguin.

MacDonagh, Oliver. 1993. *Jane Austen: Real and Imagined Worlds.* New Haven, CT: Yale University Press.

Macfarlane, Alan. 1978. *The Origins of English Individualism.* Oxford: Blackwell.

Macfarlane, Alan. 2000. *The Riddle of the Modern World: Of Liberty, Wealth, and Equality.* Basingstoke: Palgrave.

Machiavelli, Niccolò. 1513 (1964). *Machiavelli's "The Prince": A Bilingual Edition.* Trans. Mark Musa. New York: St. Martin's Press.

MacIntyre, Alasdair. 1981. *After Virtue: A Study in Moral Theory.* Notre Dame: University of Notre Dame Press.

Mackenzie, Henry. 1771. *The Man of Feeling.* http://gutenberg.org/ebooks/5083.

MacKinnon, Malcolm H. 1987. "The Longevity of the Thesis: A Critique of the Critics." In H. Lehmann and G. Roth, eds., *Weber's Protestant Ethic: Origins, Evidence, Contexts*, pp. 211–243. Cambridge: Cambridge University Press.

MacLeod, Christine. 1988. *Inventing the Industrial Revolution: The English Patent System, 1660–1800.* Cambridge: Cambridge University Press.

MacLeod, Christine. 1998. "James Watt: Heroic Invention and the Idea of the Industrial Revolution." In Maxine Berg and Kristine Bruland, eds., *Technological Revolutions in Europe: Historical Perspectives*, pp. 96–115. Cheltenham: Elgar.

MacLeod, Christine. 2007. *Heroes of Invention: Technology, Liberalism and British Identity, 1750–1914.* Cambridge: Cambridge University Press.

MacLeod, Christine, and Alessandro Nuvolari. 2006. "The Pitfalls of Prosopography: Inventors in the *Dictionary of National Biography*. *Technology and Culture* 47:757–776.

Maddison, Angus. 2001. *The World Economy: A Millennial Perspective.* Paris: Organization for Economic Cooperation and Development.

Maddison, Angus. 2007. *Contours of the World Economy, 1–2030 AD.* Oxford: Oxford University Press.

Magnusson, Lynne. 1999. *Shakespeare and Social Dialogue: Dramatic Language and Elizabethan Letters.* Cambridge: Cambridge University Press.

Mahbubani, Kishore. 2013. *The Great Convergence: Asia, the West, and the Logic of One World.* Philadelphia: Perseus.

Maine, Henry Sumner. 1861 (1905). *Ancient Law: Its Connection to the History of Early Society.* New York: Henry Holt.

Malanima, Paolo. 2013. "When Did England Overtake Italy? Medieval and Early Modern Divergence in Price and Wages." *European Review of Economic History* 17:45–70.

Malthus, Thomas Robert. 1798. *An Essay on the Principle of Population.* http://www.esp.org/books/malthus/population/malthus.pdf.

Mandeville, Bernard. 1705, 1714, 1723, 1728, 1733. *The Fable of the Bees; or, Private Vices, Publick Benefits.* 2 vols. Ed. F. B. Fay (1924). Reprint, Indianapolis: Liberty Fund, 1988.

Manin, Bernard. 1985 (1987). "On Legitimacy and Political Deliberation." *Political Theory* 15:338–368. Trans. Elly Stein and Jane Mansbridge, from "Volonté Générale ou Délibération? Esquisse d'une Theorie de la Délibération Politique," *Le Débat* (January 1985).

Mann, Thomas. 1901 (1952). *Buddenbrooks.* Trans. H. T. Lowe-Porter. New York: Vintage, 1952.

Mann, Thomas, and Jan de Vries. 1984. *European Urbanization, 1500–1800.* London: Methuen.

Mantoux, Paul. 1907 (1929). *La révolution industrielle au XVIIIe siècle. Essai sur les commencements de la grande industrie moderne en Angleterre.* Paris: Société de librairie et d'édition. Trans. Marjorie Vernon, as *The Industrial Revolution in the Eighteenth Century: An Outline of the Beginnings of the Modern Factory System in England.* London: Jonathan Cape.

March, James G. 1971. "The Technology of Foolishness." In March, ed., *Decisions and Organizations.* New York: Basil Blackwell.

Marcus, Leah S., Janet Mueller, and Mary Beth Rose, eds. 2000. *Elizabeth I: Collected Works.* Chicago: University of Chicago Press.

Marglin, Stephen A. 1974. "What Do Bosses Do? The Origins and Functions of Hierarchy in Capitalist Production." *Review of Radical Political Economics* 6 (Summer): 33–60 (pt. 1), 60–112 (pt. 2).

Margo, Robert A. 1993. "What Is the Key to Black Progress?" In McCloskey, ed. 1993, pp. 65–69.

Marlowe, Christopher. 1592. *The Jew of Malta.* In Bevington et al., eds. 2002.

Marquis, Don. 1916–1935 (1943). *The Lives and Times of Archy and Mehitabel.* Garden City, NY: Doubleday Doran.

Martin, Emmanuel. 2014. "The Economics of Peace." In Tom Palmer, ed., *Peace, War, and Liberty*, pp. 29–38. Printed for the Atlas Network. Ottawa, IL: Jameson Books.

Marvel, Seth A., Travis Martin, Charles R. Doering, David Lusseau, and M. E. J. Newman. 2013. "The Small World Effect Is a Modern Phenomenon." *Physics and Society.* October. http://arxiv.org/abs/1310.2636v1.

Marx, Karl. 1867 (1887). *Capital: A Critique of Political Economy.* Vol. 1. Ed. F. Engels. Trans. from 3rd German ed. by S. Moore and E. Aveling (1887). New York: Modern Library, n.d.

Massinger, Philip. Mid-1620s. *A New Wat to Pay Old Debts.* In Bevington et al., eds. 2002.

Mathias, Peter. 1972 (1979). "Who Unbound Prometheus? Science and Technical Change, 1600–1800." In Mathias, ed., *Science and Society, 1600–1800.* Cambridge: Cambridge University Press. Reprinted in Mathias1979, pp. 45–87.

Mathias, Peter. 1979. *The Transformation of England: Essays in the Economic and Social History of England in the Eighteenth Century.* New York: Columbia University Press.

Maurer, Noel. 2013. *The Empire Trap: The Rise and Fall of U.S. Intervention to Protect American Property Overseas, 1893–2013.* Princeton, NJ: Princeton University Press.

Maus, Katherine Eiseman. 2002. Introduction to Massinger's *A New Way to Pay Old Debts.* In Bevington et al., eds., pp. 1833–1838.

Mayer, Emanuel. 2012. *The Ancient Middle Class: Urban Life and Aesthetics in the Early Roman Empire, 100 BCE–250 CE.* Cambridge, MA: Harvard University Press.

Maynial, Edouard. 1911. *Casanova and His Time.* Trans. E. C. Mayne. London: Chapman & Hall. http://archive.org/stream/casanovahistimeoomaynrich/casanovahistimeoomaynrich_djvu .txt.

Mayshar, Joram, Omer Moav, and Zvika Neeman. 2011. "Transparency, Appropriability and the Early State." Departments of Economics, Hebrew and Tel Aviv Universities. http://www.iset .ge/files/wp_02-11_mayshar_moav_neeman_august2011.pdf.

McBrearty, Sally. 2007. "Down with the Revolution." In Mellars et al., eds., pp. 133–151.

McBurney, William H. 1965. Introduction to George Lillo, *The London Merchant.* London: Edward Arnold.

McCants, Anne E. C. 1997. *Civic Charity in a Golden Age: Orphan Care in Early Modern Amsterdam.* Urbana: University of Illinois Press.

McClelland, David C. 1961. *The Achieving Society.* New York: Free Press.

McCloskey, Deirdre N. 1970. "Did Victorian Britain Fail?" *Economic History Review* 23:446–459.

McCloskey, Deirdre N. 1972. "The Enclosure of Open Fields: Preface to a Study of Its Impact on the Efficiency of English Agriculture in the Eighteenth Century." *Journal of Economic History* 32:15–35.

McCloskey, Deirdre N. 1973. *Economic Maturity and Entrepreneurial Decline: British Iron and Steel, 1870–1913*. Cambridge, MA: Harvard University Press.

McCloskey, Deirdre N. 1975. "The Economics of Enclosure: A Market Analysis." In E. L. Jones and William Parker, eds. *European Peasants and Their Markets: Essays in Agrarian Economic History*, pp. 123–160. Princeton, NJ: Princeton University Press.

McCloskey, Deirdre N. 1976. "English Open Fields as Behavior Towards Risk." *Research in Economic History* 1 (Fall): 124–170.

McCloskey, Deirdre N. 1980. "Magnanimous Albion: Free Trade and British National Income, 1841–1881." *Explorations in Economic History* 17:303–320.

McCloskey, Deirdre N. 1981. "The Industrial Revolution, 1780–1860: A Survey." Chap. 7 of vol. 1 in Roderick Floud and McCloskey, eds., *The Economic History of Britain, 1700–Present*. 2 vols. Cambridge: Cambridge University Press, 1981.

McCloskey, Deirdre N. 1985a. *The Rhetoric of Economics*. Madison: University of Wisconsin Press.

McCloskey, Deirdre N. 1985b. *The Applied Theory of Price*. 2nd ed. New York: Macmillan.

McCloskey, Deirdre N. 1989. "The Open Fields of England: Rent, Risk, and the Rate of Interest, 1300–1815." In David W. Galenson, ed., *Markets in History: Economic Studies of the Past*, pp. 5–51. Cambridge: Cambridge University Press.

McCloskey, Deirdre N. 1990. *If You're So Smart: The Narrative of Economic Expertise*. Chicago: University of Chicago Press.

McCloskey, Deirdre N., ed. 1993. *Second Thoughts: Myths and Morals of U.S. Economic History*. New York: Oxford University Press.

McCloskey, Deirdre N. 1994. *Knowledge and Persuasion in Economics*. Cambridge: Cambridge University Press.

McCloskey, Deirdre N. 1999. *Crossing: A Memoir*. Chicago: University of Chicago Press.

McCloskey, Deirdre N. 2001. "Women's Work in the Market, 1900–2000." In Ina Zweiniger-Bargielowska, ed., *Women in Twentieth Century Britain: Economic, Social and Cultural Change*. London: Longman/Pearson Education.

McCloskey, Deirdre N. 2006a. "*Keukentafel* Economics and the History of British Imperialism." *South African Economic History Review* 21:171–176.

McCloskey, Deirdre N. 2006b. *The Bourgeois Virtues: Ethics for an Age of Commerce*. Chicago: University of Chicago Press.

McCloskey, Deirdre N. 2007. "Thrift as a Virtue, Historically Criticized." *Revue de Philosophie Economique* 8 (December): 3–31.

McCloskey, Deirdre N. 2008a. "Not by P Alone: A Virtuous Economy." In Irene van Staveren, ed, issue on ethics in economics, *Review of Political Economy* 20 (2): 181–197.

McCloskey, Deirdre N. 2008b. "How to Buy, Sell, Make, Manage, Produce, Transact, Consume with Words." Introductory essay in Edward M. Clift, ed., *How Language Is Used to Do Business: Essays on the Rhetoric of Economics*. Lewiston, NY: Mellen Press.

McCloskey, Deirdre N. 2010a. *Bourgeois Dignity: Why Economics Can't Explain the Modern World*. Chicago: University of Chicago Press.

McCloskey, Deirdre N. 2010b. "The Economics and the Anti-Economics of Consumption." In Karin Ekstrom and Kay Glans, eds., *Changing Consumer Roles*. New York: Routledge.

McCloskey, Deirdre N. 2011a. "The Rhetoric of the Economy and the Polity." *Annual Review of Political Science* 14:181–199.

McCloskey, Deirdre N. 2011b. "The Prehistory of American Thrift." In Joshua J. Yates and James Davidson Hunter, eds., *Thrift and Thriving in America: Capitalism and Moral Order from the Puritans to the Present*, pp. 61–87. New York: Oxford University Press.

McCloskey, Deirdre N. 2012a. "Happyism: The Creepy New Economics of Pleasure." *New Republic*, June 28.

McCloskey, Deirdre N. 2012b. "The Poverty of Communitarianism: Review of Sandel's *What Money Can't Buy*." *Claremont Review of Books* 12 (Fall): 57–59.

McCloskey, Deirdre N. 2013a. "What Went Wrong with Economics? A Quarter Century On." In Wilfred Dolfsma and Stefan Kesting, eds., *Interdisciplinary Economics: Kenneth E. Boulding's Engagement in the Sciences*, pp. 574–586. London: Routledge.

McCloskey, Deirdre N. 2013b. "A Sweet Talk on Free Speech." Institute for Humane Studies, November. At LearnLiberty.org.

McCloskey, Deirdre N. 2014. "Max U vs. Humanomics: A Critique of Neo-Institutionalism." *Journal of Institutional Economics*, Spring 2015, 1–27.

McCloskey, Deirdre N., and Santhi Hejeebu. 1999. "The Reproving of Karl Polanyi." *Critical Review* 13 (Summer/Fall): 285–314.

McCloskey, Deirdre, and Arjo Klamer. 1995. "One Quarter of GDP Is Persuasion." *American Economic Review* 85 (2, May): 191–195.

McCormick, Michael. 2001. *Origins of the European Economy. Communications and Commerce, A.D. 300–900.* Cambridge: Cambridge University Press.

McDougall, Walter A. 2004. *Freedom Just Around the Corner: A New American History, 1585–1828.* New York: HarperCollins Perennial.

McGuire, Robert A., and Philip R. P. Coelho. 2011. *Parasites, Pathogens, and Progress: Diseases and Economic Development.* Cambridge, MA: MIT Press.

McKay, Joseph. 2013. "Pirate Nations: Maritime Pirates as Escape Societies in Late Imperial China." *Social Science History* 37:551–573.

McKeon, Michael. 1987 (2002). *The Origins of the English Novel, 1600–1740.* 2nd ed. Baltimore: Johns Hopkins University Press.

McMahon, Darrin M. 2005. *Happiness: A History.* New York: Atlantic Monthly Press.

McNeill, William H. 1964. *Europe's Steppe Frontier, 1500–1800: A Study of Eastward Movement in Europe.* Chicago: University of Chicago Press.

McNeill, William H. 1976. *Plagues and People.* Garden City, NY: Anchor Doubleday.

McNeill, William H. 1980. *The Human Condition: An Ecological and Historical View.* Princeton, NJ: Princeton University Press.

McWhorter, John. 2008. *Our Magnificent Bastard Tongue.* New York: Gotham Books Penguin.

Mead, Walter Russell. 2007. *God and Gold: Britain, America, and the Making of the Modern World.* New York: Knopf.

Megill, Allan. 2002. *Karl Marx: The Burden of Reason.* Lanham, MD: Rowman & Littlefield.

Meisenzahl, Ralf, and Joel Mokyr. 2012. "The Rate and Direction of Invention in the British Industrial Revolution: Incentives and Institutions." In Josh Lerner and Scott Stern, eds.,

The Rate and Direction of Inventive Activity Revisited, pp. 443–479. NBER Books. Chicago: University of Chicago Press.

Mellars, Paul, Katie Boyle, Ofer Bar-Yosef, and Chris Stringer, eds. 2007. *Rethinking the Human Revolution: New Behavioural and Biological Perspectives on the Origin and Dispersal of Modern Humans.* McDonald Institute for Archaeological Research. Cambridge, UK: Oxbow Books.

Mencken, H. L. 1916. *A Little Book in C Major.* John Lane.

Mencken, H. L. 1917 (2006). *A Book of Prefaces.* Reprinted in Mencken, *Three Early Works.* New York: Barnes & Noble.

Mencken, H. L. 1949. *A Mencken Chrestomathy: His Own Selection of His Choicest Writing.* New York: Knopf.

Mendelson, E., ed. 1976. *W. H. Auden: Collected Poems.* New York: Random House.

Michaels, Walter Benn. 1987. *The Gold Standard and the Logic of Naturalism.* Berkeley: University of California Press.

Michie, Elsie B. 2000. "Austen's Powers: Engaging with Adam Smith in Debates about Wealth and Virtue." *Novel* 34 (1): 5–27.

Michie, Elsie B. 2011. *The Vulgar Question of Money: Heiresses, Materialism, and the Novel of Manners from Jane Austen to Henry James.* Baltimore: Johns Hopkins University Press.

Mielants, Eric H. 2008. *The Origins of Capitalism and the "Rise of the West."* Philadelphia: Temple University Press.

Mill, John Stuart. 1845 (1967). "The Claims of Labour." *Edinburgh Review* 81 (April): 498–525. Reprinted in John M. Robson, ed., *The Collected Works of John Stuart Mill.* Vol. 4, *Essays on Economics and Society,* pt. 1, pp. 363–390. Toronto: University of Toronto Press; London: Routledge and Kegan Paul.

Mill, John Stuart. 1859 (2001). *On Liberty.* Kitchener: Batoche Books.

Mill, John Stuart. 1848, 1871 (1970). *Principles of Political Economy and Taxation,* books 4 and 5. Ed. Donald Winch. London: Penguin.

Milton, John. 1634 (1957). "[Comus] A Mask Presented at Ludlow Castle." In Milton 1957, pp. 86–114.

Milton, John. 1644 (1957). "Areopagitica." In Milton 1957, pp. 716–749.

Milton, John. 1649 (1957). "The Tenure of Kings and Magistrates." In Milton 1957, pp. 750–780.

Milton, John. 1957. *John Milton: Complete Poems and Major Prose.* Ed. Merritt Y. Hughes. Indianapolis: Bobbs-Merrill.

Mirowski, Phillip. 2013. *Never Let a Serious Crisis Go to Waste: How Neoliberalism Survived the Financial Meltdown.* London: Verso.

Mirowski, Phillip, and D. Plehwe, eds. 2009. *The Road from Mont Pelerin: The Making of the Neoliberal Thought Collective.* Cambridge, MA: Harvard University Press.

Mises, Ludwig von. 1951. *Socialism: An Economic and Sociological Analysis.* Trans. J. Kahane, from *Die Gemeinwirtschaft: Untersuchungen über den Sozialismus* (1922, 1932). New Haven, CT: Yale University Press.

Mishra, Pankaj. 2011. "Watch This Man" (review of Niall Ferguson, *Civilization: The West and the Rest*). *London Review of Books* 33:10–12.

Mithen, Steven. 2003. *After the Ice: A Global Human History, 20,000–5,000 BC*. London: Weidenfeld and Nicolson.

Mokyr, Joel. 1983. *Why Ireland Starved: A Quantitative and Analytical History of the Irish Economy, 1800–1850*. London: Allen & Unwin.

Mokyr, Joel. 1990. *The Lever of Riches: Technological Creativity and Economic Progress*. Oxford: Oxford University Press.

Mokyr, Joel. 2002. *The Gifts of Athena*. Princeton, NJ: Princeton University Press.

Mokyr, Joel, ed. 2003. *The Oxford Encyclopedia of Economic History*. 6 vols. Oxford: Oxford University Press.

Mokyr, Joel. 2009. "Intellectual Property Rights, the Industrial Revolution, and the Beginnings of Modern Economic Growth." *American Economic Review* 99 (2): 349–355.

Mokyr, Joel. 2010. *The Enlightened Economy: Britain and the Industrial Revolution, 1700–1850*. New Haven, CT: Yale University Press.

Mokyr, Joel. 2011. "The Economics of Being Jewish." *Critical Review* 23:195–206.

Mokyr, Joel. 2013. "Is Technological Progress a Thing of the Past?" *VOX*, September 8. http://www.voxeu.org/article/technological-progress-thing-past.

Mokyr, Joel. 2014. "What Today's Economic Gloomsayers Are Missing." *Wall Street Journal* August 8.

Mokyr, Joel. Forthcoming (2016). *A Culture of Growth: Origins of the Modern Economy*.

Montesquieu, Charles-Louis de Secondat, Baron de. 1748. *De l'esprit des lois* (*The Spirit of the Laws*) 1748. In *Complete Works*, trans. 1777. http://oll.libertyfund.org/titles/montesquieu-complete-works-vol-1-the-spirit-of-laws.

Moore, Barrington. 1998. "Rational Discussion: Comparative Historical Notes on Its Origins, Enemies, and Prospects." In Moore, *Moral Aspects of Economic Growth and Other Essays*, pp. 144–157. Ithaca, NY: Cornell University Press.

Moore, Rosemary. 2000. *The Light in Their Consciences: The Early Quakers in Britain, 1646–1666*. University Park: Pennsylvania State University Press.

More, Thomas. 1516 (2010). *Utopia*. Norton Critical Editions. New York: Norton.

Moretti, Franco. 2013. *The Bourgeois: Between History and Literature*. London: Verso.

Morrill, John. 2001. "The Stuarts, 1603–1688." In K. O. Morgan, ed., *The Oxford History of Britain*, pp. 327–398. Rev. ed. Oxford: Oxford University Press.

Morris, Ian. 2010. *Why the West Rules—For Now*. New York: Farrar, Straus, Giroux,

Morris, Ian. 2014. "In the Long Run, Wars Make Us Safer and Richer." *Washington Post*, April 25

Mortenson, Peter. 1976. "The Economics of Joy in *The Shoemaker's Holiday*." *Studies in English Literature* 16:241–52.

Mote, F. W. 1999. *Imperial China, 900–1800*. Cambridge, MA: Harvard University Press.

Moynahan, Brian. 2002. *The Faith: A History of Christianity*. New York: Doubleday.

Mueller, John. 1999. *Capitalism, Democracy, and Ralph's Pretty Good Grocery*. Princeton, NJ: Princeton University Press.

Mueller, John. 2011. *War and Ideas: Selected Essays*. New York: Routledge.

Mueller, John D. 2010. *Redeeming Economics: Rediscovering the Missing Element*. Wilmington, DE: Intercollegiate Studies Institute.

Muldrew, Craig. 1998. *The Economy of Obligation: The Culture of Credit and Social Relations in Early Modern England*. New York: St. Martin's Press,

Multatuli (Eduard Douwes Dekker). 1860 (1988). *Max Havelaar; or, The Coffee Auctions of the Dutch Trading Company*. Lisse: Rebo Productions.

Mun, Thomas. 1698. *England's Benefit and Advantage by Foreign Trade, Plainly Demonstrated.* At Google Books.

Murphy, Kevin M., and Robert H. Topol. 2006. "The Value of Health and Longevity." *Journal of Political Economy* 114:871–904.

Murrell, Peter. 2009. "Design and Evolution in Institutional Development: The Insignificance of the English Bill of Rights." Department of Economics, University of Maryland.

Musson, A. E. 1978. *The Growth of British Industry*. New York: Holmes and Meier.

Myllyntaus, Timo, and Eerik Tarnaala. 1998. "When Foreign Trade Collapsed: Economic Crises in Finland and Sweden, 1914–1924." In Myllyntaus, ed., *Economic Crises and Restructuring in History: Experiences of Small Countries*, pp. 23–63. St. Katharinen, Germany: Scripta Mercaturae.

Nadler, Steven. 1999. *Spinoza: A Life*. Cambridge: Cambridge University Press.

Najita, Tetsuo. 1987. *Visions of Virtue in Togugawa Japan: The Kaitokudō Merchant Academy of Osaka*. Honolulu: University of Hawai'i Press.

Neal, Daniel. 1817. *The History of the Puritans, or Protestant Non-conformists*. Vol. 4. Ed. J. Toulmin. Revised ed.

Neal, Larry, and Jeffrey G. Williamson, eds. 2014. *The Cambridge History of Capitalism*. Vol. 1, *The Rise of Capitalism from Ancient Origins to 1848*. Cambridge: Cambridge University Press.

Nee, Victor, and Richard Swedberg. 2007. *On Capitalism*. Stanford, CA: Stanford University Press.

Needham, Joseph. 1954–2008. *Science and Civilization in China*. 27 vols. Cambridge: Cambridge University Press.

Nelson, Robert H. 2010. *The New Holy Wars: Economic Religion versus Environmental Religion in Contemporary America*. University Park: Penn State Press.

Nelson, Robert H. 2013a. "Five Moral Philosophies on Economic Growth: Fundamental Perspectives on Assessing Its Benefits and Costs." http://faculty.publicpolicy.umd.edu/nelson/publications.

Nelson, Robert H. 2013b. "The Secular Religions of Progress." *New Atlantis*, Summer.

Nelson, Robert H. 2015. *God? Very Probably: Five Rational Ways to Think about the Question of a God*. Eugene, OR: Wipf and Stock/Cascade Books.

Nettleton, George H., Arthur E. Case, and George Winchester Stone Jr., eds. 1969. *British Dramatists from Dryden to Sheridan*. 2nd ed. Cambridge, MA: Houghton Mifflin.

Neville, Peter. 1990. *A Traveller's History of Russia and the USSR*. New York: Interlink.

Niebuhr, Reinhold. 1952. *The Irony of American History*. Chicago: University of Chicago Press.

Nisbet, Robert A. 1980. *History of the Idea of Progress*. London: Heinemann.

Nordhaus, William D. 1996. "Do Real Output and Real Wage Measures Capture Reality? The History of Lighting Suggests Not." In T. F. Breshnahan and R. Gordon, eds., *The Economics of New Goods*. NBER books. Chicago: University of Chicago Press.

Nordhaus, William D. 2004. "Schumpeterian in the American Economy: Theory and Measurement." Closed access paper, National Bureau of Economic Research Working Paper W10433.

North, Douglass C. 1990. *Institutions, Institutional Change and Economic Performance*. Cambridge: Cambridge University Press.

North, Douglass C., and Robert P. Thomas. 1973. *The Rise of the Western World*. Cambridge: Cambridge University Press.

North, Douglass C., John Joseph Wallis, and Barry R. Weingast. 2009. *Violence and Social Orders: A Conceptual Framework for Interpreting Recorded Human History*. Cambridge: Cambridge University Press.

Novak, Michael. 1984. *Catholic Social Thought and Liberal Institutions: Freedom with Justice*. New York: Harper and Row.

Nozick, Robert. 1974. *Anarchy, State, and Utopia*. New York: Basic Books.

Nunziata, Luca, and Lorenzo Rocco. 2014. "A Tale of Minorities: Evidence on Religious Ethics and Entrepreneurship from Swiss Census Data." University of Padua. Forschungsinstitut zur Zukunft der Arbeit. Discussion paper 7976.

Nussbaum, Martha C. 1986. *The Fragility of Goodness: Luck and Ethics in Greek Tragedy and Philosophy*. Cambridge: Cambridge University Press.

Nussbaum, Martha C. 2006. *Frontiers of Justice: Disability, Nationality, Species Membership*. Cambridge, MA: Harvard University Press.

Nussbaum, Martha C., and Amartya Sen. 1993. *The Quality of Life*. Oxford: Clarendon Press.

Nuvolari, Alessandro 2004. "Collective Invention during the British Industrial Revolution: The Case of the Cornish Pumping Engine." *Cambridge Journal of Economics* 28:347–363.

Nye, John V. C. 1991. "Lucky Fools and Cautious Businessmen: On Entrepreneurship and the Measure of Entrepreneurial Failure." *Research in Economics History* 6 (Supplement in Honor of J. R. T. Hughes, ed. Joel Mokyr): 131–152.

Nye, John V. C. 2007. *War, Wine, and Taxes: The Political Economy of Anglo-French Trade, 1689–1900*. Princeton, NJ: Princeton University Press.

Nygren, Anders. 1930/1936 (1982). *Agape and Eros: The Christian Idea of Love*. Trans. P. S. Watson. Chicago: University of Chicago Press.

O'Brien, Patrick K. 1982. "European Economic Development: The Contribution of the Periphery." *Economic History Review* 35:1–18.

O'Brien, Patrick K. 2011. "The Contributions of Warfare with Revolutionary and Napoleonic France to the Consolidation and Progress of the British Industrial Revolution." Economic History Working Papers, 150/11. Department of Economic History, London School of Economics and Political Science.

O'Brien, Patrick K., and P. A. Hunt. 1993. "The Rise of a Fiscal State in England, 1485–1815." *Historical Research* 66:129–176.

O'Connell, Laura Stevenson. See Stevenson, Laura.

OECD. 2014. *How Was Life? Global Well-Being since 1820*. Ed. J. Van Zanden et al. OECD Publishing. http://www.oecd.org/statistics/how-was-life9789264214262-en.htm.

Ogilvie, Sheilagh. 2007. 'Whatever Is, Is Right'? Economic Institutions in Pre-industrial Europe." *Economic History Review* 60:649–684.

Ogilvie, Sheilagh. 2011. *Institutions and European Trade: Merchant Guilds, 1000–1800*. Cambridge: Cambridge University Press.

Ogilvie, Sheilagh, and A. W. Carus. 2014. "Institutions and Economic Growth in Historical Perspective." In P. Aghion and S. Durlauf, eds. *Handbook of Economic Growth*, vol. 2, pp. 403–489. Oxford: North Holland Elsevier.

Ó Gráda, Cormac. 2010. *Famine: A Short History*. Princeton, NJ: Princeton University Press.

Ó Gráda, Cormac. 2014. "Did Science Cause the Industrial Revolution?" University College Dublin, UCD Centre for Economic Research, Working Paper 14/14.

Olson, Mancur. 1993. "Dictatorship, Democracy, and Development." *American Political Science Review* 87:567–576.

Onelo, J.-P., J. Saramäki, J. Hyvönen, G. Szabó, D. Lazer,K. Kaski, et al. 2007. "Structure and Tie Strengths on Mobile Communication Networks. *Proceedings of the National Academy of Sciences* 104:7332–7336.

Origo, Iris. 1957 (1986). *The Merchant of Prato: Francesco di Marco Datini, 1335–1410*. Boston: Nonpareil.

Oschinky, Dorothea. 1971. *Walter of Henley and Other Treatises on Estate Management and Accounting*. Oxford: Clarendon Press.

Oslington, Paul. 2008. "Christianity's Post-Enlightenment Contribution to Economic Thought." In *Christian Theology and Market Economics*, ed. Ian R. Harper and Samuel Clegg, pp. 60–73. Cheltenham, UK: Elgar.

Ostrom, Elinor. 1990. *Governing the Commons: The Evolution of Institutions for Collective Action*. Cambridge: Cambridge University Press.

Ostrom, Elinor. 2010. "Beyond Markets and States: Polycentric Governance of Complex Economic Systems. *American Economic Review* 100 (June): 1–33.

Ostrom, Elinor, Roy Gardner, and James Walker. 1994. *Rules, Games, and Common-Pool Resources*. Ann Arbor: University of Michigan Press.

Pagano, Patrizio, and Massimo Sbracia. 2014. "The Secular Stagnation Hypothesis: A Review of the Debate and Some Insights." Bank of Italy, Occasional Papers. At http://www.bancaditalia.it.

Palmer, Tom G. 2012. "Bismarck's Legacy." In Palmer, ed., *After the Welfare State*, pp. 33–54. Washington, DC: Atlas Economic Research Foundation.

Palmer, Tom G. 2014. "The Political Economy of Empire and War." In Palmer, ed. *Peace, War, and Liberty*, pp. 62–82. Printed for the Atlas Network. Ottawa, IL: Jameson Books.

Park, Robert E., Ernest W. Burgess, and Robert D. McKenzie. 1925. *The City*. Chicago: University of Chicago Press.

Parker, N. Geoffrey. 1985. *The Dutch Revolt*. Rev. ed. London: Penguin.

Parker, N. Geoffrey. 1988 (1996). *The Military Revolution: Military Innovation and the Rise of the West, 1500–1800*. 2nd ed. Cambridge: Cambridge University Press.

Parker, R. A. C. 1989. *Struggle for Survival: The History of the Second World War*. Oxford: Oxford University Press.

Parkin, Tim G. 1992. *Roman Demography and Society*. Baltimore: Johns Hopkins University Press.

Parks, Tim. 2005. *Medici Money: Banking, Metaphysics, and Art in Fifteenth-Century Florence*. New York: Norton.

Parks, Tim. 2013. *Italian Ways: On and Off the Rails from Milan to Palermo*. New York: Norton.

Paton, Alan. 1948. *Cry, the Beloved Country*. London: Jonathon Cape, 1987.

Paxman, Jeremy. 1998. *The English: A Portrait of a People*. London: Michael Joseph (Penguin 1999).

Peart, Sandra J., and David M. Levy. 2005. *The "Vanity of the Philosophers": From Equality to Hierarchy in Post-Classical Economics*. Ann Arbor: University of Michigan Press.

Peart, Sandra J., and David M. Levy, eds. 2008. *The Street Porter and the Philosopher: Conversations on Analytical Egalitarianism*. Ann Arbor: University of Michigan Press.

Perdue, Peter. 2005. *China Marches West: The Qing Conquest of Central Eurasia*. Cambridge, MA: Harvard University Press.

Peterson, Christopher, and Martin E. P. Seligman. 2004. *Character Strengths and Virtues: A Handbook and Classification*. Oxford: Oxford University Press.

Peterson, Graham. 2014. Hypothesis on the Treason of the Clerks. Personal correspondence, January 1.

Pettegree, Andrew. 2014. *The Invention of News*. New Haven, CT: Yale University Press.

Petty, William. 1690 (1899). *Political Arithmetick*. In Charles Henry Hull, ed., *The Economic Writings of Sir William Petty*, vol. 1, 233–313. Cambridge: Cambridge University Press.

Pfister, Ulrich, Jana Riedel, and Martin Uebele. 2012. "Real Wages and the Origins of Modern Economic Growth in Germany, 16th to 19th Centuries." European Historical Economics Society working paper no. 17.

Phelps, Edmund S. 2013. *Mass Flourishing: How Grassroots Innovation Created Jobs, Challenge, and Change*. Princeton, NJ: Princeton University Press.

Phillips, Paul T. 1996. *A Kingdom on Earth: Anglo-American Social Christianity, 1880–1940*. University Park: Pennsylvania State University Press.

Phillips, Susan M., and J. Richard Zecher. 1993. "The Securities Exchange Commission: From Where, Where To?" In McCloskey, ed. 1993, pp. 136–141.

Phillipson, Nicholas. 2010. *Adam Smith: An Enlightened Life*. New Haven, CT: Yale University Press.

Piaget, Jean. 1932 (1965). *The Moral Judgment of the Child*. Trans. Marjorie Gabain. New York: Free Press.

Piketty, Thomas. 2014. *Capital in the Twenty-First Century*. Trans. A. Goldhammer. Cambridge, MA: Harvard University Press.

Pink, Daniel H. 2012. *To Sell Is Human: The Surprising Truth about Moving Others*. New York: Riverhead Books/Penguin.

Pipes, Richard. 1999 (2000). *Property and Freedom*. New York: Knopf.

Pirenne, Henri. 1925. *Ville du Moyen Age* (*Medieval Cities: Their Origins and the Revival of Trade*). New York: Doubleday.

Pleij, Herman. 1994. "The Rise of Urban Literature." In Erik Kooper, ed., *Medieval Dutch Literature in Its European Context*, pp. 62–77. Trans. Myra Sholtz. Cambridge Studies in Medieval Literature, 21. Cambridge: Cambridge University Press.

Plopeanu, Aurelian, Peter Foldvari, Bas van Leeuwen, and Jan Luiten van Zanden. 2012. "Where do Ideas Come From? Book Production and Patents in a Global and Temporal Perspective." Universiteit Utrecht, Center for Global Economic History, working paper no. 33.

Polanyi, Karl. 1944. *The Great Transformation*. Boston: Beacon Press.

Polanyi, Karl. 1977. *The Livelihood of Man.* Ed. H. W. Pearson. New York: Academic Press.

Pollard, Sidney. 1981. *Peaceful Conquest: The Industrialization of Europe, 1760–1970.* Oxford: Oxford University Press.

Pollock, Frederick, and F. W. Maitland, 1895. *The History of English Law before the Time of Edward I.* 2nd ed. Cambridge: Cambridge University Press.

Pomeranz, Kenneth. 2000. *The Great Divergence: China, Europe, and the Making of the Modern World Economy.* Princeton, NJ: Princeton University Press.

Popov, Vladimir. 2014. "Socialism Is Dead, Long Live Socialism!" Unpublished essay, New Economic School. http://mpra.ub.uni-muenchen.de/54294/.

Porter, Roy. 2000. *The Creation of the Modern World: The Untold Story of the British Enlightenment.* New York: Norton.

Postgate, J. N. 1992. *Early Mesopotamia: Society and Economy at the Dawn of History.* London: Routledge.

Postrel, Virginia. 2013. *The Power of Glamour: Longing and the Art of Visual Persuasion.* New York: Simon & Schuster.

Potts, Jason. 2014. "Speak Well of the Bourgeois, and Prosper"(blogpost). The Conversation, August 19. http://theconversation.com/speak-well-of-the-bourgeois-and-prosper-29824.

Poznik, G. David, et al. 2013. "Sequencing Y Chromosomes Resolves Discrepancy in Time to Common Ancestor of Males versus Females." *Science* 341 (1 August): 562–565.

Prados de la Escosura, Leandro. 2014. "Economic Freedom in the Long Run: Evidence from OECD Countries (1850–2007)." European Historical Economics Society, Working Paper no. 54. Universidad Carlos III, London School of Economics.

Prak, Maarten. 2011. "Citizenship in Pre-modern Eurasia: A Comparison between China, the Near East and Europe." Utrecht University, presented at London School of Economics. http://eprints.lse.ac.uk/39751/.

Prestona, Stephanie D., and Frans B. M. de Waal. 2002. "Empathy: Its Ultimate and Proximate Bases." *Behavioral and Brain Sciences* 25:1–72.

Pritchard, J. K., M. T. Seielstad, A. Perez-Lezaun , M. W. Feldman. 1999. "Population Growth of Human Y Chromosomes: A Study of Y Chromosome Microsatellites." *Molecular Biology and Evolution* 16:1791–1798.

Prugnolle, Franck, Andrea Manica, and François Balloux. 2005. "Geography Predicts Neutral Genetic Diversity of Human Populations." *Current Biology* 15: R159–R160.

Puccini, Giacomo, Luigi Illica, Giuseppe Giacosa. 1896 (1954). *La Bohème.* New York: G. Schirmer.

Puga, Diego, and Daniel Trefler. 2013. "International Trade and Institutional Change: Medieval Venice's Response to Globalization." Center for Monetary and Financial Studies, Madrid.

Raftis, J. Ambrose. 1964. *Tenure and Mobility: Studies in the Social History of the Mediaeval English Village.* Toronto: Pontifical Institute of Mediaeval Studies.

Ragazzini, Giuseppe, ed. 1993. *Il Nuovo Ragazzini.* 2nd edition. Bologna: Zanichelli.

Rapport, Mike. 2008. *1848: Year of Revolution.* New York: Basic Books.

Rashid, Salim. 2005. "Christianity and Capitalist Civilisation: A Reformulation." Unpublished paper presented to the Association for the Study of Religion, Economics and Culture, Kansas City, 2004.

Raskov, Danila, and Vadin Kufenko. 2014. "The Role of Old Believers' Enterprises: Evidence from the Nineteenth Century Moscow Textiles Industry." Working paper, Schriftenreihe des Promotionsschwerpunkts Globalisierung und Beschäftigung, Evangelisches Studienwerk e.V., no. 40/2014. http://hdl.handle.net/10419/97301.

Rasmusson, Arne. 1995. *The Church as Polis: From Political Theology to Theological Politics as Exemplified by Jürgen Moltmann and Stanley Hauerwas.* Notre Dame, IN: Notre Dame University Press.

Rawls, John. 1971. *A Theory of Justice.* Cambridge, MA: Harvard University Press.

Rawski, Evelyn Sakakida. 1979. *Education and Popular Literacy in Ch'ing China.* Ann Arbor: University of Michigan Press.

Razafindrakoto, Mireille, François Roubaud, and Jean-Michel Wachsberger. 2013. "Institutions, gouvernance et croissance de long terme à Madagascar : L'énigme et le paradoxe." Unpublished essay, Université Paris-Dauphine, UMR DIAL (Developpement Institutions & Mondialisation).

Reckendrees, Alfred. 2014a. "Weimar Germany: The First Open Access Order That Failed." Unpublished essay Copenhagen Business School, Department of Management, Politics, and Philosophy, Center for Business History. Freiburger Diskussionspapiere zur Ordnungsökonomik, no. 14/05. http://hdl.handle.net/10419/97511.

Reckendrees, Alfred. 2014b. "Why Did Early Industrial Capitalists Suggest Minimum Wages and Social Insurance?" Copenhagen Business School, Department of Management, Politics, and Philosophy, Center for Business History.

Reich, Robert. 2014. "How to Shrink Inequality." *Nation*, May 6.

Reinert, Sophus A. 2011. *Translating Empire: Emulation and the Origins of Political Economy.* Cambridge, MA: Harvard University Press.

Renger, Johannes. 1979. "Interaction of Temple, Palace, and 'Private Enterprise' in the Old Babylonian Economy." In E. Lipinski, ed., *State and Temple Economy in the Ancient Near East*, pp. 249–256. *Orientalia Lovaniensa analecta* 5–6. Leuven Departement Orientalistiek.

Renger, Johannes. 2003. "Trade and Market in the Ancient Near East: Theoretical and Factual Implications." *Saggi di Storia Antica* 21:15–40. In special issue, "Trade and Politics in the Ancient World," ed. C. Zaccagnini.

Richerson, Peter J., and Robert Boyd. 2004. *Not by Genes Alone: How Culture Transformed Human Evolution.* Chicago: University of Chicago Press.

Ridley, Matt. 2010. *The Rational Optimist: How Prosperity Evolves.* London: HarperCollins.

Rietbergen, Peter. 1998. *Europe: A Cultural History.* London: Routledge.

Rimbaud, Arthur. 1874 (1914, 1962). *Collected Poems.* Trans. O. Bernard. London: Penguin.

Ringmar, Erik. 2007. *Why Europe Was First: Social Change and Economic Growth in Europe and East Asia 1500–2050.* London: Anthem.

Rivkin, Andrew C. 2013. "A Film Presses the Climate, Health and Security Case for Nuclear Energy." *New York Times*, "Dot Earth" column, June 13.

Robb, Graham. 2007. *The Discovery of France: A Historical Geography.* New York: Norton.

Roland, Gérard. 2010. "The Long-Run Weight of Communism or the Weight of Long-Run History?" United Nations University, World Institute for Development Economics Research.

Röpke, Wilhelm. 1958 (1960). *Jenseits von Angebot und Nachtfrage.* Trans. Elisabeth Henderson, as *A Humane Economy: The Social Framework of the Free Market.* Chicago: Henry Regnery.

Rorty, Richard. 1983 (1990). "Postmodernist Bourgeois :Liberalism." *Journal of Philosophy* 80: 583–589. Reprinted in Rorty, *Objectivity, Relativism, and Truth: Philosophical Papers,* vol. 1, pp. 197–202. Cambridge: Cambridge University Press.

Rose, Mary Beth. 2002. *Gender and Heroism in Early Modern Literature.* Chicago: University of Chicago Press.

Rosenthal, Jean-Laurent, and R. Bin Wong. 2011. *Before and beyond Divergence: The Politics of Economic Change in China and Europe.* Cambridge, MA: Harvard University Press.

Rosling, Hans. 2010. "200 Countries, 200 Years, 4 Minutes." Video at http://www.gapminder .org/videos/200-years-that-changed-the-world-bbc/.

Rosling, Hans. 2013. "Don't Panic—the Facts about Population." Video at http://www.gap minder.org/videos/dont-panic-the-facts-about-population/.

Rossi, Guido, and Salvatore Spagano. 2014. "From Custom to Law—Hayek Revisited." Unpublished essay, Edinburgh School of Law and Department of Economics and Business, University of Catania. http://mpra.ub.uni-muenchen.de/56643/.

Rothschild, Emma. 2001. *Economic Sentiments: Adams Smith, Condorcet, and the Enlightenment.* Cambridge, MA: Harvard University Press.

Rotter, Julian B. 1966. "Generalized Expectancies for Internal vs. External Control of Reinforcement." *Psychological Monographs* 80.

Rubin, Jared. 2008. "Printing and Interest Restrictions in Islam and Christianity: An Economic Theory of Inhibitive Law Persistence." Unpublished paper, Department of Economics, California State University at Fullerton.

Rubin, Jared. 2014. "Printing and Protestants: An Empirical Test of the Role of Printing in the Reformation." *Review of Economics and Statistics* 96:270–296.

Runciman, W. G. 2009. *The Theory of Cultural and Social Selection.* Cambridge: Cambridge University Press.

Ruskin, John. 1851–1853 (1900). *The Stones of Venice.* New York: Peter Fenelon Collier.

Ruskin, John. 1866. "Work," in *Crown of Wild Olives.* Reprinted New York: Hurst, n.d.

Sachdev, Ameet. 2013. "When Online Upstarts Rattle the Playing Field." *Chicago Tribune,* October 13.

Sachs, Jeffrey D., and Laurence J. Kotlikoff. 2012. "Smart Machines and Long-Term Misery." National Bureau of Economic Research. Closed access Working Paper No. 18629.

Sahlins, Marshall. 1972 (2004). *Stone Age Economics.* New York: Aldine de Gruyter. 2nd ed., London: Routledge.

Sala-i-Martin, Xavier. 2002. "The Disturbing `Rise' of Global Income Inequality." Closed access paper, National Bureau of Economic Research no. 8904.

Sala-i-Martin, Xavier. 2006. "The World's Distribution of Income: Falling Poverty and Convergence," *Quarterly Journal of Economics* 121:351–397.

Sala-i-Martin, Xavier, and Maxim Pinkovskiy. 2010. "Parametric Estimations of the World Distribution of Income." *VOX* 22 (January 22). http://www.voxeu.org/article/parametric -estimations-world-distribution-income.

Samuelson, Paul A. 1947. *The Foundations of Economic Analysis*. Cambridge, MA: Harvard University Press.

Sandberg, Lars. 1979. "The Case of the Impoverished Sophisticate: Human Capital and Swedish Economic Growth before World War I." *Journal of Economic History* 39:225–241.

Saunders, Peter. 2013. "Researching Poverty: Methods, Results, and Impact." *Economic and Labour Relations Review* 24:205–218.

Sawyer, Peter H. 1962 (1971). *The Age of the Vikings*. 2nd ed. London: Edward Arnold.

Schama, Simon. 1987. *The Embarrassment of Riches: An Interpretation of Dutch Culture in the Golden Age*. Berkeley: University of California Press.

Schlesinger, Stephen, and Stephen Kinzer. 1982. *Bitter Fruit: The Story of the U.S. Coup in Guatemala*. Garden City, NY: Doubleday.

Schmidtz, David, and Jason Brennan 2010. *A Brief History of Liberty*. Chichester, UK: Wiley-Blackwell.

Schneider, Anna. 1920. *Die Anfänge der Kulturwirtschaft: Die sumerische Tempelstadt*. Essen: G. D. Baedeker.

Schoeck, Helmut. 1958 (1977). "Individuality vs. Equality." In Felix Morley, ed., *Essays on Individuality*, pp. 145–175. Indianapolis: Liberty Press.

Schor, Juliet B. 1998. *The Overspent American: Why We Want What We Do Not Need*. New York: Basic Books.

Schumpeter, Joseph A. 1912 (1934). *The Theory of Economic Development*. English trans. from 1926 German edition. Cambridge, MA: Harvard University Press.

Schumpeter, Joseph A. 1942 (1950). *Capitalism, Socialism and Democracy*. 3rd. ed. New York: Harper and Row, 1950.

Schumpeter, Joseph A. 1949. "Science and Ideology." *American Economic Review* 39 (2): 346–359.

Scott, James C. 2009. *The Art of Not Being Governed: An Anarchist History of Upland Southwest Asia*. New Haven, CT: Yale University Press.

Scruton, Roger. 1994. *Modern Philosophy: A Survey*. London: Sinclair-Stevenson.

Searing, James. 2002. "'No Kings, No Lords, No Slaves': Ethnicity and Religion among the Sereer-Safèn of Western Bawol (Senegal), 1700–1914." *Journal of African History* 43:407–429.

Searle, John R. 2010. *Making the Social World: The Structure of Human Civilization*. Oxford: Oxford University Press.

Sellar, Walter C., and R. J. Yeatman. 1931 (1932). *1066 and All That: A Memorable History of England*. (Bound with *And Now All This*.) New York: Blue Ribbon Books.

Sellers, Charles G. 1991. *The Market Revolution: Jacksonian America, 1815–1846*. Oxford: Oxford University Press.

Sellers, Charles G. 1996. "Capitalism and Democracy in American Historical Mythology." In Melvyn Stokes and Stephen Conway, eds., *The Market Revolution in America: Social, Political, and Religious Expressions, 1800–1880*, pp. 311–329. Charlottesville: University of Virginia Press.

Sen, Amartya. 1985. *Commodities and Capabilities*. Amsterdam: Elsevier Science.

Sewell, William H. 1994. *A Rhetoric of Bourgeois Revolution: The Abbe Sieyes and What Is the Third Estate?* Durham, NC: Duke University Press.

Shackle, George L. S. 1972 (1992). *Epistemics and Economics: A Critique of Economic Doctrines.* Cambridge: Cambridge University Press.

Shaftesbury, Anthony Ashley Cooper, 3rd Earl. 1699, 1732 (2001). *Characteristics of Men, Manners, Opinions, Times,* 6th ed. Ed. D. Den Uyl. Indianapolis: Liberty Fund.

Shaw, George Bernard. 1912. Introduction to *Hard Times* (London: Waverly). Portion reprinted in Charles Dickens, *Hard Times,* ed. George Ford and Sylvère Monod, pp. 333–340. Norton Critical Edition, 2nd ed. New York: Norton, 1990.

Shields, Carol. 2000. *Dressing Up for the Carnival.* London: Fourth Estate.

Shields, Carol. 2002. *Unless.* London and New York: Fourth Estate. Paperback, 2003.

Shils, Edward. 1957. "Dream and Nightmares: Reflections on the Criticism of Mass Culture." *Sewanee Review* 65:587–608.

Shilts, Wade. 1999. "Imagining Delay: 'Limited Liability' and the Binding of Legal Uncertainty in Nineteenth-Century Britain." PhD diss., University of Iowa.

Shilts, Wade. 2004. "Accounting, Engineering, or Advertising? Limited Liability, the Company Prospectus, and the Language of Uncertainty in Victorian Britain." *Essays in Economic and Business History* 30:47–62.

Shilts, Wade. 2007. "Making McCloskey's *Rhetoric* Empirical: Company Law and Tragedies of the Commons in Victorian Britain." In Edward Clift, ed., *Transdisciplinary Readings: Essays in Rhetoric and Economics.* Lewiston, NY: Mellen Press.

Short, Doug. 2012. "Real GDP per Capita: Another Perspective on the Economy." *Advisor Perspectives.* http://www.advisorperspectives.com/dshort/updates/Real-GDP-Per-Capita.php.

Shorto, Russell. 2013. *Amsterdam: A History of the World's Most Liberal City.* New York: Doubleday.

Silver, Morris. 1983a. *Prophets and Markets: The Political Economy of Ancient Israel.* Boston: Kluwer-Nijhoff.

Silver, Morris. 1983b. "Karl Polanyi and Markets in the Ancient Near East: The Challenge of the Evidence. " *Journal of Economic History* 53:795–829).

Silver, Morris. 1994. *Economic Structures of Antiquity: Contributions in Economics and Economic History.* Westport, CT: Greenwood Press.

Simmel, Georg. 1907 (2004). *Philosophie des Geldes,* 2nd rev. ed. (1st ed., 1900). Trans. as *The Philosophy of Money.* Ed. David Frisby. Trans. Frisby, T. Bottomore, and K. Mengelberg. 3rd enlarged ed. London: Routledge.

Simmel, Georg. 1908 (1955). "Der Streit." Chap. 4 of *Sociologie.* Trans. K. H. Wolff (from 3rd ed. of 1923) as *Conflict.* Bound as *Conflict and The Web of Group Affiliations,* with a translation by R. Bendix of another chapter of *Sociologie.* New York: Free Press.

Simmons, Phil. 2011. "The 25th Anniversary of the Chernobyl Accident." School of Economics, Business & Public Policy, University of New England, Armidale, Australia. At Australian Agricultural and Resource Economics Society.

Simon, Julian L. 1981 (1996). *The Ultimate Resource.* Princeton, NJ: Princeton University Press. 2nd ed., *The Ultimate Resource 2.*

Simone, Maria Rosa di. 2003. "Admission." In Hilde de Ridder-Symoens and Walter Rüegg, eds., *A History of the University in Europe: Universities in Early Modern Europe (1500–1800),* pp. 285–325. Cambridge: Cambridge University Press.

Singer, Peter. 1993. *Practical Ethics.* 2nd ed. Cambridge: Cambridge University Press.

Sinyavsky, Andrei D. (pseud. Abram Tertz). 1959 (1960). *On Socialist Realism.* Trans. G. Dennis. New York: Vintage.

Skinner, Quentin. 1969. "Meaning and Understanding in the History of Ideas." *History and Theory* 8 (1): 3–53. Reference is to the reprint in Tully, ed. 1989.

Skwire, Sarah. 2013. "'Without Respect of Persons': Gender Equality, Theology, and the Law in the Writing of Margaret Fell." Presented at "Equality and Public Policy," a conference sponsored by the George Washington Forum on American Ideas, Politics & Institutions.

Sluijter, Eric J. 1991. "Didactic and Disguised Meanings? Several Seventeenth-Century Texts on Painting and the Iconological Approach to Northern Dutch Paintings of This Period." In David Freedberg and Jan de Vries, eds., *Art in History/History in Art: Studies in Seventeenth-Century Dutch Culture*, pp. 175–207. Santa Monica, CA: Getty Center for the History of Art and the Humanities.

Smiles, Samuel. 1859 (1958). *Self-Help; with Illustrations of Character and Conduct.* London. https://archive.org/details/selfhelpwithilloosmilgoog.

Smiley, Jane. 1998. *The All-True Travels and Adventures of Lidie Newton.* New York: Fawcett Books.

Smith, Adam. 1759 (1790). *The Theory of Moral Sentiments* [*TMS*]. Glasgow Edition. Ed. D. D. Raphael and A. L. Macfie. Indianapolis: Liberty Classics, 1976, 1982.

Smith, Adam. 1762–1766. *Lectures on Jurisprudence.* Glasgow Edition. Ed. R. L. Meek, D. D. Raphael, and P. G. Stein. Oxford: Oxford University Press, 1978, 1982.

Smith, Adam. 1776. *An Inquiry into the Nature and Causes of the Wealth of Nations* [*WN*]. Glasgow edition. Ed. R. H. Campbell, A. S. Skinner, and W. B. Todd. 2 vols. Indianapolis: Liberty Classics, 1976, 1981.

Smith, Adam. 1977. *Correspondence of Adam Smith.* Glasgow Edition. Ed. E. C. Mossner and I. S. Ross. Oxford: Oxford University Press.

Smith, Adam. 1980. *Essays on Philosophical Subjects.* Glasgow Edition. Ed. W. P. D. Wightman and J. J. Bryce. Oxford: Oxford University Press.

Smith, Fred L., Jr. N.d. "Ego-Paganism–Eco-Socialism Severe Threats to Americas Future." Council for National Policy. http://www.cfnp.org/Page.aspx?pid=330.

Smith, Vernon L. 2007. *Rationality in Economics: Constructivist and Ecological Forms.* Cambridge: Cambridge University Press.

Smollett, Tobias. 1766. *Travels Through France and Italy.* In *The Complete Works of Tobias Smollett*, vol. 2. London 1869. At Google Books.

Snell, Daniel C. 1997. *Life in the Ancient Near East, 3100–332 B.C.E.* New Haven, CT: Yale University Press.

Sng, Tuan-Hwee, and Chiaki Moriguchi. 2014. "Asia's Little Divergence: State Capacity in China and Japan before 1850." Unpublished paper, Center for Economic Institutions, Institute of Economic Research, Hitotsubasi University, Japan.

Sobel, Dava. 1995. *Longitude: The True Story of a Lone Genius Who Solved the Greatest Scientific Problem of His Time.* New York: Penguin.

Sombart, Werner. 1913 (1915). *Der Bourgeois: Zur Geistesgeschichte des modernen Wirtschaftsmenschen.* Trans. M . Epstein, as *The Quintessence of Capitalism: A Study of the History and Psychology of the Modern Business Man.* New York: Dutton. At Google Books.

Sowell, Thomas. 1987 (2007). *A Conflict of Visions: Ideological Origins of Political Struggles.* Rev. ed. New York: Basic Books.

Sowell, Thomas. 2015. *Basic Economics: A Common Sense Guide to the Economy.* 5th ed. New York: Basic Books.

Spaulding, Robert. 2014. "Upstream and Down River: Changing Directions in the Rhine Trade, 1680–1820." Paper presented to the Transnational Rhine Conference, Akademie der Wissenschaften, Mainz, October 30.

Sprat, Thomas. 1667 (1958). *The History of the Royal Society.* Ed. Jackson Cope and Harold Jones. St. Louis: Washington University Studies.

Stackhouse, Max L., and Lawrence M. Stratton. 2002. *Capitalism, Civil Society, Religion, and the Poor.* Wilmington, DE: Intercollegiate Studies Institute.

Stark, Rodney. 2001 (2003). *One True God: Historical Consequences of Monotheism.* Princeton, NJ: Princeton University Press.

Staveren, Irene van. 2001. *The Values of Economics: An Aristotelian Perspective.* London: Routledge.

Steele, David Ramsay. 2001. "The Mystery of Fascism." *Liberty* (November), pp. 31–42. http://la-articles.org.uk/fascism.htm.

Steele, Richard. 1722 (1969). *The Conscious Lovers.* In Nettleton, Case, and Stone 1969.

Stevenson, Laura. 1976. "Anti-Entrepreneurial Attitudes in Elizabethan Sermons and Popular Literature." *Journal of British Studies* 15:1–20.

Stewart, Dugald. 1793 (1980). "Account of the Life and Writings of Adam Smith, LL.D." Pp. 269–351 in W. P. D. Wightman and J. J. Bryce, *Essays on Philosophical Subjects.* Glasgow Edition. Oxford: Oxford University Press.

Stigler, George J. 1982. *The Economist as Preacher and Other Essays.* Chicago: University of Chicago Press.

Stone, Lawrence, and Jeanne C. Fawtier Stone. 1984. *An Open Elite? England 1540–1880.* Oxford: Oxford University Press.

Stone, Robert. 2013. *Pandora's Promise.* Documentary film. Transcript from CNN airing at http://transcripts.cnn.com/TRANSCRIPTS/1311/07/se.01.html.

Storr, Virgil Henry. 2006. "Weber's Spirit of Capitalism and the Bahamas' Junkanoo Ethic." *Review of Austrian Economics,* 19 (4):

Storr, Virgil Henry. 2008. "The Market as a Social Space: On the Meaningful Extraeconomic Conversations That Can Occur in Markets." *Review of Austrian Economics* 21 (2008): 135–150.

Storr, Virgil Henry. 2013. *Understanding the Culture of Markets.* New York: Routledge.

Strauss, Leo. 1953. *Natural Right and History.* Chicago: University of Chicago Press.

Strietman, Elsa. 1996. "Finding Needles in a Haystack: Elements of Change in the Transition from Medieval to Renaissance Drama in the Low Countries." In Martin Gosman and Rina Walthaus, eds., *European theatre 1470–1600: Traditions and Transformations,* pp. 99–112. Groningen: Egbert Forsten.

Sturkenboom, Dorothée. 2004. "Prepared Remarks to the Symposium." Symposium on "Dutch Identity: Virtues and Vices of Bourgeois Society." Erasmus University, Rotterdam. May 6.

Summers, Lawrence H. 2014. "Lawrence H. Summers on the Economic Challenge of the Future: Jobs." *Wall Street Journal,* July 7.

Sun (Wu) Tzu, P. Ca. 500 BCE. *The Art of War*. Trans. Lionel Giles (1910). http://chinapage
.com/sunzi-e.html.

Suprinyak, Carlos Eduardo. 2011. "Trade, Money, and the Grievances of the Commonwealth :
Economic Debates in the English Public Sphere during the Commercial Crisis of the Early
1620's." Universidade Federal de Minas Gerais. http://econpapers.repec.org/paper/cdptex
dis/td427.htm.

Surowiecki, James. 2008. "The Open Secret of Success: Toyota Production System." *New Yorker*,
May 12.

Sutch, Richard. 1991. "All Things Reconsidered: The Life-Cycle Perspective and the Third Task
of Economic History." *Journal of Economic History* 51 (June): 1–18.

Swedberg, Richard. 2009. *Tocqueville's Political Economy*. Princeton, NJ: Princeton University
Press.

Sylla, Richard, and Gianni Toniolo, eds. 1992. *Patterns of European Industrialization: The Nineteenth Century*. London: Routledge.

Tacitus, Cornelius. 98 CE. *Germania*. Ed. D. R. Stuart. New York: Macmillan, 1916.

Tacitus, Cornelius. 98 CE. *The Agricola and the Germania*. Trans. H. Mattingly and S. A. Handford. Harmondsworth: Penguin, 1948, 1970.

Tacitus, Cornelius. c. 113 CE. *Annales*. Ed. C. D. Fisher. At http://perseus.tufts.edu/hopper/.

Taleb, Nassim Nicholas. 2007. *The Black Swan: The Impact of the Highly Improbable*. New York:
Random House.

Tallis, Raymond. 2011. Review of Terrence Deacon, *Incomplete Nature*, and Michael S. Gaz-
zanga, *Who's in Charge? Wall Street Journal*, November 12.

Tanner, Kathryn. 2005. *Economy of Grace*. Minneapolis: Fortress.

Taylor, A. J. P. 1955 (1967). *Bismarck: The Man and the Statesman*. New York: Knopf, Vintage
Books.

Taylor, Charles. 1989. *Sources of the Self: The Making of the Modern Identity*. Cambridge, MA:
Harvard University Press.

Taylor, Charles. 2004. *Modern Social Imaginaries*. Durham, NC: Duke University Press.

Taylor, Charles. 2007. *A Secular Age*. Cambridge, MA: Harvard University Press.

Tedin, Ola. 2012. "The Swedish Media and the 'Tooth Fairy State.'" *The [Swedish] Local*. May 25.

Temple, Sir William. 1673 (1972). *Observations upon the United Provinces of the Netherlands*.
Ed. G. Clark. Oxford: Oxford University Press.

Terry, Judith. 1988. "Seen but Not Heard: Servants in Jane Austen's England." *Persuasions* 10:
104–116.

Thomas, Keith. 2009. *The Ends of Life: Roads to Fulfilment in Early Modern England*. Oxford:
Oxford University Press.

Thompson, Augustine. 2005. *Cities of God: The Religion of the Italian Communes, 1125–1325*.
University Park: Pennsylvania State University Press. "Introduction" at http://www.psupress
.org/books/SampleChapters/0-271-02477-1sc.html.

Thompson, F. M. L. 1963. *English Landed Society in the Nineteenth Century*. London: Routledge
& Kegan Paul.

Thomson, Erik. 2005. "Swedish Variations on Dutch Commercial Institutions, 1605–1655."
Scandinavian Studies 77:331–346.

Tickle, Phyllis. 2008. *The Great Emergence: How Christianity Is Changing and Why*. Grand Rapids, MI: Baker Books.

Tilly, Charles. 1990. *Coercion, Capital, and European States*. Cambridge, MA: Blackwell.

Titow, J. Z. 1972. *Winchester Yields: A Study in Medieval Agricultural Productivity*. Cambridge: Cambridge University Press.

Tocqueville, Alexis de. 1840 (1945). *Democracy in America*. Two vols. Trans. P. Bradley. New York: Knopf. Vintage paperback, 1954.

Tocqueville, Alexis de. 1856 (1955). *The Old Régime and the French Revolution*. Translated by S. Gilbert from the 1858 French edition. Garden City, NY: Anchor Doubleday.

Todeschini, Giacomo. 2008. "The Theological Roots of Medieval/Modern Merchants' Self-Representation." In Jacob and Secretan, eds. 2008, pp. 17–48.

Todorov, Tzvetan. 2000 (2003). *Hope and Memory: Lessons from the Twentieth Century*. Trans. D. Bellos. Princeton, NJ: Princeton University Press.

Tolstoy, Leo. 1868–1869 (1933). *War and Peace*. Trans. Louise Maude and Aylmer Maude, 1922–1923. World's Classics. Oxford: Oxford University Press.

Tolstoy, Leo. 1869. "Some Words about *War and Peace*." *Russian Archive*, reprinted following the Second Epilogue in the Maude translation, pp. 538–548.

Tomasello, Michael. 2014. *A Natural History of Human Thinking*. Cambridge, MA: Harvard University Press.

Tomasi, John. 2012. *Free Market Fairness*. Princeton, NJ: Princeton University Press.

Toscani, Frederik. 2013. "Why High Human Capital Makes Good Revolutionaries: The Role of the Middle Classes in Democratisation." University of Cambridge Working Papers in Economics, No. 1332.

Toulmin, Stephen. 1992. *Cosmopolis: The Hidden Agenda of Modernity*. Chicago: University of Chicago Press.

Toynbee, Arnold. 1884 (1887). *Lectures on the Industrial Revolution in England*. 2nd ed. London: Rivington's.

Trevor-Roper, Hugh. 1940 (1962). *Archbishop Laud: 1573–1645*. London: Macmillan. (Reprinted, London: Phoenix Press, 1986.)

Troesken, Werner. 2014. Review of Leslie Rosenthal, *The River Pollution Dilemma in Victorian England*. EH.net (August). http://eh.net/book_reviews/the-river-pollution-dilemma-in-victorian-england-nuisance-law-versus-economic-efficiency/.

Trollope, Anthony. 1867–1868. *Phineas Finn: The Irish Member*. Oxford: Oxford University Press, 1982.

Trollope, Anthony. 1874. *Phineas Redux*. Oxford: Oxford University Press, 1983.

Trump, Donald, with Tony Schwartz. 1987. *Trump: The Art of the Deal*. New York: Warner Books.

Tufte, Edward R. 1982. *The Visual Display of Quantitative Information*. Cheshire, Connecticut: Graphics Press.

Tully, James ed. 1989. *Meaning and Context: Quentin Skinner and His Critics*. Princeton, NJ: Princeton University Press.

Tunzelmann, G. Nick von. 1978. *Steam Power and British Industrialization to 1860*. Oxford: Clarendon Press.

Tunzelmann, G. Nick von. 2003. "Technology." In Mokyr, ed. 2003.

Tunzelmann, G. Nick von, and Qing Wang. 2007. "Capabilities and Production Theory." *Structural Change and Economic Dynamics* 18:191–211.

Turnbull, Colin M. 1972. *The Mountain People*. New York: Simon & Schuster.

Union of Utrecht. 1579. English trans. at http://constitution.org/cons/dutch/Union_Utrecht _1579.html.

Van der Beek, Karine. 2013. "England's Eighteenth Century Demand for High-Quality Workmanship: Evidence from Apprenticeship, 1710–1770." Human Capital and Economic Opportunity Workshop, Economic Research Center, University of Chicago and Ben-Gurion University of the Negev.

Van der Welle, Jojakim Adriaan. 1962. *Dryden and Holland*. Groningen: Wolters.

Van Zanden, J., et al., eds. 2014. *How Was Life? Global Well-Being since 1820*. OECD Publishing. http://www.oecd.org/statistics/how-was-life9789264214262-en.htm.

Vargas Llosa, Álvaro. 2013. *Global Crossings: Immigration, Civilization, and America*. Oakland, CA: Independent Institute.

Veenhof, K. R. 1972. *Aspects of Old Assyrian Trade and Its Terminology*. Leiden: E. J. Brill.

Vidal-Robert, Jordi. 2013. "War and Inquisition: Repression in Early Modern Spain." Centre for Competitive Advantage in the Global Economy, Department of Economics, University of Warwick.

Viner, Jacob. 1959. "Five Lectures on Economics and Freedom Delivered at Wabash College." In Viner 1991, pp. 39–77.

Viner, Jacob. 1970. "Satire and Economics in the Augustan Age." In Viner 1991, pp. 303–323.

Viner, Jacob. 1991. *Essays on the Intellectual History of Economics*. Ed. Douglas A. Irwin. Princeton, NJ: Princeton University Press.

Viroli, Maurizio. 2014. *Redeeming "The Prince": The Meaning of Machiavelli's Masterpiece*. Princeton, NJ: Princeton University Press.

Voigtländer, Nico, and Hans-Joachim Voth. 2013. "Gifts of Mars: Warfare and Europe's Early Rise to Riches." *Journal of Economic Perspectives* 27:165–186.

Voltaire. 1733. "Tenth Letter: On Commerce." http://www.constitution.org/volt/phltr_10.htm

Wagner, Richard E. 1994. "*ORDO* Liberalism and the Social Market Economy." In H. Geoffrey Brennan and A. M. C. Waterman, eds., *Economics and Religion: Are They Distinct?*, pp. 121–138. Dordrecht: Kluwer.

Wahrman, Dror. 1995. *Imagining the Middle Class: The Political Representation of Class in Britain, c.1780–1840*. Cambridge: Cambridge University Press.

Wakefield, Andre. 2009. *The Disordered Police State: German Cameralism as Science and Practice*. Chicago: University of Chicago Press.

Wallerstein, Immanuel. 1974. *The Modern World-System*. Vol. 1, *Capitalist Agriculture and the Origins of the European World-Economy in the Sixteenth Century*. New York/London: Academic Press.

Wallerstein, Immanuel. 1983 (1995). *Historical Capitalism* (1983). Bound with *Capitalist Civilization* (1995). London: Verso.

Wallis, John, and Douglass C. North. 1986. "Measuring the Transactions Sector in the American Economy." In S. Engerman and R. Gallman, eds., *Long-Term Factors in American Economic Growth*. Chicago: University of Chicago Press.

Walton, Gary M. 1993. "Fulton's Folly." In McCloskey, ed. 1993, pp. 145–150.

Walzer, Michael. 1983. *The Sphere of Justice: A Defense of Pluralism and Equality.* New York: Basic Books.

Walzer, Michael. 2008. "Of Course It Does." In "A Templeton Conversation: Does the Free Market Corrode Moral Character?" John Templeton Foundation Big Questions. https://www.templeton.org/market/.

Wang Fuzhi. 1691 (2000). "The Justification of Social and Cultural Divisions" (brief selection from *On Reading "The Comprehensive Mirror"*). In W. T. deBary and R. Lufrano, eds., *Sources of Chinese Tradition.* Vol. 2, *From 1600 through the Twentieth Century*, pp. 32–34. 2nd ed. New York: Columbia University Press.

Ward-Perkins, Bryan. 2000. "Why Did the Anglo-Saxons Not Become More British?" *English Historical Review* 115:513–533.

Ward-Perkins, Bryan. 2005. *The Fall of Rome and the End of Civilization.* Oxford: Oxford University Press.

Waterman, Anthony M. C. 1991. *Revolution, Economics and Religion: Christian Political Economy, 1798–1833.* Cambridge: Cambridge University Press.

Waterman, Anthony M. C. 1994. "Whately, Senior, and the Methodology of Classical Economics." In H. Geoffrey Brennan and A. M. C. Waterman, eds., *Economics and Religion: Are They Distinct?*, pp. 41–60. Dordrecht: Kluwer.

Waterman, Anthony M. C. 2012. "Adam Smith and Malthus on High Wages." *European Journal of the History of Economic Thought* 19:409–429.

Waterman, Anthony M. C. 2014a. "Theology and the Rise of Political Economy in Britain in the Eighteenth and Nineteenth Centuries." In Paul Oslington, ed., *The Oxford Handbook of Christianity and Economics*, pp. 94–122. Oxford: Oxford University Press.

Waterman, Anthony M. C. 2014b. "Inequality and Social Evil: Wilkinson and Pickett on The Spirit Level." *Faith and Economics* 63 (Spring): 38–49.

Watson, Andrew M. 1983. *Agricultural Innovation in the Early Islamic World.* Cambridge: Cambridge University Press.

Watt, Ian. 1957. *The Rise of the Novel: Studies in Defoe, Richardson and Fielding.* Berkeley: University of California Press.

Weatherford, Jack. 2004. *Genghis Khan and the Making of the Modern World.* New York: Crown.

Weber, Max. 1904–1905 (1958). *The Protestant Ethic and the Spirit of Capitalism (Die protestantische Ethik und der Geist des Kapitalismus).* Trans. T. Parsons (1930), from 1920 German edition. New York: Scribner's.

Weber, Max. 1923 (1981). *General Economic History.* Trans. Frank Knight. New Brunswick, NJ: Transaction Books (original English pub., Glencoe, IL: Free Press, 1927).

Wheeler, Michael. 2005. "Religion." In Janet Todd, ed., *Jane Austen in Context*, pp. 406–414. New York: Cambridge University Press.

White, James Boyd. 1984. *When Words Lose Their Meaning: Constitutions and Reconstitutions of Language, Character, and Community.* Chicago: University of Chicago Press.

Whitehead, Alfred North. 1911. *Introduction to Mathematics.* London: Williams and Norgate.

Whitford, David. 2005. "The Most Famous Story We Never Told." *Fortune*, September 19.

Wiener, Martin. 1981. *English Culture and the Decline of the Industrial Spirit*. Cambridge: Cambridge University Press.

Wierzbicka, Anna. 2006. *English: Meaning and Culture*. Oxford: Oxford University Press.

Wierzbicka, Anna. 2010. *Experience, Evidence, and Sense: The Hidden Cultural Legacy of English*. Oxford: Oxford University Press.

Wilde, Oscar. 1891 (1930). "The Soul of Man under Socialism." in Wilde, *Plays, Prose Writings, and Poems*, ed. H. Pearson, pp. 257–288. London: Dent.

Willey, Basil. 1964. *The English Moralists*. New York: Norton.

Williams, James Estel. 2014. "The Riom Trial: Marshal Petain's Attack on the Third Republic." MA Thesis, Department of History, University of Louisville, KY. http://ir.library.louisville.edu/cgi/viewcontent.cgi?article=2574&context=etd.

Williamson, Jeffrey. 1993. "How Tough are Times in the Third World?" In McCloskey, ed. 1993, pp. 11–18.

Williamson, Oliver E. 1999. "Public and Private Bureaucracies: A Transaction Cost Economics Perspective." *Journal of Law, Economics and Organization* 15:306–342.

Wills, Gary. 1992. *Lincoln at Gettysburg: The Words that Remade America*. New York: Simon & Schuster.

Willsher, Kim. 2014. "François Hollande Feels the Squeeze in the Town Where He Was Once Idolised." *Observer*, March 22. http://www.theguardian.com/world/2014/mar/23/francois-hollande-tulle-elections-france.

Wilson, Bart J. 2010. "Social Preferences Aren't Preferences." *Journal of Economic Behavior & Organization* 73:77–82.

Wilson, Bart J., Taylor Jaworski, Karl E. Schurter, and Andrew Smyth. 2012. "The Ecological and Civil Mainsprings of Property: An Experimental Economic History of Whalers' Rules of Capture." *Journal of Law, Economics and Organization* 28:617–656.

Wilson, Charles. 1965. *England's Apprenticeship, 1603–1763*. London: Longmans.

Wilson, Charles. 1968. *The Dutch Republic and the Civilisation of the Seventeenth Century*. World University Library. New York: McGraw-Hill.

Wiltshire, John. 2009. "Why Do We *Read* Jane Austen?" In Susannah Carson, ed., *A Truth Universally Acknowledged: 33 Great Writers on Why We Read Jane Austen*, pp. 163–174. New York: Random House.

Wood, Gordon S. 2004. *The Americanization of Benjamin Franklin*. New York: Penguin.

Wood, James. 1999. *Broken Estate: Essays on Literature and Belief*. New York: Random House.

Woolf, Virginia. 1925. "Jane Austen." In *The Common Reader*, First Series. New York: Harcourt Brace Jovanovich, 1953.

Wootton, David. 2005. Review of Keith Thomas, *The Ends of Life*. *Times Literary Supplement*. February 29.

Wormell, Jeremy. n.d Review of Niall Ferguson, *The World's Banker: A History of the House of Rothschild*, with Ferguson's response. *Reviews in History*, no. 213. http://www.history.ac.uk/reviews/review/213.

Wright, Louis B. 1935. *Middle-Class Culture in Elizabethan England*. Chapel Hill: University of North Carolina Press.

Wrightson, Keith. 2000. *Earthly Necessities: Economic Lives in Early Modern Britain*. New Haven, CT: Yale University Press.

Wrigley, E. A. 1988. *Continuity, Chance and Change*. Cambridge: Cambridge University Press.

Yeats, William Butler. 1928 (1992). *The Poems*. Ed. Daniel Albright. London: Everyman.

Yoffee, Norman. 2005. *Myths of the Archaic State: Evolution of the Earliest Cities, States, and Civilizations*. Cambridge: Cambridge University Press.

Zagorin, Perez. 2003. *How the Idea of Religious Toleration Came to the West*. Princeton, NJ: Princeton University Press.

Zamagni, Stefano. 2010. "Catholic Social Thought, Civil Economy, and the Spirit of Capitalism." In Daniel K. Finn, ed., *The True Wealth of Nations: Catholic Social Thought and Economic Life*, pp. 63–93. Oxford: Oxford University Press.

Zamora, Daniel. 2014. "Interview [in French] in *Ballast*." Trans. S. Ackerman, as "Can We Criticize Foucault?" *Jacobin: A Magazine of Culture and Polemic*, https://www.jacobinmag.com/2014/12/foucault-interview/.

Zamoyski, Adam. 1987. *The Polish Way: A Thousand-Year History of the Poles and Their Culture*. London: John Murray.

Zeeman, Michael. 2004. "Prepared Remarks to the Symposium." Symposium on "Dutch Identity: Virtues and Vices of Bourgeois Society." Erasmus University, Rotterdam. May 6.

Zelizer, Viviana A. 2005. *The Purchase of Intimacy*. Princeton, NJ: Princeton University Press.

Ziliak, Stephen, and Deirdre N. McCloskey. 2008. *The Cult of Statistical Significance: How the Standard Error Costs Us Jobs, Justice, and Lives*. Ann Arbor: University of Michigan Press.

Zola, Émile. 1882–1883 (1992). *The Ladies Paradise*. Reprint of trans. by H. Vizetelly, 1886. Introduction by Kirstin Ross. Berkeley: University of California Press.

INDEX

Abbasid Caliphate, 435, 482

absolute advantage: contrasted with comparative advantage, 513; and foreign trade, 75. *See also* mercantilism

Abu-Lughod, Janet L: East misses, 438

accounting, 201, 320; double-entry, 322; ethics in banking, 542; of sins, 322; spiritual, 447

accumulation of capital: "accumulate, accumulate," in Marx, 96; "accumulate, accumulate," in Weber, 101, chap. 21; as conservative trope, 39; diminishing returns to, 101; "endless," in Aristotle and Weber, 279, 280, 312, 323; "endless," in Marx, 96, 106; in financial capital, Piketty on, 48; financial capital and growth, 105; routine, 94, 103, 133

Acemoglu, Daron, 652n25; bias in cross-time return to human capital, 661n7; cross-sections, 665n7; human capital and betterment, 662n7; human capital as cause, 662n7; illiberalism, 462; institutions and growth, 120; justice in Somalia, 584; neo-institutionalism, 665n15; property and 1688, 296; property rights, xxii–xxvi, 111; theory of change, 519; use of Mantoux, 98; *Why Nations Fail*, Marxian on, 97

Acheulean hand axe, 57, 101, 637

Ackerman, Bruce, xxii

Ackroyd, Peter: Venice, 460

acupuncture, 77

Adams, Henry, 410

Adams, John (economist), 116

Adams, John (founding brother), 261

Adams, Robert M.: temple theory of Mesopotamia, 549

Addison, Joseph, chap. 27, 255; attitude towards bourgeoisie, 258–259, 592; *Cato*, 261–262; dangers, 264; "honest," 239; *The Spectator*, 258; the Stones on, 264

Adhia, Nimish: Indian attitudes, 254

administrative university, 32, 555; hierarchy of, 480

affirmation of ordinary life: Taylor's phrase, 374, 410

Afghanistan: corruption, 665n5; poverty, 5

Aflaq, Michel, 625

Africa, Sub-Saharan: early iron, 77; early trade in, 93, 106, 545; European imperialism in, 89; gain from trade with Europe in, 142; genetic diversity, 70–71, 660n30; omitted by North and others, 521; optimism about, 52, 71, 74; Portuguese and, 473; recent performance, 290, 626; Searing on hill-dwellers in, 656n20; as trope of poverty, 38

Agee, James: sharecroppers, 42–43

age-heaping, 316

Agincourt, 323–324

A'Hearn, Brian: numeracy, 316

Ahl, Helene: acknowledged, xxxix

airplanes: for scouting in war, 682n5; Wright monopoly, 419

air pollution, 68; horses and, 618; ideological reflex, 623

materialism, 642–643; mistaken about capital, xiii; 1950s modernization theory, 484; monopoly, 460; moralized economy, 645; policy, 386; on polishing of ethics, 701n9; procedural right, 197; rhetoric, 175; supply chain, 566; *The Theory of Moral Sentiments* and *The Bourgeois Virtues*, 644; transcendence, 198; trickle up, 40; unsocial passion, 638; vanity, 457; virtues, 191. *See also* Boettke, Peter; Fleischacker, Samuel; Levy, David; Peart, Sandra; Smithian growth

Smith, Brock: early growth, 533

Smith, Daniel Scott, 516

Smith, Fred L., Jr.: environmentalism, 29

Smith, Vernon: group experiments, 282, 652n27; origin of property, 112; property without kings, 112

Smith, Wilfred Cantwell: propositional belief, 672n5

Smithian growth, 481; Dutch standard, 12; and Schumpeterian, 206

Smollett, Tobias: bourgeois noblemen, 442

Smyth, Andrew: property without kings, 112

Sng, Tuan Hwee: Chinese imperial administration, 480

Sobel, Dava: longitude, 652n32

social democracy: assumption of prior knowledge of betterment, 95

socialism: and envy, 644; and the family, 577; and growth, 595; in US, 24. *See also* envy; regulation

sociological change: and psychological change, xxvii. *See also* Weber, Max

Sokoloff, Kenneth. *See* Engerman-Sokoloff hypothesis on Latin America

Solman, Paul: acknowledged, xxxviii

Sombart, Werner: Arabic numerals, 316; calculation, 271; creative destruction, 618; German sociological Romanticism, 676n19; prudence, 273

Somers, Margaret, 551; Polanyist, 551; state provision, 551

Song dynasty: Goldstone on, 98; and Great Enrichment, 435; industrial revolution of, 362, 402; Jones on, 533, 534; and merchants, 281; and Mongols, 107

Soto, Hernando de, 144, 537

South Africa: licensing of business, 463; long-run optimism about, 64–65; mercantilist economic policy in, 75;

old Afrikaner zero sum, 463; unemployment, 63

Southey, Robert, 601

Sowell, Thomas: analytic egalitarianism, 699n6; profit and socialism, 567

Spagano, Salvatore: black letter law, 114

Spanish: usage of "honest," 673n4

Spaulding, Robert: Rhine tolls, 132

Spectator, The, 258; quoted, 249–250, 260. *See also* Addison, Joseph; Steele, Richard

spelling modernization in this book, 653n38

Spinoza, Baruch, 647

Sprat, Thomas: envy of Holland, 291

Stackhouse, Max: God and technology, 451

stage theory, 93; Braudel on, 107; Elias on, 250; Fiske on, 585

stagnation: Japanese poet on, 282

stagnationism, 626; recent economic observers on, 61; theory of the 1940s, 61, 64, 626, 659n2, 659n9

Stark, Rodney: church of power, 682n16; on de Stefano, 681n30; religion and ideas, 353–354; quotes R. Niebuhr on Dutch sectarians, 681n31

state capitalism, 601; effects on poor, 74

stationary state, 17, 101; Mill on, 648

status function: allegory, 127; Searle, 123

Staveren, Irene: economic ethics, 696n1

Steel, Richard, chap. 27, 255

Steele, David Ramsay: socialism, 108

Steele, Richard: attitude towards bourgeoisie, 592; *The Conscious Lover* and the cit, 265; *The Spectator*, 258; the Stones on, 264

Steinbeck, John, 42, 634; Okies in war economy, 45

Steinfeld, Robert, 569

Stendhal, 599

Stephenson, George: railway entrepreneur, 314

Stevenson, Laura (O'Connell), 310–313; quotes Deloney, 678n12; quotes Perkins, 678n19

Stewart, Alan: on Bacon, 677n14

Stewart, Dugald: Smith, 182; Smith conservative, 184

Stigler, George: ideas and interest, 181, 524

Stiglitz, Joseph: full information, 438

Stikkers, Kenneth: spiritual enrichment, 656n12

stocking frame, patent on, 175

Stoléru, Lionel: Foucault on equality, 52

Stone, George Winchester: on *The London Merchant*, 675n12
Stone, Lawrence and Jeanne: Addison and Steele, 264
Stone, Robert: nuclear power, 659n24, 660n26
Storr, Virgil: acknowledged, xxxviii; Austrian economics, 360; entangling, 557; *Geist* and Barbados, 693n9; Katrina, 664n2
Stowe, Harriet Beecher: and the market, 571
St. Paul of Tarsus: Christian fatalism, 385; on hierarchy, xxxv; novelty, 469
Strauss, Leo: natural rights, 668n2
Strauss, Richard: Kerman on, 614, 615, 616
Strietman, Elsa: *Everyman*, 448
Stringer, Chris, 663n20
strong ties, 393–394
Stuart, D. R.: edition of Tacitus, 679n2
Stubbs, John, 390
Sturkenboom, Dorothée: Dutch Spectator, 674n14
Sub-Saharan Africa: growing, 71; as result of genetic diversity, 71; results of genetic diversity, 70
subsidy: favoritism, xxxiii; South African, 606; sports stadiums, 678n9; and trade test, xxxiii, 564; Venezuela, 625
Summers, Lawrence: technological pessimism, 61; uncles of, 651n9
Suprinyak, Carlos Eduardo: early mercantilism, 514
Surowiecki, James: Toyota betterment, 682n21
Sutch, Richard: economics and history, 662n14
Swedberg Richard: Protestant ethic, 278; quotes Tocqueville, 675n6
Sweden: accounting in public administration, 271; attitude towards market in recent fiction, 298; as capitalist, 24, 459; condition of the working class in, compared with US, 50; educational services and the state in, 551; environmentalism of, 29; former poverty, 9, 10; grew without an empire, 90; ideology of equality in, 348; "national home," 577; Protestant entrepreneurship, 410, 508; as rich country, 5, 6, 290; social democracy in, 545, 620, 621, 641; social ethics in, xxiv; Temple war and trade, 288; unionism in, 56

sweet talk: bulk in economy, 491, 492, 493, 494; defined as persuasion, 490; future share, from opportunity cost of, 498; in North, Wallis, and Weingast, 518; opportunity cost of, 495; place in culture, 499; in prudence-only theories, 519; supports betterment, 503, chap. 51
Swift, Gustavus Franklin: entrepreneurship in meat, 539
Switzerland: Great Depression, 53; liberalism, xv; republic, 336
Sylla, Richard: Gerschenkron and substitutes, 695n1

Tacitus, Publius Cornelius: German honor, 444; *Germani*, 327; honor in work, 450; objectivity, 274
Taine, Hippolyte: on Defoe, 674n5; poverty in France in 1879, 9
Taleb, Nassim Nicholas: prediction, 361, 653n44
Tallis, Raymond: summarizes Gazzaniga, 125
Tanner, Kathryn: grace and economics, 688n9
Tarkington, Booth, 591; critique of bourgeoisie, 591, 610
Tarnaala, Eerik, 655n17
Tarr, Joel, 659n21
Taveneaux, René: on Jansenism, 682n8
Tawney, R. H.: influence on Acemoglu and Robinson, 97
Taylor, A. J. P.: quotes Bismarck, 672n18; welfare state, 606
Taylor, Charles: ethic of being, 197; eudaimonism, 380; intersubjectivity as conjective, 664n18; mea culpa for not reading him earlier, 374; rise of individualism, 668n10, 27; social imaginary, as rhetoric, 647
Taylor, Scott: acknowledged, xxxviii
technological unemployment, 56, 61, 497–498; Cowen on, 62–63; Ibsen on, 57, 58. *See also* job protection
technology: from elite, xxix; science and, 649. *See also* Great Enrichment; Mokyr, Joel
Tedin, Ola: Swedish state, 701n2
Temple, Sir William: Dutch calculation, 271; Dutch charity, 338; Dutch honesty, 228; Dutch honor, 329; Dutch shipping, 351; Dutch toleration, 351; English "honesty," 240

Zeeman, Michael: Dutch tolerance, 349
Zelizer, Viviana: entangling, 557
zero-sum: aristocratic society, 22, 433, 434; in Balzac and Dickens, 608; before Great Enrichment, 434; betterment, 297; decline of idea of, 503; England in 1600, 463; envy, 634; Epictetus, 201; good Christians and, 381, 512; Horatio Alger, 314; Malthus, 14; modern mercantilism, 513; poor, 74, 535; in *The Shoemaker's Holiday*, 309. *See also* mercantilism; win-win

Ziliak, Stephen: statistical significance, 675n10
Zimbabwe, 74, 290, 625
Zola, Émile, 42; Caillebotte, 590; consumerism, 609; creative destruction, 60; entry of the department store, 59–60; *Germinal*, 42, 591; *The Ladies' Paradise*, 59
zoning and building codes, 51, 144, 605, 625, 641; Italian, 137
Zuckerberg, Mark: entrepreneur, 96
Zuidhof, Peter-Wim: social spheres, 696n1
Zunz, Oliver, 312